READINGS IN

Attitude Theory and Measurement

Edited by

MARTIN FISHBEIN

Department of Psychology
University of Illinois

John Wiley & Sons, Inc.
New York · London · Sydney

Preface

The concept of attitude has played a major role in the history of social psychology. From its relatively simple beginning as a state of preparedness or a set to make a particular overt response, the concept has grown into its present-day formulation as a complex, multidimensional concept consisting of affective, cognitive, and conative components. As Gordon Allport pointed out more than thirty years ago, ". . . attitude is probably the most distinctive and indispensable concept in contemporary American social psychology. No other term appears more frequently in experimental and theoretical literature." Despite the enormous growth of social psychology, and the diversity of interest of contemporary social psychologists, Allport's words are as true today as they were in 1935. In addition, the attitude concept has come to play an increasingly important part in almost all of the behavioral sciences and many of the applied disciplines.

Because of the enormity of the attitude literature, and the proliferation of sources in which it appears, the study of attitudes has become difficult for all but the most dedicated students. Perhaps even more difficult, however, are the problems that confront the teacher attempting to prepare a course in the attitude area. Not only is he likely to be overwhelmed by the sheer quantity and diversity of the literature, but he will soon be appalled by its relative inaccessibility to his students. It was primarily the latter problem that led to the preparation of this book.

The initial plan was to bring together a collection of articles that would represent the three major facets of the study of attitude, that is, theory, measurement, and change. It soon became obvious, however, that no single volume could adequately sample all of the attitude literature. Since it has always been my opinion that a complete understanding and analysis of attitude change is impossible without first having a thorough knowledge of attitude theory and measurement, I decided to restrict the book to these latter two topics. Even though this restriction greatly reduced the number of articles that were considered, many excellent articles discussing attitude theory and measurement have also had to be excluded.

The selection of articles has been guided by several criteria. First, and foremost, I have deliberately emphasized those articles that have already demonstrated their lasting significance to an understanding of the attitude concept. Every attempt has been made to present the original contributions of those authors whose names repeatedly occur in any review of the attitude literature.

Second, although approximately half the book is concerned with attitude measurement, an attempt was made to select only those articles that are primarily concerned with the theory underlying attitude measurement rather than with the measurement process per se. It should be noted that in order to make the book maximally useful to all students, many commendable articles that involve extremely complex mathematical analyses have been omitted.

Third, an attempt was made to sample as wide a variety of historical and contemporary approaches to attitude theory and measurement as was possible.

Clearly, even within the limits established by these criteria, I have undoubtedly included articles that some instructors may find of little value, and have omitted others that some of my colleagues will regard as indispensable. It is unfortunate that at least three of these omissions (the contributions of Leon Festinger, Bert Green, and Eckard Hess) have been necessitated by copyright laws. Although I am indebted to many colleagues for recommendations and advice that guided the selection of articles, the responsibility for the remainder of the omissions and commissions is solely my own.

I am also indebted to the many authors (and publishers) who did grant permission to reprint their articles and, in particular, to those who graciously allowed me to edit their articles. I hope that my modification has in no way reduced the significance or meaningfulness of their contributions. Similarly, I hope my use of editorial license to include some of my own views has not detracted from the quality of the remainder of the selections.

I thank also my colleagues and students at the University of Illinois who have continually provided support and encouragement. In addition, I must thank two very special women: my secretary, Marlys Brown, who assisted me throughout every phase of the project and who capably handled almost all of the administrative details; and my wife, Deborah, who, in her usual competent manner, managed to bear with me while I was working on this book.

Martin Fishbein

Urbana, Illinois
April 1967

Contents

B. Multidimensional Measurement Techniques

C. Alternative Measurement Techniques

D. Problems and Prospects in Attitude Measurement

PART III.
ATTITUDE THEORY

A. Consistency Theories

B. Behavior Theories

C. Problems, Prospects, and Alternatives in Attitude Theory

READINGS IN

Attitude Theory and Measurement

PART I

Historical Foundations

1. Attitudes

GORDON W. ALLPORT

The concept of attitude is probably the most distinctive and indispensable concept in contemporary American social psychology. No other term appears more frequently in experimental and theoretical literature. Its popularity is not difficult to explain. It has come into favor, first of all, because it is not the property of any one psychological school of thought, and therefore serves admirably the purposes of eclectic writers. Furthermore, it is a concept which escapes the ancient controversy concerning the relative influence of heredity and environment. Since an attitude may combine both instinct and habit in any proportion, it avoids the extreme commitments of both the instinct-theory and environmentalism. The term likewise is elastic enough to apply either to the dispositions of single, isolated individuals or to broad patterns of culture. Psychologists and sociologists therefore find in it a meeting point for discussion and research. This useful, one might almost say peaceful, concept has been so widely adopted that it has virtually established itself as the keystone in the edifice of American social psychology. In fact several writers (cf. Bogardus, 1931; Thomas and Znaniecki, 1918; Folsom, 1931) define social psychology as the scientific study of attitudes.

As might be expected of so abstract and serviceable a term, it has come to signify many things to many writers, with the inevitable result that its meaning is somewhat indefinite and its scientific status called into question. Among the critics (e.g., Bain, 1927-1928; McDougall, 1933; Symonds, 1927), McDougall has been the most severe:

American social psychologists and sociologists

• Excerpted from an article in C. Murchison (Ed.), *Handbook of Social Psychology*, Clark University Press, Worcester, Mass., 1935, with permission of the author and the publisher.

have recently produced a voluminous literature concerning what they call "social attitudes"; the term is used to cover a multitude of facts of many kinds including almost every variety of opinion and belief and all the abstract qualities of personality, such as courage, obstinacy, generosity and humility, as well as the units of affective organization which are here called "sentiments." I cannot see how progress in social psychology can be made without a more discriminating terminology (1933, p. 219).

It is undeniable that the concept of "attitude" has become something of a factotum for both psychologists and sociologists. But, in spite of all the animadversions of critics, the term is now in nearly universal use and plays a central rôle in most of the recent systematic studies in social psychology. It is therefore a concept which students must examine with unusual care.

HISTORY OF THE CONCEPT OF ATTITUDE

Like most abstract terms in the English language, *attitude* has more than one meaning. Derived from the Latin *aptus,* it has on the one hand the significance of "fitness" or "adaptedness," and like its by-form *aptitude* connotes a subjective or mental state of preparation for action. Through its use in the field of art, however, the term came to have a quite independent meaning; it referred to the outward or visible posture (the bodily position) of a figure in statuary or painting. The first meaning is clearly preserved in modern psychology in what are often referred to as "mental attitudes"; and the second meaning in "motor attitudes." Since mentalistic psychology historically precedes response psychology, it is only natural to find that mental attitudes are given recognition earlier than motor attitudes. One of the earliest

3

psychologists to employ the term was Herbert Spencer. In his *First Principles* (1862) he wrote:

Arriving at correct judgments on disputed questions, much depends on the attitude of mind we preserve while listening to, or taking part, in the controversy: and for the preservation of a right attitude it is needful that we should learn how true, and yet how untrue, are average human beliefs (Vol. 1, pp. 1, i).

Similarly in 1868 Alexander Bain wrote:

The forces of the mind may have got into a set track or attitude, opposing a certain resistance as when some one subject engrosses our attention, so that even during a break in the actual current of the thoughts, other subjects are not entertained (p. 158).

Somewhat later, when psychologists were forsaking their exclusively mentalistic point of view, the concept of *motor attitudes* became *popular*. In 1888, for example, N. Lange developed a motor theory wherein the process of a perception was considered to be in large part a consequence of muscular preparation or "set." At about the same time Münsterberg (1889) developed his action theory of attention, and Féré (1890) maintained that a balanced condition of tension in the muscles was a determining condition of selective consciousness. In 1895 Baldwin proposed motor attitudes as the basis for an understanding of emotional expression, and later writers, such as Giddings (1896) and Mead (1924-1925) expanded still further the rôle of motor attitudes in social understanding.

In recent years it is uncommon to find explicit labeling of an attitude as either "mental" or "motor." Such a practice smacks of body-mind dualism, and is therefore distasteful to contemporary psychologists. In nearly all cases today the term appears without a qualifying adjective, and implicitly retains both its original meanings: a mental aptness and a motor set. Attitude connotes *a neuropsychic state of readiness for mental and physical activity.*

Attitudes in Experimental Psychology

Perhaps the first explicit recognition of attitudes within the domain of laboratory psychology was in connection with a study of reaction-time. In 1888 L. Lange discovered that a subject who was consciously prepared to press a telegraph key immediately upon receiving a signal reacted more quickly than did one whose attention was directed mainly to the incoming stimulus, and whose consciousness was not therefore directed primarily upon the expected reaction. After Lange's work, the task-attitude, or *Aufgabe,* as it came to be called, was discovered to play a decisive part in nearly all psychological experiments. Not only in the reaction experiment, but in investigations of perception, recall, judgment, thought, and volition, the central importance of the subjects' *preparedness* became universally recognized. In Germany, where most of the experimental work was done, there arose a swarm of technical expressions to designate the varieties of mental and motor "sets" which influence the subjects' trains of thought or behavior during the experiment. In addition to the *Aufgabe,* there was the *Absicht* (conscious purpose), the *Zielvorstellung* (or idea of the goal), the *Bezugsvorstellung* (idea of the relation between the self and the object to which the self is responding), the *Richtungsvorstellung* (or idea of direction), the *determindierende Tendenz* (any disposition which brings in its train the spontaneous appearance of a determined idea), the *Einstellung,* a more general term (roughly equivalent to "set"), the *Haltung* (with a more behavioral connotation), and the *Bewusstseinslage* (the "posture or lay of consciousness"). It was perhaps the lack of a general term equivalent to "attitude" that led the German experimentalists to discover so many types and forms.

Then came the lively controversy over the place of attitudes in consciousness. The *Würzburg* school was agreed that attitudes were neither sensation, nor imagery, nor affection, nor any combination of these states. Time and again they were studied by the method of introspection, always with meager results. Often an attitude seemed to have no representation in consciousness other than a vague sense of need, or some indefinite and unanalyzable feeling of doubt, assent, conviction, effort, or familiarity. (Cf. Fearing, 1931; Titchener, 1909.)

As a result of the *Würzburg* work all psychologists came to accept attitudes, but not all believed them to be impalpable and irreducible mental elements. Marbe's conception of the *Bewusstseinslage* as an "obvious fact of consciousness, whose contents, nevertheless, either do not permit at all of a detailed characterization, or are at any rate difficult to characterize" became a particular bone of contention. In general, the followers of Wundt believed that attitudes could be accounted for adequately as *feelings,* particularly as some blend of striving and excitement. Clarke (1911), a pupil of Titchener, found that attitudes in large part *are* represented in consciousness through imagery, sensation, and affection, and that where no such states are reported there is presumably merely a decay or abbreviation of these same constituents.

However they might disagree upon the nature of attitudes in so far as they appear in consciousness, all investigators, even the most orthodox, came to admit attitudes as an indispensable part of their psychological armamentarium. Titchener is a case in point. His *Outline of Psychology* in 1899 contained no reference to attitude; ten years later, in his *Textbook of Psychology,* several pages are given to the subject, and its systematic importance is fully recognized:

Behind everything lies a cortical set, a nervous bias, perhaps inherited and permanent, perhaps acquired and temporary. This background may not appear in consciousness at all; or it may appear as a vague, conscious attitude (passive imagination), or again as a more or less definite plan, aim, ambition, intention (active imagination). Whether conscious or not, the nervous disposition determines the course of consciousness (1916, Section 119).

The meagerness with which attitudes are represented in consciousness resulted in a tendency to regard them as manifestations of brain activity or of the unconscious mind. The persistence of attitudes which are totally unconscious was demonstrated by Müller and Pilzecker (1900), who called the phenomenon "perseveration." The tendency of the subject to slip into some frame of mind peculiar to himself led Koffka (1912) to postulate "latent attitudes." Washburn (1916) characterized attitudes as "static movement systems" within the organs of the body and the brain. Other writers, still more physiologically inclined, subsumed attitudes under neurological rubrics: traces, neurograms, incitograms, brain-patterns, and the like.

Psychoanalytic Influence

The contribution of the Würzburger and of all other experimental psychologists was in effect the demonstration that the concept of attitude is indispensable. The discovery that attitudes are to a large degree unconscious, however, tended to discourage them from a further study of the problem. Once a phenomenon has been driven, as it were, to take refuge in nervous tissue, and identified with cortical sets and brain fields, the psychologist, at least the introspectionist, is disinclined to pursue it further. The tendency of experimental orthodoxy is to admit the crucial part played by attitudes in all mental operations, but to consign them to the mysterious limbo of "motivation" and there to leave them.

It was the influence of Freud, of course, that resurrected attitudes from this obscurity and endowed them with vitality, identifying them with longing, hatred and love, with passion and prejudice, in short, with the onrushing stream of unconscious life. Without the painstaking labors of the experimentalists attitudes would not today be an established concept in the field of psychology, but also without the influence of psychoanalytic theory they would certainly have remained relatively lifeless, and would not have been of much assistance to social psychology which deals above all else with full-blooded phenomena. For the explanation of prejudice, loyalty, credulity, patriotism, and the passions of the mob, no anemic conception of attitudes will suffice.

Attitudes in Sociology

For a number of years sociologists have sought to supplement their cultural concepts with a psychology which might express in *concrete* terms the mechanisms through which culture is carried. At first, under the influence of Bagehot, Tarde, and Baldwin, a somewhat vaguely postulated instinct of imitation (or suggestion) was thought adequate. Somewhat later the basis was sought in a more varied native equipment of men. It is interesting to note that of the first two textbooks in social psychology, both published in the year 1908, the one, by Ross, marks the demise of the "simple and sovereign" psychology of imitation-suggestion, and the other, by McDougall, marks the commencement of the still more vigorous social psychology of instincts.

The instinct-hypothesis did not satisfy social scientists for long, for the very nature of their work forced them to recognize the importance of custom and environment in shaping social behavior. The instinct-hypothesis has precisely the contrary emphasis. What they required was a new psychological concept which would escape on the one hand from the hollow impersonality of "custom" and "social force," and on the other from nativism. Being committed to *some* psychological doctrine and dissatisfied with instincts they gradually adopted the concept of *attitude.*

The case of Dewey may be taken as fairly typical. In 1917 he professed to see in the doctrine of instincts an adequate basis for a social psychology. Five years later (1922) he no longer found instincts suitable and sought to replace them with a concept that would

. . . express that kind of human activity which is influenced by prior activity and in that sense acquired; which contains within itself a certain ordering or systematization of minor elements of action; which is projective, dynamic in quality, ready for overt manifestation; and which is operative in some subdued subordinate form even when not obviously dominating activity (p. 41).

To express this complex type of mental organization he chose "habit," but admitted as its equivalent either "disposition" or "attitude."

The credit for instituting the concept of attitude as a permanent and central feature in sociological writing must be assigned to Thomas and Znaniecki (1918), who gave it systematic priority in their monumental study of Polish peasants. Before this time the term had made only sporadic appearances in sociological literature, but immediately afterward it was adopted with enthusiasm by scores of writers.

According to Thomas and Znaniecki the study of attitudes is *par excellence* the field of social psychology. Attitudes are individual mental processes which determine both the actual and potential responses of each person in the social world. Since an attitude is always directed toward some object it may be defined as a "state of mind of the individual toward a value." Values are usually social in nature, that is to say they are objects of common regard on the part of socialized men. Love of money, desire for fame, hatred of foreigners, respect for a scientific doctrine, are typical attitudes. It follows that money, fame, foreigners, and a scientific theory are values. A social value is defined as "any datum having an empirical content accessible to the members of some social group and a meaning with regard to which it is or may be an object of activity" (p. 21). There are, to be sure, numerous attitudes corresponding to every social value; there are, for example, many views or attitudes regarding the church or the

state. There are also numerous possible values for any single attitude. The iconoclast may direct his attacks quite at random upon all the established social values, or the Philistine may accept them all uncritically. To a large extent, of course, new social values are created by the attitudes which are common to many men, but these attitudes themselves depend upon pre-existing social values. Hence in the social world, as studied by the sociologist, both values and attitudes must have a place. Primarily it falls to the ethnologist and philosopher to examine values; but it is social psychology which is "precisely the science of attitudes."

The authors draw a distinction between attitudes of temperament and of character; the former include what psychologists have been accustomed to speak of as instincts and innate aptitudes; the latter are the acquired operations of the socialized mind—the plans, interests, and sympathies which characterize the average citizen. The authors admit likewise a distinction between natural attitudes (toward the physical environment), which are of slight interest to social psychology, and the social attitudes proper which are far more numerous and which constitute the distinctive subject-matter of the new science.

Following closely in the same vein of thought, Faris (1925) proposed additional refinements. He would distinguish between conscious and unconscious attitudes, between mental and motor attitudes, between individual and group attitudes, and between latent and kinetic attitudes. Park (see Young, 1931), who is likewise in essential agreement with this school of thought, suggests four criteria for an attitude:

1. It must have definite orientation in the world of objects (or values), and in this respect differ from simple and conditioned reflexes.

2. It must not be an altogether automatic and routine type of conduct, but must display some tension even when latent.

3. It varies in intensity, sometimes being predominant, sometimes relatively ineffective.

4. It is rooted in experience, and therefore is not simply a social instinct.

Bernard (1930) has recently prepared a synthesis of the conceptions found in current sociological writing:

Social attitudes are individual attitudes directed toward social objects. Collective attitudes are individual attitudes so strongly interconditioned by collective contact that they become highly standardized and uniform within the group. . . . The attitude is originally a trial response, i.e., interrupted, preparatory or substitute behavior arising within an incompleted adjustment response, but it may become the permanent set of the organism. It ranges from concrete muscular response to that which is abstract, inner or neural. . . . Attitudes form the basis of all language and communication. In them is implicit all finished social behavior and through them practically all social adjustment is consummated. . . . Public opinion is the highest form of collective attitudes.

Conclusion

This brief review of the history of the concept of attitude has established three important facts:

1. After the breakdown of intellectualistic psychology the phenomena of "determination" came slowly but certainly to be admitted to unquestioned standing in experimental psychology. *Attitudes* came into fashion.
2. Under the influence of psychoanalytic theory the dynamic and unconscious character of attitudes became more fully recognized.
3. In sociological writing there was a gradual turning of interest to attitudes considered as the concrete representations of culture.

The effect of these three convergent trends within the past fifteen years has been the creation of a vigorous doctrine of attitudes, which today is bearing most of the descriptive and explanatory burdens of social psychology. Whether the concept is being overworked to such an extent that it will be discarded along with the past shibboleths of social science remains to be seen. It seems more probable that the ever increasing number of critical and analytical studies will somehow succeed in refining and preserving it.

ATTITUDES AS A FORM OF READINESS

Let us now consider a representative selection of definitions and characterizations of attitude.

[An attitude is] readiness for attention or action of a definite sort (Baldwin, 1901-1905).

Attitudes are literally mental postures, guides for conduct to which each new experience is referred before a response is made (Morgan, 1934, p. 47).

Attitude = the specific mental disposition toward an incoming (or arising) experience, whereby that experience is modified, or, a condition of readiness for a certain type of activity (*Dictionary of Psychology*, Warren, 1934).

An attitude is a complex of feelings, desires, fears, convictions, prejudices or other tendencies that have given *a set or readiness to act* to a person because of varied experiences (Chave, 1928).

. . . a more or less permanently enduring state of readiness of mental organization which predisposes an individual to react in a characteristic way to any object or situation with which it is related (Cantril, 1934).

From the point of view of Gestalt psychology a change of attitude involves a definite physiological stress exerted upon a sensory field by processes originating in other parts of the nervous system (Köhler, 1929, p. 184).

An attitude is a tendency to act toward or against something in the environment which becomes thereby a positive or negative value (Bogardus, 1931, p. 62).

By attitude we understand a process of individual consciousness which determines real or possible activity of the individual counterpart of the social value; activity, in whatever form, is the bond between them (Thomas and Znaniecki, 1918, p. 27).

The attitude, or preparation in advance of the actual response, constitutes an important determinant of the ensuing social behavior. Such neural settings, with their accompanying consciousness, are numerous and significant in social life (F. H. Allport, 1924, p. 320).

An attitude is a mental disposition of the human individual to act for or against a definite object (Droba, 1933).

[An attitude] denotes the general set of the organism as a whole toward an object or situation which calls for adjustment (Lundberg, 1929).

[Attitudes] are modes of emotional regard for objects, and motor "sets" or slight, tentative reactions toward them (Ewer, 1929, p. 136).

An attitude, roughly, is a residuum of experience, by which further activity is conditioned and controlled. . . . We may think of attitudes as acquired tendencies to act in specific ways toward objects (Krueger and Reckless, 1931, p. 238).

When a certain type of experience is constantly

repeated, a change of set is brought about which affects many central neurons and tends to spread over other parts of the central nervous system. These changes in the general set of the central nervous system temper the process of reception. . . . In terms of the subjective mental life these general sets are called attitudes (Warren, 1922, pp. 360 f.).

An attitude is a disposition to act which is built up by the integration of numerous specific responses of a similar type, but which exists as a general neural "set," and when activated by a specific stimulus results in behavior that is more obviously a function of the disposition than of the activating stimulus. The important thing to note about this definition is that it considers attitudes as broad, generic (not simple and specific) determinants of behavior (G. W. Allport, 1929).

We shall regard attitudes here as verbalized or verbalizable tendencies, dispositions, adjustments toward certain acts. They relate not to the past nor even primarily to the present, but as a rule, to the future. Sometimes, of course, it is a hypothetical future. . . . The "attitude" is primarily a way of being "set" toward or against things (Murphy and Murphy, 1931, p. 615).

It is not difficult to trace the common thread running through these diverse definitions. In one way or another each regards the essential feature of attitude as a *preparation or readiness for response.* The attitude is incipient and preparatory rather than overt and consummatory. It is not behavior, but the precondition of behavior. It may exist in all degrees of readiness from the most latent, dormant traces of forgotten habits to the tension or motion which is actively determining a course of conduct that is under way.

A Definition of Attitudes

It is not easy to construct a definition sufficiently broad to cover the many kinds of attitudinal determination which psychologists today recognize, and at the same time narrow enough to exclude those types of determination which are not ordinarily referred to as attitudes. The definitions considered above contain helpful suggestions, and yet none alone is entirely satisfactory. The chief weakness of most of them seems to be their failure to distinguish between attitudes, which are often very general, and habits, which are always limited in their scope.

Any attempt at a definition exaggerates the degree of agreement which psychologists have reached, but is justified if it contributes toward securing greater agreement in the future. The following definition has the merit of including recognized types of attitudes: the *Aufgabe,* the quasi-need, the *Bewusstseinslage,* interest and subjective value, prejudice, stereotype, and even the broadest conception of all, the philosophy of life. It excludes those types of readiness which are expressly innate, which are bound rigidly and invariably to the stimulus, which lack flexibility, and which lack directionality and reference to some external or conceptual object. *An attitude is a mental and neural state of readiness, organized through experience, exerting a directive or dynamic influence upon the individual's response to all objects and situations with which it is related.*

POSITIVE AND NEGATIVE ATTITUDES

An attitude characteristically provokes behavior that is acquisitive *or* avertive, favorable *or* unfavorable, affirmative *or* negative toward the object or class of objects with which it is related. This double polarity in the *direction* of attitudes is often regarded as their most distinctive feature. It has a central place in Bogardus' definition (1931, p. 52): "An attitude is a tendency to act toward or against some environmental factor which becomes thereby a positive or negative value." Likewise, Thurstone defines an attitude as "the affect for or against a psychological object" (1932).

This point of view is a modern version of an ancient dialectic. For centuries the opposed categories of "attraction" and "repulsion" have in one form or another played a decisive part in psychological theory. Empedocles assumed as the explanation of all activity the two contrasting immaterial principles of Love and Hate. The same opposed forces are prominent in the psychological theories of Mantegazza, Brentano, and Lindworsky. On a physiological plane one again encounters the dialectic of attraction and repulsion in the opposition of the flexors and extensors (Sherrington), in facilitation and inhibition (Münsterberg), in resistance and conductance (Troland), in outreaching and withdrawing behavior (Watson), in alliance and combat (Tarde), in acquisitive and avertive tendencies (Kempf), in adient and abient responses (Holt), and in pleasure and pain. One recent textbook of social psychology bears the subtitle,

The Psychology of Attraction and Repulsion (Smith, 1930), and the same pair of concepts underlie the sociological system of Roguin (1931, 1932). It is no wonder that many writers find it possible to classify all attitudes as either *positive* or *negative*. It is undoubtedly true that the majority fit easily into these categories.

And yet some attitudes are not readily classified. What shall one do, for example, with a detached, impersonal, or judicial attitude, or with an attitude of neutrality? Complacency, amusement, tolerance, and openmindedness are not easily reduced to "affect for or against" an object. Two bridge-players may have the same "degree of affect" toward the game, and yet differ qualitatively in their attitudes toward it. Two radicals may be equally in favor of change, but disagree in the *modus operandi* of reform. Two people equally well disposed toward the church may differ in their sacramental, liturgical, esthetic, social, Protestant, or Catholic interpretation of the church. Is the degree of positive or negative affect aroused by the concept of "God" as significant as the *qualitative* distinctions involved in theistic, deistic, pantheistic, agnostic, intellectualistic, or emotional attitudes? When one speaks of attitudes toward sex, it is obviously only the qualitative distinctions that have any intelligible meaning. What is a "serene and benevolent mind"? Certainly not one devoid of attitudes, nor yet one that is a battle-ground of tendencies "for" and tendencies "against." All of these objections to the unidimensional view argue strongly for the recognition of the *qualitative* nature of attitudes.

There is, however, one way of meeting these objections, namely, by reducing attitudes to small enough components. If they are divided up into artificialized units, the unidimensional conception is saved. The two radicals, for example, who are equally "against" the present social system, but who differ in their policies, may conceivably be compared in respect to the attraction or repulsion they show for each of the disputed policies. The bridge-enthusiasts who differ in their attitudes toward the game *can* be compared quantitatively in their attitudes for or against conversation during the play. Church-goers may be found to vary quantitatively in the degree to which they favor every specific practice: baptism by immersion, intincture, genuflection, or the use of vestments. And even the man who has a neutral attitude may be found to have a positive and measurable attachment to the *ideal* of neutrality. If such rigid

analyses are pursued, all of the complex, qualitative attitudes can be broken down and measured in *fragments*. The price one must pay for bi-polarity and quantification in such cases is, of course, extreme, and often absurd, *elementarism*.

THE MEASUREMENT OF ATTITUDES

The interest of American social psychologists in fact-collecting and statistical methods has resulted in a rapid advance in the empirical study of attitudes, with the result that attitudes today are measured more successfully than they are defined. As has often been pointed out, the situation is not unlike that in the field of intelligence testing where practicable tests are an established fact, although the nature of intelligence is still in dispute. In recent years there has been a decline of interest in the measurement of intelligence (Goodenough, 1934) and an increase of interest in the measurement of attitudes. It seems as though militant testing, having won victories on one field of battle, has sought a new world to conquer. The numerous methods available for measuring attitudes have been often reviewed and do not require restatement here. The present abbreviated account, which confines itself to three methods, may be supplemented by the more complete summaries of Bain (1930), Droba (1932, 1934a), Katz and Allport (1931), Fryer (1931), Murphy and Murphy (1931), Stagner (see Black, 1933, pp. 115-127), Sherman (1932), and Symonds (1931).

The Census of Opinions

The simplest method for determining how common an attitude (really an *opinion*) may be in a certain population is by counting ballots or by tabulating answers to a questionnaire. Roughly, this method may be said to "measure" the range and distribution of public opinion, although it does not, of course, determine the intensity of the opinion of any given individual upon the issue in question. The application of this method may be illustrated by reference to a recent poll, widely reported in the newspapers, concerning pacifistic and militaristic attitudes among 22,627 students in seventy colleges. Thirty-nine per cent of these students declared that they would participate in no war whatsoever, 33 per cent would take part only if the United States were invaded, and 28 per cent were ready to fight for any cause that might lead the nation to declare war. A critic might remark that such a result expresses only "verbal" opinion, or at the most merely temporary attitudes, which would change under the pressure of propaganda. Whatever may be the force of this objection, it applies equally to *all* of the methods now existing for determining the strength and nature of personal attitudes.

A far more elaborate census of students' attitudes was made by Katz and Allport (1931). In this study 4248 students in Syracuse University responded to a questionnaire containing many hundreds of items. The students did not write their opinions, but under each topic checked one of several alternative opinions with which they felt themselves to be most closely in agreement. Obviously this method does not provide a true scale of measurement, since the alternative items are not scaled in respect to their intensity. The results obtained, however, can be turned readily into a study of the *percentages* of students who favor each of the opinions contained in the questionnaire.

The a priori Scale

The so-called *a priori* scale is essentially a test devised on the basis of logical rather than empirical considerations. It is an economical method, widely used, and easy to apply, but in recent years it has been severely criticized. There are various forms of the *a priori* scale, but they are all alike in that their scoring is arbitrary. Sometimes the author presents a series of questions, each of which may have, say, five alternative answers from which the subject must select one. These alternative answers are conceived by the author to lie on a single continuum and to be equally spaced from the most favorable to the least favorable. To each item the author arbitrarily assigns a value of 1, 2, 3, 4, or 5, according to his opinion of its significance. Another variation allows the subject to place in rank order all of the alternatives according to his preference; these rank orders are then treated as though they were *equal* intervals in the scale. The statistical pitfalls of *a priori* scales have been pointed out by Thurstone (1927-1928).

As an example of a widely used scale of this type may be mentioned the test for "social distance" devised by Bogardus (1925*a*, 1925*b*, 1927). In this test the subject is asked the degree of intimacy he would willingly sanction between himself and members of various races. The degrees of intimacy listed in one form of

the test together with their "scale values" are as follows:

1—to close kinship by marriage
2—to my club as personal chums
3—to my street as neighbors
4—to employment in my occupation in my country
5—to citizenship in my country
6—as visitors only to my country
7—would exclude from my country

The weakness of the scale becomes at once apparent when it is realized that the distance between each of these degrees of intimacy is not necessarily comparable. The psychological difference between relationship in marriage and in a club is likely to be far greater than that existing between club relations and neighborly relations. It becomes therefore misleading to assign equally progressing arithmetical units to unequal attitudinal differences. Another difficulty arises in the assumption that each higher degree of intimacy necessarily implies all those that are lower; but there are cases where admission to neighborly relations, for example, is less distasteful than admission to one's occupation.

The Psychophysical (Rational) Scale

The most significant event in the history of the measurement of attitudes was the application of psychophysical methods by Thurstone. To apply psychophysical methods it is necessary first to conceive of an attitude as a "degree of affect" for or against an object or a value with which the scale is concerned. If this assumption is granted, it becomes possible to study the degree of favor or disfavor which each subject in a population has toward certain objects or values, such as the church, war, moving pictures, or government ownership. Within the past few years a large number of such scales have been devised and made available for general use (Thurstone and associates, 1929).

The scoring values for all of these scales are determined by combining the efforts of many judges who have arranged all the statements included in each scale according to their *discriminable* differences. If judges, by and large, agree that two statements express about the same degree of favor or disfavor it is obviously unnecessary to keep both statements in the scale; if the statements are widely different it is possible by comparing the judges' sorting of each statement in relation to all other statements to determine its position. The final, rational scale results when forty or fifty statements are secured whose distance from one another on a single continuum are known. This distance is essentially the discriminable difference between the statements as they appear to the standardizing group of judges. There are various methods by which the discriminable differences may be determined. The commonest is the "method of equal-appearing intervals." The directions for its use involve the following steps:

1. Specify the attitude variable to be measured.

2. Collect a wide variety of opinions relating to it, from newspapers, books, or from individuals.

3. Assemble on cards approximately one hundred such typical opinions.

4. Require at least 200-300 judges to sort these cards into piles (eleven being a convenient and commonly employed number), each pile representing equidistant degrees of the attitude according to each judge's estimation.

5. Calculate the scale value for each of the items by computing the median of the scale values assigned to it by the judges, and the dispersion of the judgments around the median.

6. Retain such statements as have small dispersions, and are on the whole equally spaced. Give approximately equal representation to each of the intervals secured. Clarity and brevity of wording may furnish additional bases for selection.

7. In applying the scale, the subject checks every statement with which he agrees, and his score is the mean scale-value for all the statements he has endorsed.

The most useful procedure in constructing such scales is to follow the models offered in the Thurstone-Chave (1929) or Peterson-Thurstone (1933) scale. Directions for uniform wording have been suggested by Droba (1932), Wang (1932), Kulp (1933), and Stagner (see Black, 1933, pp. 115-127). Further details concerning the construction and use of psychophysical scales may easily be traced through the literature (Black, 1933; Dockeray, 1932; Thurstone, 1927-1928, 1929, 1932; Remmers, 1934).

As revolutionary as the rational scale undoubtedly is, certain criticisms must be made against the method as it is at present employed:

1. As has already been indicated above, attitudes are not necessarily arranged naturally upon a single continuum; they are often discrete and highly individual (cf. Katz and Allport, 1931).

2. There is also the question whether scale values for statements derived from one population of judges is applicable to other populations of subjects (Rice, 1930). For example, can the judgments of adults concerning the significance of a statement dealing with moving pictures be incorporated in a test that is to be administered to children?

3. Likert (1932-1933) has shown that the simple a priori method of scoring in arbitrary units (1 to 5) when applied to these rational scales may yield results as reliable as do the psychophysical scores themselves. The agreement between the two methods is approximately .90. This fact may give comfort to investigators who wish to avoid the more complex procedures.

Thurstone's strictures upon the logic of a priori scales are undoubtedly sound, but they do not necessarily invalidate these scales when only practical results are desired. Suppose, for instance, that a psychologically minded chairman wishes to determine at a certain meeting the temper of his audience in reference to some issue under discussion. He can quickly prepare and quickly (if roughly) score an a priori scale; whereas the preparation of a more carefully standardized test would be impracticable and unnecessarily fine-grained for his purposes.

Conclusions

The success achieved in the past ten years in the field of the measurement of attitudes may be regarded as one of the major accomplishments of social psychology in America. The rate of progress is so great that further achievements in the near future are inevitable. But there are inherent limitations in all methods of testing. Unless these are kept in mind the zeal for measurement may overstep reasonable bounds.

1. Measurement can deal only with attitudes that are *common*, and there are relatively few attitudes that are common enough to be profitably scaled. In forcing attitudes into a scale form violence is necessarily done to the unique structure of man's mind. Attitude scales should

be regarded only as the roughest approximations of the way in which attitudes actually exist in the mental life of individuals.

2. Each person possesses many contradictory attitudes, and for this reason his mental set at the moment of submitting to a scale may tell only a part of the story. Furthermore, attitudes often change, and an investigation made under one set of conditions may not for long present a true picture of the attitudes of any given group. Stagner (see Black, 1933) reports a meeting of farmers in a village in northern Wisconsin who, under the influence of a persuasive speaker, voted unanimously one afternoon to call a milk strike. The same group met in the evening to hear a speaker with opposed views. They then voted unanimously not to strike.

3. Rationalization and deception inevitably occur, especially when the attitudes studied pertain to the moral life or social status of the subject. The difficulty of obtaining reliable information concerning attitudes toward sex is a case in point. So great is the tendency to protect oneself that even anonymity is not a guarantee. Lack of insight, ignorance, suspicion, fear, a neurotic sense of guilt, undue enthusiasm, or even a knowledge of the investigator's purpose may invalidate an inquiry.

BIBLIOGRAPHY

Allport, E. H. 1924. *Social psychology*. Boston: Houghton Mifflin. Pp. xiv + 453.

Allport, G. W. 1929. The composition of political attitudes. *Amer. J. Sociol.*, 35, 220-238.

Bain, A. 1868. *Mental science*. New York: Appleton. Pp. 428.

Bain, R. 1927-1928. An attitude on attitude research. *Amer. J. Sociol.*, 33, 940-957.

Bain, R. 1930. Theory and measurement of attitudes and opinions. *Psychol. Bull.*, 27, 357-379.

Baldwin, J. M. 1901-1905. *Dictionary of philosophy and psychology*. (3 vols.) New York: Macmillan. Pp. xxiv + 644; xvi + 892; xxvi + 542; viii + 543-1192.

Bernard, L. L. 1930. Attitudes, social. In *Encyclopedia of the social sciences*, Vol. 2, ed. by E. R. A. Seligman and A. Johnson. New York: Macmillan. Pp. 305-306.

Black, J. D. (Ed.) 1933. *Research in social psychology of rural life*. (Bull. 17.) New York: Soc. Sci. Res. Council. P. 130.

Bogardus, E. S. 1925a. Social distance and its origins. *J. Appl. Sociol.*, 9, 216-226.

Bogardus, E. S. 1925b. Measuring social distances. *J. Appl. Sociol.*, 9, 299-308.

Bogardus, E. S. 1927. Race friendliness and social distances. *J. Appl. Sociol.*, 11, 272-287.

Bogardus, E. S. 1931. *Fundamentals of social psychology*. (2nd ed.) New York: Century. P. 444.

Cantril, H. 1934. Attitudes in the making. *Understanding the Child*, 4, 13-15.

Chave, E. J. 1928. A new type scale for measuring attitudes. *Relig. Educ.*, 23, 364-369.

Clarke, H. M. 1911. Conscious attitudes. *Amer. J. Psychol.*, 32, 214-249.

Dewey, J. 1917. The need for social psychology. *Psychol. Rev.*, 24, 266-277.

Dewey, J. 1922. *Human nature and conduct*. New York: Holt. Pp. vii + 336.

Dockeray, D. C. 1932. *General psychology*. Englewood Cliffs, N. J.: Prentice-Hall. Pp. xxi + 581.

Droba, D. D. 1932. Methods for measuring attitudes. *Psychol. Bull.*, 29, 309-323.

Droba, D. D. 1933. The nature of attitude. *J. Soc. Psychol.*, 4, 444-463.

Droba, D. D. 1934. Social attitudes. *Amer. J. Sociol.*, 39, 513-524.

Ewer, B. C. 1929. *Social psychology*. New York: Macmillan. Pp. ix + 435.

Faris, E. 1925. The concept of social attitudes. *J. Appl. Sociol.*, 9, 404-409.

Fearing, F. 1931. The experimental study of attitude, meaning, and the process antecedent to action by N. Ach and others in the Wurzburg laboratory. In *Methods in social science*, ed. by S. Rice. Chicago: Univ. Chicago Press. Pp. 715-728.

Féré, C. 1890. Note sur la physiologie de l'attention. *Rev. Phil.*, 30, 393-405.

Folsom, J. K. 1931. *Social psychology*. New York: Harper. Pp. xviii + 701.

Fryer, D. 1931. *The measurement of interests*. New York: Holt. Pp. xxxvi + 488.

Giddings, F. H. 1896. *The principles of sociology*. New York: Macmillan. Pp. xxvi + 476.

Goodenough, F. 1934. Trends in modern psychology. *Psychol. Bull.*, 31, 81-97.

Katz, D., and Allport, F. H. 1931. *Students' attitudes*. Syracuse, N. Y.: Craftsman Press. Pp. xxviii + 408.

Koffka, K. 1912. *Zur Analyse der Vorstellungen und ihren Gesetze*. Leipzig: Quelle and Meyer. Pp. x + 392.

Köhler, W. 1929. *Gestalt psychology*. New York: Liveright. Pp. xi + 403.

Krueger, E. T., and Reckless, W. C. 1931. *Social psychology*. New York: Longmans, Green. Pp. vii + 578.

Kulp, D. H., Jr. 1933. The form of statements in attitude tests. *J. Sociol. Soc. Res.*, 18, 18-25.

Lange, L. 1888. Neue Experimente über den Vorgang der einfachen Reaktion auf Sinneseindrücke. *Phil. Stud.*, **4**, 479-510.

Lange, N. 1888. Beiträge zur Theorie der sinnlichen Aufmerksamkeit und der aktiven Apperception. *Phil. Stud.*, **4**, 390-422.

Likert, R. 1932-1933. Technique for the measurement of attitudes. *Arch. Psychol.*, **22** (140), 55.

Lundberg, G. A. 1929. *Social research.* New York: Longmans, Green. Pp. x + 379.

McDougall, W. 1921. *An introduction to social psychology.* (14th ed.) Boston: Luce. P. 418.

McDougall, W. 1933. *The energies of men.* New York: Scribner's. Pp. ix + 395.

Mead, G. H. 1924-1925. Genesis of self and social control. *Int. J. Ethics,* 251-277.

Morgan, J. J. B. 1934. *Keeping a sound mind.* New York: Macmillan. Pp. ix + 440.

Müller, G. E., and Pilzecker, A. 1900. Experimentelle Beiträge zur Lehre vom Gedächtniss. *Z. Psychol.*, **1**, xiv + 300.

Münsterberg, H. 1889. *Beiträge zur experimentellen Psychologie.* Vol. I. Freiburg: Mohr. P. 188.

Murphy, G., and Murphy, L. B. 1931. *Experimental social psychology.* New York: Harper. P. 709.

Peterson, R. C., and Thurstone, L. L. 1933. *Motion pictures and the social attitudes of children.* New York: Macmillan. Pp. xvii + 75.

Remmers, H. H. (Ed.) 1934. Studies in attitudes. *Stud. Higher Educ.,* Purdue Univ., No. xxvi. P. 112.

Rice, S. A. 1930. Statistical studies of social attitudes and public opinion. In *Statistics in social studies.* Philadelphia: Univ. Pennsylvania Press. Pp. 171-192.

Roguin, E. 1931 and 1932. *Sociologie.* (2 vols.) Lausanne: Charles Pach. Pp. iv + 651; xxxix + 789.

Ross, E. A. 1908. *Social psychology.* New York: Macmillan. Pp. xvi + 372.

Sherman, M. 1932. Theories and measurement of attitudes. *Child Develpm.*, **3**, 15-28.

Smith, J. 1930. *Social psychology.* Boston: Badger. P. 468.

Spencer, H. 1862. *First principles.* (Reprinted from 5th London ed.) New York: Burt. Pp. xv + 483.

Symonds, P. M. 1927. What is an attitude? *Psychol. Bull.*, **24**, 200 f.

Symonds, P. M. 1931. *Diagnosing personality and conduct.* New York: Century. Pp. xvi + 602.

Thomas, W. I., and Znaniecki, F. 1918. *The Polish peasant in Europe and America.* Vol. I. Boston: Badger. P. 526.

Thurstone, L. L. 1927-1928. Attitudes can be measured. *Amer. J. Sociol.*, **33**, 529-554.

Thurstone, L. L. 1929. Theory of attitude measurement. *Psychol. Rev.*, **36**, 222-241.

Thurstone, L. L. 1932. The measurement of social attitudes. *J. Abnorm. Soc. Psychol.*, **26**, 249-269.

Thurstone, L. L., and Chave, E. J. 1929. *The measurement of attitude.* Chicago: Univ. Chicago Press. Pp. xii + 97.

Titchener, E. B. 1909. *Experimental psychology of the thought processes.* New York: Macmillan. Pp. ix + 318.

Titchener, E. B. 1916. *A text-book of psychology.* (New ed.) New York: Macmillan. Pp. xvii + 564.

Wang, C. K. A. 1932. Suggested criteria for writing attitude statements. *J. Soc. Psychol.*, **3**, 367-373.

Warren, H. C. 1922. *Elements of human psychology.* Boston: Houghton Mifflin. Pp. x + 416.

Warren, H. C. (Ed.) 1934. *Dictionary of psychology.* Boston: Houghton Mifflin. Pp. ix + 372.

Washburn, M. F. 1916. *Movement and mental imagery.* Boston: Houghton Mifflin. Pp. xv + 252.

Young, K. (Ed.) 1931. *Social attitudes.* New York: Holt. P. 375.

2. The Measurement of Social Attitudes

L. L. THURSTONE

It is an honor and a privilege for me to have this opportunity of addressing the Midwestern Psychological Association. I wish that I could do justice to the occasion and express my appreciation by an address that is worth listening to. I have selected among the few subjects that are available to me one that may be of fairly general interest while it still involves many theoretical and psychological problems. I shall discuss the measurement of social attitudes. In doing so I shall review the development of the measurement methods that are applicable to attitudes and I shall also discuss some of the criticisms and questions that have recently been raised about this subject.

Several years ago when I was teaching conventional psychophysics, it seemed to me that psychophysics was really a very dull subject in spite of the fact that it did offer the satisfaction of clean and quantitative logic. This type of satisfaction is rare in psychological investigation and consequently psychophysics has stood out as a very dignified topic in psychology in spite of the fact that its intrinsic subject matter has been, on the whole, rather trivial. These depreciative statements about psychophysics can be readily amplified by referring to the conventional publications in this subject. You will then find that one of the elaborate parts of the subject is the determination of limens. There is a great deal of hairsplitting about just how a limen should be determined with the greatest possible precision. In determining a limen you fit a phi-gamma curve and then there is more hairsplitting as to whether you should adjust the errors of observation in the proportions or in the stimulus magnitudes.

• Reprinted from *Journal of Abnormal and Social Psychology*, 1931, **26**, 249-269, with permission of the American Psychological Association. This article was originally presented as an address for the Midwestern Psychological Association, May 9, 1931.

Then you will find the several psychophysical methods compared as to which gives the most reliable limen determination. And then you can find short-cuts for these methods by which you can determine somebody's limen very quickly when you are in a hurry for a limen. Now, it seems strange that I have never seen a psychologist who really cared much about any particular person's limen for anything!

I venture the guess that not more than perhaps half a dozen psychologists in this room have ever needed or wanted somebody's limen for anything with a high degree of precision. And I don't believe that the proportion would be much higher in a group of Eastern psychologists.

Of course we are interested to know the order of magnitude of errors in visual discrimination as compared with those of various forms of auditory discrimination. Even in a rough pitch discrimination test we are determining a limen in a sense, but these problems never involve any profundities of curve fitting for the limen of an individual subject. Why then does psychophysics bother so much about methods, and short-cuts for these methods, which are never used on individual subjects except when an individual serves as a specimen for some type of situation in which the methods must be adapted to the conditions of each problem anyway? This bothered me also in teaching the subject and I came to share the distrust of my students in the significance of the whole subject.

One way in which to retain the satisfactions that can be found in the logic of this subject is to change its content. We have tried this and it has seemed to some of us that psychophysics thereby takes on an entirely new aspect. Instead of asking a person, "Which of these two little cylinders is the heavier?" (apologies to Mr. Boring for the stimulus error)—instead of asking a person which of two cylinders is the heavier, we might as well ask him something interesting, such as, "Which of these two nationalities do you in general prefer to associate with?" or, "Which of these two offenses do you consider to be in general the more serious?" or, "Which of these two pictures or colored designs do you like better?" Questions of this sort of discrimination might be multiplied indefinitely and if they could be handled with some sort of psychophysical logic it is clear that we should have here the possibilities of objective description of more psychological significance than the sensory limen.

The first objection that I encountered is that the very term psychophysics should be strictly limited to the field of sensory discrimination and that the questions that I prefer to ask should not be regarded as of the dignity of psychophysics—they should be relegated to the field of mental tests and questionnaires. I find justification for extending the use of psychophysics even to questions that are interesting by referring to Titchener. He says: "Fechner was chiefly interested in the intensive aspect of mental processes, and among mental processes in sensation. His example has led other inquirers to give a disproportionate amount of attention to the laws of sensation intensity." It is unfortunate that Mr. Titchener did not happen to ask his students to judge the relative merits of handwriting specimens or of English compositions or to make social judgments because then I am sure that we should now have the permission to use psychophysical methods in a wide variety of problems.

Furthermore, if, instead of printing our questions on a piece of paper we should rig up an elaborate automatic contraption for exposing these questions, running the said contraption by an electric motor, and spreading plenty of kymographs and telegraph keys and speech keys and time markers all around the room, then I am sure that our studies would qualify as experimental psychology. But since we ask the subject to indicate his response with a pencil instead of by a telegraph key, our investigations have been outside the pale of experimental psychology.

When the constant method is used in its complete form so that every stimulus serves in turn as a standard, then it becomes the method of paired comparison. There was no quantitative logic for handling the method of paired comparison so as to obtain measurement which satisfied the criterion of internal consistency. This difficulty was overcome by finding an equation that satisfied this criterion. It has been referred to as the law of comparative judgment. With this rational equation and the method of paired comparison we have made several studies involving social stimuli and in which the subjects were asked to express various kinds of judgments other than mere comparison of physical magnitudes.

In one of these experiments a list of twenty nationalities was presented to several hundred students (1). The nationalities were arranged in pairs so that every nationality was paired with every other one in the list. The students were asked to underline one nationality of each pair to indicate which of the two nationalities they would rather associate with. The returns were tabulated in the form "proportion of the subjects who prefer nationality A to nationality B." With these experimental proportions and by the law of comparative judgment, the scale separation was calculated for each pair. By means of these data it was possible to construct a linear scale of attitude to which each nationality was allocated. At the top of the list is the American, next come other English speaking countries, and at the bottom of the list are nationalities or races other than our own. This order is what one should expect, but the scale values could not be predicted.

In general the scaling is accomplished on the principle that if the group of subjects very generally prefers A to B, then the proportion of the subjects who vote for A will be high, perhaps close to unity (2). If, on the other hand, the two nationalities are about equally well liked by the group, then there will be about as many subjects who vote for A as there are subjects who vote for B. Hence, the proportion above described will be close to .50 and the two nationalities will have zero separation, that is, they will have the same scale value.

In an experiment of this sort the criterion of internal consistency consists in the discovery that by assigning one scale value to each of the nationalities we can reconstruct all of the experimentally independent proportions. With twenty nationalities in the list we have twenty scale values and these must be sufficient to lock the 190 experimentally independent proportions within the known probable errors of the given proportions.

One of the criticisms of this procedure has

been that the entries in the list are not true nationalities. For example, in the list occur such entries as Jew, Negro, South American. It is not necessary to restrict ourselves to accepted anthropological classifications in these experiments. We are measuring the degree of affect for or against the social objects listed. This is legitimate even if some of the classifications are races rather than nationalities, or religions, or groups of nationalities. For example, it is conceivable that some of the students disliked South Americans in general without knowing much about them and without stopping to debate whether these South Americans whom they disliked were one or twenty nationalities. The category is a conversational one which lends itself to the expression of affect and it therefore serves our purposes even if the psychological or affective category does not fit the accepted anthropological or political classifications. There is of course nothing to prevent the use of other classifications so long as the categories lend themselves to the expression of the likes and dislikes of people generally.

Another criticism that has been offered against experiments of this type is that it would make a difference if the question were worded differently. For example, in the form here described the question was "Which of these two nationalities or races would you rather associate with?" Now, so runs the objection, what would happen if the question were "Which would you rather have as a fellow student?", "Which would you rather have for a neighbor?", "Which would you rather have your sister marry?" and "Which would you rather do business with?" (3). Fortunately, this question could be answered by an experiment. Fifteen hundred blanks were used in which there were three hundred blanks with each of the five questions. These were arranged in random order so that it was a matter of chance which of the five forms was given to each of the fifteen hundred subjects in the experiment. When the blanks had been filled in, they were sorted out into five piles according to the question on the blank. The twenty nationalities were then allocated to a scale separately for each of the five questions. The twenty nationalities were found to be in the same rank order in the scales which were constructed on the basis of the five questions. This proves that the scale value of a nationality is determined primarily not by the detailed form of the question but rather by the general degree of like or dislike of the subjects for each nationality. This general like or dislike is what we have called the potential action toward the object or attitude.

On the other hand, if the question had been "Which nationality would you rather have as a servant?" it is quite conceivable that the scale values might have been different, because such a question is not calculated to bring out the attitude of the subject toward the nationality with regard to social equality. If the question asked which of the nationalities is the more intelligent, which is physically superior, which is more emotional, which is the taller, it is quite certain that the scale values would have been different.

The generalization of the last experiment might be made by noting that a subject could be half way through the blank, responding by underlining one of each pair, and still not remember what the question was that he was answering by his underlining. This means merely that the subject gets a set of checking preferences without recalling the cognitive detail of the question. The question has then served its usefulness by giving the subject a set of expressing his attitudes rather than some intellectual judgment about the nationalities in question. The scale value of each nationality measures the affective value of the nationality for the group of subjects.

It is obvious that the scale value of each nationality in these experiments is a description of the group of subjects as much as it is a description of the nationalities. If the same experiment were repeated with Italian students or with Russian students, the scale values of the nationalities would undoubtedly be radically different.

This suggests the possibility of measuring cultural similarities or dissimilarities. Suppose that these paired comparison schedules were filled in by university students in ten different countries. The scale value of each of the twenty nationalities would be calculated separately for each of the ten countries. We could then calculate the correlation coefficient for the scale values of the twenty nationalities in two countries, for example, the German and the French students. If the correlation coefficient were high it would indicate a similarity in the nationality preferences of the two groups of students. If the correlation were low it would measure dissimilarity of the two groups of students as to their national preferences. If country C is very much hated by A and liked by B, then that difference would be measurable by the difference in the scale value for nationality C in the scales for groups A and B. In this way, international affiliations and antipathies might be described in a quantitative manner. Of course differences might appear in different occupational groups and in different regions of the same country.

Suppose that one group of subjects likes all of the twenty nationalities about equally well. Then the twenty nationalities would have the same scale value. Suppose that another group of subjects has very decided likes and dislikes among the twenty nationalities. Some of the nationalities would then have high scale values while others would have conspicuously low scale values. In other words, the spread in scale values would be much greater for the second group than for the first group. The intolerance of a group is measured by the spread in scale values. In this manner it would be possible to measure the tolerance of different countries for other countries. These measurements of international tolerance might conceivably have considerable social interest.

Some of our experiments have been set up so as to measure the effect of social stimuli on the international attitudes of high school children. We have worked with a number of motion picture films as stimuli (4). In Genoa, Illinois, the film *Four Sons* was shown in the local theater and 131 children in grades 7 to 12 inclusive were given free tickets. Several days before the performance they were asked to fill in a paired comparison schedule of nationality preferences. The Germans were included in this list. The morning after the performance the children again filled in the same schedule. It was assumed that the attitudes of the children did not change toward the twenty nationalities during the course of a week or ten days between the two schedules except for the possible effect of the film on their attitude toward Germans. The film made the children much more friendly toward Germans. This experiment and others of the same general type demonstrate that the effect of a single social stimulus on the international attitudes of the subjects can be measured.

The same general technique has been used for measuring attitude toward crimes (5). In such experiments a list of crimes was arranged in the same paired forms and the subjects were asked to indicate for each pair which of the two crimes they considered to be the more serious. In this manner it was found in one town that the attitudes of children toward gambling were considerably affected by seeing the picture *Street of Chance*. The film had the effect of making the children regard gambling as a more serious offense after seeing the picture. These experiments with motion pictures have been effectively conducted by Miss Ruth Peterson.

The question has been raised as to the degree of permanence of these effects. In order to answer this question we have repeated the schedules of comparison in several towns after an interval of four to five months. The attitudes have returned about half way toward their original values in four months, but these effects vary of course with the film used and the frequency of other social stimuli. In one town the effect lasted without diminution for five months.

When a series of social stimuli has been allocated to an affective continuum by the method of paired comparison we have the scale separations but we do not have a rational origin for the affective continuum. This is a problem for which Mr. Horst has found a very ingenious solution. It is of some psychological interest to locate a series of stimuli to an affective continuum in such a manner that the measurements refer to a datum of affective neutrality. The solution by Mr. Horst consists in asking a group of subjects to compare one stimulus A which is likely to be favorably regarded with another stimulus B which is likely to be considered unfavorable. The subject is asked this question, "Would you be willing to endure the disadvantage B in order to have the advantage A?" The proportion of subjects who are willing to accept B in order to have A allocates the affective origin between the two stimuli. The same procedure can of course be extended to a whole series of stimuli so that the location of an affective datum in the series can be tested by the criterion of internal consistency.

Another method of measuring attitude is to use a *statement scale* (6). This consists in a series of opinions which are submitted to the subject for endorsement or rejection. These statements or opinions have been so selected that they constitute an evenly graduated series and so that a scale value can be given to each opinion. If the opinions A, B, C, D are four successive opinions in such an evenly graduated scale about prohibition, for example, then the following conditions would be satisfied. If one person endorses opinion A and another person endorses opinion B, then a group of observers should find some difficulty in saying which of the two opinions is more favorable to prohibition. Let us suppose that three-fourths of the observers would say that opinion A is more favorable to prohibition than opinion B. Then this degree of difficulty in judging which of them is the more favorable to prohibition constitutes a measure of the separation between the two statements of opinion on the attitude scale. Now, if opinion C is so chosen that three-fourths of the observers say that B is more favorable to prohibition than C, then the scale separation between A and B is the same as the separation between B and C. In this manner a series of statements is selected from a large number so that the apparent increment in attitude from one statement to the next is the same for the whole series.

With a scale value assigned to each statement or opinion, it is of course easy to calculate the median scale value of all the statements that any given individual has endorsed. This median scale value is the score of that person on the attitude scale. The meaning of these scores can be illustrated further as follows. Suppose that three individuals, X, Y, Z, have attitude scores on prohibition which are equally spaced. Then the difference or increment in attitude between X and Y would seem to be the same as the difference in attitude between Y and Z. In other words, it would be just as difficult to discriminate between X and Y as to which is the more favorable to prohibition as it is difficult to discriminate between Y and Z. This is the basis for the construction of the attitude scales. The psychophysical experimental methods by which the attitude scales are constructed so as to satisfy these requirements are beyond the scope of this paper.

The statement scale enables one to make several types of measurement of which the following are examples.

The attitude of an individual subject can be measured by means of a statement scale. The paired comparison procedure enables us to compare groups of subjects but the statement scale procedure is preferable for measuring the attitudes of individual subjects. The range of statements that the individual endorses gives some indication of his tolerance. It is possible to plot a frequency distribution of the attitudes of a group of people toward labor unions, for example. This distribution has a central tendency or average and it has a measurable dispersion. Two groups of people may then be found to have the same average score on a disputed issue but one of the two groups may be more heterogeneous than the other. The degree of heterogeneity in attitude of a group of people is directly measured by the standard deviation of the frequency distribution of their attitude scores. This is an important aspect of group comparisons which can be reduced easily to measurement in terms of the dispersion of the scores.

In two small towns, West Chicago and Geneva, Illinois, an experiment was arranged so that a film favorable to the Chinese was shown in one town and a film unfavorable to the Chinese was shown in the other town (7). The two films were *Welcome Danger* which is thought to be unfriendly to the Chinese and which has been so criticized by the Chinese themselves, and *Son of the Gods* which is generally thought to be friendly in its interpretation of Chinese culture. The films were shown in the local theaters and the children were given free tickets to the performances. In each town the children were asked to fill in a statement scale about the Chinese several days before seeing the film and also the morning after seeing it. The results show a very decided shift in favor of the Chinese in Geneva where *Son of the Gods* was shown. In West Chicago there was a small opposite effect where the children saw the film, *Welcome Danger*. The effect of a single social stimulus, such as a motion picture film, on the international attitudes of school children can be described by the statement scale as well as by the paired comparison method.

The statement scale is constructed by asking a group of one hundred judges to sort out a list of opinions into a series of eleven successive piles to represent attitudes from one extreme to the other. The question was raised early in our experiments whether the attitudes of the judges themselves would influence the final scale values of the statements in the scale. For this reason Mr. Hinckley set up an experiment for measuring attitude toward the Negro. He had 114 statements about the Negro. At one extreme were the opinions that the Negro is the equal of the white man and should have equal social privileges. At the other extreme were the opinions that the Negro is inferior to the white man and should not have the same social privileges. Three groups of judges were used, namely, one group of white college students friendly toward the Negro, one group of white college students who thought the Negro was definitely inferior, and one group of educated Negroes. The whole list of 114 statements was scaled separately for the three groups of judges. The result was that the three scales so constructed were practically identical, thus proving that the attitudes of the judges have no serious effect on the measuring function of the statement scale.

It is possible to apply the statement scale method to the measurement of social trend. This will be illustrated in terms of attitude toward the Germans and the French. A collection of quotations from newspaper editorials has been made by Mr. Russell. His quotations cover the twenty year period 1910-1930. A group of judges sorted the editorial quotations into a series of eleven piles ranging from No. 1 expressing extreme admiration for the Germans to No. 11 expressing extreme contempt for them. The scale value of each quotation was calculated. Then the average scale value of all the quotations from the year 1910 was determined. It is the mean attitude toward the Germans for that year. The average scale value of all the quotations from year 1911 was determined and it is the mean attitude toward the Germans for that year. In this manner the mean attitude toward the Germans was represented quantitatively so that this social trend for a period of 20 years could be inspected in a single graph.

For this particular issue the curve shows the expected depression in the average scale value for the Germans during the years of the war and a corresponding rise in average scale value for the French during the same period. Of course the curves so plotted represent only the attitudes of the editorials of one large newspaper. Mr. Russell is now making this type of inquiry for four newspapers, namely the *New York Times,* the *World,* the *Chicago Daily News,* and also the *Chicago Tribune.* The curves for these four newspapers are similar. They all show a return of attitudes toward the pre-war values with interesting deviations that correspond to popularly discussed issues at various times. The newspapers also show some differences in the rapidity with which their editorials return toward pre-war attitudes for Germany. We have here the possibility of measuring the changes in attitudes as represented in the press during past times even though the

attitude scales were not available for these periods. It will be interesting to study by these quantitative methods the rapidity with which international attitudes have changed before and after each of the recent modern wars by analyzing the foreign press for a few years before and after each war. It will also be of interest to correlate these rates of change with other social facts such as facility of communication, similarity of language and culture, and the like. Perhaps this will be a psychophysical contribution to the methods of history.

Many of the criticisms and questions that have appeared about attitude measurement concern the nature of the fundamental concepts involved and the logic by which the measurements are made. I shall consider a few of these questions briefly.

One of the most frequent questions is that a score on an attitude scale, let us say the scale of attitude toward God, does not truly describe the person's attitude. There are so many complex factors involved in a person's attitude on any social issue that it cannot be adequately described by a simple number such as a score on some sort of test or scale. This is quite true, but it is also equally true of all measurement.

The measurement of any object or entity describes only one attribute of the object measured. This is a universal characteristic of all measurement. When the height of a table is measured, the whole table has not been described but only that attribute which was measured. Similarly, in the measurement of attitudes, only one characteristic of the attitude is described by a measurement of it.

Further, only those characteristics of an object can be measured which can be described in terms of "more" or "less." Examples of such description are: one object is longer than another, one object is hotter than another, one is heavier than another, one person is more intelligent than another, more educated than another, more strongly favorable to prohibition, more religious, more strongly favorable to birth control than another person. These are all traits by which two objects or two persons may be compared in terms of "more" or "less."

Only those characteristics can be described by measurement which can be thought of as linear magnitudes. In this context, linear magnitudes are weight, length, volume, temperature, amount of education, intelligence, and strength of feeling favorable to an object.

Another way of saying the same thing is to note that the measurement of an object is, in effect, to allocate the object to a point on an abstract continuum. If the continuum is weight, then individuals may be allocated to an abstract continuum of weight, one direction of which represents small weight while the opposite direction represents large weight. Each person might be allocated to a point on this continuum with any suitable scale which requires some point at which counting begins, called the origin, and some unit of measurement in terms of which the counting is done.

The linear continuum which is implied in all measurement is always an abstraction. For example, when several people are described as to their weight, each person is in effect allocated to a point on an abstract continuum of weight. All measurement implies the reduction or restatement of the attribute measured to an abstract linear form. There is a popular fallacy that a unit of measurement is a thing—such as a piece of yardstick. This is not so. A unit of measurement is always a *process* of some kind which can be repeated without modification in the different parts of the measurement continuum.

Not all of the characteristics which are conversationally described in terms of "more" or "less" can actually be measured. But any characteristic which lends itself to such description has the possibility of being reduced to measurement.

We admit that an attitude is a complex affair which cannot be wholly described by any single numerical index. For the problem of measurement this statement is analogous to the observation that an ordinary table is a complex affair which cannot be wholly described by any single numerical index. So is a man such a complexity which cannot be wholly represented by a single index. Nevertheless we do not hesitate to say that we measure the table. The context usually implies what it is about the table that we propose to measure. We say without hesitation that we measure a man when we take some anthropometric measurement of him. The context may well imply without explicit declaration what aspect of the man we are measuring, his cephalic index, his height or weight or blood pressure or what not. Just in the same sense we shall say here that we are measuring attitudes. We shall state or imply by the context of people's attitudes that we are measuring. The point is that it is just

as legitimate to say that we are measuring attitudes as it is to say that we are measuring tables or men.

Whenever a common word is adopted for scientific use, it nearly always suffers some restriction in its connotation in favor of greater precision of meaning. This has happened in many sciences, so that it is by no means peculiar to psychological terms. Consider, for example, such words as elasticity, momentum, force, which are after all common ordinary words, but as they are used by the physicist they are very much restricted and more precise while still retaining the essential ordinary idea. So it is in psychology with terms like sensation, perception, illusion, meaning, idea, and concept. Now when we turn scientific logic and experimental psychophysical procedures to the subject of attitudes, we find it necessary to restrict here also the rather loose conversational meaning of this term in order to make it at all suitable for scientific discourse.

Our present definition of the term may be briefly stated as follows: *Attitude is the affect for or against a psychological object.* Affect in its primitive form is described as appetition or aversion. Appetition is the positive form of affect, which in more sophisticated situations appears as liking the psychological object, defending it, favoring it in various ways. Aversion is the negative form of affect, which is decribed as hating the psychological object, disliking it, destroying it, or otherwise reacting against it. Attitude is here used to describe *potential action* toward the object with regard only to the question whether the potential action will be favorable or unfavorable toward the object. For example, if we say that a man's attitude toward prohibition is negative, we mean that his potential actions about prohibition may be expected to be against it, barring compromises in particular cases. When we say that a man's attitude toward prohibition is negative, we have merely indicated the affective direction of his potential action toward the object. We have not said anything about the particular detailed manner in which he might act. In this sense the term attitude is an abstraction in that it cannot be described without inserting the cognitive details that are irrelevant, but this is also true of many of the simplest concepts in daily use.

The affect about an object may be of strong intensity, or it may be weak. The positive and negative affect therefore constitutes a linear continuum with a neutral point or zone and two opposite directions, one positive and the other negative. Measurement along this affective continuum is of a discriminatory character with the discriminal error as a unit of measurement.

Against this restricted definition of attitude as the affective character of potential action about a psychological object there have been raised several questions. It has been pointed out that the emotional experiences of the past constitute an integral part of a man's attitude. If we should use the term in that inclusive manner, we should say that a man's attitude toward religion consists in part of his childhood experience with Sunday schools. The man might then say that his attitude toward religion is that he went to church when he was a child. I should prefer to say that such a fact is really not a part of his attitude toward religion but that it may help to *explain* how he got that way. It is quite conceivable that two men may have the same degree or intensity of affect favorable toward a psychological object and that their attitudes would be described in this sense as identical but that they arrived at their similar attitudes by entirely different routes. It is even possible that their factual associations about the psychological object might be entirely different and that their overt actions would take quite different forms which have one thing in common, namely, that they are about equally favorable toward the object.

In these discussions the term psychological object has its customary meaning. It may refer to a physical object, or it may refer to an idea, a plan of action, a form of conduct, an ideal, a moral principle, a slogan, or a symbol. In fact, it may refer to any idea about which the subject may express positive or negative affect.

There comes to mind the uncertainty of using an opinion as an index of attitude. The man may be a liar. If he is not intentionally misrepresenting his real attitude on a disputed question, he may nevertheless modify the expression of it for reasons of courtesy, especially in those situations in which frank expression of attitude may not be well received. This has led to the suggestion that a man's action is a safer index of his attitude than what he says. But his actions may also be distortions of his attitude. A politician extends friendship and hospitality in overt action toward a Negro while hiding an attitude that he expresses more truthfully to an intimate friend. Neither his opinions nor his overt act constitutes in any sense an infallible guide to the subjective inclinations and preferences that constitute his attitude. Therefore we must remain content to use opinions or other forms of action merely as indexes of attitude. It must be recognized that there is a discrepancy, some error of measurement as it were, between the opinion or overt action that we use as an index and the attitude that we infer from such an index.

But this discrepancy between the index and "truth" is universal. When you want to know the temperature of your room, you look at the thermometer and use its reading as an index of temperature just as though there were a single temperature reading which is the "correct" one for the room. If it is desired to ascertain the volume of a glass paperweight, the volume is postulated as an attribute of the piece of glass, even though volume is an abstraction. The volume is measured indirectly by noting the dimensions of the glass or by immersing it in water to see how much water it displaces. These two procedures give two indexes which may not agree exactly. In every situation involving measurement there is postulated an abstract continuum such as volume or temperature, and the allocation of the thing measured to that continuum is accomplished by indirect means through one or more indexes. Truth consists only in the relative consistency of the several indexes, since it is never directly known. We are dealing with the same type of situation in attempting to measure attitude. We postulate an attitude variable which is like practically all other measurable attributes in the nature of an abstract continuum, and we must find one or more indexes which will satisfy us to the extent that they are internally consistent. Only to the extent that different indexes are consistent can we be justified in postulating the attitude as a trait, for a trait is never directly measured.

If we should find that what a man says has absolutely no relation to what he does, then such inconsistency would constitute a serious limitation on the legitimacy of the abstraction of attitude. However, when we actually carry out such comparisons, we do find that the correlation is positive between verbally expressed attitudes and overt action. The correlation is not perfect, but it is certainly positive. Discrepancies will arise, as when a subject expresses himself as favorable to prohibition although he himself violates it. But if the correlation is tabulated for a large group of people, it is found that the attitude scores for those who vote for prohibition are markedly different from those who vote against it, and a similar positive correlation is found between attitude scores and overt action about drinking. The reason for limiting ourselves to verbal expressions of attitude is that they can be evaluated with more certainty, and they are much more available than a list of overt acts. This type of correlation between attitude and overt action was the subject of a recent study by Mr. Stouffer.

In order to deal with overt actions as expressive of attitudes in a feasible manner Mr. Rosander has prepared lists of situations with alternative overt acts. He asks the question, "In the following situations, which of the given alternatives are you most likely *to do?*" Then follows description of a situation with a number of alternative overt acts. For example, in a situation scale on the Negro occurs the following:

The congregation of the church you attend has always been white. One Sunday morning a Negro attends the services.

    a. You do nothing about it.

    b. You complain to the minister.

    c. You welcome the Negro to the church.

    d. You shake hands with him and ask him to come again.

    e. You sound out opinion to find how many want to keep out Negroes.

    f. You tell the fellow he had better move along.

    g. You ask the minister to tell him that he is not wanted.

    h. You tell the fellow he had better leave before you throw him out.

    i. You defend the Negro against some who complain of his presence.

    j. You give the Negro friendly warning that perhaps he had better not come back.

The various overt responses are to be scaled in a manner analogous to the procedure for the statements of opinion. It is quite probable that these two types of scale, the opinion scale and the situation scale, will be highly correlated.

We take for granted that people's attitudes are subject to change. When we have measured a man's attitude on any issue such as pacifism,

we shall not declare such a measurement to be in any sense an enduring or constitutional constant. His attitude may change, of course, from one day to the next, and it is our task to measure such changes, whether they be due to unknown causes or to the presence of some known persuasive factor, such as the reading of a discourse on the issue in question. However, such fluctuations may also be attributed in part to error in the measurements themselves. In order to isolate the errors of the measurement instrument from actual fluctuations in attitude, we must calculate the standard error of measurement of the scale itself, and this can be accomplished by methods already well known in mental measurement.

We shall assume that an attitude scale is used only in those situations in which one may reasonably expect people to tell the truth about their convictions or opinions. If a denominational school were to submit to its students a scale of attitude about the church, one might find that some students would hesitate to make known their convictions if they deviate from the orthodox beliefs of their school. At least, the findings could be challenged if the situation in which attitudes were expressed contained pressure or implied threat bearing directly on the attitude to be measured. Similarly, it is difficult to discover attitudes on sex liberty by a written questionnaire, because of the well-nigh universal pressure to conceal such attitudes when they deviate from supposed conventions. It is assumed that attitude scales will be used primarily in those situations that offer a minimum of pressure on the attitude to be measured. Such situations are common enough.

However, it is sometimes of considerable interest to inquire what the distribution of attitude may be in a group which is known to be influenced by social pressure or taboo. If, for example, a group of college students are asked to express their attitude on the subject of sex liberty, the results might indicate conformity with conventional standards. Such a result might be interpreted to mean that the students agree with conventional ideals in regard to sex liberty, or the results might be challenged as reflecting only the social taboo against deviations from the conventional standards. If, on the other hand, the results should be a distribution of unconventional attitudes, the interpretation would be more conclusive in that the expressed attitude appears in spite of the known taboo. It goes without saying that the distribution of attitude on any social issue and with any particular group must be interpreted in terms of the known factors that may influence judgment.

The question has been raised whether the concept of attitude as here used and as measured by an attitude scale is not hypothetical rather than "real." It is just as hypothetical as the concept of intelligence, which is measured by what it supposedly does. But these concepts are hypothetical in the same sense that the concepts force, momentum, volume, are hypothetical in physical science. No one has ever seen or touched a force or a momentum or a volume. They are measured by what they supposedly do. The legitimacy of these abstractions can be tested only in the consistency by which they operate in experience. Not infrequently these hypothetical entities are discarded either, first, because they lead to inconsistencies in experience or, second, because they have to be multiplied in number so that they become as numerous as the effects that they are intended to explain or facilitate in analysis. As long as biologists insisted on the definition of instincts in terms of overt acts, they found that the instincts had to be as numerous as the overt acts to be accounted for, and then the instinct abstraction lost its usefulness. The instincts probably could be defined more successfully in terms of the other end of the psychological act. The concept of intelligence is a useful though hypothetical entity. It is postulated that intelligence is that which is dynamically common to a large group of overt acts. The degree of this hypothetical power which we call intelligence is estimated in terms of overt performances, and the term is successful to the extent that different forms of adaptive overt performance are positively correlated. The greater confidence with which we handle such a hypothetical entity as force is completely contained in the higher degree of consistency with which the hypothetical force is measured in different forms of its expression. We are here dealing with a similar hypothetical entity, attitude toward a social or psychological object. It is part of the convenience of language to speak of a force as though it were the "cause" of the movement of a particle, and just so we speak of intelligence as the cause of conduct that is regarded as particularly adaptive, and we speak of attitude as the cause of that conduct which is favorable or unfavorable toward a psychological object.

The consistency by which the term "attitude" may be established as useful is to be found in the indorsements of different opinions. Consider these two opinions about the church: "I find the services of the church both restful and inspiring," and "I think the church is a divine institution." One of these statements concerns the effect of the church service on the individual subject. The other expresses a belief in the divine character of the church. Considered objectively and logically, there should be no necessary correspondence between these two statements. They are declarations about totally different things, objectively regarded. But among all the people who indorse the first statement there will be a large proportion who also indorse the second statement. That which these two objectively entirely different statements have in common is the postulated favorable affect of the subject toward the psychological object, the church. To the extent that such consistencies in indorsements can be found, we are justified in postulating a common core and in naming it.

An example of the opposite kind may serve better to illustrate the justification for postulating the common factor of attitude. Consider the statement, "Going to church will not do anyone any harm." You find by actually trying it that the pious people indorse this statement. They can hardly do otherwise. On the other hand, some of the hard-boiled atheists also indorse it if they don't think that churchgoing is going to be specially harmful. Here you have people from both ends of the affective continuum indorsing the same statement. If all of our opinions behaved that way upon statistical analysis, we would have no attitude scales, and we would not even be able to postulate the attitude continuum. But fortunately most of the opinions that we now write behave much better than that one did. This criterion we have called the criterion of irrelevance.

Perhaps the nature of the underlying concept of attitude can be finally best illustrated by an extreme example that I have found useful on several occasions. Suppose that you would all be given a list of statements about communism with the request that you check those statements that you think are true, and suppose that you were in a sufficiently docile mood to undertake the task. Some of the statements are very frankly favorable to communism, some are even extreme, others straddle the question with neutral assertions, others are derogatory, and some are bitter denunciations of the communists.

Now I shall venture the guess that the large majority of this audience would register strong denunciation of communism. Since these statements have been scaled on an affect continuum, I could plot the frequency distribution of your attitudes toward communism, and it would probably be strongly skewed with a mode at the anti-end of the scale. Here you would have given me a clear indication that you react against this social object or symbol that has been placed before you.

But now suppose that I should turn on you with the request that you all write out a statement of what it is that you have been talking about, just what these doctrines are that you have so universally denounced. I should then not be at all surprised if some of you would have difficulty in telling me just what the doctrines of communism are toward which you have reacted so strongly. Those of you who would venture to write such statements would undoubtedly differ widely in what you say that you have expressed yourself about. Now the important point for the purpose of attitude measurement is that your vagueness in supplying cognitive detail does not in the least invalidate your expression of attitude. Even though you might differ in your detailed description of the communism symbol, you might all agree that it is bad, that those who subscribe to such a symbol should be sent to jail, and that such doctrines should be kept out of the country. We have here a clear registration of affective value, a strong negative affective valuation of a symbol, and that is all that we are trying to find when we measure social attitudes. Of course, it would be socially interesting and perhaps important that we should get together on what it is that we feel so strongly about, but for the purposes of attitude measurement we have done our task when the positive or negative affect has been recorded in terms of the discriminal dispersion as a unit of measurement.

I must make it clear that in discussing these various issues, such as religion, communism, birth control, municipal ownership, race prejudice, pacifism, and so on, I am not advancing any doctrines whatever. I have personal convictions on some of these issues, and so does everybody else, but in these studies we are concerned merely with the description of the degree of affect for or against various social symbols by psychophysical methods. In giving each person a positive or negative score on a disputed social issue, we do not say anything whatever as to whether his attitude is good or bad, whether his attitude should be censured or encouraged. That is a matter of interpretation in each issue, and it is not the scientific problem with which we are concerned.

In closing, I shall mention only one other question that has appeared on several occasions. It has been suggested that the attitude scales might be used in order to eliminate undesirable students from colleges and universities. They might be given an attitude scale on patriotism or on religion or on something else that is supposed to tell whether a person is desirable or not from any particular point of view. In the first place, you would immediately make liars of many applicants who differ with you in their political or religious convictions on the issue in question. We have not yet combined the attitude scales with the lie detector, although such experiments are contemplated. But even if it were possible to ascertain the political and religious attitudes of people under conditions which would detect when they are lying, it would be a vicious policy for any educational institution to adopt.

It has been proposed that attitude scales might be used to determine whether a course of instruction in social science has had the desired effect. To be sure, one of the important results of social science instruction is change in social attitude. But to make the passing of a course contingent on taking the so-called right attitude on any particular social issue would be preposterous. I am unalterably opposed to any such policy for judging progress in social science courses.

I have reviewed some of our attempts to extend the experimental methods and the logic of psychophysics beyond the field of sensory discrimination to which it has been limited by psychological tradition. It has been stated by economists and by other social scientists that affect cannot be measured, and some of the fundamental theory of social science has been written with this explicit reservation. Our studies have shown that affect can be measured. In extending the methods of psychophysics to the measurement of affect, we seem to see the possibility of a wide field of application by which it will be possible to apply the methods of quantitative scientific thinking to the study of feeling and emotion, to aesthetics, and to social phenomena.

BIBLIOGRAPHY

1. Thurstone, L. L., "Experimental Study of Nationality Preferences," *Journal of General Psychology,* July-Oct., 1928, pp. 405-425.
2. Thurstone, L. L., "A Law of Comparative Judgment," *Psychological Review,* July, 1927, pp. 273-286.
3. Eggan, Frederick R., "An Experimental Study of Attitude toward Races and Nationalities," Chicago, 1928, unpublished Master's Thesis.
4. Thurstone, L. L., "A Scale for Measuring Attitude toward the Movies," *Journal of Educational Research,* 1930, Volume 22, pp. 89-94.

   Thurstone, L. L., "The Measurement of Change in Social Attitude," *Journal of Social Psychology,* 1931, **2**, 230-235.

   Thurstone, L. L., "The Influence of Motion Pictures on Children's Attitudes," *Journal of Social Psychology,* 1931, **2**, 291-305.

   Thurstone, L. L., "The Effect of a Motion Picture Film on Children's Attitudes toward Germans," unpublished manuscript.
5. Thurstone, L. L., "The Influence of Motion Pictures on Children's Attitudes," *Journal of Social Psychology,* 1931, **2**, 291-305.
6. Thurstone, L. L., and Chave, E. J., *The Measurement of Attitude,* Chicago, University of Chicago Press, 1929.
7. Thurstone, L. L., "Measurement of Change in Social Attitude," *Journal of Social Psychology,* 1931, **2**, 230-235.

3. Attitudes versus Actions

RICHARD T. LaPIERE

By definition, a social attitude is a behaviour pattern, anticipatory set or tendency, predisposition to specific adjustment to designated social situations, or, more simply, a conditioned response to social stimuli.[1] Terminological usage differs, but students who have concerned themselves with attitudes apparently agree that they are acquired out of social experience and provide the individual organism with some degree of preparation to adjust, in a well-defined way, to certain types of social situations if and when these situations arise. It would seem, therefore, that the totality of the social attitudes of a single individual would include all his socially acquired personality which is involved in the making of adjustments to other human beings.

But by derivation social attitudes are seldom more than a verbal response to a symbolic situation. For the conventional method of measuring social attitudes is to ask questions (usually in writing) which demand a verbal adjustment to an entirely symbolic situation. Because it is easy, cheap, and mechanical, the attitudinal questionnaire is rapidly becoming a major method of sociological and socio-psychological investigation. The technique is simple. Thus from a hundred or a thousand responses to the question "Would you get up to give an Armenian woman your seat in a street car?" the investigator derives the "attitude" of non-Armenian males towards Armenian females. Now the question may be constructed with elaborate skill and hidden with consummate cunning in a maze of supplementary or even irrelevant questions yet all that has been obtained is a symbolic response to a symbolic situation. The words "Ar-

menian woman" do not constitute an Armenian woman of flesh and blood, who might be tall or squat, fat or thin, old or young, well or poorly dressed—who might, in fact, be a goddess or just another old and dirty hag. And the questionnaire response, whether it be "yes" or "no," is but a verbal reaction and this does not involve rising from the seat or stolidly avoiding the hurt eyes of the hypothetical woman and the derogatory stares of other street-car occupants. Yet, ignoring these limitations, the diligent investigator will jump briskly from his factual evidence to the unwarranted conclusion that he has measured the "anticipatory behavior patterns" of non-Armenian males towards Armenian females encountered on street cars. Usually he does not stop here, but proceeds to deduce certain general conclusions regarding the social relationships between Armenians and non-Armenians. Most of us have applied the questionnaire technique with greater caution, but not I fear with any greater certainty of success.

Some years ago I endeavored to obtain comparative data on the degree of French and English antipathy towards dark-skinned peoples.[2] The informal questionnaire technique was used, but, although the responses so obtained were exceedingly consistent, I supplemented them with what I then considered an index to overt behavior. The hypothesis as then stated *seemed* entirely logical:

Whatever our attitude on the validity of "verbalization" may be, it must be recognized that any study of attitudes through direct questioning is open to serious objection, both because of the limitations of the sampling method and because in classifying attitudes the inaccuracy

• Reprinted from *Social Forces*, 1934, **13**, 230-237, with permission of the author and the publisher.

1 See Daniel D. Droba, "Topical Summaries of Current Literature," *The American Journal of Sociology*, 1934, p. 513.

2 "Race Prejudice: France and England," *Social Forces*, September, 1928, pp. 102-111.

of human judgment is an inevitable variable. In this study, however, there is corroborating evidence on these attitudes in the policies adopted by hotel proprietors. Nothing could be used as a more accurate index of color prejudice than the admission or non-admission of colored people to hotels. For the proprietor must reflect the group attitude in his policy regardless of his own feelings in the matter. Since he determines what the group attitude is towards Negroes through the expression of that attitude in overt behavior and over a long period of actual experience, the results will be exceptionally free from those disturbing factors which inevitably affect the effort to study attitudes by direct questioning.

But at that time I overlooked the fact that what I was obtaining from the hotel proprietors was still a "verbalized" reaction to a symbolic situation. The response to a Negro's request for lodgings might have been an excellent index of the attitude of hotel patrons towards living in the same hotel as a Negro. Yet to ask the proprietor "Do you permit members of the Negro race to stay here?" does not, it appears, measure his potential response to an actual Negro.

All measurement of attitudes by the questionnaire technique proceeds on the assumption that there is a mechanical relationship between symbolic and non-symbolic behavior. It is simple enough to prove that there is no *necessary* correlation between speech and action, between response to words and to the realities they symbolize. A parrot can be taught to swear, a child to sing "Frankie and Johnny" in the Mae West manner. The words will have no meaning to either child or parrot. But to prove that there is no *necessary* relationship does not prove that such a relationship may not exist. There need be no relationship between what the hotel proprietor says he will do and what he actually does when confronted with a colored patron. Yet there may be. Certainly we are justified in assuming that the verbal response of the hotel proprietor would be more likely to indicate what he would actually do than would the verbal response of people whose personal feelings are less subordinated to economic expediency. However, the following study indicates that the reliability of even such responses is very small indeed.

Beginning in 1930 and continuing for two years thereafter, I had the good fortune to travel rather extensively with a young Chinese student and his wife.[3] Both were personable, charming, and quick to win the admiration and respect of those they had the opportunity to become intimate with. But they were foreign-born Chinese, a fact that could not be disguised. Knowing the general "attitude" of Americans towards the Chinese as indicated by the "social distance" studies which have been made, it was with considerable trepidation that I first approached a hotel clerk in their company. Perhaps that clerk's eyebrows lifted slightly, but he accommodated us without a show of hesitation. And this in the "best" hotel in a small town noted for its narrow and bigoted "attitude" towards Orientals. Two months later I passed that way again, phoned the hotel and asked if they would accommodate "an important Chinese gentleman." The reply was an unequivocal "No." That aroused my curiosity and led to this study.

In something like ten thousand miles of motor travel, twice across the United States, up and down the Pacific Coast, we met definite rejection from those asked to serve us just once. We were received at 66 hotels, auto camps, and "Tourist Homes," refused at one. We were served in 184 restaurants and cafes scattered throughout the country and treated with what I judged to be more than ordinary consideration in 72 of them. Accurate and detailed records were kept of all these instances. An effort, necessarily subjective, was made to evaluate the overt response of hotel clerks, bell boys, elevator operators, and waitresses to the presence of my Chinese friends. The factors entering into the situations were varied as far and as often as possible. Control was not, of course, as exacting as that required by laboratory experimentation. But it was as rigid as is humanly possible in human situations. For example, I did not take the "test" subjects into my confidence fearing that their behavior might become self-conscious and thus abnormally affect the response of others towards them. Whenever possible I let my Chinese friend negotiate for accommodations (while I concerned myself with the car or luggage) or sent them into a restaurant ahead of me. In this way I attempted to "factor" myself out. We sometimes patronized high-class establishments after a hard and dusty day on the road and stopped at inferior auto camps when in our most presentable condition.

[3] The results of this study have been withheld until the present time out of consideration for their feelings.

In the end I was forced to conclude that those factors which most influenced the behavior of others towards the Chinese had nothing at all to do with race. Quality and condition of clothing, appearance of baggage (by which, it seems, hotel clerks are prone to base their quick evaluations), cleanliness and neatness were far more significant for person to person reaction in the situations I was studying than skin pigmentation, straight black hair, slanting eyes, and flat noses. And yet an air of self-confidence might entirely offset the "unfavorable" impression made by dusty clothes and the usual disorder to appearance consequent upon some hundred miles of motor travel. A supercilious desk clerk in a hotel of noble aspirations could not refuse his master's hospitality to people who appeared to take their request as a perfectly normal and conventional thing, though they might look like tin-car tourists and two of them belong to the racial category "Oriental." On the other hand, I became rather adept at approaching hotel clerks with that peculiar crabwise manner which is so effective in provoking a somewhat scornful disregard. And then a bland smile would serve to reverse the entire situation. Indeed, it appeared that a genial smile was the most effective password to acceptance. My Chinese friends were skillful smilers, which may account, in part, for the fact that we received but one rebuff in all our experience. Finally, I was impressed with the fact that even where some tension developed due to the strangeness of the Chinese it would evaporate immediately when they spoke in unaccented English.

The one instance in which we were refused accommodations is worth recording here. The place was a small California town, a rather inferior auto-camp into which we drove in a very dilapidated car piled with camp equipment. It was early evening, the light so dim that the proprietor found it somewhat difficult to decide the genus *voyageur* to which we belonged. I left the car and spoke to him. He hesitated, wavered, said he was not sure that he had two cabins, meanwhile edging towards our car. The realization that the two occupants were Orientals turned the balance or, more likely, gave him the excuse he was looking for. "No," he said, "I don't take Japs!" In a more pretentious establishment we secured accommodations, and with an extra flourish of hospitality.

To offset this one flat refusal were the many instances in which the physical peculiarities of the Chinese served to heighten curiosity. With few exceptions this curiosity was considerately hidden behind an exceptional interest in serving us. Of course, outside of the Pacific Coast region, New York, and Chicago, the Chinese physiognomy attracts attention. It is different, hence noticeable. But the principal effect this curiosity has upon the behavior of those who cater to the traveler's needs is to make them more attentive, more responsive, more reliable. A Chinese companion is to be recommended to the white traveling in his native land. Strange features when combined with "human" speech and action seems, at times, to heighten sympathetic response, perhaps on the same principle that makes us uncommonly sympathetic towards the dog that has a "human" expression in his face.

What I am trying to say is that in only one out of 251 instances in which we purchased goods or services necessitating intimate human relationships did the fact that my companions were Chinese adversely affect us. Factors entirely unassociated with race were, in the main, the determinant of significant variations in our reception. It would appear reasonable to conclude that the "attitude" of the American people, as reflected in the behavior of those who are for pecuniary reasons presumably most sensitive to the antipathies of their white clientele, is anything but negative towards the Chinese. In terms of "social distance" we might conclude that native Caucasians are not averse to residing in the same hotels, auto-camps, and "Tourist Homes" as Chinese and will with complacency accept the presence of Chinese at an adjoining table in restaurant or cafe. It does not follow that there is revealed a distinctly "positive" attitude towards the Chinese, that whites prefer the Chinese to other whites. But the facts as gathered certainly preclude the conclusion that there is an intense prejudice towards the Chinese.

Yet the existence of this prejudice, very intense, is proven by a conventional "attitude" study. To provide a comparison of symbolic reaction to symbolic social situations with actual reaction to real social situations, I "questionnaired" the establishments which we patronized during the two year period. Six months were permitted to lapse between the time I obtained the overt reaction and the symbolic. It was hoped that the effects of the actual experience with Chinese guests, adverse or otherwise, would have faded during the intervening time. To the hotel or restaurant a questionnaire was mailed with an accompanying letter purporting to be a special and personal plea for response. The questionnaires all asked the same question, "Will you accept members of the Chinese race as guests in your establishment?" Two types of questionnaire were used. In one this question was inserted among similar queries concerning Germans, French, Japanese, Russians, Armenians, Jews, Negroes, Italians, and Indians. In the other the pertinent question was unencumbered. With persistence, completed replies were obtained from 128 of the establishments we had visited; 81 restaurants and cafes and 47 hotels, auto-camps, and "Tourist Homes." In response to the relevant question 92 per cent of the former and 91 per cent of the latter replied "No." The remainder replied "Uncertain; depend upon circumstances." From the woman proprietor of a small auto-camp I received the only "Yes," accompanied by a chatty letter describing the nice visit she had had with a Chinese gentleman and his sweet wife during the previous summer.

A rather unflattering interpretation might be put upon the fact that those establishments who had provided for our needs so graciously were, some months later, verbally antagonistic towards hypothetical Chinese. To factor this experience out responses were secured from 32 hotels and 96 restaurants located in approximately the same regions, but uninfluenced by this particular experience with Oriental clients. In this, as in the former case, both types of questionnaires were used. The results indicate that neither the type of questionnaire nor the fact of previous experience had important bearing upon the symbolic response to symbolic social situations.

It is impossible to make direct comparison between the reactions secured through questionnaires and from actual experience. On the basis of the above data (see Table 1) it would appear foolhardy for a Chinese to attempt to travel in the United States. And yet, as I have shown, actual experience (Table 2) indicates that the American people, as represented by the personnel of hotels, restaurants, etc., are not at all averse to fraternizing with Chinese within the limitations which apply to social relationships between Americans themselves. The evaluations which follow are undoubtedly subject to the criticism which any human judgment must withstand. But the fact is that, although they began their travels in this country with considerable trepidation, my Chinese friends soon lost all fear that they might receive a rebuff. At first somewhat timid and considerably dependent upon me for guidance and support, they came in time to feel fully self-reliant and would approach new social situations without the slightest hesitation.

The conventional questionnaire undoubtedly has significant value for the measurement of "political attitudes." The presidential polls conducted by the *Literary Digest* have proven that. But a "political attitude" is exactly what the questionnaire can be justly held to measure;

TABLE 1. *Distribution of Results from Questionnaire Study of Establishment "Policy" Regarding Acceptance of Chinese as Guests*

Replies are to the question: "Will you accept members of the Chinese race as guests in your establishment?"

	Hotels, etc., Visited		Hotels, etc., not Visited		Restaurants, etc., Visited		Restaurants, etc., not Visited	
Total	47		32		81		96	
	1*	2*	1	2	1	2	1	2
Number replying	22	25	20	12	43	38	51	45
No	20	23	19	11	40	35	37	41
Undecided: depend upon circumstances	1	2	1	1	3	3	4	3
Yes	1	0	0	0	0	0	0	1

* Column (1) indicates in each case those responses to questionnaires which concerned Chinese only. The figures in columns (2) are from the questionnaires in which the above was inserted among questions regarding Germans, French, Japanese, etc.

TABLE 2. *Distribution of Results Obtained from Actual Experience in the Situation Symbolized in the Questionnaire Study*

Conditions	Hotels, etc.		Restaurants, etc.	
	Accompanied by investigator	Chinese not so accompanied at inception of situation	Accompanied by investigator	Chinese not so accompanied at inception of situation
Total	55	12	165	19
Reception very much better than investigator would expect to have received had he been alone, but under otherwise similar circumstances	19	6	63	9
Reception different only to extent of heightened curiosity, such as investigator might have incurred were he alone but dressed in manner unconventional to region yet not incongruous	22	3	76	6
Reception "normal"	9	2	21	3
Reception perceptibly hesitant and not to be explained on other than "racial" grounds	3	1	4	1
Reception definitely, though temporarily, embarrassing	1	0	1	0
Not accepted	1	0	0	0

* When the investigator was not present at the inception of the situation the judgments were based upon what transpired after he joined the Chinese. Since intimately acquainted with them it is probable that errors in judgment were no more frequent under these conditions than when he was able to witness the inception as well as results of the situation.

a verbal response to a symbolic situation. Few citizens are ever faced with the necessity of adjusting themselves to the presence of the political leaders whom, periodically, they must vote for—or against. Especially is this true with regard to the president, and it is in relation to political attitudes towards presidential candidates that we have our best evidence. But while the questionnaire may indicate what the voter will do when he goes to vote, it does not and cannot reveal what he will do when he meets Candidate Jones on the street, in his office, at his club, on the golf course, or wherever two men may meet and adjust in some way one to the other.

The questionnaire is probably our only means of determining "religious attitudes." An honest answer to the question "Do you believe in God?" reveals all there is to be measured.

"God" is a symbol; "belief" a verbal expression. So here, too, the questionnaire is efficacious. But if we would know the emotional responsiveness of a person to the spoken or written word "God" some other method of investigation must be used. And if we would know the extent to which that responsiveness restrains his behavior it is to his behavior that we must look, not to his questionnaire response. Ethical precepts are, I judge, something more than verbal professions. There would seem little to be gained from asking a man if his religious faith prevents him from committing sin. Of course it does—on paper. But "moral attitudes" must have a significance in the adjustment to actual situations or they are not worth the studying. Sitting at my desk in California I can predict with a high degree of certainty what an "average" business man in an average Mid-

Western city will reply to the question "Would you engage in sexual intercourse with a prostitute in a Paris brothel?" Yet no one, least of all the man himself, can predict what he would actually do should he by some misfortune find himself face to face with the situation in question. His moral "attitudes" are no doubt already stamped into his personality. But just what those habits are which will be invoked to provide him with some sort of adjustment to this situation is quite indeterminate.

It is highly probable that when the "Southern Gentleman" says he will not permit Negroes to reside in his neighborhood we have a verbal response to a symbolic situation which reflects the "attitudes" which would become operative in an actual situation. But there is no need to ask such a question of the true "Southern Gentleman." We knew it all the time. I am inclined to think that in most instances where the questionnaire does reveal non-symbolic attitudes the case is much the same. It is only when we cannot easily observe what people do in certain types of situations that the questionnaire is resorted to. But it is just here that the danger in the questionnaire technique arises. If Mr. A adjusts himself to Mr. B in a specified way we can deduce from his behavior that he has a certain "attitude" towards Mr. B and, perhaps, all of Mr. B's class. But if no such overt adjustment is made it is impossible to discover what A's adjustment would be should the situation arise. A questionnaire will reveal what Mr. A writes or says when confronted with a certain combination of words. But not what he will do when he meets Mr. B. Mr. B is a great deal more than a series of words. He is a man and he acts. His action is not necessarily what Mr. A "imagines" it will be when he reacts verbally to the symbol "Mr. B."

No doubt a considerable part of the data which the social scientist deals with can be obtained by the questionnaire method. The census reports are based upon verbal questionnaires and I do not doubt their basic integrity. If we wish to know how many children a man has, his income, the size of his home, his age, and the condition of his parents, we can reasonably ask him. These things he has frequently and conventionally converted into verbal responses. He is competent to report upon them, and will do so accurately, unless indeed he wishes to do otherwise. A careful investigator could no doubt even find out by verbal means whether the man fights with his wife (frequently, infrequently, or not at all), though the neighbors would be a more reliable source. But we should not expect to obtain by the questionnaire method his "anticipatory set or tendency" to action should his wife pack up and go home to Mother, should Elder Son get into trouble with the neighbor's daughter, the President assume the status of a dictator, the Japanese take over the rest of China, or a Chinese gentleman come to pay a social call.

Only a verbal reaction to an entirely symbolic situation can be secured by the questionnaire. It may indicate what the responder would actually do when confronted with the situation symbolized in the question, but there is no assurance that it will. And so to call the response a reflection of a "social attitude" is to entirely disregard the definition commonly given for the phrase "attitude." If social attitudes are to be conceptualized as partially integrated habit sets which will become operative under specific circumstances and lead to a particular pattern of adjustment they must, in the main, be derived from a study of humans behaving in actual social situations. They must not be imputed on the basis of questionnaire data.

The questionnaire is cheap, easy, and mechanical. The study of human behavior is time consuming, intellectually fatiguing, and depends for its success upon the ability of the investigator. The former method gives quantitative results, the latter mainly qualitative. Quantitative measurements are quantitatively accurate; qualitative evaluations are always subject to the errors of human judgment. Yet it would seem far more worth while to make a shrewd guess regarding that which is essential than to accurately measure that which is likely to prove quite irrelevant.

Sym v Non-sym beh.

4. Verbal Stereotypes and Racial Prejudice

DANIEL KATZ and KENNETH W. BRALY

One outstanding result of investigations of racial prejudice is the uniformity in the patterns of discrimination against various races[1] shown by Americans throughout the United States. People in widely separated parts of the country show a high degree of agreement in their expressions of relative liking or disliking of different "foreign" groups.

In an early study Bogardus asked 110 businessmen and schoolteachers about the degrees of social intimacy to which they were willing to admit certain ethnic groups. The degrees of social distance employed were: to close kinship through marriage, to my club as personal chums, to my street as neighbors, to employment in my occupation, to citizenship in my country, to my country as visitors only, and exclusion from my country. By weighting these seven classifications Bogardus obtained the following preferential rating of 23 ethnic groups:

Canadians	22.51
English	22.35
Scotch	20.91
Irish	19.38
French	18.67
Swedes	16.20
Germans	14.95
Spanish	14.02

• Adapted by the authors from "Racial Stereotypes of 100 College students," *Journal of Abnormal and Social Psychology*, 1933, **28**, 280-290, and "Racial Prejudice and Racial Stereotypes," *ibid.*, 1935, **30**, 175-193, with permission of the American Psychological Association, Inc. This article originally appeared in T. M. Newcomb and E. L. Hartley (Eds.), *Readings in Social Psychology*, 1st Edition, Holt, Rinehart and Winston, New York, 1947, and is reprinted with permission of the author, the publisher, and the American Psychological Association.

---

[1] The term *race* is here used in the popular, not the scientific, sense, and covers reference to racial, religious, and national groupings.

Italians	8.87
Indians	7.30
Poles	6.65
Russians	6.40
Armenians	6.16
German-Jews	5.45
Greeks	5.23
Russian-Jews	4.94
Mexicans	4.57
Chinese	4.12
Japanese	4.08
Negroes	3.84
Mulattoes	3.62
Hindus	3.08
Turks	2.91

The Bogardus study was carried out on the Pacific Coast but studies made in other parts of the United States indicate the same pattern of preferences for the various groups. In the Middle West, for example, Thurstone constructed a scale on the basis of the likes and dislikes of 239 students. The resulting rank order and scale values for 21 ethnic groups follows:

American	0.00
English	—1.34
Scotch	—2.09
Irish	—2.18
French	—2.46
German	—2.55
Swede	—2.90
South American	—3.64
Italian	—3.66
Spanish	—3.79
Jew	—3.92
Russian	—4.10
Pole	—4.41
Greek	—4.62
Armenian	—4.68
Japanese	—4.93
Mexican	—5.10
Chinese	—5.30

Hindus . . . . —5.35
Turk . . . . —5.82
Negro . . . . —5.86

How is the agreement about "foreign" groups to be interpreted? The first possibility is that the foreign groups possess varying degrees of undesirable qualities upon which most Americans base their preferential ratings. But it is obvious that there are wide individual differences within any nationality group—that is, not all Englishmen are alike, nor are all Frenchmen, nor are all Russians. It is also obvious that few Americans have had much opportunity to know a large number of people from the many nationalities they dislike. It is also highly probable that if we were basing our judgments wholly upon what we know from actual contact with individual Spaniards, we would have differing impressions of what Spaniards are really like, because we would not all have met the same type of Spaniard. Hence a more valid interpretation of the agreement of Americans about foreign groups is that it represents the prejudgments or prejudices, absorbed from the stereotypes of our culture.

Thus the preferential disliking reported by Bogardus and Thurstone may reflect attitudes toward race names and may not arise from animosity toward the specific qualities inherent in the real human beings bearing a given racial label. We have learned responses of varying degrees of aversion or acceptance to racial names and where these tags can be readily applied to individuals, as they can in the case of the Negro because of his skin color, we respond to him not as a human being but as a personification of the symbol we have learned to look down upon. Walter Lippmann has called this type of belief a stereotype—by which is meant a fixed impression which conforms very little to the facts it pretends to represent and results from our defining first and observing second.

THE PRESENT STUDY[2]

To explore the nature of racial and national stereotypes more fully, the following procedures were employed:

1. Twenty-five students were asked to list as many specific characteristics or traits as were thought typical of the following ten groups: Germans, Italians, Irish, English, Negroes, Jews,

2 This study was made in 1932.

Americans, Chinese, Japanese. Turks. No traits were suggested to the students. This list was then supplemented by characteristics commonly reported in the literature. The result was a final check-list of 84 descriptive adjectives.

2. One hundred Princeton undergraduates were then asked to select the traits from this prepared list of 84 adjectives to characterize the ten racial and national groups. Specific directions used in the experiment follow in part:

Read through the list of words on page one and select those which seem to you to be typical of the Germans. Write as many of these words in the following spaces as you think are necessary to characterize these people adequately. If you do not find proper words on page one for all the typical German characteristics, you may add those which you think necessary for an adequate description.

This procedure was then repeated for other national and racial groups. When the student had finished this he was asked to go back over the ten lists of words which he had chosen and to mark the five words of each list which seemed most typical of the group in question.

3. Another group of students was asked to rate the list of adjectives on the basis of the desirability of these traits in friends and associates. The students making this judgment had no knowledge that the characteristics were supposed to describe racial groups. The traits or adjectives were rated from 1 to 10 on the basis of their desirability.

4. Still another group of students was asked to put in rank order the ten racial and national groups on the basis of preference for association with their members. The group which the subject most preferred to associate with was placed first and the group with which he preferred to associate least was placed tenth or last.

RESULTS

Stereotyped Conceptions of Ten Ethnic Groups

Table 1 presents the twelve characteristics most frequently assigned to the ten races by the 100 students. This table summarizes the traits which students rechecked as the five most typical characteristics of each race.

The traits most frequently assigned to the Germans seem consistent with the popular stereotype to be found in newspapers and magazines. Their science, industry, ponderous and

TABLE 1. *The Twelve Traits Most Frequently Assigned to Each of Various Racial and National Groups by 100 Princeton Students*

Traits Checked, Rank Order	Number	Percent	Traits Checked, Rank Order	Number	Percent
GERMANS			Sly	20	20
Scientifically-minded	78	78	Loyal to family ties	15	15
Industrious	65	65	Persistent	13	13
Stolid	44	44	Talkative	13	13
Intelligent	32	32	Aggressive	12	12
Methodical	31	31	Very religious	12	12
Extremely nationalistic	24	24			
Progressive	16	16	**AMERICANS**		
Efficient	16	16	Industrious	48	48
Jovial	15	15	Intelligent	47	47
Musical	13	13	Materialistic	33	33
Persistent	11	11	Ambitious	33	33
Practical	11	11	Progressive	27	27
			Pleasure-loving	26	26
ITALIANS			Alert	23	23
Artistic	53	53	Efficient	21	21
Impulsive	44	44	Aggressive	20	20
Passionate	37	37	Straightforward	19	19
Quick-tempered	35	35	Practical	19	19
Musical	32	32	Sportsmanlike	19	19
Imaginative	30	30			
Very religious	21	21	**NEGROES**		
Talkative	21	21	Superstitious	84	84
Revengeful	17	17	Lazy	75	75
Physically dirty	13	13	Happy-go-lucky	38	38
Lazy	12	12	Ignorant	38	38
Unreliable	11	11	Musical	26	26
			Ostentatious	26	26
ENGLISH			Very religious	24	24
Sportsmanlike	53	53	Stupid	22	22
Intelligent	46	46	Physically dirty	17	17
Conventional	34	34	Naïve	14	14
Tradition-loving	31	31	Slovenly	13	13
Conservative	30	30	Unreliable	12	12
Reserved	29	29			
Sophisticated	27	27	**IRISH**		
Courteous	21	21	Pugnacious	45	45
Honest	20	20	Quick-tempered	39	39
Industrious	18	18	Witty	38	38
Extremely nationalistic	18	18	Honest	32	32
Humorless	17	17	Very religious	29	29
			Industrious	21	21
JEWS			Extremely nationalistic	21	21
Shrewd	79	79	Superstitious	18	18
Mercenary	49	49	Quarrelsome	14	14
Industrious	48	48	Imaginative	13	13
Grasping	34	34	Aggressive	13	13
Intelligent	29	29	Stubborn	13	13
Ambitious	21	21			

TABLE 1 (Continued)

Traits Checked, Rank Order	Number	Percent	Traits Checked, Rank Order	Number	Percent
CHINESE			Imitative	17	18
Superstitious	34	35	Alert	16	17
Sly	29	30	Suave	16	17
Conservative	29	30	Neat	16	17
Tradition-loving	26	27	Treacherous	13	14
Loyal to family ties	22	23	Aggressive	13	14
Industrious	18	19			
Meditative	18	19	TURKS		
Reserved	17	17	Cruel	47	54
Very religious	15	15	Very religious	26	30
Ignorant	15	15	Treacherous	21	24
Deceitful	14	14	Sensual	20	23
Quiet	13	13	Ignorant	15	17
			Physically dirty	15	17
JAPANESE			Deceitful	13	15
Intelligent	45	48	Sly	12	14
Industrious	43	46	Quarrelsome	12	14
Progressive	24	25	Revengeful	12	14
Shrewd	22	23	Conservative	12	14
Sly	20	21	Superstitious	11	13
Quiet	19	20			

methodical manner, and intelligence were pointed out by over one fourth of the students. Scientifically-minded was the most frequently assigned characteristic, as many as 78 percent of the group ascribing this trait to the Germans.

Italians received the common characterization of the hot-blooded Latin peoples: artistic, impulsive, quick-tempered, passionate, musical and imaginative. The greatest agreement was shown on the artistic qualities of the Italians with 53 percent of the students concurring in this belief.

The characteristics ascribed to the Negroes are somewhat similar to the picture of the Negro as furnished by the *Saturday Evening Post*: highly superstitious, lazy, happy-go-lucky, ignorant, musical, and ostentatious. The greatest degree of agreement for a single trait for any racial group was reached when 84 percent of the students voted the Negroes superstitious. Laziness was given as a typical characteristic by three fourths of the students, but the other traits mentioned above had much lower frequencies of endorsement. It may be noted in passing that for a northern college, Princeton draws heavily upon the South for her enrollment so that this characterization of Negroes is not exclusively a Northern description.

In the case of the Irish no single trait of the 84 presented could be agreed upon as a typical Irish characteristic by half the students. Forty-five percent, however, thought pugnacity typical and 39 per cent agreed upon quick-tempered. Witty, honest, very religious, industrious, and extremely nationalistic were the other adjectives selected by a fifth or more of the students.

The characterization of the English savors more of the English "gentleman" than of the general stereotype of John Bull. The leading characteristic is sportsmanship with an endorsement from 53 percent of the students. Forty-six percent of the students favored intelligence as typical of the English, 34 percent conventionality, 31 percent love of traditions, and 30 percent conservatism. Other adjectives were reserved, sophisticated, courteous, and honest.

The qualities of the competitive business world are used to describe the Jews. They are pictured as shrewd, mercenary, industrious, grasping, ambitious, and sly. Fifteen percent of the students did include Jewish loyalty to family ties. The greatest agreement (79 percent) was shown for shrewdness.

The traits ascribed to Americans show a certain objectivity on the part of the students in describing themselves, for the description given is not greatly at variance with the stereotype held by non-Americans. Americans are described as industrious, intelligent, materialistic, ambitious, progressive, and pleasure-loving. As in the case of the Irish the degree of agreement on these traits is relatively low. Almost one half did assign industry and intelligence to Americans, and a third gave materialistic and ambitious as the most descriptive adjectives.

Apparently the general stereotype for the Chinese among eastern college students is fairly indefinite, for the agreement on typical Chinese characteristics is not great. Three of the 100 students could give no characteristics for the Chinese. Of the 97 who did respond 35 percent thought the Chinese superstitious, 30 percent thought them sly, 30 percent regarded them as conservative. The next most frequently ascribed traits were love of tradition, loyalty to family ties, industry, and meditation.

The picture of the Japanese seems more clear-cut with some recognition of the westernization of Japan. Emphasis was placed upon intelligence, industry, progressiveness, shrewdness, slyness, and quietness. The Japanese are the only group in which intelligence leads the list as the most frequently assigned characteristic. Forty-eight percent of the students filling in this part of the questionnaire gave intelligence as a typical Japanese trait.

Thirteen students could select no characteristics for the Turks. Fifty-four percent of those responding gave cruelty. Other traits selected described the Turks as very religious, treacherous, sensual, ignorant, physically dirty, deceitful, and sly.

Preferential Ranking of the Ten Groups

The adjectives used to described the ten groups are a rough index of the esteem in which they are held. More precise measures were furnished (1) by the direct ranking of the ten racial and national names in order of preference (Table 2), and (2) by the desirability of the typical traits attributed to the ten groups (Table 3).

The scores in Table 3 are the average total value of the traits assigned to the various races, computed as follows: For every race the average rating of a trait was multiplied by the number of times it was assigned to that race. The ratings of all the traits assigned to one race were added and divided by the total

TABLE 2. Average Rank Order of Ten Racial Groups: Preferential Ranking

Nationality	Average Rank Order
Americans	1.15
English	2.27
Germans	3.42
Irish	3.87
Italians	5.64
Japanese	5.78
Jews	7.10
Chinese	7.94
Turks	8.52
Negroes	9.35

TABLE 3. The Ranking of Ten Races on the Basis of the Rating of Their Alleged Typical Traits by 65 Students

Nationality	Average Value of Assigned Traits
Americans	6.77
English	6.26
Germans	6.02
Japanese	5.89
Irish	5.42
Jews	4.96
Chinese	4.52
Italians	4.40
Negroes	3.55
Turks	3.05

number of assignments of traits to that race. This division would have been unnecessary if all the 100 students in the original group assigning traits had assigned five traits to every race. In some cases, however, a student made less than five assignments.

When we compare the ranking of the ten groups on the basis of preference for association with their members with their standing based on the desirability of traits attributed to them, we find a few changes in relative placement. The Italians drop from fifth to eighth place; the Irish drop two places, while the Japanese move up two places; and the Jews, Chinese, and Negroes move up one place. In other words, the Italians are regarded more highly and the Japanese are held in lower esteem than the qualities imputed to them would justify.

It also is true that the ethnic groups are bunched much more closely together on the scores based on assigned traits than on the preference ranking. The preference ranking accorded to Americans is five times as desirable as that accorded to the Japanese, but the difference in rating Americans and Japanese on the basis of imputed characteristics is nowhere nearly as great. In part this is an artifact of our method, but in part it is due to the fact that prejudice exceeds the rationalization of undesirable racial characteristics. Nonetheless there is marked similarity between the relative ranking on the basis of preference for group names and the average scores representing an evaluation of typical traits.

Thus racial prejudice is part of a general set of stereotypes of a high degree of consistency and is more than a single specific reaction to a race name. The student is prejudiced against the label Negro because to him it means a superstitious, ignorant, shiftless person of low social status. The whole attitude is more than a simple conditioned response to the race name: it is a pattern of rationalizations organized around the racial label.

This does not mean that the rationalized complex is justified by objective reality—that is, that Negroes really are the type of people described by the stereotype. In fact the clearness or vagueness of the stereotyped conception bear little relation to the degree of prejudice expressed against a group as determined by its preferential ranking.

Relative Clearness and Consistency of Pattern of Stereotypes

Table 4 shows the clearness of the stereotypes about the ten groups in terms of the degree of agreement in assigning typical characteristics to them.

TABLE 4. The Least Number of Traits Which Must Be Taken to Include 50 Percent of the Possible Assignments for Each Race

Races, Rank Order	Number of Traits Required
Negroes	4.6
Germans	5.0
Jews	5.5
Italians	6.9
English	7.0
Irish	8.5
Americans	8.8
Japanese	10.9
Chinese	12.0
Turks	15.9

Table 4 lists the least number of traits which have to be included to find 50 percent of the 500 possible votes cast by the 100 students in the case of every racial and national group. It will be remembered that each student was allowed to select 5 of the 84 traits presented and that there were 100 students. If there were perfect agreement, 2.5 traits would have received 50 percent of the votes. Perfect disagreement or chance would mean that 42 traits would be necessary to give half of the votes. Table 4 shows that in the case of Negroes we can find 50 percent of the votes or selections of traits in 4.6 traits. The agreement here is very high and even in the case of the Turks where 15.9 traits must be included to give 50 percent of the possible 500 assignments or selections the voting is far from a chance selection.

Thus in Table 4 we have a comparison of the definiteness of the ten racial stereotypes. The most definite picture is that of the Negroes. The Germans and the Jews also give consistent patterns of response, while the Chinese, Japanese, and Turks furnish the least clear cut stereotypes.

Though the belief in the undesirable qualities of a national group bolsters the prejudice against the group, it is not necessary to have a well worked out set of such rationalizations to obtain expressions of extreme prejudice. In fact Table 4 shows little relation between degree of disliking and the definiteness of the stereotyped picture. Negroes and Turks both are held in the lowest esteem, yet they represent opposite extremes in sharpness of stereotype. Students agreed among themselves most closely in characterizing Negroes and disagreed most in characterizing Turks. But they were in agreement in putting both groups at the bottom of the list as least desirable as companions or friends.

SUMMARY

1. Ten ethnic groups were placed in rank order by Princeton students on the basis of preference for association with their members. The preferential ranking was similar in its main outline to the results reported by investigators in all parts of the United States. Minor exceptions occurred in the case of the Jews and Japanese, who were placed somewhat lower and higher, respectively, than in other studies.

2. Students not only agreed in their prefer-

ential ranking of ethnic groups, but they also agreed in the types of characteristics attributed to these groups. In fact the conception of "foreign" groups is so stereotyped that it cannot be based upon actual contact with or direct knowledge of the groups in question.

3. The clearness or definiteness of the stereotyped picture is not related to the degree of prejudice. The greatest prejudice is expressed against Negroes and Turks. The stereotyped picture of the Negro is very clear-cut while that of the Turk is the vaguest of any of the ten groups included in the study.

4. A list of 84 traits given as the typical characteristics of the ten nationalities by a group of students was rated by another group of students on the basis of their desirability in associates. From these ratings scores were assigned to the ten nationalities, the relative weight of which agreed closely with the preferential ranking. Racial prejudice is thus a generalized set of stereotypes of a high degree of consistency which includes emotional responses to race names, a belief in typical characteristics associated with race names, and all evaluation of such typical traits.

5. Attitudes and Cognitive Organization

FRITZ HEIDER

Attitudes towards persons and causal unit formations influence each other. An attitude towards an event can alter the attitude towards the person who caused the event, and, if the attitudes towards a person and an event are similar, the event is easily ascribed to the person. A balanced configuration exists if the attitudes towards the parts of a causal unit are similar (1).

It is tempting to generalize from this statement and to omit the restriction to causal unit formation. Do units in general interact with attitudes in a similar way?

In trying out this hypothesis we shall understand by attitude the positive or negative relationship of a person p to another person o, or to an impersonal entity x which may be a situation, an event, an idea, or a thing, etc. Examples are: to like, to love, to esteem, to value, and their opposites. A positive relation of this kind will be written L, a negative one $\sim L$. Thus, pLo means p likes, loves, or values o, or, expressed differently, o is positive for p.

The relation "unit" will be written U. Examples are: similarity, proximity, causality, membership, possession, or belonging. pUx can mean, for instance, p owns x, or p made x; $p \sim Ux$ means p does not own x, etc. Other relations which, in many ways, seem to function like units are: p is familiar with, used to, or knows well o or x, and p is in situation x. In lumping together all these relations we are, of course, aware of the dissimilarities between them. Only in a first approximation can they be treated as belonging to one class.

The hypothesis may be stated in greater detail thus: (a) A balanced state exists if an entity has the same dynamic character in all possible respects (e.g., if p admires and at the same time

likes o); in other words, if pLo or $p \sim Lo$ is true for all meanings of L. (We may anticipate here that the analogous statement for pUo does not seem to hold in a general way.) (b) A balanced state exists if all parts of a unit have the same dynamic character (i.e., if all are positive, or all are negative), and if entities with different dynamic character are segregated from each other. If no balanced state exists, then forces towards this state will arise. Either the dynamic characters will change, or the unit relations will be changed through action or through cognitive reorganization. If a change is not possible, the state of imbalance will produce tension.

The first part of the hypothesis refers to influence of dynamic relations or attitudes on each other. Since the different dynamic relations are not included in each other logically ("p likes o" does not imply "p admires o"), the same o or x can be positive in one respect and negative in another. An example in point is the conflict between duty and inclination. A tendency exists to make the different dynamic relations agree with each other by means of cognitive restructuring (excuses or rationalizations). Another example would be the tendency to admire loved persons and to love admired persons.

More numerous are the possibilities to which the second part of the hypothesis refers. They can be grouped according to the entities making up the configurations: (a) person and non-person (p, x); (b) two persons (p, o); (c) two persons and a non-person (p, o, x); (d) three persons (p, o, q). Many of the examples seem to substantiate the hypothesis. Examples which do not fit may eventually lead to greater insight into the nature of the dynamic characters and of the unit relations. All examples refer to p's life space. This is true even of oLp which therefore means: p thinks that o likes or admires p.

• Reprinted from *Journal of Psychology*, 1946, **21**, 107-112, with permission of the author and the publisher.

(a) *p and x*. Since the own person (*p*) is usually positive, a balanced state will exist if *p* likes what he is united with in any way, or if he dislikes the *x* he is segregated from. The cases $(pLx) + (pUx)$ and $(p \sim Lx) + (p \sim Ux)$ are balanced. Examples: *p* likes the things he made; *p* wants to own the things he likes; *p* values what he is accustomed to.

(b) *p and o*. Analogously, the two balanced states for *p* and *o* will be: $(pLo) + (pUo)$ and $(p \sim Lo) + (p \sim Uo)$. Examples: *p* likes his children, people similar to him; *p* is uneasy if he has to live with people he does not like; *p* tends to imitate admired persons; *p* likes to think that loved persons are similar to him.

pUo is a symmetrical relation, i.e., pUo implies oUp. That they belong to a unit is true for *p* and *o* in the same way, though their rôles in the unit may be different (for instance, if *U* is a causal unit). However, pLo is non-symmetrical since it does not imply oLp. It is in line with the general hypothesis to assume that a balanced state exists if pLo and oLp (or $p \sim Lo$ and $o \sim Lp$) are true at the same time. Attraction or repulsion between *p* and *o* are then two-way affairs; the relation is in symmetrical harmony. pLo is a non-symmetrical relation logically, but psychologically it tends to become symmetrical. Examples: *p* wants to be loved by an admired *o*; *p* dislikes people who despise him. oLp is similar to pLo in its relation to pUo. Examples: *p* likes to meet people who, he is told, admire him.

(c) *p, o, and x*. The combinations become more numerous with three entities making up the configurations. Only a few possibilities can be mentioned. We shall always give the balanced state in symbols before stating the examples which refer to it.

$(pLo) + (pLx) + (oUx)$. Both *o* and *x* are positive and parts of a unit. Examples: *p* admires clothes of loved *o*; *p* wants to benefit his friend *o*; *p* likes to think that his friend benefits him. A seeming exception is the case of envy. If *o* owns *x* (oUx) and *p* likes *x* (pLx), $p \sim Lo$ may often follow. This exception can be derived from the fact that ownership is a one-many relation. A person can own many things but each thing can, ordinarily, be owned only by one person. Therefore "*o* owns *x*" excludes "*p* owns *x*," or oUx implies $p \sim Ux$. Since pLx may tend toward pUx, conflict is introduced.

Implications between unit relations often lead to conflict. Lewin's three cases of inner conflict rest on implications. Approach to a positive valence may imply withdrawal from another positive valence. Withdrawal from a negative valence may imply approach to another negative valence. Finally, approach to a positive valence may imply approach to a negative valence if both are located in the same region. Analogously, one can talk of three cases of outer conflict between persons. pUx may imply $o \sim Ux$ (for instance, if *U* means ownership), and if both want *x*, conflict (competition) will arise. In the same way conflict appears if *p* and *o* want to get away from *x* but only one of them can do so (if $p \sim Ux$ implies oUx, and vice versa). Lastly, it may happen that *p* likes *x* and *o* hates it, but *p* and *o* have to move together (pUx implies oUx, e.g., in marriage). They either can both have *x*, or both not have it.

Trying out variations of the triad $(pLo) + (pLx) + (oUx)$, we find that $(pLo) + (pLx) + (oLx)$ also represents a balanced case. Examples: *p* likes what his friend *o* likes; *p* likes people with the same attitudes. This case is not covered by the hypothesis unless we treat *L* as equivalent to *U*. Actually, in many cases the effects of *L* and *U* in these configurations seem to be the same. Furthermore, this case shows the psychological transitivity of the *L* relation. A relation *R* is transitive if aRb and bRc imply aRc. Thus, *p* tends to like *x* if pLo and oLx hold. As in the case of the symmetry of the pLo relation, we again have to stress the difference between logical and psychological aspect. Logically, *L* is not transitive but there exists a psychological tendency to make it transitive when implications between *U* relations do not interfere with transitivity. The relation *U*, too, seems to be in this sense psychologically transitive. $(pUo) + (oUx)$ can lead to pUx; *p* feels responsible for what people belonging to him do.

Taking into account these considerations, we can reformulate the hypothesis: (a) In the case of two entities, a balanced state exists if the relation between them is positive (or negative) in all respects, i.e., in regard to all meanings of *L* and *U*. (b) In the case of three entities, a balanced state exists if all three possible relations are positive in all respects.

The question arises whether, with a triad, one can make any generalizations about balanced cases with negative relations. For instance, $(pLo) + (o \sim Ux) + (p \sim Lx)$ is balanced. Examples: *p* likes *o* because *o* got rid of something *p* dislikes. In this case two entities, *p* and *o*, are related positively to each other, while both are related negatively to the third entity x. This holds generally: the triad of relations is in balance, if two relations are negative and one positive. This statement can be derived from the assumption that L and U are, in a balanced configuration, exchangeable, symmetrical, and transitive. L and U can then be treated as formally analogous to an identity relation. The "balanced" cases with three terms are for this relation: $a = b$, $b = c$, $a = c$; $a = b$, $b \neq c$, $a \neq c$; $a \neq b$, $b \neq c$, $a \neq c$. By substituting L or U for the identity sign one obtains the balanced cases for these relations, though the case with three negative relations does not seem to constitute a good psychological balance, since it is too indetermined.

Therefore, the second part of the hypothesis must be stated as follows: (b) In the case of three entities, a balanced state exists if all three relations are positive in all respects, or if two are negative and one positive.

$(pLo) + (oLx) + (pUx)$. Examples: p likes o because o admired p's action; p wants his friend o to like p's production; p wants to do what his friends admire.

$(pUo) + (pLx) + (oLx)$. Examples: p wants his son to like what he likes; p likes x because his son likes it.

(d) p, o, and q. Among the many possible cases we shall only consider one. $(pLo) + (oLq) + (pLq)$. Examples: p wants his two friends to like each other. This example shows, as the parallel case with x instead of q, the psychological transitivity of the L relation.

However, the transitivity of the L relation is here restricted by implications between unit relations when L represents a one-one love relation. p does not want his girl friend o to fall in love with his boy friend q because oLq in this case implies $o \sim Lp$, which conflicts with pLo. Jealousy, as well as envy and competition, is derived from implications between unit relations.

After this discussion of the different possibilities there are several more points worth mentioning which refer to examples of different groups. One is the problem of self evaluation. High self regard of p can be expressed by pLp, low self regard by $p \sim Lp$ (though the two p's in these expressions are not strictly equivalent). All of the examples so far considered presupposed pLp. However, one also has to take into account the possibility of $p \sim Lp$. As to be expected, it plays a rôle contrary to that of pLp. Examples: if p has low self regard he might reject a positive x as too good for him; if p has guilt feelings he will think he ought to be punished; if his friend admired his product he will think it only politeness. A negative action attributed to himself will produce $p \sim Lp$, etc.

The equivalence of the L and U relations seems to be limited by the fact that often the U relation is weaker than the L relation. One can assume, that pLx brings about pUx (p wants to have a thing he likes) more often than pUx produces pLx (p gets to like a thing which belongs to him). Again $(pLo) + (oLx)$ usually will lead to pLx (transitivity), but $(pUo) + (oUx)$ will not do so if there holds at the same time $p \sim Lo$.

We saw that one can derive forces towards actions, or goals, from the configurations. It can also happen, that the choice of means to a goal is determined by these patterns. If p wants to produce oLx, and he knows that oLp holds, he can do so by demonstrating to o the relation pLx, because $(oLp) + (pLx)$ will lead to oLx. If p wants to bring about oLp, and he knows that oLx holds, he can produce pUx, for instance, he will perform an act o approves of.

An examination of the discussed examples suggests the conclusion that a good deal of inter-personal behavior and social perception is determined—or at least co-determined—by simple cognitive configurations. This fact also throws light on the problem of the understanding of behavior. Students of this problem often mentioned the aspect of rationality which enters into it. Max Weber and others pointed out one kind of rationality in behavior, namely, the rationality of the means-end relation. Choosing the appropriate means to gain an end makes for a "good," a "rational" action, and we can understand it. In Lewin's concept of hodological space this kind of rationality is elaborated. However, understandable human behavior often is not of this sort, but is based on the simple configurations of U and L relations. Since they determine both behavior and perception we can understand social behavior of this kind.

REFERENCE

Heider, F. Social perception and phenomenal causality, *Psychol. Rev.* 1944, **51**, 358-374.

6. The Behavior of Attitudes

LEONARD W. DOOB

There is no question that the subject of attitude and attitude measurements is important in sociology and social psychology. Social scientists continue to discuss the nature of attitudes in articles like this, to conduct experiments which show that behavior is affected by attitude, and to measure attitudes for theoretical or practical purposes. The problem of what an attitude is and how it functions, nevertheless, persists and—as many writers on attitudes likewise point out in their introductory paragraph—little explicit agreement is apparent in the published literature.

The purpose of this paper is not to criticize other definitions or usages of the term but systematically, if partially, to relate the concept of attitude to what is known as behavior theory (10).[1] Almost all writers, no matter what their bias, agree that attitudes are learned. If this is so, then the learning, retention, and decline of an attitude are no different from the learning of a skill, a piece of prose, or a set of nonsense syllables; and they must also involve the problems of perception and motivation.

Immediately it is necessary to raise and answer the question as to why a simple, commonsense, ubiquitous concept like attitude should be translated into semi-technical jargon. There are at least two answers to the question. The first and less important answer involves scientific methodology: it is thought desirable to bring as many terms as possible relating to

a field of research (in this instance, human behavior) within one universe of discourse. Misunderstandings result from using one set of concepts to describe perception, learning, and motivation on one level and another set on a different level. Even if some sociologists who use the concept "attitude" are not attracted by the terminology of behavior theory and if they remain inclined merely to assume perception, learning, and motivation without inquiring into the details of the processes, unified knowledge concerning human behavior requires that there be a connection between what the sociologist studies or measures and what the psychologist studies or measures. Secondly and of crucial importance, a tentative translation of a term from one level to another and into an already and perhaps better developed theoretical system is fully justified if thereby inadequacies on the higher level can be pointed out. Murray and Morgan (16), for example, have recently shed new light on the nature of attitude by incorporating the closely related concept of sentiment into the former's previous conceptualization of personality.

The procedure to be followed in this paper is as follows:

1. A definition of attitude in behavioral terms will be given. It is felt that such a definition represents an advance beyond the stage of defining an attitude as the subjective counterpart of something in the environment, as a predisposition within the organism, or as being what the attitude scale measures. The psychological implications of the definition will be made clear.

2. The consequences of this definition and the theoretical structure it assumes will then be summarized briefly by calling attention to the factors which should be known to make a completely adequate analysis of attitudes.

3. Illustrative research employing the con-

• Excerpted from an article in *Psychological Review*, 1947, **54**, 135-156, with permission of the author and the American Psychological Association.

[1] The writer is deeply grateful especially to Neal E. Miller as well as to Irvin L. Child, John Dollard, and Mark A. May for their constructive criticisms. He has promiscuously and deliberately borrowed some of their ideas and, as an insignificant token of his gratitude, herewith absolves them of any responsibility for the final product.

cept of attitude will be critically examined in terms of these factors. Such a detailed examination seems preferable to surveying the attitude literature in general terms.

DEFINITION OF ATTITUDE

Attitude is defined as *an implicit, drive-producing response considered socially significant in the individual's society.* This definition states, in effect, that from the psychological point of view attitude is an implicit response with drive strength which occurs within the individual as a reaction to stimulus patterns and which affects subsequent overt responses. Since psychologists and other social scientists sometimes disagree concerning the nature and attributes of an implicit response of this type, the definition is therefore elaborated and broken down typographically into the phrases and clauses requiring further definition, elaboration, and discussion:

"An attitude is:

(1) "an implicit response

(2) "which is both (*a*) anticipatory and (*b*) mediating in reference to patterns of overt responses,

(3) "which is evoked (*a*) by a variety of stimulus patterns (*b*) as a result of previous learning or of gradients of generalization and discrimination,

(4) "which is itself cue- and drive-producing,

(5) "and which is considered socially significant in the individual's society."

1. *"An attitude is an implicit response. . . ."* By an implicit response is meant a response occurring within the individual and not immediately observable to an outsider. Motor "attitudes" like the physical set of the runner before the starter's gun is fired, therefore, are not included within the universe of discourse being analyzed because they are not entirely implicit and hence are instrumental rather than mediating acts. The semantic connection of such sets with the concept of attitude employed by social scientists is considered to be largely fortuitous from an historical standpoint.

Overt behavior that is observable to an outsider may be affected by the evoked attitude but is not here defined as the attitude itself. Attitude refers to the individual's immediate but implicit response to a stimulus pattern

and his consequent tendency to respond still further as a result of that implicit response. Such an implicit response may be conscious or unconscious, distinctly verbal or vaguely proprioceptive. What is expressed results not from the attitude alone but represents, as will be indicated, another response in a behavior sequence—an overt one—which is a function of the attitude-response and other tendencies within the individual.

2(*a*). *"An attitude is an implicit response which is . . . anticipatory . . . in reference to patterns of overt responses. . . ."* An anticipatory response—called also an antedating response by Hull (10, p. 74)—is one which originally preceded another rewarded response and which, as a result of being associated with or producing this reward, has been reinforced so that it occurs before its "original time in the response series" (14, p. 49). If an individual, for example, dislikes a fruit or a person, he tends to avoid eating the fruit or meeting the person. Originally the avoidance occurred only after actual contact had been established and after that contact had proven to be punishing and the withdrawal to be rewarding. When a thorough investigation reveals no actual prior contact, some process of generalization or discrimination must have occurred since all behavior has antecedents. The possibility of exceptions under different psychological conditions must be noted, even in these trivial illustrations: the fruit may be eaten anyhow if the individual is very hungry and the person may be met and greeted if social circumstances so require.

The conditions under which a response moves up in the behavior sequence and becomes anticipatory have so far been determined concretely in relatively simple situations. It has been shown (14, p. 79), for example, that the closer the response is in the series leading to the reward, the more likely it is to be learned and then subsequently to antedate other responses not leading to the reward. This principle suggests why few objects or individuals in society fail to arouse attitudes. Originally the individual has had to react to them or has been taught to react to them in the course of being socialized. One of the responses leading to the goal response (which by definition involves reward or the avoidance of punishment) has implicit components, is reinforced, and is here called an attitude.

2(*b*). *"An attitude is an implicit response*

which is . . . mediating in reference to patterns of overt responses. . . ." Whereas the anticipatory character of attitude indicates its temporal relation to a goal, its mediating attribute calls attention to its functional connection with that goal. A mediating response is made in an attempt to increase the likelihood of the occurrence of reward rather than punishment in connection with a goal response. In reasoning, for example, implicit responses intervene between the original stimulus pattern and the goal response and may assist the individual in achieving that goal. Attitudes can be evoked so easily because as mediating responses involving only language, imagery, or proprioceptive reactions they need not conflict with the overt behavior of the individual or with his environment.

The mediating function of attitude has led May to suggest that attitude is "a kind of substitute goal response" which "arises when the goal response cannot be immediately and easily made" (13). This attribute, which has also been suggested by other writers (e.g., 2, pp. 425-426 and 17, pp. 28-29), does seem to characterize certain attitudes. The individual who dislikes another person is restrained or restrains himself from hurting his antagonist; instead he makes an implicit response involving aggression and feelings of avoidance or repulsion. It is felt, however, that all attitudes cannot be so characterized. The liked object, for example, evokes an implicit response which facilitates rather than acts as a substitute for overt behavior in reference to it. Overt behavior, in short, may be mediated by attitudes almost immediately and there need not necessarily be a conflict or a restraint before the attitude is evoked.

Three consequences arise immediately from this conceptualization of attitude. In the first place, it appears psychologically futile—as Sherif and Cantril have indicated (20, pp. 304-305)—to attempt to classify attitudes. Responses can be characterized in so many different ways that a simple dichotomy or trichotomy usually must be willfully stretched if it is to include all types of behavior. The response defined as attitude might be called positive or negative or be said to involve approach or withdrawal were it not for the fact that these terms then require further definition which cannot be consistently or usefully applied to all situations. Both approach and avoidance, for example, may be but are not necessarily involved in

what has been called a neutral attitude or in any attitude for that matter. It seems better, in short, to apply *socially* useful labels to attitude as the need arises, in order to indicate the direction in which the individual thereby is oriented; but it should be clearly recognized that the labels have social and not psychological significance. A psychologically important distinction, however, is that between general and specific attitudes (3), a distinction which refers to the stimulus patterns evoking the response or to the evoked responses.

In the second place, reference is made in the definition to "patterns of overt responses." For reasons hereafter suggested, overt behavior can seldom be predicted from knowledge of attitude alone. Under varying conditions within the individual, a given attitude can mediate a repertoire of overt responses. A favorable attitude toward a social institution, for example, can mediate innumerable responses connected with what is considered to be the welfare of that institution.

Then, thirdly, this definition of attitude emphasizes its acquired or learned character. There are no psychic rays which enable the investigator, even though he be equipped with a poll or a scale, to determine the 'strength' of an attitude, the overt responses with which it has become associated, or its present functioning within the personality. Such knowledge can be obtained only from knowing approximately under what conditions the attitude was acquired in the first place and the extent to which it secures present and future reinforcement. The learning process, therefore, is crucial to an understanding of the behavior of attitudes.

The nature of that process cannot be ignored in a treatise on attitude as it has been by Sherif and Cantril: "Just what the psychological or physiological mechanisms of this learning may be are irrelevant to the present discussion," they write in their articles on "The Psychology of 'Attitudes'" (20, p. 302). It is difficult to see how psychologists can call these mechanisms "irrelevant" and still contend, as the authors do in the introduction to the same articles, that the "task" of the psychologist is to "give an adequate account of the psychological mechanisms involved in the formation of an attitude in any individual" (20, p. 295). The authors rest their case by stating that they "do not need to take sides in favor of any learning theory" (20, p. 307). Of course, as they write, "the primary stage in the formation of attitudes is a perceptual stage," which is merely saying that there must be a stimulus and that the stimulus must be perceived before there can be any kind of learning.

In contrast, Allport (1, pp. 810-812) has set the problem of the genesis of attitudes in terms which explicitly suggest the need for learning theory. His often quoted summary of the literature indicates that attitudes may be formed through "the integration of numerous specific responses of a similar type"; "individuation, differentiation, or segregation" of experiences; "trauma"; and the adoption of "ready-made" attitudes of others. The genesis of almost any attitude is undoubtedly more or less unique. Society sets the rewards and punishments regarding much of overt behavior; the individual being socialized then is forced into the learning situation; although he reacts to the situation uniquely, one of the end products—the attitude—he may share in large degree with others.

3(a). *"An attitude is an implicit response . . . which is evoked by a variety of stimulus patterns. . . ."* The stimuli evoking an attitude may be in the external world or within the individual. The latter range from a verbal response to an autonomic disturbance or a drive. The existing literature on attitudes testifies to the fact that the stimuli may be various. Such is the assumption behind any attitude scale in which a variety of situations is judged or behind a distinction like that between specific and general attitudes.

The arousal of an attitude involves two traditional problems in psychology, those of perception and learning. The two are interrelated and can be separated only for purposes of analysis. Perception indicates that the individual is responding because he has previously paid attention to or been oriented toward certain stimuli which then affect his sense organs and thus evoke his attitude. Learning in this connection emphasizes the reasons in the past history of the individual which have brought about the bond between the stimulus pattern and the attitude.

Gestalt psychologists especially point out that paying attention and then perceiving occur in many instances as a result of the individual's set to respond: letter boxes are not noticed unless the person has a letter to post, etc. Writers on attitude are fond of recalling that the tradition of set is somewhat hoary in academic psychology, in order to demonstrate their own respectability and their acquaintance with long German terms like *Bewusstseinslage.* In other words, perceiving depends upon drive or set (which orients the individual to respond to certain stimuli and then to respond to them in a particular way) as well as upon the arrangements of the external stimuli. Attitude may be included among the sets determining both the orientation of the individual as well as the kind of perceptual response he makes: The southerner notices incipient aggression in a Negro which a northerner will overlook.

It must be recognized, however, that in some situations the individual's attitude is not evoked until the stimulus has been actually perceived: It affects perception after its arousal but does not orient him originally in the direction of the stimuli involved. The southerner who has learned to discriminate incipient hostility from genuine docility among Negroes can make the discrimination when confronted with a Negro. It is on the basis of this discrimination that his attitude toward the Negro is or is not aroused. If he goes about the streets looking for hostility in Negroes, he may be set to make the discrimination not necessarily by his attitude toward Negroes or by his ability to detect such behavior but by some particular drive which has been previously aroused and which may or may not involve Negroes. To say that he searches for aggression solely because of his attitude toward Negroes is to fail to distinguish him from another southerner who has a more or less identical attitude (so far as content and even "affect" are concerned) but who has no "chip on his shoulder." In this case the sensible problem remains of accounting for the "chip."

In controlled experimental situations dedicated to observing the behavior of attitudes, the attention of the subjects is secured by the experimenter not through arousing the attitude being studied but through the evocation of some other drive. Subjects perceived the autokinetic phenomenon of Sherif (19) or they looked at Seeleman's photographs of white and colored individuals (18) because they had agreed to cooperate with the experimenter. This was the drive which oriented them in the experimental situation. Then their attitudes were aroused and these attitudes affected both their perceptual responses and the reports they gave the experimenters. Later on in the experiments, their evoked attitudes may have had sufficient drive strength also to orient them selectively.

3(*b*). *"An attitude is an implicit response . . . which is evoked . . . as a result of previous learning or of gradients of generalization and discrimination. . . ."* The previous section has indicated the possible relation between perception and the evocation of an attitude and therein it was suggested that an attitude can almost always be aroused by a variety of stimuli. Here it is stated that previous learning determines whether or not particular stimulus patterns will evoke the attitude. Some stimuli come to arouse an attitude after a relatively simple process of conditioning has occurred. As a result of being originally present in the situation, for example, the wrapper of the disliked fruit or the signature of the disliked person may produce an anticipatory response which mediates the goal response of avoiding it or him. Other stimuli evoke or fail to evoke an attitude not because of their presence or absence in previous situations but because they fall along a stimulus gradient of generalization or discrimination. If an individual likes or dislikes one particular Negro, there is stimulus discrimination; if all Negroes are involved, there is stimulus generalization along a gradient, for example, of skin color; if only certain "types" of Negroes arouse the attitude, there is generalization and discrimination.

Frequently attitudes are thought to be puzzling and mysterious because they can be aroused when the psychologist, the sociologist, the layman, and the individual least expect them to be. The stimulus pattern, for example, may be a word or a sentence, or some other symbol (like a flag, a face, or a gesture) which represents only a portion of the original stimulus pattern. The behavior of attitudes under these circumstances, however, becomes more intelligible when the implications of the "gradient of generalization and discrimination" are understood. This gradient is especially efficacious in the case of attitude since language can readily perform the function of mediating generalization and discrimination. Cofer and Foley (7), for example, are able *a priori* to list over fifty gradients along which generalization or discrimination from a single word can conceivably occur in purely formal (*i.e.*, in non-idiosyncratic) manner. The word "Negro," for example, through previous learning may become the one part of the original stimulus pattern which evokes an attitude

regarding Negroes. Without any difficulty there can be a semantic gradient including words like "colored," "African," and the various epithets and appellations applied to this group. Through a slightly more complicated process, eventually "zoot suit" may arouse the same attitude: if the individual has associated this type of clothing with Negroes, the response of seeing such clothing or hearing its name evokes the internal response of "Negro" which in turn has the property of arousing the attitude. This phenomenon has been called secondary stimulus generalization or acquired cue value. Similarly, thinking can aid generalization and discrimination.

Cantril in his work on attitudes fails to comprehend this stimulus gradient involved in most if not all learning and conditioning. He states, for example, that what he calls "a standard of judgment" must not be "confused with a conditioned response" (5, p. 25). What he means by "a standard of judgment" or a "frame of reference" he never makes operationally clear, although they seem to be related to attitude since they are employed profusely in his two articles on the subject. It may be that terms like these—to use Cantril's own words in reference to "conditioning"—are "so loosely employed" that they "explain nothing at all" (5, p. 55). His conception of a conditioned response is indeed narrow: "a specific reaction to a specific stimulus" (5, p. 25). In spite of a general, noncommittal reference in a footnote to a standard book on conditioning (that of Hilgard and Marquis) and an irrelevant quotation from A. N. Whitehead, this simplification of behavior theory leads him to conclude that such a theory is "by no means adequate to explain the apparent meaningfulness of man's experience" (5, p. 56). More specifically, for example, he maintains that the "analysis of the backgrounds of the people who became panicky listening to the Hallowe'en broadcast [of Orson Welles in 1938] clearly shows that in no way had they been specifically conditioned against Martian invaders' mowing down people on this planet" (5, p. 25). The point of Cantril's study (4), however, is to discover the previously existing attitudes and traits which made people prone to panic or sanity. After discovering many of them with admirable ingenuity, he gives a commonsense "explanation" of the behavior; i.e., he uses his particular vocabulary to describe what happened (4, pp. 190-201). His failure to apply

Chapter 8 of Hilgard and Marquis (8) to his own data prevents him from realizing that at the time of the broadcast people had learned to respond with anxiety to various stimuli as a result, for example, of the "war scare" associated with the Munich crisis (cf. 4, pp. 159-160). Certain Americans, some of whose socio-economic and psychological characteristics Cantril has indicated, apparently generalized from these stimuli to a broadcast which of course they had not previously experienced but which nevertheless was sufficiently similar to other stimulus patterns previously evoking the anxiety. Such individuals "jumped the gun" by behaving—after their attitudes had been aroused by Mr. Welles and his associates—as they would have in the face of genuine catastrophe.

From experiments in other fields of behavior, Hull states that the amplitude of a response "diminishes steadily with the increase in the extent of deviation . . . of the evocation stimulus . . . from the stimulus originally conditioned . . ." (10, p. 185) and that "the strength of the connections at other points of the zone can be determined only from a knowledge of the strength of the receptor-effector connection . . . at the point of reinforcement and the extent of the difference . . . between the position of the conditioned stimulus . . . and that of the evocation stimulus . . . on the stimulus continuum connecting them" (10, p. 187). Whether or not the principle holds true of attitudes has not been tested, so far as this writer knows. To test it, it would be necessary to know "the stimulus originally conditioned," the gradient along which the various "evocation stimuli" are located, and whether or not in fact these latter stimuli have never been previously reinforced or extinguished. This could be done only by means of a careful life history of various individuals and by some objective measurement of the strength of the attitude.

At any rate, this generalization of Hull has an important bearing on the strength of attitude. The "strength" of an attitude is almost as ambiguous as the concept of attitude itself. One type of strength that seems important for predicting future behavior of the individual is the *afferent-habit strength* of the attitude, i.e., the strength of the bond between the stimulus pattern and the response which is here defined as attitude. In these terms the afferent-habit strength of an attitude is a function of the number of previous reinforcements as well as the position along the gradient occupied by a particular stimulus pattern.

4. *"An attitude is an implicit response . . . which is itself cue- and drive-producing. . . ."* Like all implicit responses, attitudes can be said to have stimulus-value, i.e., they arouse other responses. The responses they evoke may indeed be various. They may produce a perceiving response, as has been suggested, and in this sense determine to what other stimuli the individual subsequently responds. They may produce linguistic responses, thoughts, images, or stereotypes. They eventually have an effect upon overt behavior. Here again reference must be made to the habit strength of the attitude, only this time it is a bond between attitude as a stimulus and a response pattern (implicit or overt), rather than between a stimulus pattern and attitude as a response. This phenomenon will be called the *efferent-habit strength* and, like the afferent-habit strength, it too can be strengthened or weakened through learning. The stimulus-value of attitude suggests why investigators have discovered so many different phenomena—aside from overt behavior—associated with attitude.

The definition of attitude refers to the distinction made by Miller and Dollard (14, pp. 22-23) between the cue- and drive-producing characteristics of a stimulus. The numbers used in counting, they point out, have cue value: the number "six" is a response to the cue of "five" and in turn acts as a cue to elicit "seven." An attitude has cue-value in the sense that it acts as a stimulus to produce another response, but it also is a drive in the sense that its tension is reduced through subsequent behavior leading to a reward. It is proper, consequently, to refer to the *drive strength* of an attitude as well as to the strength of the bond between the attitude and the responses it evokes. An individual, for example, who has not been thinking of food is shown a picture of a type of food he likes. The picture may be said to evoke his favorable attitude toward the food which is a drive whose goal response is eating. If the secondarily evoked response pattern is only salivation and the thought or statement of how he likes the food, the drive may be considered relatively weak. But if he drops what he is doing and goes out to eat immediately after seeing the picture, the drive is relatively strong.

The strength of an attitude, therefore, may refer to its afferent-habit strength, its efferent-habit strength, or its drive strength. Knowledge of an attitude's direction or content is not equivalent to measuring its strength. The attitude possessed by two people, for example, may be more or less identical in formal content as measured by an attitude scale, but its role in determining overt behavior may be quite diverse. In one individual it may be evoked by a restricted stimulus pattern (specific attitude), it may not be frequently evoked (a weak afferent-habit), or the entire pattern of additional implicit and overt responses may be restricted (a weak drive). Any one or more of these conditions may be different in the second individual. Thus the role of the patriotic attitude in the average citizen is different from the way it functions within a professional patriot. Or within the same individual the patriotic attitude may be more easily and variously aroused and lead more certainly to a greater number of responses during a war than when there is peace.

The fate of an attitude over time—whether it persists or changes—is obviously a function of complicated processes within the individual. At least three factors are involved. The first is the reward or punishment associated with the goal response. An attitude will persist when it is constantly reinforced or it will change when it is partially or wholly extinguished. Its afferent- and efferent-habit strength is then increased or decreased. The efferent-habit strength is a direct function of the frequency with which the attitude has mediated rewarding or non-rewarding behavior as well as of the immediacy and amount of the reward or non-reward. Afferent-habit strength depends ultimately upon efferent-habit strength since reinforcement or non-reinforcement results not from the arousal of the attitude but from the behavior mediated by the attitude; it also depends on the frequency with which particular stimulus patterns have aroused the mediating attitude and the distinctiveness of those patterns. In Hull's words (9), attitudes have the property of "pure stimulus acts" within a single individual: they are responses which are reinforced "because they, as stimuli, evoke *other* acts . . . which will bring about a reinforcing state of affairs. . . ."

Secondly, there is the factor of conflict with competing drives which may determine the fate of an attitude. The afferent- and efferent-habit strength of an attitude may be great, but its drive strength may be weak in comparison with other attitudes or drives aroused by the same or different stimulus patterns. The individual,

for example, may not express his attitude in overt behavior because its expression would be contrary to his general philosophy; but his attitude persists. Finally, there is forgetting which may involve other psychological processes besides extinction through non-reinforcement.

It is possible, consequently, to have an attitude play a less significant role in a personality by diminishing the number of stimuli which evoke it, by having the attitude aroused less frequently, by weakening its drive strength, by setting up stronger competing drives, or by punishing the overt behavior which it mediates. Since the afferent-habit strength is affected by the final goal response, moreover, it follows that the attitude's strength in this respect can remain more or less constant even though its efferent-habit strength vis-à-vis a particular response pattern is weakened: it is only necessary that some reinforcement be obtained by having the attitude mediate other goal responses. The prejudiced individual, for example, can retain his prejudice not by always behaving identically in response to a given stimulus pattern in his society but by behaving differently and with more or less equal satisfaction.

There is a voluminous literature on the subject of attitude change, a good part of which is called experimental (cf. 15, pp. 946-980). In general, the approach has been to subject a group of individuals to a collection of stimuli (like a course in race relations, a motion picture, propaganda analysis, or a visit to an ethnic group in a large American city). Their changes in attitude (if any) are ascertained by comparing their scores on an attitude scale before and after being subjected to the stimuli. Sometimes the changes are compared with those of a control group which has not been so stimulated. It must be said that this type of approach is socially useful but psychologically sterile: it is important to know that lectures or visits do or do not affect students but, except for sporadic attempts to correlate attitude change with obvious factors like intelligence and "intensity" of the attitude at the outset, no effort has been made to suggest precisely why the attitudes do or do not change. They change, it is said, "because" the student heard the lecture or met a Negro or saw a motion picture. Obviously the word "because" is misleading. All that has been demonstrated is a correlation, not a causal connection. Two people with approximately the same attitude and subject to approximately the same stimulus pattern, for example, will be affected differently because different responses, including or excluding the attitude, are evoked within them. Or the overt effect may be the same for different reasons: in one, the afferent strength of the attitude may be altered only in respect to particular stimulus patterns and not to others; whereas in another, the drive strength of the attitude may be reduced. To maintain, therefore, that a course or a contact produces attitude change in a group of individuals (with a large or small sigma) is to state an historically limited conclusion which certainly may be socially useful at a given moment. It is like indicating that the abolition of a slum area diminishes the delinquency rate; it does, but thereby little insight is gained into the nature of delinquency (e.g., why there are delinquents from non-slum areas). Research on attitude change, consequently, is likely to produce superficial generalizations which, being derived so uniquely from particular phenomena, can be applied to future situations only with extreme difficulty.

The psychological aspects of this definition of attitude, finally, can shed some light on another traditional problem: the relation between attitude and stereotype. Numerous studies, especially those of Katz and Braly (11) and of Child and Doob (6), have demonstrated the close connection between the two. The term "stereotype" is loosely employed. Like attitude, it seems to be an implicit response—this is what Lippmann (12) many years ago must have meant by defining it as "the picture in our heads." It becomes an attitude, however, only when it is also drive-producing. An individual, for example, has a favorable attitude toward Great Britain, it is said in oversimplified fashion, because he considers the British "patriotic." If the oversimplified explanation be accepted as valid, some learning process in the past must be presumed. A word like "good" must first have produced a "favorable" response since it was conditioned to a stimulus pattern like parent or food which for other reasons evoked that response. Then "patriotic" became associated with "good" for reasons to be found in the individual's milieu and also evoked that response. "Great Britain" as a stimulus came to produce the response of "patriotic" (the stereotype), a bit of learning doubtlessly also socially conditioned. "Patriotic" thus is a stimulus-producing response which, finally, evokes the "favorable" response to which it has been previously linked. In this instance, the stereotype evoked by "Great Britain" is a mediating response in a long response sequence and does evoke a drive. In like manner, most people in our society reply to the question, "Is the earth round or flat?" by means of some stereotype which produces the word "round." The stereotype appears to have cue- but essentially no drive-value and hence is not an attitude, although the question itself may arouse another implicit response with drive-value (attitude): to reply incorrectly to a simple question is usually non-rewarding.

5. *"An attitude is an implicit response . . . which is considered socially significant in the individual's society."* If attitudes are defined as implicit, drive-producing responses, it is obvious that they thereby are placed within the psychological sub-class of such responses but that simultaneously they are not distinguished from other responses in this group. The other psychological qualifications which have been discussed—their anticipatory and mediating character, the variety of stimuli which evoke them, and the variety of responses they evoke—are also common to other responses which, according to conventional usage, may not be considered attitudes. The rat's aversion to a grid on which it has been shocked is doubtless implicit, it is anticipatory and mediating in avoiding the shock, it can be evoked by a gradient of stimuli, and it has drive value resulting in other responses which serve perhaps to allay its anxiety; but it is ordinarily not useful to call such a response an attitude. Similarly the human being's favorable disposition toward cream cheese or a style of hat may or may not be called an attitude. Psychologically, therefore, attitude is not and—it is deliberately maintained—should not be distinguished from the larger sub-class of responses to which it appears to belong.

The distinction between attitude and other types of responses can be made not on a psychological but on a social basis: its socially evaluated significance must be considered. The rat's aversion to the grid is not an attitude unless it plays an important part in its behavior in other situations involving rats; from the human standpoint, it is not at all socially significant. The liking of cream cheese or a hat may or may not be considered socially significant: from an overall point of view, it is doubtless trivial and hence not an attitude, although it undoubtedly is of importance to cheese producers and hat manufacturers as well as their clients. The words "socially significant" must be left unspecific, since social values fluctuate from society to society and, within a particular society, over time and in various groups. Almost always the socially significant in a society is evaluated or, more simply, is called "good" or "bad" to indicate its actual or potential effect on people. A useful test to decide whether an implicit response with drive-value is an attitude is to discover whether that response is labelled desirable or undesirable by the individual's contemporaries. In any segment of society at a given moment, people are likely to acquire attitudes because they are subject to similar learning conditions.

ANALYSIS OF ATTITUDES

An ideally thorough analysis of an attitude requires knowledge (quantitative if possible) of the following factors, if its behavior and role in determining overt behavior in various situations are to be understood:

1. *Goal response:* the response pattern or patterns which the attitude anticipates and mediates and which determine its reinforcement or extinction.

2. *Perception:* the drive orienting the individual to pay attention to the stimulus pattern evoking the attitude.

3. *Afferent-habit strength:* the strength of the bond between the attitude and the evoking stimulus patterns, including the gradients of generalization and discrimination.

4. *Efferent-habit strength:* the strength of the bond between the attitude and the evoked responses, including overt ones.

5. *Drive strength:* the drive strength of the stimuli produced by the attitude.

6. *Interaction:* the strength of the other attitudes, drives, etc. with which the attitude interacts to evoke overt behavior.

7. *Social significance:* the evaluation in the society of the attitude and its direction (*e.g.*, whether positive, negative, or neutral; favorable, unfavorable, or ambivalent; friendly or unfriendly; desirable or undesirable; good or bad).

BIBLIOGRAPHY

1. Allport, G. W. Attitudes. In *A handbook of social psychology* (Murchison, C., Ed.). Worcester: Clark Univ. Press, 1935. Chap. 17.
2. Bernard, L. L. *An introduction to social psychology.* New York: Henry Holt, 1926.
3. Cantril, H. General and specific attitudes. *Psychol. Monogr.,* 1932, no. 192.
4. Cantril, H., Gaudet, H., and Herzog, H. *The invasion from Mars.* Princeton: Princeton Univ. Press, 1940.
5. Cantril, H. The psychology of social movements. New York: Wiley, 1941.
6. Child, I. L., and Doob, L. W. Factors determining national stereotypes. *J. soc. Psychol.,* 1943, **17**, 203-219.
7. Cofer, C. N., and Foley, J. P., Jr. Mediated generalization and the interpretation of verbal behavior: I. prolegomena. *Psychol. Rev.,* 1942, **49**, 513-540.
8. Hilgard, E. R., and Marquis, D. G. *Conditioning and learning.* New York: Appleton-Century, 1940.
9. Hull, C. L. Fractional antedating goal reactions as pure stimulus acts. Paper delivered before Monday Night Meeting of the Institute of Human Relations, October 24, 1941.
10. Hull, C. L. *Principles of behavior.* New York: Appleton-Century, 1943.
11. Katz, D., and Braly, K. W. Racial prejudice and racial stereotypes. *J. abnorm. and soc. Psychol.,* 1935, **30**, 175-193.
12. Lippman, W. *Public opinion.* New York: Macmillan, 1922.
13. May, M. A. A stimulus-response interpretation of "attitudes." Unpublished paper.
14. Miller, N. E., and Dollard, J. *Social learning and limitation.* New Haven: Yale Univ. Press, 1941.
15. Murphy, G., Murphy, L. B., and Newcomb, T. B. *Experimental social psychology.* New York: Harpers, 1937.
16. Murray, H. A., and Morgan, C. D. A clinical study of sentiments. *Genet. psychol. Monogr.,* 1945, no. 32.
17. Richards, I. A. *Science and poetry.* New York: Norton, 1926.
18. Seeleman, V. The influence of attitude upon the remembering of pictorial material. *Arch. Psychol.,* 1940, no. 258.
19. Sherif, M. A. A study of some social factors in perception. *Arch. Psychol.,* 1935, no. 187.
20. Sherif, M. A., and Cantril, H. The psychology of "attitudes." *Psychol. Rev.,* 1945, **52**, 295-319; 1946, **53**, 1-24.

7. Behavior Theory and the Behavior of Attitudes: Some Critical Comments

ISIDOR CHEIN

I. INTRODUCTION

In his paper on "The Behavior of Attitudes" (2) Professor Doob has contributed a lucid and thorough analysis of the concept of *attitude,* one which will no doubt have considerable impact on social psychologists and on the status of social psychology. It is desirable to examine his argument carefully and to encourage the fullest discussion of it because, as will be explained shortly, it constitutes an interesting test of behavior theory and because, if his conclusions are accepted, they may have serious implications for social psychology.

In brief, Professor Doob examines attitudes in the light of behavior theory[1] (the theory of behavior developed by Hull and his associates) and comes to the conclusion that it would be tempting to propose (if such a proposal had any prospects of success) that the concept of attitude be dropped from social science, that the concept serves a quasi-scientific need, and that when the concept will finally be abandoned, it "will be a happy day for social science, since this event will signify the emergence of a more integrated and scientific system of human behavior.[2]

• Excerpted from an article in *Psychological Review*, 1948, **55**, 175-188, with permission of the author and the American Psychological Association.

[1] We may perhaps register a mild protest at the appropriation of "behavior theory" for a particular theory of behavior, but we shall retain this usage in the present paper.

[2] It should be noted that Doob's main dissatisfaction with the concept of attitude is not on the ground of its vagueness and lack of precise definition. This type of criticism of many psychological concepts occurs with sufficient frequency, however, to justify some comment on it. The present writer, at least, does not consider the demonstration that

II. THE NATURE OF *ATTITUDE*

Doob defines an attitude as "(1) an implicit response (2) which is both (*a*) anticipatory and (*b*) mediating in reference to patterns of overt responses, (3) which is evoked (*a*) by a variety of stimulus patterns (*b*) as a result of previous learning or of gradients of generalization and discrimination, (4) which is itself cue- and drive-producing, (5) and which is considered socially significant in the individual's society."

a term is ambiguously and inconsistently used as sufficient reason for discrediting it in scientific discourse. Words that have real referents are necessarily as ambiguous as their referents are vaguely apprehended. To abandon a word because it is not precisely defined is to give up the scientific quest before it has begun. One begins by vaguely observing something (whether it be *matter,* or *intelligence,* or *attitude*) and gradually sharpens one's observation until the word designating this observed something is more and more precisely defined. Science, after all, begins in ignorance.

Sometimes the process of sharpened observation leads to the discovery that the word designates a null class, that it has no real referent, and that the original vague observation was illusory. This Doob does not attempt to show with regard to *attitude.* Sometimes the process of sharpened observation leads to the discovery that the word designates a class of referents which are included in the referents of another word and which are not distinguishable from the latter. Such a discovery leads to greater unification of science, and this Doob attempts to do with regard to *attitude.* Such attempts should, however, be regarded with great caution. To be prematurely carried away by them is to give up the investigation of a separate and possibly real phenomenon.

It follows from our conception of the evolution of scientific definitions that an argument with regard to a definition is not merely a quibble over words; not if the definition is to be regarded (as it should be) as the best possible summary, in the light of available knowledge, of the essential nature of a real referent.

The bulk of Doob's paper is devoted to the explanation and amplification of this definition and of the related points of behavior theory. Some highlights of the definition are, in the light of Doob's discussion, as follows: An attitude is a learned response; it may be evoked by any one of a variety of stimulus patterns; the latter need not have been directly associated with the response, but may through a process of secondary conditioning have become associated with a stimulus which has been directly associated with the response, or they may be sufficiently similar to the latter stimulus to evoke the same response; an attitude is itself not merely a *response,* but also a *stimulus* which may evoke any one of a variety of learned responses; it is, moreover, the kind of stimulus which is tension producing and, consequently, some of the learned responses to it (*i.e.,* goal responses) have the effect of reducing the tension (reward); it cannot itself be observed by an outsider, but the responses to which it gives rise are observable; it is no different from any other learned, implicit, cue- and drive-producing response such as a rat's aversion to a grid on which it has been shocked; but it may be arbitrarily distinguished from other such responses on non-scientific grounds (social significance). Other points of Doob's definition and elaboration will also be commented on in the following discussion.

By way of contrast and to serve as background in our discussion of Doob's concept, we present an alternative conception of the nature of attitude, an alternative which we prefer and which we believe will be a recognizable version of the common usage of the term.

An attitude, according to this conception, is *a disposition to evaluate certain objects, actions, and situations in certain ways.* For purposes of the present definition, evaluation requires words; the *disposition* to evaluate need not, however, be verbalized. An attitude may be conscious (recognized and known by its "possessor") or it may be unconscious. It may be momentary or persistent. If it persists, it becomes salient in situations to which it is pertinent; otherwise it may be relatively unobservable, except through its effects. It may pertain to matters socially significant or insignificant. The evaluations involved may correspond to, or differ from, the evaluations of most members of the culture or subculture or the "coded" cultural and institutional values. They may or may not have strong personal pertinence, self-reference, or ego-involvement. They may or may not be associated with strong impelling motives. The disposition to evaluate in certain ways is generated by such factors as one's available knowledge concerning the object, action, or situation, one's comprehension of the interrelatedness and interrelations of phenomena and of the consequences of actions, one's time perspective, one's motives and motivational displacements or substitutions, one's conscious and unconscious patterns of phenomenal equivalences (symbolisms in the psychoanalytic sense), one's introjected moral values, and the interaction of these factors in relation to other attitudes. Various aspects of this conception will also be elaborated upon in the course of the following discussion.

From the viewpoint of this second conception of the nature of attitude, when Doob writes that "The rat's aversion to a grid on which it has been shocked is doubtless implicit, it is anticipatory and mediating in avoiding the shock, it can be evoked by a gradient of stimuli, and it has drive value resulting in other responses which serve perhaps to allay its anxiety; but it is ordinarily not useful to call such a response an attitude," we may add that not only would it be not useful to call such a response (or response pattern) an attitude, but that it would be wrong. Rats may have aversions, but they do not have dispositions to evaluate which, in this case, would require a disposition to verbalize the aversion.

It should be noted that, although the two conceptions are assuredly different, there are many points of agreement or near agreement. Both would, for example, agree that (1) a person is not born with his attitudes, (2) the learning process plays a major role in the development of attitudes, (3) attitudes involve problems of perception and motivation, (4) as a result of a particular attitude a person may be more likely to perceive certain objects than others, (5) some attitudes affect perception after their arousal even though they may not have oriented the person originally in the direction of the perceived objects, (6) specific behavior cannot be safely predicted from a knowledge of attitude alone, and (7) people may act contrary to their attitudes.

III. POINTS OF INCONSISTENCY IN DOOB'S DEFINITION

The most important inconsistency has to do with the term in Doob's definition which asserts that an attitude is a response. Elsewhere, however, he writes that, "The individual . . . may not express his attitude in overt behavior because its expression would be contrary to his general philosophy; *but his attitude persists*" (italics added). Now, by any ordinary usage of the word "response," a response occurs and is gone; it does not persist. In other words, if an attitude can persist, it cannot be a response. Doob may, of course, have in mind a class of persistent responses, but such responses do not seem to belong in the stimulus-response formula and, hence, in behavior theory. In all S–R psychologies one looks for a stimulus which immediately precedes the response, and to admit responses which keep going (perhaps for many years) is certainly to change the psychological significance of the stimulus term in the S–R formula.

Despite his definition of an attitude as a response, Doob often seems on the verge of thinking of an attitude as a habit or an established stimulus-response "bond." Thus he defines the strength of an attitude in terms of the strengths of the stimulus-response bonds in which it is involved. This would give meaning to Doob's statement that an attitude may persist, for, while the response may be momentary, the bond presumably persists. It may be more sensible, therefore, to think of an attitude as the *habit* rather than as the response.

But an attitude cannot be both a response and a habit; it must be one or the other or neither. It is our inclination to say neither. For in customary usage it seems that there may be both persistent and momentary (possibly but not necessarily, recurrent) attitudes. And it seems to us that both have more in common with each other than either does, respectively, with a habit or a response.

Closely related to the question of whether an attitude is a response is the question of the relation of attitude to set. In our own conception, attitudes are a species of set. Doob also concedes that "Attitude may be included among the sets determining both the orientation of the individual as well as the kind of perceptual response he makes." Sets may also be momentary or persistent (and hence our previous question as to whether an attitude is best conceived of in relation to habits or responses or to neither applies to set as well), but, even if we concede that all sets are responses, the important thing about a set is not that it is a response, but the selective function that it plays. In other words,

in playing up the response aspect of attitude, Doob is missing the boat.

That Doob seems to have some kind of antipathy to set is suggested by the following passage: "Writers on attitude are fond of recalling that the tradition of set is somewhat hoary in academic psychology, in order to demonstrate their own respectability and their acquaintance with long German terms like *Bewusstseinslage*." Perhaps this antipathy accounts for Doob's insistence that an attitude is implicit, i.e., not "overt behavior that is observable to an outsider." His sole justification for the criterion of implicitness is his opinion that "The semantic connection of such sets [motor 'attitudes' like the physical set of the runner before the starter's gun is fired] with the concept of attitude employed by social scientists is . . . largely fortuitous from an historical standpoint." But if attitudes are a species of set, then the connection is by no means an historical accident; because, apart from the question of whether any set can be said to have no motor aspects, sets which are manifestly motor and other sets have much in common, at least in a functional sense.

The matter is of some importance because, in making implicitness a defining attribute of attitude, Doob introduces a quite dispensable source of ambiguity. There is, of course, no sharp line of demarcation between *implicit* and *explicit* as Doob defines these terms; observability varies in degree. This implies that it must in many instances be difficult to decide (by Doob's definition) whether or not one is dealing with an attitude. How unobservable must an attitude be before one ceases to refer to it as an attitude? Also, it must often be difficult to distinguish between an overt *manifestation* of an attitude and an overt *consequence* of it. For instance, is a *moue* of distaste a manifestation or a consequence? If it should be decided that it is a manifestation, then by Doob's definition, whatever it is a manifestation of *is not* an attitude; but if it is regarded as a consequence, then what it is a consequence of *is* an attitude. Insofar as we may arbitrarily regard it as either manifestation or consequence, then we may arbitrarily decide that we are or are not dealing with an attitude.

As the final item in this section we shall raise the question of whether an attitude is properly defined as anticipatory. Doob follows Hull in defining an anticipatory response as "one which originally preceded another rewarded response and which, as a result of being associated with or producing this reward, has been reinforced so that it occurs before its 'original time in the response series.' " Doob's illustrations are singularly unilluminating with regard to attitudes as anticipatory responses. Thus, in the case of an individual disliking another person, we are told: "Originally the avoidance occurred only after actual contact had been established and after the contact had proven to be punishing and the withdrawal to be rewarding." It is clear that the avoidance response may occur more quickly as a result of learning than it did originally, but it is not clear how it can be regarded as an anticipatory response since, being the goal response, it is always necessarily the last in the series. Doob, as a matter of fact, explicitly states that an attitude precedes (leads to) the goal response. Perhaps, of course, the attitude is the dislike rather than the avoidance (the latter being regarded, perhaps, as a response to the former) and it is the dislike which moves up in the response series. The dislike presumably (at least by the definition) does not become an attitude until it does move up in the response series, but it is not at all clear why a dislike which arises more quickly should be called an attitude while one which arises less quickly (and is in fact the same dislike) should not be called an attitude. Moreover Doob goes on to say that, "When a thorough investigation reveals no actual prior contact, some process of generalization or discrimination must have occurred since all behavior has antecedents." In other words, not only does an attitude occur before its original time in the response series, but it seems that it may occur in a response series in which it has never previously occurred at all; if mere temporal placement may define anticipation, then this is anticipation with a vengeance.

Again the matter is of some importance because making an attitude, by definition, anticipatory, leads to various difficulties. It precludes, for instance, the possibility of functional or dynamic contemporaneity between the attitude and the pertinent goal response. Even if an attitude may be said to persist, Doob's position implies that whatever effect an attitude may have has already taken place by the time the goal response occurs. Yet, to take one example, a young man may have an attitude about kissing girls even while acting in accordance with, or contrary to, his attitude;

and his enjoyment of the process and later reactions to it may continue to be influenced by his attitude. Doob's formulation raises the problem which confronts all attempts to deal with dynamics in historical, as distinguished from ahistorical (cf. 1) terms, namely, how something which no longer exists (and it no longer exists because it antedates its effects) can influence something which is now going on.

IV. POINTS NOT REQUIRED BY BEHAVIOR THEORY

Doob's definition requires that attitudes play a mediating role and he explains that "A mediating response is made in an attempt to increase the likelihood of the occurrence of reward rather than punishment in connection with a goal response." This qualification imposes, without any apparent justification, a restriction upon the concept of attitude which is not in accord with current usage. And while we cannot discern any reason for the restriction, there are several reasons for objecting to it.

In the first place, attitudes may *decrease* the likelihood of goal responses being rewarding. For instance, a student who cheats on an examination may find his "achievement" rather empty as a consequence of his attitude regarding honesty. In the second place, by defining attitudes as mediating, they are functionally placed *between* the person and his goal responses. Yet attitudes play a role in the very selection of goal responses. For example, partly as a function of his attitudes concerning personal integrity, a student may not have the alternative of handing in a term paper which he himself has not written. It is misleading to say that such attitudes are attempts to increase the likelihood of reward in connection with goal responses when, actually, they play a role in defining what is rewarding.

As a second item we shall deal with Doob's analysis of attitude strength. Despite our differences with this analysis, we regard it as an extremely important contribution to the psychology of attitudes, for it makes some important and hitherto neglected distinctions. It should be noted, therefore, that our objections are not to the distinctions but to the framework of behavior theory within which they are made.

Doob distinguishes between *"afferent-habit*

strength of the attitude," its *"efferent-habit strength,"* and its *"drive strength."* He defines the first as "the strength of the bond between the stimulus pattern and the response which is here defined as attitude"; the second as the strength of the "bond between attitude as a stimulus and a response pattern (implicit or overt), rather than between a stimulus pattern and attitude as a response"; and the third he characterizes as follows: "An attitude has cue-value in the sense that it acts as a stimulus to produce another response, but it also is a drive in the sense that its tension is reduced through subsequent behavior leading to a reward." While he never quite defines "drive *strength*," it seems clear that this term signifies the degree of impulsion to tension reducing behavior.

Afferent and efferent habit strengths are both described in terms of the strength of stimulus-response bonds. What Doob means by the *strength* of such a bond is indicated when he writes: ". . . it may not be frequently evoked (a weak afferent habit). . . ." The translation from *strength* to *frequency* of *evocation* is illuminating. Mere frequency of evocation is obviously irrelevant except in relation to the frequency of occurrence of the stimulus pattern. But if it is evoked once by a given stimulus pattern, why not all the time? To answer this question in terms of habit strength is sheer tautology. The obviously correct answer is that conditions (inner and outer) surrounding the bond are different from time to time. It follows that the relative frequency of evocation is a function of the surrounding conditions rather than of "the strength of the bond" and that, in this respect at least, all bonds are equally strong.[3]

[3] It may, of course, be argued that Doob's translation of bond strength into frequency of evocation was merely a careless slip and that it does not do justice to behavior theory. If bond strength can be defined independently of frequency of evocation, then it may perhaps be said that the latter is a function of both the bond strength and conditions surrounding the bond. Such a definition may apparently be found in terms of the frequency (and quality?) of the reinforcement involved in establishing the bond. We say that it may *apparently* be found because, actually, the effect of such a definition is to make "bond strength" a verbal synonym of "frequency of reinforcement." One may, perhaps, argue that such a definition is really a hypothesis that (*a*) there really is such a variable as bond strength, (*b*) it is a function of frequency of reinforcement, and (*c*) it may be measured in terms of the latter. Unless, however, some way is presented to verify (*a*) and (*b*), the hypothesis is empty and

If "bonds" may be said to differ in strength, the strength would have to be measured in terms of what it takes to disrupt them rather than in terms of frequency of occurrence. But if the amount of effort needed to undo a "bond" is a measure of its strength, it follows that its strength is a function of the knowledge, skill, strategy, and/or appropriateness with which these efforts are marshalled against it. It becomes apparent that its strength does not reside solely in the bond. This does not mean that such strength is scientifically insignificant, any more than *mass* is insignificant because it does not inhere in physical objects. It does mean that in dealing with the strength of attitudes one's perspective has to take in more than the learning process and the "bonds" themselves.

With regard to "drive strength," it is at present a moot point whether the "drives" associated with some attitudes come from the attitudes themselves or whether the motivational force comes from factors beyond the attitudes themselves. The present writer is inclined to favor the second of these possibilities. One may find attitude and drive varying independently. Many of one's attitudes toward food may, for instance, remain unchanged as one goes through the hunger cycle. One may have an attitude with regard to, say, the marital difficulties of two relative strangers and what

(*c*) simply establishes "bond strength" and "frequency of reinforcement" as verbal synonyms.

A test of the hypothesis might be provided by showing that the relative frequency of evocation varies as a function of frequency of reinforcement despite the constancy of surrounding conditions. Unfortunately, we have no way of holding the inner conditions, at least, constant. Let us, however, grant for purposes of discussion the successful performance of such an experiment, with positive results. Such results would require a peculiar assumption to explain them. Since all surrounding conditions are being held constant, variation in frequency of evocation could only be a function of *variation* in the bond (because for a given status of the bond it either will or will not produce the response under given stimulation). And this variation in the bond cannot be a function of some variable factor acting on the bond, since it is agreed that all other factors are constant. In other words, we would have to assume that the bond has acquired an inner life as a result of which it waxes and wanes independently of what is going on around it. We might then argue whether such a waxing and waning is best described in terms of an invariant adjective, a-given-degree-of-strength. But, for our own part, we would rather not make this assumption until we absolutely have to.

seems to be the same attitude with regard to identical difficulties between one's two closest friends. Does the lack of impulsion to do anything about it in the first case as compared to the strong impulsion to do something in the second case signify that these are really two different attitudes of different drive strengths? Or does the drive in the second case derive from one's concern about one's friends, the attitude to the marital difficulties being in both cases the same? Or, to take another instance, the attitude of regarding one's own ethnic group as superior to other ethnic groups, does this attitude derive its motivational force (e.g., to resist any overt contradiction of the attitude) from within itself, or does it derive its force from such motives as the need to maintain one's level of self-esteem?

We have already stressed the point that our objections to Doob's distinctions between the three types of "attitude strength" are not to the distinctions themselves, but to the conceptual framework within which they are made. The distinctions have two definite values. In the first place, they throw light on what may happen when ratings of the strengths of attitudes are made. Roughly corresponding to Doob's "afferent-habit strength," these ratings may reflect the degree of confidence that the attitude actually exists (e.g., ratings of low intensity may correspond to "Sometimes I feel this way and sometimes I don't—I'm not sure how I feel!" Or, "I am ambivalent about it —I feel both ways—I'm not sure how I feel"); or, roughly corresponding to Doob's "efferent-habit strength," these ratings may reflect one's degree of conviction that something ought to be done and one's readiness to support such action; or, finally, roughly corresponding to Doob's "drive strength," they may reflect the intensity of one's urge to do something oneself. The implication is clear that, in obtaining ratings of the intensity of attitudes, one should if possible specify the dimension of intensity involved.

In the second place, the issue of attitude strength aside, Doob's analysis is valuable in that it calls attention to the fact that an attitude is not completely described until we know its perceptual-cognitive content (the object, action, or situation to which it is pertinent), its action implications (one's beliefs about what should be done about, or with regard to, the object), and its motivational force (the strength of the motives with which it is bound up). But one cannot separate the cognitive

from the action aspects as Doob does when he treats "afferent-habit strength" as involving a different "bond" from "efferent-habit strength." If two people have attitudes toward a common object, but differ on what they believe should be done with regard to that object, it seems both simpler and more accurate to say that they have different attitudes toward that object than to say that they have a common afferent habit and different efferent habits. Nor can one give unqualified assent to Doob's statement that "Afferent-habit strength depends ultimately on efferent-habit strength since reinforcement or nonreinforcement results not from the arousal of the attitude but from the behavior mediated by the attitude." For if one could disrupt the "afferent habit," the "efferent habit" would automatically go with it, there being nothing to arouse it. In other words, it is just as true to say that the efferent-habit depends on the afferent-habit. The two are, in fact, inseparable.

In passing, we may note Doob's remark that a stereotype "becomes an attitude . . . only when it is drive-producing." It seems to us that a better formulation would be that a stereotype is not an attitude because, taken by itself, it has no action implications (i.e., it involves no opinion or belief concerning what should be done about the object of the stereotype). It is part of an attitude and may be used to gauge attitudes only insofar as one may assume action implications. In Doob's language, it is an afferent habit which does not necessarily have any efferent habits associated with it. Insofar as it creates a likelihood of accepting certain action implications, it is a condition of an attitude. Concretely one may think of certain people as being "dirty," but if one is indifferent toward people's dirtiness this is not an attitude. Associated drives, on the other hand, are not at all necessary to have an attitude. One may, for instance, have an attitude toward the caste system in India without being at all impelled to do something about it.

V. POINTS REQUIRED BY BEHAVIOR THEORY

Doob takes Sherif and Cantril (3) to task for saying that it is possible to discuss attitudes without committing oneself to any particular learning theory. In a sense, a proponent of behavior theory has to take such a position because behavior theory is built around a particular learning theory. If it is to offer an interpretation of any psychological phenomenon, it must do so in terms of its particular theory of the learning process.

Concerning the genesis of attitudes, we have already indicated in presenting our alternative to Doob's conception of the nature of an attitude our agreement with the proposition that the learning process plays a major rôle. This is, by no means, complete agreement, for Doob admits only the learning process (and only a particular kind of learning process, at that). To hold the latter position, it seem to us, is to take insufficient account of creative cognitive processes, both of thought and perception. Such processes, we believe, also play a role in the generation of attitudes. It consequently seems to us that a more satisfactory formulation of the relation of learning to attitude would be: The residues of past learning play a rôle in determining how a given situation or object is perceived and what a person wants in the situation or with regard to the object. The latter, in turn, play a rôle in determining the attitudes which are generated and the salience of already existing attitudes. The important dynamic fact is how the person perceives the situation and what he wants in it rather than the fact that learning had previously taken place.

In this connection, we believe that there is an intellectual trap in the commonly accepted principle that if some psychological process is not learned, then it must be innate and, if it is not innate, then it must be learned. We believe that new insights do arise, and we see no good reason why novel features of current situations should not be perceived or why previously unnoticed features of repeatedly experienced situations may not be perceived for the first time. We also see no reason why such cognitive novelties should not play a significant rôle with relation to attitude despite an absence of associated learning. The atom bomb was something new to most people; they had no established responses to it; but it exercised immediate and profound effects on the attitudes of many of them.

In line with behavior theory, Doob takes the position that "Some stimuli come to arouse an attitude after a relatively simple process of conditioning has occurred. . . . Other stimuli evoke or fail to evoke an attitude not because of their presence or absence in previous situations but because they fall along a stimulus gradient of generalization or discrimination." The recognition of such gradients is of course a great improvement over the oversimplification of early conditioning theories, but from our point of view, this is still insufficient.

The proponents of the more sophisticated conditioning theories still act as if new perceptions never occur or, if they do occur, as if they have no dynamic significance since, being new, they are not directly or indirectly associated with past learning. Suppose, for example, that a new perception occurs which just doesn't happen to fall along some generalization or discrimination gradient. Will a person remain completely unaffected by it? We think not. Nor can one argue that it is impossible for a perception not to fall along such a gradient without also assuming that these gradients are completely preestablished. Otherwise how can a new gradient ever come into being?

This point is particularly emphasized when these gradients are themselves interpreted as resulting solely from secondary conditioning. The Gestalt psychologists have presented enough evidence on structural processes in perceptual grouping to raise doubts as to the sufficiency of secondary conditioning in this context. It is necessary, therefore, to appeal to some supplementary principle as Doob does when he turns to similarity as a factor involved in producing generalization gradients. But if similarity is interpreted in terms of a doctrine of identical elements or identical neural pathways, the viewpoint is again committed to the assumption that there can be no novel perceptual processes, an assumption which we are not prepared to accept. If, on the other hand, similarity is interpreted in other terms, then something more is involved in the generalization gradients besides the learning process itself.

BIBLIOGRAPHY

1. **Chein, I.** The genetic factor in ahistorical psychology. *J. gen. Psychol.,* 1947, **36,** 151-172.
2. **Doob, L. W.** The behavior of attitudes. *Psychol. Rev.,* 1947, **54,** 135-156.
3. **Sherif, M. A., and Cantril, H.** The psychology of "attitudes." *Psychol. Rev.,* 1945, **52,** 295-319; 1946, **53,** 1-24.

8. The Personal Setting of Public Opinions: A Study of Attitudes Toward Russia

M. BREWSTER SMITH

Underlying the rapid growth of public opinion research in the last decade has been the fruitful conception of public opinion as a sum or resultant of the opinions of individual members of the public. Such a conception leads immediately to the question, "What are Smith, Jones, Brown, and all the other members of the public actually thinking on a given subject?"—a question to which the techniques of the sampling survey are providing increasingly adequate answers. When our interest extends to the formative and directing influences on public opinion, the same approach leads us to ask, "Why do Smith, Jones, etc. think as they do?" "Depth interviewing" and its modifications have been developed to press this attack. If we are to take seriously the productive assumption that public opinion is most effectively studied on the individual level, an important source of insights into the dynamics of opinion should be found in the study of opinions as they reflect the personalities of the individuals who hold them. The relatively few studies that have made forays into this area have not attempted a systematic formulation of the ways in which opinions are grounded in the personality.

To develop and test such a coherent psychological approach to public opinion, the intensive methods of clinical personality study and the broader but shallower methods of the polling survey were brought to a focus in a cooperative study of attitudes toward Russia.[1] The study as a whole will be reported elsewhere. Here some of the main findings of a part of the project—a panel survey of attitudes toward Russia among a cross-section of adult men in a New England community—will be described with two ends in view: first, to illustrate the main lines of an attempt to formulate systematically the nature of opinion and its relation to personality factors, and second, to throw some incidental light on the important problem of American attitudes toward Russia.

The initial formulations underlying the opinion surveys emerged from the related clinical study of a small number of individuals, whose personalities and opinions were investigated in the course of over thirty hours of individual interviewing and testing. Our objective in the opinion surveys was to refine and test the generality of formulations that had proved important in understanding the opinions of the individual cases studied by intensive methods.

A "panel" representing adult men in the community was interviewed personally at the men's homes, first in March and then in May, 1947.[2] The first series of interviews, which systematically explored the men's attitudes toward Russia, comprised 319 men. Of these, 250 were re-interviewed in order to obtain information about their personalities. The smaller group taking part in both interviews did not differ markedly in demographic characteristics from the initial group.

Two general approaches were employed in the design of the interviews and in their

• Reprinted from *Public Opinion Quarterly*, 1947, 11, 507-523, with permission of the author and the publisher.

[1] This study was made possible by support from the Harvard Laboratory of Social Relations. The writer is particularly indebted to Dr. J. S. Bruner for his participation and guidance in the planning and analysis of the survey phase of the project.

[2] We are indebted to Dr. Alvin Zander and Dr. Seth Arsenian for their kind cooperation in facilitating the field work. Mrs. Betty Lopez, Mr. David Schneider, Mr. Henry Riecken, and the author trained the interviewers, and Mrs. Lopez supervized the interviewing.

analysis. The first of these sought to provide a systematic *descriptive analysis* of attitudes toward Russia. Here the attempt was made to delineate an "anatomy" of attitudes that would provide an adequate basis for the "physiology" of a subsequent *functional analysis*. The latter was concerned with the interplay of opinions and other manifestations of the personality.

PRINCIPAL CONCEPTS OF A DESCRIPTIVE ANALYSIS

Descriptively we may fruitfully distinguish how a respondent *feels* about Russia—the *affective* aspect of his attitudes, and what he *thinks* about it—their *cognitive* aspect. On the affective side, there are the familiar factors of *direction,* defined in terms of his approval or disapproval of Russia as a whole or of such features as he may differentiate, and *intensity,* his degree of concern. On the cognitive side, the *informational context* of his attitudes may be distinguished as the structure of his beliefs and knowledge that affect his opinions, and their *time perspective* as his expectations concerning future developments in regard to Russia.

Both the cognitive and affective elements of a person's attitudes patently have much to do with what he wants to *have done* about Russia. The latter aspect we singled out as the individual's *policy orientation:* the measures toward Russia that he supports and opposes. Policy orientation has the most direct political relevance of the various descriptive categories, but is probably bound more closely than the others to the issues of the moment. All of these categories seem necessary for an adequate description of the attitudes comprising public opinion. A brief consideration of some of our findings may serve to indicate the utility of this scheme, as well as to introduce some necessary elaborations.

Direction, Intensity, and Organization

Probably the first problem to be faced in a description of public opinion toward Russia is its direction: are people favorable or unfavorable? As one might expect, the direction of opinion was found to vary according to the aspect of the problem in question. Direction was therefore studied in terms of the lines along which attitudes toward Russia were commonly differentiated. In most respects, unfavorable opinions prevailed. The extent of disapproval

showed marked variation, however, and in regard to Russia's part in World War II, the proportion of respondents who indicated unqualified approval considerably exceeded the disapproving group.

Aspect of Russia	Per Cent Indicating Approval
Russia's part in World War II[3]	46%
Russia's international role[4]	14
Russian system of government[5]	6

One need not rest, however, with the statement that attitudes are predominantly favorable in some respects and unfavorable in others. The different aspects of Russia involved in the men's attitudes had different weight in determining their over-all evaluation of Russia and their policy orientation. Table 1 shows, for example, that when the respondents were asked to pick out what was most important (among 12 things listed) in making them feel about Russia the way they did, only 9 per cent cited "the part Russia played in World War II," as compared with 23 per cent who selected "Russia's part in spreading world Communism" and 21 per cent who mentioned "the lack of freedom and democracy inside Russia."

Attitudes toward Russia can therefore be conceived as hierarchically *organized*. The aspects in regard to which Russia was likely to be viewed with relative favor turn out only rarely to have had determinative importance for the respondents. This finding suggests the danger of looking to poll results from single questions for an assessment of the over-all direction of opinion. It is vital to know whether direction of opinion in regard to a given aspect is consequential or trivial in the organization of the respondent's attitudes. The conception of the

[3] The question was: "Looking back on it now, what would you say about Russia's part in the war?" Data are for respondents indicating unqualified approval.
[4] Based on the card question: "Now, about Russia's part in the world today—do you think it has been mostly good, more good than bad, about half good and half bad, more bad than good, or mostly bad?" Data are for respondents giving the first two answers.
[5] Based on the question: "How do you feel about the Russian system of government? What is good and what is bad about it?" Data are for respondents giving favorable answers, with or without qualification. All three questions were asked in the March, 1947, survey.

TABLE 1. *Relative Importance Attributed by Respondents to Various Aspects of Russia**

Aspects of Russian Foreign Relations		52%
Russia's part in spreading world Communism	23%	
The possibility of war with Russia	11	
The part Russia played in World War II	9	
Russia's treatment of small countries	9	
Aspects of Russian Internal Affairs		46
The lack of freedom and democracy inside Russia	21	
The lack of free enterprise inside Russia	12	
Russia's treatment of the church and religion	7	
Russia's concern for the welfare of her people	5	
The equality given all races and minority groups in Russia	1	
Russian planning and efficiency	**	
Russian backwardness and inefficiency	**	
Russia's point of view on morality and the family	0	
No opinion		2
Total		100%
Number of respondents		250

* The question asked in May, 1947, was: "As you know, we're interested in the way people look at Russia, what they see in her. I wonder if you could tell me which of these things you think is most important in making you feel about Russia the way you do?" [Show card.]
** Less than 0.5 per cent.

hierarchical organization of a person's attitudes makes it possible to speak consistently of his being favorable to Russia in some respects and unfavorable in others, at the same time that we ascribe to him a generally favorable—or unfavorable—attitude toward Russia.

It is not enough to know the direction of attitudes toward Russia; we must also know their intensity. It seems likely, in fact, that the just-considered hierarchical organization of a person's over-all attitude depends directly on the intensity of his component attitudes. Thus, those features of Russia about which he feels most strongly determine his over-all evaluation of Russia and have most to do with his policy orientation toward the country. Support for this plausible view is found in the survey data. When asked which things were most important and which next most important in making them feel as they did about Russia, some respondents indicated two aspects both of which could be classed under "Russian foreign relations" (see Table 1 for the classification), while others named aspects both in the area of "Russian internal affairs." When these extreme groups are compared in respect to the inten-

sity of their attitudes toward Russia's international role, 75 per cent of the former group as against 56 per cent of the latter are found to have said that they were at least "quite a lot" concerned.[6] In this case, then, intensity of opinion was higher with respect to the dominant area in the organization of the respondents' attitudes. If we want to find the keystones of opinion on a topic, according to this view, we should look for the areas in which the intensity of opinion is highest.

Time Perspective

A study limited to the affective side of opinion—its direction and intensity—would give at best an incomplete understanding of opinion phenomena. The person's beliefs and expectations form the premises for his evaluation and policy orientation. In this regard, the complex pattern of expectations that constitutes the

[6] The question, asked in the May survey, was: "How concerned are you about Russia's part in the world today—a great deal, quite a lot, not so much, or none at all?" There were 71 and 59 respondents in the two groups, respectively.

time perspective of a person's attitudes is of major importance. For some, the meaningful future extends little beyond the practical concerns of tomorrow. The opinions of such persons with narrow time perspective surely take form under different influences and have different meaning from those of persons whose broad time perspective includes a careful balancing of future possibilities. Another important distinction is between "short run" and "long run" perspectives. In the long run perspective, the constraint of reality may be more lax than in the short run, while the implications of threat or benefit to the individual are less immediate. Discrepancies between the two views may therefore be expected.

Results from our survey seem to require this distinction between the short and long run. When the respondents were asked,

"Do you think the United States and Russia will get along together better, worse, or about the same in the next few years?"

44 per cent said relations would get "better," while only 15 per cent indicated that they would get "worse." These optimistic findings must be contrasted with the results for the following question:

"Do you expect the United States to fight in another war within the next 50 years? [If 'yes,' 'perhaps,' or 'don't know'] Are there any particular countries that you think we might fight against?"

Here 51 per cent of the sample said they definitely expected another war, and named Russia as the probable enemy, while an additional 13 per cent thought that if there were to be another war it would be with Russia.

Rather than providing a relatively unbiased assessment of expectations in regard to possible war with Russia, this question appears to have tapped the stereotyped assumption of the inevitability of future wars, a belief that entails little personal threat when held in the relatively remote time perspective of the long run. The high proportion who mentioned Russia as the probable enemy did not necessarily foresee war with Russia; rather, they expected another war eventually and regarded the country with which American relations were most problematic as the most likely candidate. In the short run, nearly half of the respondents expected improvement in relations between the countries at the time of the survey.

Informational Context

Time perspective is only a part of the important cognitive aspect of attitudes. There remains to be considered their informational context—the entire complex of beliefs and knowledge that bears on a person's opinions. At the core of the informational context of our respondents' attitudes toward Russia lay the picture of Russia that they had formed for themselves. The degree of factually correct information—or *informational level*—is only one aspect of the informational context, and not the most important one.

Several questions revealed the prevalent stereotype of Russia among our respondents as one of a dictatorship engaged in spreading world Communism for purposes of self-aggrandizement. The economic aspect of Communism took a relatively secondary place, while considerations of social welfare figured scarcely at all. Beliefs concerning moral and religious practices were marginal to the stereotype, but those that prevailed were still mostly unfavorable in purport. The picture of Russia formed by our respondents was of course intimately related to the direction and policy orientation of their attitudes.

In regard to informational *level*, however, as estimated from scores on a series of seven "fact questions on Russia," there was practically no relation to the direction of their opinions about Russia's international role nor to their policy orientation. On the other hand, the better informed men were distinctly more optimistic in their time perspective in regard to relations with Russia. They were less likely to pick Russia as a probable enemy in a future war, and, as Table 2 illustrates, they were more likely to expect United States-Soviet relations to improve.

Results such as these call into question the conclusion of Walsh in 1944 that "the decisive factor in American opinion toward Russia appears to be neither class, nor religion, nor political preference, but information."[7] If we re-examine the data as summarized by Walsh, we find that it is again time perspective—expectations about post-war relations—that is

[7] Cf. W. B. Walsh, "What the American People Think of Russia," *Public Opinion Quarterly,* **8,** No. 4 (1944).

TABLE 2. Expectations about United States-Soviet Relations, in Relation to Informational Level

Question: "Do you think the United States and Russia will get along together better, worse, or about the same in the next few years?"	Well-Informed Respondents	Poorly Informed Respondents
Relations will get *better*	53%	35%
Relations will stay the *same*	28	36
Relations will get *worse*	14	16
No opinion	5	13
Total	100%	100%
Number of respondents	155	164

related to informational level. It may have been that the extent of information about Russia was also related to the direction and policy orientation of opinion at that time, but the poll results that he quotes do not provide the necessary data. The present scheme has the merit of calling attention to distinguishable aspects of attitudes that warrant separate consideration.

Policy Orientation

The cognitive and affective aspects of attitudes both underlie their policy orientation, which we have defined as the measures, in this case toward Russia, that the respondent supports and opposes. From the standpoint of the individual as well as from that of political relevance, policy orientation represents in a very real sense the point or focus of his attitudes. Behind the persistent tendency of most people to evaluate the salient features of their world is the need to know where one *stands,* to know in at least a rudimentary way the course of action one would take if the occasion should demand it. In the case of political attitudes on topics of public concern, policy orientation consists for the most part in alignment in terms of publically defined issues.

At the time of our first survey (just before the President's "Truman Doctrine" speech), the following question provided the principal information on our respondents' policy orientation:

"Some people say that the United States should try to do everything possible to cooperate with Russia and others say that we've got to be tough with Russia. Which do you agree with most?"

Fully 53 per cent said that the United States should be "tough" with Russia, while only a third (33 per cent) favored a policy of "cooperation." In itself, such a finding is not too informative. Further questions revealed, for example, that the majority could not further specify the policies they would favor, while many of those favoring "cooperation" appeared to have had relatively stern policies in mind. In addition, the supporters of a "tough" policy proved to be less easily dislodged from their position, and were more likely to indicate that policy toward Russia would make a difference in their vote for a presidential candidate. Such matters of lability and passivity of policy orientation need investigation to give meaning to the bare proportions found in support of different policies.

Illustrative Relationships

The descriptive features of attitudes that have been distinguished cannot of course be conceived in isolation. The study of their relationships is itself informative, and raises significant problems for functional interpretation. Two examples may serve to emphasize the complexity of the processes involved.

Intensity of concern about Russia was found to be associated with a high level of information about Russia. Among the relatively well-informed respondents, 71 per cent said they were at least "quite a lot" concerned about Russia's part in the world today, in comparison to 52 per cent among the poorly-informed group. The respondents who were higher in intensity were found to have had more frequent and adequate contact with the press, radio, and magazines. Presumably the relationship is a reciprocal one: knowledge leads to concern, while concern leads to receptivity to information. This reciprocal relation between intensity and informational level has an important consequence: holders of the most narrowly stereotyped unfavorable views were not particularly likely to show the intensity that their beliefs might be supposed to warrant. The ignorance underlying their unfavorable stereotypes was part of a complex interaction that also involved their relative lack of concern about Russia.

Another close relationship held between the direction of a person's opinions and the nature of the beliefs forming his informational context. There is good evidence that the interplay here was also reciprocal. The influence of beliefs on the direction of opinion needs no special supporting evidence. The reverse influence is neatly documented by Table 3. There it may be seen that respondents who were relatively favorable toward Russia were more likely than unfavorable respondents to decide erroneously that Russia declared war on Japan shortly before the first atomic bomb. In this case it seems quite clear that the direction of opinion was causally prior to the belief. It is unlikely that many of the respondents had heard or read the erroneous assertion as a fact, while virtually all of the respondents must have been aware

of the true succession of events when they were occurring. In all likelihood, those who answered the question incorrectly had no belief on the matter prior to the asking of the question, and created on the spur of the moment a belief consistent with the direction of their attitudes.

FUNCTIONAL ASPECTS OF ATTITUDES TOWARD RUSSIA

One cannot pursue the study of attitudes far, however, without inquiring about their function in personality. The correspondence, for example, between the informational context and direction of an attitude can only be understood in terms of the values activating the individual's over-all view of Russia. That is to say, the correspondence between the conception of Russia as a dictatorship and unfavorable attitudes is only "natural" in a public sharing democratic values to which dictatorship is repugnant. Several ways in which attitudes are enmeshed with personality factors emerged from the study. They may reflect or express the person's central values (their *value* function). They may show consistency with his characteristic ways of reacting (their *consistency* function), or perhaps gratify indirectly his basic needs (their *gratification* function). They may form part of his attempt to construct for himself a stable and meaningful world within which he can order his life (their *meaning* function). Finally, they may serve to express

TABLE 3. *Beliefs Concerning Russian Entry into the War against Japan, in Relation to Direction of Opinion toward Russia*

Belief	Favorable Respondents*	Unfavorable Respondents*
Russia declared war in 1941	4%	4%
Russia declared war shortly before the first atomic bomb was dropped	49	35
Russia declared war shortly after the first atomic bomb was dropped	38	45
Russia never declared war	4	9
Don't know	5	7
Total	100%	100%
Number of respondents	45	109

* The question, asked in March, 1947, was, "Now about Russia's part in the world today—do you think it has been mostly good, more good than bad, about half good and half bad, more bad than good, or mostly bad?" Data for the first two and the last two categories are compared here.

TABLE 4. Intensity of Attitudes toward Russia, in Relation to Breadth of Interests

Question: "How concerned are you about Russia's part in the world today? . . ."	Respondents with Broad Interests*	Respondents with Narrow Interests*
. . . a great deal	40%	23%
. . . quite a lot	40	28
. . . not so much	19	43
. . . none at all	1	4
No opinion	0	2
Total	100%	100%
Number of respondents	73	110

* The question, asked in May, 1947, was: "By and large, do you usually prefer to be with people who are quite a lot concerned about what is going on in the world, or with people who are mostly interested in their homes and families?"

his identification with and promote his acceptance by his favored social groups (their *conformity* function).

Personal Values and Attitudes toward Russia

The nature of a person's central values was found to be important for his attitudes toward Russia in several respects. In the first place, the scope of his interests is of primary importance in determining the intensity of his attitudes toward Russia. Secondly, the particular values that he holds dear sensitize him to corresponding aspects of Russia and provide him with standards of judgment. Finally—a consequence of the second point—the nature of his value system has much to do with the hierarchical organization of his attitudes toward Russia.

As might be expected, men with broader interests were much more likely than others to show a relatively high level of intensity in their concern about Russia. We took as one rough index of breadth of interests whether a respondent said that he usually preferred "to be with people who are quite a lot concerned about what is going on in the world, or with people who are mostly interested in their homes and families." Men who gave the former response were also more likely than others to place high value on participation in community affairs and on taking an interest in national and world affairs. As Table 4 shows, 80 per cent of the men with broader interests said that they were at least "quite a lot" concerned about Russia's part in the wold. Only 51 per cent of the group with narrower interests, on the other hand, showed this level of intensity. Intensity of atti-

tudes toward Russia thus formed part of a more general tendency to take an interest in the world beyond hearth and home. A respondent may have prided himself on a range of interests that involved concern about Russia; or, his broader range of interests may have led him to enrich his information about Russia to an extent that he saw its relevance to values that were important to him.

The part played by the person's central values in determining the hierarchical organization of his attitudes toward Russia may be illustrated by the case of the value of *liberty*. Respondents who gave a response classifiable under this value when asked what things in life were most important to them[8] (62 cases) were compared with all others (188 cases) in regard to the aspect of Russia that they said had most to do with their feelings. Of the group stressing liberty, 36 per cent selected "the lack of freedom and democracy inside Russia," compared with 17 per cent of the remaining respondents—and this was the only notable difference in the responses of the two groups. The degree to which a value is important to the individual can thus determine which aspect of Russia plays the key part in the organization of his attitudes.

[8] The question was: "We've been talking about some of your present opinions. We are also interested in finding out what sorts of things people think are important in life. I have a question here about what you think is important in life. It's a little hard to put in words right off, I know, but from your experience, what would you say are the most important things to you? What sort of things mean the most to you?"

The correspondence between a person's central values and the features of Russia around which his attitudes are organized is, however, by no means direct. Some values of greatest importance to him may fail entirely to *engage* with his conceptions of Russia. A good example of this was the value of economic security. The most frequent responses elicited by the open-ended question on personal values referred to economic security—matters like a steady job, good pay, etc. A naive application of the present approach might therefore lead one to expect that individual economic security as espoused by Russia would play an important part in the attitudes toward Russia formed by the men stressing this value. Actually, nothing of the kind was observed. There was no association between economic security as a value and emphasis on corresponding aspects of Russia.

Two facts that are probably sufficient to account for this finding have major implications for a general formulation of the relation between personal values and the organization of attitudes. In the first place, the information in terms of which the respondents might have seen the relevance of Russia to economic security was simply not available in the current media of communication. While it is probably true that the holding of a value sensitizes a person to perceive and digest information that pertains to it, there is a limit to the extent that he will actively seek out information that is not readily available. In this case, the resultant informational context furnished no basis for the *engagement* of the value. Secondly, the value of economic security was likely to entail a rather narrow scope of interests, in the form in which it was important to most of our respondents. Men who cited it as a central value were likely to show relatively little interest in current events or community participation. Their interests tended to center more exclusively around the daily concerns of a minimal existence. There was therefore small occasion for them to apply the value of economic security in their judgments of Russia.

For a value to enter into a person's attitudes on a topic, then, there are at least two necessary conditions: the scope of the value must be broad enough to apply to the topic, and the information available to the person must contain at least some basis for engaging his value. Taking these limitations into consideration, we may tentatively extend our principle of the organization of attitudes. It was previously suggested that the hierarchical organization of a person's attitudes on a complex topic depends directly on their relative intensity. Now we may say that *intensity is a function of the extent to which a personal value is engaged and of the importance of this engaged value in the hierarchy of the person's central values.*

Other functional relationships to the personality doubtless also enter into the determination of intensity. Here it may be noted that the present statement goes far to clarify the reciprocal relationship found to exist between informational level and intensity. A more adequate informational context permits the person's values to engage more fully with Russia.

Personality Traits and Attitudes toward Russia

A person's attitudes are formed so as to be consistent with his characteristic modes of reaction, and may be pressed into service for the indirect gratification of underlying personality strivings. Although there is a serious limit to the kinds of personality data obtainable from door-to-door interviews, one can, nevertheless, get at some important personality factors in field interviewing. An illustration of the consistency of personality traits with attitudes toward Russia is a case in point.

People characteristically respond to a frustrating situation, according to Rosenzweig,[9] in one of three ways: they may turn aggressively on others ("extrapunitive reaction"), or on themselves ("intrapunitive reaction"), or they may ignore the frustration ("impunitive reaction"). It seemed likely that these characteristic types of reaction might carry over into their opinions. A rough indicator of the first two of these tendencies was provided by responses to the following question:

"When things go wrong, are you more likely to get sore at other people or to feel bad and blame yourself for the situation?"

Table 5 compares the men who said that they usually "get sore at" others with those who said they blamed themselves. It may be seen that those who blame others—the "extrapunitive" group—were somewhat more likely than the "intrapunitive" respondents to blame Russia for United States-Soviet disagreements and to support a "tough" United States policy toward

9 Cf. S. Rosenzweig, "Types of Reaction to Frustration," *Journal of Abnormal and Social Psychology*, **29**, No. 3 (1934).

TABLE 5. Opinions about Russia, in Relation to Reported Reaction to Frustration

Opinion	Tends to Blame Others	Tends to Blame Self
Blames Russia for U.S.-Soviet disagreement*	74%	63%
Expects U.S.-Soviet relations to stay the same or deteriorate	76	49
Favors "tough" U.S. policy toward Russia	67	57
Number of respondents	46	127

* The question, asked in May, 1947, was: "Do you think that the present disagreements between the United States and Russia are *entirely* Russia's fault, *mostly* Russia's fault, the fault of the *United States,* or do you think that *both* countries are equally to blame?" Data are for respondents giving the first two answers. The other questions have already been quoted.

Russia. This is what one would expect if their attitudes were to be consistent with the rest of their personality tendencies. They were also considerably more likely to expect United States-Soviet relations to stay the same or deteriorate. The latter finding appears to have been an *indirect* consequence of the distinguishing personality characteristic. Perhaps a greater tendency to blame oneself and the groups with which one was closely identified required a defensive sanguineness from the intrapunitive group. Or, on the other hand, those who saw the United States as at least partly implicated in the blame may have been more likely to think the disagreements between the countries remediable.

Attitudes toward Russia as a Source of Meaning and Stability

On *a priori* grounds one might suppose that a person's attitudes toward any topic serve the important function of sorting out his world of experience into a predictable order that can provide the background for an orderly existence. It is necessary to postulate some such function in order to interpret the constraint that knowledge places on wishful thinking. The present data on attitudes toward Russia provide several illustrations of the tendency of a person's beliefs and expectations to conform to the direction of his attitude. But, not surprisingly, the more informed respondents were less likely to let their feelings enter into their beliefs. For example, of the well-informed group (155 cases), 55 per cent said that they expected the world to become more commu-

nistic, compared with 41 per cent of the poorly informed group (164 cases). Here was an expectation that was surely distasteful to a large majority of the respondents but was accepted by a majority of the well-informed.

That knowledge imposes a constraint on wishful thinking is an obvious fact, but one which should not be neglected. This constraint would seem to depend on the likelihood that beliefs subject to contradiction in the normal course of experience may jeopardize the stability of one's world picture. It is possible to fend off some of the implications of experience, but the need for stability places limits on the development of one's private world.

This formulation leads to an hypothesis regarding the balance between differentiation and consistency in a person's attitudes. An undifferentiated attitude, depicting Russia as all black or all white, has the advantage of simplicity, posing fewer problems of decision than one compounded of shades of gray. But in order that a person's picture of the world may seem trustworthy and have the stability desirable in a map from which he takes his bearings, it must also take into account the situation as he understands it. The extent that a person's attitudes are differentiated, then, may represent the compromise between the need for simplicity and the need for adequacy that best fulfills his requirement of a stable and meaningful conception of his world.

Social Conformity and Attitudes toward Russia

The functional relationships thus far illustrated propose relatively basic relations be-

TABLE 6*

Evaluation of Russia's International Role	Own Opinions	Estimate of Friends' Opinions
Mostly good or more good than bad	11%	7%
About half good and half bad	29	21
More bad than good or mostly bad	59	66
No opinion	1	6
Total	100%	100%
Number of respondents	250	250

* Data are for the May, 1947, survey.

tween the structure and content of attitudes and personality factors. But the content of a person's attitudes may also be taken over more or less bodily from his associates or from prestigeful persons as a way of expressing identification with them and facilitating their acceptance. This pressure toward conformity is rooted in the person's basic needs for acceptance and approval. It is not, however, the sole or perhaps even the principal source of influence promoting relative uniformity of opinion within face-to-face groups. In addition there is the fact that members of such groups are likely to have common informational contexts on a topic, both because they share similar sources of information and because members of the group are themselves major sources of information for one another. Furthermore, they are also likely to have acquired from one another and from similar life experiences a relatively similar value outlook.

The survey findings were in keeping with the supposition that conformity plays an important role in the determination of a person's attitudes. Our data also suggest the interesting possibility that the need for conformity may favor *shifts* in the total distribution of opinion. A simple comparison of the men's own opinions with those that they ascribe to their friends reveals a tendency for the friends to be considered slightly more anti-Russian (Table 6).

Such a finding may be characteristic of a state of affairs in which the "anti" position is more strongly and vociferously held than the "pro" —as our data indicate was certainly the case in regard to Russia at the time of the survey. To the extent that the need for approval creates real pressure toward conformity, conformity must be toward the opinions of others

as *the person understands them.* When one direction of opinion has relatively higher "audibility" than the other, conformity may be expected to lead not merely toward uniformity but toward uniformity in the direction of the more audible opinion.

CONCLUSION

While the individual attitudes underlying public opinion on any topic are indeed complex, their complexity need not preclude systematic analysis. All too often, investigations of public opinion have proceeded to devise questions about this or that aspect of a public issue on a hit-or-miss basis. A framework for the description of attitudes is clearly needed.

The descriptive scheme that has been developed here in connection with attitudes toward Russia should prove generally useful. Cognitive and affective elements as well as policy orientation can be fruitfully distinguished in most political attitudes. A systematic approach of this sort throws into perspective important relationships among attitudinal features from which a more adequate understanding of opinion processes may be attained.

Such an adequate understanding, however, requires insight into the functions that opinions serve in the psychological economy of the person who holds them—the ways in which opinions are embedded in personality. We have illustrated in connection with attitudes toward Russia a first approximation toward an analysis of these functions. Further investigations embodying a functional approach should add to the understanding of the dynamics of opinion on particular topics and in different publics, and be a promising source of advance in the theory of public opinion.

PART II

Attitude Measurement

A. Standardized Measurement Techniques

9. Measuring Social Distances

EMORY S. BOGARDUS

This study is supplementary to one already reported upon under the caption "Social Distance and its Origins."[1] Social distance, it may be repeated, refers to the degrees and grades of understanding and feeling that persons experience regarding each other. It explains the nature of a great deal of their interaction. It charts the character of social relations.

The measurement of social distances is to be viewed simply as a means for securing adequate interpretations of the varying degrees and grades of understanding and feeling that exist in social situations. The measurement exercise and its results indicate the main points for intensive inquiry into human experiences.

In the experiment described here, a modification of a plan first suggested by Dr. Robert E. Park was used. One hundred and ten persons claiming racial descent as indicated in Table 1 took part. These individuals were all mature persons of experience, being of two groups, either young business men, or public school teachers.

Document 1 is a marked copy of the form that was used. The first sentence was read slowly to the members of each group and its chief points carefully explained. Each person was then asked to proceed with the marking, putting a cross under each one of the seven groupings to which he would admit Armenians, for example, and so on down the list of races without stopping.

One of the first questions to be raised is: In how many groupings in our country may the members of any race, as a class, be admitted, (as judged by the ratings of the 110 judges using

• Reprinted from *Journal of Applied Sociology*, 1925, **9**, 299-308, with permission of the author and the publisher.

[1] *Journal of Applied Sociology*, January-February, 1925, pp. 216-226.

TABLE 1. Racial Descent

English	60
Germans	31
Irish	28
French	24
Scotch	22
Dutch	15
Scotch-Irish	17
Welch	6
Canadian	4
Chinese	3
Swedish	3
Norwegian	3
Japanese	2
Jew-German	2
Spanish	2
Jew-Russian	1
Filipino	1
Pole	1
Indian	1

the arithmetic mean)? By referring to Document 1 it will be seen that the Armenians would be admitted by the specific person who made it out to only one group, namely, the visitors' group, while the English would be admitted in five groups. In the first case the index to the social contact range is 1.00; and in the second instance, 5.00. The social contacts open to the English immigrant are five times as various as those open to the Greek. The Greeks, it may be noted, would be admitted to no groups within the United States, and thus the social contact range (S. C. R.) index in their case would be .00.

Reference to the second column of Table 3 shows that according to the 110 raters the social contact range varies from 1.18 for the Turks to 4.60 for the English, while the social contact range accorded the Italians is 2.26, which is intermediate between the extremes.

DOCUMENT 1

Social Distance

According to my first feeling reactions I would willingly admit members of each race (as a class, and not the best I have known, nor the worst members) to one or more of the classifications under which I have placed a cross (x).

	7 / 1	6 / 2	5 / 3	4 / 4	3 / 5	2 / 6	1 / 7
	To close kinship by marriage	To my club as personal chums	To my street as neighbors	To employment in my occupation in my country	To citizenship in my country	As visitors only to my country	Would exclude from my country
Armenians						x	
Bulgarians						x	
Canadians	x	x	x	x	x		
Chinese						x	
Czecho-Slovaks						x	
Danes				x	x		
Dutch				x	x		
English	x	x	x	x	x		
French	x	x	x	x	x		
French-Canadians	x	x	x	x	x		
Finns				x	x		
Germans	x	x	x	x	x		
Greeks							x
Hindus							x
Hungarians						x	
Indians (Amer.)				x	x		
Irish	x	x	x	x	x		
Italians				x	x		
Japanese							x
Jew-German						x	
Jew-Russian						x	
Koreans							x
Mexicans						x	
Mulattos							x
Negroes							x
Norwegians	x	x	x	x	x		
Portuguese						x	
Filipinos						x	
Poles						x	
Roumanians	x	x	x	x	x		
Russians						x	
Serbo-Croatians						x	
Scotch	x	x	x	x	x		
Scotch-Irish	x	x	x	x	x		
Spanish						x	
Syrians							x
Swedish				x	x		
Turks							x
Welch	x	x	x	x	x		

1. Your father's races ....*English* ....
2. Your mother's races ....*Scotch-Irish* ....

A significant correlation is at once obvious between racial membership of the raters and the extent of social contact range is to be noted in Table 3.[2] Where the racial membership is low and the range high, as in the case of the Canadians, the relationship of the Canadians to the English and other "high" races among the raters is the chief explanation. Sometimes, as indicated by subsequent interviews with the raters, a fellow-feeling was aroused primarily by a racial group name, such as French-Canadian.

The S. C. R. index does not indicate merit or traits of the respective races, but rather something of the extent of the social contacts open to each race. The smaller the range of contacts accorded a race, the less, presumably, the opportunities for accommodation and assimilation. The social contact range all indicates something regarding the racial attitudes of the raters. In this way the attitudes of different groups of raters can be compared. For example, the 110 raters participating in this experiment may be divided into two groups, one of the business men and the other of public school teachers. Table 2 gives a comparison

TABLE 2. *Comparison of Social Contact Range Indexes Accorded Different Races by Business Men and by Public School Teachers (Samples)*

Races	By Business Men	By Public School Teachers
Armenians	1.26	1.97
Chinese	.80	1.61
English	4.33	4.71
Germans	3.03	3.67
Hindus	.56	1.58
Japanese	.63	1.71
Negro	.83	1.58
Turk	.60	1.51

of the S. C. R. indexes accorded certain selected races.

From these figures it will be seen that the business men did not accord as wide a range of social contacts as the teachers to the respective races. The experiences of business men may be of a different character; at any rate, the need for a study of the experiences of the two

groups is the chief observation to be made. Each of the social contact range indexes is a question mark; each raises important questions concerning the experiences of the raters and the relationships of the raters to the races that are being judged.

A further examination of the original record sheets shows a certain grading of the seven-fold classification of groups within which races may be permitted social contacts (see Document 1). If a race as a class is admitted to the intermarriage group it is usually admitted to the next four, involving personal "chum," neighborhood, occupational, and citizenship contacts. If not admitted to the intermarriage group, a race may still be admitted to the personal "chum" and other regular contact groupings within the country; and so on. Moreover, if debarred from citizenship, it is also debarred from all the groups on the left-hand; if debarred from the "visitors only" classification, then it is forbidden entrance to all the left-hand groups; and if excluded entirely from the country, then it is excluded from all other group contacts. In other words, the order of the seven-fold classification from left to right seems to constitute (further experimentation is needed) a gradation in social contact distance. If this be true, then an index may be worked out. The "best" index would be the lowest or .00, that is, no groups removed from the individual rater, and the "poorest" would be the highest, 6.00, or six groups removed.

Column 3 in Table 3 gives the arithmetic mean of the ratings regarding social contact distance of the 110 persons participating. The Canadians are given the closest "contact" possibilities with a social contact distance (S. C. D.) index of .30, while the Turks are put the farthest away with a S. C. D. index of 4.80. In other words, when we compare the S. C. D. index with the S. C. R. index a high correlation is evident, that is, the best, or highest S. C. R. indexes parallel with minor variations the best, or lowest, S. C. D. indexes.[3] A long "contact range" is paralleled by a short "contact distance," and vice versa. That is to say, the Canadian immigrant is doubly fortunate, and the Turkish immigrant is doubly unfortunate, for the Canadian immigrant is not only admitted to a large range of group contacts, but he is admitted to the most intimate groups; the

---

[2] Because of lack of space, the actual correlation figures are omitted.

[3] Again, for lack of space reasons, correlation figures are not given.

TABLE 3. *Recording Social Distance*

(Arithmetic mean of ratings by 110 judges in each case)

	Racial Descent of Raters	Social Contact Range Index	Social Contact Distance Index	Social Contact Quality Index
Armenians	0	1.77	3.51	6.16
Bulgarians	0	1.49	3.97	4.62
Canadians	4	4.55	.30	22.51
Chinese	3	1.38	4.28	4.12
Czecho-Slovak	0	1.84	3.46	6.20
Danes	0	3.44	1.48	14.82
Dutch	15	3.65	1.12	16.06
English	60	4.60	.27	22.35
French	24	4.08	1.04	18.67
French-Canadian	0	3.60	1.41	16.81
Finns	0	2.42	2.84	9.48
Germans	31	3.49	1.89	14.95
Greeks	0	1.56	3.89	5.23
Hindus	0	1.30	3.35	3.08
Hungarians	0	1.80	3.45	5.76
Indians (Amer.)	1	1.90	3.65	7.30
Irish	28	4.16	.93	19.38
Italians	0	2.26	2.98	8.87
Japanese	2	1.41	4.30	4.08
Jew-German	2	1.78	3.83	5.45
Jew-Russian	1	1.59	4.13	4.94
Koreans	0	1.28	4.55	3.54
Mexicans	0	1.53	4.02	4.57
Mulattos	0	1.26	4.44	3.62
Negroes	0	1.37	4.10	3.84
Norwegians	3	3.39	1.67	14.78
Portuguese	0	1.94	3.95	6.77
Filipinos	1	1.61	3.90	5.15
Poles	1	1.90	3.57	6.65
Roumanians	0	1.71	3.74	5.47
Russians	0	1.78	3.57	6.40
Serbo-Croatians	0	1.42	4.43	3.98
Scotch	22	4.24	.69	20.91
Scotch-Irish	17	4.12	.75	23.05
Spanish	2	2.81	2.28	14.02
Syrians	0	1.72	4.00	5.83
Swedish	3	3.71	1.44	16.20
Turks	0	1.18	4.80	2.91
Welsh	6	4.15	1.18	18.72

Turk, on the other hand, is admitted only to a small range of contacts and these are of the most remote and least intimate types.

Again, if the 110 raters be divided into two groups of business men and of teachers, the former are found to put nearly all the races a greater distance away than the latter do.

Reference to Table 3 will show as in connection with the S. C. R. indexes that the S. C. D. indexes parallel the racial descent numbers of the 110 raters. The "English descent" raters would not only admit English immigrants to the largest range of contacts but also to contacts of closest intimacy. Serbo-Croatians, for exam-

TABLE 4. Highest and Lowest S. C. R. Indexes (Samples)

Highest		Lowest	
English	4.60	Turk	1.18
Canadians	4.55	Mulatto	1.26
Scotch	4.24	Koreans	1.28
Irish	4.16	Hindus	1.30
Welsh	4.15	Negro	1.37
Scotch-Irish	4.12	Serbo-Croatians	1.42

TABLE 5. Highest and Lowest S. C. D. Indexes (Samples)

Lowest		Highest	
Canadians	.30	Turk	4.80
English	.40	Mulatto	4.44
Scotch	.69	Serbo-Croatians	4.43
Scotch-Irish	.75	Japanese	4.30
Irish	.93		

ple, are not represented among the raters at all; they are given few contact opportunities and these of remote types. The chief significance of

TABLE 6. Comparison of Social Contact Distance Indexes Accorded Different Races by Business Men and by Teachers (Samples)

Races	By Business Men	By Teachers
Armenians	4.16	3.27
Chinese	4.83	4.01
English	.63	.14
Germans	1.76	1.53
Hindus	5.40	2.97
Japanese	5.16	4.02
Negro	4.63	3.86
Turk	5.23	4.57

the S. C. D. indexes is that they raise questions regarding the nature of the personal experiences of each of the 110 raters whereby they admit some races to close proximity and put others "far away."

Since the S. C. R. and S. C. D. indexes are largely quantitative, the question arises whether or not a qualitative index may be derived. By

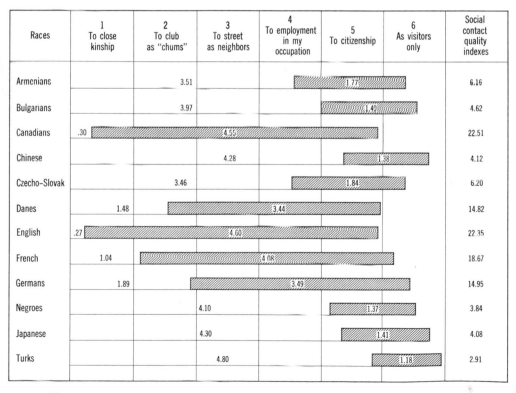

Races	1 To close kinship	2 To club as "chums"	3 To street as neighbors	4 To employment in my occupation	5 To citizenship	6 As visitors only	Social contact quality indexes
Armenians		3.51		1.77			6.16
Bulgarians		3.97		1.40			4.62
Canadians	.30		4.55				22.51
Chinese			4.28		1.38		4.12
Czecho–Slovak		3.46		1.84			6.20
Danes	1.48		3.44				14.82
English	.27		4.60				22.35
French	1.04		4.08				18.67
Germans	1.89		3.49				14.95
Negroes		4.10			1.37		3.84
Japanese		4.30			1.41		4.08
Turks			4.80			1.18	2.91

Figure 1. Social contact indexes (samples) for selected races based on reactions of 110 raters. Figures over light lines indicate the social distances before contacts are permitted to the given races. Figures within black bars denote range of the social contacts that are permitted each race.

assigning arbitrary values to the worth of the social contacts in each of the seven classifications (Document 1), namely, a value of 7 for grouping 1; 6, for grouping 2; and so on, it is possible to work out what may be called a social contact quality (S. C. Q.) index. By referring to Document 1· it will be seen that the S. C. Q. index for both the Armenians and Bulgarians is 2, but for the English it is 25, the sum of the "quality" units in each of the first five groups. The S. C. Q. indexes, therefore, might run from 25 (for any race might be put in each of the first five groupings) down to 1 (the contact quality value given to grouping 7).

TABLE 7. *Highest and Lowest Social Quality Indexes (Samples)*

Highest		Lowest	
Canadians	22.51	Turks	2.91
Scotch-Irish	23.05	Hindus	3.08
English	22.35	Mulattoes	3.62
Scotch	20.91	Koreans	3.54
Irish	19.38	Negroes	3.84

The arithmetic mean of the S. C. Q. indexes of the 110 raters for each of the races is given in the fourth column of Table 3. The five highest and the five lowest S. C. Q. indexes are given in Table 7, with the Canadians at the top, and the Turks at the bottom, as in the case of S. C. R. indexes. The S. C. Q. indexes take into consideration more factors than either of the other indexes; they may be considered as representing a summary of the factors included in both the other indexes. As in the case of the other indexes, they call for personal experience data from each of the raters as a means of interpretation. They also require extensive experimentation, especially in connection with the assignment of the values assigned to each of the seven groupings.

Figure 1 is an attempt to visualize the S. C. R. indexes, the S. C. D. indexes, and the S. C. Q. indexes, in one picture. The range of contacts is indicated by the length of the black lines; the social contact distance by the dotted lines; and the social contact quality by the figures to the right.

10. *Attitudes Can Be Measured*

L. L. THURSTONE

1. THE POSSIBILITY OF MEASURING ATTITUDE

The purpose of this paper[1] is to discuss the problem of measuring attitudes and opinions and to offer a solution for it. The very fact that one offers a solution to a problem so complex as that of measuring differences of opinion or attitude on disputed social issues makes it evident from the start that the solution is more or less restricted in nature and that it applies only under certain assumptions that will, however, be described. In devising a method of measuring attitude I have tried to get along with the fewest possible restrictions because sometimes one is tempted to disregard so many factors that the original problem disappears. I trust that I shall not be accused of throwing out the baby with its bath.

In promising to measure attitudes I shall make several common-sense assumptions that will be stated here at the outset so that subsequent discussion may not be fogged by confusion regarding them. If the reader is unwilling to grant these assumptions, then I shall have nothing to offer him. If they are granted, we can proceed with some measuring methods that ought to yield interesting results.

• Reprinted from *American Journal of Sociology*, 1928, **33**, 529-554, with permission of the University of Chicago Press. This is one of a series of papers by the staff of the Behavior Research Fund, Illinois Institute for Juvenile Research, Chicago. Series B, No. 110.

[1] The original manuscript for this paper has enjoyed a great deal of friendly criticism, some of which turns on matters of terminology and some on the assumptions which are here stated. In order to keep this paper within reasonable length, the description of the detailed psychophysical methods used and the construction of several attitude scales are reserved for separate publication. This paper concerns then only an outline of one solution to the problem of measuring attitude.

It is necessary to state at the very outset just what we shall here mean by the terms "attitude" and "opinion." This is all the more necessary because the natural first impression about these two concepts is that they are not amenable to measurement in any real sense. It will be conceded at the outset that an attitude is a complex affair which cannot be wholly described by any single numerical index. For the problem of measurement this statement is analogous to the observation that an ordinary table is a complex affair which cannot be wholly described by any single numerical index. So is a man such a complexity which cannot be wholly represented by a single index. Nevertheless we do not hesitate to say that we measure the table. The context usually implies what it is about the table that we propose to measure. We say without hesitation that we measure a man when we take some anthropometric measurements of him. The context may well imply without explicit declaration what aspect of the man we are measuring, his cephalic index, his height or weight or what not. Just in the same sense we shall say here that we are measuring attitudes. We shall state or imply by the context the aspect of people's attitudes that we are measuring. The point is that it is just as legitimate to say that we are measuring attitudes as it is to say that we are measuring tables or men.

The concept "attitude" will be used here to denote the sum total of a man's inclinations and feelings, prejudice or bias, preconceived notions, ideas, fears, threats, and convictions about any specified topic. Thus a man's attitude about pacifism means here all that he feels and thinks about peace and war. It is admittedly a subjective and personal affair.

The concept "opinion" will here mean a verbal expression of attitude. If a man says that we made a mistake in entering the war against Germany, that statement will here be spoken of as an opinion. The term "opinion" will be restricted to verbal expression. But it is an expression of what? It expresses an attitude, supposedly. There should be no difficulty in understanding this use of the two terms. The verbal expression is the *opinion*. Our interpretation of the expressed opinion is that the man's *attitude* is pro-German. An opinion symbolizes an attitude.

Our next point concerns what it is that we want to measure. When a man says that we made a mistake in entering the war with Germany, the thing that interests us is not really the string of words as such or even the immediate meaning of the sentence merely as it stands, but rather the attitude of the speaker, the thoughts and feelings of the man about the United States, and the war, and Germany. It is the attitude that really interests us. The opinion has interest only in so far as we interpret it as a symbol of attitude. It is therefore something about attitudes that we want to measure. We shall use opinions as the means for measuring attitudes.[2]

There comes to mind the uncertainty of using an opinion as an index of attitude. The man may be a liar. If he is not intentionally misrepresenting his real attitude on a disputed question, he may nevertheless modify the expression of it for reasons of courtesy, especially in those situations in which frank expression of attitude may not be well received. This has led to the suggestion that a man's action is a safer index of his attitude than what he says. But his actions may also be distortions of his attitude. A politican extends friendship and hospitality in overt action while hiding an attitude that he expresses more truthfully to an intimate friend. Neither his opinions nor his overt acts constitute in any sense an infallible guide to the subjective inclinations and preferences that constitute his attitude. Therefore we must remain content to use opinions, or other forms of action, merely as indices of attitude. It must be

[2] Professor Faris, who has been kind enough to give considerable constructive criticism to the manuscript for this paper, has suggested that we may be measuring opinion but that we are certainly not measuring attitude. It is in part a terminological question which turns on the concept of attitude. If the concept of attitude as here defined is not acceptable, it may be advisable to change the terminology provided that a distinction is retained between (1) the objective index, which is here called the statement or opinion, and (2) the inferred subjective inclination of the person, which is here called the attitude variable.

recognized that there is a discrepancy, some error of measurement as it were, between the opinion or overt action that we use as an index and the attitude that we infer from such an index.

But this discrepancy between the index and "truth" is universal. When you want to know the temperature of your room, you look at the thermometer and use its reading as an index of temperature just as though there were no error in the index and just as though there were a single temperature reading which is the "correct" one for the room. If it is desired to ascertain the volume of a glass paper weight, the volume is postulated as an attribute of the piece of glass, even though volume is an abstraction. The volume is measured indirectly by noting the dimensions of the glass or by immersing it in water to see how much water it displaces. These two procedures give two indices which might not agree exactly. In almost every situation involving measurement there is postulated an abstract continuum such as volume or temperature, and the allocation of the thing measured to that continuum is accomplished usually by indirect means through one or more indices. Truth is inferred only from the relative consistency of the several indices, since it is never directly known. We are dealing with the same type of situation in attempting to measure attitude. We must postulate an attitude variable which is like practically all other measurable attributes in the nature of an abstract continuum, and we must find one or more indices which will satisfy us to the extent that they are internally consistent.

In the present study we shall measure the subject's attitude as expressed by the acceptance or rejection of opinions. But we shall not thereby imply that he will necessarily *act* in accordance with the opinions that he has indorsed. Let this limitation be clear. The measurement of attitudes expressed by a man's opinions does not necessarily mean the prediction of what he will do. If his expressed opinions and his actions are inconsistent, that does not concern us now, because we are not setting out to predict overt conduct. We shall assume that it is of interest to know what people *say* that they believe even if their conduct turns out to be inconsistent with their professed opinions. Even if they are intentionally distorting their attitudes, we are measuring at least the attitude which they are trying to make people believe that they have.

We take for granted that people's attitudes are subject to change. When we have measured a man's attitude on any issue such as pacifism, we shall not declare such a measurement to be in any sense an enduring or constitutional constant. His attitude may change, of course, from one day to the next, and it is our task to measure such changes, whether they be due to unknown causes or to the presence of some known persuasive factor such as the reading of a discourse on the issue in question. However, such fluctuations may also be attributed in part to error in the measurements themselves. In order to isolate the errors of the measurement instrument from the actual fluctuation in attitude, we must calculate the standard error of measurement of the scale itself, and this can be accomplished by methods already well known in mental measurement.

We shall assume that an attitude scale is used only in those situations in which one may reasonably expect people to tell the truth about their convictions or opinions. If a denominational school were to submit to its students a scale of attitudes about the church, one should hardly expect intelligent students to tell the truth about their convictions if they deviate from orthodox beliefs. At least, the findings could be challenged if the situation in which attitudes are expressed contains pressure or implied threat bearing directly on the attitude to be measured. Similarly, it would be difficult to discover attitudes on sex liberty by a written questionnaire, because of the well-nigh universal pressure to conceal such attitudes where they deviate from supposed conventions. It is assumed that attitude scales will be used only in those situations that offer a minimum of pressure on the attitude to be measured. Such situations are common enough.

All that we can do with an attitude scale is to measure the attitude actually expressed with the full realization that the subject may be consciously hiding his true attitude or that the social pressure of the situation has made him really believe what he expresses. This is a matter for interpretation. It is something probably worth while to measure an attitude expressed by opinions. It is another problem to interpret in each case the extent to which the subjects have expressed what they really believe. All that we can do is to minimize as far as possible the conditions that prevent our subjects from telling the truth, or else to adjust our interpretations accordingly.

When we discuss opinions, about prohibition for example, we quickly find that these opinions are multidimensional, that they cannot all be represented in a linear continuum. The various opinions cannot be completely described merely as "more" or "less." They scatter in many dimensions, but the very idea of measurement implies a linear continuum of some sort such as length, price, volume, weight, age. When the idea of measurement is applied to scholastic achievement, for example, it is necessary to force the qualitative variations into a scholastic linear scale of some kind. We judge in a similar way such qualities as mechanical skill, the excellence of handwriting, and the amount of a man's education, as though these traits were strung out along a single scale, although they are of course in reality scattered in many dimensions. As a matter of fact, we get along quite well with the concept of a scale in describing traits even so qualitative as education, social and economic status, or beauty. A scale or linear continuum is implied when we say that a man has more education than another, or that a woman is more beautiful than another, even though, if pressed, we admit that perhaps the pair involved in each of the comparisons have little if anything in common. It is clear that the linear continuum which is implied in a "more and less" judgment may be conceptual, that it does not necessarily have the physical existence of a yardstick.

And so it is also with attitudes. We do not hesitate to compare them by the "more and less" type of judgment. We say about a man, for example, that he is more in favor of prohibition than some other, and the judgment conveys its meaning very well with the implication of a linear scale along which people or opinions might be allocated.

2. THE ATTITUDE VARIABLE

The first restriction on the problem of measuring attitudes is to specify an attitude variable and to limit the measurement to that. An example will make this clear. Let us consider the prohibition question and let us take as the attitude variable the degree of restriction that should be imposed on individual liberty in the consumption of alcohol. This degree of restriction can be thought of as a continuum ranging from complete and absolute freedom or license to equally complete and absolute restriction, and it would of course include neutral and indifferent attitudes.

In collecting samples from which to construct a scale we might ask a hundred individuals to write out their opinions about prohibition. Among these we might find one which expresses the belief that prohibition has increased the use of tobacco. Surely this is an opinion concerning prohibition, but it would not be at all serviceable for measuring the attitude variable just mentioned. Hence it would be irrelevant. Another man might express the opinion that prohibition has eliminated an important source of government revenue. This is also an opinion concerning prohibition, but it would not belong to the particular attitude variable that we have set out to measure or scale. It is preferable to use an objective and experimental criterion for the elimination of opinions that do not belong on the specified continuum to be measured, and I believe that such a criterion is available.

This restriction on the problem of measuring attitudes is necessary in the very nature of measurement. It is taken for granted in all ordinary measurement, and it must be clear that it applies also to measurement in a field in which the multidimensional characteristics have not yet been so clearly isolated. For example, it would be almost ridiculous to call attention to the fact that a table cannot be measured unless one states or implies what it is about the table that is to be measured; its height, its cost, or beauty or degree of appropriateness or the length of time required to make it. The context usually makes this restriction on measurement. When the notion of measurement is applied to so complex a phenomenon as opinions and attitudes, we must here also restrict ourselves to some specified or implied continuum along which the measurement is to take place.

In specifying the attitude variable, the first requirement is that it should be so stated that one can speak of it in terms of "more" and "less," as, for example, when we compare the attitudes of people by saying that one of them is more pacifistic, more in favor of prohibition, more strongly in favor of capital punishment, or more religious than some other person.

Figure 1 represents an attitude variable, militarism-pacifism with a neutral zone. A person who usually talks in favor of preparedness, for example, would be represented somewhere to the right of the neutral zone. A person who is more interested in disarmament would be represented somewhere to the left of the neutral zone. It is possible to conceive of a frequency distribution to represent the distribution of attitude in a specified group on the subject of pacifism-militarism.

Consider the ordinate of the frequency distribution at any point on the base line. The point and its immediate vicinity represent for our purpose an attitude, and we want to know relatively how common that degree of feeling for or against pacifism may be in the group that is being studied. It is of secondary interest to know that a particular statement of opinion is indorsed by a certain proportion of that group. It is only to the extent that the opinion is representative of an attitude that it is useful for our purposes. Later we shall consider the possibility that a statement of opinion may be scaled as rather pacifistic and yet be indorsed by a person of very pronounced militaristic sympathies. To the extent that the statement is indorsed or rejected by factors other than the attitude-variable that it represents, to that extent the statement is useless for our purposes. We shall also consider an objective criterion for spotting such statements so that they may be eliminated from the scale. In our entire study we shall be dealing, then, with opinions, not primarily because of their cognitive content but rather because they serve as the carriers or

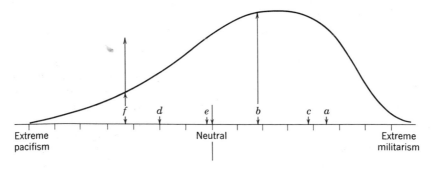

Figure 1

symbols of the attitudes of the people who express or indorse these opinions.

There is some ambiguity in using the term attitude in the plural. An attitude is represented as a point on the attitude continuum. Consequently there is an infinite number of attitudes that might be represented along the attitude scale. In practice, however, we do not differentiate so finely. In fact, an attitude, practically speaking, is a certain narrow range or vicinity on the scale. When a frequency distribution is drawn for any continuous variable, such as stature, we classify the variable for descriptive purposes into steps or class intervals. The attitude variable can also be divided into class intervals and the frequency counted in each class interval. When we speak of "an" attitude, we shall mean a point, or a vicinity, on the attitude continuum. Several attitudes will be considered not as a set of discrete entities, but as a series of class intervals along the attitude scale.

3. A FREQUENCY DISTRIBUTION OF ATTITUDES

The main argument so far has been to show that since in ordinary conversation we readily and understandably describe individuals as more and less pacifistic or more and less militaristic in attitude, we may frankly represent this linearity in the form of a unidimensional scale. This has been done in a diagrammatic way in Figure 1. We shall first describe our objective and then show how a rational unit of measurement may be adopted for the whole scale.

Let the base line of Figure 1 represent a continuous range of attitudes from extreme pacifism on the left to extreme militarism on the right.

If the various steps in such a scale were defined, it is clear that a person's attitude on militarism-pacifism could be represented by a point on that scale. The strength and direction of a particular individual's sympathies might be indicated by the point a, thus showing that he is rather militaristic in his opinions. Another individual might be represented at the point b to show that although he is slightly militaristic in his opinions, he is not so extreme about it as the person who is placed at the point a. A third person might be placed at the point c to show that he is quite militaristic and that the difference between a and c is very slight. A similar interpretation might be ex-

tended to any point on the continuous scale from extreme militarism to extreme pacifism, with a neutral or indifference zone between them.

A second characteristic might also be indicated graphically in terms of the scale, namely, the range of opinions that any particular individual is willing to indorse. It is of course not to be expected that every person will find only one single opinion on the whole scale that he is willing to indorse and that he will reject all the others. As a matter of fact we should probably find ourselves willing to indorse a great many opinions on the scale that cover a certain range of it. It is conceivable, then, that a pacifistically inclined person would be willing to indorse all or most of the opinions in the range d to e and that he would reject as too extremely pacifistic most of the opinions to the left of d, and would also reject the whole range of militaristic opinions. His attitude would then be indicated by the average or mean of the range that he indorses, unless he cares to select a particular opinion which most nearly represents his own attitude. The same sort of reasoning may of course be extended to the whole range of the scale, so that we should have at least two, or possibly three, characteristics of each person designated in terms of the scale. These characteristics would be (1) the mean position that he occupies on the scale, (2) the range of opinions that he is willing to accept, and (3) that one opinion which he selects as the one which most nearly represents his own attitude on the issue at stake.

It should also be possible to describe a group of individuals by means of the scale. This type of description has been represented in a diagrammatic way by the frequency outline.

Any ordinate of the curve would represent the number of individuals, or the percentage of the whole group, that indorses the corresponding opinion. For example, the ordinate at b would represent the number of persons in the group who indorse the degree of militarism represented by the point b on the scale. A glance at the frequency curve shows that for the fictitious group of this diagram militaristic opinions are indorsed more frequently than the pacifistic ones. It is clear that the area of this frequency diagram would represent the total number of indorsements given by the group. The diagram can be arranged in several different ways that will be separately discussed. It is sufficient at this moment to realize that, given a valid scale of opinions, it would be possible to compare several different groups in their attitudes on a disputed question.

A second type of group comparison might be made by the range or spread that the frequency surfaces reveal. If one of the groups is represented by a frequency diagram of considerable range or scatter, then that group would be more heterogeneous on the issue at stake than some other group whose frequency diagram of attitudes shows a smaller range or scatter. It goes without saying that the frequent assumption of a normal distribution in educational scale construction has absolutely no application here, because there is no reason whatever to assume that any group of people will be normally distributed in their opinions about anything.

It should be possible, then, to make four types of description by means of a scale of attitudes. These are (1) the average or mean attitude of a particular individual on the issue at stake, (2) the range of opinion that he is willing to accept or tolerate, (3) the relative popularity of each attitude of the scale for a designated group as shown by the frequency distribution for that group, and (4) the degree of homogeneity or heterogeneity in the attitudes of a designated group on the issue as shown by the spread or dispersion of its frequency distribution.

This constitutes our objective. The heart of the problem is in the unit of measurement for the base line, and it is to this aspect of the problem that we may now turn.

4. A UNIT OF MEASUREMENT FOR ATTITUDES

The only way in which we can identify different attitudes (points on the base line) is to use a set of opinions as landmarks, as it were, for the different parts or steps of the scale. The final scale will then consist of a series of statements of opinion, each of which is allocated to a particular point on the base line. If we start with enough statements, we may be able to select a list of twenty or thirty opinions so chosen that they represent an evenly graduated series of attitudes. The separation between successive statements of opinion would then be uniform, but the scale can be constructed with a series of opinions allocated on the base line even though their base line separations are not uniform. For the purpose of drawing frequency distributions

it will be convenient, however, to have the statements so chosen that the steps between them are uniform throughout the whole range of the scale.

Consider the three statements a, c, and d, in Figure 1. The statements c and a are placed close together to indicate that they are very similar, while statements c and d are spaced far apart to indicate that they are very different. We should expect two individuals scaled at c and a respectively to agree very well in discussing pacifism and militarism. On the other hand, we should expect to be able to tell the difference quite readily between the opinions of a person at d and another person at c. The scale separations of the opinions must agree with our impressions of them.

In order to ascertain how far apart the statements should be on the final scale, we submit them to a group of several hundred people who are asked to arrange the statements in order from the most pacifistic to the most militaristic. We do not ask them for their own opinions. That is another matter entirely. We are now concerned with the construction of a scale with a valid unit of measurement. There may be a hundred statements in the original list, and the several hundred persons are asked merely to arrange the statements in rank order according to the designated attitude variable. It is then possible to ascertain the proportion of the readers who consider statement a to be more militaristic than statement c. If the two statements represent very similar attitudes we should not expect to find perfect agreement in the rank order of statements a and c. If they are identical in attitude, there will be about 50 per cent of the readers who say that statement a is more militaristic than statement c, while the remaining 50 per cent of the readers will say that statement c is more militaristic than statement a. It is possible to use the proportion of readers or judges who agree about the rank order of any two statements as a basis for actual measurement.

If 90 per cent of the judges or readers say that statement a is more militaristic than statement b ($p_{a>b} = .90$) and if only 60 per cent of the readers say that statement a is more militaristic than statement c ($p_{a>c} = .60$) then clearly the scale separation ($a — c$) is shorter than the scale separation ($a — b$). The psychological scale separation between any two stimuli can be measured in terms of a law of comparative judgment which the writer has recently formulated.[3]

The detailed methods of handling the data will be published in connection with the construction of each particular scale. The practical outcome of this procedure is a series of statements of opinions allocated along the base line of Figure 1. The interpretation of the base-line distances is that the apparent difference between any two opinions will be equal to the apparent difference between any other two opinions which are spaced equally far apart on the scale. In other words, the shift in opinion represented by a unit distance on the base line seems to most people the same as the shift in opinion represented by a unit distance at any other part of the scale. Two individuals who are separated by any given distance on the scale *seem* to differ in their attitudes as much as any other two individuals with the same scale separation. In this sense we have a truly rational base line, and the frequency diagrams erected on such a base line are capable of legitimate interpretation as frequency surfaces.

In contrast with such a rational base line or scale is the simpler procedure of merely listing ten to twenty opinions, arranging them in rank order by a few readers, and then merely counting the number of indorsements for each statement. That can of course be done providing that the resulting diagram be not interpreted as a frequency distribution of attitude. If so interpreted the diagram can be made to take any shape we please by merely adding new statements or eliminating some of them, arranging the resulting list in a rough rank order evenly spaced on the base line. Allport's diagrams of opinions[4] are not in any sense frequency distributions. They should be considered as bar-diagrams in which are shown the frequency with which each of a number of statements is indorsed. Our principal contribution here is an improvement on Allport's procedure. He is virtually dealing with rank orders, which we are here trying to change into

measurement by a rational unit of measurement. Allport's pioneering studies in this field should be read by every investigator of this problem. My own interest in the possibility of measuring attitude by means of opinions was started by Allport's paper, and the present study is primarily a refinement of his statistical methods.

The unit of measurement for the scale of attitudes is the standard deviation of the dispersion projected on the psychophysical scale of attitudes by a statement of opinion, chosen as a standard. It is a matter of indifference which statement is chosen as a standard, since the scales produced by different standard statements will have proportional scale values. This mental unit of measurement is roughly comparable to, but not identical with, the so-called "just noticeable difference" in psychophysical measurement.

A diagram such as Figure 1 can be constructed in either of at least two different ways. The area of the frequency surface may be made to represent the total number of votes or indorsements by a group of people, or the area may be made to represent the total number of individuals in the group studied. Allport's diagrams would be made by the latter principle if they were constructed on a rational base line so that a legitimate area might be measured. Each subject was asked to select that one statement in the list most representative of his own attitude. Hence at least the sum of the ordinates will equal the total number of persons in the group. I have chosen as preferable the procedure of asking each subject to indorse all the statements with which he agrees. Since we have a rational base line, we may make a legitimate interpretation of the area of the surface as the total number of indorsements made by the group. This procedure has the advantage that we may ascertain the range of opinion which is acceptable to each person, a trait which has considerable interest and which cannot be ascertained by asking the subject to indorse only one of the statements in the list. The ordinates of the frequency diagram can be plotted as proportions of the whole group. They will then be interpreted as the probability that the given statement will be indorsed by a member of the group. In other words, the frequency diagram is descriptive of the distribution of attitude in the whole group, and at each point on the base line we

[3] For a more detailed discussion of this law see my article "The Law of Comparative Judgment," *Psych. Rev.* (July, 1927). For the logic of the psychological S-scale see "Psychophysical Analysis," *Amer. J. Psych.* (July, 1927).

[4] Floyd H. Allport and D. A. Hartman, "Measurement and Motivation of Atypical Opinion in a Certain Group," *Amer. Pol. Sci. Rev.*, XIX (1925), 735-760.

want an ordinate to represent the relative popularity of that attitude.

5. THE CONSTRUCTION OF AN ATTITUDE SCALE

At the present time three scales for the measurement of opinion are being constructed by the principles here described.[5] These three scales are planned to measure attitudes on three different variables, namely, pacifism-militarism, prohibition, and attitude toward the church. All three of these scales are being constructed first by a procedure somewhat less laborious than the direct application of the law of comparative judgment, and if consistent results are obtained the method will be retained for other scales.

The method is as follows. Several groups of people are asked to write out their opinions on the issue in question, and the literature is searched for suitable brief statements that may serve the purposes of the scale. By editing such material a list of from 100 to 150 statements is prepared expressive of attitudes covering as far as possible all gradations from one end of the scale to the other. It is sometimes necessary to give special attention to the neutral statements. If a random collection of statements of opinion should fail to produce neutral statements, there is some danger that the scale will break in two parts. The whole range of attitudes must be fairly well covered, as far as one can tell by preliminary inspection, in order to insure that there will be overlapping in the rank orders of different readers throughout the scale.

In making the intial list of statements several practical criteria are applied in the first editing work. Some of the important criteria are as follows:

1. The statements should be as brief as possible so as not to fatigue the subjects who are asked to read the whole list.

2. The statements should be such that they can be indorsed or rejected in accordance with their agreement or disagreement with the attitude of the reader. Some statements in a ran-

dom sample will be so phrased that the reader can express no definite indorsement or rejection of them.

3. Every statement should be such that acceptance or rejection of the statement does indicate something regarding the reader's attitude about the issue in question. If, for example, the statement is made that war is an incentive to inventive genius, the acceptance or rejection of it really does not say anything regarding the reader's pacifistic or militaristic tendencies. He may regard the statement as an unquestioned fact and simply indorse it as a fact, in which case his answer has not revealed anything concerning his own attitude on the issue in question. However, only the conspicuous examples of this effect should be eliminated by inspection, because an objective criterion is available for detecting such statements so that their elimination from the scale will be automatic. Personal judgment should be minimized as far as possible in this type of work.

4. Double-barreled statements should be avoided except possibly as examples of neutrality when better neutral statements do not seem to be readily available. Double-barreled statements tend to have a high ambiguity.

5. One must insure that at least a fair majority of the statements really belong on the attitude variable that is to be measured. If a small number of irrelevant statements should be either intentionally or unintentionally left in the series, they will be automatically eliminated by an objective criterion, but the criterion will not be successful unless the majority of the statements are clearly a part of the stipulated variable.

When the original list has been edited with these factors in mind, there will be perhaps 80 to 100 statements to be actually scaled. These statements are then mimeographed on small cards, one statement on each card. Two or three hundred subjects are asked to arrange the statements in eleven piles ranging from opinions most strongly affirmative to those most strongly negative. The detailed instructions will be published with the description of the separate scales. The task is essentially to sort out the small cards into eleven piles so that they *seem* to be fairly evenly spaced or graded. Only the two ends and the middle pile are labelled. The middle pile is indicated for neutral opinions. The reader must decide for each statement which of five subjective degrees

5 Three attitude scales are now in course of preparation by Mr. E. J. Chave, of the Divinity School, University of Chicago, on attitudes toward the church; by Mrs. Hattie Smith on attitudes about prohibition; and by Mr. Daniel Droba on attitudes about pacifism-militarism. The latter two will be published as Doctor's dissertations.

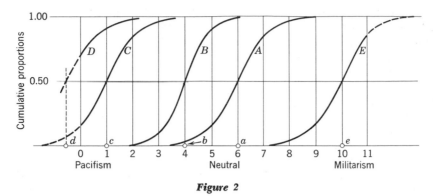

Figure 2

of affirmation or five subjective degrees of nega-tion is implied in the statement or whether it is a neutral opinion.

When such sorting has been completed by two or three hundred readers, a diagram like Figure 2 is prepared. We shall discuss it with the scale for pacifism-militarism as an example. On the base line of this diagram are repre-sented the eleven apparently equal steps of the attitude variable. The neutral interval is the interval 5 to 6, the most pacifistic interval from 0 to 1, and the most militaristic interval from 10 to 11. This diagram is fictitious and is drawn to show the principle involved. Curve *A* is drawn to show the manner in which one of the statements might be classified by the three hundred readers. It is not classified by anyone below the value of 3, half of the readers classify it below the value 6, and all of them classify it below the value 9. (The scale value of the statement is that scale value below which just one half of the readers place it.) In other words, the scale value assigned to the statement is so chosen that one half of the readers consider it more militaristic and one half of them consider it less militaristic than the scale value assigned. The numerical calcu-lation of the scale value is similar to the cal-culation of the limen by the phi-gamma hypothesis in psychophysical measurement.

It will be found that some of the statements toward the ends of the scale do not give com-plete ogive curves. Thus statement *C* is incom-plete in the fictitious diagram. It behaves as though it needed space beyond the arbitrary limits of the scale in order to be completed. Its scale value may, however, be determined as that scale value at which the phi-gamma curve through the experimental proportions crosses the 50 per cent level, which is at *c*. Still other statements may be found, such as *D*, which

have scale values beyond the arbitrary range of the scale. These may be assigned scale val-ues by the same process, though less accurately.

The situation is different at the other end of the scale. The statement *E* has a scale value at *e*, but owing to the limit of the scale at the point 11 the experimental proportion will be 1.00 at that point. If the scale continued be-yond the point 11 the proportions would con-tinue to rise gradually as indicated by the dotted line. The experimental proportions are all necessarily 1.00 for the scale value 11, and hence these final proportions must be ignored in fitting the phi-gamma curves and in the loca-tion of the scale values of the statements.

6. THE VALIDITY OF THE SCALE

(a) The scale must transcend the group mea-sured. One crucial experimental test must be applied to our method of measuring attitudes before it can be accepted as valid. A measuring instrument must not be seriously affected in its measuring function by the object of meas-urement. To the extent that its measuring function is so affected, the validity of the in-strument is impaired or limited. If a yardstick measured differently because of the fact that it was a rug, a picture, or a piece of paper that was being measured, then to that extent the trustworthiness of that yardstick as a measur-ing device would be impaired. Within the range of objects for which the measuring in-strument is intended, its function must be independent of the object of measurement.

We must ascertain similarly the range of applicability of our method of measuring atti-tude. It will be noticed that the *construction* and the *application* of a scale for measuring attitude are two different tasks. If the scale is to be regarded as valid, the scale values of the statements should not be affected by the opinions of the people who help to construct it. This may turn out to be a severe test in practice, but the scaling method must stand such a test before it can be accepted as being more than a description of the people who construct the scale. At any rate, to the extent that the present method of scale construction is affected by the opinions of the readers who help to sort out the original statements into a scale, to that extent the validity or universality of the scale may be challenged.

Until experimental evidence may be forthcoming on this point, we shall make the assumption that (the scale values of the statements are independent of the attitude distribution of the readers who sort the statements.) The assumption is, in other words, that (two statements on a prohibition scale will be as easy or as difficult to discriminate for people who are "wet" as for those who are "dry.") Given two adjacent statements from such a scale, we assume that the proportion of "wets" who say that statement *a* is wetter than statement *b* will be substantially the same as the corresponding proportion for the same statements obtained from a group of "drys." Restating the assumption in still another way, we are saying that it is just as difficult for a strong militarist as it is for a strong pacifist to tell which of two statements is the more militaristic in attitude. If, say, 85 per cent of the militarists declare statement *A* to be more militaristic than statement *B,* then, according to our assumption, substantially the same proportion of pacifists would make the same judgment. If this assumption is correct, then the scale is an instrument independent of the attitude which it is itself intended to measure.

The experimental test for this assumption consists merely in constructing two scales for the same issue with the same set of statements. One of these scales will be constructed on the returns from several hundred readers of militaristic sympathies and the other scale will be constructed with the same statements on the returns from several hundred pacifists. If the scale values of the statement are practically the same in the two scales, then the validity of the method will be pretty well established.[6]

[6] The neutrality point would not necessarily be represented by the same statement for both militarists and pacifists, but the scale separations between all pairs of statements should be practically the same for the two conditions of standardization.

It will still be necessary to use opinion scales with some discretion. Queer results might be obtained with the prohibition scale, for example, if it were presented in a country in which prohibition is not an issue.

(b) An objective criterion of ambiguity. Inspection of the curves in Figure 2 reveals that some of the statements of the fictitious diagram are more ambiguous than others. The degree of ambiguity in a statement is immediately apparent, and in fact it can be definitely measured. The ambiguity of a statement is the standard deviation of the best fitting phi-gamma curve through the observed proportions. The steeper the curve, the smaller is the range of the scale over which it was classified by the readers and the clearer and more precise is the statement. The more gentle the slope of the curve, the more ambiguous is the statement. Thus of the two statements *A* and *B* in the fictitious diagram the statement *A* is the more ambiguous.

In case it should be found that the phi-gamma function does not well describe the curves of proportions in Figure 2, the degree of ambiguity may be measured without postulating that the proportions follow the phi-gamma function when plotted on the attitude scale. A simple method of measuring ambiguity would then be to determine the scale distance between the scale value at which the curve of proportions has an ordinate of .25 and the scale value at which the same curve has an ordinate of .75. The scale value of the statement itself can also be defined, without assuming the phi-gamma function, as that scale value at which the curve of proportions reaches .50. If no actual proportion is found at that value, the scale value of the statement may be interpolated between the experimental proportions immediately above and below the .50 level. In scaling the statements whose scale values fall outside the ten divisions of the scale, it will be necessary to make some assumption regarding the nature of the curve, and it will probably be found that for most situations the phi-gamma function will constitute a fairly close approximation to truth.

(c) An objective criterion of irrelevance. Before a selection of statements can be made for the final scale, still another criterion must be applied. It is an objective criterion of irrelevance. Referring again to Figure 1, let us consider two statements that have identical scale values at the point *f.* Suppose, further, that

these two statements are submitted to the group of readers represented in the fictitious diagram of Figure 1. It is quite conceivable, and it actually does happen, that one of these statements will be indorsed quite frequently while the other statement is only seldom indorsed in spite of the fact that they are properly scaled as implying the same degree of pacifism or militarism. The conclusion is then inevitable that the indorsement that a reader gives to these statements is determined only partly by the degree of pacifism implied and partly by other implied meanings which may or may not be related to the attitude variable under consideration. Now it is of course necessary to select for the final attitude scale those statements which are indorsed or rejected primarily on account of the degree of pacifism-militarism which is implied in them and to eliminate those statements which are frequently accepted or rejected on account of other more or less subtle and irrelevant meanings.

An objective criterion for accomplishing this elimination automatically and without introducing the personal equation of the investigator is available. It is essentially as follows: Assume that the whole list of about one hundred statements has been submitted to several hundred readers for actual voting. These need not be the same readers who sorted the statements for the purpose of scaling. Let these readers be asked to mark with a plus sign every statement which they indorse and to reject with a minus sign every statement not to their liking.

If we want to investigate the degree of irrelevance of any particular statement which,

for example, might have a scale value of 4.0 in Figure 3, we should first of all determine how many readers indorsed it. We find, for example, that 260 readers indorsed it. Let this total be represented on the diagram as 100 per cent, and erect such an ordinate at the scale value of this statement. We may now ascertain the proportion of these 260 readers who *also* indorsed each other statement. If the readers indorse and reject the statements largely on the basis of the degree of pacifism-militarism implied, then those readers who indorse statements in the vicinity of 4.0 on the scale will not often indorse statements that are very far away from that point on the scale. Very few of them should indorse a statement which is scaled at the point 8.0, for example. If a large proportion of the 260 readers who indorse the basic statement scaled at 4.0 should also indorse a statement scaled at the point 8.0, then we should infer that their voting on these two statements has been influenced by factors other than the degree of pacifism that is implied in the statements. We can represent this type of analysis graphically.

Every one of these other statements will be represented by a point on this diagram. Its *x*-value will be the scale value of the statement, and its *y*-value will be the proportion of the 260 readers who indorsed it. Thus, if out of the 260 readers who indorsed the basic statement there were 130 who also indorsed statement No. 14, which has a scale value of, say, 5.0, then statement No. 14 will be represented at the point *A* on Figure 3.

If the basic statement, the degree of irrelevance of which is represented in Figure 3, is

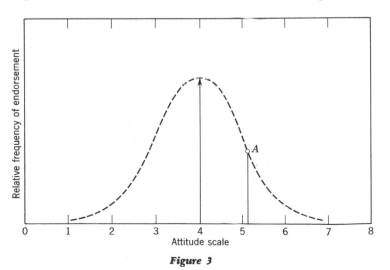

Figure 3

an ideal statement, one which people will accept or reject primarily because of the attitude on pacifism which it portrays, then we should expect the one hundred statements to be represented by as many points hovering more or less about the dotted line of Figure 3. The diagram may of course be more contracted or spread out, but the general appearance of the plot should be that of Figure 3. If, on the other hand, the basic statement has implications that lead to acceptance or rejection quite apart from the degree of pacifism which it conveys, then the proportion of the indorsements of the statements should not be a continuous function of their scale distance from the basic statement. The one hundred points might then scatter widely over the diagram. This inspectional criterion of irrelevance is objective and it can probably be translated into a more definite algebraic form so as to eliminate entirely the personal equation of the investigator.

Two other objective criteria of irrelevance have been devised. They will be described in connection with the attitude scales now being constructed.

7. SUMMARY OF THE SCALING METHOD

The selection of the statements for the final scale should now be possible. A shorter list of twenty or thirty statements should be selected for actual use. We have described three criteria by which to select the statements for the final scale. These criteria are:

1. The statements in the final scale should be so selected that they constitute as nearly as possible an evenly graduated series of scale values.

2. By the objective criterion of ambiguity it is possible to eliminate those statements which project too great a dispersion on the attitude continuum. The objective measure of ambiguity is the standard deviation of the best fitting phi-gamma curve as illustrated in Figure 2.

3. By the objective criteria of irrelevance it is possible to eliminate those statements which are accepted or rejected largely by factors other than the degree of the attitude-variable which they portray. One of these criteria is illustrated in Figure 3.

The steps in the construction of an attitude scale may be summarized briefly as follows:

1. Specification of the attitude variable to be measured.

2. Collection of a wide variety of opinions relating to the specified attitude variable.

3. Editing this material for a list of about one hundred brief statements of opinion.

4. Sorting the statements into an imaginary scale representing the attitude variable. This should be done by about three hundred readers.

5. Calculation of the scale value of each statement.

6. Elimination of some statements by the criterion of ambiguity.

7. Elimination of some statements by the criteria of irrelevance.

8. Selection of a shorter list of about twenty statements evenly graduated along the scale.

8. MEASUREMENT WITH AN ATTITUDE SCALE

The practical application of the present measurement technique consists in presenting the final list of about twenty-five statements of opinion to the group to be studied with the request that they check with plus signs all the statements with which they agree and with minus signs all the statements with which they disagree. The score for each person is the average scale value of all the statements that he has indorsed. In order that the scale be effective toward the extremes, it is advisable that the statements in the scale be extended in both directions considerably beyond the attitudes which will ever be encountered as mean values for individuals. When the score has been determined for each person by the simple summation just indicated, a frequency distribution can be plotted for the attitudes of any specified group.

The reliability of the scale can be ascertained by preparing two parallel forms from the same material and by presenting both forms to the same individuals. The correlation between the two scores obtained for each person in a group will then indicate the reliability of the scale. Since the heterogeneity of the group affects the reliability coefficient, it is necessary to specify the standard deviation of the scores of the group on which the reliability coefficient is determined. The standard error of an individual score can also be calculated by an analogous procedure.

The unit of measurement in the scale when constructed by the procedure here outlined is not the standard discriminal error projected by a single statement on the psychological continuum. Such a unit of measurement can be obtained by the direct application of the law of comparative judgment, but it is considerably more laborious than the method here described. The unit in the present scale is a more arbitrary one, namely, one-tenth of the range on the psychological continuum which covers the span from what the readers regard as extreme affirmation to extreme negation in the particular list of statements with which we start. Of course the scale values can be determined with reliability to fractional parts of this unit. It is hoped that this unit may be shown experimentally to be proportional to a more precise and more universal unit of measurement such as the standard discriminal error of a single statement of opinion.

It is legitimate to determine a central tendency for the frequency distribution of attitudes in a group. Several groups of individuals may then be compared as regards the means of their respective frequency distributions of attitudes. The differences between the means of several such distributions may be directly compared because of the fact that a rational base line has been established. Such comparisons are not possible when attitudes are ascertained merely by counting the number of indorsements to separate statements whose scale differences have not been measured.

In addition to specifying the mean attitude of each of several groups, it is also possible to measure their relative heterogencity with regard to the issue in question. Thus it will be possible, by means of our present measurement methods, to discover for example that one group is 1.6 more heterogeneous in its attitudes about prohibition than some other group. The heterogeneity of a group is indicated perhaps best by the standard deviation of the scale values of all the opinions that have been indorsed by the group as a whole rather than by the standard deviation of the distribution of individual mean scores. Perhaps different terms should be adopted for these two types of measurement.

The tolerance which a person reveals on any particular issue is also subject to quantitative measurement. It is the standard deviation of the scale values of the statements that he indorses. The maximum possible tolerance is of course complete indifference, in which all of the statements are indorsed throughout the whole range of the scale.

If it is desired to know which of two forms of appeal is the more effective on any particular issue, this can be determined by using the scale before and after the appeal. The difference between the individual scores, before and after, can be tabulated and the average shift in attitude following any specified form of appeal can be measured.

The essential characteristic of the present measurement method is the scale of evenly graduated opinions so arranged that equal steps or intervals on the scale *seem* to most people to represent equally noticeable shifts in attitude.

11. The Method of Constructing an Attitude Scale

RENSIS LIKERT

I. THE SELECTION OF STATEMENTS

Each statement should be of such a nature that persons with different points of view, so far as the particular attitude is concerned, will respond to it differentially. Any statement to which persons with markedly different attitudes can respond in the same way is, of course, unsatisfactory.

The results obtained in constructing the present scales demonstrate the value of the following criteria. These criteria were kept in mind in collecting the statements for the original Survey of Opinions.

1. It is essential that all statements be expressions of *desired behavior* and not statements of *fact*. Two persons with decidedly different attitudes may, nevertheless, agree on questions of fact. Consequently, their reaction to a statement of fact is no indication of their attitudes. For example, a person strongly pro-Japanese and a person strongly pro-Chinese might both agree with the following statements:

"The League of Nations has failed in preventing Japan's military occupation of Manchuria."

or

"Japan has been trying to create in Manchuria a monopoly of trade, equivalent to closing the 'open-door' to the trade of other countries."

To agree with them or believe them true is in no way a measure of attitude.

Rice (27, p. 184) has clearly stated the im-

portance of recognizing this criterion when in discussing the Thurstone technique he says:

What is the possibility that the acceptance or rejection by a subject of a statement upon the completed scale may represent a rational judgment concerning the truth or falsity of the statement made? It would seem to exist. If so, the validity of the statement as an index of attitude is destroyed or impaired.

In dealing with expressions of desired behavior rather than expressions of fact the statement measures the present attitude of the subject and not some past attitude. The importance of dealing with present rather than past attitudes has been emphasized by Thurstone (38) and Murphy (22, p. 615). A very convenient way of stating a proposition so that it does involve desired behavior is by using the term *should*.

2. The second criterion is the necessity of stating each proposition in *clear, concise, straight-forward statements*. Each statement should be in the simplest possible vocabulary. No statement should involve double negatives or other wording which will make it involved and confusing. Double-barreled statements are most confusing and should always be broken in two. Often an individual wishes to react favorably to one part and unfavorably to the other and when the parts are together he is at a loss to know how to react. Thus in the following illustration a person might well approve one part and disapprove another part:

"In order to preserve peace, the United States should abolish tariffs, enter the League of Nations, and maintain the largest army and navy in the world."

To ask for a single response to this statement makes it meaningless to the subject. This state-

* Excerpted from the Appendix of "A Technique for the Measurement of Attitudes," *Archives of Psychology*, 1932, No. 140, 44-53, with the permission of the author and the Columbia University Press.

ment should be divided into at least three separate statements.

The simplicity of the vocabulary will, of course, vary with the group upon whom the scale is intended to be used, but it is a desirable precaution to state each proposition in such a way that persons of less understanding than any member of the group for which the test is being constructed will understand and be able to respond to the statements. Above all, regardless of the simplicity or complexity of vocabulary or the naïveté or sophistication of the group, each statement *must avoid every kind of ambiguity*.

3. In general it would seem desirable to have the questions so worded that the modal reaction to some is more toward one end of the attitude continuum and to others more in the middle or toward the other end. In this manner, the modal value of the responses to the different questions in the attitude scale will range fairly well across the attitude continuum. There is no need, however, to have questions whose modal reactions are at either extreme of the continuum.

4. To avoid any space error or any tendency to a stereotyped response it seems desirable to have the different statements so worded that about one-half of them have one end of the attitude continuum corresponding to the *left* or *upper* part of the reaction alternatives and the other half have the same end of the attitude continuum corresponding to the *right* or *lower* part of the reaction alternatives. For example, about one-half the statements in the Internationalism scale have the international extreme corresponding with "Strongly approve" while the other half has it corresponding with "Strongly disapprove." These two kinds of statements ought to be distributed throughout the attitude test in a chance or haphazard manner.

5. If multiple choice statements are used, the different alternatives should involve *only a single attitude variable* and not several.

II. CONSTRUCTING THE SCALE

It is usually desirable to prepare and select more statements than are likely to be finally used, because after trying the statements upon a group, some may be found to be quite unsatisfactory for the intended purpose. For this reason after selecting a good number of statements they should be given to the group or a part of the group whose attitudes we wish to measure. The sample used should be sufficiently large for statistical purposes.

For purposes of tabulation and scoring, a numerical value must be assigned to each of the possible alternatives. If five alternatives have been used, it is necessary to assign values of from one to five with the three assigned to the undecided position on each statement. The ONE end is assigned to one extreme of the attitude continuum and the FIVE to the other; this should be done consistently for each of the statements which it is expected will be included in the scale. Thus if we arbitrarily consider the "favorable to the Negro" extreme FIVE and the "unfavorable to the Negro" extreme ONE, the alternative responses to the following statements would be assigned the values shown in Table 1.

Some may object to the designation made, saying that the terms "favorable" and "unfavorable" are ambiguous or that the favorable attitude is just opposite to that here considered favorable.

So far as the measurement of the attitude is concerned, it is quite immaterial what the extremes of the attitude continuum are called; the important fact is that persons do differ quantitatively in their attitudes, some being more toward one extreme, some more toward the other. Thus, as Thurstone has pointed out in the use of his scales, it makes no difference whether the zero extreme is assigned to "appreciation of" the church or "depreciation of" the church, the attitude can be measured in either case and the person's reaction to the church expressed.

The split-half reliability should be found by correlating the sum of the odd statements for each individual against the sum of the even statements. Since each statement is answered by each individual, calculations can be reduced by using the sum rather than the average.

An objective check ought then to be applied to see (1) if the numerical values are properly assigned and (2) whether the statements are "differentiating." One possible check is item analysis which calls for calculating the correlation coefficient of each statement with the battery. If a negative correlation coefficient is obtained, it indicates that the numerical values are not properly assigned and that the ONE and FIVE ends should be reversed. If a zero or very low correlation coefficient is obtained, it indicates that the statement fails to measure

TABLE 1

Numerical Value	"How far in our educational system (aside from trade education) should the most intelligent Negroes be allowed to go?
1	(*a*) Grade school.
2	(*b*) Junior high school.
3	(*c*) High school.
4	(*d*) College.
5	(*e*) Graduate and professional schools."

"In a community where the Negroes outnumber the whites, a Negro who is insolent to a white man should be:

5	(*a*) Excused or ignored.
4	(*b*) Reprimanded.
3	(*c*) Fined and jailed.
2	(*d*) Not only fined and jailed, but also given corporal punishment (whipping, etc.).
1	(*e*) Lynched."

"All Negroes belong in one class and should be treated in about the same way."

	STRONGLY APPROVE	APPROVE	UNDECIDED	DISAPPROVE	STRONGLY DISAPPROVE
Value	(1)	(2)	(3)	(4)	(5)

"Where there is segregation, the Negro section should have the same equipment in paving, water, and electric light facilities as are found in the white districts."

	STRONGLY APPROVE	APPROVE	UNDECIDED	DISAPPROVE	STRONGLY DISAPPROVE
Value	(5)	(4)	(3)	(2)	(1)

that which the rest of the statements measure. Such statements will be called undifferentiating. Thurstone (38) refers to them as irrelevant or ambiguous. By "undifferentiating" we merely mean that the statement does not measure what the battery measures and hence to include it contributes nothing to the scale. A statement which is undifferentiating for a scale measuring one attitude continuum may be quite satisfactory for a scale measuring another attitude continuum. The following are some of the reasons why a statement may prove undifferentiating:

1. The statement may involve a different issue from the one involved in the rest of the statements, that is, it involves a different attitude continuum.

2. The statement may be responded to in the same way by practically the entire group. For example, the response to the following statement was practically the same upon the part of all students—some two thousand—to whom it was given: "Should the United States repeal the Japanese Exclusion Act?"

3. The statement may be so expressed that it is misunderstood by members of the group. This may be due to its being poorly stated, phrased in unfamiliar words, or worded in the form of a double-barreled statement.

4. It may be a statement concerning fact which individuals who fall at different points on the attitude continuum will be equally liable to accept or reject.

It is, of course, desirable in constructing an attitude scale that the experimenter exercise every precaution in the selecting of statements so as to avoid those that are undifferentiating. However, item analysis can be used as an objective check to determine whether the members of a group react differentially to the statement in the same manner that they react differentially to the battery; that is, item analysis indicates whether those persons who fall toward one end of the attitude continuum on the battery do so on the particular statement and vice versa. Thus item analysis reveals the satisfactoriness of any statement so far as its inclusion in a given attitude scale is concerned.

No matter for what *a priori* reasons the experimenter may consider a statement to belong in a scale, if the statement, when tried on a group, does not measure what the rest of the statements measure, there is no justification for keeping that statement in the battery. After all, we are interested in measuring the attitudes of the members of the group, not those of the experimenter.

There is no reason to expect that the logical analysis of the person who selects the statements will necessarily be supported by the group. Quite often, because of a lack of understanding of the cultural background of the group, the experimenter may find that the statements do not form the clusters or hierarchies that he expected. It is as important psycho-

logically to know what these clusters are as it is to be able to measure them.

The degree of inclusion, i.e. the size of the correlation coefficient between the item and the battery, required for a particular statement will no doubt be a function of the purpose for which the attitudes are being measured. If a general survey type of study is being undertaken the degree of inclusion required will be less than when a more specialized aspect of attitudes is being studied. A similar relationship is to be noted in the measurement of intelligence.

The only difficulty in using item analysis is that the calculation of the necessary coefficients of correlation is quite laborious. The criterion of internal consistency was tried and the results obtained were found to be comparable with the results from item analysis. Table 2 shows a comparison of the results obtained from item analysis and the criterion of internal consis-

TABLE 2. Comparison of the Results Obtained from the Application of the Criterion of Internal Consistency and Item Analysis to the Negro Scale for Groups "A" and "B" Combined (N = 62)

Column 1	Column 2	Column 3	Column 4	Column 5
1	.69	1.7	2	5
2	.64	1.5	6	6
3	.51	1.7	10	11
4	.18	0.4	14	14
5	.62	1.3	7	8
6	.40	0.7	11	13
7	.12	0.1	15	15
8	.39	1.1	12	10
9	.26	0.9	13	12
10	.65	2.7	5	1
11	.60	1.2	8	9
12	.54	1.4	9	7
13	.67	2.3	4	2
14	.74	2.0	1	3
15	.68	1.6	3	4

rho (Column 4 vs. Column 5) = +.91)

Column 1—Statement numbers.

Column 2—Coefficient of correlation between the score on the individual statement and the average score on all fifteen statements.

Column 3—Difference between the average score of the highest 9 individuals and the lowest 9 individuals.

Column 4—Order of excellence as determined by item analysis based upon the coefficients of correlation shown in Column 2.

Column 5—Order of excellence as determined by the criterion of internal consistency based upon the differences shown in Column 3.

TABLE 3. *Criterion of Internal Consistency Applied to the Internationalism Scale for Group "D"* (N = 100)

STATEMENT NUMBERS

		Three-Point Statements														Five-Point Statements								
		1	2	3	4	5	6	7	8	9	10	11	12	13	14	15	16	17	18	19	20	21	22	23	24
HIGH GROUP																									
Individual No.	Score																								
85	108	4	4	4	4	4	4	4	4	4	4	4	4	5	5	5	5	5	5	5	5	5	5	5	5
65	104	4	4	3	4	4	4	4	4	4	4	4	4	5	5	5	5	5	5	5	5	5	5	5	4
13	102	4	4	4	4	4	4	4	4	4	4	4	4	5	5	3	5	5	5	5	5	5	3	3	5
10	101	4	4	4	4	4	4	4	4	4	4	4	4	4	3	3	4	5	5	5	5	5	4	5	5
71	101	2	4	4	4	4	4	2	4	4	4	4	4	5	3	4	5	5	5	5	5	5	5	5	5
98	100	4	4	4	4	4	4	4	4	4	4	4	4	5	3	5	4	5	5	3	5	5	5	3	4
27	98	4	2	4	4	4	4	4	4	4	4	4	4	4	5	3	5	5	5	4	4	5	2	5	5
60	98	4	4	4	4	4	4	2	4	2	4	4	4	5	5	3	4	5	5	3	5	5	4	5	5
64	98	4	4	4	4	4	4	4	4	2	4	4	4	4	3	4	3	5	5	5	5	5	4	5	4
Sum of 9-high		34	34	35	36	36	36	32	36	32	36	36	36	42	37	35	40	45	45	40	44	45	35	41	42
Sum of 9-low		18	20	20	28	24	29	21	20	22	21	34	23	21	24	22	15	31	22	15	22	24	17	14	22
D		16	14	15	8	12	7	11	16	10	15	2	13	21	13	13	25	14	23	25	22	21	18	27	20
D/9		1.8	1.6	1.7	.9	1.3	.8	1.2	1.8	1.1	1.7	.22	1.4	2.3	1.4	1.4	2.8	1.6	2.6	2.8	2.4	2.3	2.0	3.0	2.2
Order		1.5	5	3.5	10	7	11	8	1.5	9	3.5	12	6	6.5	11.5	11.5	2.5	10	4	2.5	5	6.5	9	1	8
(3-point statements and 5-point statements treated separately)																									
LOW GROUP																									
17	49	2	2	2	2	2	2	4	4	2	2	2	2	1	2	1	1	2	2	1	2	4	2	1	2
77	54	2	2	2	2	2	4	2	2	2	3	4	2	2	3	3	1	4	2	1	2	2	2	1	2
22	60	2	2	2	2	4	4	2	2	2	2	4	2	4	3	1	3	4	2	2	2	4	2	1	2
35	61	2	2	2	4	3	3	2	2	4	4	4	3	2	2	3	1	3	2	3	1	3	2	2	2
53	62	2	2	2	4	4	2	2	2	2	2	4	2	2	3	2	2	2	3	1	3	1	1	1	1
69	62	2	2	4	2	2	4	2	2	2	2	4	2	2	3	3	2	4	1	1	4	5	2	1	4
94	63	2	2	2	4	3	4	2	2	4	2	4	4	2	2	3	2	4	2	2	3	2	2	2	2
21	64	2	2	2	2	2	4	3	2	2	2	4	2	2	3	3	2	4	4	2	3	2	2	2	4
88	64	2	4	2	4	2	2	2	2	2	2	4	4	4	3	3	1	4	4	2	2	1	2	3	3
Sum of 9-low		18	20	20	28	24	29	21	20	22	21	34	23	21	24	22	15	31	22	15	22	24	17	14	22

tency. It will be noted that the relation between the order of excellence for the different statements as determined by item analysis and the criterion of internal consistency as expressed by rho is + .91. Since the criterion of internal consistency is much easier to use than item analysis and yet yields essentially the same results, its use is suggested.

In using the criterion of internal consistency the reactions of the group that constitute one extreme in the particular attitude being measured are compared with the reactions of the group that constitute the other extreme. In practice approximately ten per cent from each extreme was used. Table 3 shows the criterion of internal consistency applied to the Internationalism scale for Group D. This criterion acts as an objective check upon the correct assigning of numerical values in that if the numerical values are reversed on a particular statement the extreme high group will score low on that statement and the extreme low group will score high, i.e. we will obtain a negative difference between the two extreme groups on that question. Furthermore, if a statement is undifferentiating it will not differentiate or discriminate the two extreme groups, i.e., the high group will not score appreciably higher than the low group upon that statement.

Finally, on the basis of the results obtained from item analysis or the criterion of internal consistency and having due regard for all the factors concerned, one should select the most differentiating statements for the final form or forms of the attitude test. If, through this selection of the more differentiating statements, statements concerning a particular aspect of the attitude being measured are eliminated, then, obviously, the final scale can only be said to measure the attitude continuum represented by the remaining statements. For example, if it is found by the use of these objective checks that statements concerning the economic status of the Negro involve an attitude continuum other than that of statements having to do with the social equality of the Negro, the former should not be mixed with the latter. On the contrary, two attitude scales should be constructed. If, on the other hand, these two groups of statements are found to involve the same attitude continuum, they can be combined into a single scale. As previously stated, the degree of inclusion required or desired will generally be a function of the purpose for which the attitude scales are being used.

A sufficient number of statements should be used in each form to obtain the desired reliability. In preparing the final form or forms, it would be desirable to apply the fourth criterion stated under "The Selection of Statements."

Because a series of statements form a unit or cluster when used with one group of subjects which justifies combining the reactions to the different statements into a single score, it does not follow that they will constitute a unit on all other groups of persons with the same or different cultural backgrounds. For example, an examination of the statements in the Imperialism scale will reveal that it contains statements having to do with imperialism both in China and Latin America, and while it is true that these statements form a sufficient cluster to justify their being treated as a unit with the groups used, still with other groups of persons with markedly different attitudes toward China or Latin America it is probable that this single scale would have to be divided into two or more scales.

The ease and simplicity with which attitude scales can be checked for split-half reliability and internal consistency would seem to make it desirable to determine the reliability and examine the internal consistency of each attitude scale for each group upon which it is used. It is certainly reasonable to suppose that just as an intelligence test which has been standardized upon one cultural group is not applicable to another so an attitude scale which has been constructed for one cultural group will hardly be applicable in its existing form to other cultural groups.

BIBLIOGRAPHY

Murphy, G., and Murphy, L. B. *Experimental Social Psychology*. New York: Harper, 1931.

Rice, S. A. Statistical studies of social attitudes and public opinion. In Rice, S. A. (Ed.), *Statistics in social studies*. Philadelphia: University of Pennsylvania Press, 1930, 131-192.

Thurstone, L. L., and Chave, E. J. *The measurement of attitude*. Chicago: University of Chicago Press, 1929.

12. A Basis for Scaling Qualitative Data

LOUIS GUTTMAN

1. INTRODUCTION

In a great deal of research in the social and psychological sciences, interest lies in certain large classes of qualitative observations. For example, research in marriage is concerned with a class of qualitative behavior called marital adjustment, which includes an indefinitely large number of interactions between husband and wife. Public opinion research is concerned with large classes of behavior like expressions of opinion by Americans about the fighting ability of the British. Educational psychology deals with large classes of behavior like achievement tests.

It is often desired in such areas to be able to summarize data by saying, for example, that one marital couple is better adjusted than another marital couple, or that one person has a better opinion of the British than has another person, or that one student has a greater knowledge of arithmetic than has another student. There has been considerable discussion concerning the utility of such orderings of persons. It is not our intention in this paper to review such discussions, but instead to present a rather new approach to the problem which seems to afford an adequate basis for quantifying qualitative data.

This approach has been used successfully for the past year or so in investigating morale and other problems in the United States Army by the Research Branch of the Morale Services Division of the Army Service Forces. While this approach to quantification leads to some interesting mathematics, no knowledge of this mathematics is required in actually analyzing data. Simple routines have been established which require no knowledge of statistics, which take less time than the various manipulations now

used by various investigators (such as critical ratios, biserial correlations, factor analysis, etc.), and which give a complete picture of the data not afforded by these other techniques. The word "picture" might be interpreted here literally, for the results of the analysis are presented and easily assimilated in the form of a "scalogram," which at a glance gives the configuration of the qualitative data.

Description of the practical procedures, as well as the mathematical analysis, must be postponed to other papers. The present paper is devoted to a non-technical discussion of what we mean by a scale.

2. THE NOTIONS OF VARIABLE, FUNCTION, AND SIMPLE FUNCTION

First, a word about what is meant by a variable, whether qualitative or quantitative. We use the term in its conventional logical or mathematical sense, as denoting a set of values. These values may be numerical (quantitative) or non-numerical (qualitative).[1] We shall use

[1] In conventional courses in undergraduate college mathematics it is not ordinarily pointed out that a great deal of mathematics deals with purely qualitative variables. Notions of metrics and quantitative variables can be arrived at by sequences of qualitative classifications. In fact, this is the manner in which our approach to scaling derives a scale ordering.

The reader who is interested might look at a recent departure in textbooks for an introductory course in college mathematics (M. Richardson, *Fundamentals of Mathematics*, Macmillan, 1941). This book gives a simple, entertaining, and mature introduction to the foundations of mathematics. Its emphasis is on understanding, rather than on manipulation. It covers fundamental topics like point sets, the concept of number, and others that are rarely mentioned in ordinary undergraduate curricula and yet are mainstays of mathematical theory. It is only that most of us have been exposed exclusively to certain algebraic manipula-

• Reprinted from *American Sociological Review*, 1944, **9**, 139-150, with permission of the author and the American Sociological Association.

the term "attribute" interchangeably with "qualitative variable." The values of an attribute (or of a quantitative variable, too, for that matter) may be called its *subcategories,* or simply *categories.*

An example of an attribute is religion. A person may have the value "Catholic," "Buddhist," "Jewish," "Mormon," "atheist," or some other value of this variable. There is no particular intrinsic ordering among these values. Another example is expression of an opinion. A person may say, "I like the British," "I don't like the British," or "I don't know whether or not I like the British." Another example is, a person may be observed to smile at another person upon meeting him, or he may be observed not to smile.

Quantitative variables are readily recognized and need no discussion here.

A variable y is said to be a single-valued function of a variable x if to each value of x there corresponds a single value of y. Thus, if y has the distinct values $y_1, y_2, \ldots, y_m$, and if x has the distinct values, $x_1, x_2, \ldots, x_n$, where m and n may be different, y is called a single-valued function of x if a table of correspondence can be set up like, for example, the following:

x	x_1	x_2	x_3	$\ldots$	x_n
y	y_3	y_5	y_{m-2}	$\ldots$	y_2

For each value of x there is one and only one value of y. (The converse need not hold: for the same value of y there may be two or more values of x.) Obviously, if y is to be a single-valued function of x, then we must have $m \leqslant n$.

In particular, suppose y is an attribute, say like the above attribute about expression of liking for the British. Then $m = 3$, and we may denote by y_1 the statement, "I like the British"; by y_2, the statement, "I don't like the British"; and by y_3, "I don't know whether or not I like the British." If x is a quantitative variable which takes on more than m values ($n > m$), and if we can divide the x values into m intervals

which will have a one-to-one correspondence with the values of y, then we shall say the attribute y is a *simple* function of x. For example, suppose x takes on the ten values 0, 1, 2, 3, 4, 5, 6, 7, 8, 9. Then the correspondence table might be as follows:

x	0	1	2	3	4	5	6	7	8	9
y	y_1	y_1	y_1	y_3	y_3	y_2	y_2	y_2	y_2	y_2

Or we might show this graphically by plotting the x values on a straight line, and cutting it into intervals, as in Figure 1. For statistical

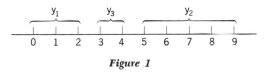

Figure 1

variables, another representation is in terms of a bar chart of frequencies, and this is what we use for convenience in §10 and §11 below.

3. THE DEFINITION OF SCALE

For a given population of objects, the multivariate frequency distribution of a universe of attributes will be called a *scale* if it is possible to derive from the distribution a quantitative variable with which to characterize the objects such that each attribute is a simple function of that quantitative variable. Such a quantitative variable is called a scale variable.

Perfect scales are not to be expected in practice. The deviation from perfection is measured by a *coefficient of reproducibility,* which is simply the empirical relative frequency with which the values of the attributes do correspond to the proper intervals of a quantitative variable. In practice, 85 percent perfect scales or better have been used as efficient approximations to perfect scales.

A value of a scale variable will be called a *scale score,* or simply a *score*. The ordering of objects according to the numerical order of their scale scores will be called their scale order.

Obviously, any quantitative variable that is an increasing (or decreasing) function of a scale variable is also a scale variable. For example, in the illustration in §2, consider x to be a scale variable. Any constant could be subtracted from or added to each of the x scores, and y would remain a simple function of the transformed x. Thus, the scores 0, 1, 2, 3, 4, 5, 6, 7, 8, 9 could

---

tions that we conceive such manipulations to be the essence of mathematics. A more sophisticated view is to regard mathematics as unveiling necessary relationships that arise from classifications. Much useless discussion of mathematics as a "tool" in social research could be saved by recognition of the fact that qualitative classifications lead to just as rigorous implications as do quantitative.

be replaced by the respective scores —5, —4, —3, —2, —1, 0, 1, 2, 3, 4. Or the x scores could be multiplied by any constant, or their square roots or logarithms could be taken—any transformation, continuous or discontinuous, could be used, as long as the rank order correlation between the original x and the transformed variable remained perfect. All such transformations will yield scale variables, each of which is equally good at reproducing the attributes.

Therefore, the problem of metric is of no particular importance here for scaling. For certain problems like predicting outside variables from the universe of attributes, it may be convenient to adopt a particular metric like a least squares metric, which has convenient properties for helping analyze multiple correlations. The interesting mathematics involved here will be discussed in another paper. However, it must be stressed that such a choice of metric is a matter of convenience; any metric will predict an outside variable as accurately as will any other.

In practice, the rank order has been used as a scale variable. (It is in fact a least squares metric for a rectangular distribution of scale scores.)

4. THE UNIVERSE OF ATTRIBUTES[2]

A basic concept of the theory of scales is that of the universe of attributes. In social research, a universe is usually a large class of behavior such as described in the introduction above. The universe is the concept whose scalability is being investigated, like marital adjustment, opinion of British fighting ability, knowledge of arithmetic, etc. The universe consists of all the attributes that define the concept. Another way of describing the universe is to say it consists of all the attributes of interest to the investigation which have a common content, so that they are classified under a single heading which indicates that content.

For ease in focusing, let us take an example from opinion research where it is desired to observe the population of individuals in a standardized manner by a checklist of questions. The behavior of interest to the investigation is responses of individuals to such questions. Suppose the universe of attributes consists of all possible questions which could be asked in such a list concerning the fighting ability of the British. Such questions might be: "Do you think the British Army is as tough as the German Army?"; "Do you think the R.A.F. is superior to the Luftwaffe?"; etc. (We do not pause here for problems of wording, interpretation, and the like. The reader is urged rather to focus on the general outline we are trying to establish.) There may be an indefinitely large number of such questions which belong in the universe; and in a particular investigation, ordinarily only a sample of the universe is used.

An attribute belongs to the universe by virtue of its content. The investigator indicates the content of interest by the title he chooses for the universe, and all attributes with that content belong in the universe. There will, of course, arise borderline cases in practice where it will be hard to decide whether or not an item belongs in the universe. The evaluation of the content thus far remains a matter that may be decided by consensus of judges or by some other means. This has been recognized before, although it need not be regarded as a "sin against the Holy Ghost of pure operationalism."[3] It may well be that the formal analysis for scalability may help clarify uncertain areas of content. However, we have found it most useful at present to utilize informal experience and consensus to the fullest extent in defining the universe.

An important emphasis of our present approach is that a criterion for an attribute to belong in the universe is *not* the magnitude of the correlations of that item with other attributes known to belong in the universe. It will be seen (in §10 below) that attributes of the same type of content may have any size of intercorrelations, varying from practically zero to unity.[4]

---

2 The words *population* and *universe* are ordinarily used interchangeably in statistical literature. For scales, it is necessary to refer both to a complete set of objects and to a complete set of attributes, so it will be convenient to reserve *population* for the former, and *universe* for the latter. In social research, the objects are usually people, so that *population* is appropriate for them.

3 Clifford Kirkpatrick, "A Methodological Analysis of Feminism in Relation to Marital Adjustment," *American Sociological Review*, June 1939, 4:325-334.

4 That correlations are no criterion for content has been quite well known. See, for example, R. F. Sletto, *Construction of Scales by the Criterion of Internal Consistency*, Sociological Press, Hanover, N.H., 1937.

5. THE POPULATION OF OBJECTS

Defining the universe of attributes is a problem similar to the standard problem of defining the population of objects or individuals[5] of interest to the investigation. An investigator must always delimit the population with which he is working. For example, in the case of opinion about the British as fighters, he must decide *whose* opinions he wishes to ascertain. Is he interested in everyone in the world, or just in everyone in the United States? Is he interested in everyone in the United States, or just in adults? If just in adults, how is an adult to be defined? Here, too, decisions will sometimes be difficult as to whether a particular individual belongs in a population or not, and decisions must be made somehow before the investigation begins, else the investigator will not know whom to observe.

6. METHODS OF OBSERVATION

Let us assume that somehow we have a universe of attributes and a population of individuals defined. Next, observations are made as to the behavior of the population with respect to the universe. (In practice this will often be done only with samples. A sample of individuals from the population will have their behavior observed on a sample of attributes from the universe.) How the observations are to be made is of no concern to us here. In opinion research and other fields, questionnaires and schedules have been used. But any technique of observation which yields the data of interest to the investigation may be used. Such techniques for the social and psychological sciences might be case histories, interviews, introspection, and any other technique from which observations may be recorded. The important thing is not how the observations were obtained, but that the observations be of central interest to the investigation.

Use of a questionnaire implies that the investigator is interested in a certain type of universe of verbal behavior. Participant observation may imply that the investigator is interested in a certain type of universe of non-verbal behavior. Such distinct universes may each be investigated separately. It may often be of interest to see how well one universe correlates

with another, but such a correlation cannot be investigated until each universe is defined and observed in its own right.

The examples of scales to be given later in this paper happen to comprise observations made by means of questionnaires. It should not be inferred, however, that scaling refers only to that technique. *Scaling analysis is a formal analysis, and hence applies to any universe of qualitative data of any science, obtained by any manner of observation.*

7. THE PURPOSE OF SCALING

Obviously it is very clumsy to record the large number of observations ordinarily involved in a universe of attributes for a population of individuals. The recording requires a table with one row for each individual and one column for each attribute. (The table may theoretically be indefinitely large.) It would be convenient if we could represent the observations in a more compact manner which would enable us to reproduce such a table whenever desired. A compact representation, if it could be obtained, would have two great advantages: first, a mnemonic advantage, for a compact representation would be easier to remember than would be a large table; and second, if it were desired to relate the universe to other variables it would be easier to do so by means of the compact representation than by using the large multivariate distribution of the attributes in the universe. From these are derived other advantages which will become apparent as the reader's familiarity with scales grows.

A particularly simple representation of the data would be to assign to each individual a numerical value and to each category of each attribute a numerical value such that, given the value of the individual and the values of the categories of an attribute, we could reproduce the observations of the individual on the attribute. This will be possible only for restricted types of data, where each attribute in the universe can be expressed as a simple function of the same quantitative variable, that is, where the universe of attributes forms a *scale* for the population of individuals.

8. AN EXAMPLE OF A DICHOTOMOUS SCALE

As may be expected, the universe of attributes must form a rather specialized configuration for

5 For convenience, since the examples in this paper concern populations of human beings, we shall talk entirely in terms of such populations.

the population of individuals if it is to be scalable. Before describing a more general case, let us give a little example. (A sociological interpretation of this apparently mathematical example is given in §15 below.) Consider a mathematics test composed of the following problems:

(*a*) If *r* is the radius of a circle, then what is its area?

(*b*) What are the values of *x* satisfying the equation

$$ax^2 + bx + c = 0?$$

(*c*) What is de^x/dx?

If this test were given to the population of members of the American Sociological Society, we would perhaps find it to form a scale for that population. The responses to each of these questions might be reported as a dichotomy, right or wrong. There are $2 \times 2 \times 2 = 8$ possible types for three dichotomies. Actually, for this population of sociologists we would probably find only four of the possible types occurring. There would be the type which would get all three questions right, the type which would get the first and second questions right, the type which would get only the first question right, and the type which would get none of the questions right. Let us assume that this is what would actually happen. That is, we shall assume the other four types, such as the type getting the first and the third questions right but the second question wrong, would not occur. In such a case, it is possible to assign to the population a set of numerical values like 3, 2, 1, 0. Each member of the population will have one of these values assigned to him. This numerical value will be called the person's score. From a person's score we would then know precisely to which problems he knows the answers and to which he does not know the answer. Thus a score of 2 does not mean simply that the person got two questions right, but that he got two particular questions right, namely, the first and second. A person's behavior on the problems is reproducible from his score. More specifically, each question is a *simple function* of the score, as is shown in §10 below.

9. THE MEANING OF "MORE" AND "LESS"

Notice that there is a very definite meaning to saying that one person knows more mathematics than another with respect to this sample. For example, a score of 3 means more than

a score of 2 because the person with a score of 3 knows everything a person with a score of 2 does, and more.

There is also a definite meaning to saying that getting a question right indicates more knowledge than getting the same question wrong, the importance of which may not be too obvious. People who get a question right all have higher scale scores than do people who get the question wrong. As a matter of fact, we need no knowledge of which is a right answer and which is a wrong answer beforehand to establish a proper order among the individuals. For convenience, suppose the questions were given in a "true-false" form,[6] with suggested answers $2\Pi r$, $(-b \pm \sqrt{b^2 - 4ac})/2a$, and xe^{x-1} for the respective questions. Each person records either a T or an F after each question, according as he believes the suggested answers to be true or false. If the responses of the population form a scale, then we do not have to know which are the correct answers in order to rank the respondents (only we will not know whether we are ranking them from high to low or from low to high). By the scale analysis, which essentially is based on sorting out the joint occurrences of the three items simultaneously, we would find only 4 types of persons occurring. One type would be $F_1T_2F_3$, where the subscripts indicate the questions; that is, this type says F to question 1, T to question 2, and F to question 3. The other three types would be $F_1T_2T_3$, $F_1F_2T_3$, and $T_1F_2T_3$. These types could be shown in a chart (a "scalogram") where there is one row for each type of person and one column for each category of each attribute. Without going into details, the scale analysis would establish an order among the rows and among the columns which would finally look as shown in Figure 2.

Figure 2

Or, alternatively, both rows and columns might be completely reversed in order. Each

6 We shall assume that no one gets an answer right by guessing. In a later paper it will be shown how scale analysis can actually pick out responses that were correct merely by guessing. But for this, much more than three items are necessary.

response to a question is indicated by a check mark. Each row has three checkmarks because each question is answered, either correctly or incorrectly. The "parallelogram" pattern in the chart[7] is necessary and sufficient for a set of *dichotomous* attributes to be expressible as simple functions of a single quantitative variable.

From this chart we can deduce that F_1, T_2, and F_3 are all correct answers, or are all incorrect answers. That is, if we were now told that F_1 is a correct answer, we would immediately know that T_2 and F_3 are also correct answers. This means that we can order the men according to their knowledge even if we do not know which are the correct answers and which are the incorrect answers, only we do not know whether we are ordering them from highest to lowest or from lowest to highest. Except for direction, the ordering is a purely formal consequence of the configuration of the behavior of the population with respect to the items. The importance of this fact will become more apparent in more complicated cases where the attributes are not dichotomous but have more than two categories. We do not take the space here to expand on this point, but merely state that the scale analysis automatically decides, for example, where an "undecided" response to a public opinion poll questionnaire belongs, whether it is above "yes," below "no," in between, equivalent to "yes," or equivalent to "no."

10. THE BAR CHART REPRESENTATION

Another way of picturing the dichotomous scale of the sample of three items would be as follows: suppose that 80 percent of the population got the first question right, 40 percent got the second question right, and 10 percent got the third question right. The univariate distributions of the three respective items could be shown by the bar chart in Figure 3.

The bars show the percentage distributions for the respective questions. The multivariate distribution for the three questions, *given that they form a scale for the population,* can also be indicated on the same chart, since all those who are included in the group getting a harder question right are also included in the group

[7] Such a chart, where one column is used for each *category* of each attribute, we call a *scalogram.* The scalogram boards used in practical procedures are simply devices for shifting rows and columns to find a scale pattern if it exists.

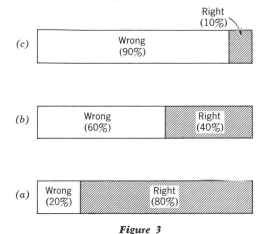

Figure 3

getting an easier question right. Thus, we could draw the bar chart over again, but connect the bars with dashed lines in the fashion shown in Figure 4. Here we can see how the three ques-

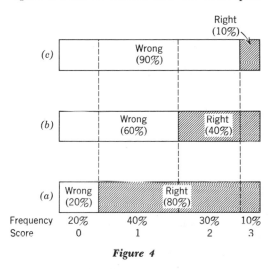

Figure 4

tions are simple functions of the scores. From the marginal frequencies of the separate items, *together with the fact that the items form a scale,* we are enabled to deduce that 10 percent of the people got a score of 3. The 10 percent who got the hardest question right are included in those who got the easier questions right. This is indicated by the dashed line on the right, between the scores 2 and 3, which carries the same 10 percent of the people (those with a score of 3) through the three bars. The 40 percent who got the second question right include the 10 percent who got the hardest question right and 30 percent out of those who got the hardest question wrong, but all 40 percent got the easiest question right. This leaves us 30 percent who got just the first and second questions right. And so on. Thus we can think of an ordering of the persons along a horizontal axis, and each item can be thought of as a *cut* on that axis. All those above the cutting point get the question right and all those below the cutting point get the question wrong. Thus there is a one-to-one correspondence between the categories of an item and segments of the axis. Or we can say that each attribute is a simple function of the rank order along the axis.

It is because all the items in the sample can be expressed as simple functions of the same ordering of persons that they form a scale. Each item is perfectly correlated with or reproducible from the ordering along the axis. However, the point correlations between the items are not at all perfect. For example, the four-fold table between the second and third items is as shown in the table.

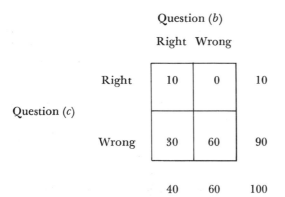

Question (b)

Right   Wrong

		Right	Wrong	
	Right	10	0	10
Question (c)				
	Wrong	30	60	90
		40	60	100

The point correlation between the two items is .41. As a matter of fact, the point correlation between two dichotomous items may be anything from practically zero to unity, and yet they may both be perfect functions of the same quantitative variable. That this may be paradoxical might be explained by inadequate treatment of qualitative variables in conventional courses and textbooks on statistics.[8]

[8] *Technical Footnote.* A tetrachoric coefficient for the four-fold table above, assuming a bivariate normal distribution, would be unity. However, this is *not* the correlation between the items. It does not tell how well one can predict one item from the other. The tetrachoric coefficient expresses instead the correlation between two quantitative variables of which the items are functions, provided the assumptions of normality are true. The reason the tetrachoric is unity in this case is that the quantitative variables of which the items are functions are one and the same variable,

An important feature of this four-fold table is the zero frequency in the upper right-hand corner cell. Nobody who got the third question right got the second question wrong. Such a zero cell must always occur in a four-fold table between two dichotomous items which are simple functions of the same quantitative variable.

11. ANOTHER EXAMPLE OF A SCALE

Now let us give an example of a more complicated scale. Suppose we were interested in finding out how much desire soldiers may express now about going back to school after the war is over. Suppose that out of the universe of attributes which define this desire we select the following sample of four questions to be presented on a questionnaire.

1. If you were offered a good job, what would you do?
   (a) I would take the job
   (b) I would turn it down if the government would help me go to school
   (c) I would turn it down and go back to school regardless
2. If you were offered some kind of job, but not a good one, what would you do?
   (a) I would take the job
   (b) I would turn it down if the government would help me go to school
   (c) I would turn it down and go back to school regardless
3. If you could get no job at all, what would you do?
   (a) I would not go back to school
   (b) If the government would aid me, I would go back to school
   (c) I would go back to school even without government aid
4. If you could do what you like after the war is over, would you go back to school?
   (a) Yes
   (b) No

Let us suppose the responses of the men to these questions form a scale in the manner shown in Figure 5.

namely, the scale variable. Notice, however, that the distribution of the scale variable according to the rank order is not at all normal. One of the contributions of scaling theory is to do away with untested and unnecessary hypotheses about normal distributions. It is the point correlation that is involved in the mathematical analysis of scaling, not the tetrachoric.

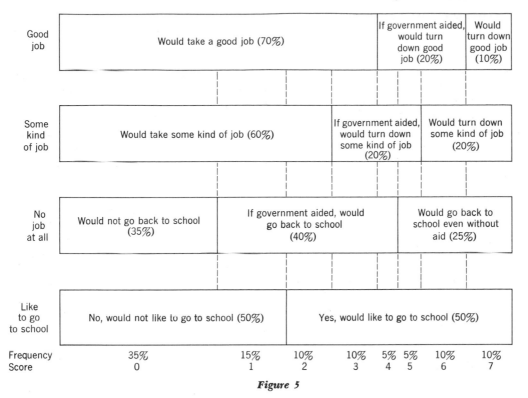

Figure 5

We now know how to read such a chart. Ten percent of the men said they would turn down a good job to go back to school; 20 percent said they would turn down a good job only if the government aided them; 70 percent said they would take a good job; and so on. The 10 percent who said they would turn down a good job are included in the 20 percent who said they would turn down some kind of a job, and the 20 percent are included in the 25 percent who said they would go back to school if they got no job at all, and these 25 percent are included in the 50 percent who said they would like to go back to school.

For three trichotomous and one dichotomous questions there are $3 \times 3 \times 3 \times 2 = 54$ possible types. In order for these to form a scale, it can be shown that at most eight types can occur. The chart shows the eight types, which have been scored from 0 through 7. The chart shows the characteristic of each type. For example, the type with the score 3 includes all men with the following four values: they say that they would take a good job if it were offered to them rather than go back to school; that they would turn down some kind of job if the government would aid them to go back to school; that they would go back to school if the government

would aid them if they could get no job at all; and that they would like to go back to school. Thus, by reading the categories crossed by the dashed lines which enclose each type, we can read off the characteristics of the type.

Notice that each of the four attributes is a simple function of the scale scores. For example, the "good job" question has its categories correspond with the following three intervals of the scale scores: 0-3, 4-6, 7.

The question might be raised as to how often will scales be found in practice. Isn't even a fair approximation to a structure like that in the above chart too much to hope for to be found in real life? Towards an answer to this, we can only cite thus far our experience with research in the Army. Literally dozens of sufficiently perfect scales have been found in various areas of attitude, opinion, and knowledge. The example given above of desire to go to school is a fictitious version of a set of similar questions that have actually proved scalable for the Army. Many varieties of data have been found scalable, and many have not. Those data which proved scalable could then be related to other variables very easily. Those that were not scalable required a more complicated analysis to handle them properly.

12. ON SAMPLING THE UNIVERSE OF ATTRIBUTES

An important property of a scalable universe is that the ordering of persons based on a sample of items will be essentially that based on the universe. If the universe is a scale, what the addition of further items would do would be merely to break up each type given by the sample into more differentiated types. But it would not interchange the order of the types already in the sample. For example, in Figure 5 above, type 6 would always have a higher rank order than type 5. People in type 6 might be ordered within the type into more subcategories; people within type 5 might be ordered into more subcategories; but all subcategories within 6 would remain of higher rank than all those in type 5. This may be seen in reverse, for example, by deleting one of the questions and noticing that all that is accomplished is to collapse the number of types to a smaller number so that two neighboring types may now become indistinguishable; but any types two steps apart would still remain in the same order with respect to each other.

Hence, we are assured that if a person ranks higher than another person in a sample of items, he will rank higher in the universe of items. This is an important property of scales, that *from a sample of attributes we can draw inferences about the universe of attributes.*

One of the criteria for selecting a sample of items is to choose a sample with enough categories to provide a desired amount of differentiation between individuals. Thus if individuals are desired to be differentiated say only into 10 groups, items should be chosen which will yield 10 types.[9] The shape of the distribution of the rank orders in a sample of attributes will of course depend upon the sample. One sample of attributes may give one shape distribution; another sample may give another shape distribution. This need not be a matter of concern, since our primary interest lies in the ordering of people, not the relative frequency of each position.

It might be asked how can one know the universe forms a scale if all one knows is a sample from the universe. At present it seems quite clear that in general the probability of finding a sample of attributes to form a scale by chance for a sample of individuals is quite negligible, even if there are as few as three dichotomous items in the sample and as many as one hundred individuals.[10] It seems quite safe to infer in general that if a sample of attributes is selected without knowledge of their empirical interrelationships and is found to form a scale for any sizeable random sample of individuals, then the universe from which the attributes are selected is scalable for the entire population of individuals.

13. SCALING AND PREDICTION

It is important to distinguish between two closely related topics, scaling and prediction. Finding that a universe of attributes is scalable for a population means that it is possible to derive a quantitative variable from the multivariate distribution such that each attribute is a simple function of that variable. We might phrase this otherwise by saying that each attribute is (perfectly) predictable from the quantitative variable.

This is the converse of the ordinary problem of prediction. In an ordinary problem of prediction, there is an outside variable, independently defined, that is to be predicted *from the attributes.* For example, it might be desired to predict the income of a student five years after he graduates from college, from his present knowledge of mathematics. To do this, an experimental sample would have to be obtained where salaries five years after college are known for each person and where responses to each item on the mathematics test are known. If the criterion of least-squares is adopted, then the best prediction on the basis of the sample would be the multiple regression of income on

---

[9] We are of course not considering problems of reliability in the sense of repeated observations of the same attributes. For convenience, we are tacitly assuming perfect reliability.

[10] *Technical Footnote.* To work out the complete probability theory would require two things: first, a definition of a sampling process for selecting items, and second, a definition of what is meant by a scale not existing. A definition of the sampling process is difficult because items are ordinarily developed intuitively. Stating a null hypothesis that a scale does not exist leads to many possible analytical formulations, for different limiting conditions may be imposed upon the multivariate distribution of the items. For example, should the marginal frequencies be considered fixed in all samples, should the bivariate frequencies be considered fixed, etc.? These are questions which may become clearer as the theory of scaling develops, and in return may clarify our conceptions of what observation of social phenomena implies.

the three items in the sample. The multivariate distribution of the three items and the outside variable would give the necessary data for computing the regression, curvilinear or linear, which would be best for predicting the outside variable. If we wished to predict some other outside variable from the same items, a new multiple regression would have to be worked out from the multivariate distribution of the three items and the new outside variable. In general, the first of these regressions would ordinarily be expected to differ from the second. In general, weights to be used to predict one outside variable from a set of attributes will differ from those used to predict another outside variable; a new multiple regression must be worked out for each outside variable.

This emphasizes an important property of scales. If the items have a multivariate distribution that is scalable, it can easily be seen that no matter what the outside variable may be, the same prediction weights may be given to the items. The correlation of any outside variable with the scale scores is precisely the same as the multiple correlation of that outside variable with the items in the scale. Thus we have an outstanding property of scaling, namely, that *it provides an invariant quantification of the attributes for predicting any outside variable.* No matter what prediction purpose is to be served by the attributes, the scale scores will serve that purpose.

14. ON "ITEM ANALYSIS"

Let us repeat the distinction just made. In scaling we reproduce the attributes from a quantitative variable. In prediction, we predict a variable from the attributes. This is a sharp difference which enables us to avoid much of the confusion that seems to prevail in the previous literature on scale construction. It seems to have been felt that items in a universe are merely stepping stones from which to obtain scores. It seems to have been felt that it was an embarrassing deficiency to lack a particular variable to predict from the items—that as a necessary evil one had to resort to methods of internal consistency to derive scores.

This accounts for current "item analysis" approaches to scaling. These use procedures that are typically as follows. A trial set of weights is assigned the categories, yielding a trial set of scores. Then each item is examined to see how well it by itself discriminates between these

scores, that is, how well the scores can be predicted *from the item*. Those items which individually discriminate best are retained, and the others eliminated.

The misleading character of such procedures can be seen by inspection of the examples of scales in §10 and §11 above. We have pointed out that the intercorrelations between attributes in a scale can be as close to zero as one pleases. It can also easily be seen that the correlation ratio of the scale *scores* with any single item can also be as close to zero as one pleases. The predictability of the scale variable from an attribute does not tell whether or not the attribute is predictable from the scale variable.

The use of the "item analysis" procedures in connection with scales seems to be an unfortunate carry-over from the problem of ordinary prediction of an outside variable. In such a prediction problem, the items are truly but stepping stones to enable predictions to be made. It is known[11] that item analysis affords a first approximation to multiple correlation (or the discriminant function), and an item is of interest only insofar as it aids in the multiple regression.

Our emphasis for scaling is quite different. In scaling, we are interested in each and every attribute in the universe on its own merits. If we were not, we would not work with the universe. The attributes are the important things; and if they are scalable, then the scores are merely a compact framework with which to represent them.

If a compact framework is found, it has the additional important property of being an efficient device for predicting any outside variable in the best manner possible from the given universe of attributes.

15. THE RELATIVITY OF SCALES

An interesting problem associated with scales is: why does a universe form a scale for a given population? For example, take the sample of three mathematics questions given above. Why should these three questions be scalable? There is no necessary logical reason why a person must know the area of a circle before he can know what a derivative is, and in particular the derivative of e^x. The reason for a scale emerging

[11] See, for example, Louis Guttman, "An Outline of the Statistical Theory of Prediction," in Paul Horst et al., *The Prediction of Personal Adjustment*, Social Science Research Council, 1941.

in this case seems largely cultural. Our educational system is such that the sequence with which we learn our mathematics in our high schools and colleges is first to get things such as areas of circles, then algebra, and then calculus. And the amount of drill that we have on each of these topics is probably also in that order. It would be quite possible, however, for the proverbial "man from Mars" to come to this earth and study calculus without having to learn the area of a circle, so that he might not be a scale type, according to the scale presented above; or a student may have had some personal incident which somehow impressed upon him with great force the derivative of e^x, but in the ordinary course of circumstances would have forgotten it even more readily than he forgot the area of a circle.

The scale analysis will pick out such deviants or non-scale types. Of course, if these non-scale types are too numerous, we shall not say that a scale exists. In practice we find scales, although never perfect scales, only because there has been sufficient uniformity of experience for the population of individuals so that the attributes mean essentially the same thing to the different individuals. As a matter of fact a study of the deviants is an interesting by-product of the scale analysis. Scale analysis actually picks out individuals for case studies.

A universe may form a scale for a population at a given time and may not at a later time. For example, the items in the scale of expression of desire of American soldiers to go back to school after the war may not prove to be scalable if they were asked once more at the close of the war.

A universe may form a scale for one population of individuals, but not for another. Or the attributes may form scales for two populations in different manners. For example, a sample of items of satisfaction with Army life which formed a scale for combat outfits in the Air Force did not form a scale for men in the technical schools of the Air Force. The structure of camp life for these two groups was too different for the same items to have the same meaning in both situations.

If a universe is scalable for one population but not for another population, or forms a scale in a different manner, we cannot compare the two populations in degree and say that one is higher or lower on the average than another with respect to the universe. They differ in more than one dimension, or in kind rather than in degree. It is only if two groups or two individuals fall into the same scale that they can be ordered from higher to lower. A similar consideration holds for comparisons in time. An important contribution of the present theory of scaling is to bring out this emphasis quite sharply.

16. SUMMARY

1. The multivariate frequency distribution of a universe of attributes for a population of objects is a scale if it is possible to derive from the distribution a quantitative variable with which to characterize the objects such that each attribute is a simple function of that quantitative variable.

2. There is an unambiguous meaning to the order of scale scores. An object with a higher score than another object is characterized by higher, or at least equivalent, values on each attribute.

3. There is an unambiguous meaning to the order of attribute values. One category of an attribute is higher than another if it characterizes objects higher on the scale.

4. It can be shown that if the data are scalable, the orderings of objects and of categories are in general unique (except for direction). Both orderings emerge from analysis of the data, rather than from *a priori* considerations.

5. The predictability of any outside variable from the scale scores is the same as the predictability from the multivariate distribution with the attributes. The zero order correlation with the scale score is equivalent to the multiple correlation with the universe. Hence, *scale scores provide an invariant quantification of the attributes for predicting any outside variable whatsoever.*

6. Scales are relative to time and to populations.

   (*a*) For a given population of objects, a universe may be scalable at one time but not at another, or it may be scalable at two periods of time but with different orderings of objects and categories.

   (*b*) A universe may be scalable for one population but not for another, or it may be scalable for two populations but with different orderings of objects and categories.

(c) Comparisons with respect to degree can be made only if the same scaling obtains in both cases being compared.

7. From the multivariate distribution of a sample of attributes for a sample of objects, inferences can be drawn concerning the complete distribution of the universe for the population.

(a) The hypothesis that the complete distribution is scalable can be adequately tested with a sample distribution.

(b) The rank order among objects according to a sample scale is essentially that in the complete scale.

(c) The ordering of categories in a sample scale is essentially that in the complete scale.

8. Perfect scales are not found in practice.

(a) The degree of approximation to perfection is measured by a *coefficient of reproducibility*, which is the empirical relative frequency with which values of the attributes do correspond to intervals of a scale variable.

(b) In practice, 85 percent perfect scales or better have been used as efficient approximations to perfect scales.

9. In imperfect scales, scale analysis picks out deviants or non-scale types for case studies.

13. Cross-Cultural Comparability in Attitude Measurement via Multilingual Semantic Differentials

CHARLES E. OSGOOD

The world is rapidly shrinking—politically, socially, and psychologically. Recent developments in the technology of transportation and communication are annihilating both space and time. These same developments are making it possible to conduct social and behavioral science research on an international scale that is certainly rewarding scientifically and perhaps essential practically, if we are to survive along with our technology. Indeed, there are many hypotheses about human nature that demand cross-national designs, if we are to successfully disentangle what is common to the human species from what is specific to a particular language or culture.

But comparisons across cultures are extremely difficult for what anthropologists call nonmaterial traits—things such as values, customs, attitudes, feelings, and meanings. Many years ago Edward Sapir and Benjamin Lee Whorf phrased what would now be called the hypothesis of psycholinguistic relativity. According to this hypothesis, how we perceive, how we think and even how we formulate our basic philosophies depend upon the structure of the language we speak. If this were literally and completely true, then comparisons across language barriers would be impossible. The Sapir-Whorf hypothesis has been shown to apply to certain aspects of language—for example, the way in which the lexicon of any language arbitrarily

• Reprinted from I. Steiner and M. Fishbein (Eds.), *Current Studies in Social Psychology*, Holt, Rinehart and Winston, New York, 1965, with permission of the author and the publisher. This article is a slightly abridged version of a paper read before the International Congress of Psychology, August 23, 1963. Professors William K. Archer, ethnolinguist, and Murray S. Miron, psycholinguist, were coinvestigators in the research, which was supported by the Human Ecology Fund.

carves up the world denotatively does influence the perceptual and conceptual processes of its users. But, our research is making it clear that there are other aspects of language—particularly the way it represents affect and the way affect mediates metaphor and symbolism—for which universality rather than relativity seems to be the rule.

Let me begin by asking you to do the impossible—to imagine a space of some unknown number of dimensions. This will be our hypothetical semantic space. Just like all self-respecting spaces, this one has an origin, which we define as complete "meaninglessness"—this is like the neutral grey center of the color space. If we think of the meaning of any word or concept as being some particular point in this space, then we could represent it by a vector out from the origin to that point (for example, x and y in Figure 1). The longer the vector, the further out in semantic space (concept x), the more "meaningful" the concept; the shorter the vector, the nearer the origin of the space (concept y), the less intensely meaningful the concept—this being analogous to saturation in the color space. Vectors may also vary in their direction within this n-dimensional space, and we equate direction with the "quality" of meaning—like the way colors may vary in hue, including the white to black axis. It should also be noted that if we are dealing with an Euclidean space—which is the simplest assumption about Nature to start with—then the less the distance between the endpoints of vectors in our semantic space, the more similar in meaning should be the concepts they represent.

One more analogy with the color space will prove useful to us: Just as complementary colors are defined as points equidistant and in opposite directions from the origin of the color space, which when mixed together in equal proportions cancel each other out to neutral grey, so we may think of verbal opposites as defining straight lines through the origin of the semantic space and cancelling each other out to meaningless when mixed. As a matter of fact, this is exactly the way dictionary-makers define pure or logical opposites in language— their meanings cancel each other out, component for component.

Now imagine a whole set of different straight-line "cuts" through this space, as suggested by the fine lines in Figure 1. Each would be defined by a different pair of opposites—*hard-soft, excitable-calm, good-bad, fair-unfair, hot-cold, noisy-quiet, large-small,* and so forth— creating a veritable pincushion of qualitative dimensions. In order to locate a particular person's meaning of a particular concept, say "white rose buds," we might now play a special game of "Twenty Questions" with him: (1) Is this concept *beautiful* or *ugly?* It is *beautiful*—so it must be in the upper half of the total space. (2) Is it *hard* or *soft?* It is *soft* —so it must be upward and to the right. (3) Is it *noisy* or *quiet?* It is *quiet*—so it must be in the octants away from us rather than near us in Figure 1. Thus, with only three binary questions, we could decide in which of eight octants of the space was "white rose buds"; or, if each straight-line "cut" were scaled into seven dis-

criminable steps, for example, from *extremely beautiful* through neutral to *extremely ugly,* as we have actually done in our work, then each decision would reduce uncertainty by six-sevenths, and only three "cuts" would differentiate a space having 343 discrete regions.

But to talk about "directions" in any space one has to have some reference coordinates. Is the up-down, north-south, east-west of the semantic space to be completely arbitrary, or is there some "natural" built-in structuring, analogous to the gravitational and magnetic determinants of geophysical space? This question is an empirical one, and the logical tool is some variant of factor analysis. We need to take large and representative samples of scales defined by verbal opposites, determine their patterns of correlation when used in judging varied samples of concepts by large and varied samples of subjects, and see if in fact they do fall into "natural" clusters or factors. We will want to determine if these factors are orthogonal, at right angles to each other, and if they are stable, that is, repeatable over independent samples of people, concepts and scales.

When a group of people judge a set of concepts against a set of semantic scales, a cube of data is generated, as shown in Figure 2. The rows are defined by scales, the columns by the concepts being judged, and the "slices" from front to back by the subjects doing the judg-

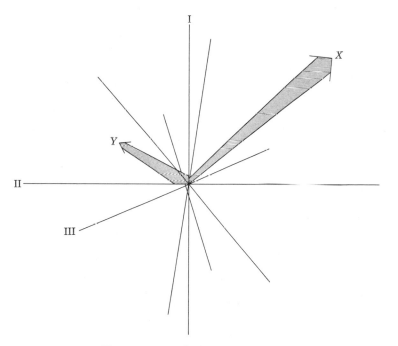

Figure 1. Hypothetical semantic space.

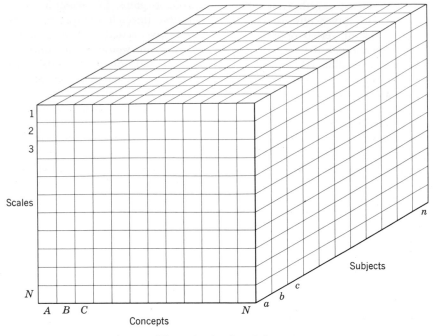

Figure 2. A cube of data.

ing. Each cell represents with a single value how a particular subject rated a particular concept against a particular scale. We are usually, but not necessarily, interested in the correlations among the scales; we may obtain these correlations across subjects or across scales or across both simultaneously. We may do separate analyses for single subjects or single concepts, or we may collapse either the subject dimension (if we are interested in cultural meanings) or the concept dimension (if we are interested in concept class characteristics). In other words, there are many ways we can slice this semantic cake, and each is appropriate for answering a different kind of question.

During the past decade or more we have analysed many such data cubes collected from English-speaking Americans. Much of this work has been summarized by Osgood, Suci, and Tannenbaum (1957). Despite deliberate and independent variations in the rules for sampling scales and concepts and in the kinds of subjects used, three dominant, orthogonal factors have kept reappearing: An "evaluative" factor (represented by scales like *good-bad, kind-cruel,* and *honest-dishonest*), a "potency" factor (represented by scales like *strong-weak, hard-soft* and *heavy-light*) and an "activity" factor (represented by scales likes *active-passive, fast-slow* and *hot-cold*). What this means is that

there are at least three "directions" in the semantic space that are regions of relatively high density, in the sense of containing many highly correlated scales representing similar modes of qualifying. Evaluation, potency and activity appear to be the most salient modes of qualifying experience. Of course, there are additional factors, other dimensions of the semantic space—indeed, a long train of them of decreasing importance and increasing uniqueness.

Is this basic evaluation-potency-activity framework common to all people? Within the English-speaking American community we have made many comparisons—between old people and young, between males and females, between Eisenhower Republicans and Stevenson Democrats, and even between schizophrenics and normals. The results of all these and many more comparisons can be stated quite succinctly: In no case has there been convincing evidence for differences in the underlying factors. But is it possible that this semantic system is restricted to Americans who speak the English language? Let me now tell you something about our attempt to determine if this affective meaning system varies with language and culture or is, indeed, panhuman.

In the course of our earlier work we had already made a number of cross-cultural comparisons—involving Japanese, Koreans, Greeks, and Navajo, Zuni, and Hopi Indians in the American Southwest—and the similarities in factor structure were striking. But, for the most part, these studies involved simply translating American English scales into the various languages under investigation, and we were open to the criticism that we were forcing people of other language/culture communities to operate within the limits imposed by our own semantic system. During the past four years we have been trying to test the generality of the affective semantic system under the most rigorous conditions we could devise. With the cooperation of senior social scientists and their associates in some fifteen countries around the world and a staff at the University of Illinois, we have been collecting basic semantic data cubes "from scratch," so to speak, testing the generality of the factor systems, and, on the basis of the generality revealed, constructing comparable semantic measuring instruments.

We start with a list of 100 familiar concepts that have been selected by linguists and anthropologists as being "culture fair" and that have survived a stringent translation test with bilinguals in all of the six language families represented in our sample. (We have been working with Japanese, Cantonese in Hong Kong, Kannada in Southern India, Hindi in Northern India, Farsi in Afghanistan and Iran, Arabic in Lebanon, Turkish, Finnish, Serbo-Croatian in Yugoslavia, Polish, and a number of Western Indo-European languages: Dutch, Flemish, French, Swedish, and English.) This original list of 100 translation-equivalent concepts, like "house," "man," "sky," "hand," "future," "dog," and "anger," is the only point at which translation is involved and could influence the results. From this point on, everything is done in the native language, with native monolingual subjects and with indigenous research personnel.

The first step is to have 100 young high-school-level boys in each country give the first qualifiers (adjectives, in English) that occur to them when each of the 100 concepts is given as a stimulus—for example, to the word for "tree" in his language one boy might say *tall*, another *green,* another *big,* and so forth. This basketful of 10,000 qualifiers (100 subjects times 100 concepts) is shipped to Illinois, where, using IBM and Illiac high-speed computers, we determine a rank order of these various ways of qualifying experience in terms of their total frequency of usage, diversity of usage across the 100 nouns, and independence of usage with respect to each other—in other words, we are looking for the most characteristic, productive and independent qualitative dimensions in each language. Even at this level, similarities begin to emerge. Not only are the rank-frequency distributions of qualifiers statistically similar, but when the ranked qualifiers in various languages are translated into English and correlated, the correlations are all in the .50 to .70 range and highly significant. In other words, despite the difficulty of "mapping" one language into another in translation, the dominant modes of qualifying experiences, of describing aspects of objects and events, tend to be very similar, regardless of what language one uses or what culture he happens to have grown up in.

The 60 or 70 highest ranked qualifiers are shipped back to the field, where their opposites are elicited and they are made into bipolar scales—the highest ranked 50 surviving this process being kept. Then another group of young males rate the original 100 concepts against these 50 scales, 200 subjects being divided into subgroups of 20 judging subsets of 10 concepts because this task is so time-consuming. Thus we generate a cube of semantic data, 100 concepts times 50 scales times 20 subjects, in each language/culture community. These data are returned to Illinois, where standard correlation, factor analysis and rotation procedures are applied by our computers. Such analyses of each cube of data yield a unique solution for each language/culture community; nevertheless, it is gratifying to be able to report that for the 12 communities carried through this stage so far, evaluation, potency and activity are identifiable as the first three factors in magnitude—and usually in that order.

The most crucial test of factorial similarity is to put the data from all countries into the same mathematical space. Since we have neither identical subjects nor identical scales, we must do this by assuming that our 100 translation-equivalent concepts are identical, and by correlating across them. To the extent that these 100 concepts are *not* identical in meaning across our language/culture communities—and we can be sure that they are not identical—then all this can do is introduce "noise" into our system and reduce our correlations, that is, work against us. In the first such test that we ran, we selected the three highest-loading scales on the first three factors of the unique analysis of seven countries (63 scales in all), intercorrelated them across 100 common concepts, and then factored the correlation matrix by usual procedures. The results clearly indicated that evaluation, potency, and activity factors are truly pancultural. The three dominant factors do not represent particular language/culture communities, but rather common semantic dimensions.

What is the purpose of all this busy work in many lands and many tongues? The first, purely scientific purpose has been to demonstrate that human beings the world over, no matter what their language or culture, do share a common meaning system, do organize experiences along similar symbolic dimensions. In contradiction to Benjamin Lee Whorf's notion of "psycholinguistic relativity," here is at least one aspect of language behavior that is universal. A second, more practical purpose of this research is to develop and apply instruments for measuring "subjective culture"—meanings, attitudes, values, customs and the like—instruments that can be shown to be comparable across languages and thereby break through the language barrier. The demonstration of common semantic factors makes it completely feasible to construct efficient "semantic differentials" for measuring the meanings of critical concepts cross-culturally, with reasonable confidence that the yardstick being employed is something better than a rubber band. It is now possible to ask questions like: "How does the meaning of the self vary from culture to culture?" "How do attitudes toward leadership and authority vary around the world?" "Is a common subjective culture developing among the world's elites?"—and be reasonably sure that the answers are not artifacts of translation.

Now, given this long introduction, let me turn directly to the matter of measuring attitudes cross-culturally. Despite the plethora of definitions of "atitude," there seems to be general consensus that (a) they are learned and implicit, (b) that they may be evoked either by perceptual signs or linguistic signs (c) that they are predispositions to respond evaluatively to these signs, and (d) that the evaluative predisposition may fall anywhere along a scale from "extremely favorable" through "neutral" to "extremely unfavorable."

In all of the general factor analyses of affective meanings we have done to date, the first

and dominant factor—usually accounting for about twice as much variance as any other—has always been clearly identifiable as Evaluation. Furthermore, being a bipolar factor, graded in intensity in both directions from a neutral point, it meets the criterion of reflecting predispositions from "extremely favorable" through "neutral" to "extremely unfavorable." It is also clear that, in the general mediation theory of meaning of which our semantic differential measuring operations are part, meanings of concepts are implicit reactions to either perceptual or linguistic signs, and they are learned. The evaluative factor of semantic differentials thus seems to meet all the criteria for a measure of attitude, and it is therefore tempting to simply define "attitude" toward any concept as its projection onto the evaluative factor in the total meaning space.

We do have some empirical justification for this identification. My colleague during the early development of semantic differential technique, Dr. Percy Tannenbaum, compared E-factor scores for subjects judging the concepts "the Negro," "the church," and "capital punishment" with their scores on special Thurstone attitude scales devised to tap each of these attitudes. Reliabilities of the E-factor scores proved to be slightly higher, actually, than those of the Thurstone scales. More important, the E-factor scores for the concepts correlated with their corresponding Thurstone scale scores as highly as reliabilities could allow. In other words, it would appear that whatever the specific Thurstone scales were measuring—and they were designed to measure attitude—the E factor was measuring equally well.

But if this is the case, then the E factor of the semantic differential has an obvious advantage: it applies exactly the same set of evaluative scales to all three concepts, "Negro," "church" and "capital punishment," whereas in the Thurstone technique unique statements must be selected and scaled for each concept whose attitude is being assessed. The E factor of the semantic differential thus has the advantage of being potentially general across the concepts being studied. If such generality is an advantage within a single language/culture community it becomes absolutely essential if we are to measure attitudes comparably, across differences in both languages and cultures. One can imagine the difficulties there would be in trying to translate and show scale equivalence for statements like "I would not admit a Negro to my social club," or "I go to church every Sunday."

You will recall that the factors obtained from different language/culture communities were found to be truly pancultural in the direct, mathematical sense that the scales from these different language/culture communities were found to be highly correlated when used in rating the standard 100 concepts. We will now take the four scales for each community which load highest and most purely on the pancultural evaluative factor and use their composite value for each concept, transposed to a + 3 to — 3 scale, as an *SD-attitude-score*— that is, a semantic-differential-determined attitude score for each concept. The scales used in this analysis, both in the native language and in approximate English translation, are given in Table 1. You will note that although

they are not—in many cases translation equivalents, they do maintain a common evaluative feeling-tone.

Before presenting some illustrative results, I would like to offer a few words of caution about interpretation. First, these data were collected in the course of the "tool-making" phases of our work and hence the concepts were not selected for their relevance to attitude measurement. Second, due to the large number of judgments involved in the concept-on-scale task, subgroups of 20 subjects judged subgroups of 10 concepts; therefore, the N in each case is only 20. In our work with American subjects we have found factor-score differences as small as half a scale unit to be significant at beyond the .05 level for N's of this magnitude, but to be on the safe side I would use a full scale unit as a significance criterion here. Third, there

TABLE 1. *Scales Contributing to SD-Attitude-Scores for Seven Language/Culture Communities*

	Native Language	English Translation
American English	nice-awful sweet-sour good-bad happy-sad	
Dutch	prettig-naar gezellig-ongezellig mooi-lelijk gelukkig-ongelukkig	pleasant-unpleasant cozy-cheerless pretty-ugly happy-sad
Belgian Flemish	aangenaam-onaangenaam plezierig-vervelend gezellig-ongezellig prachtig-afschuwelijk	agreeable-disagreeable pleasant-boring cozy-cheerless magnificent-horrible
French	sympathique-antipathique rassurant-effrayant gai-triste gentil-méchant	likeable-repugnant calm-frightened happy-sad nice-awful
Finnish	hauska-ikava valoisa-synkka makea-hapan onneton-onnellinen	nice-awful light-gloomy sweet-sour happy-sad
Japanese	気持よい — 気持悪い 快よい — 不快な 有難い — 迷惑な ようこばしい — 悲しい	pleasant-unpleasant comfortable-uncomfortable thankful-troublesome happy-sad
Indian Kannada	ದಯಾಳು – ಕ್ರೂರ ಒಳೆಯ – ಕೆಟ್ಟ ಸುಂದರ – ವಿಕಾರ ಕಾಟಾಳು – ಒರಟು	merciful-cruel good-bad beautiful-ugly delicate-rough

TABLE 2. SD-Attitude Scores for Some "Attitude Objects" among Standard 100 Concepts

Concepts	Language/Culture Communities						
	American	Dutch	Flemish	French	Finnish	Japanese	Kannada
Work	0.5	0.7	—0.2	0.9	0.3	1.0	1.0
Wealth	1.3	0.5	1.2	0.9	—0.1	0.9	0.4
Doctor	1.6	1.0	—0.7	0.8	0.3	1.0	1.0
Luck	1.6	1.6	1.6	1.5	1.2	2.5	1.0
Peace	2.0	1.4	2.3	2.1	1.1	2.3	0.8
Policeman	0.8	—0.4	—0.3	—0.4	—0.5	0.0	1.0

appear to be real differences in scale-checking style between language/culture groups; in the present case, the Flemish-speaking Belgians have SD-attitude-scores beyond plus or minus 1.5 in polarization for 56 of the 100 concepts, whereas the Finns and the Kannada-speaking Indians have only 6 and 9 concepts respectively reaching this degree of polarization. It is also true that inconsistencies in attitudinal direction among the individual subjects in a group will tend to cancel the composite scores toward neutrality, but since we are here interested in *cultural meanings,* not individual, this will not concern us. Finally, you should keep in mind the fact that the subjects are unmarried males of junior high-school age.

With these caveats in mind, let us turn to some results. Table 2 reports SD-attitude-scores for some concepts among our sample of 100 that are usually considered objects of attitude. Attitude toward "work" is most favorable for the Kannada-speaking Indians of Mysore and the Japanese, but actually slightly negative for the Flemish-speaking Belgians. The concept of "wealth" is quite positive in evaluation for Americans and Flemings but negative for Finns. Flemish and Finnish subjects have neutral or slightly negative attitudes toward "doctor," in contrast to the very favorable American attitude. For some reason—unknown to me at least—the Japanese have an extremely positive feeling about "luck." "Peace" is favored highly by everyone, and about equally if we take into account the differences in average polarization; but only for Indians and Americans is "policeman" a positive concept.

Table 3 presents sets of concepts that are universally favorable, neutral, or unfavorable— insofar as our small sample of seven language/ culture communities can be considered an ade-

quate sample of the universe! "Girl," "love," "marriage" and "mother" are highly favorable notions, as are "pleasure," "freedom," "success," "sympathy," and "friend"—all of which is not too surprising. The list of universally unfavorable concepts reads like a catalogue of human misery: the emotional states of "pain," "anger," "guilt," and "fear"; the conditions of "danger," "punishment," and "crime"; the specific threats posed by "thief," "snake," and "poison"; and then, at last, "battle," "defeat" and "death." Yet, among these generally unfavorable notions, there are some interesting deviations: note the rather mild disapproval registered by the Indians (even taking into account their generally reduced polarization), as compared with the intensely negative attitudes of the Japanese; note also the relative lack of concern of the French for things like "pain," "danger," and "death" as compared with the Flemish-speaking Belgians.

It is interesting, but perhaps not surprising, that the evaluatively neutral concepts are all natural objects and phenomena. "Stone," "root," "rope," "knot," and "cloud" surely are not objects about which people are likely to have strong attitudes, nor are the natural phenomena of "wind" and "heat" (unless they are in excess, in which case they usually have special names like "tornado"). But this is not necessarily the case. The first set of concepts in Table 4 might have been expected to be attitudinally neutral, too, but they are not for all people in our sample. The linguistically and culturally close Dutch and Flemings have a highly favorable attitude toward "Wednesday"; all Indo-European language communities (Americans, Dutch, Flemish, and French) place a high valuation on "chair," in contrast to the non-Indo-European groups (Finnish, Japanese

TABLE 3. Concepts Having Favorable, Neutral, and Unfavorable SD-Attitude-Scores Among Standard 100 Concepts

Concepts	Language/Culture Communities						
Favorable	Ameri-can	Dutch	Flemish	French	Finn-ish	Japa-nese	Kan-nada
Girl	2.1	2.0	2.3	1.9	1.4	1.1	1.1
Love	2.2	2.1	2.2	2.0	1.8	1.3	1.4
Marriage	2.3	1.9	2.0	2.0	1.7	1.4	1.1
Mother	2.1	2.1	2.1	2.3	1.1	1.9	1.7
Pleasure	1.8	1.9	2.3	2.2	1.3	2.0	1.1
Friend	1.8	1.4	2.0	1.5	1.1	1.5	1.8
Freedom	2.3	2.0	2.1	1.9	1.9	2.2	1.6
Sympathy	1.3	1.3	2.1	2.1	1.4	0.8	1.0
Music	1.6	1.7	1.9	1.3	1.2	1.4	1.9
Sleep	1.8	1.2	1.7	1.2	1.4	1.6	0.4
Sun	1.6	1.8	1.7	2.1	1.2	1.7	0.9
Success	1.5	2.1	2.1	1.7	0.5	2.2	1.0
Neutral							
Wind	0.6	—0.3	—1.0	0.6	0.1	0.4	0.3
Heat	0.4	0.5	0.3	0.8	0.0	0.3	0.4
Stone	0.0	—0.6	0.2	0.2	—0.4	0.4	—0.8
Cloud	1.3	0.5	0.1	—0.5	0.2	0.5	0.7
Root	0.6	0.0	—0.1	0.1	—0.4	0.5	0.9
Rope	0.2	0.3	0.5	—0.1	—0.7	0.6	0.7
Knot	0.2	0.0	0.0	0.8	0.0	0.0	0.5
Unfavorable							
Pain	—1.4	—1.8	—2.3	—1.0	—1.2	—1.9	—0.7
Anger	—1.9	—1.1	—2.2	—1.3	—1.3	—1.5	—1.3
Guilt	—1.2	—1.3	—2.2	—1.3	—0.9	—2.1	—0.5
Fear	—1.4	—1.4	—2.0	—1.4	—1.4	—1.5	—0.3
Danger	—1.6	—1.8	—2.1	—0.9	—1.1	—2.0	—0.8
Punishment	—0.9	—1.1	—2.3	—1.6	—1.7	—1.1	—1.1
Crime	—1.9	—1.8	—1.9	—1.9	—1.5	—2.5	—0.6
Thief	—1.9	—2.0	—2.2	—1.4	—1.4	—2.5	—1.3
Snake	—0.5	—1.1	—1.6	—1.4	—0.4	—2.0	—0.5
Poison	—1.7	—1.6	—2.3	—1.6	—1.4	—2.2	—0.9
Battle	—1.8	—1.4	—1.7	—1.7	—1.8	—2.1	—0.5
Defeat	—1.5	—1.5	—1.7	—1.5	—1.4	—1.3	—0.4
Death	—0.9	—1.6	—2.0	—0.3	—1.3	—1.2	—0.9

and Kannada); the Kannada-speaking Indians have, for them, an extremely positive feeling toward the "moon," while the Japanese feel similarly about "tree." Just why such affective investments should exist, I do not know, but I suspect they are reflections of uniquenesses in subjective culture and should be of interest to cultural anthropologists.

Other comparisons in this table—which I have titled "Attitudinal Bits to Conjure With" —may have similar interest. The second set of concepts, all referring to human and kin clas-sifications, display close similarities among the Indo-European language groups, who, I believe, also share the same kinship system. We also note that attitudes toward "women" are higher than toward "men" everywhere except in Japan —however, keep in mind that our subjects were boys between 14 and 16 years of age. The set of future-oriented concepts, "hope," "future," and "purpose," display an interesting pattern—they are all positively evaluated by Americans, French and Japanese, but are essen-tially neutral attitudinally for the Dutch,

TABLE 4. Attitudinal Bits to Conjure With

Concept	Language/Culture Community						
	American	Dutch	Flemish	French	Finnish	Japanese	Kannada
Wednesday	0.6	1.4	1.5	0.6	0.3	0.8	0.4
Chair	1.2	1.4	1.6	1.4	0.3	0.9	0.8
Moon	1.2	1.1	1.0	1.1	0.6	1.3	2.0
Tree	0.8	0.9	1.1	1.4	0.1	2.0	0.8
Husband	1.2	1.7	2.0	1.4	0.2	1.5	1.3
Father	1.9	1.2	1.4	2.2	1.0	1.9	1.4
Man	1.1	1.1	1.4	1.8	0.5	1.3	0.8
Woman	1.9	1.9	1.8	2.4	1.1	1.2	1.1
Mother	2.1	2.1	2.1	2.3	1.1	1.9	1.7
Girl	2.1	2.0	2.3	1.9	1.4	1.1	1.1
Hope	1.9	0.7	0.6	1.3	0.7	1.3	0.3
Future	1.4	0.7	0.5	1.2	0.3	1.1	0.5
Purpose	1.1	0.6	0.6	1.1	0.3	1.0	0.5
Hunger	—1.5	—1.3	—1.9	—0.3	—1.0	—1.2	0.5
Need	0.5	0.4	—2.7	0.0	0.1	0.9	0.7
Meat	1.6	0.7	1.5	0.7	—0.1	0.8	0.2
Bread	1.6	1.0	1.5	1.4	0.4	1.4	0.7
Fruit	1.5	1.4	2.2	1.5	0.7	1.7	1.5
Food	1.8	1.6	1.4	1.5	0.6	1.6	0.9
Laughter	1.9	1.2	1.9	1.6	1.1	1.2	0.2

Flemings, Finns, and Indians. Does this necessarily imply that Americans, French and Japanese are more hopeful about the future and more purposefully striving toward it?

The next set of concepts suggests a paradoxical kind of denial mechanism: The Indians in Mysore rate "hunger" and "need" relatively positively, and yet (with the exception of "fruit") have relatively neutral attitudes toward the food concepts; on the other hand, the well-off Americans, Flemings, and Dutch have the most negative attitudes toward "hunger" (and the Flemings particularly toward "need"), yet display consistently positive attitudes toward the food concepts. It is as if those that have are most gratified with having and most concerned about being deprived! But, in the end, there is "laughter"; Americans and Flemings hold this form of social commentary in the highest esteem—Indians the least.

REFERENCE

Osgood, C. E., Suci, G. J., and Tannenbaum, P. H. *The Measurement of Meaning*. Urbana: University of Illinois, 1957.

B. Multidimensional Measurement Techniques

14. Psychological Scaling without a Unit of Measurement

CLYDE H. COOMBS

I. INTRODUCTION

The concept of measurement has generally meant the assignment of numbers to objects with the condition that these numbers obey the rules of arithmetic (1). This concept of measurement requires a ratio scale—one with a non-arbitrary origin of zero and a constant unit of measurement (3). The scales which are most widely made use of in psychology are regarded as interval scales in that the origin is recognized to be arbitrary and the unit of measurement is assumed to be constant. But this type of scale should be used only if it can be experimentally demonstrated by manipulation of the objects that the numbers assigned to the objects obey the laws of addition. The unit of measurement in psychology, however, is obtained by a combination of definitions and assumptions, which, if regarded as a first approximation and associated with a statistical theory of error, serves many practical purposes. But because we may sometimes question the

* Excerpted from *Psychological Review*, 1950, 57, 145-158, with permission of the author and the American Psychological Association. This paper is a condensation of some of the ideas contained in a chapter of a general theory of psychological scaling developed in 1948-1949 under the auspices of the Rand Corporation and while in residence in the Department and the Laboratory of Social Relations, Harvard University. Development of the theory before and after the sojourn at Harvard was made possible by the support of the Bureau of Psychological Services, Institute for Human Adjustment, Horace H. Rackham School of Graduate Studies, University of Michigan.

meaning of the definitions and the validity of the assumptions which lead to a unit of measurement, it is our intent in this paper to develop a new type of scale not involving a unit of measurement. This type of scale is an addition to the types set up by S. S. Stevens (3). Stevens recognized ratio, interval, ordinal, and nominal scales. The type which we shall develop falls logically between an interval scale and an ordinal scale. We shall make no assumption of equality of intervals, or any other assumption which leads to a unit of measurement. We shall find, however, that on the basis of tolerable assumptions and with appropriate technique we are able to *order* the magnitude of the intervals between objects. We have called such a scale an "ordered metric." We shall develop the concepts first in an abstract manner with a hypothetical experiment and then illustrate the ideas with an actual experiment. Under the limitations of a single paper we shall not present the psychological theory underlying some of the concepts and we shall place certain very limiting conditions on our hypothetical data in order to simplify the presentation.

II. THE PROBLEM

When we set up an attitude scale by any of a variety of methods, for example the method of paired comparisons and the law of comparative judgment, we order statements of opinion on the attitude continuum and assign a number to each statement. We recognize in this instance that the origin for the numbers is arbitrary. We then follow one of several possible procedures (determining which statements an individual will indorse, for example) to locate the positions of individuals on this same continuum. Because both individuals and stimuli have positions on this continuum we shall call it a joint distribution, joint continuum, or J scale. In general, with a psychological continuum, we might expect that for one individual the statements of opinion, or stimuli, have different scale positions than for another individual. Thurstone (4) has provided the concept of stimulus dispersion to describe this variability of the scale positions on a psychological continuum. We have recently (2) discussed an equivalent concept for the variability of scale positions which an individual may assume in responding to a group of stimuli. These two concepts have been basic to the development of a general theory of scaling to which this paper is an introduction.

For didactic purposes we shall achieve brevity and simplicity for the presentation of the basic ideas underlying an ordered metric scale if we impose certain extreme limiting conditions on the variability of the positions of stimuli and individuals on the continuum. These conditions are that the dispersions of both stimuli and individuals be zero. In other words these conditions are that each stimulus has one and only one scale position for all individuals and that each individual has one and only one scale position for all stimuli. For purposes of future generalization we shall classify these conditions as Class 1 conditions. Stimuli will be designated by the subscript j and the position of a stimulus will be designated the Q_j value of the stimulus on the continuum. The position of an individual on the continuum will be designated the C_i value of an individual i.

If we conceive of the attribute as being an attitude continuum, the C_i value of an individual is the Q_j value of that statement of opinion which perfectly represents the attitude of that individual. In this case the C_i value of an individual is his ideal or norm. We shall assume that the degree to which a stimulus represents an individual's ideal value is dependent upon the nearness of the Q_j value of the stimulus to the C_i value of the individual.

We shall then make the further assumption that if we ask an individual which of two statements he prefers to indorse he will indorse that statement the position of which is nearer to his own position on the continuum.

Thus if asked to choose between two stimuli j and k, the individual will make the response

$$j > k \qquad (1)$$

if

$$|Q_j - C_i| < |Q_k - C_i|$$

where $j > k$ signifies the judgment "stimulus j preferred to stimulus k."

Under the extreme limiting conditions we have imposed on the C_i and Q_j values the method of paired comparisons would yield an internally consistent (transitive) set of judgments from each individual, though not necessarily the same for each, and each different set of such judgments could be represented by a unique rank order for the stimuli for that individual. We shall call the rank order of the stimuli for a particular individual a qualitative I scale, or, in general, an I scale.

Thus if an individual placed four stimuli in the rank order A B C D as representing the descending order in which he would indorse them, then, this would be equivalent to the consistent set of judgments A > B, A > C, A > D, B > C, B > D, C > D; where the symbol ">" signifies "prefer to indorse," as before. The order, A B C D, is the qualitative I scale of this individual. Hence for Class 1 conditions it is sufficient to collect the data by the method of rank order; the greater power of the method of paired comparisons would be unnecessary and wasted.

Let us assume now that we have asked each of a group of individuals to place a set of stimuli in rank order with respect to the relative degree to which he would prefer to indorse them. Our understanding of the results that would follow will be clearer if we build a mechanical model which has the appropriate properties. This is very simply done by imagining a hinge located on the J scale at the C_i value of the individual and folding the left side of the J scale over and merging it with the right side. The stimuli on the two sides of the individual will mesh in such a way that the quantity $|C_i - Q_j|$ will be in progressively ascending magnitude from left to right. The order of the stimuli on the folded J scale is the I scale for the individual whose C_i value coincides with the hinge.

It is immediately apparent that there will be classes of individuals whose I scales will be qualitatively identical as to *order* of the stimuli and that these classes will be bounded by the midpoints between pairs of stimuli on the J scale. For example, suppose that there are four stimuli, A B C D, whose Q_j values or positions on a joint continuum are as shown in Fig. 1 and that there is a distribution function of the positions of individuals on this same continuum as indicated.

If we take the individual whose position is at X in Figure 1, the I scale for that individual is obtained by folding the J scale at that point and we have the scale shown in Figure 2.

The qualitative I scale for the individual at X is A B C D.

If we take the individual in position Y as shown in Figure 1 and construct his I scale, we have the scale shown in Figure 3.

The qualitative I scale for the individual at Y is C D B A.

Consider all individuals to the left of position X on the J scale in Figure 1. The I scales of all such individuals will be quantitatively different for different positions to the left of X.

For every one of them, however, the *order* of the stimuli on the I scale will be the same, A B C D. We shall regard these I scales as being qualitatively the same. As a matter of fact, the I scales of individuals to the right of X continue to be qualitatively the same until we reach the midpoint between stimuli A and B. For an individual immediately to the right of this midpoint the qualitative I scale will be B A C D. I scales immediately to the right of the midpoint AB will continue to be qualitatively the same, B A C D, until we reach the midpoint between stimuli A and C. Immediately past this midpoint the qualitative I scale is B C A D. Continuing beyond this point a complicating factor enters in which we shall discuss in a later section under metric effects.

The distinction which has been made here between quantitative and qualitative I scales is of fundamental importance to the theory of psychological scaling. In almost all existing experimental methods in psychological scaling we do not measure the magnitudes $|C_i - Q_j|$,

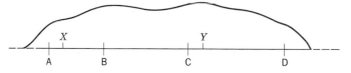

Figure 1. *A joint distribution of stimuli and individuals.*

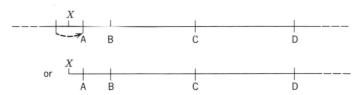

Figure 2. *The I scale of an individual located at X in the joint distribution.*

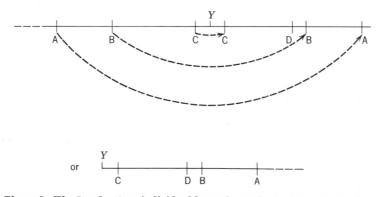

Figure 3. *The I scale of an individual located at Y in the joint distribution.*

but only observe their ordinal relations for a fixed C_i.[1] The kind of information which is obtained by the experimenter is essentially qualitative in nature.

As we shall see, data in the form of I scales may tell us certain things:

(1) whether there is a latent attribute underlying the preferences or judgments;

(2) the order of the stimuli on the joint continuum;

(3) something about the relative magnitudes of the distances between stimuli;

(4) the intervals which individuals are placed in and the order of the intervals on the continuum; and

(5) something about the relative magnitudes of these intervals.

III. A HYPOTHETICAL PROBLEM

Let us now conduct a hypothetical experiment designed merely to illustrate the technique. Of course this experiment, if actually conducted, would not turn out as we shall construct it, because we shall assume the extreme limiting conditions on Q and C values that were previously imposed.

Let us imagine that we have a number of members of a political party and that we have four individuals who are potential presidential candidates. Let us ask each member of the party to place the four candidates, designated A, B, C, and D, in the rank order in which he would prefer them as President. With four stimuli the potential number of qualitatively different rank orders is 24—the number of permutations of four things taken four at a time. If there were no systematic forces at work among the party members we would get a distribution of occurrences of these 24 I scales which could be fitted by a Poisson or Binomial distribution, everything could be attributed to chance, and the experiment would stop there. Instead, let us imagine for illustrative purposes a different result equally extreme in the opposite direction. Let us imagine that from the N individuals doing the judging only seven qualitatively

[1] The ordinal relations of $|C_i - C_j|$ may also be obtained experimentally for a fixed Q_j, over a set of C_i. We call such scales S scales by analogy with I scales. For sake of simplicity they are not treated here but actually the treatment for I scales and S scales is identical if the roles of stimuli and individuals are merely interchanged.

different I scales were obtained and these were the following:

I_1	A B C D
I_2	B A C D
I_3	B C A D
I_4	C B A D
I_5	C B D A
I_6	C D B A
I_7	D C B A

The significance of the deviation of such results as these from pure chance would be self-evident. Consequently we would look at these seven I scales to see if there was some systematic latent attribute represented by a joint continuum such that individual differences and stimulus differences on such a continuum could account for these manifest data. Studying the set of seven I scales we observe that two of them are identical except in reverse order, A B C D and D C B A. Furthermore we see that in going from one to the next, two adjacent stimuli in the one have changed positions in the next. These are the characteristics of a set of I scales which have been generated from a single J scale. Seven I scales is the maximum number that one can obtain from a single quantitative J scale of four stimuli under the conditions of Class 1. The systematic latent attribute underlying this set of I scales is represented by the J scale which generates them. Our objective, then, is to recover this J scale and discover its properties or characteristics.

To recover the J scale we proceed as follows. Every complete set of I scales has two and only two scales which are identical except in reverse order. These are the I scales which arise from the first and last intervals of the J scale. Consequently these two I scales immediately define the ordinal relations of the stimuli on the J scale, in this case A B C D (the reverse order, of course, is equally acceptable). From the seven I scales we can order on the J scale the six midpoints between all possible pairs of stimuli. In going down the ordered list of I scales as previously determined, the pair of adjacent stimuli in one I scale which have changed places in the next I scale specify the midpoint on the J scale which has been passed.

Thus in the first interval (Figure 4), we have all the individuals to the left of the midpoint between stimuli A and B. The second I scale is B A C D, and as stimuli A and B have changed places in going from the I_1 scale to

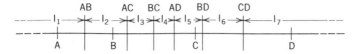

Figure 4. An example of how the midpoints of four stimuli may section the joint distribution into seven intervals, each characterized by an I scale.

the I_2 scale we have passed the midpoint AB. In going from I_2 to I_3 stimuli A and C exchange orders on the two I scales and hence the midpoint between A and C is the boundary between I_2 and I_3. If we continue this process we see that the order of the six midpoints is as follows: AB, AC, BC, AD, BD, CD. These six boundaries section the joint distribution into seven intervals which are ordered as also are the stimuli. From the order of the six midpoints in the case of four stimuli we have one and only one piece of information about metric relations on the joint continuum. Because midpoint BC precedes AD we know that the distance between stimuli C and D is greater than the distance between stimuli A and B. We shall discuss these points and characteristics in more detail in the section on metric effects. There are then an infinite variety of quantitatively different J scales which would yield this same set of seven I scales—but there is only one qualitative J scale. The J scale in Figure 4 meets the conditions necessary to yield the manifest data.

It must be emphasized that all *metric* magnitudes in Figure 4 are arbitrary except that the distance from stimulus A to B is less than the distance from stimulus C to D.

With the qualitative information obtained in this experiment about the latent attribute underlying the preferences for presidential candidates the next task is the identification of this attribute. Here all the experimenter can do is to ask himself what it is that these stimuli have and the individuals have to these different degrees as indicated by their ordinal and metric relations. One might find in this hypothetical case that it appears to be a continuum of liberalism, for example, or of isolationism. One would then have to conduct an independent experiment with other criteria to validate one's interpretation.

IV. METRIC EFFECTS

While the data with which we deal in the vast majority of scaling experiments are quali-

tative and non-numerical there are certain relations between the manifest data and the metric relations of the continuum. These relations have not all been worked out and general expressions have yet to be developed. The complexity of the relations very rapidly increases with the number of stimuli; therefore to illustrate the effect of metric we shall take the simplest case in which its effect is made apparent, the case of four stimuli.

With four stimuli, A, B, C, and D, there are 24 permutations possible. Thus it is possible to find 24 qualitatively different I scales. Also, obviously, each of these 24 orders could occur as a J scale which could give rise to a set of I scales. Half of the J scales may be regarded as merely mirror images of the other half. Thus if we have a J scale with the stimuli ordered B A D C and identify the continuum as liberalism-conservativism, then, in principle, we also have the J scale with the stimuli ordered C D A B and would identify it as conservativism-liberalism. Hence there are only twelve J scales which may be regarded as qualitatively distinguishable on the basis of the order of the four stimuli. I scales which are mirror images of each other, though, are definitely not to be confused. They may well represent entirely different psychological meanings. The direction of an I scale is defined experimentally—the direction of a J scale is a matter of choice.

Each J scale of four stimuli gives rise to a set of seven qualitative I scales. We are interested in knowing, of course, whether the J scale deduced from a set of I scales obtained in an experiment is qualitatively unique. The answer to this appears to be yes and immediately obvious when it is recognized that a set of I scales generated from a J scale has two and only two I scales which are mirror images of each other; that these two I scales must have been generated from the intervals on the opposite ends of the J scale, and that the order of the I scales within a set is unique. These statements are still to be developed as formal mathematical proofs and hence must be regarded as tentative conclusions.

However, a given qualitative J scale does not give a unique *set* of I scales. For example, with four stimuli, we may have the qualitative J scale A B C D. This order of four stimuli on a J scale can yield *two different sets* of I scales as follows:

Set 1	Set 2
A B C D	A B C D
B A C D	B A C D
B C A D	B C A D
B C D A ——————	C B A D
C B D A	C B D A
C D B A	C D B A
D C B A	D C B A

It will be noticed that these two sets of seven I scales from the same qualitative J scale are identical except for the I scale from the middle interval. This arises from the following fact. There are six midpoints for the four stimuli on the J scale. These are as follows: AB, AC, AD, BC, BD, CD. The order and identity of the first two and the last two are immutable; they must be, in order: AB, AC, . . . , . . . , BD, CD. But the order of the remaining two midpoints is not defined by the qualitative J scale but by its quantitative characteristics. If the interval between stimuli A and B is greater than the interval between C and D, then the midpoint AD comes before the midpoint BC and the set of seven I scales will be set 1 listed above. If the quantitative relations on the J scale are the reverse and the midpoint BC comes before AD, then the set of seven I scales which will result are those listed in set 2 above.

Thus we see that in the case of four stimuli, a set of I scales will uniquely determine a qualitative J scale and will provide one piece of information about the metric relations. For five or more stimuli the number of pieces of information about metric relations exceeds the minimum number that are needed for ordering the successive intervals. *However,* the particular pieces of information that are obtained might not be the appropriate ones for doing this. It is interesting to note here that this is a new type of scale not discussed by Stevens. This is a type of scale that falls between what he calls ordinal scales and interval scales. In ordinal scales nothing is known about the intervals. In interval scales the intervals are equal. In this scale, which we call an ordered metric, the intervals are not equal but they may be ordered in magnitude.

As the number of stimuli increases, the variety of different *sets* of I scales from a single qualitative J scale increases rapidly. This means that a great deal of information is being given about metric relations. For example a J scale of five stimuli yields a set of eleven I scales

$$\left(\text{in general } n \text{ stimuli will provide } \binom{n}{2} + 1 \right.$$

$$\left. \text{different I scales from one J scale} \right).$$ Depending on the relative magnitudes of the four intervals between the five stimuli on the J scale, the same qualitative J scale may yield *twelve different sets* of I scales. This means that for a given order of five stimuli on a J scale there are twelve experimentally differentiable quantitative J scales. Previously, in the case of four stimuli, we found only two differentiable quantitative J scales for a given qualitative J scale.

The particular set of I scales obtained from five stimuli *may* provide up to five of the independent relations between pairs or intervals. For example, suppose we have the qualitative J scale A B C D E. Among the twelve possible sets of I scales which could arise are the following two, chosen at random:

Set 1	Set 2
A B C D E	A B C D E
B A C D E	B A C D E
B C A D E	B C A D E
B C D A E	B C D A E
C B D A E ——————	B C D E A
C D B A E ——————	C B D E A
D C B A E ——————	C D B E A
D C B E A	D C B E A
D C E B A	D C E B A
D E C B A	D E C B A
E D C B A	E D C B A

Let us see what information is given by each of these sets about the relative magnitudes of the intervals between the stimuli on the J scales. Consider set 1 first. The order of the ten midpoints of the five stimuli according to set 1 is as follows: AB, AC, AD, BC, BD, CD, AE, BE, CE, DE. We know immediately, from the fact that the midpoint BC comes after AD, that the interval between stimuli A and B ($\overline{AB}$) is greater than the interval between stimuli C and D ($\overline{CD}$). We have summarized this in the first row of the table below. The other rows contain the other metric relations which can be deduced from set 1.

SET 1

Order of Midpoints	Relative Magnitude of Intervals on J Scale
AD, BC	$\overline{CD} < \overline{AB}$
CD, BE	$\overline{BC} < \overline{DE}$
BD, AE	$\overline{AB} < \overline{DE}$
CD, AE	$\overline{AC} < \overline{DE}$

Or, in brief form, the I scales contained in set 1 indicate that the following relations must hold between stimuli on the J scale.

$$\overline{CD} < \overline{AB} < \overline{DE}$$
$$\overline{AB} + \overline{BC} < \overline{DE}$$

In the same manner we may study the implications of set 2 for the metric relations between stimuli on the J scale. The midpoints for this set are in the following order: AB AC AD, AE, BC, BD CD, BE, CE, DE.

SET 2

Order of Midpoints	Relative Magnitude of Intervals on J Scale
AD, BC	$\overline{CD} < \overline{AB}$
CD, BE	$\overline{BC} < \overline{DE}$
AE, BD	$\overline{DE} < \overline{AB}$
AE, BC	$\overline{CE} < \overline{AB}$

Or, in brief, the relative magnitudes of the intervals between stimuli on the J scale are known to the following extent.

$$\overline{BC} < \overline{DE} < \overline{AB}$$
$$\overline{DE} + \overline{CD} < \overline{AB}$$

The different implications of these two sets of I scales for the metric relations on the J scale may be illustrated by sketching two quantitative J scales which have the appropriate metric relations (Figure 5).

The two sets of I scales which are illustrated here were only two of twelve possible different sets which could be generated from a single *qualitative* J scale of five stimuli. Each of the twelve sets of I scales would imply a different set of quantitative relations among the distances between stimuli on the J scale. The two sets of I scales used here happened to differ from each other in three of their particular members. If we take the twelve potential sets and make frequency distribution of the number of pairs of sets which have 1, 2, 3, 4, or 5 particular I scales different or 10, 9, 8, 7, or 6 I scales in common, we get the distribution shown in the table.

Number of Identical Ordinal Positions in a Pair of Sets with the Same Qualitative I Scale	Number of Such Pairs of Sets
10	18
9	24
8	17
7	6
6	1
	$66 = \binom{12}{2}$

The surface has not even been scratched on the generalizations which can be developed. Enough has been presented here to provide a general idea of the type of information which can be derived.

V. SUMMARY

We have presented a new type of scale called an ordered metric and have presented the experimental procedures required under certain limiting conditions to secure such a scale.

We have pointed out that the information which could be obtained under these conditions is as follows:

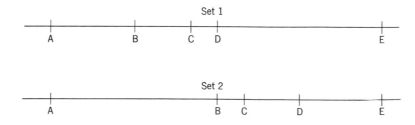

Figure 5. An example of two joint distributions with the same order of stimuli but different metric relations obtained from different sets of I scales.

1. The discovery of a latent attribute underlying preferences.

2. The order of the stimuli on the attribute continuum.

3. Something about the relative magnitudes of the distances between pairs of stimuli.

4. The sectioning of the continuum into intervals, the placing of people in these intervals, and the ordering of these intervals on this attribute continuum.

5. Something about the relative magnitudes of these intervals.

These were illustrated with a hypothetical example.

REFERENCES

1. Campbell, N. R. Symposium: Measurement and its importance for philosophy, in *Action, perception, and measurement,* The Aristotelian Society, Harrison and Sons, Ltd., 1938.
2. Coombs, C. H. Some hypotheses for the analysis of qualitative variables. *Psychol. Rev.,* 1948, **55**, 167-174.
3. Stevens, S. S. On the theory of scales of measurement. *Science,* 1946, **103**, 677-680.
4. Thurstone, L. L. The law of comparative judgment. *Psychol. Rev.,* 1927, **34**, 273-286.

15. Latent Structure Analysis

PAUL F. LAZARSFELD

The present paper will analyze one special procedure by which it is possible to make what one might call inferential classifications. Any number of well-known topics are covered by this provisional name tag: a person's attitude as inferred from his behavior, the intention of a document as inferred from certain linguistic characteristics, the morale of a group as inferred from its various performances, and many others.

The matter can be reformulated in the following way. Empirical observations locate our objects in a manifest property space. But this is not what we are really interested in. We want to know their location in a latent property space. *Our problem is to infer this latent space from the manifest data.* This reformulation of the relation between concept formation and classification by indicators has a number of advantages. One of them deserves special attention.

In any empirical classification guided by conceptual considerations we try to overcome the accidental elements inherent in the use of indicators. Suppose we want to order people according to how they feel about the role of government in economic affairs. We might ask them a series of questions as to public ownership of railroads, mines, banks, etc. It is reasonable to assume that the more someone favors *laissez faire* the fewer of these items he will answer *pro* public ownership. Still we know that many individual idiosyncrasies will creep into the answers. A strong laissez faire person has just read about a mine accident and under this impact he gives a *pro* public ownership response to the mine item; a strong interventionist happens to know a very fine bank president and therefore excludes the bank item from his list of *pro* responses. In the manifest property space we are at the mercy of these vagaries. But in the latent space, as we shall see, we can take them into account and thus achieve a more "purified" classification.

We are now ready to turn to the one question which has still been left unanswered: how is the probability relation between the observed indicators and the intended classification established? How do we move from the manifest to the latent property space?

THE LOGICAL FOUNDATION OF LATENT STRUCTURE ANALYSIS: A SYNOPSIS OF THE MAIN ISSUES

Inferential classifications with the help of a set of indicators are nothing new in the world of science. A doctor who uses a series of tests to see whether a patient has tuberculosis, a psychoanalyst who uses free associations to retrace a childhood experience, a chemist who observes various reactions to identify the nature of some substance—all use what might be called diagnostic procedures. They know, or believe they know, laws and regularities which link their manifest indicators with their latent space. Their diagnosis applies previous knowledge to a specific new case.

Some Initial Clarifications

But there exists a second type of procedure where, so to say, the acquisition of general knowledge and its application to a specific case are performed simultaneously. This happens if the starting point of an investigation is a statistical one and if our attention is mainly focused on the covariation of indicators in a large number of cases. The present section is devoted to a clarification of this idea. It will help if we sketch the course of the following discussion by raising a number of questions and offering some preliminary answers.

• Excerpted from S. Koch (Ed.) *Psychology: A Study of a Science,* Vol. 3, McGraw-Hill, New York, 1959, with permission of the author and the publisher.

1. With what kinds of manifest material shall we deal? They are qualitative, but to further simplify matters, they will be dichotomies through most of this report. Thus our examples will be "yes" or "no" answers to an observation. Does a man agree or disagree with a statement? Is he native or foreign born? Is a city above or below the national suicide rate?

We shall call any piece of such information an "item." In each case we shall have an *item list* in which items are numbered in an arbitrary but fixed way. The number of items in this list coincides with the dimensionality of the manifest property space.

One alternative of each dichotomy will arbitrarily be called positive (+), the other negative (—). Often a judicious use of these designations will help in intuitively grasping the material as a whole. Each object in our study will be characterized by a *response pattern* of the following kind:

Response to Item No.

1	2	3	...	m
+	—	+	...	+

The term response pattern is taken from questionnaire practice but is used here in a metaphorical sense. The items might all be derived from observation, e.g., the behavior of a person in various situations, and the objects might be collectivities and not individuals.

2. A whole group of "respondents" will be characterized by their *response frequencies:* they are the proportion of the group who answer each item i affirmatively (p_i), two items (p_{ij}), three items (p_{ijk}), etc. A barred index will be used to indicate a negative response. Thus $p_{1\bar{2}3}$ is the proportion of people who give an affirmative answer to items 1 and 3 and a negative answer to item 2. The whole set of these response frequencies is called a "dichotomous system" and its nature is very important for a more detailed study of latent structure analysis. For our present purpose, acquaintance with the symbolism will suffice.

3. How are we to represent a latent space? In the traditional way by a system of coordinate axes, i.e., a so-called cartesian frame of reference. In this section we shall restrict ourselves to one-dimensional latent spaces to facilitate exposition. But assessing the number of dimensions in the latent space is possible. A one-dimensional space is, of course, a straight line. We shall often call it a *latent continuum*.

4. What is the relation between the manifest items and the latent continuum? It involves probabilities. Thus we shall assume that there exists a curve—preferably a mathematically simple one—which relates to each point of the latent continuum a specific probability that a given item has a positive response. Suppose that our latent continuum deals with socioeconomic status, and three of our items are ownership of a yacht, presence of running warm water, and presence of two living rooms in the house of the respondent. Common sense would let us suspect that the corresponding probability relation will be somewhat like Figure 1. The graph

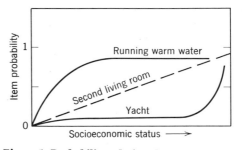

Figure 1. Probability relations between the intended classification by socioeconomic status and the observed frequency of three indicators.

intimates that very quickly as we go up the social scale almost every family will have running warm water; only the upper crust is likely to own yachts, while the probability of more space in addition to bedrooms increases fairly proportionally with socioeconomic status. The truth of these surmises is not relevant here. What matters is the way they are expressed through Figure 1. Of course we have not yet stated precisely what we mean by probability, and we are still in the dark as to how we would define and know a respondent's socioeconomic status. These two points soon will be taken up in considerable detail.

The curves of probabilities in Figure 1 we shall call *trace lines;* they trace the probability for an item as a "respondent" moves along the latent continuum. If the latter is a two-dimensional one then the probabilities form a trace surface. In full generality we shall talk of *latent traces*. Notice that a trace line is defined for each item separately. Later a crucial problem will be what to think about the probability of joint responses to several items occurring simultaneously at each point of the latent space.

5. How are we to understand the term "probability" used all through the preceding pages? A traditional example of how to look at

probability is as follows: we take a sample of people aged fifty and find out how many die within the next year; we compute the proportion of people who died between the ages of fifty and fifty-one. Then we generalize this ratio and say that it is the probability of dying at the age of fifty within one year. This operation can be refined as far as we want to go. We might say, for instance, that the probability of business executives' dying within a year at the age of fifty is greater than the corresponding probability for office clerks. The class for which such probabilities are computed and then generalized is usually called the reference class of the probability (3).

This same procedure, however, can be used in still another way. Suppose we ask an individual, Mr. Brown, repeatedly whether he is in favor of the United Nations; suppose further that after each question we "wash his brains" and ask him the same question again. Because Mr. Brown is not certain as to how he feels about the United Nations, he will sometimes give a favorable and sometimes an unfavorable answer. Having gone through this procedure many times, we then compute the proportion of times Mr. Brown was in favor of the United Nations. This we could also call the probability of Mr. Brown's being in favor of the United Nations. But now the reference class is not many Mr. Browns having been asked this question once, but one Mr. Brown having been asked the question many times.

There is one interesting consequence of this version of the probability notion. A specific Mr. Brown, for instance, might feel that it is his duty to be in favor of the United Nations. Therefore, if he is asked a question when he is sober, his probability—or, if you please, his propensity—to be in favor of the United Nations might be rather high. Under the influence of alcohol, however, his hostility to the international organization might come out. Therefore, his probability under the influence of alcohol could be different than his probability if he were sober.

How can we know trace lines? This is, of course, the central problem of latent structure analysis. The remainder of the present section will provide some preparation, consideration, and examples for developing an appropriate answer.

The whole configuration of trace lines for all items and the location of each object in the latent space is called the latent structure. It is

a typical example of what is often called a "mathematical model," a construct which is derived from actual data together with certain general reflections on the purpose these data serve. In our case the situation is as follows: from our manifest data we actually know the frequencies in which the various response patterns occur in a given population; what we want to know are the *latent parameters* of the model, the coefficients which characterize the latent traces, and the distribution of the population within the latent space. We therefore need equations which link the manifest frequencies to the latent parameters. From these so-called *accounting equations* we then can compute all the elements in the model. The name given to these equations is meant to indicate that with the knowledge of the full latent structure, we can account for everything known about the manifest data.

In order to clarify this basic idea, it is best to discuss in some detail two empirical operations with which most research students are well acquainted. By a slight extrapolation they become basic elements of latent structure analysis. The situation is somewhat similar to what was just mentioned about the concept of probability. Probabilities are formal extrapolations from the empirical notion of relative frequencies. In our case we are referring to item analysis which forms the basis of the notion of trace lines, and to the "explanation" of statistical relations which becomes the basis for the accounting equations.

We turn first to item analysis and trace lines.

Item Analysis and Item Curves

Every graduate student who takes a course in applied psychology knows about item analysis. If he wants to develop an attitude or a performance test he knows that he should proceed in the following way. He is permitted to start with many questionnaire items which he hopes will be indicative of what in the end he wants to "measure." But then he is supposed to distinguish between good items and bad items. This he is taught to do in the following way: he forms a "raw" score by adding up for each respondent the number of items which are answered in the "correct" way. Then he plots each single item against this raw score. (This we shall call the *item curves.*) The items which have a high association with the raw score are acceptable. The items which have a low association are considered inappropriate and should be eliminated. We will now give an example of such an item analysis, but we will refine it in two ways:

1. We shall plot *two* items against the raw score.

2. We shall not only plot each item separately, but we shall investigate *how the association between the two items is related to the raw score.*

Item Analysis Applied Simultaneously to More Than One Item

Our material comes from a public relations study where 560 respondents were asked questions regarding their attitudes to the oil industry. Do oil companies treat their workers fairly; do they make too much profit; are they wasteful of our natural resources, etc.? To each question the respondent could give one of five answers, which ranged from firmly favorable to firmly unfavorable (from the oil industry's point of view). There were ten questions in all and eight of them were combined into an arbitrary score in the following way: a firmly favorable answer was given a weight of 4 and so on down to the firmly unfavorable, which got a weight of 0. Then all the weights were added so that a respondent's general attitude score could range from 0 to 32. This score was used as the "outside continuum" or base variable. Against it the probabilities (proportion) of answers to the remaining two questions were plotted. These two were:

Item 1. Do the big oil companies control too much of the oil business?

Item 2. Is the oil industry wasteful of our natural resources?

A positive reply (from the industry point of view) was one in which a respondent expressed at least some disagreement (score class 3 and 4). The joint positive response required such disagreement with both items. In Table 1 we now have the data for the item curves for each item alone and for the joint responses. The vertical marginals of the five partial fourfold tables indicate the item curve of item 1. In the lowest general attitude group, 17 out of 106, or 16 per cent, give an affirmative response. In the group farthest to the right, 84 out of 103, or 84 per cent, do so. The horizontal marginals indicate the item curve for the second item; the corresponding figures are 31 per cent and 79 per cent. Thus item 1 (concern with economic control) is more expressive of the "underlying" classification than item 2 (concern with natural resources). Figure 2 shows the item curves for items 1 and 2 and adds a third: the proportion of people who give a positive answer to both items. These proportions are based on the left upper corner figures of each of the five fourfold tables in Table 1. Note that the item curve for both items is more concave (seen from the top) than either of the curves for items 1 and 2 separately.

The items in our attitude tests have obviously been selected by the investigator as indicators of an underlying continuum. The item curves are a crude representation of the relation between these indicators and the intended classification. But what about the relation among the indicators? The reader will remember that we came to the general expectation that indicators will be statistically related to each other because they have their links with the underlying continuum in common. In terms of prob-

TABLE 1. The Interrelation of Two Test Items for Five Subclasses of Respondents Classified According to a General Attitude Score Derived from Eight Other Questions*

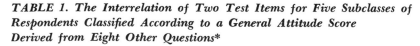

	Item 2 +	Item 2 −			Item 2 +	Item 2 −			Item 2 +	Item 2 −			Item 2 +	Item 2 −			Item 2 +	Item 2 −	
Item 1 +	3	14	17	Item 1 +	15	27	42	Item 1 +	35	26	61	Item 1 +	40	18	58	Item 1 +	67	17	84
Item 1 −	30	59	89	Item 1 −	32	61	93	Item 1 −	34	29	63	Item 1 −	13	21	34	Item 1 −	12	7	19
Total	33	73	106		47	88	135		69	55	124		53	39	92		79	24	103

General Attitude Score	0 to 16	17 to 20	21 to 23	24 to 26	27 to 32

* A response favorable to the oil industry is indicated by a + sign.

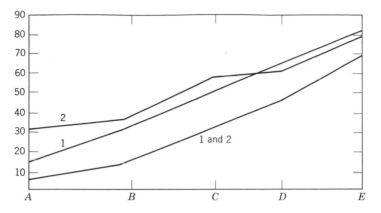

Figure 2. Item curves corresponding to Table 1.

ability notions we can now put it this way: the probability of joint occurrence p_{12} will not be $p_1 p_2$—the chance result of two independent probabilities—but, rather, p_{12} will be greater than $p_1 p_2$. In the empirical data we shall expect a positive association in the fourfold table, which cross-tabulates the reply to two items. This turns out to be the case in our public relations example, as can be seen from Table 2.

Table 2 is obtained by adding the five partial tables in Table 1.

TABLE 2. The Interrelation of Items 1 and 2 of Table 1, for All 560 Respondents

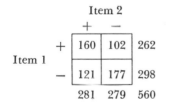

		Item 2 +	Item 2 −	
Item 1	+	160	102	262
Item 1	−	121	177	298
		281	279	560

Here $p_{12} = 160/560 = .29$, whereas $p_1 \cdot p_2$ is only $(.47)(.50) = .24$. Still, using rather informal language, we can say that the responses to two items of a test show positive relations because they were chosen as indicators of an underlying property. But this argument can be turned around. *If a class of people are alike in an underlying property, then the indicators of this property should not be statistically related in this class.* In our example we can submit this idea to a crude test. Our general score was supposed to be a crude measure of the general attitude of the respondent to the oil industry. By dividing the respondents into five classes, as in Table 1, we get groups of people who among themselves have a rather similar attitude.

In general our expectation is borne out. We now have five partial fourfold tables: the asso-

ciation is negative in one, practically zero in two, and positive in two. The five tables can be looked upon as chance variations from an association which is actually zero. Extrapolating the results of Table 1, we can say that if by an appropriate score, the underlying property of a population is kept constant, then the indicators of the property are statistically unrelated.[1]

The essence of our example is this. On the basis of their raw scores, we divided our respondents into five classes. Within these classes raw scores are relatively similar, and this similarity is understood to correspond to the similarity of individuals within a class in their general attitude toward the oil industry. Just as individuals within a class have a similar attitude, individuals in different classes have dissimilar attitudes. This dissimilarity manifests itself in the differences between probabilities of affirmative responses in the different classes. *Within* each class the probabilities for all people are the same for any one item; of course, different items will generally have different probabilities of affirmative response within a given class. Considering the responses to a single item by individuals in one class, we still find a mixture of positive and negative responses. After all, the

[1] Whether the association or correlation between items 1 and 2 in such subclassifications can be considered a result of chance can be tested by x^2 procedures. It should be desirable to obtain more such examples, because the present one points to an interesting possibility. The five associations go uniformly from negative to positive as we move from low to high general scores. If this turns out to be the case in other tests, we would be confronted with a result in test psychology which deserves further investigation and interpretation. For our present purpose this matter is irrelevant, because we use our concrete data only to lead up to an axiomatic idealization.

class does not determine the response; it only determines the probability of each response. The variability of response is supposed to stem from accidental elements. Quite irrespective of their attitude toward a specific industry, some people happen to be more concerned with the preservation of natural resources, others are more worried about the growth of economic monopoly. Biographical and other reasons might account for such a difference; in any case, these idiosyncratic elements are assumed to be unrelated to each other. Within a class which is homogeneous in regard to its basic attitude, the answers to specific items are assumed to be unrelated. This was not quite the case in our concrete example but was enough so that an extrapolation seems indicated. *We shall define a homogeneous class as one in which this statistical independence of indicators prevails.*

This leads us to investigate the characteristics of a group of respondents which can be considered a mixture of subgroups where, within the subgroups, a set of indicators are statistically independent of each other.

The "Mixture" Phenomenon and Its Role in the Explanation of Statistical Relations

We start with a simple case. Suppose that in each of three groups two items are statistically independent. Table 3 should be looked upon as an idealization (and simplification) of Table 1. We "mix" these three groups and form a new one by adding box by box the corresponding numbers on the left side of Table 3. On the right side we now find an association between the two items, which did not exist in the three partial tables to the left. Where does this asso-

ciation come from? We understand this best if we look at the margins of the three left-side parts of Table 3. In Class I the probability of a positive response is much lower on *both* attributes than in Class III. If in the combined population we select successive respondents, they will sometimes come from Class I and sometimes from Class III. In the former case, they will be more likely to give negative responses on both attributes; in the latter case, both responses are more likely to be positive. *The statistical association between the two items in the total population is thus accounted for by the fact that each attribute by itself is positively related to the general attitude of the respondents which distinguishes the three subclasses.* This was, of course, also the case in our previous example of the public relations study of the oil industry. Table 1 shows that, for all the items, the probability of a positive response increases with the general attitude score. The positive association between the two items in Table 2 is therefore accounted for by the fact that they are both indicators of an underlying attitude or, more precisely, the probability of positive responses is positively related to the general attitude score. The resulting association in Table 3 is noticeable but not very strong. Therefore we increase the marginal differences between the three homogeneous classes and mix again. Now the resulting association is much more marked. How is this finding to be explained in the light of the previous discussion? It will be remembered that the marginals in the partial subtables correspond to the "item curves" of the two items. In Table 4 they are clearly much steeper than in Table 3. This

TABLE 3

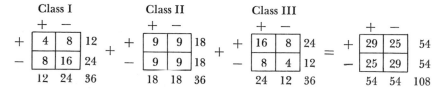

	Class I				Class II				Class III							
	+	**−**			**+**	**−**			**+**	**−**				**+**	**−**		
+	4	8	12	**+**	**+**	9	9	18	**+**	**+**	16	8	24	**=**	**+**	29	25	54
−	8	16	24		**−**	9	9	18		**−**	8	4	12		**−**	25	29	54
	12	24	36			18	18	36			24	12	36			54	54	108

TABLE 4

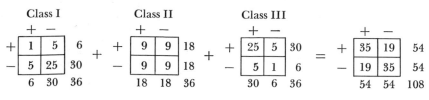

	Class I				Class II				Class III							
	+	**−**			**+**	**−**			**+**	**−**				**+**	**−**		
+	1	5	6	**+**	**+**	9	9	18	**+**	**+**	25	5	30	**=**	**+**	35	19	54
−	5	25	30		**−**	9	9	18		**−**	5	1	6		**−**	19	35	54
	6	30	36			18	18	36			30	6	36			54	54	108

means that now the two items have a much stronger relation to the underlying continuum than before. As a result the interrelation between the two indicators on the right side of Table 4 is much stronger than in Table 3.[2]

So far our emphasis has been on the mixing of homogeneous subgroups and the resulting associations between indicators. But Tables 1, 3, and 4 can also be read in the opposite direction, from right to left. We then start with an existing association between indicators; we "unmix" the population under study and end by showing the homogeneous subgroups in which the associations disappear. Actually, this is always done if, in empirical research, a statistical finding is to be explained. We want to remind the reader of the three major types of such explanations.

Type 1. A good example is available from political research. In a presidential election educated people vote more frequently than the uneducated. We can classify people into three groups, however, according to their interest in elections. Then on each interest level we can set up a fourfold table between voting and education (graduation from high school forming the point where higher education begins). We then find that with each increase in interest the proportion of voters increases, as well as the proportion of people having higher education. *Within* interest groups, however, there is practically no relation between education and voting. Interest, therefore, accounts for the original relation in terms of what is usually called an "intervening" variable. The whole structure can be represented by the following scheme where arrows stand for a vague idea of causation.

Education → Interest → Voting

The original two variables are underscored. Their association is *interpreted* through the role of "interest." The interpretation is tested by showing that the original association disappears within subgroups which are homogeneous in regard to interest.[3]

[2] The reader should satisfy himself that many other combinations could occur. Suppose, e.g., that we made Class III in Tables 3 and 4 much larger than Class I. Then, in the resulting fourfold table, both items and their joint occurrence would show higher frequencies.

[3] Cf. [1]. There a characteristic counterexample is included. Men vote more frequently than women. This cannot be accounted for by interest. Even

Type 2. The second major type of accounting is usually known as the controlling of *spurious factors.*

Examples are almost proverbial: fires where many fire engines come out cause more damage; does this mean that fire engines are dangerous? Obviously not. Large fires bring out many engines and cause much damage. The arrow scheme corresponding to this case would be as follows:

If the size of the fire is "kept constant" there would be no positive relation between equipment and damage.

In both types of accounting the statistical test is the same, and it is the one which we have carefully analyzed above. The ultimate relation between two attributes is owing to the fact that they are both related to a third property; once this property is kept constant the original relation disappears. The difference between type 1 and type 2 lies in the sequence of variables involved. In both cases we start with an association between two factors: education and voting in the first example, equipment and damage in the second. But in type 1 the explanatory factor intervenes between the two original variables; whereas in type 2 it antecedes the damage as well as the number of engines the fire brings out.

Type 3. The third type of accounting is usually less discussed because its outcome seems so obvious from a substantive point of view. Still it is the most important one for the present purpose, and all our initial examples belong here. When we deal with indicators of a supposed underlying property, there exists no necessary time relation between the intended classification and its overt manifestations. Rather the relation here is one of generality and specificity. Still, the test of whether we are really dealing with appropriate indicators is the same as before; we want to know *whether the underlying property does account for the interrelation between the manifest indicators.* We would look for a way to classify people according to the underlying characteristic and assume that if this is held constant no further statistical

within the same interest group men vote more than women.

relation should exist between the various indicators.

The most obvious way to make this test is to see whether people who are alike on the majority of the indicators show any appreciable relation between the remaining ones. This we did with our oil study example. Another approach would be to use a rating scale. For instance, people could be asked to rate their political interest on a scale from 1 to 10. Then they could be divided into fairly homogeneous classes according to this self-rating. If we then have an itemized interest test, we could raise this question: does the self-rating account for the interrelation between the test items? The answer would be in the positive if, on each level of self-rating, the items were not statistically associated. The arrow scheme corresponding to that of the previous example would be:

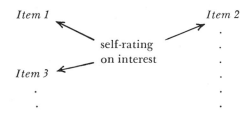

It is hoped that we have given enough examples so that the reader has a clear picture of the following two related facts:

1. There exists a uniform operation of accounting for an empirical relation between two properties. It consists of studying this relation for subclasses of the original population, these subclasses being formed by the introduction of additional properties. The substantive nature of these "accounting properties" and their relation with the original data make for the main types of accounting procedures as they occur in the practice of research.

2. These various accounting procedures are all in fact inversions of the "mixture phenomenon" described above. In mixtures of homogeneous groups, indicators show statistical associations: they are due to the covariation of the indicators *between* these subclasses. Inversely, associations between indicators in empirical populations can be accounted for by dividing them into homogeneous subgroups: the variables along which this "unmixing" can be done "explain" the statistical associations originally found.

We can now relate all these considerations to latent structure analysis.

The Accounting Equations and the Principle of Local Independence

We are prepared to answer the question which we first raised at the end of the historical survey in the first section. There we came to the conclusion that the problem of disposition concepts boiled down to the task of *relating a manifest to a latent property space*. The manifest space was given by the observed properties of our objects, which for our present purpose, we have reduced to dichotomies. We came to use the word "item" for an indicator and the term "response" for its observed presence or absence. A "response pattern" was a point in such a dichotomous property space.

The latent space corresponds to our intended classification, which, as we saw, was variously called in the literature "an underlying characteristic," "a trait," "a disposition," etc. It was not necessary to assume anything about this latent space; the number of its dimensions was not specified, nor did they need to be of any particular mathematical form, dichotomous, continuous, or whatever. But when we came to this point of our discussion we left it undecided how we would achieve this latent classification, in view of the fact that we have only manifest observations available. What solution does latent structure analysis propose for this problem?

It defines the latent space as that classification which accounts for the statistical interrelations between the manifest observed indicators. It is the classification which "unmixes" a given population into homogeneous subgroups. The many consequences of this definition must now be spelled out.

The latent space is not known in advance but is *defined by its accounting role*. When we discussed examples of item curves, we first divided people by some index (e.g., a rating on the number of positive responses) into fairly homogeneous classes and then studied empirically how the indicators were related in the various subclasses; Table 1 was a typical example. But *in latent structure analysis we do not have an empirically provided general classification against which the occurrence frequencies or probabilities of the different items can be plotted. The underlying classification is derived from the statistical behavior of the indicators themselves.* The sequence of affirmative response proportions for a given item over all homogeneous "latent" classes becomes its item curve; it is now called a trace line to stress that it is not directly given but derived from empirical data.

Accounting Equations

Let us assume that we have c homogeneous classes and n items. Let us assume further that these homogeneous classes are ordered in some way. (In Table 3, for instance $c = 3$, and the three classes are ordered from left to right.) Let us now focus on two specific items, say, the two items in the scheme just mentioned. The response frequencies of the two items in the composite population (exemplified by the right side of Table 3) can be derived from the following equations:

$$p_1 = \sum_{x=1}^{c} v^x p_1{}^x$$

$$p_2 = \sum_{x=1}^{c} v^x p_2{}^x$$

$$p_{12} = \sum_{x=1}^{c} v^x p_1{}^x p_2{}^x$$

This is in algebraic form the box-by-box summation we have carried out in all our mixing examples. The superscript in $p_1{}^x$ shows from what class x the "latent probabilities" have been taken; v^x is the proportion of the whole population in class x. Suppose now the joint frequencies on the left were given and the task consisted in computing the response frequencies in the homogeneous subclasses. We could not solve it because there are fewer equations than unknowns. Obviously, however, we could add more equations by adding more items. Not only would that give us more equations of the type just mentioned, but it would also add an additional type: we could now set up equations for higher-order frequencies, for instance,

$$p_{123} = \sum_{x=1}^{c} v^x p_1{}^x p_2{}^x p_3{}^x$$

In general there always occurs a point where we have enough equations to solve the whole problem. Equations of this type are called *accounting equations* because they permit us to derive parameters of the latent structure from the manifest data. These accounting equations are, in a way, the mathematical summary of everything we have said so far. Let us review, therefore, how they are related to the different elements of our discussion.

First, they formalize algebraically the diagnostic procedure by which we make the inference from the manifest data to the latent position of a respondent. An indicator or test item is introduced because we have a more or less vague idea how it is likely to be related to what we want to find out about each of our respondents. We assume that if we could by some manipulation put people into various positions of this intended classification, their response probability would vary according to this general image. The latent probabilities give precise expression to the relation between the latent and the manifest space. They are tantamount to a diagnosis for any manifest response pattern which might be empirically observed.

But, of course, we cannot move respondents into various positions; we observe each respondent only once. Instead, we have a variety of respondents whom we assume—in the spirit of the whole model—to be actually at different places in the latent structure. As a matter of fact, we make an even stronger assumption: for the purpose of our model, we assume that all our respondents are alike but for one fact, that they are different in regard to the latent property. This is the second element in the whole analysis.

A third element is the following trend of reasoning. Even if we knew where a respondent belongs in the latent space, we would have to make him respond repeatedly to each item so that we could ascertain empirically his response probability. But again we must remember that each respondent is observed only once on each of the items. This difficulty is surmounted by the idea that in an empirical population we are most likely to have many people who are at the same point in the latent space. Now we consider such respondents to be, for our purpose, identical; therefore, the proportion of affirmative answers in such a homogeneous group can be taken to be the same as we would have obtained if we had observed one member of each of these groups repeatedly.

Let us get this series of constructions clearly in our minds by visualizing the process in reverse order. We could get all our trace lines by the following procedure:

1. We imbue one respondent, by some kind of manipulation, with various amounts of the latent property.

2. At each point, we make him respond to each item repeatedly with "brainwashing" inserted between any two trials. This would give us, at each point of the latent space, the prob-

ability of an affirmative response for our "typical" subjects.

3. The totality of these probabilities, attached to each point of the latent space, would be the trace of an item—in the one-dimensional case, the trace line.

Now the steps (1) and (2) are replaced by the fact that at each point of the latent space we have many respondents; we substitute their response frequencies for the probabilities we are looking for. But remember that even this is a fiction. Although we are convinced that our whole populaton can be subclassified into such homogeneous groups, when we deal with concrete respondents we do not know at what point of the latent space they are. Here we take advantage of the accounting equations just explained and developed. What we actually know are the response frequencies of a mixed population to a number of items in all their combinations. Therefrom we can compute the response probabilities in the postulated homogeneous subclasses. As a matter of fact, we learn, as a by-product of this computation, what proportion of our respondents is in each of these latent classes.

But notice that even now there is one topic which we have not discussed at all, namely, the single respondent. We do not know at which point of the latent space he is located. This is a matter which we will take up only in the next section. What we now know is the latent structure, the proportion of people in each class and the conditional probabilities of giving an affirmative response to each item in these classes.

This whole web of assumptions and deductions can be fruitfully divided into three sections. One has to do with rather conventional ideas which are accepted wherever probability notions are introduced; the idea, for instance, that for the purpose of a specific investigation different people can be considered as alike, and that the proportion having a property is an estimate of the probability that a single one of them will exhibit it. Although the logical foundations of this idea are by no means simple, we need not justify them here because of their general acceptance in all model building.

A second group of our ideas has to do with the problem of unmixing: deriving the probabilities in homogeneous subclasses from the response frequencies of a mixed population. This is straightforward algebra and does not require any further logical foundation. Actually, it is the most characteristic and novel aspect of latent structure analysis. Here the accounting equations come in.

Finally, we have the principle of *local independence*. (The term has been suggested by Frederick Mosteller.) It covers the phase of our discussion in which an intended classification (an underlying, intervening variable) is *defined* as the one which divides a given population into homogeneous subgroups. The principle of local independence identifies the "measurement" problem with the mixing phenomenon or, rather, its inversion—unmixing. For this, no further foundation can be introduced. The principle is proposed as a mathematical axiom which formalizes the basic assumption of what we have called index formation in the social sciences. If an investigator chooses a number of indicators for the purpose of diagnosis, for the purpose of putting people or social objects into an intended classification, he does assume—knowingly or not—that the statistical relations between these indicators are essentially owing to the fact that they are all related to the intended latent property. For a group of people, therefore, who are alike in regard to this latent property, all the indicators will be statistically unrelated. This principle partakes of the common characteristics of all axioms which are introduced into a theory—and no theory exists without at least one axiom.[4]

The idea of making the principle of local independence the nub of index construction, even of concept formation in the social sciences, is the central logical feature of latent structure analysis. Together with conventional probability notions and some newly developed but quite orthodox algebra, all procedures and all empirical findings derive from it.

THE NINE STEPS OF LATENT STRUCTURE ANALYSIS

A latent structure analysis of necessity involves a certain sequence of operations which can be cast into a schedule of nine steps.

Summary of the Nine Steps

First we must think about the form of models which might reasonably be appropriate. This means that we want to consider systems of manifest and latent variables such that their interrelations mirror the interrelations between

---

[4] Frederic Lord in discussing the principle of local independence has aptly stated that it is "almost indispensable for any theory of measurement." Cf. (2).

indicators in the data and the concept which is the real object of concern. Having considered these questions in a general way, we must state our assumptions in explicit mathematical form (step 1). Then we can write the accounting equations, which give the relations between manifest and latent parameters, in the particular form which the chosen model imposes on them (step 2). Next we must ask what conditions or restrictions are put on the interrelations within the data by the assumptions of the model (step 3). These "conditions of reducibility" are useful in a number of ways: first, they are explicit statements of relations which must hold among the manifest parameters, so that by means of simple operations on the data, and without solving the accounting equations, we can determine whether the assumed model is appropriate for the given data. Second, the conditions of reducibility are useful in evaluating how closely the data are in accord with the requirements of the model. Third, the conditions of reducibility contribute to an understanding of the model and to the question of the solvability of the accounting equations.

This question of the solvability of the accounting equations may be asked more specifically in the form: given the manifest parameters, are there a sufficient number of conditions imposed by the model to make it possible to identify the latent parameters? (step 4) Having answered this question, we proceed to its logical corollary: if the equations are solvable, how does one actually solve them? (step 5)

Up to this point everything is algebra. Now the data must be introduced, and we are forced to do some arithmetic. A "fitting procedure" (step 6) in latent structure analysis is usually a shuttling back and forth between data and latent parameters—using data of lower order to identify certain latent parameters, from these computing what the data would have been if they had fitted the (partially identified) model perfectly, then combining these "fitted data" with higher-order manifest data to compute further latent parameters. A fitting procedure has two goals: (a) a set of latent parameters and (b) a set of "fitted manifest parameters" which are perfectly in agreement with the demands of the model and at the same time are as close as possible to the actual data. How close a fit was achieved requires some evaluation (step 7). Two questions must be answered here: Are the differences between the actual and the fitted parameters small enough? Do the differences appear to be randomly distributed, or do they fall into some pattern which suggests that a somewhat different latent structure model would be more appropriate? If this is the case, we must again start from scratch, except for what we have learned by the experience. But if we are satisfied with the fit, there is still some work to be done.

We want to know how the respondents who give a particular response pattern are distributed over the latent space (step 8). And it is of interest to ask about the most likely or the most typical location of individuals who gave a particular response pattern, and in some way to assign a *score* to each respondent, or to each response pattern. Similarly we may ask how much each item contributes to the diagnostic process, and perhaps we may wish to give each item a score indicating its ability to discriminate between individuals at different points of the latent space (step 9).

REFERENCES

1. Lazarsfeld, P. F., Berelson, B., and Gaudet, H. *The people's choice.* (2d ed.) New York: Columbia Univ. Press, 1948. Pp. 45-49.
2. Lord, F. The relation of test score to the trait underlying the test. *Educ. psychol. Measmt.,* 1953, **13**, 517-549.
3. Nagel, E. Principles of the theory of probability. *Int. Encycl. unified Sci.,* 1939, **1**, No. 6, p. 23.

16. The Perception of Social Attitudes

SAMUEL J. MESSICK

The attitudes of others may be perceived as organized in different ways by different groups of people. Consider an attitude area composed of attitude toward war, attitude toward capital punishment, and attitude toward the treatment of criminals (correction vs. punishment). Certain people may perceive others as varying from an extreme humanitarian to a correspondingly extreme nonhumanitarian viewpoint. In such a situation some particular person might be seen as being antiwar, anticapital punishment, and procriminal correction in the sense that one attitude directly implies the other and that no alternatives are possible (see Figure 1). Such a

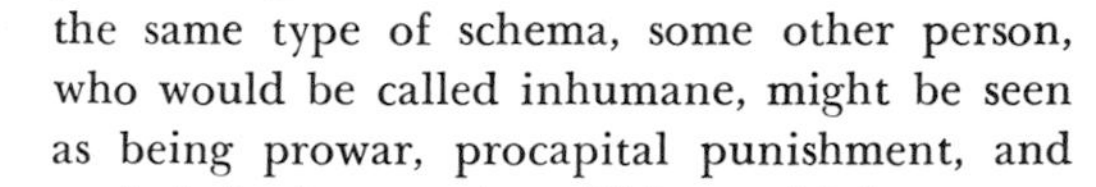

Type A
$$-W \text{————————} +W$$
$$-C.P. \text{————————} +C.P.$$
$$+Corr. \text{————————} -Corr.$$

Figure 1. Conceptualization of the attitudes toward war, toward capital punishment, and toward treatment of criminals as a unidimensional system.

person might be called a "humanitarian." In the same type of schema, some other person, who would be called inhumane, might be seen as being prowar, procapital punishment, and anticriminal correction. This would be a one-dimensional system, since the attitudes are not perceived separately but as one composite "humane-inhumane" attitude. People with such a

• Reprinted from *Journal of Abnormal and Social Psychology*, 1956, **52**, 57-66, with the permission of the author and the American Psychological Association. This study was supported in part by the Office of Naval Research contract N6onr-270-20 with Princeton University and also in part by funds from the National Science Foundation. The opinions and conclusions expressed are, of course, those of the author and do not represent the views of the Office of Naval Research or of the National Science Foundation. The initial portion of this study was carried out when the author was an Educational Testing Service Psychometric Fellow at Princeton University.

point of view could not conceive of a person who was both antiwar and procapital punishment.

Another group of people may perceive the attitudes of others as being structured in a different way (see Figure 2). In this type of struc-

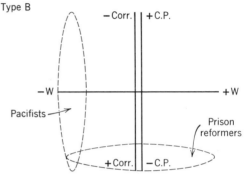

Figure 2. Conceptualization of the attitude toward capital punishment combined with the attitudes toward correction of criminals while the attitude toward war is seen as an independent dimension.

ture capital punishment of extreme criminals is equated with punishment of criminals in general as a deterrent to crime, but war is seen as something independent. This dimensional configuration provides a "frame of reference" in which Type B finds it possible to conceive of people in each of the four quadrants. In this perceived structuring, two pacifists could be conceived of as having widely different views toward capital punishment. Although they are both viewed as being against war, one could be seen as in favor of capital punishment as a protection to society and a deterrent to crime and the other as against it because "it is just as uncivilized as war." Type B would also feel it possible for two people to be violently anti-capital punishment and yet have different views toward war, because war is considered to be essentially independent of attitudes toward criminals. It would be difficult under these circumstances, however, for Type B to conceive of a person who was in favor of punishing minor criminals and at the same time against capital punishment for extreme criminals.

In Type C war and capital punishment are equated as two means of taking human life, but criminal correction is seen as something independent (Figure 3). Thus, Type C might con-

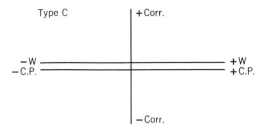

Figure 3. Conceptualization of attitudes toward war and capital punishment combined as two means of taking human life while the attitude toward correction of criminals is seen as independent.

ceive of two religious conscientious objectors as being against both war and capital punishment because killing is involved, and yet one may be considered procorrection for humanitarian reasons and the other propunishment because evildoers must pay.

For Type D these three attitudes are viewed as being independent of each other, and it is possible for this group to conceive of people in each of the octants (Figure 4). Of course, the dimensions in any of the above types may be related in various ways—the lines drawn at angles instead of perpendicularly.

It must not be construed from the above discussion that a given group of people perceive

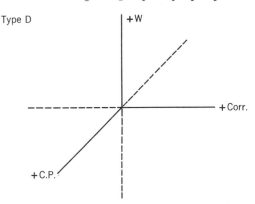

Figure 4. Conceptualization of the attitudes toward war, toward capital punishment, and toward the correction of criminals as three completely independent dimensions.

the attitudes of others in only one way. The above types may be considered to be "points of view," and it is certainly possible for an individual to hold several different points of view with respect to the attitudes of others, depending upon the characteristics of the "other" people considered. Some individuals may be able to conceive of a different attitude structure for every group of people specified, because they perceive different types of people in different ways. However, it is also possible that these individuals perceive one particular attitude structure more often than another, and that in the absence of specific knowledge or a detailed characterization of the other person, they may ascribe to his attitudes this modal structure, It is this modal, or dominant, way in which individuals generally structure the attitudes of others with which the present study is concerned.

In psychophysics multidimensional scaling methods (12, 13) have been developed which yield dimensional configurations for psychophysical judgments. These methods may be promising for the analysis of attitudes. The fundamental concept involved in these techniques is psychological distance, a construct that has been widely used by many psychological theorists. Psychological distance in the attitude realm can be thought of in terms of the degree of agreement or disagreement shown between two statements. If a person who strongly agrees with one statement would also be likely to agree strongly with another, then these two statements can be considered to be psychologically close together. If a person who strongly agrees with one statement would not be very likely to agree with the other, then those two statements can be considered to be psychologically far apart. If the psychological distances among attitude statements can be analyzed in a Cartesian space, it will be possible to obtain a configuration of the way in which an individual perceives attitudes as being structured in a given domain.

THE PROBLEM AND AN APPROACH TO ITS SOLUTION

As was seen in the introduction, it is possible on a priori grounds to structure the attitudes of others in terms of several different, yet reasonable, dimensional arrangements. The actual attitude arrangements perceived by individuals, however, has seldom been investigated, mainly because of a lack of appropriate methods. Knowledge of the ways in which individuals perceive attitudes as being structured in others is important psychologically, since such perceptions affect an individual's understanding of others, his relationships and adjustments with others, and his actions toward others. It might be possible to obtain some information about these perceived attitude structures by utilizing multidimensional scaling techniques.

The purpose of this study, then, is first of all to see whether a set of perceived attitude relationships can be adequately represented in dimensional terms and, secondly, to see if two groups, which probably differ with respect to these attitudes, perceive them as being structured in different ways. The adequacy of the dimensional representation can be evaluated in terms of the requirements of the multidimensional psychophysics model (see 7, 13, 18). This model provides for a Euclidean dimensionalization of the data, and if the data do not have Euclidean properties, one of the requirements of the model will not be met, i.e., the matrix of distance scalar products (see 7, 18), which must be positive semi-definite for Euclidean distances, will be found to have large negative roots. Therefore, if large negative roots are found, the suitability of the model is in question, and dimensions should not even be extracted. Unfortunately, however, statistical tests for the size of latent roots are not available, so arbitrary acceptance regions must be set (7, 13). Under such conditions, it might sometimes be possible for a matrix to be dimensionalized when it is actually non-Euclidean. Even in this case, however, there are indications of the unsuitability of the model, for a forced Euclidean description of non-Euclidean distances would lead to an increase in dimensionality. Thus, whenever the number of dimensions extracted approaches the number of stimuli, not only is the fruitfulness of the approach in that area in doubt, but the suitability of the model is also in question.

Multidimensional scaling methods have been utilized by Richardson [method of triadic combinations (10)] and Torgerson [method of complete triads (13)] which could be applied for this purpose. These methods are essentially extensions of the method of paired comparisons to the multidimensional case. The method of complete triads could be applied to attitude statements as it stands, but it has the undesirable property that for n statements

$n(n-1)(n-2)/2$ judgments would be required from each S. The task becomes prohibitive with more than 10 statements. It would be more reasonable to apply a multidimensional extension of the method of successive intervals (3, 11), which would require only $n(n-1)/2$ judgments. The procedure for such a method would require S to arrange $n(n-1)/2$ pairs of stimuli on a distance continuum according to the degree of similarity of the members of each pair. This question of similarity or relatedness can be approached in the attitude realm by asking for a judgment of the agreement or disagreement shown between two statements. The judgment involved can be set up in terms of the attitudes of some *other* person in the following way: S is asked to imagine the type of person who would strongly agree with Statement A and then to decide how this same person would also feel about Statement B. In this way, S is asked to estimate the attitude relationships of others, and the multidimensional analysis of these data will provide a dimensional configuration of these perceived attitude relationships. Minimal information about the "other" person is provided in this procedure, i.e., he is characterized only as being in complete agreement with a single statement. Perhaps, in this highly unstructured situation, this agreement will act as a cue to the complex characterization which S most often ascribes to other people in general, and S will respond in terms of this modal, or dominant, characterization.

Since there is a persistent correlation between a person's own attitudes and his estimates of the attitudes of others (5, 14, 16), the procedure suggested here for investigating the structure of perceived attitudes bears certain similarities to projective instruments. However, such correlations characteristically range from .4 to .6. Such a relationship seems to indicate the possibility of assessing a person's own attitudes by giving him the seemingly objective task of estimating the opinions of others, but this is not the intent of the present experiment. The suggested procedure as it stands does not necessarily yield the structure of S's own attitudes or the actual structure of attitudes in others, but it does yield information about the ways in which people *perceive* attitudes "out there" in others. Two groups were used in the present experiment, which were thought to be diverse with respect to the attitudes involved. Any differences in the attitude configurations obtained from these groups might possibly be traced not only to differences in perception but also to differences in the *Ss'* actual attitudes which had been projected into the situation. Since the primary concern of the present study was with the perception of attitudes, the directions and the task were so formulated as to minimize the effects of projection. The success of this intention and the projective aspects of the task as formulated will be considered in a later section.

METHOD

In the present study a multidimensional method of successive intervals (1, 6) was applied to a set of attitude statements in an attempt to discover the number and the nature of the relevant dimensions perceived. The attitude statements were chosen from three of Thurstone's scales—attitude toward war, attitude toward capital punishment, and attitude toward the treatment of criminals. The procedure was applied using two diverse groups in an attempt to discover any differences which may exist in the structuring of these perceived relationships. The groups chosen for this purpose were a theological seminary class and an Air Force officer candidate class.

The Stimulus Statements and Their Experimental Presentation

Seven statements were selected from each of the three Thurstone scales on attitude toward war (9), attitude toward the treatment of criminals (17), and attitude toward capital punishment (8). These statements, which were selected in such a way as to be fairly evenly distributed over the favorable-unfavorable continuum for each of the three attitudes, are listed below.

1. On the whole, wars do the world some good.

2. Peace and war are both essential to progress.

3. War is sometimes necessary because right is more important than peace.

4. War has some benefits, but it's a big price to pay for them.

5. Although war is terrible, it has some value.

6. War is hardly necessary in the modern world.

7. There is no conceivable justification for war.

8. All criminals are victims of circumstances and deserve to be helped.

9. One way to deter men from crime is to make them suffer.

10. Correction is more effective than punishment in preventing crime.

11. Harsh imprisonment merely embitters a criminal.

12. Criminals must be punished.

13. Petty offenders can be reformed without punishment.

14. Failure to punish the criminal encourages crime.

15. The death penalty should be given for major crimes.

16. Capital punishment is good because it deters others from crime.

17. I think capital punishment is necessary but I wish it were not.

18. Until we find a more civilized way to prevent crime we must have capital punishment.

19. No thinking individual can believe in capital punishment as a method of preventing crime.

20. Criminals are pathological people who should be corrected, not executed.

21. The death of a comrade in prison embitters all the inmates against the state.

In this procedure, it is not at all necessary to use previously scaled attitude statements. Any other set of statements, scaled or otherwise, which was thought to be of possible relevance to the domain in question could have been used. The selection of previously used items for the present investigation was for the purpose of gaining some incidental information about the claimed unidimensionality of the Thurstone scales.

The statements were arranged in booklet form in order to make the task more amenable to group presentation. One statement was printed at the top of each page, followed by a list of statements at the left. To the right of each of these statements appeared a series of 11 boxes, with the first box labeled "Strongly Disagree," the sixth box labeled "Neutral," and the eleventh box labeled "Strongly Agree." The *S* was asked to imagine the type of person who would strongly agree with the statement at the top of the page and then to decide how this same person would also feel about each of the statements on the left. The *S* was then to indicate the extent of this person's agreement or disagreement with each statement by placing a cross in one of the boxes to the right. In constructing the booklet the order of appearance of the statements on each page and the order of the pages in the booklet was determined by random number techniques.

The Judgments Required

The multidimensional method of successive intervals requires that the subject arrange all possible pairs $[n(n-1)/2 = 210]$ of the 21 statements on a distance continuum according to the degree of relatedness or agreement shown between the members of each pair. In order to obtain judgments about perceived attitudes, the question of relatedness was set up in terms of the attitudes of some other person as described above. In terms of the multidimensional model this task can be considered as asking S to estimate the distance between Statements A and B, while located at A and looking at B. The reverse judgment for each pair of statements was also obtained in the present experiment, i.e., S was also asked to imagine the type of person who would strongly agree with Statement B and then to decide how this same person would also feel about Statement A. This task may be considered as judging the distance from Statement B to Statement A, while located at B and looking at A. Thus, the procedure requires two judgments for each of the 210 pairs of statements, making a total of 420 judgments required from each subject.

The two judgments of the same distance taken from opposite directions were obtained in the present experiment in order to see whether the data met one of the basic requirements of the multidimensional scaling model. The multidimensional attitude scaling model is an interpoint-distance model, i.e., attitude statements and people are represented in the same space by points. The extent of the individual's agreement or disagreement with the statements in the space is represented by the distance between the person and the statement. The person agrees with items close to him in any direction and disagrees with items far away. One property of this model, then, is that the probability of an affirmative response to any statement decreases as the distance between the statement and the person increases, without regard to direction. Statements selected by Thurstone scaling methods such as equal-appearing intervals, paired comparisons, or suc-

cessive intervals usually have this property. Such statements are commonly referred to as "point" statements, and the multidimensional scaling model can be properly applied only to such items. The requirement that the probability of an affirmative response should vary inversely with distance independent of direction is another way of saying that the distance between two points in Euclidean space should be the same in both directions.

In the present experiment, then, an attempt was made to see whether judgments of the same distance taken from opposite directions would come out similar. The two judgments elicited for each pair of statements were considered as independent estimates, and scale values were obtained for both the distances AB and BA for each pair. If the multidimensional scaling requirement that the distance between two points be the same in both directions is met by the data, the differences between corresponding AB and BA distances should be small. Systematic groupings of large differences would probably indicate the type of asymmetric relationships that might reasonably be expected to occur with cumulative items (4) as opposed to the symmetric relationships expected from point items. If a few large differences occur, then, the statements involved in these differences should be deleted from the study on the grounds of a failure to meet certain requirements of the model. However, great care should be exercised in evaluating these differences, since a few large discrepancies might occur by chance alone. Also, large differences would be expected for statement pairs at either extreme of the similarity scale, since such scale values are based on only a few cases and, hence, are very unstable.

The Subjects

The two diverse groups selected for this experiment were a seminary class and an Air Force officer candidate class. The seminary group consisted of 40 third-year male students at the Princeton Theological Seminary in Princeton, New Jersey. A regularly scheduled class hour had been made available for the purposes of this experiment, and the enlisting of Ss was put on a purely voluntary basis. Forty volunteers were obtained from the class, and the rest of the students were permitted to leave the room.

The Air Force group consisted of 82 male officer candidates who had just finished the first half of their O.C.S. training at Lackland Air Force Base, San Antonio, Texas.

No direct measure of the actual attitudes of these two groups was obtained in the present investigation for several reasons. Instead, attitude differences were inferred from the widely different backgrounds of the Ss. It seemed reasonable that factors which had led to such divergent career choices might also be reflected in divergent attitudes, especially in an attitude area dealing with war and punishment. However, the main reason why these actual attitudes were not "measured" in the present study was that it would have made it difficult, if not impossible, to obtain the cooperation of suitable populations of Ss, but other reasons did exist.

An investigation of the actual attitudes of these groups would have to be set up in multidimensional terms, not only to be comparable to the analysis of perceived attitudes, but also because some important differences between groups are probably reflected in relationships among dimensions rather than in responses to single scales. On the surface, then, the proper approach would appear to be to obtain responses to the three Thurstone scales, intercorrelate items, and factor-analyze. However, the vector model of factor analysis and the interpoint distance model of multidimensional scaling are not directly comparable (6), so the actual and perceived attitude structures could not be compared anyway.

RESULTS[1]

Each attitude booklet contained responses to 210 AB statement combinations and to 210 BA combinations. Each response, which was signified by a cross in one of a series of 11 boxes, indicated the judged extent of the imaginary other person's agreement with Statement B. This set of responses, 420 per booklet, constituted the raw data, which were analyzed separately for the seminary and Air Force groups.

The Seminary Group Data

The 420 combinations of statements were scaled by a graphical successive-intervals technique developed by Gertrude W. Diederich and described in (6). The 210 scale values for the AB statement-pairs represented the 210

possible distances among the 21 statements, all distances being estimated in one specified direction. The scale values for the 210 BA statement pairs represented the same distances, estimated in the opposite direction. There was adequate agreement between corresponding AB and BA values, so the two estimates were averaged for each distance. The general multidimensional scaling procedure described by Messick and Abelson (7) was then used to obtain a multidimensional configuration for these interstatement distances.

The end product of the multidimensional scaling procedure is a matrix of projections, which is analogous to the factor matrix of multiple-factor analysis. The rank of this matrix is equal to the dimensionality, r, of the Euclidean space defined by the experimentally obtained distances, and the elements of the matrix represent the projections of the statements on a set of r orthogonal axes placed at the centroid of the statements (13, 18). In the present experiment, this matrix of projections was of Rank 2, and when the two-dimensional configuration was plotted, two distinct streaks of points were evident. The structure was translated slightly in order to place the origin at the intersection of the streaks and then was rotated orthogonally until the largest streak of points was in a horizontal position. This particular orientation has the advantage of producing the maximum number of zero projections for this two-dimensional space, thus permitting a simple psychological interpretation. The rotated, translated configuration obtained from the seminary group appears in Figure 5.

The horizontal dimension in this figure contains all 14 statements from the scales of attitude toward the treatment of criminals and attitude toward capital punishment, and thus it represents a "propunishment vs. antipunishment" dimension. Statements 9, 12, 14, 15, 16, and to a slightly lesser extent 17 and 18 define the propunishment end of the continuum, and Statements 8, 10, 11, 13, 19, 20, and 21 define the antipunishment end. A "war" dimension is located obliquely to the "punishment" dimension at an angle of approximately 60°, with Statements 1, 2, 3, 4, and 5 lying in the prowar direction and Statements 6 and 7 in the antiwar direction. The 60° angle between the dimensions indicates a positive correlation between the prowar and propunishment attitudes perceived by the seminary group.

[1] The data, along with a complete description of analytical procedures, appear in the writer's dissertation (6).

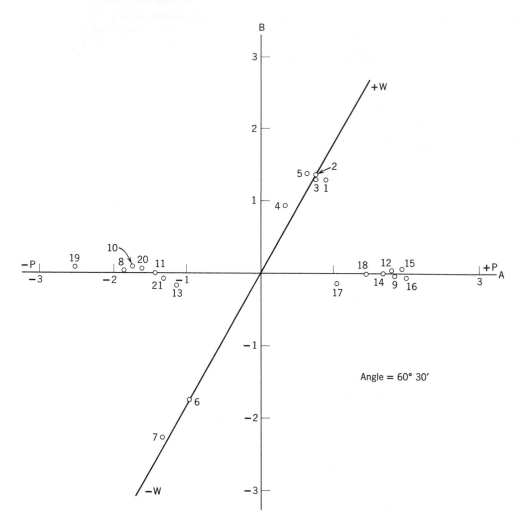

Figure 5. Dimensional configuration of 21 attitude statements for the theological seminary group.

The Air Force Group Data

The graphical scaling technique used to analyze the seminary data is a simple, quick iterative routine which yields a very good approximation to a computationally laborious least-squares solution for successive intervals, which was also developed by Diederich (see 6). After the seminary data had already been analyzed graphically, an IBM routine for the computational procedure was developed, so the Air Force data were treated according to the punched-card technique (15). When the 420 scale values obtained in this way were examined, it was again found that there was adequate agreement between corresponding AB and BA values, so the two estimates were averaged for each distance. The resulting 210 averages represented all possible distances

among the 21 statements. The general multidimensional scaling technique (7) was used to obtain the configuration of the statements, and the matrix of projections was again found to be of Rank 2.

Two distinct streaks of points were again evident in the two-dimensional configuration, and the structure was translated slightly and rotated orthogonally to the same orientation as for the seminary data. This rotated, translated configuration for the Air Force group appears in Figure 6. The horizontal factor in this figure represents a punishment dimension, having Statements 9, 12, 14, 15, 16, 17, and 18 in the propunishment direction and Statements 8, 10, 11, 13, 19, 20, and 21 in the antipunishment direction. A war dimension is located oblique to the punishment dimension at an

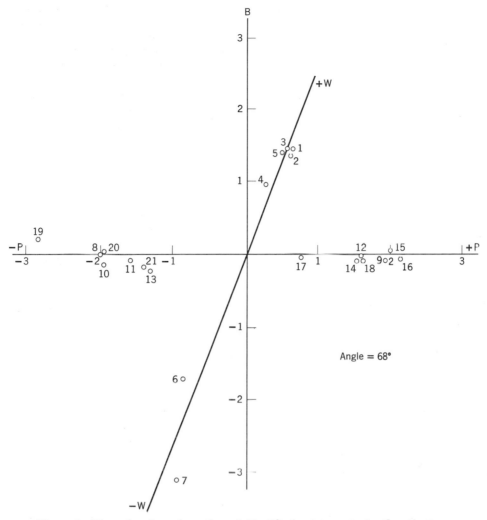

Figure 6. Dimensional configuration of 21 attitude statements for the Air Force officer candidate group.

angle of approximately 68°, with Statements 1, 2, 3, 4, and 5 lying in the prowar direction and Statements 6 and 7 in the antiwar direction. The 68° angle between these dimensions indicates a positive correlation between perceived prowar and propunishment attitudes for the Air Force group.

The two configurations described above can be considered to be adequate dimensional representations of the experimentally obtained distances, since, apart from small residuals, only two dimensions were necessary to account for relationships among 21 stimuli, and no indications of non-Euclidean properties were found, i.e., there were no markedly negative latent roots.

A Comparison of the Structures Obtained from the Seminary and Air Force Groups

A comparison between the final rotated structures obtained from the seminary and Air Force groups (Figure 5 vs. Figure 6) indicates an extremely high amount of agreement. It is quite evident from these figures that the two structures are essentially identical. The angle between the two dimensions in the seminary structure is 60°, while in the Air Force structure the angle is 68°. This shift in axis position is in an expected direction in terms of the probable differences between the "actual" attitudes of the Air Force and seminary groups. One might expect a theological seminary population to be more "humanitarian" than a military population. If this is the case, the "actual" attitudes of the seminary group would be expected to exhibit a higher correlation between antiwar and antipunishment attitudes than the "actual" attitudes of the Air Force group. If the "actual" attitudes of the Ss in this particular experimental situation affect attitutes as perceived in others, then the shift in axes toward a higher correlation for the seminary than for the Air Force group is in an expected direction. However, the angular difference of 8° is probably not significant.

DISCUSSION

The dimensional configurations obtained from both the seminary and Air Force groups certainly demonstrate that perceived relationships among attitudes toward war, capital punishment, and the treatment of criminals can be adequately represented in dimensional terms. Apparently, then, individuals do think of these attitudes as having a definite structure, and when asked to make judgments concerning attitude statements, they respond in terms of such dimensional frames of reference. The configuration obtained from both the Air Force and seminary groups is essentially the same as Type B given in Figure 2, with the war dimension drawn obliquely to the punishment dimension. Within this frame of reference, the two groups find it possible to conceive of people in each of the four quadrants, but it should be noted that certain kinds of people would be almost inconceivable to them. For instance, both groups would have difficulty in conceiving of a person who was in favor of capital punishment of extreme criminals and at the same time against punishing minor criminals.

The finding of an underlying structure in an attitude domain, when considered along with some of the specific properties of the structure, has important implications for attitude measurement and theory. Since one of the more reasonable ways to measure multidimensional attributes is to apply appropriate unidimensional scales along each of the dimensions involved, dimensional configurations such as those found in the present experiment would aid considerably, first of all, in determining the number and the nature of the relevant dimensions and, secondly, in selecting and evaluating the appropriate unidimensional scales. It is striking that the attitude statements in both

the Air Force and seminary structures form straight lines, indicating a unidimensionality in the original Thurstone scales, at least for the items considered in the present experiment. Similar studies investigating the linearity of other scales would be interesting and very important in justifying the use of these scales in attitude measurement. Another important aspect of these configurations is the fact that the scales on attitude toward capital punishment and attitude toward the treatment of criminals, which are admittedly similar in content but nevertheless had been independently established by equal-appearing interval techniques, should be perceived as precisely the same unidimensional continuum. This finding has important theoretical implications, since it suggests that different attitude variables, which had been separately abstracted on a priori grounds, can be reasonably thought of in terms of a single dimension. These results, however, pertain only to "perceived" attitudes and, no matter how suggestive they are, the structure of "actual" attitudes should be investigated before such a finding is incorporated into attitude theory. It well may be, for instance, that the "actual" attitudes of the Ss in the present experiment were three-dimensional, even though the groups *perceived* the attitudes in others in terms of a two-dimensional configuration. In other words, the results of the present study are immediately applicable to considerations of the ways in which individuals conceive of attitudes as being structured "out there," but further research is necessary before they may be applied to considerations of individuals' own attitudes. In any event, multidimensional analysis applied in attempts at a systematic understanding of the psychology of attitudes offers the hope that the host of trait names and labels in the attitude area can be represented in terms of a limited number of variables.

The high correlation between the configurations obtained from the Air Force and seminary groups indicates a definite similarity in the ways in which these groups perceive attitudes in this particular domain as being structured. It is not unreasonable that perceived attitude structures should be similar for two diverse groups, since similar frames of reference are important for efficient communication, but the essential identity of the two structures requires comment. Previous studies (5, 14, 16) have shown a persistent correlation between a person's own attitudes and his estimates of the attitudes of others. If the seminary and Air Force groups differ, as they probably do, with respect to attitudes toward war and punishment, the seemingly projective nature of the task of estimating the opinions of others would lead one to expect a difference between the structures obtained in the multidimensional analysis. However, the above studies are not really comparable to the present experiment, since they involved estimates of group opinion obtained from subjects who were themselves members of the group. Also, as Campbell (2, p. 23) has pointed out, ". . . in a group of any size, the respondent has an uneven acquaintanceship, and probably associates more with those of tastes like his own. Basing his estimates of group opinion upon his own experience in the group, his error may be in part a 'sampling bias' as well as biased perception."

The information supplied the subject in the present experiment was such as to be favorable to objective perception and unfavorable to projection. In one sense the information supplied was minimal; the other person, whose attitude relationships were to be estimated, was characterized only by complete agreement with a single statement. In the absence of a detailed characterization of the other person, the S evidently ascribed to his attitudes some kind of modal or average structure. It might be argued that minimal information is a favorable condition for eliciting projective responses, but the information supplied in the present case, although minimal in characterizing the other person, was quite specific concerning isolated aspects of his attitudes. A great deal of specific information is given to the subject when he is told that another person strongly agrees with the statement, "There is no conceivable justification for war," and it is not difficult to evaluate objectively the extent of this person's agreement with the statement, "On the whole, wars do the world some good."

Projection is favored by conditions of insufficient or conflicting information, but when specific and relevant information is available concerning a particular judgment, an objective response is probably favored.

SUMMARY

The primary purpose of this study was to see whether a set of perceived attitude relationships could be adequately represented in dimensional terms and, if so, to discover the number and the nature of the relevant dimensions involved. A secondary purpose was to investigate judgments made by two diverse groups in order to discover whether they perceive attitudes as being structured in different ways. Accordingly, a multidimensional method of successive intervals, which is a Euclidean distance model, was applied to judgments of attitude relationships. The procedure required S to arrange all possible pairs of a set of attitude statements on a distance continuum according to the degree of similarity of the members of each pair.

Seven statements were selected from each of the three Thurstone scales on attitude toward war, capital punishment, and the treatment of criminals, and these 21 statements were set up in booklet form for group presentation. The attitude booklets were administered to 40 third-year, male students at a theological seminary, and to 82 male Air Force officer candidates.

The multidimensional attitude structures perceived by the two diverse groups were essentially identical, the relationships among statements of the three attitudes being adequately represented in terms of two oblique dimensions, a war dimension and a punishment dimension. Apparently individuals do perceive attitudes, at least in this particular attitude area, in terms of a definite structure, and when called upon to make judgments concerning attitude relationships, they respond in terms of this dimensional frame of reference.

REFERENCES

1. Abelson, R. P. A technique and a model for multidimensional attitude scaling. *Publ. Opin. Quart.*, Winter, 1954-1955, 405-418.
2. Campbell, D. T. The indirect assessment of social attitudes. *Psychol. Bull.*, 1950, **47**, 15-38.
3. Gulliksen, H. A least squares solution for successive intervals assuming unequal standard deviations. *Psychometrika*, 1954, **19**, 117-139.
4. Guttman, L. A basis for scaling qualitative data. *Amer. sociol. Rev.*, 1944, **9**, 139-150.
5. Katz, M. R. A hypothesis on anti-Negro prejudice. *Amer. J. Sociol.*, 1947, **53**, 100-104.

6. Messick, S. J. The perception of attitude relationships: a multidimensional scaling approach to the structuring of social attitudes. Unpublished doctoral dissertation, Princeton Univer., 1954. Also, Princeton: Educational Testing Service, 1954.

7. Messick, S. J., and Abelson, R. P. The additive constant problem in multidimensional scaling. *Psychometrika*, 1956, **21**, 1-16.

8. Peterson, R. C. *Scale for the measurement of attitude toward capital punishment*. Chicago: Univer. of Chicago Press, 1931.

9. Peterson, R. C. *Scale for the measurement of attitude toward war*. Chicago: Univer. of Chicago Press, 1931.

10. Richardson, M. W. Multidimensional psychophysics. *Psychol. Bull.*, 1938, **35**, 659-660.

11. Saffir, M. A comparative study of scales constructed by three psychophysical methods. *Psychometrika*, 1937, **2**, 179-198.

12. Torgerson, W. S. A theoretical and empirical investigation of multidimensional scaling. Unpublished doctoral dissertation, Princeton Univer., 1951.

13. Torgerson, W. S. Multidimensional scaling: I. Theory and method. *Psychometrika*, 1952, **17**, 401-419.

14. Travers, R. M. W. A study in judging the opinions of groups. *Arch. Psychol.*, N. Y. No. 266, 1941.

15. Tucker, L. R., Messick, S., and Garrison, H. A punched card procedure for the method of successive intervals. Princeton: Educational Testing Service, 1954.

16. Wallen, R. Individual's estimates of group opinion. *J. soc. Psychol.*, 1943, **17**, 269-274.

17. Wang, C. K. A., and Thurstone, L. L. *Scale for the measurement of attitude toward the treatment of criminals*. Chicago: Univer. of Chicago Press, 1931.

18. Young, G., and Householder, A. S. Discussion of a set of points in terms of their mutual distances. *Psychometrika*, 1938, **3**, 19-22.

17. A Technique and a Model for Multi-Dimensional Attitude Scaling

ROBERT P. ABELSON

The majority of techniques for scaling attitudinal judgments or responses produce scales which are one-dimensional. The scale consists of a single continuum of opinion along which are located a succession of opinion items (or of people. This continuum generally ranges between pro- and anti- the attitudinal object. Examples of such one-dimensional techniques are Thurstone scales,[1] Likert scales,[2] paired comparisons scales,[3] successive intervals scales,[4] and Guttman scales.[5] It is apparent that in all of these methods the property of one-dimensionality has been forced on the scale by the choice of items and by the analytical method and by no means necessarily represents the dimensionality of the set of all commonly held attitudes in the domain. It is certainly true that in many attitude areas (religion, for example), different individuals may be favorable (or unfavorable) in different ways, on different levels, or for different reasons. For each of these scaling methods there exist procedures[6]

to determine the internal consistency of "scalability" of the final scale. If the scale is internally consistent, it is one-dimensional. But if it is not internally consistent, then items must be rewritten or discarded or the scoring manipulated in some fashion. The methods do not provide for multi-dimensionality of the material as an alternative to one-dimensionality, and this is an unfortunate limitation on the power of scaling methods. Lazarsfeld's latent class analysis[7] is non-dimensional, since it results in the specification of a number of discrete nominal classes of people which have no necessary relation to each other along one or more psychological continua. Coombs, meanwhile, has proposed ranking methods which are intended to yield multi-dimensional ordinal scales, but there is considerable doubt as to the practicality of the methods.[8] He cannot handle fallible data as yet. Anything but perfectly reliable judgments prevent the occurrence of a solution. Factor analysis has been used gingerly,[9] but is subject to some reservations.[10] Thus, in the study of attitudes,

• Reprinted from *Public Opinion Quarterly*, Winter, 1954-1955, 405-418, with permission of the author and the publisher. This study was conducted at Yale University as part of a coordinated program of research on attitude and opinion change, financed by a grant from the Rockefeller Foundation.

1 Thurstone, L. L., and E. J. Chave, *The Measurement of Attitude*. Chicago: Univ. of Chicago Press, 1929.

2 Likert, A., "A Technique for the Measurement of Attitudes," *Arch. Psychol.*, 1932, *No. 140.*

3 Thurstone, L. L., "Psychophysical Analysis," *Amer. J. Psychol.*, 1927, **38**, 268-389.

4 Saffir, M., "A Comparative Study of Scales Constructed by Three Psychophysical Methods," *Psychometrika*, 1937, **2**, 179-198.

5 Guttman, L., "The Cornell Technique for Scale and Intensity Analysis," *Educ. psychol. Measmt.*, 1947, **7**, 247-279.

6 Green, B. F., "Attitude Measurement," in G. Lind-
zey (Ed.), *Handbook of Social Psychology, Vol. I*, Cambridge: Addison Wesley Press, 1954.

7 Lazarsfeld, P. F., "The Logic and Mathematical Foundation of Latent Structure Analysis," in S. A. Stouffer, et al., *Measurement and Prediction*. Princeton: Princeton Univ. Press, 1950.

8 Coombs, C. H., "Theory and Methods of Social Measurement," in L. Festinger and D. Katz (Eds.), *Research Methods in the Behavioral Sciences*. New York: Dryden Press, 1953.

9 Eysenck, H. J., "Primary Social Attitudes as Related to Social Class and Political Party." *Brit. J. Soc.*, 1951, **2**, 198-209. Harris, C. W., "A Factor Analysis of Selected Senate Roll Calls," *Educ. Psychol. Measmt.*, 1948, **8**, 583-592.

10 Ferguson, G. A., "The Factorial Interpretation of Test Difficulty," *Psychometrika*, 1941, **6**, 323-329. Guttman, L., "The Problem of Attitude and

there is a dearth of satisfactory methods which permit a multi-dimensional analysis.

In psychophysics, however, multi-dimensional scaling methods have recently come into prominence (Richardson, Attneave, Torgerson).[11] These methods scale physical stimuli in a multi-dimensional psychological space. The fundamental concept involved is that of psychological *distance*. There is nothing to prevent the transference of multi-dimensional method from the psychophysical to the attitude domain. Social *distance* is a well-known social-psychological phrase.[12] Psychological distance is a concept employed in approach and avoidance gradient theory[13] and in Lewin's field theory.[14] We think we know what we mean by psychological distance. If psychological distances can be analyzed as though they were physical distances, it will be possible to obtain a "map" of the way in which an individual structures the similarities and differences among attitudes in a given domain. On such a map, short (psychological) distances would represent (psychological) similarity, or agreement, and long distances would represent dissimilarity, or disagreement. Multi-dimensional scales based upon the interpretation of dissimilarities or disagreements as distances have already been constructed with non-psychophysical stimuli (Klingberg,[15] and Osgood and Suci[16]).

There is a theorem due to Young and Householder which permits a multi-dimensional map to be constructed from a set of interpoint distances d_{jk} between each point j and every other point k.[17] Torgerson has given procedures for

obtaining the coordinates of n stimuli from the inter-stimulus distances when the data from which the distances are computed is not completely reliable.[18] The dimensionality of the space into which the stimuli are scaled is not fixed in advance; it is determined by the data, although an attempt is made to limit the dimensionality if the data is willing.

ANALYTICAL TECHNIQUE

Scaling Methods for Obtaining Inter-Stimulus Distances

N subjects judge the subjective dissimilarity of objects j and k on an m-point scale. A judgment of 1 indicates maximal similarity, a judgment of m indicates maximal dissimilarity, and the other integers cover the range in between.

It is desired to find S_{jk}, the scale value of the dissimilarity or distance between j and k. With n stimuli there are $\frac{1}{2} n(n-1)$ judgments to be made by each subject.

To construct a scale for one subject, take the judgment directly and call it S_{jk}. This procedure is bound to be insensitive and not highly reliable; however, precedent for treating integer judgments as though they formed a true interval scale (i.e., where the interval from 1 to 2 is equal to the interval from 2 to 3, etc.) is provided by Stephenson and by Osgood and Suci. Maps for single individuals were actually computed in connection with the experimental study reported in this paper. They are somewhat unstable due to the unreliability of single judgments, but are by no means unreasonable.

If the number of subjects is between 1 and 25 or thereabouts, equal-appearing intervals scaling can be used; that is, the median judgment of the N subjects for a stimulus pair is taken as S_{jk}. If, in computing the medians, the upper boundary of the first category is assigned the value 1 and the upper boundary of the mth category is assigned the value m, the scale values will have a possible range from $\frac{1}{2}$ to $m - \frac{1}{2}$.

With as many as 25 subjects (or, if they are available, many more than that) the method of successive intervals is a superior way to find the scale values from the m-category judgments. Variations of the method of successive intervals

Opinion Measurement," in S. A. Stouffer, et al., *Measurement and Prediction*, Princeton: Princeton Univ. Press, 1950.

[11] Richardson, M. W., "Multidimensional Psychophysics," *Psychol. Bull.*, 1938, **35**, 659-660. (Abstract). Attneave, F., "Dimensions of Similarity," *Amer. J. Psychol.*, 1950, **63**, 516-556.

[12] Bogardus, E. S., "Measuring Social Distances," *J. Appl. Sociol.*, 1925, **9**, 299-308.

[13] Miner, N., "Comments on Theoretical Models Illustrated by the Development of a Theory of Conflict," *J. Personal.*, 1951, **20**, 82-100.

[14] Lewin, K., *Principles of Topological Psychology*, New York: McGraw-Hill, 1936.

[15] Klingberg, F. L., "Studies in Measurement of the Relations Among Sovereign States," *Psychometrika*, 1941, **6**, 335-352.

[16] Osgood, C. E., and Suci, G. J., "A Measure of Relation Determined by Both Mean Difference and Profile Information," *Psychol. Bull.*, 1952, **49**, 251-262.

[17] Young, G., and A. S. Householder, "Discussion

of a Set of Points in Terms of Their Mutual Distances," *Psychometrika*, 1938, **3**, 19-22.

[18] Torgerson, W. S., "Multidimensional Scaling: I. Theory and Method," *Psychometrika*, 1952, **17**, 401-419.

have been offered by Saffir, Mosier, Edwards, Thurstone and Edwards, Gulliksen,[19] and in slightly different form, by Attneave and Garner and Hake.[20] Of these treatments, that of Thurstone and Edwards is perhaps the most readable, while that of Gulliksen is the most precise.

In both the equal-appearing and successive intervals methods, the scale values are determined save for an arbitrary constant. It is blandly assumed that zero is where it ought to be on the scale; that is, that a true psychological distance of zero would actually be represented as such by the scaling method. For the equal-appearing intervals method the range of scale values is from $\frac{1}{2}$ to $(m - \frac{1}{2})$. But with the successive intervals method, it is possible to get negative scale values by certain methods. If this happens it is imperative to add a constant to all values in such a way that the smallest scale value is some small arbitrarily chosen positive number. With this precaution, it is usually safe to set S_{jk}, the scale value, equal to d_{jk}, the distance. A more detailed discussion of the additive constant problem is presented elsewhere.[21] The entire multi-dimensional scaling procedure using successive intervals analysis is presented in great detail by Messick.[22]

EXPERIMENTAL STUDY

The Stimuli

Twelve statements relating to war, armaments and communism were used in the study. The statements are listed below.

19 Mosier, C. I., "A Modification of the Method of Successive Intervals," *Psychometrika*, 1940, **5**, 101-107; Edwards, A. L., "The Scaling of Stimuli by the Method of Successive Intervals," *J. Appl. Psychol.*, 1952, **36**, 118-122; Thurstone, L. L., and Edwards, A. L., "An Internal Consistency Check for the Method of Successive Intervals," *Psychometrika*, 1952, **17**, 169-180; Gulliksen, H., "A Least-Squares Solution for Successive Intervals Assuming Unequal Standard Deviations," *Psychometrika*, 1954, **19**, 117-139.

20 Garner, W. R., and H. W. Hake, "The Amount of Information in Absolute Judgments," *Psychol. Rev.*, 1951, **58**, 446-459; Attneave, F. A., "Method of Graded Dichotomies for the Scaling of Judgments," *Psychol. Rev.*, 1949, **56**, 334-340.

21 Messick, S., and Abelson, R. P., "The Additive Constant Problem in Multidimensional Scaling," *Psychometrika*, 1956, **21**, 1-16.

22 Messick, S., "The Perception of Attitude Relationships; A Multi-Dimensional Scaling Approach to the Structuring of Social Attitudes," Ph.D. Thesis, Princeton Univ., 1954.

Abbreviation

1. A very tough American policy toward Russia is a good idea, even if it leads to war. (Tough)
2. We should not fight Russia unless she commits direct aggression with her armed forces. (Fight only)
3. War is the only means of ridding the world of Communism. (Rid)
4. Concessions of territory to the Communists would be desirable if this prevented war. (Concessions)
5. There are many effective means to fight Communism without war. (Effective means)
6. War is a necessary and useful instrument. (War)
7. Peaceful relations with Russia should be sought by bargaining across the conference table. (Bargaining)
8. Communism is a greater force for good in the world than we have been led to believe. (Pro-Communism)
9. America should increase her present armaments enormously. (Arm)
10. War is tragic and terrible. (Peace)
11. America should reduce her present armaments substantially. (Disarm)
12. Communism is a false, dangerous ideology. (Anti-Communism)

The key statements in the study are numbers 6, 8, 9, 10, 11, and 12. These provide the endpoints for three anchoring dimensions—a Communism dimension, a War dimension, and an Armaments dimension. The other statements are felt to be anchored in these dimensions. A further hypothesis is that the Armaments dimension is a function of the War dimension and the Communism dimension. That is to say, armaments are instrumental to the value of Anti-Communism and to either the value of War or the value of Peace (depending on how one looks at it), and thus do not lead to an independent third dimension. It is probable that the dimensionality of an attitude map is equal to the number of independent value

TABLE 1

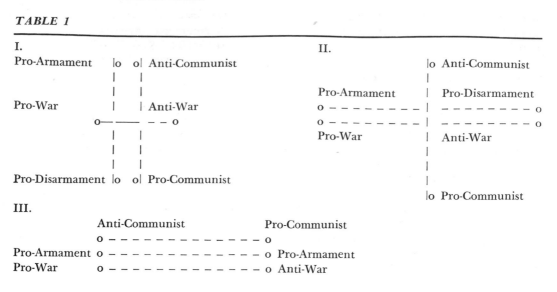

(The circles indicate the statements and the dotted lines hypothetical dimensions along which statements intermediate between the extremes would lie.)

systems covered by the attitude statements used, with statements instrumental to those values not increasing the dimensionality. (In the present study, it turns out that two factors are indeed sufficient.) Considering only the six anchoring stimuli, one might hypothesize three major typologies of final attitude map. These types are sketched in Table 1.

Type I might be called the Popular Conception: Armament is equated with Anti-Communism; Armament is unrelated to (at right angles to) a Pro-War attitude.

Type II would correspond to a Quaker philosophy: Armament is equated with being Pro-War, and Disarmament with being Anti-War; Armament is unrelated to Anti-Communism.

The armament dimension might lie at an intermediate angle between those depicted by Types I and II. Armaments could be seen as being both Anti-Communist and Pro-War, and as such, might constitute a conflicted attitudinal object.

Type III represents one solution to this possible dilemma—it is the solution provided by a preventive war: Anti-Communists are seen to be Pro-War, and Armaments are directly instrumental to both.

In order to decide whether these hypothesized typologies actually can be found in various samples of respondents, judgments were elicited from a group of one hundred Yale students (presumably representing a popular political position) and from a sampling in the New York area—fourteen students who are affiliated with the Socialist Party. (The political position of the Socialist Party is Anti-Communist but pacifistic.)

Method

Each subject was given the following instructions:

"For each pair of statements, say A and B, imagine two people having a discussion in which one of the two people makes statement A and the other person makes statement B. Make a judgment of the extent to which you feel that these two people are in agreement. Use an eight-point scale. A rating of 1 indicates maximum agreement, a rating of 8 indicates extreme disagreement, and 2, 3, 4, 5, 6, and 7 indicate intermediary degrees of agreement between these two extremes."

The subjects were also asked to state their own agreement or disagreement with each of the twelve statements on an eight-point scale. In addition to the similarity judgments and the personal agreements, thirteen political and social attitude items were administered. From the twenty-eight subjects scoring most politically conservatively were selected two random samples of fourteen subjects each to compare with the Socialist sample of fourteen subjects. A two-dimensional map was computed for each of these three groups.

RESULTS: I. COMPARISON OF DIFFERENT GROUPS

For each group, the set of median judgments of psychological similarity were manipulated according to Torgerson's procedure to produce the two-dimensional map. For purposes of comparability of the three groups, each map was translated and rotated in such a way that the war dimension lay along the x-axis with its mid-point at the origin.

The maps for the Socialist group and one of the two Conservative groups are presented in Figure 1.

Several interesting conclusions may tentatively be drawn from the mappings, although they do not conform very closely to the patterns hypothesized beforehand.

1. The maps are reliable. The two Conservative groups are more like each other than either is like the Socialists. (Thus the map for the second Conservative group has been omitted.)

2. The Socialists view Pro-War and Anti-Communist statements as being correlated. The angle between these two dimensions is 42°. For the two conservative groups, this angle is 61° and 67°, respectively, representing considerably less correlation.

3. The Armaments dimension is more closely associated with the War dimension for the Conservative groups than for the Socialist group.

4. The Socialists view statements 2 and 5 differently than do the Conservatives. Statement 2 is: "We should fight Russia only if attacked directly by her armed forces." Statement 5 is: "There are many effective means to fight Communism without War." The Socialists see these statements as farther removed from

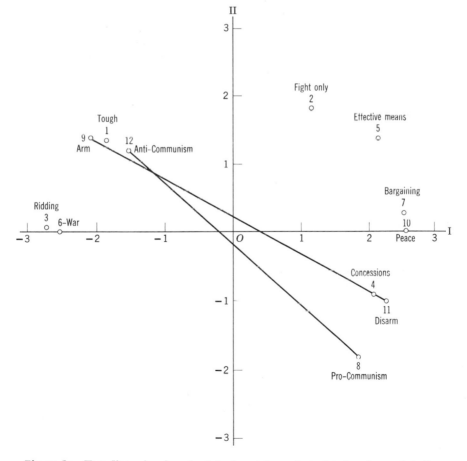

Figure 1a. Two-dimensional map of twelve statements (rotated and translated)—Socialists.

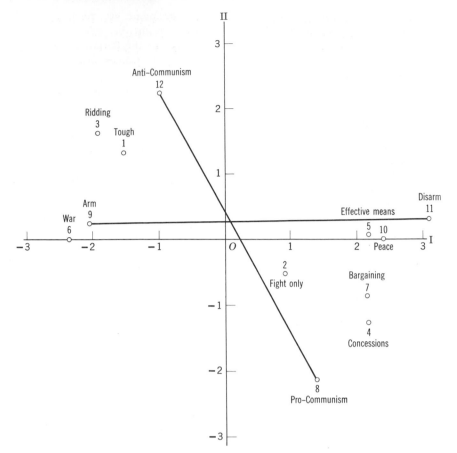

Figure 1b. *Two-dimensional map of twelve statements (rotated and translated)—Conservatives I.*

a simple Anti-War statement than do the Conservatives.

5. If the variance of the loadings in the Pro-War—Anti-War direction and the variance of the loadings in the direction orthogonal to this are calculated, the results are as shown in Table 2.

For the Socialists, a greater proportion of the variance is due to considerations associated with War and Peace. It might be inferred from this that War vs. Peace is proportionately more important to the Socialists than to the Con-

servatives. For the Socialists, the statements which contribute variance independent of this are chiefly No. 2 and No. 5. For the Conservatives, the independent variance is contributed mainly by the Pro- and Anti-Communist statements.

Results: Contour Maps

In the attitude maps discussed above, no mention was made of the groups' own personal agreements or disagreements with each single statement. It is possible to incorporate this

TABLE 2

	Variance Due to War Dimension	Variance Independent of War Dimension	Proportion Due to War Dimension
Socialists	18.08	4.83	0.789
Conservatives I	15.32	5.57	0.734
Conservatives II	15.12	5.42	0.736

information into the map directly. Each statement in the space can be assigned a "valence." Then the valence (with a sign and a magnitude) of any arbitrary point $P(x, y)$ in the space can be computed from the formula

$$V(P) = \sum_{j=1}^{n} \frac{V(j)}{1 + d^2{}_{Pj}} \qquad (1)$$

where $V(P)$ is the valence at the point P, $V(j)$ is the valence of statement j, and d_{Pj} is the distance from statement j to point P. The denominator is written $(1 + d^2{}_{Pj})$ so that the valences do not tend to infinity as the point P moves close to a statement j. In the present form, the valence at such a point will be the valence of j plus the individual contributions from the more distant points. This formulation assumes that there can be a discrepancy between the valence of a statement and the valence of the point in the psychological space which it occupies. Equation (1) is analogous to the equation for the electrical potential at a point in a field of electrical charges, except that $(1 + d^2)$ is used in place of simply d. Valence is analogous to potential.[23]

Carrying the analogy further, one can draw contours of equal valence in the attitude space. Of particular interest is the contour of zero valence, since it represents the locus of all potential statements toward which the subjects are neutral.

In the present study the valence of each statement for each experimental group was chosen as the median agreeableness M_j of the statement. Since a median of 4.0 presumably represents indifference (ratings of agreeableness were made on an eight-point scale), the formula employed was

$$V(j) = 4.0 - M_j \qquad (2)$$

Contour maps were constructed from Equations (1) and (2), aided by graphical interpolation. The maps for two of the three groups are presented in Figure 2. These are the same maps as in Figure 1, with contour lines added.

In reading these contour maps, a "hill" (a concentration of contours of high valence) is to be interpreted as a region in the attitude domain within which all statements or potential statements are highly regarded by the group.

[23] This model is reminiscent of Lewin's "life space" in that we have a cognitive map with valences operative within its boundaries. The map is a map of cognitions and not of the physical world, however. We have attempted here to build more quantative detail into such a map.

The valleys (concentrations of contours of low valence), are regions wherein all statements or potential statements are highly disfavored by the group. Detailed consideration of the possible significance of these contour maps leads to several sorts of propositions, of which four are presented here:

1. The steepness of the hills and valleys (the degree of bunching together of the contours) is an indicator of the *tension* in a region. Where the contour of zero valence lies in the middle of a region of high tension, strong *conflict* exists. (It is not possible to tell on the basis of the contour map alone whether such conflict is among the members of the group or applies intrapersonally to all members of the group.)

2. When two or more widely separated high hills exist, the domain can be said to be *unintegrated*. Vacillation in the attention of the group from the region of one hill to the region of the other hill or hills is likely.

3. If there is a large discrepancy between the valence of a statement and the valence of the surrounding region, particularly if the discrepancy involves valences of different signs, the situation is unstable; there is a *predisposition toward change* of the domain. That is, local *tension* (as defined in Proposition 1) exists. The change could come about through a change in valence of the statement or a change in its position, or else through compensatory changes in the valences and positions of nearby statements. This proposition suggests some of the ways in which multi-dimensional scaling might prove useful in attitude-change research.

4. The contour of zero valence, in general, intersects the line drawn between the opposite poles of any value dimension (e.g., War vs. Peace). The point of intersection divides the range of alternatives along that value dimension into those which the group approves and those which the group disapproves.

In applying these propositions to empirical contour maps, it is necessary to realize that a great many assumptions are involved in the construction and interpretation of these maps. The most doubtful assumptions are these:

(*a*) All attitude statements in the domain with strong valences have been represented among the list of statements given to the subjects for judgment. (The inclusion of important new statements might seriously alter the contours.)

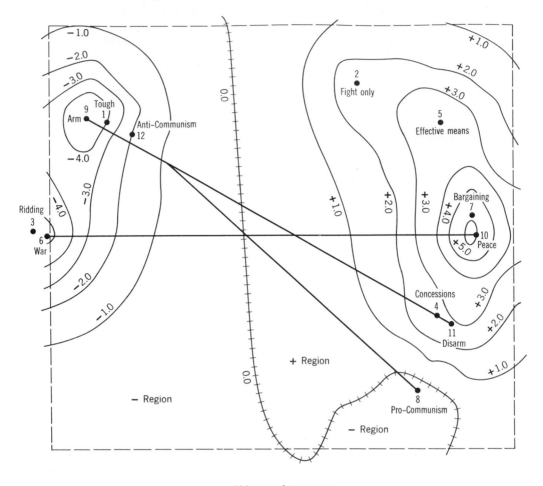

Valences of statements

1.	−2.8	7.	+3.2
2.	+2.1	8.	−1.8
3.	−3.4	9.	−3.3
4.	+0.2	10.	+3.3
5.	+3.2	11.	+2.7
6.	−3.6	12.	+1.5

Figure 2a. Contour map—Socialists.

(*b*) The statements in the domain are related to each other in the spontaneous thinking of the subjects and are not merely an aggregate of items thought to be logically related *by the experimenter* and represented to the subjects as a domain. (Thought processes of the "logic-tight compartment" type would not allow for the action of valences at a distance, though the present model assumes such action.)

Further qualifications which are probably less serious than (*a*) or (*b*) are these:

(*c*) Sampling errors and judgmental variabil-

ity are involved in the original similarity judgments and estimates of valence.

(*d*) The valence estimates are based on degree of agreement with the statements: no account is taken of the intensity of agreement.

(*e*) There is no guarantee that Euclidean geometry is appropriate to attitude scaling.

(*f*) The analytical procedure is only an approximation; while two dimensions may be generally adequate for the statements on the average, two or three statements may require a third dimension. It is furthermore possible that something analogous to the specificity of tests

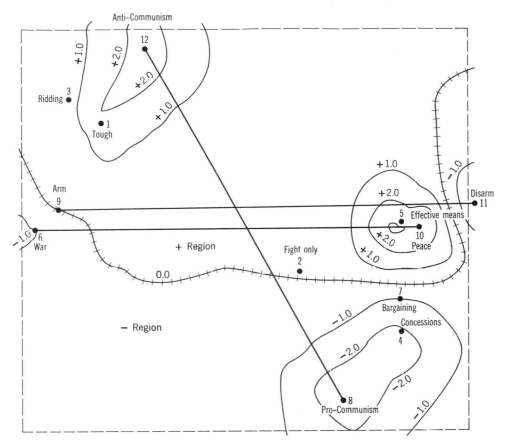

Valences of statements

1.	+1.6	7.	+0.4
2.	+0.2	8.	−2.9
3.	−0.8	9.	+1.2
4.	−3.1	10.	+3.4
5.	+1.8	11.	−3.4
6.	−2.2	12.	+2.9

Figure 2b. Contour map—Conservatives I.

in factor analysis should have been postulated. Each statement would then lie partially in a dimension of its own.

(g) Equation (1) might not be the best choice.

In spite of all these limitations, the maps at hand seem to be reasonably interpretable on the basis of the above propositions.

On the basis of Proposition 1, one infers that the Conservative groups are in greatest conflict over the statements concerning Peace, Bargaining, and Disarmament. The Socialists, on the other hand, show little or no conflict; only the statement concerning Communism lies on the opposite side of the zero valence contour near

a region of high tension. There are, nevertheless, three regions of very high tension surrounding the statements respectively concerning War, Armament, and Peace.

Proposition 2 suggests that the region of positive valence is much more highly integrated for the Socialists than for the Conservatives. However, notice that in the regions of negative valence, neither of the groups is completely integrated. It would be nice to be able to make the statement: "The Socialists know quite well what they are for, but are not of one mind as to what they are against, whereas the Conservatives know very well what they are against, but are not sure what they are for." This statement is almost, but not quite justified by the maps.

The attitude statements which are unstably located according to the terms of Proposition 3 are Nos. 3, 7, and 9 for the Conservatives I, Nos. 7 and 11 for the Conservatives II, and Nos. 4, 8, and 12 for the Socialists. The valences of all of these statements are substantially discrepant from the valences of the localities in which they lie.

Proposition 4 leads to very interesting results. Considering first the War vs. Peace value dimension, we find that the Conservative groups will accept all positions varying along this dimension except those that are very close to War. The Socialists, however, will only accept those that cover the half of the continuum nearest to Peace. On the Arm-Disarm dimension, the Conservatives will accept anything except a substantial reduction of armaments, whereas the Socialists highly favor a substantial reduction of armaments and would presumably accept at most a very slight increase of armaments. On the Anti-Communist through Pro-Communist dimension, the Conservatives approve of all positions on the Anti-Communist end and also of a small segment past the mid-point. On the other hand, the Socialists disapprove of positions at both extreme ends, favoring only a more neutral set of positions nearer the Pro-Communist end (although it must be remembered that the Anti-Communist statement is unstably located by the Socialists.)

SUMMARY

A mathematical technique for obtaining multi-dimensional attitude maps is discussed. It can be used with any number of subjects. The attitude space is to be thought of as a frame of reference in which various attitudes are embedded because of their meaningful connections with the values which anchor the frame of reference. The subjects are requested to judge the similarity of the members of pairs of attitude statements. High similarity or meaningful connection can be represented by small psychological distance and high dissimilarity by large psychological distance. The mathematical analysis converts sets of distances into a psychological space with each statement occupying a certain coordinate position.

The technique was applied to forty-two subjects. Twelve statements dealing with war, armaments and Communism were employed. Consistent differences were found between the attitude map of a group of Socialist subjects and the maps of two groups of politically conservative subjects. There is a discussion of some of the interesting insights into the attitudes of the subjects provided by the maps. These can be uncovered by postulating a kind of Lewinian force field model in which the various statements exert attractive and repulsive forces throughout the space.

18. Systematic Differences Between Individuals in Perceptual Judgments

LEDYARD R. TUCKER

OPTIMAL DECISIONS AND DIFFERENCES IN HUMAN JUDGMENTS

Human judgments and differences between individuals in making these judgments appear to enter the process of making optimal decisions in two major areas of consideration. In the first area there is the problem of the measure to be optimized. This may be a function of values and preferences of individuals. The second area involves the nature of operating systems and the laws of relations in these systems. Differences between individuals which exist in the perception and understanding of such systems influence the perception and interpretation of information available to the person about the present state of a system, about the dynamic changes and movements taking place within a system, and in the relations between a system and its surround (or environment). Further aspects of these differences between individuals are in anticipated effects that may result from possible actions. Such judgments, undoubtedly, affect the optimality of subsequent situations.

The major emphasis in this chapter is on methods for studying the structure of individual differences in judgments. Consider two logical extremes regarding individual differences. In one we might assert that every individual is like every other individual with perhaps some random effects in his judgmental process. In the other we could contend that every individual is unrelated to every other individual in his judgmental process. The first is a neat and tidy view—too neat and tidy. The second is chaos.

* Excerpted from an article in M. W. Shelly and G. L. Bryan (Eds.), *Human Judgments and Optimality*, John Wiley and Sons, New York, 1964, with permission of the author and the publisher.

It offers no promise for solution to problems of human judgments. Truth about the relations in human judgments among individuals in a population probably lies somewhere between these extremes. Undoubtedly the judgmental processes of individuals lie in some structured field, more complex than all being alike and not so diverse as to be chaotic. Knowledge of the structure of individual differences in this field should be important to the use of human judgments in optimal decisions.

Factor Analytic Procedure for Study of Differences in Perceptual Judgments

Several recent studies have used an adaption of factor analysis to study the structure of individual differences in perceptual structure. Factor analysis is a technique originally devised to study the structure of individual differences in intelligence and abilities. Possible adaptations have been explored for application in other areas; the present use is one of the latest.

Consider the mathematical outline in Figure 1. The observed data is indicated in the table in the upper section. For the present use, pairs of stimuli are considered from a list of stimuli and a measure of the perceived difference between the stimuli in each pair is obtained for each individual. There is a column for each individual. For example, in a study by Helm and Tucker (1962), "Individual Differences in the Structure of Color-Perception," Helm obtained measures of the relative perceived differences by Torgerson's multidimensional-triad ratio-scaling procedure between pairs of colors for 10 colors painted on porcelain disks. In multidimensional scaling such measures are considered as distances between points in a space representing the structure of perception. In the procedure used interpoint distances were obtained for each in-

Observed interpoint distances

Individuals

		1	2	3	. . .	10
	1–2	$d_{1\text{-}2,1}$	$d_{1\text{-}2,2}$	$d_{1\text{-}2,3}$	. . .	$d_{1\text{-}2,10}$
	1–3	$d_{1\text{-}3,1}$	$d_{1\text{-}3,2}$	$d_{1\text{-}3,3}$	. . .	$d_{1\text{-}3,10}$
Stimulus pairs	. . .	. . . .				
	1–10	$d_{1\text{-}10,1}$	$d_{1\text{-}10,2}$	$d_{1\text{-}10,3}$	. . .	$d_{1\text{-}10,10}$
	2–3	$d_{2\text{-}3,1}$	$d_{2\text{-}3,2}$	$d_{2\text{-}3,3}$	. . .	$d_{2\text{-}3,10}$
	. . .	. . . .				
	2–10	$d_{2\text{-}10,1}$	$d_{2\text{-}10,2}$	$d_{2\text{-}10,3}$	. . .	$d_{2\text{-}10,10}$
	. . .	. . . .				
	9–10	$d_{9\text{-}10,1}$	$d_{9\text{-}10,2}$	$d_{9\text{-}10,3}$	. . .	$d_{9\text{-}10,10}$

Factor coefficients for stimulus pairs

Factors

		I	II
	1–2	$a_{1\text{-}2,\text{I}}$	$a_{1\text{-}2,\text{II}}$
	1–3	$a_{1\text{-}3,\text{I}}$	$a_{1\text{-}3,\text{II}}$
	. . .	. . . .	
Stimulus pairs	1–10	$a_{1\text{-}10,\text{I}}$	$a_{1\text{-}10,\text{II}}$
	2–3	$a_{2\text{-}3,\text{I}}$	$a_{2\text{-}3,\text{II}}$
	. . .	. . . .	
	2–10	$a_{2\text{-}10,\text{I}}$	$a_{2\text{-}10,\text{II}}$
	. . .	. . . .	
	9–10	$a_{9\text{-}10,\text{I}}$	$a_{9\text{-}10,\text{II}}$

Factor coefficients for individuals

Individuals

		1	2	3	. . .	10
Factors	I	$x_{\text{I},1}$	$x_{\text{I},2}$	$x_{\text{I},3}$	. . .	$x_{\text{I},10}$
	II	$x_{\text{II},1}$	$x_{\text{II},2}$	$x_{\text{II},3}$	. . .	$x_{\text{II},10}$

Approximation formula

$$\hat{d}_{j\text{-}k,i} = a_{j\text{-}k,\text{I}}x_{\text{I},i} + a_{j\text{-}k,\text{II}}x_{\text{II},i}$$

Figure 1. Outline of analysis model.

dividual and were recorded in a table (see Figure 1). There was a row for each pair of colors and a column for each individual.

Once a table of interpoint distances is compiled, a question can be raised about the similarity or differences of entries in the several columns. If all individuals were perceiving the differences between stimuli alike, each column would be like every other column. In matrix algebra terminology this matrix of interpoint distances would be of rank 1. A random effect would merely add random discrepancies. If there were two kinds of people with separate perceptual systems, the columns in the table of

interpoint distances could be sorted so that those in one section would be alike and those in a second section would be alike, but the columns in the two sections would differ between sections. This would be a special case of a rank 2 matrix. For example, in the study by Helm and Tucker there were 10 individuals with normal color vision, indicated by standard color vision tests, and four who were colorblind. We expected that possibly the 10 with normal color vision would form one group and the four color-blind individuals would form a second group. This expectation was borne out only in part. The color-blind individuals did tend to form a separate group, but those with normal color vision did not do so. There was considerable nonrandom variation in the results among those with normal color vision so that the columns of observations formed a progression from one type to a second. The matrix for normal color vision is a more general example of a matrix of rank 2.

The method of analysis used does not depend on finding separate groups or orders among the columns of the table of interpoint distances. It is a procedure related to principal axes factor analysis and is based on a development by Carl Eckart and Gale Young (1936) for the approximation of one matrix by another of lower rank. The tables of factor coefficients and the approximation formula in Figure 1 are laid out for a rank 2 approximation. A table of factor coefficients for stimulus pairs appears in the middle section of Figure 1, and a table for individuals appears in the bottom section. According to the approximation formula at the bottom of the figure, the coefficient for a stimulus pair on factor I is multiplied by the factor coefficient for an individual on factor I. A similar product of coefficients for factor II is formed, and the sum of these two products is obtained. This yields the approximation to the interpoint distance for the selected stimulus pair and individual. For a rank 1 approximation there would be only one column of factor coefficients for the stimulus pairs, one row of factor coefficients for the individuals, and one term or product in the approximation formula. For a rank 3 approximation there would be three columns for the stimulus pairs, three rows for the individuals, and three products in the approximation formula. In this method of analysis an approximation of each rank is tried, and the sum of squares of errors of approximation is determined. A higher ordered approximation is used if it results in a somewhat lower sum of squares of discrepancies than an approximation of rank one less. One of the unsolved problems is the development of a satisfactory decision formula for determining the rank of approximation to be used. In the color discrimination data three factors appeared to be needed to account for the facts observed. The approximation accounted for 98% of the sum of squares of the original data, and the sum of squares of discrepancies accounted for the remaining 2%.

A convenient geometric analogy interprets each row of the table of factor coefficients for individuals as giving the coordinates of points for the individuals on one dimension. Thus, if there are two rows in this table, each individual may be represented as a point in a two-dimensional space. Consider Figure 2. There is a sim-

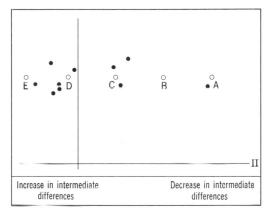

Figure 2. Factor structure for individuals. Color discrimination data.

ilar figure for individuals of normal color vision in the Helm and Tucker study. When the data for all subjects were analyzed, three dimensions were needed. However, the three-dimensional space could be viewed so that one dimension had only color-blind individuals with nonzero coordinates. Figure 2 presents the remaining two dimensions. All individuals have nearly equal positive coordinates on axis I, the vertical axis. The coordinates on axis II, the horizontal axis, range from a sizable positive value to smaller negative values. Points for the observed individuals are the blackened circles. The open circles represent hypothesized individuals and are discussed shortly. If there had been two groups of individuals, the observed points would have appeared in two corresponding clusters. The progression from one type of perception of stimulus pair differences, or interpoint distances, corresponds to a series of observed

points running from one side to the other, as in Figure 2. Both configurations can be represented in a two-dimensional space which corresponds to a rank 2 approximation of the interpoint distances. A common terminology is to equate the rank of the approximation to the dimensionality of the space and speak of a two-dimensional approximation, a three-dimensional approximation, etc.

IDEALIZED INDIVIDUALS: DEFINITION AND DESCRIPTION

Having found that it is necessary to use two dimensions to represent the judged interpoint distances between the colors by normal-visioned subjects, we are faced with an interesting and important question: what is the nature of these differences in perception? To answer this question, the hypothesized individuals indicated by open circles in Figure 2 were chosen to represent the progression of perceptions by the normal-visioned individuals. These hypothesized individuals are frequently termed "idealized individuals." For each idealized individual the coordinates in the space formed a new column of factor coefficients for individuals, and interpoint distances for stimulus pairs were computed by the approximation formula in Figure 1 by using the experimentally determined factor coefficients for stimulus pairs. If the interpoint distances for a given idealized individual have been determined, the methods of multidimensional scaling may be applied to gage the nature of the corresponding perceptual space. In this space the stimuli are represented by points at distances from one another equal to the observed interpoint distances. For example, if the distance from stimulus A to B is one unit, from stimulus B to C, four units, and from stimulus A to C, five units, these interpoint distances can be represented by placing all three stimuli on a straight line, since the distance from A to C is equal to the sum of the distances from A to B and from B to C. If the three interpoint distances were three, four, and five units, the stimuli would be at the corners of a right triangle. For more stimuli it may be necessary to use more than two dimensions in the perceptual space to represent the observed interpoint distances.

Idealized Individuals in Color Discrimination

For the color-discrimination data there was a major two-dimensional perceptual space for each of the idealized individuals, with the 10 colors forming a more or less circular pattern as expected from the selection of colors, the stimuli having been selected from one plane of the color pyramid to form a circle of the different hues. The most perfect fit to the interpoint distances by this two-dimensional pattern was found for idealized individual C. Discrepancies in interpoint distances, as approximated by the circular perceptual space for the other idealized individuals, produced an interesting progression. Idealized individual E corresponded to an overstatement of the intermediate-sized interpoint distances. For example, the interpoint distance between a red and a yellow was large for idealized individual E when compared with the distance between the red and a green. For idealized individual A the reverse tendency was indicated; the intermediate-sized interpoint distances were understated.

Implications of the individual differences among individuals of normal color vision for optimal decisions is worthy of further study. It might be found that people like idealized individual E could make sharper matches of new colors to standard colors or to colors of existing objects. People like idealized individual A might be better able to pick out complementary colors. A possible consequence is that different individuals would make better optimal decisions based on judgments of colors dependent on the task.

A STUDY OF PERCEPTION OF POLITICAL THINKING

In a second study to be reviewed Tucker and Messick (1963) used judgments of perceived similarity of political thinking of prominent people, such as Roosevelt, Dewey, Talmadge, McCarthy, Douglas, Hitler, Nehru, and Stalin. There were 20 men on the list. Each person chosen as a subject was asked to judge the amount of similarity-dissimilarity in political thinking for each pair of men. These ratings were used directly as interpoint distances. A total of 39 subjects, all undergraduates at the University of Illinois, took part in this study and were selected from a larger group who made the ratings and answered a questionnaire about their political views. In choosing the subjects, an attempt was made to obtain a wide variety of political views. The analysis of the individual differences in the ratings yielded a three-dimensional space in which the coordi-

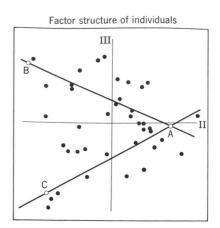

Factor structure of individuals

Figure 3. Political relations data. Interpretation for idealized individuals. A. One dimension: United States men versus foreign men. B. Two dimensions: (1) Republican-Democrat; (2) good-bad. C. Possibly seven dimensions of rather complex structure. Abstracted from Ledyard R. Tucker and Samuel Messick (1963).

nates on the first dimension bore nearly equal positive values. Figure 3 presents the plot between the second and third dimensions. An interesting feature of this plot is the approximate triangular dispersion of the points for which there is no apparent explanation. Three idealized individuals were selected, as indicated in Figure 3, A near the heaviest cluster of observed individuals, B toward the upper left, and C toward the lower left. The only trend related to the political views of the subjects is that a larger portion of the liberal democrats favoring labor are closer to idealized individual B than the other idealized individuals.

The perceptual spaces for the three idealized individuals offer interesting comparisons. For idealized individual A there was only one dimension in the perceptual space, with the men from the United States clustered at one point and the foreign men at another. One must conclude that many of the undergraduate students made only this rather crude distinction between the political figures used in the study. Idealized individual B discriminated between Republicans and Democrats and made a second discrimination that seemed to be based on an evaluative judgment. This second dimension of the perceptual space separated Joseph Stalin, Adolf Hitler, Alger Hiss, Henry Wallace, and Senator McCarthy from the rest. It must be remembered that this view is shared by a number of liberal Democrats, which may account for the inclusion of McCarthy in this dimension. The perceptual space for idealized individual C is rather complex and involves rather particularized distinctions of a larger number of dimensions. It may be that the direction in the space of individuals in Figure 3 away from the A–B line toward idealized individual C represents overstatements of intermediate differences which make many of the stimuli appear further apart and increase the dimensionality of the perceptual space.

A STUDY OF PERCEPTION OF RELATIONS AMONG PERSONALITY TRAITS

Darhl Pedersen (1962) studied for his PhD dissertation the perceived personality trait relationships of two samples of 50 undergraduate students plus 160 others who answered the questionnaires. The central questionnaires listed a sample of 600 stimulus pairs drawn from the 1225 pairs generated from 50 trait names. Ratings were on a scale from opposite through unrelated to same. Factor coefficients for individuals determined for each sample of 50 subjects

on half the pairs judged were extended to estimates of the coefficients for all 260 subjects in the study. This permitted an evaluation of the reliability of the results determined by using different subjects and different trait pairs in the factor analysis. For three major factors the reliability correlations were more than .80. Figure 4 presents the plot between dimensions II and III for all subjects. As in the preceding studies, the points were all positive on dimension I. Again, as in the political relations data, three idealized individuals were chosen, and the nature of the perceptual space was investigated. The space for idealized individual A, for which the coordinate on dimension I was high, appeared to be the standard stereotype for relations between the traits. Idealized individual B had a high coordinate on dimension II and represented a distortion of the stereotype wherein many items, for which the stereotypical view was that the adjectives in each item were unrelated, the distortion was to judge the adjectives more opposite in meaning. We might speculate about the relations between this di-

Factor structure of individuals

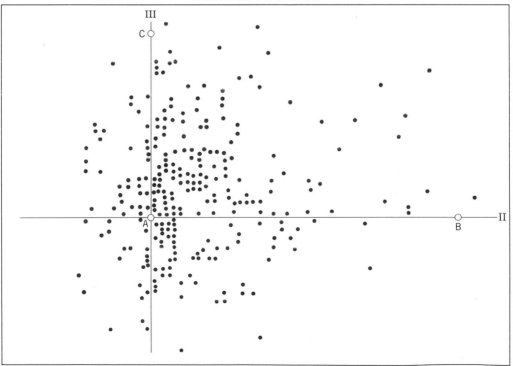

Figure 4.   Trait relations data. Interpretation for idealized individuals. A. Standard stereotype of trait relations. B. Response set increasing dissimilarity between related trait pairs. C. Authoritarian point of view. Abstracted from Darhl M. Pedersen, 1962.

mension and the dimension differentiating people with normal color vision and the dimension toward idealized individual C in the political relations study. All three dimensions appear to represent transformation of the intermediate relations.

Dimension III in Pedersen's study is especially interesting. There are indications that it represents the view of people with authoritarian personalities. Pedersen obtained a number of measures on the subjects in his study, and correlations were calculated between these measures and the individual coefficients on the three dimensions of individual differences. Correlations with all outside variables for dimensions I and II were quite low. However, dimension III correlated negatively with ability measures and scientific interest (in the Kuder Preference Record) and positively with content scores on authoritarianism, as measured by the California F Scale and derived questionnaires. Shifts in the perceptual space involved the traits characterized by the following adjectives: dishonest, weak, passive, submissive, rational, predictable, aggressive, domineering, defensive, and uninteresting. Important among these shifts is that domineering became positively related to honest, stable, and rational and negatively related to others, such as tense, selfish, and insensitive. Being rational was less like being intelligent and more like being unpredictable, domineering, active, interesting, and brave. Being aggressive shifted from being similar to selfish, tense, and unsociable toward being similar to unselfish, honest, mature, and sociable. Defensive developed a positive relation to strong, mature, interesting, honest, and graceful. Passive was no longer opposite to aggressive and developed stronger connotations. This certainly represents a change in the standard stereotype view and could lead to different perceptions of situations among people. It could also lead to different expectations regarding the results of actions taken in various situations relating to the reactions of people.

CONCLUSION

These studies form a beginning on the study of individual differences in the structures of perceptions by people. They provide a new use for several multivariate statistical methods, especially factor analysis, in the study of the structure of individual differences in areas of psychological phenomena such as perception and judgments in the world around the individuals. Numerous implications are concerned with the relation of human judgments to making optimal decisions. Not only is the variable to be optimized a function of human judgments, subject to individual differences in values and preferences, but the perception of situations is a function of human judgment and is also subject to individual differences in interpretation and perception. There is a further possibility that there are differences in the conception of the nature of laws of relations and determination in dynamic systems. These, too, should affect the making of decisions from which we hope to obtain optimal results.

REFERENCES

Eckart, C., and Young, Gale. The approximation of one matrix by another of lower rank. *Psychometrika*, 1936, **1**, 211-218.

Helm, C. E., and Tucker, L. R. Individual differences in the structure of color-perception. *Am. J. Psychol.*, 1962, **75**, 437-444.

Pedersen, Darhl M. *The measurement of individual differences in perceived personality trait relationships and their relation to certain determinants. Doctoral dissertation.* University of Illinois, 1962.

Tucker, L. R., and Messick, S. Individual differences in multidimensional scaling. *Psychometrika*, 1963, **28**, 333-367.

C. Alternative Measurement Techniques

19. The Indirect Assessment of Social Attitudes

In the problem of assessing social attitudes, there is a very real need for instruments which do not destroy the natural form of the attitude in the process of describing it. There are also situations in which one would like to assess "prejudice" without making respondents self-conscious or aware of the intent of the study. At the present time there are few if any indirect tests which could confidently be used for either of these purposes. There are, none the less, a considerable number of techniques that have been partially explored and validated. It is the purpose of this paper to survey such techniques and to present a point of view with regard to the problem of indirect measurement.

Current interest on the part of social psychologists in the indirect assessment of attitudes is perhaps primarily an aspect of the larger projective test movement in personality study. However, as will be seen in the course of this survey, there has been an interest in this approach from the very first efforts in attitude measurement (81), anticipating by some ten years the current interest in "projective techniques."

The terms "indirect" and "projective" have been used to refer to both *disguised*, and to *non-structured* measurement efforts. Using these two terms alone, one could distinguish four types of tests:

1. *Non-disguised-structured:* the classic direct

* Reprinted from *Psychological Bulletin*, 1950, 47, 15-38, with permission of the author and the American Psychological Association.

attitude tests of Thurstone (78), Likert (49), *et al.*

2. *Non-disguised-non-structured:* the free-response interview and questionnaire approaches, the biographical and essay studies.

3. *Disguised-non-structured:* the typical "projective" techniques.

4. *Disguised-structured:* tests which approximate the objective testing of attitudes.

It is with the latter two categories that the present review is concerned, although some items that properly belong in category 2 will be included where they represent deliberate efforts at "projective" attitude testing.

While a formal division of content on these two criteria suffices, the writer will, in discussion, use a third which overlaps but does not duplicate the other two. This third criterion is that of dependence upon voluntary self-description as opposed to diagnosis based upon differential performance in an objective task. Upon this latter criterion rather than "structuredness" will rest the primary distinction between our two types of methods.

DISGUISED-NON-STRUCTURED TESTS OF SOCIAL ATTITUDES

In this category are included those techniques which offer the respondent opportunity for the spontaneous expression of attitudes in an ambiguous or non-structured setting. Most of these techniques are borrowed quite directly from well established clinical tools, and will be classified on that basis.

Approaches Based on the Thematic Apperception Test

Though by no means the first, the indirect test most widely cited in previous surveys of the literature (18, 42, 54, 82) is that of Proshansky (65). He intermingled ambiguous pictures of labor situations with the more usual T.A.T. scenes. The pictures were presented to a group by means of slides, with each person being asked to write for two and one-half minutes on what he thought the slide represented. Slides were shown for only five seconds. Proshansky found that ratings made from the resulting descriptions correlated .77 and .67 with a direct verbal scale of attitudes toward labor. A more elaborate proposal for the use of a similar technique with attitudes toward Negroes and Jews has been made (51), but as yet, no results are available.

Specially designed Thematic Apperception pictures have also been used by Frenkel-Brunswik, Sanford and Levinson in their extensive study of the personality correlates of prejudice (24). In this research the purpose was not so much to measure prejudice as to get a more detailed and qualitative picture of its expression. Nevertheless, the complicated interrelationships they found qualify the use of such pictures as attitude measuring instruments. For example, many prejudiced women told warmer and more sympathetic stories to a picture of a Negro mammy than they did to pictures of an elderly white woman (23). While such a finding is consistent with personality theory, it points to the danger of an over-simplified one-to-one interpretation of such material.

Essentially identical in technique is the "Human Relations Test" developed by the staff of the College Study in Intergroup Relations (15). This consists of ten drawings, each portraying an ambiguous intergroup contact. For example, a crowded street-car scene and a basketball scene are used. The respondents are asked to write a short story about each scene, telling what happened, how it came about, and what will happen next. The test is available on printed cards or projection slides, and since it is being used by a number of cooperating colleges, and at a wide variety of age levels, there is some promise of a standardized test emerging.

Johnson (39) has successfully studied the development of Anglo-Spanish attitudes in the Southwest through stories told by children to a specially designed series of pictures. He used six carefully selected conflict situations. These were duplicated in three forms: with all Anglo characters (for use with English-American children), with all Spanish characters (for use with Spanish children), and with mixed Anglo-Spanish characters (for use with both groups). Attitudes were assessed by contrasting responses to identical situations when they involved Anglo-Spanish conflict and when depicted by their own group members only. Quantification was achieved by having two judges categorize individual responses on a number of dimensions. Reliability coefficients for six sub-groups were over .90.

Approaches Utilizing Doll Play Techniques

In the first explicit attempt to use a projective technique in the assessment of social attitudes, Dubin (19) utilized toys in a fashion similar to the "play techniques" of the clinical psychologist. Using ten adult respondents, he asked them to "construct on this table a dramatic scene or scenes of the world as you see it today" and later "Now make a dramatic scene or scenes of the world as you would like it to be." From report and pictures of these scenes, three judges were able to estimate answers on 21 direct attitude questions dealing with labor, the Negro, internationalism, etc. with an average rank order correlation of .49.

For use with children, Arnold Meier has developed an interviewing aid, the "What Would You Do?" test, which is "projective" in the present sense. Doll cut-outs including minority children are manipulated on background drawings which depict such situations as entering the home, school scenes, etc. (15).

Similar to these approaches is the "movie story game" developed by Evans and Chein (21) for use with children from eight to twelve. On a miniature stage, Negro and white dolls are manipulated, with the child being asked at various points what the identified doll would say. Particular attention is paid to the patterning of segregation responses with acquaintances and with strangers. Preliminary studies indicate effective disguise and general meaningfulness for the test.

Hartley and Schwartz (33) have combined doll-play with pictorial material in the investigation of intergroup attitudes of children five to seven years of age. Montage background compositions carried characteristic symbols of Jewish religion in one case, Catholic in another, and in a third indicated typical middle class surroundings with no indication of religion. Identical family sets of dolls were placed upon these three backgrounds, and all were available for use by the child in playing out situations, such as a birthday party, school bus, meals, etc. In the preliminary report it is indicated that children identify with some accuracy the religious symbols, and that their play indicates intergroup attitudes in a meaningful way.

Sentence Completion Tests

At the Ohio State University, Shirley Wilcox Brown is using a modification of Rotter's test (68) in investigating attitudes toward the Negro. A 40-item schedule has been prepared, in which are imbedded some 20 sentence fragments dealing specifically with the Negro problem. Examples of relevant and neutral items are as follows:

1. I feel . . .
2. Skin color . . .
3. I hate . . .
4. Maybe . . .
5. Some lynchings . . .
6. The K.K.K. . . .
7. It seems to me that segregation . . .
15. Negro body odor . . .
37. Racial intermarriage . . .

In this test, no real effort at dissembling is made. The cooperating respondent is asked to volunteer a description of his own attitudes, with no more disguise than in the direct tests. The instructions read "Complete these sentences to express *your real feelings.* Try to do every one. Be sure to make a complete sentence!" Preliminary applications of the test indicate its power to discriminate between criteria groups. Scoring has been done by both coding and rating procedures. The indications are that the test can provide a reliable measure of attitudes.

Another twist to the sentence completion notion is being used in the study of personality and prejudice among school children conducted by Else Frenkel-Brunswik and Harold E. Jones (22). Here the test avoids all mention of minority groups, but provides stereotypic statements which may be completed with names of various minority groups or others. Examples of items are:

Are there some people who are mean? WHAT PEOPLE?

It would be better if more of a certain type of people were allowed to come into the United States. WHAT PEOPLE?

Some people are poor and it is their own fault. WHAT PEOPLE?

This test has elicited mention of foreign and minority groups from about one third of the children to which it has been administered. From another third or so come one or more anti-prejudice statements. A portion of the students make no responses classifiable in either way, and are thus not effectively evaluated. Using a net score (subtracting anti-prejudice responses from the total of prejudiced ones) corrected reliability figures run around .6 to .8 and correlations with a highly reliable direct test are on the order of .5. The approach is most satisfactory for the comparison of groups of respondents, and for the evaluation of the relative salience and extremity of attitudes toward different minority groups. In addition, unique data on the uniformity of stereotyping are provided.

While these two sentence completion tests make a deliberate effort to achieve a projective or indirect character, they are not too different from any free-response questionnaire on attitudes. Compare, for example, Zeligs' approach in which school children were asked to "write the most interesting true sentence" they knew about each group, within a one minute limit (84).

Miscellaneous Non-Structured Techniques

The Rosenzweig Picture Frustration Test has also been modified for the measurement of social attitudes, a task to which it is obviously appropriate. This test requires the respondent to fill in the balloons in a series of cartoon drawings involving frustrating face-to-face intergroup contacts (6).

Probably belonging within the limits of our general category is the study by Fromme (25). He presented to the respondents five political cartoons, each with four alternative captions, covering a wide range of pro and con opinion. The respondent was asked to pick the best caption, and this choice, plus the discussion resulting, was utilized in a qualitative analysis of attitude structure.

The procedures just discussed are all indirect and "projective" in current usage of the terms. At the risk of some oversimplification, the assets they have in common may be emphasized and the stage set for contrasting them with the second group of procedures.

While tests such as these may be in part disguised, in that the experimenter does not tell the respondent his real purpose and may indeed substitute a false justification, their primary asset is that of securing an expression of attitudes in a more natural and spontaneous form, allowing opportunity for each individual to "project" upon a neutral screen his own integration of the problem. In contrast, the usual direct paper-and-pencil attitude test, requiring the endorsement of prepared items, may be said to force artificially the expression of attitudes into a preconceived and common mold. The great advantage of these non-structured tests is one of freedom, rather than of disguise. While some respondents may complete their assignments unaware of the experimenter's interest, in a tense situation one could hardly use any of the above devices expecting to get unconscious or uncensored expressions of attitude from uncooperative respondents. Essentially these tests are "voluntary" in the same sense that the usual attitude test, interest inventory, or neuroticism test is. The respondent is told (either directly or in effect) that there are no right or wrong answers, and he is placed in a situation in which a voluntary and arbitrary performance is acceptable.

DISGUISED-STRUCTURED TESTS OF SOCIAL ATTITUDES

The approaches which we will consider below differ from the ones mentioned above perhaps only in degree or in relative emphasis. Yet the distinction involved is important. The characteristics of these disguised, non-voluntary tests, can be stated in a number of ways:

The respondent participates in an objective task, in which he seeks right answers. The voluntarism of the usual projective techniques is lacking. To the respondent, the situation is similar to that of an achievement or ability test.

All respondents have a common motivation in taking the test. All, we may assume, are seeking to perform adequately on the same objective task. Attention is focused on a common goal, oblique to the experimenter's purpose.

Rather than stressing the freedom and lack of structuring, there is an attempt to diagnose attitudes from systematic bias in the performance of an objective task. The test may be highly structured—directly scorable—and still offer opportunity for unconsciously operating bias to distort behavior in a systematic and diagnosable manner.

Here is a simple formula for constructing such a test. Find a task which all your respondents will take as objective, and in which all will strive to do well. Make the task sufficiently difficult, or use a content area in which the respondents have had little experience or opportunity for reality testing. Load the test with content relative to the attitude you study. Look among the responses for systematic error, or for any persistent selectivity of performance. If such be found, it seems an adequate basis for the inference of an attitude.

To be sure, this approach has to some extent been used in the projective techniques discussed above. The T.A.T., for example, is introduced as a "test of creative imagination" (58), but little attempt is made to carry out effectively this pretense pattern. Respondents accept the task with a wide diversity of motivations, varying levels of seriousness, curiosity, and suspiciousness. And while all may be "projecting," the motivational situation is highly un-uniform, and meaningful comparisons between the responses of the serious, the suspicious, and the playful can hardly be made. Similarly, the "play technique" has been given to college men with the excuse that the experimenter was interested in "ideas for moving picture plays" and wanted the respondent to construct a "dramatic scene" (58, p. 553); and the sentence completion test has been given as an ability test (as Ebbinghaus intended it), with instructions to complete the sentences in any grammatical fashion as quickly as possible. But the disguise in these typical projective tests seems to be half-hearted, or implausible, weakened by the explicit freedom of response allowed. At best, the respondents accept the task as meaningless, or as a psychologist's mystery. It is probably common that something of the intent of the experimenter is divined, and the task completed despite this.

Information Tests

To make the model of the indirect, disguised, non-voluntary test of social attitudes more explicit, let us examine the use of an information test for attitude diagnosis. The reader has probably commented at one time or another upon the inextricable interrelationship between people's attitudes and what they take to be facts. You would all probably agree that in a detailed test of information, the direction of people's guesses or misconceptions will frequently bear a relationship to their attitudes. In a complementary fashion, a given person's knowledge is apt to reflect in its unevenness his selective awareness and retention, or his biased sources of information. Newcomb has dramatically portrayed the non-random character of right and wrong answers on an information test in his study of "The Effect of Social Climate upon Some Determinants of Information" (62). While selective awareness and divergent sources of information were primarily involved, Newcomb comments with regard to the difficult information items "the direction of guessing is altogether likely to be weighted toward the subject's attitude. If this reasoning is correct, the . . . test tends to become itself an attitude test." Coffin (14) and Smith (76) have found beliefs of factual type statements to correlate highly with related attitude tests. Indeed, in looking over the high correlations found in the literature on the relationship between information and attitudes, one is tempted to guess that some re-interpretation of them is in order. Is it not likely that many items were such that persons of liberal, tolerant attitudes found guessing easier?

Loeblowitz-Lennard and Riessman have proposed that an information test be used to measure indirectly attitudes toward Negroes and Jews (50). Hammond (31) has actually used such a test to measure attitudes toward "labor-management" and "Russia," and his work is worthy of some detailed comment here. We have mentioned that not only guessing behavior but also differential patterns of information may be diagnostic of attitudes. Hammond eliminated the latter by the "error-choice" technique, in which the respondent was forced to choose between the two alternative answers each of which was, by intent, equally wrong, but in opposite directions from the correct answer. Such items were:

"Average weekly wage of the war worker in 1945 was (1) $37.00, (2) $57.00." "Financial reports show that out of every dollar (1) 16¢, (2) 3¢ is profit."

Scoring these information guesses as attitude items gave total scores on 20 such items that differentiated a labor union group from two business clubs with almost no overlap. In spite of the small number of cases (18 union and 42 business) the critical ratios were 11.3 on the Labor-Management, and 12.5 on the Russia questionnaire. Reliabilities on the two scales were roughly estimated at .78 and .87 respectively.

What we have here is an objective test situation (which could be made more so by using more alternatives and including a correct one) in which people's errors are not random, but systematic. The presence of biased performance clearly necessitates the inference of some underlying process, which we choose to call attitude. The claim for face validity on such a test seems to be stronger than the one that can be made for either the direct or unstructured attitude test. Is not systematically biased performance in dealing with environmental actualities the essential practical meaning of attitude?

Parrish (64) has more recently used a regular multiple choice information test as an indirect indicator of attitudes, in conjunction with a direct attitude scale and a second indirect test involving estimating opinion poll results (see below). All three tests effectively reflected 12 minutes worth of anti-Kuomintang propaganda in approximately the same degree when the greater reliability of the direct test is considered. The pseudo-information test had 32 items and a reliability of .66 (using Kuder-Richardson formula 14 modified for multiple levels of response). It correlated .67 (corrected for attenuation) with the direct test (10 items, reliability .91) given at the same time (both anonymously, so there is no reason to suspect the direct test). The correlation with the public opinion estimate test was .59.

Kremen (43) attempted to evaluate the effect of student role-playing of a discrimination episode upon attitudes toward the Negro, using a multiple-choice information-type indirect test and a direct test. While neither test reflected the role playing in mean scores, her findings have importance for attitude measurement, inasmuch as role-playing *lowered* the relationship between the direct and indirect test. The results from ten sociology classes (five pairs in which the instructor and subject were the same) are presented below:

	Correlation between Direct and Indirect Tests				
Role-playing classes:	.39	.36	.20	.53	.38
Paired control classes:	.54	.70	.35	.58	.60

For all classes combined, the direct test had a reliability of .89, the indirect test .42 (Kuder-Richardson, Formula 14). The explanation of this phenomenon is not obvious from her data insofar as analysed. She does not report reliability values separately for the ten classes, although this step is planned in further analysis of the data.

R. B. Cattell (12, 13) has undertaken a large scale exploration into the "objective" measurement of attitudes, using a rationale very similar to the one presented here for non-voluntary attitude tests. In this study, a large number of ingenious methods have been tried, and others suggested.[1] The methods have been applied to a number of attitude-interests, such as playing more sociable games, excelling in one's career, and being smartly dressed, which differ greatly from the social-problem topics of most of the other studies reviewed. Two of the methods may be classified with information test approaches. His measure of "False Belief (Delusion)" (12) was presented to respondents as a multiple-choice information test. A sample item: "During the war church attendance increased greatly and, since V-J day it has: (declined slightly; tended to increase still more; stayed at its high peak; returned to its pre-war level; fallen to its lowest point since 1920)." Presumably the different responses were given different weights as in a direct test and as done by Parrish and by Kremen. Applied to a religious attitude, ten such items gave a Spearman-Brown reliability of .53, and correlated .33 with a paired-comparisons preference test, and .10 with records kept of time and money expenditure.

Cattell's other information test approach was more straight-forward. As mentioned above, we may expect that a person will reveal his attitudes not only in the direction of his "errors" but also in the selective character of the "right answers" he knows.

Cattell prepared 10-item information tests for each of a number of attitudes. The items dealt with the "knowledge required in following the course of action connected with the attitude" (12). For twelve topics, these tests, scored in terms of the number of items correct, provided Spearman-Brown reliabilities ranging from .13 to .92, with an average of .59. Correlation with records of time expended on the various activities averaged but .16. With money spent on activities the average value was .15, and with paired-comparison preferences, .16.

[1] Omitted from the present review are a number of physiological and related psychological measures, such as P.G.R., writing pressure, pulse pressure, speed of reading, fluency, and speed of decision, which Cattell also investigated.

In this approach, Cattell has resurrected an approach to the "objective" or "indirect" measurement of vocational interests which flourished during and after the first world war. Fryer (26) and others provide summaries of such research. No longer called "interest" tests, these selective vocabulary and object recognition tests are today firmly established among vocational selection and guidance tools.

Estimation of Group Opinion and Social Norms

As Travers (79), Wallen (80), and others have demonstrated, there is persistent correlation between a person's own attitude and his estimate of group opinion. While a few persons may chronically underestimate the popularity of their own opinions, the prevailing tendency is to overestimate the size of the group agreeing with one's self. Biserial correlations between endorsement of a dichotomous item and the estimation of the proportion of the group endorsing show few values below .2 and characteristically run from .4 to .6 or higher. This relationship seems to indicate the possibility of assessing a person's attitudes by giving him the entirely objective task of estimating group opinion. If one regards correlation with direct attitude expression as validation, one starts with very high single item validities indeed. If from a single item, one can predict a person's attitudes to the extent of a correlation of .40, how well might one not be able to predict from twenty such items? In several attempts along this line at the Ohio State University, conducted under the direction of the present author, the results have fallen considerably below such optimistic hopes. From combined estimates of group opinion, the best correlation obtained with a direct attitude score based on the same items runs around .60, not better than the best single item-estimate correlation. More detailed exploration of the technique is being made, however. Parrish (64) used a public opinion estimate test, with items dealing with U. S. opinion on China, the opinions of Americans with experience in China, and the opinions of the Chinese. Only the first type are directly comparable to the Travers and Wallen situation, and these did not come out the best in the item analyses. The test, containing only 10 items, had a Kuder-Richardson reliability of .53, correlating .67 with the direct test when corrected for attenuation. In this instance there was no direct duplication of content in the direct attitude test items and in the opinion estimates.

The technique is not entirely new. In 1929, Sweet, using a test designed by Goodwin Watson, found boys' estimates of group opinions valuable in diagnosing adjustment problems (77). More recently, Katz has reported results confirming the general relationship between own attitudes and estimates of group opinion, although he does not give correlation coefficients (41). As part of Section A in their "Sentiments" examination, Murray and Morgan (59) ask the respondent to guess what the majority of people believes or prefers, e.g. "what are the three most popular things to do?" Newcomb (61) made one of the first uses of the percentage estimate of group opinion, but has not reported his results in terms of the responses of individuals. It might be pointed out that the correlation involved in these studies is not necessarily to be interpreted as projection. In a group of any size, the respondent has an uneven acquaintanceship, and probably associates more with those of tastes like his own. Basing his estimates of group opinion upon his own experience in the group, his error may be in part a "sampling bias" as well as biased perception.

F. C. Bartlett (4, 5) and D. M. Carmichael (9) before the war were experimenting with the use of predictions of social events as diagnostic of attitudes. The respondent is given a situation and some background information, and then asked to make a prediction. Predictions regarding the likelihood of cooperation between social groups have been used, for example. The approach can probably be presented as a test of ability, and would seem to offer the possibility of wide variation in content. McGregor (53) has also pointed out the relationship between predictions and personal attitudes. Using predictions of another kind, Davis (17) has devised a simple test for use with children which could easily be given in an objective frame of reference, and which already has the desirable quality of asking the respondent to talk about somebody else rather than himself. (Indeed, his technique is practically identical with the first "projective" personality tests designed by Cattell (10) on the model of multiple-choice intelligence test items.) In Davis' test, situations are presented, and the respondent predicts the protagonist's action by selecting from several prepared alternatives.

Noland (63) used a projective approach toward estimating social norms with one set of items in his extensive study of absenteeism, asking "how important a cause of absenteeism do you think each of the following." These single items predicted absenteeism with a correlation of .50 or better. The value of the finding is weakened, however, by having as a criterion of absenteeism voluntary reports on the same (unsigned) questionnaire.

Tests of Ability to Do Critical Thinking

During the last three or four years of his life, John J. B. Morgan had been working on another technique that admirably meets our criteria (55, 56, 57). He used a syllogisms test, with a large number of possible conclusions provided, from which the respondent was to pick the logically correct one. Following Sells' study of atmosphere effect, the syllogisms were invalid. In spite of the invalidity of the syllogism, college students will concentrate their choices on the one or two wrong alternatives favored by the atmosphere effect. To use this phenomenon in diagnosing attitudes, Morgan gave the same syllogisms in both impersonal or abstract form (e.g., "No A's are B's. Some C's are B's. From these statements it is logical to conclude: No C's are A's, etc.") and with content ("A trustworthy man does not engage in deceitful acts. The bombing of Pearl Harbor by the Japanese was a deceitful act. From these statements it is logical to conclude: No Japanese are trustworthy, . . . etc."). By studying the shift in the popular responses from the nonsense to the meaningful form, Morgan attempted to diagnose group attitudes. While the technique needs much further study, it seems well worth such elaboration. In particular, an attempt should be made to control the effect of greater tangibility, per se, and also the intrusion of evidence from outside the syllogism which might be confounded with purely attitudinal effects. Note that in this particular study, the shifts of the group showed more tolerance for the Japanese than otherwise. Lansdell has utilized the technique for studying covert attitudes toward marriage, attempting to apply it for the diagnosis of the attitudes of a single individual (45).

Ruch, in his 1937 edition of *Psychology and Life* (69, pp. 633-634), reports briefly upon a classroom experiment in which preferences for ethnic groups were reflected in the ability to judge the validity of syllogisms about the same groups. In this instance, no choice of conclusions was offered, but rather the students judged the validity of the complete syllogism as stated. Lefford (46) has shown in more detail the disrupting influence of emotional subject matter upon such judgments.

The syllogism approach, and a number of others, have been anticipated by Goodwin Watson's *Measurement of Fair Mindedness,* published in 1925 (81). By fair-mindedness Watson seems to have meant something roughly equivalent to tolerance, critical thinking, or open-mindedness. His six sub-tests were designed to provide scores on this trait, which they did with adequate reliability. But Watson recognized that in the "errors" or lapses from fair-mindedness were clues as to the biases or attitudes of the respondents, and a secondary "analytic" scoring was made in these terms. Three of the sub-tests we would characterize as being direct[2] and of the others, we will classify two under the heading of "critical thinking," treating the third—*Moral Judgments*—below. The *Inference Test* provided statements of fact, followed by several conclusions that might be drawn, only one of which is logically justified, the others offering opportunities for the intrusion of personal biases in various directions. This test has been expanded in the Watson-Glazer Tests of Critical Thinking (28) which could be scored for various prejudices although they have not been so used as far as the present writer is aware. Gilbert (27) has made use of this same technique in a study in which high-school children were given hypothetical racial problems for which they could choose strictly logical conclusions or conclusions showing bias.

In Watson's *Arguments Test* both pro and con arguments on various topics are presented, and the respondent evaluates these for their strength as arguments. The test taps the tendency for a person to view as strong those arguments which support his own point of view. Robbins (66) has recently confirmed the principles underlying this test, although his data

are not in such form as to indicate whether or not accurate inferences as to attitudes could be made from such judgments. He found that students performed better in judging the adequacy of reasons for points of view with which they agreed than those with which they disagreed.

Tests Employing Bias in Perception and Memory

The demonstrations of systematic attitudinal bias in highly "objective" perceptual and learning tasks have provided some of the most important developments of the past 15 years for attitude theory (2, 20, 48, 73, 74). The use of errors in seeing and remembering in the diagnosis of individual attitudes epitomizes the disguised, structured, and non-voluntary assessment of attitudes.

Pioneers in the use of this approach are E. L. and R. E. Horowitz (37). In their study of the development of social attitudes among the children of a southern community they invented a number of techniques which have merited a great deal more re-use than they have seen. While designed to portray group differences, many of them should be appropriate to individual testing. Their *Aussage Test* involved exposing a complicated picture for two or three seconds, following which they tested for perception and memory through a series of standardized deliberately leading questions. For instance, the question "who is cleaning the grounds" to Picture 10 brings answers referring to a non-existent Negro in some 70% of the cases. To Picture 4, the misleading question "What is the colored man in the corner doing" brings a steadily increasing proportion (in reports from higher age groups) of menial activities for the non-existent Negro man.

Their *Perception-Span Test* involved a series of posters each having pictures of 10 items mounted upon it. These were exposed for 10 seconds, and the children asked to "tell all the pictures you can remember." While there were difficulties with perseveration and blocking, some age group differences were noted, with the younger children failing to note Negroes, and the older ones showing a selective awareness for them. A *Recall Test,* asking for the reproduction of ten words used earlier in a word association test, seemed also to indicate that in the younger years the word "Negro" was less well remembered than would be ex-

---

[2] These are the *Word Cross-out Test* in which the respondent crosses out "distasteful" words, as in Pressey's test, the *Degree of Truth Test* allowing for extreme or moderate statements of belief and disbelief and, the *Generalization Test* in which a number of statements about various groups are presented, and the respondent is to indicate whether the statement is true of "All, Most, Many, Few, or No" members of the group. (This is probably one of the first tests of "stereotyping." It might be classified as indirect if administered as an information test.)

pected. The *Pictorial Recognition Test* involving the recognition of faces previously exposed, finds the faces of whites more frequently recognized than the faces of Negroes.

Seeleman's study (71) confirms this finding with respect to individual differences within the group. Presenting sets of Negro and white photographs she tested for later recognition by asking that the previously exposed pictures be picked from a larger group. The discrepancy between memory for white and Negro faces was checked against attitudes on a direct test. Using people in the extreme quartiles on the direct test only, the test and memory-bias scores correlated .64 and .71 with different populations. In a paired-associates memory test involving complimentary phrases to be paired with white and Negro pictures, error discrepancy scores showed no correlation with the direct test, but the tendency to assign favorable phrases to the Negro (regardless of correctness) correlated .66 with the direct test in the one population for which the correlation is reported. These values are high enough to suggest that with refinement an indirect test might be achieved.

On a preliminary experiment, Murray Jarvik (22) attempted to utilize memory distortion as an indicator of attitudes. Sixth, seventh and eighth grade students in a rural school were read five minute stories and then were asked to write down all they could remember of the story. The stories had simple dramatic plots, but were full of confusing detail and lacunae with regard to specific names, characteristics, and ethnic identities. Opportunity was given for memory distortion in the direction of common stereotypes. The results were essentially negative. However, motivation and literacy were low, and the task was a part of a rather long testing program. Note also that memory distortion usually occurs over longer spans of time, and that had the test employed selective retention rather than distortion it might have been more successful.

Cattell (12, 13) utilized three techniques involving memory and perceptual distortion. His test of "Immediate Memory" was based upon selective recall for attitude relevant statements from sets of twelve presented at one-second intervals. In the total, there were over 500 statements. Spearman-Brown reliability figures for eleven attitudes ranged from .13 to .86, averaging .50. Correlations with other measures were essentially zero (with time ex-

penditure, average .01; with money expenditure, average .03; with paired-comparisons preferences, average .13; with the information test (see above), .01). In the scoring, both "facilitating" and "frustrating" statements relative to the attitude were pooled. Cattell recommends that in future research these be separated.

Cattell's "Distraction" method involved the exposure for ten seconds of statements related to the attitudes. Around the statement were scattered twelve or thirteen nonsense syllables. Subjects were held responsible for recalling the statement and the nonsense syllables. Scoring was in terms of decrement in nonsense syllable recall for statements related to a given attitude. The original hypothesis was that the stronger the attitude, the poorer the nonsense syllable learning, through distraction. Actually, the opposite effect was found. With a Spearman-Brown reliability of .64 for one attitude (being smartly dressed), the correlation with the paired-comparison preference measure was —.29, with time expenditure, —10, with money expenditure, —.08, and with the information test (discussed above) —.35. Since only ten items were involved, these values are regarded as sufficiently high to encourage further work with the method. The "Misperception" method involved the tachistoscopic exposure of attitude statements for one second, with the respondent responsible for repeating the statement and noting the misspellings. The overlooking of misspelling was regarded as a sign of strong attitude. Ten items dealing with the desire to play more sociable games provided a Spearman-Brown reliability of .43, and correlations with the paired-comparisons preference measure of .00, the expenditure of money of —.01, and the information test of —.13.

These methods of selective memory and selective distractibility have been anticipated in the indirect measurement of occupational interests by Burtt in 1923 (7, 8, pp. 334-343). In a paired-associates memory test, one half of the pairs were relevant to agricultural engineering. The ratio of memory for these pairs as opposed to memory for other pairs correlated .30 with instructors ratings as to interest and industry. In a cancellation test, in which irrelevant words were to be crossed out, different paragraph contents were employed. Differentials in efficiency of cancellation correlated .30 with the above-mentioned instructors ratings. Contrary to Cattell's findings, the greater distractibility was associated with stronger interest.

Tests Involving Ability to Judge Character

Murphy and Likert, in *Public Opinion and the Individual* (60), utilized a wealth of techniques anticipating the projective testing movement. Among these was the "Ratings from Photographs." Following the general framework of Rice's classic study on stereotypes, they provided labeled pictures of a union president, a railroad magnate, a pacifist, a Negro champion of Negro rights, etc. Respondents were asked to judge from these labeled photographs the character of the pictured person, in terms of courage, selfishness, intelligence, conceit, sympathy, practicality, and sentimentality. Contrary to expectation, they found no relationship between attitudes as measured in a variety of paper and pencil tests and these picture ratings. However, since the making of character judgments from photographs comes as near to being a paradigm of psychiatric projection as can be found in present test approaches, it might be suggested that this technique be further explored before being abandoned. In line with the tenor of the present discussion would be the suggestion that the objectivity or "pseudo-objectivity" of the task be increased, with the use of some such label as "social intelligence test" or the like.

In precisely this model is the "Faces Game" originally developed by Marion Radke (67, p. 50-51) and being used as modified by Isidor Chein and Iljana Schreiber in research of the Commission on Community Interrelations of the American Jewish Congress (16). In this test children are asked "Let's see how good you are at telling what people are like just by looking at their faces." Thirty-four sets of four pictures (two white and two Negro for all but four sets) are presented, each with a question such as "one of the girls in this row is very lazy and never bothers to do anything" or "one of the boys in this row is the best sport in his class." Two scores are provided: one *the "white salience" score* (the total mentions of white children for items either good or bad), and *the prejudice score* (the ratio of unfavorable choices of faces of the other group to total choices of other groups). The test produces significant individual and group differences, and showed retest reliabilities over a six month period of .50 and .36 for white and Negro children, respectively, on the prejudice score. For the white salience score, the values were .32 and .16. The researchers do not regard the test as satisfactory for general use as yet.

Hsü (38) had three women graduate students sort male photographs for handsomeness, and ten days later for judged membership in the Communist party. The correlations were negative (—.50 and —.21) for the two women who were anti-communist and positive (.51) for the one woman who was relatively pro-communist. After reading a *Time* report on the blockade of Berlin, the correlations for sorts on a second set of the photographs were negative for all three women. While this study does not provide in itself an adequate basis for measuring attitudes, it does hold out promise for more extensive work with character judgments from photographs.

Tests Involving Miscellaneous Abilities

Another of the excellent test approaches in the Horowitzs' study (37) was labeled the *Categories Test*. This test was modeled directly upon a typical intelligence test item. Five pictures were presented, and the question asked "Which one does not belong?" As they adapted it, the item could be answered in more than one way, and the choice indicate something of the important social categories for the child. For example, a page might contain pictures of three white boys, one white girl, and one Negro boy. In this instance, the child could use either sex or race as the dominant category. Other items provided opportunities to categorize by age and socio-economic status as well. Here again, the emphasis was on group norms rather than individual differences.

Hartley (32) has more recently used the categorization of photographs as a measure of ethnic salience. In this study, however, the task was presented in a voluntary framework, in contrast with the objective assignment presented in the *Categories Test*. In Hartley's "faces test" the respondent is told to: "Sort them out into piles. You can make as many piles as you want to, or as few as you choose. You can classify them on any basis you want to!"

In the Murray and Morgan "Study of Sentiments" (59) several of the "indirect methods, methods which conceal the examiner's intent" provide an ability test façade. The "Sentiments Examination" Section A Part 1 asks for the "most descriptive adjectives" for 48 stimulus words, "the S being led to believe that the examiner is interested in testing the range of his vocabulary." In Part 3 "The S is led to believe his verbal ability is being tested with a simile completion test," e.g. "As pathetic as a . . . ." In the "Arguments Completion Test" the respondent is asked to continue and finish an argument, the beginning of which has been described. "Being led to believe his powers of argumentation are being tested, the subject quickly becomes involved in the controversy he or she is inventing, and ends by exposing more of his own sentiments than he might otherwise have done" (59, pp. 58-60).

Tests Involving Miscellaneous Judgments

The following tests are disguised and structured, but in part at least must be classified as *voluntary,* in so far as judgments are required in situations in which there is no "objective" right answer. On the other hand, they retain the advantage of having the respondent (1) work on a task presumably less threatening than the experimenter's primary problem, and (2) report upon external values or realities, rather than upon himself directly. These studies like many already discussed, depend upon the demonstration of a judgment differential of which the respondent is presumably unaware.

In Watson's (81) "Moral Judgments" subtest, judgments of approval or disapproval are made about a variety of situations, sets of these situations being identical except for the specific persons or groups involved. For example unwarranted search is made of a suspected "radical" headquarters, on the one hand, while in a parallel item, the same type of search is carried out with a business corporation suspected of dishonesty. Scoring is done on the basis of discrepancy of judgment between the parallel situations.

Similar in title and in plan to Watson's Moral Judgments Test is the ingenious approach to Negro-White attitudes devised by Seeman (72). While he used equated comparison groups, the technique could be modified for diagnosing bias in individuals. He selected six items from a standard test of moral evaluations on marriage and sexual matters. To one group, the episode items were illustrated by pictures of white couples; to the other, with Negro illustrations. Both groups were made up of white college students. Contrary to expectation, the judgments were more lenient—less disapproval—with the Negro illustrations. Furthermore, when the two groups were subclassified according to scores on the Likert scale of attitudes toward the Negro, the major part of the differential was contributed by the more

tolerant persons rather than the more anti-Negro parts of the two groups. The intolerant extremes in this sample were more consistent, less "biased." These results are important and meaningful, but further indicate the danger of over-simplified interpretations in indirect approaches.

The readiness with which judgments of literary merit can be manipulated by the substitution of fictitious authors has been demonstrated by Farnsworth (70) and Sherif (73). Prestige seems to be one of those forces which can bias the performance of an objective task. Can we use this bias to infer attitudes? Lewis (47) seems to have had in mind some such approach. The present writer (22) deliberately set out to utilize the prestige effect to measure attitude toward five minority groups. Rather than literary passages, proverbs or mottoes were used. Rather than individual authors, the adage was attributed to the group as a whole, e.g., "American pioneer saying" or "old Jewish motto." Eighth and ninth grade students were asked to evaluate the quality of each motto separately—there being ten mottoes attributed to each group. The test yielded a general prejudice score that correlated but .30 with a direct test. Other scores were worthless. However, in view of the strength of prestige suggestion in other experiments, this approach seems worth trying further. It is quite possible that in the form given the task was trivial and the disguise thin.

Horowitz (35) illustrated the development of patriotism and conformity among children by tests in which the task was to pick "the best looking flag," or the "best place to live in" from a series of photographs of houses, etc.

As Wolff, Smith and Murray (83) have shown, reactions to group-disparagement jokes are correlated with group membership. Gordon (29) has recently tried to utilize this phenomenon in the assessment of social attitudes. Twenty-four jokes, both antagonistic and sympathetic, dealing with Negroes and Jews were rated as to their funniness on a 5-point scale. Four groups of college men were used: a Protestant fraternity, a Catholic fraternity, a Negro fraternity, a Jewish (non-Zionist) fraternity, and a Zionist club. The groups differed in their responses to these jokes but not as anticipated in all instances. The jokes sympathetic to Jews were rated highest by the two Jewish groups— but the anti-Jewish jokes failed to differentiate the groups. The anti-Negro jokes were rated lowest by the Negro group, but the pro-Negro jokes failed to differentiate. The various groups ranked the individual jokes quite similarly as to popularity, with rho's between the orders for the different groups ranging from .71 to .94. With regard to individual differences *within* the various groups, the ratings of the jokes showed no relationship to attitudes toward Negroes or Jews as revealed in a direct attitudes test or a symbol endorsement test. The tests were administered as a part of a larger testing program.

Cattell (13), in the program already referred to used a "Projection-Phantasy" test, in which the respondent picked from ten sets of ten incomplete sentences, five each which he completed. Rather than scoring the words used in completing the sentences, Cattell scored the *choice* of incomplete sentences. Each set contained one representative of each of ten different attitudes. Applied to the desire to excel in one's profession, and to the desire for more sleep and rest, this test had Spearman-Brown reliabilities of .13 and .60. Correlations with the paired-comparison preferences were .15 and .31, with time and money expenditure, .01 and .26, with information, .20 and .20. In spite of the relatively low level of these values, this method was regarded as one of the more promising.

Kalpakian's "The Construction of a Disguised Test by the Use of Photographs for the Study of Attitudes Toward Negroes" (40) represents an attempt at disguise which fails in part to meet the criteria suggested here. Like other tests reported in this section, a judgment differential of which the respondent was unaware was sought. Twenty-six matched pairs of pictures was selected—one set depicting Negroes, the other whites. The test was structured, in that a choice of responses, "Like—Indifferent —Dislike" was required for each picture. The instructions read in part "we're interested in seeing what kinds of pictures people like and don't like . . . we're not interested in the technical photographic aspects of the pictures, rather we want your reactions to what is in the pictures. That is, how do you feel about what is in each picture." Note the voluntary nature of this assignment—the respondent being told in effect that there are no right or wrong answers. Note also the absence of any clear cut assigned basis of judgment which might lend indirection (such as asking for judgments of beauty of the photograph or skill of photogra-

pher). Kalpakian did aid the disguise by placing these 52 photographs in random order among 68 irrelevant pictures. This is similar to the efforts in disguise made by those who distribute the items of one attitude scale among a variety of other types (e.g., 24). In one of Kalpakian's groups, 100 subjects were asked what they thought the purpose of the test was. Only 15 did not guess that the purpose involved attitudes toward the Negro; 51 thought this and several other attitudes were being tested; 34 judged correctly that the primary purpose was attitudes toward Negroes. On the other hand only 7 were aware of the matching of the pictures. Scored on proportion of white to Negro "likes" the test showed corrected split-half reliability coefficients between .71 and .82 in various white high school and college groups. Mean values showed a definite "white salience" for all groups. Scores correlated with both self ratings and ratings by friends, demonstrated by critical-ratio tests. The correlation with the Thurstone-Hinkley was .40, which became .80 when corrected for restricted range. In terms of the categories of this review, Kalpakian's test is similar to the "show me" and other picture tests developed by Horowitz (34). It is structured in that a limited number of response categories is provided. It is direct, substituting pictures for the ethnic labels used in statement-endorsement type of direct tests.

GENERAL CONSIDERATIONS

Validity of Indirect Tests

Most efforts to develop indirect attitude tests are predicated upon the assumption that indirect tests will under certain conditions have higher validity than direct tests. It is worthy of note that *none* of the studies reviewed here offers any evidence that this is the case. The testing of this hypothesis is certainly the next step if these preliminary efforts are thought to be sufficiently promising to justify more research.

The most usual effort at validation has involved correlating the indirect test with direct test results, under conditions in which the latter were gathered anonymously or in which there was no reason to suspect respondent dissembling (e.g., 19, 22, 29, 38, 40, 43, 60, 64, 65). Hammond (31) and Gordon (29) used environmentally selected criterion or comparison groups. Parrish's tests (64) meaningfully reflected an experience differential between two groups. These are, however, isolated instances, and even at the exploratory level, we might expect more use of criterion groups.

As has been pointed out previously, the case for *face validity* for indirect tests may often be better than for direct tests. In a number of the disguised, structured tests, the distribution of scores and measures of internal consistency demonstrates unequivocally that non-random, systematic errors, differences in perceptions, etc. exist, of which the respondents are presumably unaware. These systematic unconscious "biases" are well worth study in their own right, and seem to lie close to the functional meaning of attitude.

Attitude Measurement as Related to Attitude Definition and Theory

Research on social attitudes has been justly criticized for a lack of common definition of the concept, and for a failure to integrate definition and measurement procedures. This diversity of definition has been in odd contrast with the obvious similarity of research procedures. This paradox arises from definitional attempts which confound *explanations* of the phenomena with the process of *pointing* to the phenomena. It is the contention of the present writer that agreement on the implicit operational (or pointing) definition of attitudes is already present. As a tentative formulation the following is offered: *A social attitude is (or is evidenced by) consistency in response to social objects.* If we look at those definitions utilizing concepts of set, or readiness to respond for example, Allport's (1): "An attitude is a mental and neural state of readiness, organized through experience and exerting a directive or dynamic influence upon the individual's response to all objects and situations to which it is related"—and ask for the evidence of a "mental and neural state of readiness," the symptoms of a "directive or dynamic influence," criteria as to the "objects and situations to which it is related," these evidences will be in final analysis consistency or predictability among responses. *An individual's social attitude is a syndrome of response consistency with regard to social objects.* And even those whose behavioristic orientation leads to a rejection of such mentalistic definitions as Allport's— and who would say with Bain (3) and Horowitz (36, p. 142), "essentially . . . the attitude must be considered a response rather than a set to respond"—in research practice do not equate *isolated* responses with attitudes, but on the contrary look for the appearance of *response consistencies*. This is dramatically evidenced by Horowitz's (34) use of the appearance of consistent differentiated response to photographs of Negro and white children to mark the occurrence of race prejudice in children.

This standpoint provides a basis for the operational delimitation of specific and general attitudes. It likewise demands that if attitude measurement be integrated with definition, internal consistency among the sample responses collected by the test must be demonstrated. To the present writer, the demonstration of a single factor through factor analysis seems ideal, although time consuming. Spearman-Brown and Kuder-Richardson (44) reliability measures, Guttman's (30) "reproducibility coefficient," Loevinger's (52) "homogeneity," and Thurstone's "coefficient of irrelevance" (78) are likewise evidences of internal consistency. Item analysis against total scores (49, 75), remains one of the best practical means of improving internal consistency.

Contemporary American theories commonly hypothesize attitudes to be learned, or identify them with other cognitive phenomena such as perception and concept formation. From the operational definition suggested it would be hard to distinguish attitude from habit, which likewise is evidenced by behavior consistency. Indeed, if learning be conceived broadly enough to include the development of any response consistency, attitude formation is identical with learning. Traditionally, learning has been used in those situations in which the response consistencies represented optimal reflections of a simple, uniform environment— where increasing response consistency represented the elimination of "error." But a similar process goes on in "unsolvable" or highly complicated environments, and stereotyped modes of response are developed which are non-optimal reflections of the environment, which do not represent error-reduction. The terms perseveration, set, fixation, position habit, bias, irrational behavior, idiosyncracy, pre-judgment, non-random error, over simplification, bad habit, rigidity, all come to mind to describe this process. Presumably, this latter type of response consistency is a result of the same cognitive processes which under other conditions result in "right answer" learning. It is with these common processes that the concept of attitude is identified, although typically it is most closely associated with the acquisition of "irrational" or non-adaptive response consistencies.

In these terms it may be meaningful to compare direct and indirect efforts at attitude assessment. In both direct and indirect tests enough internal consistency has been demonstrated on some topics to justify speaking of attitudes. Likewise, in numerous instances reported here, considerable correlation has been demonstrated between responses to direct and to indirect tests, justifying the hypothesis that a common attitude lies behind them. Missing is the demonstration that this pattern of consistency extends beyond paper and pencil to the "real-life" situations which are usually in mind when the concept of "attitude" is used. While meaningful research problems exist in regard to patterns of consistency within a universe of paper and pencil responses, the bulk of the researches reviewed are predicated upon the assumption that broader consistencies exist —that overt behavioral manifestations of the attitude can be predicted.

With regard to the level of response consistency, it should be noted that direct tests uniformly have much higher reliability coefficients than do indirect ones, especially when the number of items and time of administration are considered. Of course this consistency is in part conscious, voluntary, and possibly superficial—in contrast to the involuntary "bias" in performance achieved by many indirect tests. In this sense, the indirect tests of the nonvoluntary sort do in themselves demonstrate and utilize the dramatic phenomena of attitudinal interference with tasks of learning, perceiving, remembering, and evaluating, such as are summarized by Sherif and Cantril (74, pp. 29-91). And it is such consistencies, rather than consistency in voluntary self-description, which give vitality to current usage of the concept of attitude. In this, indirect attitude tests lie closer to contemporary attitude theory than do direct tests.

SUMMARY

The efforts at indirectly measuring social attitudes have been summarized. A distinction has been offered between disguised, non-structured, types of test on the one hand, and disguised, structured, tests on the other. Because of a greater freedom from dependence upon the respondent's voluntary self description, the use of disguised, structured tests has been emphasized.

As can be seen from the survey, there is an abundance of partially tried techniques. Equally good ones can be developed from the general formula: A plausible task, (a) which your respondents will all strive to do well, (b) which is sufficiently difficult or ambiguous to allow individual differences in response, and (c) which can be loaded with content relative to the attitude you seek to measure. Test the responses of individuals for persistent selectivity in performance, for correlated or non-random errors. For example, several persons have suggested to the present writer what might be called the "photocrime" test. Here criminal scenes would be pictured in photograph and text. Sufficient ambiguity would be provided to make it a challenging problem to the amateur detective, and, incidentally, to allow the possibility of bias in the selection of the criminal from the suspects of various ethnic or social identification. A test of "common legal knowledge" might well provide a framework for carrying further some of the notions in Watson's "Moral Judgments" sub-test. The respondent might be asked to decide whether or not civil liberties had been violated in a wide range of specific situations—might be asked to decide between claimant and defendant in a number of civil suits. Here the content could easily be manipulated to get at almost any social attitude one might be interested in. It should not be too difficult to keep the respondent convinced that he dealt solely with matters of the law. We are prone to see as propaganda that with which we disagree. A "propaganda analysis test" should reveal indirectly some people's attitudes. For the build-up, give a review of some principles on how to spot propaganda, how to detect an ulterior motive, a selfish interest group, deceit, exaggeration, etc. Then have the respondent test his skill on a number of argumentative paragraphs, which he evaluates as to the extent and kind of propaganda present. The root of this notion may be found in Watson's "Arguments" sub-test.

Such devices may be multiplied, the reader can no doubt provide better ones. In some of these, the fiction of an objective test situation will be hollow indeed. In others, for example in the estimation of group opinion, we are tapping biased performance in an everyday act of social perception. We are not taking at face value the respondent's own volunteered description of himself. Rather we are studying systematic errors in the respondent's own perceptions, errors of which he himself is not aware. Not only in attitude testing but in personality study in general, distortions of performance in dealing with the environment provide objective evidence of an individual's unique picture of his world. Just as the psychophysicists were long ago forced to introduce *Vexirwersuche,* or catch trials, into introspection—to eliminate impossible negative reaction times and infinitesimal two-point thresholds—so personality testing, whether check-list or free-response, must rise above dependence on voluntary self-description. The development of structured indirect attitude tests is thought to be a step in this direction.

BIBLIOGRAPHY

1. Allport, G. W. Attitudes. Ch. 17 in C. Murchison (Ed.), *A handbook of social psychology.* Worcester, Mass.: Clark University Press, 1935.
2. Allport, G. W., and Postman, L. *The psychology of rumor.* New York: Holt, 1947.
3. Bain, R. An attitude on attitude research. *Amer. J. Sociol.,* 1928, **33**, 940-957.
4. Bartlett, F. C. *The study of society.* London: Kegan Paul, 1939.
5. Bartlett, F. C. The cooperation of social groups: a preliminary report and suggestions. *Occup. Psychol.,* 1938, **12**, 30-42.
6. Brown, J. F. Modification of the Rosenzweig picture frustration test to study hostile interracial attitudes. *J. Psychol.,* 1947, **24**, 247-272.
7. Burtt, H. E. Measuring interests objectively. *Sch. and Soc.,* 1923, **17**, 444-448.
8. Burtt, H. E. *Principles of employment psychology* (Rev. Ed.). New York: Harper, 1942.
9. Carmichael, D. M. The cooperation of social groups. *Brit. J. Psychol.,* 1938, **29**, 206-231; 329-344.
10. Cattell, R. B. *A guide to mental testing.* London: Univ. London Press, 1936.
11. Cattell, R. B. Projection and the design of projective tests of personality. *Charact. and Pers.,* 1944, **12**, 177-194.
12. Cattell, R. B., Heist, A. B., Heist, P. A., and Stewart, R. G. The objective measurement of dynamic traits. (To be published in *Educ. psychol. Msmt.,* 1950.)
13. Cattell, R. B., Maxwell, E. F., Light, B. H., & Unger, M. P. The objective measurement of attitudes. (To be published in the *Brit. J. Psychol.,* **50**, 1950.)
14. Coffin, T. E. Some conditions of suggestion and suggestibility: a study of certain attitudinal and situational factors influencing the process of suggestion. *Psychol. Monogr.* 1941, **4**, No. 241.
15. College Study in Intergroup Relations. (Lloyd Allen Cook, Director.) Study forms and technics in intergroup relations. Supplementary Sheet No. 5, Jan., 1948. (Mimeographed.) Detroit: Wayne University.
16. Commission on Community Interrelations of the American Jewish Congress. (Stuart Cook, Research Director.) The face game. Unpublished reasearch on a modified version of a test originally developed by Marian Radke. 1947-1948.
17. Davis, T. E. Some racial attitudes of Negro college and grade school students. *J. Negro Educ.,* 1937, **6**, 157-165.
18. Deri, S., Dinnerstein, D., Harding, J., and Pepitone, A. D. Techniques for the diagnosis and measurement of intergroup attitudes and behavior. *Psychol. Bull.,* 1948, **45**, 248-271.
19. Dubin, S. S. Verbal attitude scores predicted from responses in a projective technique. *Sociometry,* 1940, **3**, 24-28.
20. Edwards, A. L. Political frames of references as a factor influencing recognition. *J. abnorm. soc. Psychol.,* 1948, **36**, 34-61.
21. Evans, M. C., and Chein, I. The movie story game: a projective test of interracial attitudes for use with Negro and white children. Paper read at the 56th annual meeting of the American Psychological Association, Boston, Sept. 8, 1948.
22. Frenkel-Brunswik, E., Jones, H. E. (Directors), and Rokeach, M., Jarvik, M., and Campbell, D. T. (Staff). Unpublished research on the personality correlates of anti-minority attitudes among grade school children. A project of the University of California Institute of Child Welfare, financed by a grant from the American Jewish Committee, 1946-1947.
23. Frenkel-Brunswik, E., and Reichert, S. Personality and prejudice in women. (Unpublished manuscript.)

24. Frenkel-Brunswik, E., Levinson, D., and Sanford, R. N. The anti-democratic personality. In T. M. Newcomb and E. L. Hartley (Eds.), *Readings in social psychology*. New York: Holt, 1947.

25. Fromme, A. On use of qualitative methods of attitude research. *J. soc. Psychol.*, 1941, **13**, 429-460.

26. Fryer, D. *The measurement of interests*. New York: Holt, 1931.

27. Gilbert, H. H. Secondary science and pupil prejudice. *J. educ. res.* 1941, **35**, 294-299.

28. Glazer, E. M. An experiment in the development of critical thinking. *Teach. Coll. Contr. Educ.*, No. 843. New York: Bureau of Publications, Teachers Coll., Columbia Univ., 1941.

29. Gordon, S. Exploration of social attitudes through humor. Master's Thesis, Univ. of Illinois, 1947.

30. Guttman, L. A basis for scaling qualitative data. *Amer. sociol. Rev.*, 1944, **9**, 139-150.

31. Hammond, K. R. Measuring attitudes by error-choice; an indirect method. *J. abnorm. soc. Psychol.*, 1948, **43**, 38-48.

32. Hartley, E. L. *Problems in prejudice*. New York: Kings Crown Press, 1946.

33. Hartley, E. L., and Schwartz, S. A pictorial-doll play approach for the study of children's intergroup attitudes. Mimeographed preliminary draft. Research Institute in American Jewish Education, American Jewish Committee, Summer, 1948.

34. Horowitz, E. L. The development of attitude toward the Negro. *Arch. Psychol., N. Y.*, 1936, **28**, No. 194.

35. Horowitz, E. L. Some aspects of the development of patriotism in children. *Sociometry*, 1940, **3**, 329-341.

36. Horowitz, E. L. "Race" attitudes. In O. Klineberg (Ed.), *Characteristics of the American Negro*. New York: Harper, 1944.

37. Horowitz, E. L., and Horowitz, Ruth E. Development of social attitudes in children. *Sociometry*, 1938, **1**, 301-338.

38. Hsü, E. H. An experimental study of rationalization. *J. abnorm. soc. Psychol.*, 1949, **44** 277-278.

39. Johnson, G. G. An experimental analysis of the origin and development of racial attitudes with special emphasis on the role of bilingualism. Ph.D. Thesis, Univ. of Colorado, 1949.

40. Kalpakian, E. Y. The construction of a disguised test by use of photographs for the study of attitudes toward Negroes. Master's Thesis, Clark University, 1947. (*Clark University Bulletin*. Abstracts of Dissertations and Theses, Worcester, Mass., Oct., 1947.)

41. Katz, Martin R. A hypothesis on anti-Negro prejudice. *Amer. J. Sociol.*, 1947, **53**, 100-104.

42. Krech, D., and Crutchfield, R. S. *Theory and problems of social psychology*, New York: McGraw-Hill, 1948.

43. Kremen, E. O. An attempt to ameliorate hostility toward the Negro through role playing. Master's Thesis, The Ohio State University, 1949.

44. Kuder, G. F., and Richardson, M. W. The theory of the estimation of test reliability. *Psychometrika*, 1937, **2**, 151-160.

45. Landsdell, H. A study of distorted syllogistic reasoning as a means of discovering covert attitudes toward marriage. *Bull. Canad. Psychol. Assn.*, 1946, **6**, 98 (Abstract.)

46. Lefford, A. The influence of emotional subject matter on logical reasoning. *J. gen. Psychol.*, 1946, **34**, 127-151.

47. Lewis, H. B. An approach to attitude measurement. *Psychol. League J.*, 1938, **2**, 64-67.

48. Levine, J. M., and Murphy, G. The learning and forgetting of controversial material. *J. abnorm. soc. Psychol.*, 1943, **38**, 507-517.

49. Likert, R. A technique for the measurement of attitudes. *Arch. Psychol., N. Y.*, No. 140, 1932.

50. Loeblowitz-Lennard, H., and Riessman, F., Jr. A proposed projective attitude test. *Psychiatry*, 1946, **9**, 67-68.

51. Loeblowitz-Lennard, H., and Riessman, F., Jr. A preliminary report on social perception test—a new approach to attitude research. *Social Forces*, 1946, **24**, 423-427.

52. Loevinger, J. The technic of homogeneous tests compared with some aspects of "scale analysis" and factor analysis. *Psychol. Bull.*, 1948, **45**, 507-529.

53. McGregor, D. The major determinants of the prediction of social events. *J. abnorm. soc. Psychol.*, 1938, **33**, 179-204.

54. McNemar, Q. Opinion-attitude methodology. *Psychol. Bull.*, 1946, **43**, 289-374.

55. Morgan, J. J. B. Distorted reasoning as an index of public opinion. *Sch. and Soc.*, 1943, **57**, 333-335.

56. Morgan, J. J. B., and Morton, J. T. The distortion of syllogistic reasoning produced by personal convictions. *J. soc. Psychol.*, 1944, **20**, 39-59.

57. Morgan, J. J. B. Attitudes of students toward the Japanese. *J. soc. Psychol.*, 1945, **21**, 219-246.

58. Murray, H. A. *Explorations in personality*. New York: Oxford Univ. Press, 1938.

59. Murray, H. A., and Morgan, C. D. A clinical study of sentiments. I and II. *Genet. Psychol. Monogr.*, 1945, **32**, 3-311.

60. Murphy, G., and Likert, R. *Public opinion and the individual*. New York: Harpers, 1937.

61. Newcomb, T. M. *Personality and social change*, New York: Dryden Press, 1943.

62. Newcomb, T. M. The influence of attitude climate upon some determinants of information. *J. abnorm. soc. Psychol.*, 1946, **41**, 291-302.

63. Noland, E. W. Factors associated with absenteeism in a south central New York State industry. Ph.D. thesis on file in the Cornell University Library, 1944.

64. Parrish, J. A. The direct and indirect assessment of attitudes as influenced by propagandized radio transcriptions. Master's thesis, The Ohio State University, 1948.

65. Proshansky, H. A projective method for the study of attitudes. *J. abnorm. soc. Psychol.*, 1943, **38**, 383-395.

66. Robbins, I. Point of view and quality of thought in attitude measurement. *Improving Educational Research*, pp. 52-56. American Educ. Res. Ass. 1948 Official Report, Washington, D. C.

67. Rose, Arnold. *Studies in reduction of prejudice*. Chicago: American Council on Race Relations, 1948.

68. Rotter, J. B., and Willerman, B. The incomplete sentences tests as a method of studying personality. *J. consult. Psychol.*, 1947, **11**, 43-48.

69. Ruch, F. L. Psychology and life. (1st Ed.). Chicago: Scott, Foresman and Company, 1937.

70. Saadi, M., and Farnsworth, P. R. The degrees of acceptance of dogmatic statements and preferences for their supposed makers. *J. abnorm. soc. Psychol.*, 1934, **29**, 143-150.

71. Seeleman, V. The influence of attitude upon the remembering of pictorial material. *Arch. Psychol.*, N. Y., 1940-1941, **36**, No. 258.

72. Seeman, M. Moral judgments: a study in racial frames of references, *Amer. sociol. Rev.*, 1947, **12**, 404-411.

73. Sherif, M. A study of some social factors in perception. *Arch. Psychol.*, N. Y., 1935, No. 187.

74. Sherif, M., and Cantril, H. *The psychology of ego-involvements*. New York: Wiley, 1947.

75. Sletto, R. F. *Construction of personality scales by the criterion of internal consistency*. Hanover: The Sociological Press, 1937.

76. Smith, G. H. Beliefs in statements labeled fact and rumor. *J. abnorm. soc. Psychol.*, 1947, **42**, 80-90.

77. Sweet, L. *The measurement of personal attitudes in younger boys*. New York: The Association Press, 1929.

78. Thurstone, L. L., and Chave, E. J. *The measurement of attitude*. Chicago: Univ. Chicago Press, 1929.

79. Travers, R. M. W. A study in judging the opinions of groups. *Arch. Psychol.*, N. Y., No. 266, 1941.

80. Wallen, R. Individuals' estimates of group opinion. *J. soc. Psychol.*, 1943, **17**, 269-274.

81. Watson, G. B. The measurement of fair-mindedness. *Tech. Coll. Contr. Educ.* No. 176. New York: Teachers Coll., Columbia Univ., 1925.

82. Williams, Robin M., Jr. *The reduction of intergroup tensions*. New York: Social Science Research Council Bull., No. 57, 1947.

83. Wolff, H. A., Smith, C. E., and Murray, H. A. The psychology of humor; 1. a study of race disparagement jokes. *J. abnorm. soc. Psychol.*, 1934, **28**, 341-365.

84. Zeligs, R. Racial attitudes of children. *Sociol. soc. Res.*, 1937, **21**, 361-371.

20. *The Identification of Prejudicial Attitudes by the Galvanic Skin Response*

JOSEPH B. COOPER and DAVID POLLOCK

A. INTRODUCTION

This study was designed as an extension of two previous studies (2, 3) which provided physiological evidence in support of the view that prejudicial-attitudes are affectively fortified.

In the first of these studies, statements which described certain ethnic and national groups for which individual subjects had previously and variously expressed antipathy, neutrality, and affinity, by rating and ranking scale means, were read to those subjects in individual experimental sessions. GSRs to derogatory statements in reference to affinity groups were greater than to neutral groups in 14 of 20 cases; $p < .0594$. GSRs to complimentary statements in reference to antipathy groups were greater than to neutral groups in 19 of 20 cases; $p < .00007$.

The second study was a replication of the first, with attention solely directed to stimulus groups held in antipathy. In this study GSRs were greater to complimentary statements in reference to antipathy groups than in reference to neutral groups in 20 of 23 cases; $p < .0005$.

The design of the present study was essentially the reverse of the first two. In this study GSRs were recorded first. From these, predictions were then made of attitude content, as measured by paper and pencil scaling means.

B. THE PROBLEM

Whereas previously it had been found that individuals who expressed intense dislike for particular groups emitted excessively large GSRs to complimentary statements in reference

• Reprinted from *Journal of Social Psychology*, 1959, **50**, 241-245, with permission of the senior author and the publisher.

to those groups, it had still not been determined if relatively large GSRs were predictive of prejudicial-attitudes for an unselected sample. The question was: Does an individual's relatively large affective response to a complimentary statement in reference to a group indicate a negative content prejudicial-attitude toward that group? Operationally, affectivity level is described by GSR and prejudicial-attitude is described by paper and pencil scaling.

In view of the theoretical formulation of the problem and results of the two previously mentioned studies, an hypothesis was formulated. Its theoretical statement was: Display of excessive affectivity in response to a complementary description of a national or ethnic group is predictive of an antipathetic prejudicial-attitude toward that group. Its operational statement was: A relatively great GSR to a complimentary verbal description of a national or ethnic group is predictive of a relatively low attitude scale position for that group.

C. EQUIPMENT, SUBJECTS, AND PROCEDURE

The GSR unit of a Keeler Polygraph (Model 302) was used. This unit is equipped with a kymograph mechanism which carries coördinate-line paper upon which a pen records GSR magnitude. Rhodium palmar electrodes were used.

Attitudes were scaled by paired-comparison. The paired comparison scale contained the names of the following groups: Austrian, Canadian, English, German, Irish, Japanese, Jew, Mexican, Pole, Swede. The test-retest Spearman r reliability median was .96.

Subjects were students in two sections of general psychology. They were divided approximately evenly as to sex. Seventy-two subjects were given *GSR* tests. Of these, 19 did not respond sufficiently for inclusion within the sample. The sample *N* was 53.

Subjects were given appointment slips, each identified by number, not by name. They appeared for individual experimental sessions during class periods, each session requiring approximately 15 minutes.

Upon coming into the experimental room, the subject was shown the polygraph, and its basic characteristics were explained. The experiment itself was explained as a test of the *GSR* as a function of standard stimuli which were being read to all subjects. The subject's anonymity was assured. The subject was seated in a comfortable, wide-arm chair to the left of the polygraph. He could see the polygraphy peripherally, but could not follow the pen tracings. The experimenter stood to the right-rear of the subject. After placement of the electrodes the subject was "balanced in" by use of standard stimuli such as a hand-clap, touch on the neck, or a loudly spoken word. Final "balancing in" was accomplished while reading a complimentary statement which referred always to Irish. Thus, in the experiment proper, 9 groups were used for stimulus material.

The order of presentation of the stimulus statements was standard except for Nos. 3, 5, and 7. Since it had already been found (1) that Japanese, Jews, and Mexicans were groups toward which relatively great antipathy is shown by the local college population, they were randomized within these positions. As well, the complimentary statements descriptive of them were randomized. Thus, these three groups and the statements which described them were randomized in these three positions.

The group description statements were all of equal length, a blank at the second word position being left for insertion of the name of the appropriate group. As an example, one statement was: "The ———— are people it would be profitable to imitate, for they are superior both intellectually and morally."

The experimenter noted on the kymograph paper the beginning of the reading of a statement. After the pen had come to or about the base-line for 10 seconds another mark was made. Such a recorded limitation described a *GSR*. Thus, the area under the curve was evaluated as the summation of the rectangular spaces which were described by the parameter. In that there seems to be no accurate means for comparing *GSR*s from one subject to another, comparisons were made intra-subject, not inter-subject.

D. RESULTS

Four tests of the hypothesis were made. Each was a test of data accumulated by way of procedures just described.

1. The First Test

With reference to the three stimulus groups which were randomly rotated (Japanese, Jews, Mexicans), it was predicted that subjects whose *GSR*s to them were above their individual *GSR* means would rank them below the paired comparison median. For each of the three groups the X^2 test for two independent samples (4, p. 109) was used. They were: 8.54, 6.73, and 9.43 respectively. In each case $p < .005$.

2. The Second Test

Each subject's greatest *GSR* was identified now with reference to all 9 stimulus groups. The prediction was made that the group to which the greatest *GSR* was made would be ranked by the subject below the paired-comparison scale median. Here, 43 of the 53 subjects so ranked their greatest *GSR* groups. The binomial test (4, p. 41) result was: $z = -4.41$, $p < .00003$.

3. The Third Test

This test was the same as the second except that instead of the single greatest *GSR*, the two greatest were here identified for each subject. It was predicted that the subject would rank *both* of these groups below the paired-comparison scale median. In this instance 41 of the 53 subjects responded as predicted: $z = -3.85$, $p < .00007$.

4. The Fourth Test

The 9 stimulus groups were ranked for the sample according to *GSR* magnitude and according to paired-comparison position. It was predicted that a substantial correlation between *GSR* magnitudes and paired-comparison rank positions would obtain. The Spearman rank coefficient was .82.

E. SUMMARY AND CONCLUSIONS

This study was the third in a series designed to test the prevalently held view that when prejudicial-attitudes are brought into play they are affectively supported. The first two studies (2, 3) provided evidence in support of this view. These studies showed a consistent relationship between prejudicial-attitude strength and affectivity level. Subjects used in these first two studies were only those who had already indicated relatively strong prejudicial-attitudes toward particular social groups by way of rating and ranking scale performance.

The present study, the third, was designed as a "check" on the first two, and differed from them in two principal ways. First, the sample was random, in the sense that information with reference to subjects' prejudicial-attitudes had nothing to do with their selection. Second, GSRs were recorded first and paired-comparison scales were administered later. In the latter respect, the third study was a reversal of the procedure used in the first two.

In individual experimental sessions, 9 complimentary statements were read to subjects. Each statement referred to an ethnic or national group. The GSR was automatically recorded for each statement. At a later time subjects completed a paired-comparison scale which ranked the groups with reference to preference.

It was predicted that relatively great affectivity (as measured by relatively great GSR) would be indicative of relatively great anti-pathetic prejudicial-attitude (as measured by a relatively low position on the paired-comparison scale). Four tests of this prediction were made.

The first test indicated that relatively great and small GSRs, which are elicited by group naming complimentary statements, are respectively predictive of relatively low and high paired-comparison scale positions for those groups. The second test indicated that subjects who respond to a group-describing complimentary statement with an excessive GSR hold that group in antipathetic prejudicial-attitude position, as measured by paired-comparison scaling means. The third test indicated that the *two* groups which elicit greatest GSRs, when referred to by complimentary remarks, are *both* held in antipathetic prejudicial-attitude positions, as measured by paired-comparison scaling means. The fourth test indicated that ranking of the sample's GSR magnitudes correlate at a high order with its ranking of prejudicial-attitudes as scaled by paired-comparison.

The results of this study confirm those of two previous studies which demonstrated a relationship between prejudicial-attitude content and strength, and level of affectivity. The effect of these findings lends additional support to the contention that prejudicial-attitudes are affectively supported.

REFERENCES

1. Cooper, J. B. Prejudicial attitudes and the identification of their stimulus objects: A phenomenological approach. In publication, *J. Soc. Psychol.*
2. Cooper, J. B., and Siegel, H. E. The galvanic skin response as a measure of emotion in prejudice. *J. of Psychol.*, 1956, **42**, 149-155.
3. Cooper, J. B., and Singer, D. N. The rôle of emotion in prejudice. *J. Soc. Psychol.*, 1956, **44**, 241-247.
4. Siegel, S. *Nonparametric Statistics.* New York: McGraw-Hill, 1956.

21. The AB Scales: An Operational Definition of Belief and Attitude

MARTIN FISHBEIN and BERTRAM H. RAVEN

Many social psychologists have seen fit to distinguish between "belief" and "attitude." Generally, cognitive aspects have been attributed to "beliefs" and affective or motivational aspects have been attributed to "attitudes" (Allport, 1954; Campbell, 1961; Katz and Stotland, 1959; Krech and Crutchfield, 1948). This paper attempts further to clarify these two concepts by providing, what we consider to be, a much-needed operational distinction between "belief" and "attitude."

In a study stimulated by Festinger's (1957) theory of cognitive dissonance, it appeared that an individual's conceptions of extra-sensory perception could be affected along several dimensions (Raven and Fishbein, 1961). Pressures could be exerted upon the S's belief in ESP—"What is the probability that such a phenomenon does exist?" "Is it existent or non-existent?"—or upon his evaluation of ESP—"Is ESP 'good' or 'bad'?" The latter, consistent with Osgood et al. (Osgood, 1952; Osgood and Tannenbaum, 1955; Osgood, Suci, and Tannenbaum, 1957; Doob, 1947; and Rhine, 1958), can be seen as the evaluative dimension of a concept, or more specifically, as an "attitude." The former dimension could then be considered as the probability dimension of a concept, or more specifically, as a "belief." Having arrived at these definitions, it was necessary to determine whether the two dimensions could be measured and manipulated independently.

CONSTRUCTION OF THE INSTRUMENT

Fortunately, Osgood et al. (1957) had already demonstrated that a reliable and valid measure of attitude, i.e., the evaluative dimension, could be obtained by having subjects check positions on the series of seven-place bipolar adjective scales, e.g., "good-bad," "clean-dirty," et cetera. Since the reliability of the semantic differential had already been demonstrated, it seemed that the same technique could be used to measure the probability dimension. Thus the instrument utilized in measuring both dimensions was a modified form of Osgood's semantic differential.

The adjective pairs making up the final instrument were determined empirically by asking subjects to take prescribed orientations in responding to an adjective-rating task. Twenty-two pairs of polar adjectives, representing the two dimensions, were selected on a priori grounds. These adjectives were given to fifteen graduate psychology students, randomly assigned to four groups. These respondents were asked to rate the concept "ESP" on the polar adjective scales.

Members of Group I were told to rate the concept (ESP) the way they thought it would be rated by someone who believed that extra-sensory perception existed, and who felt that ESP was a good thing. Members of Group II were told to give their ratings the way a person with a strong negative belief and a positive attitude would rate the concept; Group III received instructions to estimate the ratings of an individual with a strong positive belief and negative attitude; while Group IV was told to give ratings for an individual with strong negative belief and negative attitude.

In this case, as in the others reported herein where semantic differential ratings were used, Ss were given the standard instructions for using the semantic differential form (Osgood, Suci, and Tannenbaum, 1957). As in Osgood's

• Reprinted from *Human Relations*, 1962, **15**, 35-44, with permission of the publisher. This study was supported by the Group Psychology Branch of the Office of Naval Research (Contract Nonr 253 (54), NR 171-350).

(Concept to be rated is inserted here)

	rational			intuitive
A	harmful	−3	+3	beneficial
A	wise	+3	−3	foolish
A	dirty	−3	+3	clean
	successful			unsuccessful
B	impossible	−3	+3	possible
	educated			ignorant
	cruel			kind
	graceful			awkward
	potent			impotent
B	false	−3	+3	true
	active			passive
B	existent	+3	−3	nonexistent
A	bad	−3	+3	good
B	probable	+3	−3	improbable
	skeptical			believing
B	unlikely	−3	+3	likely
	honest			dishonest
A	sick	−3	+3	healthy
	strong			weak

*Figure 1. The AB Scales. The scales measuring attitude are marked with **A** in the left column; those measuring belief are marked **B**. The direction of scoring is also indicated with +3 and −3. None of these was indicated on the forms actually given to the subjects.*

form, each scale had three degrees of positive, three degrees of negative, and a neutral point[1] (see Figure 1).

In analyzing the data, adjective pairs that did not clearly distinguish between belief and attitude were eliminated. That is, if a particular scale was scored positive in Groups I and II (favorable attitude groups), and negative in Groups III and IV (unfavorable attitude groups), then it was considered a good attitude scale. Similarly, a scale receiving positive scores

in Groups I and III (positive belief groups), and negative scores in Groups II and IV (negative belief groups), was considered a good belief scale. Those scales that yielded positive or negative scores in three or more groups were discarded.

With the scales thus partially refined, the procedure was repeated with a new sample of 19 undergraduate psychology students, five Ss each in Groups I, II, and III, and four Ss in Group IV. Again, nondiscriminating items were discarded.

We were now left with the final instrument, which we shall call the AB Scales (see Figure 1). This instrument consists of five belief items (probable-improbable; possible-impossible; likely-unlikely; existent-nonexistent; and true-false), five attitude items (good-bad; sick-healthy; harmful-beneficial; wise-foolish; and clean-dirty),

[1] Actually, in scoring the scales, it is easier to assign values from "1" to "7," with "4" being the neutral category, thus avoiding negative quantities during statistical treatments. A constant, equivalent of four times the number of scales, can later be subtracted from the total score. We have presented our tables in the latter form, since it more clearly represents the directional aspects of beliefs and attitudes.

and ten filler items which serve somewhat to disguise the purpose of the instrument.

As an additional test, the instrument was given to another sample of twenty undergraduate Ss, five in each of the four role-play conditions. With five adjective pairs each, attitudes and beliefs could both vary between —15 and +15. Table 1 indicates that the scales did indeed differentiate quite clearly between the four role-play conditions.

*TABLE 1. Mean Attitude and Belief Scores for Role-Play Groups**

Scale	Group I	Group II	Group III	Group IV
Attitude	+10.2	+11.2	−12.2	−13.0
Belief	+15.0	−14.2	+11.8	−15.0

* Scores could range from —15 to +15. The four groups were asked to role-play respectively: I. High belief, positive attitude; II. Low belief, positive attitude; III. High belief, negative attitude; IV. Low belief, negative attitude. There were five Ss in each group.

Needless to say, the role-play conditions could not be considered as a reasonable test of the reliability or validity of our scales. Though the role-playing served as a useful tool in the selection of scale items, the actual tests of reliability and validity were conducted in non-role-playing situations. It should be pointed out that other adjective pairs might also have been used to differentiate between belief and attitude. For example, in the first undergraduate sample, "high-low" and "kind-cruel" were also found to be good attitude scales. Since we had arbitrarily decided to limit the scale to five adjective pairs for each dimension, we selected those which seemed most sensitive, while recognizing the possibility of including a greater number of adjective pairs for even greater precision.

RELIABILITY, GENERALIZABILITY, AND INTER-ITEM CORRELATIONS

Although the reliability of Osgood's semantic differential had already been demonstrated, it was felt that a specific test of the reliability of these scales was needed. Forty-three Ss rated the concept ESP on the AB Scales during one of their regular class sessions, and re-rated the concept after a four-day delay, in the same circumstances. For these 43 subjects, the correlation between attitude scores was .900, while that for belief scores was .908. Both correlations are significant well beyond the .01 level.

To test whether the independence of belief and attitude was specific to ESP, we presented the AB Scales to a fifth sample of 121 subjects. All Ss were asked to rate the concepts "extrasensory perception," "atomic fallout," and "racial prejudice." The correlations between belief and attitude for the concepts were —.168, —.069, and +.120 respectively. Thus it appears that the independence of the belief and attitude scales is not specific to ESP. It remains for further empirical investigations to determine how general such independence is in relation to other concepts, but it appears unlikely that belief in the existence of any object should correlate with the attitude toward it.

Since Osgood had empirically determined the evaluative dimension through factor-analytic techniques, there was little question about the inter-correlations of the adjective pairs comprising the A Scale. However, the B Scale was determined through a role-play procedure, and certain of Osgood's evaluative adjective pairs were eliminated from the A Scale because they failed to discriminate between the two dimensions. It therefore seemed necessary to provide inter-item correlations for both the A and the B Scales.

Following the technique of Osgood, Suci, and Tannenbaum (1957) for obtaining an inter-correlation matrix of adjective pairs for more than one concept, correlations were obtained for 53 subjects' ratings of the concepts "extrasensory perception," "atomic fallout," and "racial prejudice." The inter-correlations of the adjective pairs comprising the A Scale were all significant at less than the .01 level, with the range being from .638 to .858. Similarly, all the inter-correlations of the adjective pairs comprising the B Scale were significant at less than the .01 level, the range being from .399 to .798. Inter-correlations between adjective pairs of the A and B Scales were generally nonsignificant, although a few significant negative correlations were obtained.

A VALIDITY TEST OF THE AB SCALES

To test the validity of the AB Scales, an attempt was made selectively to alter subjects' beliefs or attitudes through the method of differential communications. Four different articles approximately one page in length were used. These were presented as excerpts from actual articles. A different article was given to each of four groups. The groups and communications were:

1. *Positive belief group*—the communication stressed phenomena that could be "explained" only by ESP.
2. *Negative belief group*—the communication stressed the lack of controls and poor experimental design in ESP experiments.
3. *Positive attitude group*—the communication stressed the values of ESP.
4. *Negative attitude group*—the communication stressed the dangers of ESP.

In composing the articles, care was taken to avoid indication by the author of his own belief or disbelief in ESP, in the attitude-change communications. Similarly, indication of attitude in the belief-change communications was avoided. There were 41 introductory psychology students in the study of belief change and 36 introductory psychology students in the attitude-change study.

In the two experiments identical procedures were used. After being given Osgood's standard instructions for using the semantic differential, the subjects rated the concept "extra-sensory perception" on the AB Scales. The subjects in each experiment were then randomly divided into two groups, with one group receiving the

positive article (for belief in Experiment I or attitude in Experiment II) and the other group receiving the negative article. After reading the material, all Ss once again rated the concept "extra-sensory perception" on the AB Scales. The actual changes in response to differential communications should yield more acceptable evidence of the validity of the scales.

From Table 2 it can be seen that attitudes were changed differentially as a function of communications designed to change attitudes ($\chi^2 = 6.13$, $p = .02$). Similarly, the belief communications had differential effects on beliefs ($\chi^2 = 10.70$, $p = .01$). The table indicates that there was also some change in beliefs as a function of attitude communication, and some change in attitudes as a function of belief communication, but neither of these differences was significant.

Another set of findings was observed in Experiment I, the groups which received the belief communication. The results were: (*a*) the pretest means and standard deviations of the two groups *vis-à-vis* both belief and attitude were not significantly different from one another; (*b*) however, there was a positive correlation of .49 (significant at the .05 level) between belief and attitude in the negative group prior to the communication; (*c*) the correlation was maintained after the communication; and (*d*)

TABLE 2. *Number of Subjects Changing Beliefs and Attitudes on AB Scales Following Communications*

Type of Communication	Frequency Change in Belief			Frequency Change in Attitude		
	Positive	No Change	Negative	Positive	No Change	Negative
A. Communications Designed to Change Beliefs						
Positive	13	2	4	6	4	9
Negative	4	1	17	2	4	16
	χ^2 (1 df) = 10.695* $p = .01$			χ^2 (1 df) = 1.77* p = n.s.		
B. Communications Designed to Change Attitudes						
Positive	8	5	5	9	1	8
Negative	4	3	11	1	1	16
	χ^2 (1 df) = 2.81* p = n.s.			χ^2 (1 df) = 6.13* $p = .02$		

* "Positive" and "no change" cells combined. Chi-squares were corrected for continuity. *P*-values are the same when "negative" and "no change" cells are combined.

therefore, in addition to obtaining a significant belief change, there was also a significant attitude change in the negative group ($p = .008$, two-tailed sign test). Thus, though the above data demonstrated that it is possible independently to manipulate beliefs and attitudes, as here defined, and that one can obtain non-correlated measures, it seems that there are some situations in which the two may be correlated. This is of much theoretical interest in its own right, and should be investigated further.

DISCUSSION

If our independent manipulation of belief and attitude seems inconsistent with other treatments of these concepts in the literature (e.g., Campbell, 1950; Campbell, 1961; Carlson, 1956; Newcomb, 1953; Rosenberg, 1958, 1960), it would be well to keep in mind the specific definitions of "belief" and "attitude" which have been utilized thus far in this paper. In prior discussions, "attitude" was often defined as *including* "belief." For example, Krech and Crutchfield (1948) define belief as "an enduring organization of perceptions and cognitions about some aspect of the individual's world," and attitude as "an enduring organization of *motivational, emotional,* perceptual and cognitive processes with respect to some aspect of the individual's world." Accordingly, any change in the cognitive aspect of some attitudinal object would, by their definition, entail a change in the attitude toward that object. They would also consider some beliefs which do not involve any evaluation. When defined as the probability dimension, a belief can change independently of an attitude. Further, two individuals may differ in belief but have similar attitudes, or vice versa. In addition, with respect to any object of belief, it is possible to obtain a measure of the evaluative dimension, or attitude, toward that object; such evaluation may vary from negative through zero to positive.

Perhaps it will appear that this definition of belief is a very specialized one. It seems reasonable to consider the degree of belief in the existence of ESP, God, life after death, gremlins, etc., but with respect to other objects, practically everyone would agree that the objects exist. Yet, here too, there might be disagreement as to the extent of existence. For example, there is no reason to assume that a person living in a totalitarian state will believe as strongly in the existence of "the church" as individuals living in democratic societies. Similarly, people living in all-white communities may believe less strongly in the existence of "Negroes" than people who have had personal experience with Negroes.

The definition of belief thus far considers only the probability of the existence of an object. Of course, any object that exists must exist in some fashion. In understanding beliefs, should we be content simply to measure the perceived probability of existence, or should we not also be concerned with the precise nature of that existence? Such a question compels us to suggest a distinction between *belief in* an object, and *belief about* an object. Thus far, we have defined *belief in,* or more completely, *belief in the existence of,* an object. One could also consider *belief in the existence of a relationship* between that object and some other object, or some quality. Having measured belief in the existence of ESP, one might also be concerned with belief in the existence of relationships involving ESP, such as "ESP is spiritualistic," "ESP is a type of communication," "ESP leads to thought control," "ESP is beneficial." Any of these statements could be placed above the AB Scales and the belief in the existence of that particular relationship could be measured. The various *beliefs in* the relationships between an object and other objects or qualities would then be defined as *beliefs about* that object. While *belief in* refers to the existence of an object, *belief about* deals with the nature of that object, the manner in which it exists. It is obvious that individuals can thus agree in their belief in an object, but differ in their beliefs about that object, i.e., in their estimation of the various qualities and objects which might be associated with a given object. The various relationships involved in *belief about* an object are innumerable: "is part of," "has the characteristic of," "is opposed to," "leads to," "is the opposite of," et cetera. Many individuals who agree that ESP exists may disagree as to whether it is "powerful," "mystical," or "insidious." Religious controversy through the ages has obtained among individuals who were agreed as to their *belief in* God, but who were not agreed in their *beliefs about* him—as to whether or not he was "omnipotent," "omniscient," "vengeful," "had a Son," et cetera. The AB Scale which was used earlier to measure *belief in* an object could similarly be used to measure *belief about* an object, since the significant relational statements could also be measured on the belief scale. When Carlson (1956) introduced information which led subjects to associate desegregation in housing with changes in our international relations, he was, in effect, manipulating *belief about* segregation, and probably also belief about our international relations.

How, then, could one account for Carlson's finding that, for moderately prejudiced subjects, attitude toward segregated housing changed when he presented information indicating that desegregation would lead to improved American prestige abroad, and that such action was associated with "equal opportunities for all" and "broad-mindedness"? We would consider that he had altered belief in a number of relationships involving desegregation, thus he had altered *beliefs about* desegregation. Furthermore, the subjects had positive attitudes toward the various qualities and objects to which desegregation was related. From various theories of imbalance or dissonance (Festinger, 1957; Heider, 1958; Newcomb, 1953; Osgood, Suci, and Tannenbaum, 1957; Osgood, 1960; Rosenberg, 1960; Zajonc, 1960), one would expect a change in attitude which would restore balance. Heider might diagram the relationship as shown in Figure 2.

In these diagrams, *p* represents the subject; *x* represents "desegregation"; *y*, "American prestige abroad"; the arrows from *p* to *x* and *y* indicate "liking" or attitudinal relationships; the arrow from *x* to *y* indicates a unit-forming relationship. In our system, the lines *px* and *py* represent attitudes of *p* toward *x* and *y* respectively; the line *xy* represents a belief in the existence of a relationship between *x* and *y*—a belief about *x*.

From this system, it appears that balance could also have been restored by changing the attitude toward "American prestige abroad" to negative. Further, another alternative for restoring balance is for *S* not to believe in the existence of the relationship between "desegregation" and "American prestige abroad." That is, the *xy* relationship might have been changed to a negative one. This is quite likely what happened with many of Carlson's subjects who had strong negative attitudes toward desegregation and who did not change their attitudes as a result of Carlson's operations. Hypothetically, the imbalance situation could not occur if *S* did not believe in the existence of either "desegregation" or "American foreign policy."

With our scale system, these changes could be readily checked by (*a*) placing "desegregation" at the top of the scales, and measuring attitude toward and belief in "desegregation"; (*b*) placing "American prestige abroad" above the scales and measuring attitudes toward and belief in "American prestige abroad"; and (*c*) placing the phrase "desegregation improves American prestige abroad" above the scales and measuring the belief in the existence of this relationship. In addition, a measure of the attitude toward this last relationship may also be obtained.

Following these considerations, Fishbein (1961) has recently investigated the functional relationships between attitude toward an object, attitudes toward other concepts, and the beliefs about the object, i.e., the beliefs in the existence of relationships between the object and these concepts. The data are supportive of the conceptualization discussed above.

SUMMARY

In this paper a theoretical and operational basis for distinguishing "belief" and "attitude" has been suggested. "Belief" was defined as the probability dimension of a concept—"Is its existence probable or improbable?" "Attitude" was defined as the evaluative dimension of a concept—"Is it good or bad?" A set of semantic differential scales was selected through role-

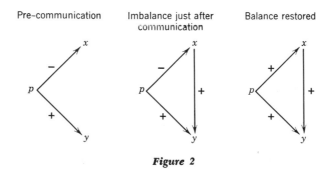

Pre-communication   Imbalance just after communication   Balance restored

Figure 2

playing procedures which yielded a set of five polar adjectives that measure belief, and five that measure attitude. Tests with several concepts showed no correlation between ratings of objects on these two sets of scales. Communications were presented to different groups of Ss which appeared to affect "attitude" and "belief" independently. In these studies, the reliability and validity of the distinction were established.

Later discussion distinguished between "belief in" a concept and "belief about" a concept, the latter being defined as belief in the existence of a number of relationships between the concept and other concepts. It was shown that a change in attitude toward a particular concept could result from a change in *belief about* that concept. Techniques for testing such influence with the new scales were suggested.

REFERENCES

Allport, G. W. (1954). *The nature of prejudice.* New York: Addison-Wesley.

Campbell, D. T. (1950). The indirect assessment of social attitudes. *Psychol. Bull.,* **47,** 15-38.

Campbell, D. T. (1961). Social attitudes and other acquired behavioral dispositions. In S. Koch (Ed.), *Psychology: A study of a science.* Vol. 6. New York: McGraw-Hill.

Carlson, E. R. (1956). Attitude change through modification of attitude structure. *J. abnorm. soc. Psychol.,* **52,** 256-261.

Doob, L. S. (1947). The behavior of attitudes. *Psychol. Rev.,* **54,** 135-156.

Festinger, L. (1957). *A theory of cognitive dissonance.* Evanston, Ill.: Row, Peterson.

Fishbein, M. (1961). An investigation of some of the theoretical and empirical relations between belief and attitude. University of California, Los Angeles. Unpublished doctoral dissertation.

Heider, F. (1958). *The psychology of interpersonal relations.* New York: Wiley.

Katz, D., and Stotland, E. (1959). A preliminary statement to a theory of attitude structure and change. In S. Koch (Ed.), *Psychology: A study of a science.* New York: McGraw-Hill, Vol. 3.

Krech, D., and Crutchfield, R. (1948). *Theory and problems of social psychology.* New York: McGraw-Hill.

Newcomb, T. M. (1946). The influence of attitude climate upon some determinants of information. *J. abnorm. soc. Psychol.,* **41,** 291-302.

Newcomb, T. M. (1953). An approach to the study of communicative acts. *Psychol. Rev.,* **60,** 393-404.

Osgood, C. E. (1952). The nature and measurement of meaning. *Psychol. Bull.,* **49,** 197-237.

Osgood, C. E., and Tannenbaum, P. H. (1955). The principle of congruity in the prediction of attitude change. *Psychol. Rev.,* **62,** 42-55.

Osgood, C. E., Suci, G. J., and Tannenbaum, P. H. (1957). *The measurement of meaning.* Urbana: University of Illinois Press.

Raven, B. H., and Fishbein, M. (1961). Acceptance of punishment and change in belief. *J. abnorm. soc. Psychol.,* **63,** 411-416.

Rhine, R. J. (1958). A concept-formation approach to attitude acquisition. *Psychol. Rev.,* **65,** 362-9.

Rosenberg, M. J. (1958). Research program on affective and cognitive aspects of attitude change. Yale University. (Annual Report, Contract Nonr-609 (27).)

Rosenberg, M. J. (1960). A structural theory of attitude dynamics. *Publ. Opin. Quart.,* **24,** 319-340.

Zajonc, R. B. (1960). The concepts of balance, congruity, and dissonance. *Publ. Opin. Quart.,* **24,** 280-296.

22. The Own Categories Procedure in Attitude Research

MUZAFER SHERIF and CAROLYN WOOD SHERIF

The Own Categories Procedure is a general method for the study of social attitudes which avoids certain limitations inherent in many available models for attitude measurement and provides more information about the individual's attitude than most of them. The procedure yields quantitative indicators of the individual's attitude and the degree of its importance to him, through the number of categories he uses and the pattern of his judgments in the categories.

In this paper, we shall first describe the procedure, then summarize the theoretical basis for its use in attitude research, as briefly as possible. Next, research findings will be described which indicate some major variables affecting the measures yielded by the procedure. Finally, the utility of the procedure in attitude research will be discussed briefly.

DESCRIPTION OF PROCEDURE

The phrase "Own Categories" reflects the translation of the conception of attitude into operational procedures. Attitude is conceived as a set of *evaluative* categories which the individual has formed (or learned) during his interaction with persons and objects in his social world. When faced with persons, objects, or events relevant to his attitude, the individual uses these categories for classifying specific items as acceptable-unacceptable, good-bad, truthful-erroneous, or other appropriate evaluative terms. In this sense, they are his "own categories" for evaluation, as contrasted with the division of a stimulus domain under labels arbitrarily imposed by an authority figure, an

• This paper was prepared for the Symposium on Attitude Measurement and Attitude Change at the International Congress of Applied Psychology, Ljubljana, Jugoslavia, 1964. It is used with the permission of the senior author.

experimenter, or a survey interviewer. They are his personal reference scale for appraising the stimulus domain in question.

To the extent that the object of the attitude is socially relevant, individuals belonging to the same group or culture will share rather similar attitudes, hence each individual's own categories are not necessarily unique to him. The bounds of their acceptances will vary within a range defining the "proper," "the acceptable," and the "desirable" way of viewing the stimulus domain and behaving toward it in their group or society. This range of positions defined as acceptable, plus a range of positions defining what is unacceptable in a group or society represents one social norm in their set of values or norms, which is an important aspect of its culture.

The Own Categories Procedure starts with preparation of a set of items relevant to an attitude. These may be objects, pictures, or verbal statements about some topic or issue. The content of the items may vary, however, the logic of the procedures need not change with the content. Major criteria in assembling the pool of items will be specified later. In research thus far, the number of items has varied from 25 to over one hundred.

The individual's task is simple and natural in any culture where sorting objects is a familiar task. He is instructed to sort the pool of items into any number of piles, or categories, that seem to him necessary, so that items within each category seem to him to "belong together." The dimension or attribute which he is to judge is specified clearly. For some research purposes, he is told to categorize them in terms of their acceptability to him.

If, however, the aim is a "disguised" or "indirect" test of his attitudes, instructions are used which do not arouse his awareness that his stand is under the scrutiny of a stranger, or researcher. Then, he is told to place the items into categories as objectively as possible in terms of how "favorable" or "unfavorable" they are toward the persons, events, issues, or objects in question. For example, he may be told to categorize statements concerning Negro citizens of the United States in terms of their "favorableness" to the status of the Negro. One extreme category is specified in instructions, e.g., "Put the statements most unfavorable to Negroes in the first pile." Otherwise, utmost caution is used to avoid hints as to the number of categories to be used, and the individual is free to distribute the items into the categories in any way he chooses.

When his task is completed to his satisfaction, the individual is usually asked to order his categories. He may be asked to label or describe them, either in terms of the explicit criterion stated in instructions or in terms of their acceptability-unacceptability to him personally. These variations depend upon the research purpose and hypotheses.

THEORETICAL BASIS OF THE PROCEDURE

The present approach started with the search for reference scales which are psychologically and socially valid for the study of attitude and attitude change. In an unpublished study in 1948 (Sherif, Volkart, and Hovland), we found that the bounds of the positions accepted and rejected on a social issue vary, even for persons upholding the same position as most acceptable. A series of studies on a variety of social issues over the last 15 years has confirmed the early finding, namely, that the ranges of the positions that an individual accepts, rejects, and toward which he remains noncommittal (when not required to evaluate every position) vary systematically according to his personal involvement in the issue (Sherif and Hovland, 1961; Sherif, Sherif, and Nebergall, 1965). There is a high probability that the individual who endorses an extreme position will rank that issue high in importance, within his scheme of personal priorities. But those adopting a moderate position with equal ardor display patterns of acceptance-rejection-noncommitment similar to their more extreme counterparts.

Specifically, we found that individuals highly involved in some stand on a social issue reject many more positions than they accept, and readily evaluate almost every position as acceptable *or* objectionable. (Their *latitudes of rejec-*

tion are approximately twice the size of their *latitudes of acceptance,* and noncommitment approaches zero.) Proportional to his lack of involvement, the number of positions the individual accepts and rejects become approximately equal and his latitude of noncommitment increases. This means that highly involved persons have a much broader latitude of rejection than persons less concerned, and that they remain noncommittal toward fewer positions, even when not required to evaluate all of them.

What psychological principles underlie these differences in the size of the individual's latitudes for acceptance, rejection, and noncommitment? We had no factual basis for positing a typology of individuals as to the range of their tolerance, nor for unmeasurable "psychodynamic mechanisms" which would account for the different patterns. We still have no such evidence. We sought a theoretical basis for the phenomena sufficiently broad to encompass the considerable factual evidence that a particular individual may tolerate differences on issues of little concern to him—to the point of self-contradiction—while seeing a matter of high personal concern in terms of "black and white." There is also evidence that the ranges for toleration and condemnation vary from one human group to another.

We found such a basis in the psychology of judgment, studied for decades in psychological laboratories in various countries. Our account of the principles essential to the present approach is necessarily brief and sketchy (cf. Sherif and Sherif, 1956; Sherif and Hovland, 1961; Sherif, Sherif, and Nebergall, 1965). Whether the object of judgment is a weight, the length of a line, the color of a person's skin, or the beauty of a girl, judgment is rendered relative to the immediate stimulus context in which it appears and to preceding contexts.

For example, quite apart from one's attitude on the issue of the segregation of public schools according to skin color or national origin, a statement such as "We must keep the future interests of school children in mind" is appraised differently when preceded by other statements opposed to segregation, on the one hand, or favoring segregation, on the other.

But not all the stimuli present or just preceding a judgment have equal weight in affecting the outcome, even in the psychophysical laboratory where the stimuli are motivationally neutral. In the orthodox psychophysical methods, the standard stimulus presented with each new stimulus for comparison is more influential than others less frequently presented, or not designated as a standard (Helson, 1959, p. 591). Such frequently presented stimuli, or those designated as standards, become anchors for the individual's judgments. Lacking an explicit standard, the individual typically uses the most extreme stimuli presented to him as anchors in sizing up the intermediate values; and the end stimuli thus contribute more than others to his judgment of a particular member of the series (Parducci, 1963).

An anchor stimulus or a designated standard enhances the accuracy of judgment for items coinciding with it in value; but it produces systematic shifts or "displacements" in judgments of objects differing from it in varying degrees. An anchor differing slightly from the object of judgment results in displacement *toward* the anchor: this is an *assimilation effect,* well known in studies of perception and now thoroughly established in judgment (cf. Sherif, Taub, and Hovland, 1958; Parducci and Marshall, 1962; Helson, 1964). With increasing discrepancies between the anchor and the object of judgment, assimilation ceases and displacement begins to occur in a direction away from the anchor: the difference between the anchor and the object is exaggerated. This is the well-known *contrast effect.* Assimilation and contrast in judgment are complementary phenomena governed by the relationships between anchor and object of judgment.

In 1950, a series of studies was initiated to clarify the differences and similarities between judgments of neutral and socially relevant items, ranging from experiments with lifted weights to studies of the scale values of attitudinal statements. On this basis, a conceptual approach was developed which does account for the distinctive patterning of latitudes of acceptance-rejection and which provides the theoretical basis of the Own Categories Procedure. The approach is based on the relationships governing assimilation-contrast effects, taking into account the following generalizations:

1. If a person has an attitude toward the stimulus domain, his judgments of specific objects in that domain are, to some extent, relative to the categories of his own reference scale, in addition to the context of immediate and preceding stimulation.

2. To the extent that the domain has high priority in his scheme of personal relatedness with his social world, his latitude of acceptance becomes an anchor or standard for his placement of other items in the domain. In other words, the range of positions acceptable to him becomes an anchor proportional to his personal involvement in upholding it.

3. To the extent that his own position becomes the most salient anchor in the situation, the individual's categorization of items is *evaluation* of the items. There is now a considerable body of research supporting this statement (Sherif, Sherif, and Nebergall, 1965). Even when instructed to heed only the stimulus attributes of the items and categorize them on an impersonal dimension, the highly involved individual performs the task in terms of his agreements-disagreements with the items, including his assessments of their truth and falsity. One may temporarily force him to follow instructions by insisting that he compare one item with another, as in the method of paired comparisons. He *can* discriminate among the items, but barring special arrangements requiring him to do so, he simply does not divorce the task of judging the items from his evaluations of them.

4. When his own stand is the anchor, other items will be displaced toward his acceptable category (assimilation) or away from it (contrast), proportional to their proximity or difference from his own stand. The additional, necessary condition for these systematic displacements is that the objects lack, in some degree, objective properties which are readily and uniformly perceived as defining membership in a particular category. For example, strongly worded statements of an extreme position on a social issue are not displaced systematically to any significant degree. They are readily identified as extreme positions in terms of the prevailing social realities. Systematic displacements are found, however, for less extreme and intermediate positions on the same issues.

With these four additions, the theoretical approach accounts for the phenomena which are used to study attitudes with the Own Categories Procedure.

RESEARCH USING THE OWN CATEGORIES PROCEDURE

Using this conceptualization, Sherif and Hovland (1953) predicted that individuals strongly involved in problems of the status of Negro citizens would (a) use fewer categories for judging statements on the issue than less involved individuals, and (b) place fewer statements in the category of items most acceptable to them than in the category most objectionable to them. Highly involved Negro students (who were the first admitted to a previously white university), active white participants in the desegregation movement, Negroes at a segregated university, a few consistently anti-Negro whites, and unselected white students were the subjects. They sorted 114 statements prepared by Hinckley as the preliminary pool for item selection for a Thurstone attitude scale. The pool contained pro-Negro and anti-Negro statements with a large number of intermediate items having high Q values (high variability). The statements were sorted by the Own Categories Procedure, either two weeks before or two weeks after the same subjects judged them using 11 categories as prescribed in the Thurstone "equal-appearing intervals" method (Hovland and Sherif, 1952).

They found that highly involved persons, judging these statements in terms of their favorableness-unfavorableness to Negroes, produced bimodal distributions of the statements into categories: intermediate categories were neglected, while a disproportionate number of items was placed in the extreme category farthest removed from the position the individual found acceptable. The bimodal distribution was greatly accentuated under the Own Categories Procedure owing to the significant tendency for highly involved persons to use fewer categories. In fact, the most militant Negro subjects used, on the average, fewer than four categories, placed 65 of the 114 statements in a single category highly objectionable to them and 27 in a category acceptable to them. In comparison, unselected white students placed 43 statements in objectionable categories, and 38 in categories they later indicated were acceptable.

Using a combined index of skewness of the judgment distribution and number of categories, Sherif and Hovland found that these two measures differentiated between their subject groups according to their personal involvement in the problem of the status of Negroes. Proportional to their involvement, their threshold for acceptance was raised, as indicated by a smaller mode in the distribution of judgments in acceptable categories. Their threshold of rejection was lowered, as indicated by the disproportionately high mode of the distribution at categories they later said were objectionable. These peaks in the distribution reveal the individual's acceptable and objectionable categories, the objectionable category being wider.

Latitude of Acceptance as Anchor in Evaluation

Carolyn Sherif (1961) compared the evaluative and nonevaluative categories of American Indian and white high school students of comparable educational level. Since the ranges of acceptable items varied according to their cultural backgrounds in several respects, it was possible to show contrasting evaluations of the same items by the Indian and white students according to their latitudes of acceptance, while demonstrating that their categorizations of neutral items did not differ.

Using the Own Categories Procedure, each individual sorted four sets of items. The Indian and white students categorized series of digits (numbers) in comparable fashion, attempting to fit the items into equal categories according to the decimal system. Their categories for *evaluating* the same digits when preceded by dollar signs differed significantly from these; and differences between the Indians and whites were significant.

Having previously conducted a cultural survey, Sherif (1963) knew that the prevailing bounds for acceptable expenditures of money differed. For example, reflecting an elaborate tradition of gift-giving in their culture, Indians considered much larger sums of money necessary for an appropriate gift than whites, but much smaller sums than whites were deemed acceptable for wearing apparel. When evaluating the series of numbers as dollar values, their latitude of acceptance was the main anchor, with the result that their evaluative categories were highly unequal when the range of prices exceeded acceptable bounds. To the extent that the price range was beyond acceptable bounds, the discrepant items were lumped together in one category as extremely objectionable.

This experiment showed that the "relativity of judgment" is not solely in terms of the immediate and preceding stimulus context of judgment, but is also affected by the individual's own categories for what is acceptable and objectionable whenever *evaluations* are rendered. For this reason, the Own Categories Procedure is suitable for assessing similarities and differences in reference scales prevailing in different cultures even when the objects of evaluation are not extremely involving to the individuals.

Salience of Attitudinal Anchors Varies with Degree of Involvement

C. Sherif's study also showed that the number of categories used varied systematically according to the individual's relative involvement with the four different sets of items. On the average, all subjects used more categories for the digits than they did for series of socially valued items. The three sets of socially valued items were ranked in personal importance by a paired comparisons procedure. The number of categories used in evaluating them differed, in turn, according to their rank in personal importance.

More categories were used for the monetary values than for descriptions of interpersonal behavior, and the fewest categories used for assessing the desirability of interpersonal contact with members of different ethnic groups. An intra-class correlation of .38 for the number of categories used by the same individuals for the four different materials was significant, but sufficiently low to indicate that most of the variance was accountable to the differing personal relevance of the item content.

A recent experiment by Glixman (1965) with different subjects and stimulus materials supports this conclusion. He reports that individuals used fewer categories in appraising descriptive statements about themselves than in sorting familiar objects, even though a much larger number of the self-descriptions was presented. He also reports correlation coefficients for individual consistency in number of categories used for three item contents which vary around .35 for his different subject samples.

It may be objected that significant differences in number of categories used by the same individuals in categorizing sets of items which differ in personal import are confounded by differences in the stimulus material itself—by the experimenter's incapacity to equate the range of the domains in question, and so on. The objection is appropriate. In this connection, a research thesis by John Reich (1963) directed by M. Sherif is pertinent.

Reich studied the own categories of mature women between the ages of 35 and 50 with

median years of schooling exceeding four years of university study. The attitude in question concerned legislative re-apportionment. Owing to the growth of urban areas, the number of representatives to the state legislature from different districts no longer represented the relative sizes of their populations. Reich secured active members of the League of Women Voters, which had dedicated its major efforts to remedying this situation, as individuals highly involved in the issue. The less involved subjects were women school teachers, who also favored re-apportionment, but were not particularly concerned with the issue, as indicated by lack of overt acts and expressions of opinion. The two samples were matched by age and education as closely as possible.

It is interesting to note that persons who were *opponents* to re-apportionment changed their stands during the study. A Federal Court ruling, stating that the legislature *must* re-apportion, shifted his anti-reapportionment subjects to a pro-apportionment position according to an out-moded formula which no one had supported up to that time. We mention this change to emphasize the fact that the individual's own categories are inevitably tied, to some extent, to the reference scales prevailing in the social realities of his time and place. Similar shifts in the positions on psychosocial scales have been observed in the United States over the past century by groups favoring and opposing a federal income tax and, more recently, desegregation of public facilities.

From a pool of 120 statements on the issue of re-apportionment, Reich chose 60 from pretests with 79 subjects. Fifteen were consistently judged as *pro,* 15 consistently as *anti,* and 30 had been judged with high variability. In categorizing these 60 statements by the Own Categories Procedure, 74 per cent of the highly involved women used four or fewer categories, while only 26 per cent of the teachers used such a small number. The less involved teachers placed about the same number of statements in favorable and unfavorable categories, but the highly involved League members placed over half of the statements in unfavorable categories, which they found extremely objectionable.

The League members saw the issue in "black and white," and mostly "black," despite the fact that they were equally well educated and highly conversant with the complexities of legislative re-apportionment. Because of their superior information on the issue, they doubtless *could* have made finer discriminations than the teachers. The fact is, that given the opportunity to categorize the positions in their own way, they did *not* make fine discriminations.

The Crucial Role of the Intermediate Items

An earlier study by La Fave and Sherif (1962) provided convincing evidence that the distinctively bimodal distributions of judgments obtained by the Own Categories Procedure occurred through systematic displacements of the intermediate items. Twenty-five items on the issue of desegregation of public facilities were selected through pre-tests in order to have five representatives in each of the following classes: Very Integrationist, Integrationist, Moderate, Segregationist, and Very Segregationist. Variability in placement of the items in the two extreme categories was low. Three samples judged the position of these 25 statements under the Own Categories instructions.

The highly involved, favorable subjects were 95 Negroes from a state Negro university in the southwest; the least involved were 144 unselected white undergraduate students in a desegregated university. In an effort to secure highly involved, anti-Negro subjects, 79 members of a college fraternity with strong ties to Southern tradition were used. The fraternity members, however, were a heterogeneous lot, as noted in the next section.

Owing to the small number of items (25), variations in number of categories used were less than in other studies previously cited. However, 92 per cent of the Negro subjects used four or fewer categories, and fully 68 per cent used three or fewer. In comparison, 46 per cent of the unselected white students used five or more categories for the 25 items. Of the Southern Fraternity members, 77 per cent used four or fewer categories.

Over 87 per cent of Negroes placed more items in categories which they labeled as favoring segregation than in those favoring desegregation. Among Southern fraternity members, the distribution was reversed by 59 per cent of the sample, that is, more judgments were made as favoring desegregation. Unselected white students distributed their judgments more evenly, 55 per cent of them placing equal numbers of items in favorable and unfavorable categories.

Tracing down the items responsible for the bimodal distributions of most Negro and a majority of Southern fraternity members, La Fave and Sherif were able to show that they occurred through systematic displacements of 13 statements which were intermediate to the extremes and had high Q values. The Negro subjects using fewer categories accumulated such statements in categories unfavorable to integration —a contrast effect relative to their own pro-integration stand. The Southern fraternity members, a majority of whom opposed integration, accumulated such statements in categories favoring integration—again a contrast effect.

This research shows the importance of one of the major requirements in preparing a pool of items for the Own Categories Procedures: the array must include, between the extremes, a large number of items which are "intermediate" in position or are ambiguous in their position with respect to the extremes. Judgments of such items are characterized by great variability. They are, in short, items which are typically discarded in the construction of most conventional attitude tests as too variable.

Studies by Zimbardo (1960) and La Fave et al. (1963) show that the characteristics of such items which make them subject to systematic displacement according to the individual's attitude are not adequately described simply as "ambiguity," and that the inclusion of adjectives with positive or negative connotation reduces variability in placement. The items which we have found most suitable are those representing positions on an issue which are not well known, positions which are the object of wide disagreement (for example, "neutrality" on a "hot" intergroup or international issue), and statements whose meaning is "indeterminate." An example of the latter is borrowed from Zimbardo's study (1960) of university students majoring in science or in the humanities, namely: "Anyone who has known a scientist personally will know why science is where it is today."

The second major requirement for preparing a pool of items is that the range or variety should be large, including extreme positions on social issues or, in cross-cultural comparisons of reference scales, covering a range beyond usual experience and tradition. This requirement reflects the fact that the particular range of values presented for judgment does affect the placement of particular items.

For example, C. Sherif (1961) found that Indian and white students used narrower categories, thus discriminated more keenly, when presented a range of items which were largely acceptable to them than when objectionable items were also included. This corresponds to the well-known tendency to see fine shades of difference when dealing with friends or allies, but to ignore many of these differences when one's friends are compared with enemies.

Comparison of Findings for Persons For and Against the Object of Attitude

In the studies reviewed thus far, the use of few categories and the bimodal distributions of items in them have been shown most decisively for individuals who uphold stands intensely favorable toward the objects. The practical reason for this deserves comment. In selecting highly involved subjects, we have relied as much as possible on their known public actions and statements on the issue in question. Particularly in relation to the Negro issue, it has not been possible to obtain subjects who publicly state and act upon an anti-Negro position.

In an effort to remedy this lack, we have used not one, but a combination of criteria for an *anti* position, including conventional paper-and-pencil tests of attitude toward the Negro, self-ratings, and observation of behavior. On the basis of these criteria, we found that only 41 of the 78 Southern fraternity members could be classified as consistently anti-Negro.

The inconsistencies we have found were traceable to self-reports of attitude *or* paper-and-pencil tests. The explanation is not complex. There is a collegiate norm which prevails among students in all but a few places which makes an open stand against the Negro simply "not the thing to do." In their self-ratings and paper-and-pencil tests, aware that the researcher is interested in their attitudes, many individuals respond in terms of the *researcher's expectations,* rather than in terms of their views— which they subsequently belie through anti-Negro statements to friends and sympathizers. "Social desirability" (Edwards, 1957) of their responses is the salient consideration in the research situation. Avoidance of this problem is a major advantage of the Own Categories Procedure, since it may be presented as a completely "objective" task to the subject.

In view of the lack in other studies, the use of overtly *anti* subjects by Katheryn Vaughan (1961) is particularly significant.

Vaughan conducted her study near the U. S.-Mexican border, where persons of Mexican origin compose a substantial portion of the population, and in another part of the same state about 600 miles north, where such persons are not common. In the vernacular, persons of Mexican origin or descent are called "Latins" (a more polite term than some others) and non-Latins are "Anglos."

Replicating the Sherif-Hovland study (1952, 1953), Vaughan compared the placements of statements about Latins, with 11 categories prescribed in instructions and with the Own Categories Procedure. She constructed a pool of 103 statements, selecting 60 which were composed of five sub-sets: two sub-sets consistently placed at the extremes, two with moderate variability but scale values on either a favorable or unfavorable side, and one sub-set with extremely high variability.

The results for the 11 instructed categories represent a striking mirror image of those found for Negro and pro-Negro whites in the Hovland-Sherif study (1952). Intermediate categories were neglected by intensely anti-Latins, their extreme category for pro-Latin statements was very broad, and a smaller mode in the distribution of judgments occurred at the extreme anti-Latin end, with which they agreed. Residents of the area with sparse Latin population, and little concern with it, distributed their judgments fairly evenly over the 11 categories.

The same trends were greatly accentuated using the Own Categories Procedure. Over 85 per cent of the anti-Latins used three or fewer categories, while almost 92 per cent of the uninvolved subjects used four or more categories. The range was 2-5 categories for involved anti-Latins and 2-11 for involved subjects, but only 8 per cent of the latter used three categories or fewer.

Vaughan at no time requested any statement as to which categories were acceptable or objectionable to the subjects; but she reports that many of the highly anti-Latin persons had great difficulty in following instructions to categorize the statements objectively as favorable-unfavorable to Latins. They kept insisting that many of the statements were "not true," and they had all sorts of "facts" to prove it. This observation represents the considerable evidence that the individual's Own Categories for acceptance-rejection do serve as the reference scale for his placements, even when he is warned not to use them, provided that the object of judgment is of importance to him.

CONCLUDING REMARKS

The Own Categories Procedure does not suffer from certain limitations of most available techniques for attitude measurement. Its logic does not derive from statistical or physical models for measurement, but from widely general principles of psychological functioning.

The task required of the individual does not presume a common culture or educational level, but is applicable with changed content to any cultural setting where objects are sorted.

It may be used in the study of attitudes without arousing the individual's awareness that *his attitude* is being explored for research purposes.

It yields quantitative measures both for the location of his acceptable and most objectionable categories and his degree of involvement in the matter. A restricted number of categories with the greatest mode in the judgment distribution at the objectionable segment and a secondary mode at the acceptable segment is typical of highly involved persons. To the extent that the individual is little involved in the matter at hand, his distribution of the items approaches more equal divisions into a greater number of categories. In this event, the acceptable and objectionable categories may be ascertained *after* he has sorted them, from the labels he uses for the various categories.

When appropriate for the research purposes, the individual may be asked directly to evaluate the objects in terms of his acceptances-rejections. By varying the stimulus material, it is possible to assess individuals' categories relative to those prevailing in their own and different cultural groups, and to predict their reactions to cultural items deviating from their latitudes of acceptance. In fact, we believe that findings on the individual's own categories will have much greater predictive value than most conventional tests yielding a single position to represent the individual's attitude.

For example, in our study of reactions to communications on the 1960 Presidential Election we found that highly committed partisans of the major parties judged a communication mildly favoring their opponent as much more extreme than it was—contrasting it to their own position by displacing it *away* from their own position. Less involved persons adopting the *same* position as most acceptable assimilated the identical communication *toward* their own position. This finding is predictable when one knows that the less involved person has a more finely differentiated set of categories and that he is noncommittal toward those in the segment of positions presented by the speaker. The highly involved person, on the other hand, has very broad categories, including one or more for objectionable positions, and this latitude of rejection covers moderate positions.

In our opinion, the use of similar theory and procedures for the study of reactions to sociocultural change and innovation is one of the most exciting among several problems to be explored through the Own Categories Procedure.

SELECTED AND SUMMARY REFERENCES

Edwards, A. L., 1957. *The Social Desirability Variable in Personality Assessment and Research.* New York: Dryden.

Glixman, A. R., 1965. Categorizing behavior as a function of meaning-domain. *J. Pers. soc. Psychol.,* **2**, 370-377.

Helson, H., 1959. Adaptation Level Theory. In S. Koch (Ed.), *Psychology: A Study of a Science.* Vol. I. *Sensory, Perceptual, and Physiological Foundations.* New York: McGraw-Hill.

Helson, H., 1964. Current trends and issues in adaptation-level theory. *Amer. Psychologist,* **19**, 26-38.

Hovland, C. I., and Sherif, M., 1952. Judgmental phenomena and scales of attitude measurement: item displacement in Thurstone scales. *J. abnorm. soc. Psychol.,* **47**, 822-832.

La Fave, L., and Sherif, M., 1962. Reference scales and placement of items with the Own Categories Technique. Paper presented to Annual Meetings, American Psychological Association, St. Louis. Norman, Oklahoma: Institute of Group Relations (mimeographed).

La Fave, L., et al., 1963. Connotation as a supplemental variable to assimilation—contrast principles psychosocial scales. Paper to American Psychological Association, Annual Meetings, Philadelphia (mimeographed).

Parducci, A., 1963. Range-frequency compromise in judgment. *Psychol. Monogr.,* **77**, 2, Whole no. 565.

Parducci, A., and Marshall, L. M. 1962. Assimilation vs. contrast in the anchoring of perceptual judgments of weight. *J. exper. Psychol.*, **63**, 426-437.

Reich, J., and Sherif, M., 1963. *Ego-Involvement as a Factor in Attitude Assessment by the Own Categories Technique.* Norman, Oklahoma: Institute of Group Relations (mimeographed).

Sherif, C. W., 1961. *Established Reference Scales and Series Effects in Social Judgment.* Austin, Texas: University of Texas.

Sherif, C. W., 1963. Social categorization as a function of latitude of acceptance and series range. *J. abnorm. soc. Psychol.*, **67**, 148-156.

Sherif, C. W., Sherif, M., and Nebergall, R. E., 1965. *Attitude and Attitude Change: The Social Judgment-Involvement Approach.* Philadelphia: W. E. Saunders Co.

Sherif, M., and Hovland, C. I., 1953. *Social Judgment: Assimilation and Contrast Effects in Communication and Attitude Change.* New Haven, Conn.: Yale University Press.

Sherif, M., and Sherif, C. W., 1956. *An Outline of Social Psychology.* New York: Harper and Row.

Sherif, M., Taub, D., and Hovland, C. I., 1958. Assimilation and contrast effects of anchoring stimuli on judgments. *J. exper. Psychol.*, **55**, 150-155.

Vaughan, K. R., 1961. *A Disguised Instrument for the Assessment of Intergroup Attitudes.* Kingsville, Texas: Texas College of Arts and Industries.

Zimbardo, P. G., 1960. Verbal ambiguity and judgmental distortion. *Psychol. Reports,* **6**, 57-58.

23. Some Studies of Social Distance

HARRY C. TRIANDIS and LEIGH M. TRIANDIS

INTRODUCTION

In all societies there are norms specifying the "correct" or "appropriate" behaviors for members when they encounter other people. For instance, some societies have what is known as a "mother-in-law taboo," a norm which states that "when you are in the presence of your mother-in-law, you hide or avoid getting close to her." Here the "person" is identified by the kin relationship, and the behavior is one of keeping physical distance.

In our society, certain kinds of people have norms of avoidance of persons who are different from themselves with respect to such characteristics as physical type (race), belief system (religion or political philosophy), occupation, nationality, and so forth. Avoidance may involve exclusion of persons with such "undesirable" characteristics from the "friendship circle," the neighborhood, the occupational group, the place of work, and sometimes from the country. The degree to which individuals are willing to accept people who differ from themselves into their own social group may be considered a measure of their "social distance" from these out-group persons. Research shows that a number of factors influence social distance judgments. The most important of these factors will be considered in this article. They include both characteristics of the persons being judged—their race, religion, nationality, occupation, and sex; and characteristics of the judges—their culture, social class, educational level, and personality traits.

THE MEASUREMENT OF SOCIAL DISTANCE

It is possible to find out what kinds of people are avoided, and how much they are

• Reprinted from I. D. Steiner and M. Fishbein (Eds.), *Current Studies in Social Psychology*, Holt, Rinehart and Winston, New York, 1965, with permission of the senior author and publisher.

avoided, by asking a person to indicate whether he would accept a particular kind of person (for example, a Negro) as an intimate friend, as a neighbor, as a fellow employee, and so on, or whether he would exclude him from such relationships. The sociologist Bogardus established a scale of social distance by employing the following items, which are listed below in the order of increasing social distance: (1) would admit to close kin by marriage; (2) would admit to my club as personal chum; (3) would admit to my street as neighbor; (4) would admit to employment in my occupation; (5) would admit to citizenship in my country; (6) would admit as a visitor only to my country; (7) would exclude from my country. Bogardus (1928) found that American white subjects maintained little social distance toward Englishmen, Canadians, and Northern Europeans, and more social distance toward Southern Europeans such as Italians and Greeks. The greatest amount of social distance was found for people who differed from the subjects with respect to racial characteristics (such as, Orientals and Negroes).

However, these results are ambiguous. When an American white subject indicates much social distance toward Negroes, it is difficult to know whether he rejects them because of their physical type or their probable lower-class background. Or, to take another example, when an American shows social distance toward Irishmen, does he object to their nationality or to their probable religion (Roman Catholic)? Triandis and Triandis (1960) avoided this ambiguity by asking their white American subjects to react to hypothetical persons who were described in greater detail than is customary in studies of social distance. Thus subjects were asked to indicate their acceptance of a Negro who is a physician, Portuguese, and a Roman Catholic. By a statistical technique called analysis of variance it was possible to find out whether the race, the occupation, the nationality, or the religion of the stimulus persons determined the social distance.

Let us clarify this procedure. The first step requires a standardization of the social distance scale. A large number of statements, such as those used by Bogardus, are presented to a group of judges. The judges are asked to indicate, on an 11-point scale, how much social distance is implied by agreement with each of the statements. Typically the statement, "I would marry this person," is given as an anchor, and defines the zero social distance point; the statement, "I would kill this person," is used as the anchor for the other end of the scale. When that is done, a judge may decide that agreement with the statement, "would exclude from the neighborhood," implies considerable social distance—say, six points on an eleven-point scale. A group of judges typically provides a distribution of such judgments for each statement. The distribution of judgments

for each statement is analyzed by a technique developed by the psychologist Thurstone, and a single scale value is derived for each statement.

Table 1 shows some social distance statements and some values obtained from such a standardization process. Suppose that an American subject is asked whether he would or would not do the various things listed in Table 1 with a "Negro Physician." Let us say that a subject indicates that he would *not* accept the Negro Physician as an intimate friend, as a close kin by marriage, as a roommate, or as a personal chum, but would accept him as a neighbor, as a family friend, in the same apartment, and so on; and would not do any of the negative things that are listed. Then the social distance of this subject toward "Negro Physicians" is 38.7.

Let us assume that a subject obtains the social distance scores shown in Table 2 when he evaluates four types of persons: Negro phy-

TABLE 1. *Scale Values of Statements Used in Two Cultures*

Statement	American Scale Value	Greek Scale Value
I would marry this person	0.00	0.00
I would accept this person as an intimate friend	11.1	13.5
I would accept this person as a close kin by marriage	21.5	28.5
I would accept this person as a roommate	29.5	—
I would accept this person as a member of my intimate social group (in Greek, *parea*)	—	31.1
I would accept this person as a personal chum in my club	31.1	—
I would accept this person as my family's friend	40.9	24.0
I would accept this person as a neighbor	38.7	—
I am going to invite this person to dinner	—	33.3
I would live in the same apartment house with this person	49.4	—
I would rent a room from this person	57.5	42.8
I would be willing to participate in the lynching of this person (in Greece: I would kill this person if I had the chance)	100.0	100.0

TABLE 2

	Negro	White	Total	
Physician	38.7	11.1	49.8 ⎫	Difference = 40.4
Unskilled laborer	68.7	21.5	90.2 ⎭	
Total	107.4	32.6		

Difference = 74.8

sicians, Negro laborers, white physicians, and white laborers.

It is intuitively clear that this subject pays more attention to the "race" of the stimulus than to the "occupation," because the difference between the "Negro" and "White" stimuli is about 75 points, while the difference between the "Physican" and "Unskilled Laborer" stimuli is only about 40.

When the analysis of variance technique is used, it is possible to learn several things:

1. Whether the subject "pays attention" to a particular characteristic. For instance, a subject might obtain the following scores:

	Negro	White
Physician	11.1	11.1
Unskilled laborer	68.7	68.7

This pattern of scores would indicate that "race" is of no relevance whatever in the determination of his social distance scores. In the analysis of variance, the characteristic "race" would be found to control no "significant amount of variance." It is desirable to compute the statistical significance of the variance of the social distance scores that is controlled by each of the characteristics of the stimulus persons so that one may disregard apparent effects that are probably accidental or undependable. The level of significance tells us whether the obtained difference in social distance scores, when shifting from the "preferred" to the "nonpreferred" value of the characteristic, is likely to have been observed by chance, or not likely to have been observed by chance. In the latter case, we may infer that the subject has been "paying attention" to the characteristic.

2. It is possible to learn the relative importance of the characteristics for the particular subject. The statistical procedure indicates how much variability in social distance scores is controlled by each of the characteristics, and also how much total variability there is in the social distance scores obtained by a particular subject. The percentage of the total variability which is controlled by a specific characteristic serves as an index of the weight of that characteristic for the subject. For example, if the total variability were 100, race might control 60 percent, occupation 30 percent, and "error" 10 percent of the total variability. We would say that the weights for race and occupation are 60 and 30. This means that race controls

twice as much variability (or makes twice as much difference) as does occupation in the determination of the subject's social distance scores.[1]

3. Finally, we can learn whether there are so-called "interactions" between the characteristics. In the first example shown above, there is an interaction between race and occupation. The subject shows some social distance toward Negroes, and some toward unskilled laborers; but he shows a particularly large amount of social distance toward the stimulus that has *both* the "nonpreferred" characteristics. The statistical technique also permits checks of the statistical significance of this interaction.

Thus, the use of this procedure permits us to learn at least three things: (1) whether the subject really pays attention to a particular stimulus characteristic, (2) whether he pays attention to combinations of characteristics, and (3) how much importance he attaches to each of the characteristics and their combinations.

THE RELATIVE IMPORTANCE OF THE CHARACTERISTICS OF THE STIMULUS PERSONS

The first study that used this technique showed that American white subjects paid some attention to all four of the characteristics used in the study and attached the following weights to them: race 77, occupation 17, religion 5, and nationality 1. (Note: these weights add to 100.) When the responses of the subjects were averaged out before the analysis, there was no evidence of any interactions but for individual subjects there were many interactions. In other words, one subject might have shown particularly large social distance

[1] To be completely correct, this procedure requires the subtraction of the error variance from the variance due to a particular source. The "correction" formula typically leads to ratios or weights that differ by less than 10 percent from the ratios obtained without the correction. In the example in the text this correction would result in weights of 45.5 and 18.2, which are still in the ratio of *about* 2 to 1. In all the work reported in this article, this correction has not been used because the "weights" obtained by the more elaborate procedure are extremely similar to the uncorrected weights. As long as one is interested in the question, "what is the order of importance of the weights," it is unnecessary to make the correction, since the corrected and uncorrected weights give the same answer.

toward "unskilled Negroes," and another toward "unskilled Jews."

Weidemann and Triandis (in preparation) did a study in which the characteristics being considered were the sex, race, religion and status of the stimulus persons. Since many of the social distance items that are appropriate for other groups (such as, admit to my street as neighbor, admit to close kin by marriage, exclude from my country) are not very appropriate for measuring attitudes toward women, the authors used a series of questions which involved placing the stimulus persons in positions of varying status. In order to control for the context in which the status differential occurred, five triads of superior, equal and subordinate status positions were used. One such triad, for example, was as follows:

Superior Status: a director of a play in which you are acting

Equal Status: another actor or actress with you

Subordinate Status: a stage hand in a play in which you are acting.

The subjects of this study were white and predominantly Christian students at the University of Illinois. The weights obtained for the male subjects were: race (white-Negro), 46; religion (Christian-Jewish), 25; sex (male-female), 28; status (superior-equal-subordinate), 1. The weights for the women were: race 60, religion 26, sex 13, and status 1. Thus the women placed more emphasis upon race and less on sex than did the men. Whites were preferred to Negroes, Christians to Jews, and men to women by both male and female subjects. Status was unimportant in determining social distance, when considered for all stimulus persons. However, interaction effects showed that both Negroes and women were rejected in positons of superior status by both male and female subjects. Although the overall social distance toward women is considerably less than that expressed toward Negroes, women were rejected more strongly than were Negroes in superior positions; that is, subjects preferred a Negro man to a white or Negro woman for superior status positions. This preference occurred for both male and female subjects but was much stronger for women (race $\times$ status = 26, sex $\times$ status = 74) than for men (race $\times$ status = 42, sex $\times$ status = 58).

SUBJECT CHARACTERISTICS: FIRST STUDY

Some subjects showed much more social distance than other subjects. Thus, social distance appears to be determined not only by societal norms, but also by the demographic and personality characteristic of the subjects.

Demographic Characteristics

Triandis and Triandis (1960) found that upper class subjects tend to show less social distance than lower class subjects; that Jewish subjects tend to show less social distance than Christian subjects; and that subjects with a Southern or Eastern European national background tend to show less social distance than subjects with a Northern or Western European background. These differences probably reflect, in part, the norms of these various societal groups and, in part, the historic factors that are related to immigration to this country.

Personality Characteristics

Some subjects, regardless of ethnic or national background, show more distance than other subjects. In the study described above, subjects who scored high on the California Fascism Scale tended to show more social distance than did subjects who scored low on that scale. The California F-scale is an instrument that reflects (inversely) the social sophistication or breadth of perspective of the subject (Kelman and Barclay, 1963).

A good deal of previous research employing the F-scale, and other scales designed to measure different aspects of the subject's personality, suggested that a person may show more social distance if he is insecure about his own merit. A secure person is capable of facing people different from himself, who may challenge his values and assumptions much more comfortably than is an insecure person. People hold many kinds of beliefs about which there can be no objective proof. The only way for them to feel sure that their beliefs are correct is to talk with other people who hold the same views. Thus, people who hold different beliefs pose a real threat to an insecure individual and he is likely to avoid them. If an individual has a narrow, unsophisticated perspective, he is likely to have a very simple system of beliefs, and "strange" people can be particularly threatening to this system (Rokeach, 1960).

To summarize, then, a person's social distance from other people is in part determined by the norms of his social goup and in part by his own personality. Norms are learned from talking to his parents, friends, and valued associates; personality is determined by both genetic predisposing factors and the childhood training experiences to which he was subjected by his parents. His general education and level of sophistication are additional factors that may broaden his perspective and make other people, who are different from himself, less threatening.

SUBJECT CHARACTERISTICS: SECOND STUDY

From these considerations, Triandis and Triandis (1962) derived two hypotheses: (1) different cultures have different norms about social distance, and (2) within a culture, the more insecure and anxious an individual is, the higher the amount of social distance he will feel towards people who are not like himself.

To test these hypotheses, Triandis and Triandis administered a questionnaire to 100 university students at the University of Athens, Greece, and to 100 students at the University of Illinois. The questionnaire presented complex stimuli varying in all possible combinations of the following characteristics: Race: White Negro; Occupation: Bank Manager-Coal Miner; Religion: Same-Different from that of the subject; and Nationality: French-Portuguese. The "same-different" religion was explained to the subjects by asking them to think of their own religion when seeing the words "same religion"; and of that religion, out of a set that included different Christian and Jewish denominations, which they considered most different from their own when seeing the words "different religion." In other words, an American Jewish subject who saw the stimulus: "Portuguese, Negro, Bank Manager, Different Religion" may have responded to "Portuguese, Negro, Bank Manager, Roman Catholic"; and a Greek Orthodox subject, looking at the *same* stimulus may have responded to a "Portuguese, Negro, Bank Manager, Conservative Jew."

The first step in the study involved separate standardizations of the social distance scales in the two cultures. The scale statements were standardized by the Thurstone successive intervals technique, described above, using a population of 100 Greek high school students.

Table 1 presents some of the statements used in the study and shows the scale values of the statements that were obtained from the American and Greek judges.

The 16 stimuli generated by the characteristics mentioned above (race, religion, occupation, and nationality) and the social distance statements were presented to a new sample of 100 Greek and 100 Illinois students. The patterns of responses obtained from the two cultures had numerous similarities. In both cultures the preferred stimulus was the "French, Bank Manager, White, Same Religion." In both cultures the "Portuguese Miner, Negro, Different Religion" stimulus was the least preferred. The average distance toward the latter stimulus was 37.1 and 33.4 for the American and the Greek subjects respectively. The average American subject would accept a "Portuguese Miner, Negro, Different Religion" person as a neighbor and the average Greek would invite him to dinner. But, it must be remembered that these average social distance scores are greatly depressed by the large number of both Illinois and Greek students who would accept *all* of the stimuli under all circumstances. Actually, although none of the subjects indicated that they would be willing to kill any of the stimulus persons, there were some who would exclude Negro or Jewish stimuli from their country and *many* who would exclude them from their neighborhoods.

The similarities between the American and Greek scores suggest that there is about the same variability in the social distance scores in the two cultures. The next question is this: Are the social distance scores determined by the same characteristics in the two cultures? The answer is no, particularly if we pay attention to the relative weights of the characteristics.

The Culture of the Subjects

The American subjects in this study gave a large weight to race; the Greeks gave a large weight to religion. The American weights were as follows: race 86; occupation 3; religion 8; and nationality $\frac{1}{2}$. The Greek weights were: race 24; occupation 5; religion 56; and nationality 0. Thus, the Americans gave large weights to race as they had done in the previous study (Triandis and Triandis, 1960), and small weights to religion (anti-Semitism) and occupation, while the Greeks gave religion the biggest weight and race and occupation smaller weights.

This finding supports the hypothesis that different cultures have different norms about social distance. The average American subject apparently focuses more on *race,* and the average Greek subject more on *religion.* This hypothesis is further strengthened by Triandis, Davis and Takezawa (in preparation). These researchers repeated the Trandis and Triandis (1962) study with German high school students and Japanese university students. For the German study they used stimuli formed from different combinations of race (Negro-white), occupation (physician-unskilled laborer), religion (Protestant-Catholic-Jewish), and nationality (German-American-Italian). The Japanese stimuli were also formed with the characteristics of race (Negroid-Caucasoid-Mongoloid), occupation (physician-unskilled laborer), religion (Protestant-Catholic), and nationality (Japanese-American-Portuguese). The same stimuli were also presented to two samples of Illinois students.

First, we might ask, what kind of results were obtained from the American students who responded to the "German study stimuli" and those who responded to the "Japanese study stimuli." Since the stimuli were a little different from those used in the previous studies, we should expect some differences. The weights obtained with the German stimuli and white American Protestant subjects were as follows: race 60; occupation 22; religion 6; and nationality 1. For the Japanese stimuli the weights were: race 57; occupation 35; religion 1; and nationality 4. Table 3 summarizes these findings. The stars indicate the level of significance of the results. When there are four stars it means that there is one chance in 10,000 that the subjects in the particular culture did *not* pay attention to the corresponding characteristic.

The results of Table 3 are fairly consistent with the previous results. The major difference occurs on the weight given to occupation. This is probably due to the fact that the difference between Bank Manager and Coal Miner employed in the Greek study is smaller than that between Physician and Unskilled Laborer employed in the German and Japanese studies. The other difference is on religion and nationality between the Greek and the Japanese studies. But here again the stimuli account for the difference. The Japanese stimuli did not include the characteristic "Jewish," hence the drop in the size of the weights from 8 to 1, and they did include the nationality "Japanese," while in the Greek study the nationalities were French and Portuguese. These results suggest that the weights depend on the extent to which one uses extreme characteristics to describe a particular dimension. Thus, weights must be considered in conjunction with the kinds of stimuli used in a particular study. However, when samples from two different cultures are given the same stimuli, differences in the weights will reflect differences in emphases that are due to the cultures of the subjects.

The German subjects provided the following weights: race 6; occupation 70; religion 12; and nationality 2. There is a spectacular difference between the American and German subjects in the weights given to race and occupation, with the American subjects giving more weight to race and less weight to occupation than do the Germans. The Germans also give more weight to religion and nationality than do the Americans. In the case of the Japanese, the weights were: race 38; occupation 50; religion 0; and nationality 3. Again the Americans give more weight to race and less weight to occupation than do the Japanese.

To sum up, there is little doubt that different cultures employ different weights in the determination of the social distance. The typical American weights are much larger for the characteristic race than for other characteristics. The typical Greek weights are larger for the characteristic religion. The typical German weights are very high for occupational status, moderately high for religion, and relatively low for race. The typical Japanese weights are very high for occupation and race, and small for nationality. It must *not* be assumed, however, that these results characterize every subject in each of these cultures. There is a great deal of variability within cultures that is attributable to the religion and social class of the subjects. For example, Triandis, Davis and Takezawa found that the weights given by different subsamples of American subjects were quite different. The American Jewish male subjects showed little social distance, and the amount they did show was mostly determined by the occupation of the stimulus persons.

TABLE 3. *Relative Weights Obtained in Three Studies of Social Distance (Each Study Employed a Different Set of Stimulus Persons)*

Characteristics	Samples					
	Greeks	American with Greek Stimuli	Germans	American with German Stimuli	Japanese	American with Japanese Stimuli
Race	24**	86****	6***	60****	38****	57****
Occupation	5*	3**	70*****	22****	50*****	35****
Religion	56***	8***	12**	6***	0	1***
Nationality	0	0.5	2*	1***	3****	4***
Stimuli used for						
Race:	Negro–White		Negro–White		Negro–White–Mongoloid	
Occupation:	Bank Manager–Coal Miner		Physician–Unskilled Laborer		Physician–Unskilled Laborer	
Religion:	Same–Different from subject		Protestant–Catholic–Jewish		Protestant–Catholic	
Nationality:	French–Portuguese		German–American–Italian		Japanese–American–Portuguese	

* $p < .05$
** $p < .01$
*** $p < .001$
**** $p < .0001$

The American Jewish female subjects showed a similar pattern, though they did give substantially larger weights to "religion" than did the male subjects.

The Personality of the Subjects

In both their American and their Greek samples, Triandis and Triandis (1962) found that subjects who obtained high social distance scores tended to answer "yes" to a wide variety of attitude questions, including items from the California F-scale and statements that were intended to be the obverse of those items. Persons who obtained high social distance scores also showed a tendency to check the most extreme positions on graphic rating scales, thus indicating either very strong agreement or very strong disagreement with attitude statements. Psychologists are not agreed concerning the meaning of "acquiescent" and "extreme" styles of response to attitude questionnaires, but such reactions are commonly believed to reflect personality factors. Through the use of analysis of variance, Triandis and Triandis were able to show that the cultural backgrounds (American or Greek) of their subjects controlled almost twice as much variance in social distance scores as did the two response styles.

In a later study (Triandis, Davis and Takezawa), several personality measures were obtained and correlated with social distance scores. American subjects who scored high on social distance tended to be low on independence of judgment (measured by a scale developed by Barron) and on tolerance for ambiguity (measured by a scale developed by Budner). German subjects who were high on social distance also showed low tolerance for ambiguity (measured by a scale developed by Brengelmann). Thus, there is a cross-cultural replication of this result, with two different kinds of scales measuring tolerance for ambiguity. This characteristic is related to the ability of the subject to "suspend judgment" until he has considerable information. Subjects who have low tolerance for ambiguity tend to "prejudge" other people on the basis of obvious group characteristics such as

their race or religion. From the Weidemann and Triandis (in preparation) study, it is worth noting that "prejudice toward women," as measured by the Nadler-Morrow (1959) Scale, correlates .30 (p < .01) with the authoritarian content of the F-Scale, corrected for response acquiescence. This suggests that the correlates of antifeminine prejudice are similar to those of anti-Negro and anti-Semitic prejudice.

The attitudes of the high social distance subjects are also of some interest. Such subjects are very likely to agree *strongly* with attitude statements such as "What youth needs most is strict discipline, rugged determination and the will to work and fight for family and country," or "In my opinion patriotism and loyalty are the first requirements of a good citizen." These statements are similar in content to some of the propaganda messages disseminated by Fascists and Nazis before the Second World War. It is interesting that the postwar young German subjects (born in 1944) tested in the Triandis, Davis and Takezawa study rejected such statements more strenuously than did the Illinois subjects tested in the same study. The attitudes of the latter subjects toward a large variety of social and political issues were measured by Triandis et al. and related to the degree of social distance shown by the subjects. It was found that high social distance subjects indicated much more conformity to existing social institutions and prevailing points of view about political behavior, and were more conservative and uncritical of these values, than did the low social distance subjects.

SUMMARY

For normal populations, such as those tested in the studies described above, social distance is greatly influenced by cultural norms concerning what is appropriate behavior towards persons who are "different." Individuals who are particularly sensitive to these norms, and who tend to conform and accept uncritically the values imparted to them by their culture, are particularly likely to show large amounts of social distance.

REFERENCES

Bogardus, E. S. *Immigration and race attitudes*. Boston: Heath, 1928.

Kelman, H. C., and Barclay, Janet. The F Scale as a measure of breadth of perspective. *J. abnorm. soc. Psychol.*, 1963, **67**, 608-615.

Nadler, E. B., and Morrow, W. R. Authoritarian attitudes toward women and their correlates. *J. soc. Psychol.*, 1959, **49**, 113-123.

Rokeach, M. *The open and closed mind.* New York: Basic Books, 1960.

Triandis, H. C., and Triandis, Leigh Minturn. Race, social class, religion and nationality as determinants of social distance. *J. abnorm. soc. Psychol.,* 1960, **61,** 110-118.

Triandis, H. C., and Triandis, Leigh Minturn. A cross-cultural study of social distance. *Psychol. monogr.,* 1962, **76,** No. 540.

Triandis, H. C., Davis, E. E., and Takezawa, S. I. Some determinants of social distance among American, German and Japanese students. Submitted for publication, 1964.

Weidemann, Sue Rowand, and Triandis, Leigh Minturn. A study of discrimination with respect to race, religion, and sex. Unpublished Senior Honors Thesis, University of Illinois, 1963. Submitted for publication, 1964.

24. Exploratory Factor Analyses of the Behavioral Component of Social Attitudes

HARRY C. TRIANDIS

In a recent statement of a theory of attitude structure and change, Katz and Stotland (1959) examined some of the directions in which research on attitudes might proceed. They pointed out that attempts to find consistent relationships between attitudes and behavior might have failed because of the use of attitudes with weak or nonexistent behavioral components. They suggest that

the assessment of attitudes should include more than the measurement of affectivity and evaluation. It should include measurement of the belief component, the behavioral component, and the linkage of attitude and its value system (p. 465).

Important contributions to the measurement of the evaluative component have been reviewed by Edwards (1957). Osgood, Suci, and Tannenbaum (1957) provided a simple procedure for the measurement of the "meaning of an object," which includes assessment of its evaluation. Zajonc (1954) has related some of the cognitive and affective elements associated with an attitude. Fishbein (1961) has examined the relationship between beliefs and attitudes, and has provided semantic-differential procedures for the measurement of the cognitive and affective components of attitudes. Peak (1955), Rosenberg (1956), and others have examined the perceived instrumentality of attitude objects for the attaining of goals and values. The behavioral component of attitudes, however, has generally been neglected. Bogardus'

• Reprinted from *Journal of Abnormal and Social Psychology*, 1964, **68**, 420-430, with permission of author and the American Psychological Association. This research was supported by a grant from the University of Illinois Research Board.

(1928) scale of a social distance involves this component. Some improvements in the psychometric characteristics of this scale have been made by Triandis and Triandis (1960, 1962), but their work also suggested that the dimensionality of the social distance scale should be examined. Although for very rough work the social distance scale may be regarded as unidimensional, more refined work requires examination of the dimensions of social behavior.

The present paper conceives of attitudes as consisting of several components, one of which is the behavioral component. It focuses on the question: "What are the main dimensions of the behavioral component of attitudes?" The isolation of dimensions underlying any theoretical construct, such as the construct "the behavioral component of attitudes," has several advantages: it permits clearer analysis and hence better understanding of the theoretical construct; it permits explicit measurement of the dimensions defining the construct, through a few items which are relatively "pure" or independent of each other; and it suggests that when behaviors that are closely related to a particular dimension are to be predicted from attitude measures, it is desirable to give more weight to the relevant dimension, and less weight to the other dimensions of the behavioral component of attitudes.

This paper presents a methodology for the analysis of the behavioral component of attitudes, and some examples of the kinds of data and results that are obtainable with this methodology.

The variables used in this exploration create a cube of data. One face of this cube consists of stimulus persons that may vary in race, religion, social class, age, sex, and various personality characteristics. The second face of the cube consists of behaviors that a person might undertake in relation to such stimulus persons —for example, have a cocktail with them, exclude them from the neighborhood, elect them to political office, etc. On the third face of the cube are the characteristics of the subjects in the investigation—their demographic, personality, and other characteristics. A fourth dimension of exploration might be the situation or behavior setting (Barker and Wright, 1954) in which the interaction takes place. In the present exploration, the situation was not specified.

The procedure was an extension of that employed by Triandis and Triandis (1960, 1962) and by Triandis (1961). A typical judgment made by a subject is exemplified by the following item:

A 50-year old, Negro, Roman Catholic, physician, male

$$1 \quad 2 \quad 3 \quad 4 \quad 5 \quad 6 \quad 7 \quad 8 \quad 9$$
would :—:—:—:—:—:—:—:—: : would not
have a cocktail with this person

The data can be analyzed in several ways. One may ask: "How are the behaviors correlated with each other?" or "How are the stimulus persons related to each other?" or "What kind of subjects give one kind of result and what kind give another?" A variety of research projects might be undertaken to explore this cube of data.

METHOD

Selection of Stimulus Persons

Previous work on social distance (Triandis, 1961; Triandis and Triandis, 1960, 1962) has used race, social class, religion, nationality, and philosophy of life as the characteristics of the stimulus persons. Studies of employability have used stimuli differing in age, sex, race, religion, social class, competence, sociability, and physical and social disability (Rickard, Triandis, and Patterson, 1963; Triandis, 1963). Factorial designs were employed, usually with two levels of each characteristic (for example, white versus Negro, highly competent versus barely competent). From these studies it was determined that race, sex, age, occupation, and religion are very important characteristics of stimulus persons and ought to be included in the first exploration of the cube of data mentioned above.

The following levels of the five characteristics were used: Race—Negro-white; Sex—male-female; Age—20-50; Occupation—physician–soda-fountain clerk; and Religion—Protestant-Roman Catholic-Jewish. Thus, the stimuli formed a $2 \times 2 \times 2 \times 2 \times 3$ factorial design. This design required 48 stimulus persons. However, since unrealistic stimuli might antagonize the subjects, the 20-year-old physicians and the Jewish-Negroes were dropped from the design. In addition to the stimuli mentioned above, four "white, male, Protestant, 50-year-old" stimuli that might be important in a subject's "person life space" were included: A person doing the same work as the subject, the subject's supervisor, a person who works for the subject, and a person who represents a labor union in the subject's place of work. A total of 34 complex stimuli were used.

Selection of Behaviors

The behaviors were selected through a content analysis of novels. A random sample of 80 American novels written after 1850 was taken from the University of Illinois library, and a random sample of 10 pages was selected from each novel. The 800 pages were carefully read and every social behavior was recorded. A social behavior was defined as a situation in which a person does something in relation to, or with, another person. A list of approximately 700 behaviors was obtained. If two behaviors were extremely similar (for example, "have a drink with" and "have a cocktail with"), one of them was dropped from the list. Behaviors that appeared only once in the sample of 800 pages and appeared to have no social significance were also dropped (for example, "Lift on my shoulders," "Push button in elevator for"). Behaviors that were judged as being too ambiguous (for example, "Astound") were also dropped. This procedure reduced the 700 behaviors to 165.

Since a further reduction in behaviors was necessary, a pretest questionnaire was administered to various psychology classes. The questionnaire required judgments of how six stimulus persons might be involved with the subject in the 165 behaviors. The six stimulus persons were specified only as to occupation, which ranged in prestige from scientist to street cleaner. Thus, 6×165 or 990 judgments had to be made on 9-point scales. The typical subject completed only about two-thirds of these judgments. Since the order of presentation was counterbalanced, approximately an equal number of subjects judged each item.

Three sets of instructions were tried in this pretest. The instructions used by Osgood et al. (1957) asked the subjects to indicate the extent of the relationship between the person (concept) and the behavior (scale). Another set of instructions asked the subjects to judge whether "it is likely" that he would behave in the way specified by the scale with the stimulus person. The third set of instructions used the word "appropriate" instead of the word "likely." For each set of instructions, the medians of the distributions of the judgments of the subjects, judging a particular person on a particular scale, were recorded. Inspection of these medians indicated no important differences between the three instructions. However, since the semantic-differential instructions tended to result in more discrimination between the high- and low-prestige stimulus persons they were adopted.

Further examination of the medians revealed that some behaviors provided very little discrimination between the six stimulus persons. The criterion of a difference between the medians of at least 2 scale units, for any pair of stimulus persons, was adopted for retention of the scale in the sample.

Finally, the distribution of the judgments of the subjects, when judging a particular stimulus person on a particular scale, was used as an indication of ambiguity. Those behaviors which provided distributions with an interquartile range of more than 5 scale units were eliminated, since ambiguity was suspected. The above two procedures reduced the number of behaviors to 105.

The 105 remaining behaviors were studied according to Guttman's (1959) facet-analysis procedures. The behaviors could be classified into two facets: One facet dealt with the kind of relationship that was implied by the behavior—subordinate, coordinate, or superordinate; the other facet with the behavior area—social, cognitive, emotional, physical, or moral. For instance, the behavior "Believe" was classified as cognitive subordination; "Make love to" as emotional coordination; "Bully" as physical superordination, etc. In order to reduce the sample and at the same time make it maximally heterogeneous, only one behavior per cell was retained. For instance, "Believe" and "Learn from" were both classified in the cognitive subordination cell, and only one of them was retained in the sample. In deciding which one to retain the experimenter used his own judgment, but an attempt was made to retain as many of the Bogardus scale items as possible. By these steps a final sample of 61 behaviors was achieved.

Subjects

Since the present research was purely exploratory, an attempt was made to sample student subjects that were as heterogeneous as possible. A class of 35 beginning introductory-psychology students took the complete questionnaire (61 behaviors × 34 stimulus persons), which required about 3 hours. A sample of 85 "sophisticated" subjects, who had almost completed the experimenter's course in social psychology (where social norms, prejudice, etc., had been discussed) were also given the questionnaire. Each of the subjects in this group completed a random third of the questionnaire in one class period. The responses of the subjects in each sample to a particular questionnaire item (stimulus person-behavior combination) were summed, and divided by the number of subjects who had responded to the item. These average judgments formed a 61 × 34 matrix (behaviors × stimulus persons). The behaviors were then correlated with each other across the 34 stimulus persons. Thus, a matrix of 61 × 61 correlations was obtained from each sample. In spite of the differences between the two samples, the correlation between the 1,830 correlation coefficients obtained from the first sample with the 1,830 corresponding coefficients obtained from the second sample was .92. Thus, neither psychological training nor the partial completion of the questionnaire by different subjects seems to have affected the correlations between the behaviors. For this reason, the data obtained from the two samples were merged.

The merged data were then divided according to the subject's sex and religion. The criterion of at least 10 subjects in a particular subsample was adopted. Analyses for the Roman Catholic and Jewish women are not available, because the number of such subjects was insufficient.

Since the research that is to be presented was conceived of as purely exploratory, no attempt was made to obtain random, or even adequate, samples of subjects. The main goal was to discover whether this kind of approach is likely to be fruitful. Much further work is required before generalizations applicable to the United States population, or some fraction of this population, can be made. In the discussion which follows, the terms "Protestant females," "Jewish males," etc., are merely being used to describe particular samples. No inferences concerning all Protestant females or all Jewish males should be made from these data. It is hoped that publication of this report will suggest similar studies to investigators having access to populations that are not available to the present investigator. If a number of similar studies, employing the present design, are undertaken, it may be possible to extrapolate to some fraction of the United States population.

In addition to the above samples, a class of 37 introductory-psychology students was given the California F Scale and the 10 highest and 10 lowest students in the distribution were invited to take the questionnaire.

Thus, the analyses that are to be reported were based on complete data (2,640 judgments) of 10 High F Scale subjects (authoritarians); 10 Low F Scale subjects (nonauthoritarians); 22 Protestant, 16 Roman Catholic, and 10 Jewish men; and 17 Protestant women—a total of 85 subjects. All subjects were white.

Treatment of the Data

The judgments of the subjects in a particular sample, for a particular stimulus person-behavior combination, were summed and divided by the appropriate N. These average judgments formed a matrix of 61 rows (behaviors) × 34 columns (stimulus persons). The rows were correlated, using Ns of 34. In this way, a matrix of 61 × 61 correlations between behaviors was obtained. Since a factor analysis of the behaviors could not be undertaken unless only $34 - 1 = 33$ behaviors were considered, the 61 behaviors were divided into two sets of 28 with an overlap of 5 marker variables. The division was done so that variables highly correlated with each other would belong to different sets. The two sets of 33 behaviors were factor analyzed independently. Furthermore, one set of 33 behaviors was factored for each of the sub-samples—authoritarians, nonauthoritarians, Protestants, Roman Catholic, and Jewish males, and Protestant females.

The highest value in each column was used as an estimate of the communality. To expedite the analysis, both the ILLIAC and 1401 IBM computers were used simultaneously, with some of the samples being processed by one and some by the other computer. Principal-axes analyses were performed on ILLIAC and centroid factor analyses on the 1401 (for which there was no principal-axes program). For the data obtained from the Protestant males, both centroid- and principal-axes analyses were performed. In all analyses seven factors were extracted. Five of these turned out to be meaningful and were rotated to simple structure by the Kaiser (1958) varimax procedure. In the Results section the method of factor analysis is indicated.

Once the factors were rotated, factor scores of the stimulus persons on each of the five factors were obtained by means of the matrix equation $F = (A'\ A)^{-1}\ A'\ Z$, where F is the matrix of the factor-score estimates, A the matrix of factor loading, A' the transposed A matrix, and Z the matrix of the scores of the stimulus persons on the behaviors in standard score form (see Harman, 1960, pp. 360-361, for complete discussion). Thus, each of the 34 stimulus persons acquired five scores, one score on each of the five factors. The entries of the missing cells corresponding to unrealistic stimuli (for example, the Negro, Jews, and 20-year-old physicians), were estimated from the entries in the adjacent cells. The characteristics of the stimulus persons were viewed as the "treatments" in an analysis of variance design, and the factor scores obtained by each of the stimulus persons on a particular factor were considered as the dependent variable. Thus, for each of the subsamples of subjects, it was possible to do five analyses of variance—one for each of the five factors—and determine the amount of variance that each of the characteristics of the stimulus persons determined on each of the five factors. The advantage of this last step in analysis is that it indicates what characteristics of the artificial stimuli, or what interactions of these characteristics, are relevant in the determination of the variance of scores on each factor.

RESULTS

The analyses of the undifferentiated samples of subjects proved unclear. When the sex and religion of the subjects are not considered, confusion of scales such as "Marry" makes the resulting factors not comparable to the factors obtained from differentiated samples. For this reason, the discussion below will focus on the results obtained from the differentiated samples.

Factors Obtained from the Protestant Male Sample

Table 1 shows the behaviors that loaded on the factors obtained from the Protestant male

TABLE 1. Factors Obtained from Protestant Male Sample

From First Set of 33 Variables			From Second Set of 33 Variables	
	Varimax Rotation Loadings			Varimax Rotation Loadings
Social Behavior	Principle-Axes Factor Analysis	Centroid Factor Analysis	Social Behavior	Centroid Factor Analysis
Factor I: Formal Social Acceptance with Subordination versus Rejection with Superordination				
Admire character of	.86	.83	Obey	.88
Cooperate in political campaign with*	.85	.83	Ask for opinion of	.88
Plead with	.83	.81	Believe	.85
Elect to political office	.81	.83	Disregard opinion of	—.84
Drop name from list of my dinner guests	—.83	—.79	Give dinner party in the honor of	.80
Exclude from first class hotel	—.74	—.80	Cooperate in political campaign with*	.76
Praise suggestions of	.77	.75	Not vote for	—.74
Invite to my club	.74	.76	Accept help from	.69
Admire ideas of	.67	.62	Not change places with	—.66
Accept this person calling me by my first name when I do not call him by his (hers)	.62	.52	Invite to a large party	.65
Be commanded by	.56	.58	Work for	.57
Accept as an intimate friend*	.54	.51	Accept as an intimate friend*	.53
Percentage of total variance accounted for	25	25		26
Factor II: Marital Acceptance versus Rejection				
Fall in love with	.96	.94	Marry*	.97
Marry*	.95	.93	Physically love	.96
Teach	.63	.58	Go out on a date with	.95
Smile at	.55	.54	Kiss the hand of	.93
Lose game when this person is my competitor	.49	.52	Love even after his (her) death	.91
Percentage of total variance accounted for	11	11		19
Factor III: Friendship Acceptance versus Rejection				
Win game in which this person is my competitor	.69	.32	Eat with	.80
Be partners with in an athletic game	.66	.76	Go fishing with	.73
Gossip with	.29	.71	Drink with	.69
Accept as an intimate friend*	.57	.44	Accept as an intimate friend*	.68
Be on a first name basis with	.44	.70	Accept as chum	.67
Percentage of total variance accounted for	7	11		13
Factor IV: Hostile Acceptance versus Social Distance				
Prohibit from voting	.49	.77	Exclude from my neighborhood*	.79
Permit to do me a favor	.64	.48	Accept as a close kin by marriage	—.72
Admit as a tourist in my country	.57	.44	Work with	—.63
Accept as an intimate friend*	—.11	—.50	Discuss moral issues with	—.50
Prohibit the admission of this person to my club	.22	.52	Accept as an intimate friend*	—.24
Percentage of total variance accounted for	11	7		9

* Marker variables.

TABLE 1 *(Continued)*

From First Set of 33 Variables			From Second Set of 33 Variables	
Social Behavior	Varimax Rotation Loadings		Social Behavior	Varimax Rotation Loadings
	Principle-Axes Factor Analysis	Centroid Factor Analysis		Centroid Factor Analysis
Factor V: Interaction with Superiors-Subordinates				
Treat as a subordinate*	—.74	—.66	Treat as a subordinate*	—.71
Admire ideas of	.46	.61	Command	—.55
Lose game to	.48	.45	Change places with	.42
Be commanded by	.41	.43	Work for	.34
Recommend the employment of in a firm in which I have "an influence"	.39	.46	Obey	.31
Percentage of total variance accounted for	6	6		5

* Marker variables.

subjects, for both sets of 33 behaviors. Factor I was called "Formal Social Acceptance with Subordination versus Formal Social Rejection with Superordination." For both sets of 33 variables, the behaviors with the high loadings implied either formal acceptance ("Cooperate in political campaign with," "Give dinner in honor of," "Vote for," etc.) or subordination ("Obey," "Admire character of," etc.). The positive pole of this factor suggests behaviors that are appropriate towards social superiors and the negative-pole behaviors that are appropriate toward social subordinates. Factor II is clearly a marital acceptance factor. Factor III suggests same-sex friendship acceptance. Factor V is a pure subordination-superordination factor, suggesting interaction with supervisors and other persons of "rank."

Factor IV obtained from the first set of 33 behaviors differs from the corresponding factor obtained from the other set of behaviors. The highest loadings included the "Prohibit from voting" behavior, but there was an insignificant loading on "Exclude from my neighborhood." Thus, it appears to be a "Hostile Acceptance with Voting Prohibition" factor. The second set of behaviors, due to a more fortunate sampling of variables in that set, seems to have yielded a fairly clear "Social Distance" factor.

The meaning of the factors may be clarified by the analyses of variance of the factor scores of the stimulus persons. Thus, for the sample of Protestant males, the analysis of variance

of factor scores on Factor I, shown in Table 2, gave the following results: Formal Social Acceptance with Subordination was more likely with white than with Negro stimulus persons ($p < .001$) and race controlled 38.4% of the variance on that factor; physicians were more accepted than soda-fountain clerks ($p < .001$) and occupation controlled 37.8% of the variance; persons of the same religion as the subject (Protestants) were more acceptable ($p < .001$) and religion controlled 4.4% of the variance; persons who were 20 years old were more acceptable ($p < .001$); same religion physicians were particularly acceptable ($p < .001$); and Roman Catholic women were much less acceptable than Roman Catholic men—the Sex × Religion interaction was significant ($p < .01$) and controlled 1.1% of the variance.[1]

Factors Obtained from Other Samples

Since the analyses of the other samples are based on relatively few cases, the data will not be presented.[2] The data suggest that there are

[1] Factor II, Marital Acceptance, showed the preference of the subjects for marital partners of the same age, race, and religion, and of the opposite sex. Factor III showed a preference for friends of the same age, sex, religion, and race. Factor IV showed prohibition from voting for 20-year-old non-Protestants, and Factor V, subordination to physicians.

[2] The results of the other samples—Tables A-H—have been deposited with the American Documentation Institute. Order Document No. 7807 from ADI Auxiliary Publications Project, Photoduplica-

TABLE 2. Five-Way Analysis of Variance of Factor Scores of Protestant Male Subjects—Orthogonal Factors

Source	df	Factor I			Factor II			Factor III			Factor IV			Factor V		
		% Variance	MS^a	F	% Variance	MS^a	F	% Variance	MS^a	F	% Variance	MS^a	F	% Variance	MS^a	F
Age (A)	1	2.5	1.99	18.09***	16.2	10.31	44.83***	8.8	5.47	24.86***	21.0	17.98	29.00***		2.50	3.13
Sex (B)	1		.24	2.18	17.9	11.38	49.48***	51.0	31.82	144.64***	10.0	8.58	13.84***	5.4	3.70	4.63*
Religion (C)	2	4.4	3.48	31.64***	1.4	.89	3.87*	4.4	2.73	12.41***		.82	1.32			
Race (D)	1	38.4	30.48	277.09***	23.6	15.06	65.48***	3.3	2.14	9.73**		2.58	4.16			
Occupation (E)	1	37.8	30.00	272.73***	8.2	5.21	22.65***		.61	2.77	5.3	4.52	7.29*	10.2	6.95	8.69**
A × B	1							3.1	1.96	8.91**						
A × E	1															
A × C	2		.25	2.27		.68	2.96	1.8	1.09	4.95*	3.9	3.35	5.40*		1.05	1.31
A × D	1	.9	.69	6.27**	7.9	5.02	21.83***	3.0	1.86	8.45**	7.9	6.74	10.87**		2.30	2.88
B × C	2	1.1	.80	7.27**					.43	1.95				14.1	9.67	12.09***
B × D	1	.6	.49	4.45*	9.2	5.89	25.61***		.56	2.55		2.13	3.44			
B × E	1					.27	1.17		.65	2.95		2.35	3.79		2.29	2.86
C × D	2		.19	1.73		.33	1.43									
C × E	2	1.5	1.22	11.09***				1.8	1.08	4.91*	3.1	2.67	4.31*		.96	1.20
D × E	1		.15	1.36					.59	2.68						
Other interactions	27		.11			.23			.22			.62			.80	
Total % variance for significant effects		87.2			84.3			77.2			51.2			29.7		

Note. Percentage of variance not entered for nonsignificant effects. *MS* and *F* not entered when *F* is less 1.

[a] For the purpose of this table, *MS*s were rounded off to two decimal places. *F*s were computed with *MS*s significant to three decimal places.

* $p < .05$.

** $p < .01$.

*** $p < .001$.

interesting differences between the subsamples. Thus, though similar factors appear across the various samples, some differences in emphasis are observable, as indicated by different loading patterns. In addition, the difference between the High and Low F Scale subjects was in the expected direction. The High F Scale subjects produced only three clear factors, while the Low F Scale subjects produced the usual five clear factors. The simpler structure obtained from the authoritarian subjects is consistent with the categorical thinking of the subjects, as discussed in the literature.

A suggestion of the nature of these factor differences, across samples, is provided by Table 3.

Congruence of Factors across Samples

In order to obtain an objective measure of the similarity of the obtained factors across the various samples, coefficients of congruence (Tucker, 1951) were computed between all possible combinations of factors. Table 3 summarizes some of the congruity coefficients, as well as the other results.

A relatively rigorous criterion for acceptance of the "existence" of a factor is a coefficient of congruence of .50 or more with some factor obtained from another sample. This criterion may be improper, since it is conceivable that a factor which is unique to one religious group may exist. However, the Formal Social Acceptance with Subordination, Social Acceptance with Condescension, and Marital Acceptance factors clearly meet this criterion. At a somewhat less rigorous criterion level, the Friendship Acceptance and Subordination factors also seem clear. The relative lack of clarity of the Social Distance factor suggests that there was conflict and nonagreement about social distance. As a result, it was unclear what behaviors, beyond nonacceptance in the neighborhood and as a kin by marriage, were considered appropriate towards persons differing in race.

DISCUSSION OF OBTAINED FACTORS

The present study was not designed to obtain factors from samples of subjects differing in religon and sex. This separation was necessary to obtain maximum clarity, and much of

tion Service, Library of Congress, Washington, D. C. 20540. Remit in advance $1.75 for microfilm or $2.50 for photocopies and make checks payable to: Chief, Photoduplication Service, Library of Congress.

the discussion deals with the data obtained from these samples. However, since the samples of subjects were so unsystematic, nonrandom, and small, no general statements can be made about the religion and sex of subjects as determinants of the obtained factors.

The study was undertaken as an exploration of the way subjects cluster social behaviors. It would have been perfectly feasible to factor the correlation matrix of the behaviors of *every single* subject and to discuss his or her way of clustering behaviors. Since this would have required 85 factor analyses (1 for each of the subjects) and presentation of the data would have been very difficult, it was decided to average the responses of homogeneous subjects. This method successfully provided a first approximation of some of the factors used to structure the social relations space.

Thus, it is likely that typical subjects, in our culture, use some combination of the factors presented in Table 3. Some of the factors that show considerable congruence across samples are probably sufficiently common to be used by most people. For example, the Formal Social Acceptance with Subordination factor seems to be widely used. The General Social Acceptance factor, typical of the authoritarian subjects only, shows poor congruence (only .65) with it, but is a very similar factor. The Social Acceptance with Condescension factor, found only with the Jewish males, shows relatively poor congruence (.62) with the Formal Social Acceptance with Subordination factor, but is also essentially the same. Thus, this factor may be said to be present in all the samples. The Marital Acceptance and Friendship Acceptance factors, although showing less congruence, are also essentially present in most of the sample. The Social Distance and Subordination-Superordination factors are less ubiquitous, but are present in some form or other in most samples.

The remaining factors are less general. However, most of the "typical scales" of Table 3 should be included in future work, in order to explore their generality.

The Formal Social Acceptance with Subordination factor appears to include behaviors that are appropriate in relation to social superiors or inferiors with whom the subject has no institutionalized relationship. By contrast, the Subordination-Superordination factor appears to group behaviors appropriate for interaction with supervisors or subordinates. The Marital Acceptance factor summarizes inter-

TABLE 3. Summary of Factors Found in Various Samples

Sample	Congruity Coefficients			Percentage of Total Variance Controlled	Typical Scales	Significant Main Effects (with Characteristics High on Factor Listed First)
	1	2	3			
Formal Social Acceptance with Subordination						
1. Nonauthoritarian subjects	.75			25	Admire ideas of	Same vs. different age (20 vs. 50 years old)
2. Protestant females	.82	.85		20	Elect to political office	Same vs. different religion
3. Protestant males	.82	.76	.86	25	Admire character of	Same vs. different race (white vs. Negro)
4. Catholic males				16		High prestige vs. low prestige occupation
Social Acceptance with Condescension						
1. Jewish males				18	Be on a first name basis with	Different vs. same age
2. Nonauthoritarian subjects	.70			25	Treat as equal / Not invite to my club	Different vs. same sex / Different vs. same religion / Different vs. same race / Low prestige vs. high prestige occupation
Friendly Superiority vs. Unfriendly Distance						
1. Jewish males				24	Win game from	Females vs. males
2. Nonauthoritarian subjects	.17			9	Not lose game to / Be partners with in athletic game	Same religion vs. different religion
Marital Acceptance						
1. Authoritarian subjects	.47			11	Marry	Same vs. different age (20 vs. 50 years old)
2. Protestant females	.73	.59		9	Fall in love with	Opposite vs. same sex
3. Jewish males	.65	.31	.71	8	Go out on a date with	Same vs. different religion
4. Protestant males				11		Same vs. different race (white vs. Negro)

TABLE 3 (Continued)

Sample	Congruity Coefficients 1	2	3	Percentage of total Variance Controlled	Typical Scales	Significant Main Effects (with Characteristics High on Factor Listed First)
Friendship Acceptance						
1. Protestant males	.44			11	Eat with	Same vs. different age (20 vs. 50 years old)
2. Catholic males				13	Be partners with in an athletic game	Same vs. different sex
					Win game from	Same vs. different religion
						Same vs. different race (white vs. Negro)
Social Distance						
1. Protestant males	.23			7	Exclude from my neighborhood	Different vs. same age (20 vs. 50 years old)
2. Catholic males				11	Prohibit from voting	Different vs. same sex
					Not accept as a close kin by marriage	Different vs. same race (Negro vs. white)
Interaction with Superiors-Subordinates						
1. Protestant males				6	Not treat as a subordinate	Different vs. same age (50 vs. 20 years old)
2. Catholic males		.40		7	Be commanded by	Same vs. different race (white vs. Negro)
					Admire ideas of	High prestige vs. low prestige occupation
General Social Acceptance						
1. Authoritarian subjects				29	Accept as an intimate friend	Not available
					Cooperate in political campaign with	
					Admit as a tourist in my country	

217

actions appropriate with the opposite sex. Race, age, and religion determined significant amounts of variance on this factor. The Friendship Acceptance factor also appears meaningful. Protestant males preferred same sex, age, religion, and race persons as friends. The Social Distance factor seems to be reflecting mostly the rejection of Negroes. This is consistent with previous findings (Triandis and Triandis, 1960, 1962).

The validity of this method of analysis can be intuitively evaluated by examining the loadings of various behaviors on a factor on which there is known sex-role differentiation. For example, a number of behaviors had different loadings on the Protestant male and female Marital Acceptance factors. The male factor had a loading of .63 on the behavior "Teach," while the female factor had a loading of —.10. This is consistent with sex-role differentiation in our culture.

GENERAL DISCUSSION

The present study has accomplished three things: It demonstrated the general methodology for the construction of Behavior Differentials, and reduced the 61 social behaviors to a more limited number of 20 to 25 behaviors that might be used in future work; it demonstrated the method of analysis of the cube of data formed by the stimulus persons, the social behaviors, and the subjects rating the stimuli on the behaviors; and it showed that the exploration of the subjects' structuring of the social relations space, by means of the Behavior Differential, is feasible and leads to "sensible" results.[3]

The present research also has implications for studies of social distance. Previous writers

[3] A related analysis may be mentioned parenthetically. When the 34 stimulus persons were correlated over the 61 behaviors and the resulting 34×34 matrix factored, four factors accounted for 94% of the observed variance. Factor I seemed to involve stimulus persons towards whom there is much cultural determination of behaviors. The low-status Negro women obtained high loadings on this factor; the low-status white women and the high-status Negroes, low loadings. Factor II was a status factor, with the 50-year-old physicians obtaining high loadings and the 20-year-old soda-fountain clerks, low loadings. Factor III contrasted the "datable" stimuli (20-year-old white women) with the other stimuli. Factor IV contrasted the unusual stimuli (for example, 50-year-old Negro woman physician) with the common stimuli.

on social distance, including the present writer, have assumed that social distance is a unidimensional construct. If this were the case, the Marital Acceptance factor would represent the least amount of social distance, the Friendship Acceptance factor the next least, and the Formal Social Acceptance factor the next least; the subjects would answer three items representing these factors as shown in Table 4. The

TABLE 4. Responses Which Would Occur to Three Items if Social Distance Were Unidimensional

	Marriage	Friendship*	Formal Acceptance†
Minimal social distance	Yes	Yes	Yes
Slight social distance	No	Yes	Yes
Moderate social distance	No	No	Yes
Substantial social distance	No	No	No

* For example, "Go fishing with."
† For example, "Vote for."

existence of response patterns such as those shown in Table 5 suggests that these three items are independent. Such patterns clearly make sense. The data also suggest that for authoritarian subjects, the correlation between "Marry"

TABLE 5. Responses Indicating Independence of Three Items

	Marriage	Friendship*	Formal Acceptance†
Subject$_1$	Yes	Yes	No
Subject$_2$	No	Yes	No
Subject$_3$	Yes	No	No

* For example, "Go fishing with."
† For example, "Vote for."

and "Vote for" was slightly negative (— .16, ns). Between "Marry" and "Elect to political office" it was — .51 ($p < .001$). Since it is inconsistent with Guttman's (1959) concept of unidimensionality to be willing to marry someone, but not be willing to accept him as a political candidate, the domain explored by the present study is clearly not unidimensional. It might be argued that Bogardus (1928) was aware of the multidimensionality of the domain of social behavior statements, and for this reason was careful to employ only very few statements falling on a single dimension. This is correct. However, when more precise work requires a scale with more than a few items, the unidimensionality of the scale breaks down. This does not mean that unidimensional social-distance scales with few items are impossible to construct and are not useful for certain kinds of research. On the contrary, such scales are adequate as long as the research does not require much refinement, as much of the work on social distance has shown.

The present research also has implications for the analysis of the relationship between attitudes and behavior. Greater precision in predicting behavior from attitudes will probably be obtained when specific behaviors, for example, choice of friends, are predicted from the relevant factor of the Behavior Differential (Friendship Acceptance), or from linear combinations of several independent, but relevant, factors underlying the behavioral component of attitudes.

REFERENCES

Barker, R. G., and Wright, H. F. *Midwest and its children: The psychological ecology of an American town.* Evanston, Ill.: Row, Peterson, 1954.

Bogardus, E. S. *Immigration and race attitudes.* Boston: Heath, 1928.

Edwards, A. L. *Techniques of attitude scale construction.* New York: Appleton-Century-Crofts, 1957.

Fishbein, M. An investigation of the relationships between beliefs about an object and the attitude toward that object. Technical Report No. 6, 1961, University of California, Los Angeles, Contract Nonr 233(54).

Guttman, L. A structural theory for intergroup beliefs and action. *Amer. sociol. Rev.,* 1959, **24**, 318-328.

Harman, H. H. *Modern factor analysis.* Chicago: Univer. Chicago Press, 1960.

Kaiser, H. F. The varimax criterion for analytic rotation in factor analysis. *Psychometrika,* 1958, **23**, 187-200.

Katz, D., and Stotland, E. A preliminary statement to a theory of attitude structure and change. In S. Koch (Ed.), *Psychology: A study of a science.* Vol. 3. *Formulations of the person and the social context.* New York: McGraw-Hill, 1959. Pp. 423-475.

Osgood, C. E., Suci, G. J., and Tannenbaum, P. H. *The measurement of meaning.* Urbana: Univer. Illinois Press, 1957.

Peak, Helen. Attitude and motivation. In M. R. Jones (Ed.), *Nebraska symposium on motivation: 1955.* Lincoln: Univer. Nebraska Press, 1955. Pp. 149-189.

Rickard, T. E., Triandis, H. C., and Patterson, C. H. Indices of employer prejudice toward disabled applicants. *J. appl. Psychol.,* 1963, **47**, 52-55.

Rosenberg, M. J. Cognitive structure and attitudinal affect. *J. abnorm. soc. Psychol.,* 1956, **53**, 367-372.

Triandis, H. C. A note on Rokeach's theory of prejudice. *J. abnorm. soc. Psychol.,* 1961, **62**, 184-186.

Triandis, H. C. Factors affecting employee selection in two cultures. *J. appl. Psychol.,* 1963, **47**, 89-96.

Triandis, H. C., and Triandis, Leigh M. Race, social class, religion, and nationality as determinants of social distance. *J. abnorm. soc. Psychol.,* 1960, **61**, 110-118.

Triandis, H. C., and Triandis, Leigh M. A cross-cultural study of social distance. *Psychol. Monogr.,* 1962, **76**(21, Whole No. 540).

Tucker, L. R. A method for synthesis of factor analysis studies. *USA Personnel Res. Sect. Rep.,* 1951, No. 984.

Zajonc, R. B. Structure and cognitive field. Unpublished doctoral dissertation, University of Michigan, 1954.

25. A Multiple-Indicator Approach to Attitude Measurement

STUART W. COOK and CLAIRE SELLTIZ

At least since LaPiere's report (1934) of the discrepancy between the actual reception accorded him and a Chinese couple and the answers to a questionnaire about accepting Chinese as guests, investigators have been concerned with the fact that different procedures designed to assess the same attitudes have often led to quite different placements of the same individuals, and that observed behavior toward a social object (person, group, etc.) is frequently not what would have been predicted from a given instrument intended to measure attitude toward that object. There have been several types of reaction to such observed discrepancies. One has been to assume that there is a "true" attitude toward the object, which one or both measures have failed to gauge correctly. A second has been to assume that there are different "classes" of attitudes toward a given object—for example, "verbal attitudes" and "action attitudes"—which should not necessarily be expected to correspond. Another has been to equate attitude with behavior, using "attitude" simply as a descriptive term summarizing observed consistencies in behavior. Still another reaction has been to think of attitude as an underlying disposition which enters, along with other influences, into the determination of a variety of behaviors toward an object or class of objects, including statements of beliefs and feelings about the object and approach-avoidance actions with respect to it.

We prefer the latter position; first, because for us, as for others (e.g., Allport, 1954) the observation of regularities in social behavior seems to point to the operation of relatively

stable underlying dispositions toward classes of objects. Further, we believe that apparent inconsistencies in social behavior may often best be understood in terms of the operation of such stable underlying dispositions in shifting relation to other influences on behavior. Finally, if validly distinguished, a dispositional concept has, by its very nature, a wider range of situational relevance—including projectability into relatively novel situations—than a simple descriptive concept equating attitude with behavior in specified situations.

We assume that two classes of variables, in addition to an individual's attitudinal disposition toward a given object or class of objects, influence his behavior in situations involving the object or symbols of the object (including the behavior constituting his responses to instruments designed to measure attitude toward the object): (a) *other characteristics of the individual,* including his dispositions toward other objects represented in the situation, values he holds that are engaged by the situation, his motivational state, his expressive style, and so on; (b) *other characteristics of the situation,* including its prescriptions as to appropriate behavior, the expectations of others in the situation with respect to the individual's behavior, the possible or probable consequences of various acts on his part, and so on.

In this view, an attitude cannot be measured directly, but must always be inferred from behavior—whether the behavior be language in which the individual reports his feelings about the attitude-object, performance of a task involving material related to the object (e.g., recall of statements which take a position with respect to the object), or actions toward a representative of the object-class (e.g., avoidance of such an individual). Lazarsfeld (1959) takes a similar position in his discussion of latent structure analysis. He points out that there is a probability relation between an indicator

• Reprinted from *Psychological Bulletin,* 1964, 62, 36-55, with permission of the senior author and the American Psychological Association. This paper was prepared as part of a program of research on the measurement of social attitudes supported by grants from the National Science Foundation and the Air Force Office of Scientific Research.

and the underlying trait of which it is taken as an indication; that is, a given trait does not invariably produce a given behavior. He stresses that, in consequence, some inconsistency will always be found between different measures of a hypothesized trait, and that the task of the investigator is to combine them into an "index" or "measurement" which represents the best inference that can be made from the manifold of empirical operations to the underlying characteristic they are assumed to reflect.

This orientation leads to emphasis on the need for a number of different measurement approaches to provide a basis for estimating the common underlying disposition, and to the expectation that data from these approaches will not be perfectly correlated. However, it seems to us that it should be possible to increase the correspondence among the indicators by careful analysis of other factors that are likely to affect response to a given measuring instrument and by efforts to reduce or control the influence of those factors. Ideally, the goal would be to develop one or more measures from which the effects of all probable response determinants other than attitude toward the relevant object would be removed. This goal, however, seems unlikely of achievement; therefore it seems to us important to work with a number of different measures, in each of which an effort is made to eliminate or control in some systematic way some identifiable influence on response other than the attitude in question. Since different influences will be controlled in different measures—and thus, conversely, different influences in addition to attitude will affect responses on the different measures—there will remain a lack of full correspondence among scores on the different measures.

Social scientists have long recognized that factors other than an individual's attitude toward an object may influence both his response to instruments designed to measure the attitude and his behavior toward the object in everyday life. Much recent work in the field of both personality and attitude measurement has been concerned with identifying the effects of such "extraneous" variables as the tendency to agree (or to disagree) with statements regardless of their content (e.g., Bass, 1955; Cronbach, 1946, 1950) or the wish to give a socially acceptable picture of oneself (e.g., Edwards, 1953, 1957; Taylor, 1961). Another interest has been in the development of indirect methods of attitude assessment (for a review of such methods, see Campbell, 1950). But attempts to develop indirect measures have, for the most part, been sporadic, and there has been little effort to examine systematically the relation of different indirect measures to each other or their relative susceptibility to such influences as agreeing response set or social norms.

Despite the general awareness of measurement problems, examination of reports of experimental research on attitudes shows the following picture: First, even investigators who hold very sophisticated theoretical positions about the nature and functions of attitudes and the conditions for attitude change commonly use only a single attitude measure—typically quite crude—in testing hypotheses derived from those theoretical positions. Second, most investigators are aware of the possibility that responses to these instruments may be influenced by factors other than the attitudes they are intended to measure. Third, efforts are made to guard against the intrusion of such factors or to rule out interpretations based on the possibility that they have been operative. These safeguards usually take one or more of the following forms: sampling (e.g., selection of groups of subjects believed to differ in susceptibility to the extraneous influences most likely to be operative in the measurement situation), experimental design (e.g., the introduction of control groups), internal analysis of the data (e.g., considering how the responses of subgroups of subjects might be expected to differ if one determinant rather than another were operative).

We do not mean to minimize the importance of such procedures. In any given study they may quite convincingly rule out the possibility that responses have been influenced by factors other than subjects' attitudes toward the object in question. Nevertheless, it seems to us that effort directed toward improving measuring instruments might be at least equally useful.

AN EXAMINATION OF DIFFERENT TYPES OF MEASURING INSTRUMENTS IN TERMS OF THE KINDS OF EVIDENCE THEY PROVIDE AS A BASIS FOR INFERENCES ABOUT ATTITUDE

In most current research on attitudes, efforts directed specifically toward improving measuring techniques are limited to such matters as assuring anonymity, attempting to separate the measurement from the experimental sessions, varying the order of presentation of items or the context in which they are embedded. If we are to go beyond such limited steps, a more systematic analysis of the characteristics of measuring instruments is needed than is yet available. This paper is a first step toward such an analysis. Our purpose is not to present a detailed review of the different kinds of instruments that have been used to measure attitudes; this has been well done by others (Campbell, 1950; Deri, Dinnerstein, Harding, and Pepitone, 1948; Weschler and Bernberg, 1950). Rather, we propose to examine broad classes of measurement techniques from the point of view of the kinds of evidence they provide and thus the nature of the inferences involved in estimating attitude. By "the nature of the inferences involved" we mean the grounds for believing that attitude toward the presumed object is a determinant of responses to the measuring instrument, and the bases for inferring the nature of the attitude from the characteristics of the responses (i.e., for considering a given response as indicative of a positive or a negative disposition toward the object).

We have found it useful to think in terms of five major groupings: (a) measures in which the material from which inferences are drawn consists of self-reports of beliefs, feelings, behavior, etc., toward an object or class of objects; (b) measures in which inferences are drawn from observed overt behavior toward the object; (c) measures in which inferences are drawn from the individual's reactions to or interpretations of partially structured material relevant to the object; (d) measures in which inferences are drawn from performance on objective tasks where functioning may be influenced by disposition toward the object; and (e) measures in which inferences are drawn from physiological reactions to the object. Not all of the measures discussed have been used as attitude tests in the formal sense, but for each of them there is reason to believe that attitude may be an important determinant of response and thus that the technique could serve as a basis for inferences about attitude.

In assessing the adequacy of an instrument as an indicator of attitude, consideration of its susceptibility to other influences is as important as consideration of the grounds for believing that underlying disposition toward the object is a determinant of response. In examining measuring instruments from the point of view of the possible influence of fac-

tors other than attitude, we shall consider two major aspects: (a) the probability that overt responses may deviate from "private" responses —that is, the ease with which an individual can alter his responses to present a certain picture of himself; (b) the probability that private responses may be influenced by determinants other than attitude, in the absence of any attempt to distort responses.

Possibilities of influence of private response by factors other than attitude are, of course, almost limitless; we shall discuss only those that seem most probable with respect to each type of instrument. Susceptibility of overt response to distortion—that is, the possibility of discrepancy between private and overt response —would seem to be a function of three characteristics of the instrument: the extent to which its purpose is apparent, the extent to which the implications of specific responses are clear, and the extent to which responses are subject to conscious control.

In discussing the susceptibility of measures to distortion of responses and techniques developed to lessen the probability of distortion, we assume that with respect to many attitudes the settings in which tests are usually administered tend to exert pressures in a constant direction. It seems reasonable to suppose that most respondents, presented with tests in an academic setting or under the auspices of some other "respectable" organization, will assume that the responses which will place them in the most favorable light are those which represent them as well adjusted, unprejudiced, rational, open minded, and democratic. Moreover, since these are ideal norms at least in much of the American middle class, the pressures specific to the test situation are likely to coincide with inner pressures toward maintaining an image acceptable to the self as well as to others. By "controversial social attitudes" we mean attitudes with respect to which such norms are operative. Some of our discussion, and especially some of our examples, concern techniques for making it easier for the individual to reveal himself as not well adjusted, not unprejudiced, etc., or for making it harder for him to portray himself, falsely, as well adjusted, unprejudiced, etc. While some assumption as to the probable direction of pressures operating in the situation is necessary for the concrete details of certain techniques, the principles involved do not hinge on the specific direction of pressures; given testing situations in which there is reason to believe that the pressures are predominantly in a different direction, the techniques can be modified accordingly. And many of the techniques require no assumption about the probable direction of pressures, being designed to reduce the effects of extraneous influences in any direction.

Measures in Which Inferences Are Drawn from Self-Reports of Beliefs, Feelings, Behaviors, etc.

By far the most frequently used method of securing material from which to make inferences about an attitude is to ask an individual to reveal—either in his own words or through acceptance or rejection of standardized items—his beliefs about the attitudinal object, how he feels toward it, how he behaves or would behave toward it, how he believes it should be treated.

The basis for inference is clear: it is axiomatic in all definitions that an individual's attitude toward an object is indicated by his beliefs, feelings, and action orientation toward it. The nature of the inference is also clear: it is assumed that the relationship between attitude and expression is a direct one and that the attitude corresponds to the manifest, common-sense implications of the stated belief or feeling. For example, a stated belief that the object has characteristics usually considered desirable is taken as reflecting a favorable disposition toward it, and a stated belief that it has characteristics usually considered undesirable is taken as reflecting an unfavorable disposition. Similarly, a report that the person avoids contact with the object is taken as indicating an unfavorable disposition toward it, while a report that he does or would willingly enter into contact with it is taken as indicating a favorable disposition.

In some definitions, attitude is considered identical with, or simply a summary of, beliefs, feelings, behavior, etc., toward the object; thus no problem of inference arises. However, in such definitions some criteria must be adopted for choosing which behavior constitutes the population of "attitudinal responses" to be sampled. The choice of such criteria would, we believe, depend upon an analysis essentially similar to our consideration of "extraneous influences" in the remainder of this paper.

Self-report measures have a number of characteristics that make them susceptible to distortion of overt responses. The purpose of the instrument is obvious to the respondent; the implications of his answers are apparent to him; he can consciously control his responses. Thus a person who wishes to give a certain picture of himself—whether in order to impress the tester favorably, to preserve his own self-image, or for some other reason—can rather easily do so. This difficulty has long been recognized, and in recent years it has been extensively investigated under the rubric of "social desirability." A number of techniques have been devised to make the purpose of the instrument or the implications of the responses less apparent; to make it easier to give answers that may be considered undesirable; and to make it harder to give, falsely, answers that may be considered desirable. Some of these techniques are focused primarily on reducing the likelihood that responses will be distorted in an attempt to meet the investigator's expectations or to please him; others are addressed to reducing the influence on responses of a desire to maintain a certain self-image as well as that of a desire to please or impress the investigator.

One of the simplest approaches to making the purpose of the instrument less apparent is the inclusion of items not relevant to the attitudinal object in which the investigator is interested. A variation of this approach is to include in each of the items a number of aspects in addition to that in which the investigator is interested; for example, if the investigator is interested in attitudes toward one or more racial groups, each item may refer to a hypothetical person characterized not only in terms of race but of age, sex, religion, occupation, etc. Approaches of either sort serve only to make the purpose of the test less obvious. They do not completely conceal or disguise it, nor can they do so within the format of self-report measures, which by definition call for the individual's own account of his reactions to the attitudinal object.

Among the simplest, and most frequently used, approaches to making it easier to give answers that may be considered undesirable are assurances of anonymity, statements to the effect that "there are no right or wrong answers" or that "people differ in their views on these things," emphasis on the importance of honest answers in order to contribute to scientific knowledge or some other presumably desirable outcome, efforts to build up rapport between questioner and respondent and to create the impression that the questioner will not disapprove of whatever views may be expressed.

Other approaches are built into the instrument itself: including items to which an unfavorable reply is likely to be considered acceptable (e.g., "Would you be willing to have a ditch digger as U. S. Congressman from your district?"—Westie, 1952, 1953), in order to break down a possible set to give uniformly favorable replies; including in the statement of a view that may be considered undesirable a qualification or a justification of it (e.g., "It is best that Jews should have their own fraternities and sororities, since they have their own particular interests and activities which they can best engage in together, just as Christians get along best in all-Christian fraternities"—Adorno, Frenkel-Brunswik, Levenson, and Sanford, 1950); wording questions in such a way that they assume the respondent holds certain views or has engaged in certain kinds of behavior (e.g., "When did you first . . . ?"—Kinsey, Pomeroy, and Martin, 1948).

Other approaches are designed to make it difficult to give, falsely, what may be considered a desirable answer. In the measurement of personality, a major effort in this direction has been the use of forced-choice tests, where the respondent is asked to indicate which of two statements, matched in terms of social desirability but differing in their implications with respect to traits or needs, is closer to his own views or more descriptive of his own behavior. This approach has not been extensively used in the measurement of attitudes.

In addition to their susceptibility to conscious distortion in order to give the picture the individual wishes to present of himself, responses to self-report measures may be influenced by another set of characteristics presumably unrelated to attitude toward the object in question—characteristics frequently labeled "response set" or "expressive style." It has long been noted that some individuals have a consistent tendency to agree (or to disagree) with items presented to them, regardless of their content; or to select, with more than chance frequency, the alternative which appears in a given position; or to give extreme (or moderate) answers.

A number of techniques have been devised to reduce the effects of such tendencies on scores that are to be taken as indicative of attitudes. Perhaps the simplest and the most common approach to the problem of influence

by a tendency to agree (or to disagree) is to vary the wording of items in such a way that for approximately half of them agreement represents a favorable response to the attitudinal object, and for half an unfavorable response. Other approaches to this problem involve setting up the instrument in such a way that responses do not take the form of expressing agreement or disagreement with one statement at a time. The instrument may consist of pairs of statements representing roughly opposed points of view on a given issue, both statements being worded positively or both worded negatively; the subject is asked to indicate which is nearer his own position, or to indicate his position on a scale running between the two statements. The following pair of items from an unpublished scale of attitudes toward freedom of speech, developed by students of Donald T. Campbell at Northwestern University, illustrate this approach:

A. Fascists and Communists are entitled to preach their beliefs in this country.
B. Only those who are in agreement with this country's philosophy of government are entitled to preach their beliefs.

In other instruments, the problem, at least in its obvious form, is avoided by using items that call for free response—open-ended questions, sentence stubs to be completed with the individual's own responses, etc.

An approach to correcting for the effects of a tendency to give extreme answers, or moderate answers, consists in providing matched pairs of items, one referring to the attitudinal object, the other referring to some control object, and scoring in terms of the discrepancy between the two responses. For example, if respondents are asked only, "Would you be willing to have a Negro bookkeeper live in the same apartment building you live in?" and are provided with a 5-point response scale, it is impossible to determine whether respondents who answer "very willing" differ from those who answer simply "willing" in attitude, in response style, or in both. Providing a parallel item with respect to a white bookkeeper and scoring on the basis of discrepancy between an individual's responses to the Negro and the white removes the effects of response style from the score (Westie, 1953).

Susceptibility of self-report measures to the two kinds of influences discussed so far—desire to present a certain picture of oneself, and response sets unrelated to the content of items —clearly leads to the possibility of distortion of responses in the obvious sense of lack of correspondence between the overt responses and the individual's private beliefs, feelings, policy views, etc. Still other factors, however, may influence his private beliefs and feelings as well as his overt responses. While private beliefs, feelings, and action orientations with respect to an object are by definition at least partially determined by the individual's attitude toward the object, they may be influenced by other factors as well—for example, by the availability of information, or by other values the individual holds. Thus, a person who has an essentially devaluing attitude toward Negroes may nevertheless have learned and state as his belief that there is no difference in the chemical composition of the blood of Negroes and whites; on the other hand, a person whose disposition toward Negroes is not devaluing may know and state as his belief that the average scholastic achievement of Negroes in the United States is lower than that of whites. A person with a devaluing attitude toward Negroes may nevertheless believe that they should not be deprived of the right to vote, because he sees this right as an essential ingredient of democracy; a person whose attitude toward Negroes is not devaluing may be opposed to laws forbidding discrimination in the sale and rental of housing because he places great store on the right of an owner to do with his property as he sees fit.

To the extent that such other influences affect different items differently, or affect only certain items, this problem has been attacked by examining responses for consistency, eliminating items which show low agreement with total scores, or eliminating those to which responses do not fall on a unidimensional scale.

A given technique may help to reduce or correct for extraneous influence from more than one source. For example, scoring in terms of discrepancy between responses to items concerning the attitudinal object and comparable items about a control object may provide a correction for the effects of other values or meanings engaged by the items as well as for response sets. Asking the respondent to choose which of two statements is closer to his views may help to eliminate the influence both of response set and of concern with the acceptability of responses, if the alternatives provided are equivalent in both respects.

Not only may a given technique serve more than one function; a given instrument may embody a number of techniques designed to reduce the influence of extraneous factors. For example, in Westie's (1953) Summated Differences Test, the subject is presented with hypothetical persons of specified race (Negro or white) and occupation (eight occupations, ranging from ditch digger to banker, plus "the average man"), and asked to indicate, on 5-point scales, his willingness to accept each of these 18 hypothetical persons in each of 24 relationships—a total of 432 items. Some of the items are such that a negative answer is likely to be considered acceptable by most people (e.g., unwillingness to vote for a machine operator, whether white or Negro, as President of the United States is not likely to be seen as an expression of "prejudice"), thus presumably breaking down a possible tendency to give uniformly favorable answers whether through an acquiescent response set or through a desire to give a picture of oneself as unprejudiced. The large number of items, and the format of the questionnaire, make it extremely unlikely that the subject can remember or check his response to a given item with respect to one racial group when he is answering the comparable item concerning the other group. Scoring on the basis of discrepancy between parallel items referring to whites and Negroes takes account both of possible response sets and of the influence of the specified occupation and the specified situation. Thus, this instrument adds to the basic social distance questionnaire a number of techniques designed to make the focus of the investigator's interest less apparent, to make it easier to give answers that might be considered undesirable, to correct for possible response sets, and to some extent to take account of other values or meanings that may affect responses.

Measures in Which Inferences Are Drawn from Observation of Overt Behavior

Many investigators have pointed out the desirability of using measures in which overt behavior toward members of a class of objects would serve as a basis for inferences about attitude toward the object-class. As with self-report measures, the basis for inference is clear; all definitions of attitude specify that behavior can be taken as an indicator of attitude. And, as in the case of self-report measures, the usual assumption is that there is a simple correspondence between the nature of the behavior and the nature of the underlying attitude; for example, that friendly behavior toward a member of a given class of objects indicates a favorable attitude toward the object-class.

There has been much less extensive development of measures of this sort than of self-report measures. Situations capable of eliciting behavior toward an attitudinal object are more difficult to devise and to standardize, and more time consuming and costly to administer, than self-report measures. Although some measures of this type have been devised, they have not been widely enough used to provide much evidence as to their specific strengths and weaknesses nor to stimulate efforts to correct for shortcomings. However, analysis of their characteristics can provide estimates as to their probable susceptibility to influences other than attitude and possibilities of reducing such susceptibility.

Attempts to develop behavioral measures have followed three general lines. One consists in presenting subjects with standardized situations that they are led to believe are unstaged, in which they believe that their behavior will have consequences, and in which the attitudinal object is represented in some way other than by the actual presence of a member of the object-class. For example, subjects may be asked to sign a petition on behalf of an instructor about to be discharged for membership in the Communist party, to contribute money for the improvement of conditions for migratory workers, to indicate whether they would be willing to have a Negro roommate. DeFleur and Westie (1958) have attempted to develop a measure of this sort which is appropriate for use in many different testing situations. In their procedure, as part of a larger program of research, white subjects viewed a number of colored photographic slides showing a young Negro man and a young white woman, or a young white man and a young Negro woman, in a social setting; subjects described the pictures and answered specific questions about them. At the close of an interview following this session the measurement procedure being discussed here was introduced. DeFleur and Westie describe the procedure as follows: The subject was told that another set of such slides was needed for further research, was asked if he (or she) would be willing to be photographed with a Negro of the opposite sex, and then was given "a standard photograph release

agreement," containing a variety of uses to which such a photograph would be put, ranging from laboratory experiments where it would be seen only by professional sociologists, to a nationwide publicity campaign advocating racial integration. The subject was asked to sign his name to each use of the photograph which he would permit. These investigators report that subjects "uniformly perceived the behavioral situation posed for them as a highly realistic request."

Such devices differ from self-report measures with similar content in that, in the behavioral measures, the subject either actually carries out the behavior (signs a petition, makes a contribution, etc.) or is led to believe that his agreement to do so will lead to real-life consequences (being asked to pose for a photograph to be put to specified uses, being assigned a Negro roommate, etc.).

Another approach is to present the subject with an admittedly staged situation and ask him to play a role—perhaps to behave as he would in such a situation in real life, perhaps to take the part of someone else or to act in some specified way. Stanton and Litwak (1955) presented actual and potential foster parents with situations of interpersonal stress in which they were instructed to behave in a given way (defined as not manifesting specified undesirable or neurotic kinds of behavior); for example, in one scene the subject was instructed that he was to play the role of a married man, having dinner with his parents; the investigator, playing the role of the man's father, treated his son like a child, criticized his wife, and put him in the wrong. These investigators found that ratings based on a half-hour's role playing were better predictors of subjects' behavior as foster parents (as rated by case workers who had sustained contact with them) than were ratings based on 12 hours of intensive interviewing by a trained social worker. Stanton, Back, and Litwak (1956) reported that a role-playing approach was successful in discovering the limits of positive and negative feelings about public housing projects on the part of slum dwellers in Puerto Rico. These investigators have stressed the importance of designing the scene specifically to elicit responses relevant to the particular behavior or attitude in which the investigator is interested.

A third behavioral approach, used in the study of attitudes toward social groups, has been to ask for sociometric choices among individuals some of whom are members of the object group, preferably under circumstances that lead the participants to believe that such choices will have consequences in the form of subsequent assignment in some situation. Early applications of this technique to the study of intergroup attitudes were made in studies by Moreno (see 1943) and by Criswell (1937, 1939), in which patterns of choices by school children were analyzed in terms of the development of cleavage along racial lines. Subsequently, sociometric techniques have been used in research evaluating the effects of certain experiences on attitudes (e.g., Mann, 1959a; Mussen, 1950a, 1950b) and of the relations among different aspects of attitudes (e.g., Mann, 1959b).

There are differences among these three kinds of behavioral measures—situations appearing to the subject to be unstaged, role playing, and sociometric choice—in characteristics that affect the probability that overt responses will correspond to responses that would be shown if the individual were not concerned with presenting (to others or to himself) a certain picture of himself. Let us consider first the extent to which their purpose is apparent to the respondent. To the extent that the purportedly unstaged situations are accepted as genuine, the respondent will not see them as designed to get information about his attitudes; thus one possible source of pressure to give responses that are likely to be considered desirable is eliminated. Nevertheless, the implications of his behavior as revealing certain characteristics may be apparent to him; even if he accepts a question about his willingness to pose with a Negro or to have a Negro roommate as genuine, he may be aware that a positive answer will have the effect of presenting him as unprejudiced, a negative answer as prejudiced. Thus, even in the absence of awareness that he is being tested, an individual may be motivated to give a response that differs from his spontaneous private one, in order to present himself to the questioner as unprejudiced or to maintain his own image of himself as one who behaves in an unprejudiced way. The sociometric choice method would appear to be similar in these respects, though it may perhaps be assumed that, in the absence of special influences calling attention to racial or ethnic group membership, the implications of the choices are less likely to be apparent. In the case of role playing, the extent to which the purpose of the situation and the implications of responses are clear presumably depends on the convincingness with which the situation can be presented as a measure of some other characteristic, such as acting ability.

All of these behavioral approaches have characteristics that may operate to make it easier to respond in ways that may be considered undesirable. In many situations it is possible to justify a negative response on neutral or acceptable grounds: one does not believe in signing petitions, or he does not like to have his picture taken, or he prefers Persons A and B to X and Y because they share his interest in music. Or, in the role-playing situation, his behavior is shaped not by his own reactions toward the attitudinal object but by interest in the dramatic requirements of the situation. (To the extent that these alternative explanations are real possibilities, however, they introduce other problems about interpretation of the behavior as an indicator of the attitude in which the investigator is interested.)

Some characteristics of the behavioral approaches may reduce the probability that the individual will modify his behavior in order to present an acceptable picture of himself. When responses are expected to have real-life consequences, the anticipation of such consequences may counterbalance the wish to make a good impression. In a social distance questionnaire, if one wishes to present himself (to the tester, or to himself, or both) as unprejudiced, there is little effective pressure against saying that one would be willing to work with a Negro, or to have a Negro roommate; but if the question is posed in a context where a positive reply is seen as leading to assignment of a Negro as a co-worker or a roommate, one must weigh his willingness to accept that consequence against his wish to appear unprejudiced. In role playing, the pressure for quick response to unanticipated stimulus situations probably operates to lessen conscious control of behavior in order to produce a desired impression. Faced with the necessity of doing or saying something to keep the situation going, the individual may not have time to consider the impression he is making; to the extent that this is so, this approach may be thought of as reducing the individual's conscious selection of his response.

Thus behavioral measures seem to be less susceptible than simple self-report measures to distortion of response in the interest of presenting a certain picture of the self. But they are at least as susceptible as self-report measures to the effects of other extraneous influences. It has sometimes been suggested that the model of behavioral measures would be apparently unstaged situations in which a member of the object-class is present. But it is clear that behavior in everyday life situations (which this model seeks to approximate) is not determined exclusively by attitude toward the presumed attitudinal object. In the case of behavior toward minority groups, for example, social custom is a major determinant; in communities with segregated transportation systems, almost all white people—regardless of their attitudes toward Negroes or toward segregation—sit in the white section, whereas in communities with unsegregated transportation systems, very few white people—regardless of their attitudes—refuse to sit next to Negroes. Other values may override attitudes toward the presumed object; an individual who feels physical revulsion at the experience of eating with Negroes may nevertheless do so because he has come to believe that the ideals of democracy, or religious principles of brotherhood, or the position of the United States in the eyes of the world, require that all men be treated as equals. Finally, other characteristics of the object individuals may predominate over their ethnic identification in determining response to them. Thus, LaPiere (1934) concluded that the factors which most influenced the behavior of hotel and restaurant personnel to the Chinese couple with whom he was traveling "had nothing to do with race"; rather, it was the quality and condition of their clothing, the appearance of their baggage, their cleanliness and neatness, and above all, their self-confident and pleasant manner, that determined reactions. Observations such as this suggest that, to the extent that one is interested in tapping generalized dispositions toward a given group rather than in predicting behavior in specific situations, behavioral measures that call for response to a symbolic representation of the group may be less subject to influence by extraneous factors than measures that call for response to members of the group who are physically present.

Campbell (1961) has suggested an approach to the use of behavior measures which is based on the premise that different situations have different thresholds for the manifestation of hostile, avoidant, or discriminatory behavior. He suggests that, in order to secure evidence about an individual's attitude, it is necessary to place him in a number of situations with differing thresholds—ranging, for example, from eating with a Negro at a business men's luncheon club (assumed to be a situation with a low threshold for nondiscriminatory behavior—in other words, one in which it is easy to behave in an unprejudiced way) to renting one's house to a Negro (assumed to have a high threshold for nondiscriminatory behavior). The lowest-threshold situation in which an individual exhibits discriminatory behavior would indicate his position on a scale of attitude with respect to the group in question. Such a procedure would be effective in taking account of pressures that are constant for all, or most, individuals; it would not, it seems to us, rule out the effects of differences in the strength for different individuals of such influences as concern with social approval, other values seen as relevant to the situation, etc.

Measures in Which Inferences Are Drawn from the Individual's Reaction to or Interpretation of Partially Structured Stimuli

The characteristic common to techniques in this category is that, while there may be no attempt to disguise the reference to the attitudinal object, the subject is not asked to state his own reactions directly; he is ostensibly describing a scene, a character, or the behavior of a third person. He may be presented with a photograph of a member of the object-class (usually a person of a given social group) and asked to describe his characteristics; or he may be presented with a scene in which members of the object-class are present and asked to describe it, to tell a story about it, to predict the behavior of one of the characters, etc. The stimulus material may be verbal rather than pictorial; for example, the subject may be asked to complete sentence stubs referring to a hypothetical third person.

The bases for inferences about attitudes are those common to all projective tests: assumptions that perception of stimuli that are not clearly structured is influenced by the perceiver's own needs and dispositions; that, asked to provide an explanation or interpretation for which the stimulus presented gives no clear clue, the subject must draw on his own experience or his own dispositions or his own definitions of what would be probable or appropriate; that, asked to attribute behavior to others, especially under speed conditions, the most readily accessible source of hypotheses is the individual's own response disposition. As in self-report and behavioral tests, the usual assumption is that the expressed response corresponds directly to the individual's attitude; for example, that attribution of desirable characteristics to a member of a given group represents a favorable attitude toward that group, that interpretation of a scene as one in which there is hostility toward a member of a given group represents a hostile attitude toward the group, that attribution of a positive (or a negative) response to a hypothetical third person with respect to a given object reflects a positive (or a negative) disposition toward the object in question.

A major reason for the development of such techniques is the assumption that, by disguising the purpose of the instrument and the implications of responses, they lessen the probability of distortion of responses in the interest of presenting a certain picture of the self. They are presented to the respondent not as measures of attitudes but as tests of imagination, verbal fluency, ability to judge character, social sensitivity, or some such characteristic. To the extent that the respondent accepts these explanations, he presumably is unaware not only of the purpose of the test but of the implications of his responses as revealing his own attitudes. Even if the subject does realize that he is expressing his own attitude, it is assumed that it may be easier to express views that may be considered undesirable if one does not explicitly acknowledge them as his own. In some instances the questions asked are nonevaluative, so that the implications of one or another response are quite unlikely to be apparent to the respondent; for example, "What is the [nonexistent] colored man in the corner doing?" (Horowitz and Horowitz, 1938).

Questions have been raised, however, about the validity of the assumption that responses, even though spontaneous and undistorted, reflect the individual's own attitude toward the object. While it seems clearly established that an individual's response may reflect his own disposition, it is not certain that it necessarily does so. Given a scene in which the roles of Negro and white are ambiguous, an individual who describes the Negro as being in a menial position may be reflecting his own devaluing disposition toward Negroes; on the other hand, he may simply be reporting the arrangement most commonly observed in our culture. Similarly, the responses he attributes to a hypothetical third person may be based either on his own response disposition or on his estimate of how most people would react in such a situation.

Attempts to secure evidence as to whether responses to instruments of this type do in fact reflect the individual's own attitudes have followed two lines: examination of the correspondence between estimates of attitude based on these measures and estimates based on other measures (usually of the self-report type); and examination of data secured from instruments of this sort in the light of predictions about patterns of results.

Several studies have found significant correspondence between results of measures of this type and scores on self-report measures. Proshansky (1943) found high correlations between scores based on a standard self-report scale for measuring attitude toward organized labor and scores based on descriptions of briefly-exposed ambiguous pictures of relevant social situations. Riddleberger and Motz (1957) found that subjects who scored high and those who scored low on a self-report measure of attitude toward Negroes differed in their explanations of how the people in a pictured interracial group had met. Sommer (1954), using a modified form of Brown's (1947) adaptation of the Rosenzweig Picture-Frustration Test, was able to identify with considerable success not only individuals who scored high and those who scored low on a self-report scale of attitude toward Negroes but a subgroup who had been instructed to respond to the Picture-Frustration Test as if they were unprejudiced, even though their self-report scores were unfavorable.

However, in view of the assumption that an important characteristic of tests of this type is their relative lack of susceptibility, as compared with self-report measures, to efforts to present a certain picture of the self, correspondence with scores based on self-report measures is a dubious criterion. Getzels (1951), recognizing this fact, approached the problem by predicting conditions under which speeded completions of third-person sentence stubs would differ from completions, by the same respondents, of the same sentence stubs presented in the first person. He made two predictions: (a) that first- and third-person responses would differ on items subject to strong social norms not fully internalized by all members of the group and would not differ on items not subject to such norms; and (b) that in the case of the former items, more socially acceptable answers would be given on the first-person form than on the third-person form. Both predictions were strongly supported. Getzels recognized the possibility that responses to the third-person form might be based on estimates of how most people would respond rather than on the subjects' own response dispositions. Accordingly, he asked the subjects to estimate how most people would respond to the items about Negroes, and found no difference between the average estimates made by those whose third-person responses had been favorable and those whose third-person responses had been unfavorable.

A number of techniques involving perception —in a more literal sense—of ambiguous or unstructured material may be considered in this category. For example, a number of psychologists have been investigating the possible relation of attitudes to perception of stimuli presented under stereoscopic conditions of binocular rivalry. Bagby (1957), presenting pairs of cards differing in cultural content (e.g., a bullfighter and a baseball player) to subjects from Mexico and the United States, found that Mexicans tended to see the card with Mexican content, North Americans those with content familiar in the United States. Pettigrew, Allport, and Barnett (1958), presenting to residents of South Africa pairs of pictures of individuals from different racial groups, found that Afrikaners deviated most consistently from other groups in their responses, overusing the "European" and "African" categories, underusing "Colored" or "Indian."

A study by Bray (1950) made use of unstructured visual material in a different way. Taking off from Sherif's (1935) finding that estimates of movement in the autokinetic phenomenon are markedly influenced by the estimates given by others, Bray investigated the effects of estimates by confederates who were identified as members of minority groups. He had the hypothesis that the extent and direction of such effects would be influenced by the subject's attitude toward the minority group. Here the unstructured perceptual material did not refer to the attitudinal object, but simply provided an opportunity for expressing indirectly a response to the attitudinal object—the physically present, minority-group member.

Again, there are problems about the nature of the inferences that can be drawn. Bray, for example, did not find the direct relationship he

had predicted between attitude toward the minority group (as measured by self-report scales) and responses to the minority-group members' estimates. In the case of binocular rivalry, in what way, if at all, does attitude influence perception? Does one see the picture with the most familiar content? Does one see the member of the racial group toward which he is most favorable, or the one toward which he is most hostile, or of which he is most afraid?

Questions such as these point both to the need for further research on the usefulness of these techniques as measures of attitude and to potentially fruitful lines of investigation of the relation between attitudes and response to various kinds of materials under various conditions.

Measures in Which Inferences Are Drawn from Performance of "Objective" Tasks

Approaches in this category present the respondent with specific tasks to be performed; they are presented as tests of information or ability, or simply as jobs that need to be done. The assumption common to all of them is that performance may be influenced by attitude, and that a systematic bias in performance reflects the influence of attitude.

For example, the subject may be asked to memorize material, some of which is favorable to the attitudinal object, some unfavorable, perhaps some neutral or irrelevant. The assumption is that material congenial with the subject's own position will be learned more quickly and remembered longer. Some empirical support is available for this assumption; for example, in a study by Levine and Murphy (1943), using material about the Soviet Union, and one by Jones and Kohler (1958) using statements about segregation. Or the subject is given a test of "information," in which at least some of the items referring to the attitudinal object either have no correct answers or are so unfamiliar that it can be assumed that few if any respondents will know the correct answers; alternative responses believed (by the investigator) to indicate relatively favorable or relatively unfavorable dispositions toward the object are provided. The assumption here is that, when forced to make a guess on ostensibly factual questions where he has no objective basis for an answer, the subject is likely to choose the alternative most consistent with his own attitudinal disposition. This assumption, too, is supported by some empirical evidence; for example, studies by Hammond (1948) and Weschler (1950) of attitudes toward labor and toward Russia, and by Rankin and Campbell (1955) of attitude toward Negroes. Or the task may be a test of "reasoning," in which syllogisms or other logical forms are presented, and the subject is asked to indicate which of a number of conclusions can appropriately be drawn. Items referring to the attitudinal object are paralleled by similar items with neutral or abstract content; scoring is on the basis of the number and direction of errors on the attitudinally relevant items as compared with the control items. The assumption is that reasoning may be swayed by attitudinal disposition, and thus that errors on the attitudinal relevant items reflect the individual's own position, if the parallel neutral items have been answered correctly. Watson (1925), Morgan (1945), and Thistlethwaite (1950), among others, have developed instruments of this type. Thistlethwaite found a significant difference between Northern and Southern college students in frequency of errors on items dealing with Negroes (as compared with errors on the neutral items), and no corresponding difference on items dealing with Jews, women, or patriotism.

Other measures place the emphasis on the material being judged or on the outcome to be achieved rather than on the ability involved in achieving it. For example, the subject is asked to sort items about the attitudinal object in terms of their position on a scale of favorableness-unfavorableness, ostensibly in order to help in the construction of a Thurstone-type scale. The assumption here is that the rater's own attitude toward the object—especially if it is extreme—influences his judgments of the favorableness of statements about the object. Despite the earlier belief that ratings of items for Thurstone scales are not affected by the raters' own attitudes, a number of recent studies (e.g., Hovland and Sherif, 1952) have found such effects.

It seems reasonable to suppose that most subjects accept these tasks at face value; presumably only someone with rather sophisticated knowledge of research techniques in the social sciences would be aware of their attitudinal implications. Thus it seems reasonable to suppose that they may be relatively impervious to distortion in the interest of presenting a desired picture of the self.

Again, however, there are questions about the nature of the inferences to be drawn. If a subject shows marked and consistent bias, it seems reasonable to infer that he has an attitude toward the object strong enough to affect his performance. If he does not show consistent bias, however, are we to infer that his attitude is not strong, or not consistent? In other words, how sensitive are such measures? Is it possible that individuals with equivalent attitudes differ in the extent to which their performance on such tasks is influenced by those attitudes?

Another problem has to do with the direction in which attitude influences the response, and, conversely, with the nature of the inference to be drawn from a given response. Responses may reflect either wishes or fears; a member of the Communist party may overestimate the number of Communists in the United States, but so may a member of the John Birch Society. A person who underestimates the number of Negro doctors in the United States may do so on the basis of his feeling that Negroes do not have the ability to become doctors, or he may do so on the basis of his belief that opportunities for Negroes to obtain medical training are limited.

Judgments of the favorableness or unfavorableness of statements are subject to a similar problem of interpretation. Hovland and Sherif (1952), working with items about Negroes, found that ratings by Negro subjects and by white subjects who actively supported desegregation differed from ratings by "average" and by anti-Negro white subjects. However, other investigators (e.g., Manis, 1960; Weiss, 1959), working with statements about different attitudinal objects, found that subjects with extreme attitudes —whether favorable or unfavorable—showed similar patterns of ratings, which differed from those made by subjects with moderate attitudes.

As with the preceding category, these problems of interpretation point to the need for caution in inferring the attitude of a given individual from a single test of this sort, but they seem to point also to the probable usefulness of further empirical investigation of the relation of scores based on such measures to those based on tests providing other grounds for inference.

Another group of measures presented as objective tasks or tests of ability focus on the extent to which the attitudinal object figures prominently in the subject's organization of his environment, that is, its salience for him. The kinds of data appropriate for inference about the salience of an attitudinal object differ in some respects from the kinds appropriate for inference about the nature or direction of the attitude. Measures of salience have been developed primarily with respect to attitudes toward social groups. They are of two types: techniques for assessing the tendency to classify individuals in terms of group membership, and techniques for assessing the tendency to subordinate individual differences to group identification.

One technique for assessing the tendency to classify individuals in terms of group membership, originated by Horowitz and Horowitz (1938), may be presented as a test of concept formation. It consists in presenting to a subject sets of photographs of individuals differing in race, sex, age, and socioeconomic status and asking him to select those which "belong together." For example, one set may contain photographs of three white boys, one white girl, and one Negro boy. If the subject replies that the white girl does not belong, this is taken to mean that for him sex is a more important basis for classification than race; if he replies that the Negro boy does not belong, the inference is that race is a more important category for him than sex.

Another technique for assessing the tendency to classify individuals in terms of group membership, presented as a test of memory, involves the clustering, in recall, of verbal symbols for which alternative classificatory principles are available. This technique rests on the finding from studies of verbal behavior that when words drawn from various categories are presented in random order, subjects tend to recall them in clusters, with several words representing a given category being recalled together even though they were not next to each other in the list presented. In studying the salience of race as a basis for classification, a subject would be presented, in random order, with names of people from several different occupational categories—for example, baseball players, musicians, political figures, actors, one name in each category being that of a Negro. The extent to which names of Negroes are grouped together in recall would provide the basis for inference as to the salience of race as a basis for classifying individuals.

A measure of the tendency to subordinate individual differences to group identification, originated by Horowitz and Horowitz (1938), consists in showing the subject a number of photographs of individuals of different ethnic groups and then asking him to identify, from a larger number of photographs, those he has already seen. The task is presented as one involving perception and/or memory. Scoring is in terms of the proportion of correct responses to individuals of a given social group as compared with the proportion of correct responses with respect to individuals of other groups. The inference here is that accuracy in identifying whether or not pictures of specific individuals of a given social group have previously been seen is decreased by the tendency to subordinate individual differences to group identification.

Seeleman (1940-1941), using pictures of whites and Negroes, found a high correlation between scores on this measure and scores on a self-report questionnaire designed to measure attitude toward Negroes, with the less-favorable subjects less accurate in identifying whether the Negro pictures had previously been exposed. The question whether there is, in general, a correlation between salience of an attitudinal object and favorableness of disposition toward it is an interesting problem for empirical investigation.

Measures in Which Inferences Are Drawn from Physiological Reactions to the Attitudinal Object or Representations of It

At the opposite extreme from measures relying on a subject's verbal report of his beliefs, feelings, etc., are those relying on physiological responses not subject to conscious control. These may be measures of a subject's reaction—for example, galvanic skin response (GSR), vascular constriction—to the presence of a member of the object group or to pictorial representations of situations involving members of the object group. For example, Rankin and Campbell (1955) compared GSRs obtained when the experimenter was a Negro with those obtained when the experimenter was white; Westie and DeFleur (1959) recorded GSR, vascular constriction of finger, amplitude and duration of heartbeat, and duration of heart cycle, while the subjects were viewing pictures of whites and Negroes in social situations. Hess and Polt (1960) have photographed pupillary constriction in response to unpleasant stimuli and pupillary dilation in response to pleasant stimuli.

Or the measures may involve responses, such as salivation, blinking, vascular constriction, that have been conditioned to a verbal stimulus, and, by a process of semantic generalization, appear in response to words or concepts that are similar in meaning to the original stimulus. For example, Volkova (1953) has reported a series of experiments in Russia in which subjects were conditioned to salivate in response to the word GOOD; subsequently, such statements as "The Young Pioneer helps his comrade" brought maximum salivation, while such statements as "The Fascists destroyed many cities" brought minimum salivation.

In the case of unconditioned physiological responses to the presence or the representation of the attitudinal object, the basis for inference comes directly from the concept of attitude. Just as all definitions of attitude include beliefs, feelings, and overt behavior as indicators of attitude, so do all definitions, explicitly or implicitly, include physiological responses. It is assumed that the magnitude of the physiological reaction is directly and positively related to the extent of arousal or the intensity of feeling; thus, the greater the physiological response, the stronger and/or more extreme the attitude is presumed to be. Here again, however, there are problems in inferring the nature of the attitude being reflected. Most measures of physiological reaction give direct indications only of the extent of arousal; they do not reveal whether the corresponding emotion is pleasurable or unpleasurable. In general, in attempts to assess attitudes toward social groups via measurement of physiological responses, it has been assumed that the range of affect is not from strongly favorable to strongly unfavorable but rather from accepting, or neutral, to strongly unfavorable; thus the inference has been drawn that the greater the physiological response, the more unfavorable the attitude. If Hess' technique of photographing pupillary constriction-dilation can be adapted to the study of attitudes, it would provide a much firmer basis for inferences about the direction of attitude, since the reaction being measured shows a differential response to pleasant and unpleasant stimuli.

In the case of the conditioned physiological responses, the basis for inference is somewhat different, stemming from learning theory. A response that has been conditioned to a given stimulus tends to generalize to stimuli that are similar. Thus, if a response that has been conditioned to the concept "good" appears when the attitudinal object is presented, the inference is that the subject considers the object good— that is, that his attitude toward it is favorable; if the response does not appear when the attitudinal object is presented, the inference is that the subject does not consider it good—that is, that his attitude toward it is not favorable.

The purpose of the physiological measures may or may not be apparent to the subject. In the Westie and DeFleur (1959) study, for example, subjects presumably realized that the physiological measures were being used as indicators of their reactions to the interracial pictures. In the Rankin and Campbell (1955) experiment, on the other hand, subjects were led to believe that they were taking part in a word-association study and that it was their GSRs to the stimulus words (rather than to the Negro and white experimenters) that were being investigated. Whether or not the purpose is clear to the subject, the fact that the responses measured are not subject to conscious control would seem to eliminate the possibility of modification of responses in order to present a certain picture of the self.

However, physiological responses may be quite sensitive to influences other than those in which the investigator is interested—both to other aspects of the stimulus material and to other environmental influences. It is difficult to control the experimental situation so completely that other factors are ruled out as possible determinants of the response.

Again, questions such as these point to the need for extreme caution in drawing inferences about the attitude of a given individual from a measure of this type. But, again, they point to encouraging possibilities for empirical research and to the opportunity to greatly increase our understanding of attitudes and their relation to various kinds of response, by the use of instruments yielding different types of evidence.

REFERENCES

Adorno, T. W., Frenkel-Brunswik, Else, Levenson, D. J., and Sanford, R. N. *The authoritarian personality*. New York: Harper, 1950.

Allport, G. W. The historical background of modern social psychology. In G. Lindzey (Ed.), *Handbook of social psychology*. Vol. 1. *Theory and method*. Cambridge, Mass.: Addison-Wesley, 1954. Pp. 3-56.

Bagby, J. W. A cross-cultural study of perceptual predominance in binocular rivalry. *J. abnorm. soc. Psychol.*, 1957, **54**, 331-334.

Bass, B. M. Authoritarianism or acquiescence? *J. abnorm. soc. Psychol.*, 1955, **51**, 616-623.

Bray, D. The prediction of behavior from two attitude scales. *J. abnorm. soc. Psychol.*, 1950, **45**, 64-84.

Brown, J. F. A modification of the Rosenzweig Picture-Frustration Test to study hostile interracial attitudes. *J. Psychol.*, 1947, **24**, 247-272.

Campbell, D. T. The indirect assessment of social attitudes. *Psychol. Bull.*, 1950, **47**, 15-38.

Campbell, D. T. Social attitudes and other acquired behavioral dispositions. In S. Koch (Ed.), *Psychology: A study of a science.* Vol. 6. *Investigations of man as socius: Their place in psychology and the social sciences.* New York: McGraw-Hill, 1961.

Criswell, Joan H. Racial cleavages in Negro-white groups. *Sociometry*, 1937, **1**, 87-89.

Criswell, Joan H. Social structure revealed in a sociometric retest. *Sociometry*, 1939, **2**, 69-75.

Cronbach, L. J. Response sets and test validity. *Educ. psychol. Measmt.*, 1946, **6**, 475-494.

Cronbach, L. J. Further evidence on response sets and test design. *Educ. psychol. Measmt.*, 1950, **10**, 3-31.

DeFleur, M. L., and Westie, F. R. Verbal attitudes and overt acts: An experiment on the salience of attitudes. *Amer. sociol. Rev.*, 1958, **23**, 667-673.

Deri, Susan, Dinnerstein, Dorothy, Harding, J., and Pepitone, A. D. Techniques for the diagnosis and measurement of intergroup attitudes and behavior. *Psychol. Bull.*, 1948, **45**, 248-271.

Edwards, A. L. The relationship between the judged desirability of a trait and the probability that the trait will be endorsed. *J. appl. Psychol.*, 1953, **37**, 90-93.

Edwards, A. L. *The social desirability variable in personality assessment and research.* New York: Dryden Press, 1957.

Getzels, J. W. The assessment of personality and prejudice by the method of paired direct and projective questions. Unpublished doctoral dissertation, Harvard University, 1951.

Hammond, K. R. Measuring attitudes by error-choice: An indirect method. *J. abnorm. soc. Psychol.*, 1948, **43**, 38-48.

Hess, E. H., and Polt, J. M. Pupil size as related to interest value of visual stimuli. *Science*, 1960, **132**, 349-350.

Horowitz, E. L., and Horowitz, Ruth E. Development of social attitudes in children. *Sociometry*, 1938, **1**, 301-338.

Hovland, C. I., and Sherif, M. Judgmental phenomena and scales of attitude measurement: Item displacement in Thurstone scales. *J. abnorm. soc. Psychol.*, 1952, **47**, 822-832.

Jones E. E., and Kohler, Rika. The effects of plausibility on the learning of controversial statements. *J. abnorm. soc. Psychol.*, 1958, **57**, 315-320.

Kinsey, A. C., Pomeroy, W. B., and Martin, C. E. *Sexual behavior in the human male.* Philadelphia, Pa.: Saunders, 1948.

LaPiere, R. T. Attitudes vs. actions. *Soc. Forces*, 1934, **14**, 230-237.

Lazarsfeld, P. F. Latent structure analysis. In S. Koch (Ed.), *Psychology: A study of a science.* Vol. 3. *Formulations of the person and the social context.* New York: McGraw-Hill, 1959.

Levine, J. M., and Murphy, G. The learning and forgetting of controversial material. *J. abnorm. soc. Psychol.*, 1943, **38**, 507-517.

Manis, M. The interpretation of opinion statements as a function of recipient attitude. *J. abnorm. soc. Psychol.*, 1960, **60**, 340-344.

Mann, J. H. The effect of inter-racial contact on sociometric choices and perceptions. *J. soc. Psychol.*, 1959, **50**, 143-152.   (*a*)

Mann, J. H. The relationship between cognitive, affective and behavioral aspects of racial prejudice. *J. soc. Psychol.*, 1959, **49**, 223-228.   (*b*)

Moreno, J. L. *Who shall survive?* (Orig. publ. 1934) (Rev. ed.) Beacon, N. Y.: Beacon House, 1943.

Morgan, J. J. B. Attitudes of students toward the Japanese. *J. soc. Psychol.*, 1945, **21**, 219-227.

Mussen, P. H. The reliability and validity of the Horowitz Faces Test. *J. abnorm. soc. Psychol.*, 1950, **45**, 504-506.   (*a*)

Mussen, P. H. Some personality and social factors related to changes in children's attitudes toward Negroes. *J. abnorm. soc. Psychol.*, 1950, **45**, 423-441.   (*b*)

Pettigrew, T. F., Allport, G. W., and Barnett, E. O. Binocular resolution and perception of race in South Africa. *Brit. J. Psychol.*, 1958, **49**, 265-278.

Proshansky, H. M. A projective method for the study of attitudes. *J. abnorm. soc. Psychol.*, 1943, **38**, 393-395.

Rankin, R. E., and Campbell, D. T. Galvanic skin response to Negro and white experimenters. *J. abnorm. soc. Psychol.*, 1955, **51**, 30-33.

Riddleberger, Alice B., and Motz, Annabelle B. Prejudice and perception. *Amer. J. Sociol.*, 1957, **62**, 498-503.

Seeleman, Virginia. The influence of attitude upon the remembering of pictorial material. *Arch. Psychol., N. Y.*, 1940-1941, **36** (No. 258).

Sherif, M. A study of some social factors in perception. *Arch. Psychol., N. Y.*, 1935, No. 187.

Sommer, R. On the Brown adaptation of the Rosenzweig P-F for assessing social attitudes. *J. abnorm. soc. Psychol.*, 1954, **49**, 125-128.

Stanton, H., Back, K. W., and Litwak, E. Role-playing in survey research. *Amer. J. Sociol.*, 1956, **62**, 172-176.

Stanton, H. R., and Litwak, E. Toward the development of a short form test of interpersonal competence. *Amer. sociol. Rev.*, 1955, **20**, 668-674.

Taylor, J. B. What do attitude scales measure: The problem of social desirability. *J. abnorm. soc. Psychol.*, 1961, **62**, 386-390.

Thistlethwaite, D. Attitude and structure as factors in the distortion of reasoning. *J. abnorm. soc. Psychol.*, 1950, **45**, 442-458.

Volkova, B. D. Some characteristics of conditioned reflex formation to verbal stimuli in children. *Sechenov physiol. J. USSR*, 1953, **39**, 540-548.

Watson, G. B. The measurement of fairmindedness. *Teachers Coll. Columbia U. Contr. Educ.*, 1925, No. 176.

Weiss, W. The effects on opinions of a change in scale judgments. *J. abnorm. soc. Psychol.*, 1959, **58**, 329-334.

Weschler, I. R. An investigation of attitudes toward labor and management by means of the error-choice method. *J. soc. Psychol.*, 1950, **32**, 51-67.

Weschler, I. R., and Bernberg, R. E. Indirect methods of attitude measurement. *Int. J. Opin. attit. Res.*, 1950, **4**, 209-228.

Westie, F. R. Negro-white status differentials and social distance. *Amer. sociol. Rev.*, 1952, **17**, 550-558.

Westie, F. R. A technique for the measurement of race attitudes. *Amer. sociol. Rev.*, 1953, **18**, 73-78.

Westie, F. R., and DeFleur, M. L. Autonomic responses and their relationship to race attitudes. *J. abnorm. soc. Psychol.*, 1959, **58**, 340-347.

D. Problems and Prospects in Attitude Measurement

26.   Judgmental Phenomena and Scales of Attitude Measurement: Item Displacement in Thurstone Scales

CARL I. HOVLAND and MUZAFER SHERIF

In his influential study *The Measurement of Attitude,* Thurstone states as a major requirement for attitude scales that the scale values of statements be independent of the position held by the judges who do the initial categorization: ·

If the scale is to be regarded as valid, the scale values of the statements should not be affected by the opinions of the people who help to construct it. This may turn out to be a severe test in practice, but the scaling method must stand such a test before it can be accepted as being more than a description of the people who construct the scale. At any rate, to the extent that the present method of scale construction is affected by the opinions of the readers who help to sort out the original statements into a scale, to that extent the validity or universality of the scale may be challenged (19, p. 92).

The first research study of the Thurstone assumption was carried out by· Hinckley (8) on

• Reprinted from *Journal of Abnormal and Social Psychology,* 1952, **47**, 822-832, with permission of the junior author and the American Psychological Association. The present study, the first of several on the topic of judgmental phenomena and scales of attitude measurement, was done as part of a coordinated program of research on opinion and attitude change being conducted at Yale under a grant from the Rockefeller Foundation to whom acknowledgement is gratefully made (cf. Hovland, C. I., Changes in attitude through communication, *J. abnorm. soc. Psychol.,* 1951, **46**, 424-437).

attitudes toward Negroes. Opinion statements were categorized by two groups of white judges, one with anti-Negro attitudes and the other with pro-Negro attitudes, and by a group of Negro judges. Scale values were determined by the method of equal-appearing intervals. Hinckley found that the average scale values for the two white groups were highly correlated ($r = .98$) despite their difference in attitude on the issue and that the scale values for the anti-Negro white judges were also closely correlated with those for the Negro judges ($r = .93$). On the basis of these results Hinckley concluded that "the scale which we have constructed for measuring attitude toward the social position of the Negro is not influenced in its measuring function by the attitudes of the subjects used in the construction" (8, p. 293). Substantially similar results were obtained in a later study by Pintner and Forlano (14), who used the Attitude toward Patriotism scales which had also been derived by the method of equal-appearing intervals.

That the attitudes and opinions of the judges have no effect on the placement of items is in sharp conflict with the results of studies in the fields of perception and judgment. These studies indicate that judgments *are* greatly influenced by motivational and attitudinal factors operative at the time. Thus in the studies by Asch, Block, and Hertzman (2) where subjects judged photographs, political figures, professions, and slogans along such dimensions as intelligence, honesty, and social usefulness, judgments were made "in accordance with an underlying attitude of acceptance or rejection." Other studies indicate that category intervals are directly affected by attitudinal factors. As long ago as 1914 Fernberger (7) showed that changes in attitude bring about changes in the range of judgments of equality, hence in the size of category intervals. A series of studies by Volkmann (20), Rogers (16), and McGarvey (13) showed that category intervals are caused to expand or shrink by the experimental introduction of anchoring agents beyond or within the scale and that "anchoring can be achieved by appropriate verbal instructions, without the use of anchoring stimuli" (21, p. 287).

Displacement of judgments along a scale seems a general phenomenon when the stimuli carry strong social and personal value. For example, Cartwright found that the S's estimation of equivalence of statements was affected by his own position. "The size of the range of equivalence related to a 'radical' and to a 'conservative' differed, depending upon S's own political attitudes" (3, p. 195). "For the radical S, the judgments of 'radical' extend 7.5 units while the judgments of 'conservative' extend 10 units. For the conservative S, on the other hand, the judgments of 'radical' extend 8.5 units, while the judgments of 'conservative' extend only 5.2 units" (3, p. 189).

In studying the response of Negro youth to the social value placed on light skin color, Johnson (10) found a tendency for self-ratings to be a shade or more lighter than they appear to the tester. This was shown even more definitively in the study by Marks (12) who matched each Negro S's skin color with an objective hue. The tendency was to displace one's own coloring as much as objective fact allowed in the direction of the desired norm of light brown. A dark individual, rating himself close to average, would displace individuals lighter than himself to lighter than average categories. In contrast, a light individual would judge the majority of the group as dark. While the relative position of each S is kept the same by different raters, the absolute position varies from rater to rater.

It is interesting to note that in Cartwright's study the Ss were more discriminating in accepting items at their own end of the scale, and lumped together items at the extreme opposite to their own stand, while in the study of Marks the displacements of items (skin color) were in the direction of the desired skin color. It is apparent that the direction of item displacement will depend upon both the stimulus material and the S's motivation in relation to it.

More recently Hinckley himself, in collaboration with Rethlingshafer, added further substantiating evidence of the effect of the judge's own attitude upon his judgments. Starting with the general assumption that "men judging heights of men on a scale of short to tall would be influenced in their scale values by their own heights" (9, p. 257), these investigators found that "the judgment of the average height of all men is influenced by the height of the man making the judgment. The 'meaning' of the social value terms of 'short' and 'tall' is in part determined by the height of the judge. The 'egocentric' influence is also controlled by the objective facts, particularly in judging the extreme heights" (9, p. 262).

Thus we have the paradox that some leading texts in social psychology say in the chapter on perception and judgment that judgments are greatly affected by the individual's attitudes and motives, while in the chapter on scaling methods they state that judgments of the meaning of items are unaffected by the position of the judges who do the sorting. Analysis of prior attitude scale studies suggests a possible explanation for the discrepancy: the utilization of too narrow a range of individuals, with the consequent elimination of the extreme Ss who would show variation and displacement of judgments most clearly. In the Pintner and Forlano study, the question may be raised as to whether intense personal involvement was achieved on the issue of patriotism during the thirties, and the authors report that "No group could be called unpatriotic" (14, p. 41). In the Hinckley study (8), on the other hand, considerable personal involvement in the issue would be expected, particularly on the part of the Negro judges. But the report suggests that here again the range may have been unintentionally narrowed by a procedure he intended only to eliminate "careless" subjects:

One tendency which revealed itself in the sorting of the subjects was the bunching of statements in one or more piles to the apparent detriment of the other piles. This phenomenon of bunching at the extremes was noticed in the case of *certain* of the *white subjects,* but was *especially noticeable* in the Negro subjects. Since the 114 statements are distributed with fair uniformity over the entire scale, *marked bunching is a sign of careless sorting*. If more than a fourth of the statements are assigned to any one pile, it will leave less than three-fourths to distribute over the remaining ten piles. Furthermore, the individual who sorts the statements in this fashion often ignores some of the piles completely. *On the assumption that this bunching was due to poor discrimination and carelessness every case having 30 or more statements in any one pile was automatically eliminated from consideration, and the results were not recorded* (8, p. 283).[1]

From the studies of judgment cited above it would be predicted that this piling up of statements in certain categories by some of the white Ss and, in a more noticeable way, by the Negro Ss may be due to the effect of the Ss' strong attitudes on the topic. It may be that by eliminating these Ss the investigator eliminated, at the same time, those who had the most accentuated attitudes on the issue. It is interesting, in connection with this hypothesis, that even after all Ss placing 30 or more statements in any category were eliminated, there was still "a slight tendency for Group I, which is prejudiced against the Negro, to judge a given statement to be more favorable to the Negro than Group II [favorable to the Negro] judged it" (8, p. 293).

PROBLEM

The previous studies of the Thurstone scale do not appear to the writers to have fully settled the issue of whether or not scale values are affected by the attitude of the judges, since there does not appear to be sufficient evidence that adequate representation was made of Ss at the extremes, with intense involvement in the issues being judged. We were, therefore, interested in reinvestigating the problem under conditions which would provide the maximum opportunity for the operation of the types of factors which have been found important in the field of perception and judgment. It is hoped that such a study will be a contribution to a *rapprochement* between the areas of judgment and of attitude measurement.

Accordingly, the Hinckley experiment was duplicated using attitudes toward Negroes, but with means of insuring that the Negro and pro-Negro white judges were not selected in any way which might exclude those with the

[1] Italics ours.

strongest attitudes on the issue, as we thought possible with the Hinckley procedure of eliminating individuals who placed 30 or more items in any one category. Moreover, checks were incorporated to evaluate his inference that such individuals were "careless."

On the assumption that the set of 114 statements used by Hinckley represents a wide range of positions, with some clearly *pro* and others clearly *con*, and that a large number are of a neutral character, a favorable situation exists for studying how internal factors such as motives and attitudes affect the placement of the rather unstructured and ambiguous middle-position statements. The literature on judgment and perception cited earlier clearly suggests the general hypothesis that the position of a judge on an issue in which he has strong personal involvement will constitute an "anchor" for his judgments, whether or not his attitude is specifically called for in the instructions. The specific hypothesis for the present study may be stated in summary form as follows[2]:

1. Judges with extremely pro or con attitudes will show a tendency to concentrate their placement of items into a small number of categories.

2. Judges with an extreme position and strong personal involvement will be highly discriminating in accepting items at their own end of the scale. They will correspondingly display a strong tendency to lump together statements at the end of the scale which they reject. The former tendency can be described as a raised *threshold of acceptance* and the latter as a lowered *threshold for rejection*.

3. A greater degree of displacement will occur for the "neutral" items and a smaller degree for the sharply defined pro and con statements at the extremes.

In less technical terminology these hypotheses state that individuals with strong personal in-

[2] These hypotheses are formulated in relation to the placement of items in categories along a scale prescribed by the experimenter. Such scales and categories may be referred to as "imposed" scales and "imposed" categories. We have also extended these hypotheses by allowing each S to define his own scale by choosing the number of categories he personally considered necessary to distinguish the different positions in the issue. Results using these methods, obtained in conjunction with the present experiment, will be reported in a separate paper.

Studies in addition to those already cited which bear on our hypotheses include 1, 4, 11, 15 and 17.

volvement will tend to see issues pretty much "in all black and white" rather than with fine distinctions, and that statements even mildly critical of their position will be judged to be more hostile by them than by more neutral individuals.

METHOD

Procedure

The problem presented above requires a design satisfying the following: (a) a topic which has strong personal involvement for Ss chosen to represent the *pro* or *con* stand on the issue, (b) clear differentiation of Ss with respect to their position on the issue, (c) administration of the judging task without giving any hints that an attitude study is involved, and (d) checks to determine whether heavy concentration of statements in any category is due to "carelessness." For these reasons, the Attitude Toward Negro scale was considered to be the most appropriate topic, and through the kindness of Professor Hinckley we were able to secure the original 114 statements he used concerning the social position of Negroes. These statements had been selected to include the entire range from very favorable to very unfavorable on the issue and to be distributed in a fairly representative way over the range.

The prime consideration in each step of the procedure was that all means be taken to insure careful and uniform administration to relatively small groups of Ss in each session and to be certain that Ss understood the instructions at each point. In every case the experiment was administered by graduate assistants who had been thoroughly briefed concerning the procedure, who had themselves carried out the instructions under close supervision, and who had in most cases practiced the procedure on a trial group. A special point was made to select administrators who would appear to Ss to be "one of them." The groups were kept small in number whenever possible, in order that administrators could easily but unobtrusively observe Ss while instructions were being carried out. On the whole the sorting was administered in large rooms, chiefly in laboratory space, in order to give each S ample room to spread out the statements before him.

Categorization of items. The first task for the Ss consisted of sorting the statements into piles. Each of the 114 statements was mimeographed on a 3 × 5 in. card. To facilitate later tabu-

lation, an arbitrary code number unrelated to the content of the item was assigned to each statement and stamped on the back of the card. No S asked a question concerning any possible connection between the statement and the code number. As a further precaution, the cards were shuffled beforehand so that S would not be able to get an idea about the exact number of statements. It was thought that the knowledge of the exact number of statements might tempt him to divide the total number of cards by the number of categories to give him a fixed guide for the number to be assigned to each category.

Deliberately, no mention of attitude measurement was introduced in the instructions until the sorting phase was completed. It was only after the sorting was completed by S that instructions aiming to tap his attitude on the issue were introduced. To insure this, the instructions pertaining to sorting and those requiring the checking of S's particular stand on the issue were put on different sheets, and those relating to the attitudinal aspect were not passed out until the sortings were completed. This temporal sequence was employed in line with our basic hypothesis that, whether or not the attitude of Ss was explicitly activated, the Ss would reveal it in their behavior when faced with appropriate stimuli.

After receiving the envelope containing the 114 statements, Ss were given the appropriate instructions for sorting. The instructions for the actual procedure of sorting were identical with those used by Thurstone and Chave (19), Hinckley (8), and others. The Ss were given 3 to 4 minutes to read the following instructions aloud:

You are given a number of statements expressing opinions in regard to the social position of Negroes. These cards are to be sorted into different piles.

You will find it easier to sort them if you look over a number of cards, chosen at random, before you begin to sort.

You are given eleven cards with roman numbers on them: I, II, III, IV, V, VI, VII, VIII, IX, X, XI. Please arrange these before you in regular order. Under Card I, put those statements which are most *unfavorable* in regard to the social position of Negroes. Under Card XI, put those statements which are most *favorable* in regard to the social position of Negroes. Under each of the other 9 cards, between I and XI, put those statements which correspond to that step in the 11 piles.[3]

This means that when you are through sorting you will have 11 piles of statements arranged in order from I, the *lowest*, to XI, the *highest*.

Use your judgment as to where each statement should be placed in the 11 piles. Do not be concerned about the number of cards in each pile.

When you are through sorting, please put a rubber band around each of the 11 piles of cards, placing the numbered card on top of each pile.

If you complete the sorting before others, please remain quietly in your seat until final announcements are made by the experimenter.

After the appropriate instructions for sorting were read aloud, the administrator answered any questions concerning the sorting to be sure that instructions were understood. Administrators were, however, cautioned not to use examples relating to Negroes to clarify the instructions. For example, as an instance of a very unfavorable statement on an issue, administrators used "Organized religion is the greatest single detriment to the advancement of civilization in the world today"; or, as an example of a very favorable statement on an issue, "Organized religion is the only hope for the salvation of the world."

When the instructions for sorting were clear to the Ss, the sorting began. During this time, the administrator distributed rubber bands to each S and performed other tasks so that he would be in a position to see that each S was conscientiously performing the task according to instructions, without seeming to be observing the placement of specific cards. The sorting process consumed about 55 minutes. The Ss were reminded to remain in their seats and

keep their cards with them until all Ss had finished sorting.

Obtaining the judge's own attitudes. The second instruction sheet, which concerned the Ss' agreement and disagreement with the piles of statements they had sorted, was then distributed. After sorting, the following instructions were given for the purpose of tapping Ss' attitudes on the issue:

Now that you have completed the sorting of cards into piles, pick up that pile of cards which comes closest to your view on the issue (that is, the social position of Negroes). On the numbered card on top of that pile, please write the word "agree." After writing the word "agree" on this pile, please write *one* of the following to indicate the degree of agreement with that pile: (*a*) "very strongly," (*b*) "strongly," or (*c*) "mildly."

Now pick up that *pile* of cards which is most objectionable from your point of view. On the numbered card on top of that pile, please write the word "disagree." After writing the word "disagree" on this pile, please write *one* of the following to indicate the degree of disagreement with that pile: (*a*) "very strongly," (*b*) "strongly," or (*c*) "mildly."

When you have completed the above, please replace the 11 piles of cards, each carefully separated by its rubber band, in the envelope.

This is part of a scientific research project. The results of each person's sorting will be treated as scientific data and will be confidential.

Check on the "carelessness" hypothesis. The chief purpose of the next procedural step was to have the Ss estimate the proportion of statements which they judged to be "very unfavorable," "unfavorable," "neutral," "favorable," and "very favorable" to Negroes to determine whether or not there would be general correspondence between actual proportions of cards sorted into various piles and the Ss' estimates of these proportions when the cards were out of sight. This step is critical for the problem at hand. If there is a general correspondence between the patterns of these percentages filled in by S without the actual sight of the objective piles he has made and the actual proportions into which he sorted the cards, the explanation for disproportionately large piles (of 30 or more statements) as due to "carelessness" appears inadequate. Correspondence be-

---

[3] Probably for this issue, it would have been preferable to use I as the favorable and XI as the unfavorable end. The few sortings done by Negro Ss under individual supervision showed a tendency to switch I to the favorable end unless reminded that I represented the unfavorable end. Therefore, special care was taken in the experimental sessions (especially with Negro Ss) to repeat several times that I was the unfavorable, XI the favorable end of the scale. To provide maximum comparability we conformed to Hinckley's use of I as the most unfavorable end. A small number of Ss consistently reversed the two extremes and these data were recopied in the standard direction.

tween the actual proportions in the piles and the percentages filled in by Ss at a later time would indicate a consistency in evaluation of the stimulus material at two time intervals which would not be expected if the sorting were casual and random.

The estimates of sortings were obtained after all Ss had replaced the statements in their envelopes. The administrator passed out a 3 × 5 in. card to each S *individually* so that he could check to be sure that the sorted piles were in the envelopes. The administrator explained the task orally as follows:

Now that you have sorted the statements into piles in terms of their stand regarding Negroes, please estimate the percentage of statements which in your judgment were "very unfavorable" to Negroes, "unfavorable" to Negroes, "neutral," "favorable" to Negroes, and "very favorable" to Negroes. Write the per cent for each of these stands printed on the card from "very unfavorable" to "very favorable" in the appropriate space under the column headed "% of statements regarding Negroes." The five percentages which you write should add up to 100%. You will note that there is a question at the bottom of the card to be answered on the back. I believe the other items are self-explanatory.

Supplementary attitude measurement with white judges. It was important to have a clearer differentiation of groups than that afforded by the rather crude list of six statements used for this purpose by Hinckley. In the case of Negro Ss, the intensity of agreement and disagreement with the piles of statements they had sorted and the obvious attitude of Negro Ss sufficed. But for the white Ss, a further check on their attitudes was obtained by administration of the Likert Negro Scale[4] as the final step in the session. The scale was not administered to Negro Ss because discussion with Negro pretest Ss revealed a strong animosity toward filling out a form prepared entirely from the white point of view. In fact, some Negro Ss spontaneously remarked that the statements to be sorted were prepared from the white standpoint.

Subjects

The final procedure presented above was decided upon after pretesting on both white

4 See Likert, R. A technique for the measurement of attitudes. *Arch. Psychol., N. Y.*, 1932, No. 140.

and Negro Ss ($N = 100$). Ten Ss made the sortings individually under close supervision with the view of getting detailed hints for the procedure.

The main concern in the selection of the final experimental Ss was to insure groups of Ss who would represent differentiated segments on the scale ranging from an extremely favorable position to an extremely unfavorable position in regard to the issue of the social position of Negroes. For this purpose, groups and institutions were selected which would insure a likelihood of obtaining such differentiated positions on the scale.

Negro groups. It followed that Negro Ss should be used to represent the pro end of the scale. A total of 103 were used. Fifty-four were enrolled as graduate students or were attending the summer session at the University of Oklahoma. These more mature Negroes may be taken as the most self-consciously pro group in this study. Since these individuals were attending the University in the year following the Supreme Court decision ending segregation at the University, they had a sense of mission and an accentuated identification as members of their group. Many were brought to the university by the National Association for the Advancement of Colored People, which has encouraged Negroes on the campus to form active social groups. As a group, these students had had more actual contact with discrimination practices than the younger Negro Ss.

The younger group of Negro Ss was made up of 49 undergraduates at a state university for Negroes; hence, their age and educational level are lower than that of the University of Oklahoma group. While segregation and awareness of anti-Negro feeling had been a part of their life, they had grown up largely in a Negro environment. Since this university is also located in a Negro community, this relatively "sheltered" condition is continued in academic life.

White groups: 1. Pro-Negro. Because validity derived from the stands taken in actual life was the desired criterion governing selection of subject groups, two small groups of white Ss who had actually participated in pro-Negro activities were chosen. Members of these groups, totaling 19, had been among the leaders in local campaigning at the University of Oklahoma (by student polls, newspaper work, etc.) for an end to segregation. One group was selected by the director of the YMCA as among those individuals who were thus active. Another group had been organized around this issue. Thus, for these very pro-Negro white Ss, personal information as well as details of the stand of their groups were available.

2. *"Average" subjects.* Here results from a number of different colleges throughout the South were secured. These included two in an area in southeastern Oklahoma popularly known as "Little Dixie." In general, students attending these schools are from a lower socioeconomic level than those attending the state university. The educational level of the area is relatively low. Affiliation with fundamentalist religious groups is common. The students in these colleges are, for the most part, preparing to become teachers. From one, 53 Ss were chosen from classes in elementary English. From the other, 58 students who had not been exposed to courses in either psychology or sociology, were used.

Three colleges and universities from the state of Georgia were also secured. Sixty-four Ss were obtained, distributed about equally through the three institutions. In all, 194 white judges were used.

3. *Anti-Negro subjects.* It was hoped to secure a group of strongly anti-Negro Ss. The major difficulty in finding strongly anti-Negro Ss lay in the fact that no groups organized strictly around such a stand were available. Further, pretesting revealed a strong tendency on the part of college students to express more liberal attitudes than would probably have been expressed at the time of the original Hinckley study. A number of such Ss who were believed to be somewhat less liberal on this issue were obtained from living units at the University of Oklahoma. But it finally appeared necessary to use the Ss in the total white sample who expressed the most anti-Negro attitudes on the evaluation cards and on the Likert questionnaires.

RESULTS

Categorization of Statements by Various Groups

One method of analyzing any differences between the major groups of Ss in the degree to which items are displaced is to determine the number of statements placed in each of the eleven categories. Results on these distributions are shown in Figure 1 for (a) Negro Ss, (b) strongly pro-Negro white Ss (leaders in the anti-segregation movement), and (c) "average" white Ss from six Southern colleges. To permit comparison of the results for the last group with those obtained by Hinckley, his procedure of eliminating all individuals placing 30 or more statements into any single category was also studied. Data are also presented for a group of 17 Ss who appeared to have the most anti-Negro attitudes within the white group. These 17 Ss had indicated disagreement with the pile of statements most favorable to Negroes and had markedly anti-Negro Likert scale scores (below 50).

It will be observed that the Negro group shows a heavy piling up of statements in the extreme categories, indicating displacement of neutral statements to the extreme position. This displacement is particularly noticeable for category I at the anti-Negro end, a position with which these Ss strongly disagree. The distribution of responses of the pro-Negro white group is similar to that for Negroes but a little less extreme. The dotted line at 30 indicates the frequency which Hinckley used to eliminate Ss. Over three-fourths of the Negro Ss and two-thirds of the pro-Negro white Ss would be eliminated by applying the Hinckley criterion.

The data for the average white group show considerably less piling up at the ends. When the Hinckley elimination procedure is followed the distribution is relatively flat. The differences in the distributions for the Negro and average white are highly significant statistically.

The results for the anti-Negro Ss are not strikingly different from those for the average white Ss. But it will be noted that as compared with the white Ss they tend to show a slightly greater tendency to concentrate items at the *positive* end of the scale.

Scale Values for the Various Criterion Subgroups

Another method of studying displacement of items is to investigate the distributions of scale values obtained for the various subgroups. These are the data on which Thurstone, Hinckley, and others base their main case for the validity of their scaling procedure. Inspection of the original 114 items reveals that all of the statements are not equally appropriate for white and Negro Ss. For example, items like "I would not patronize a hotel that ac-

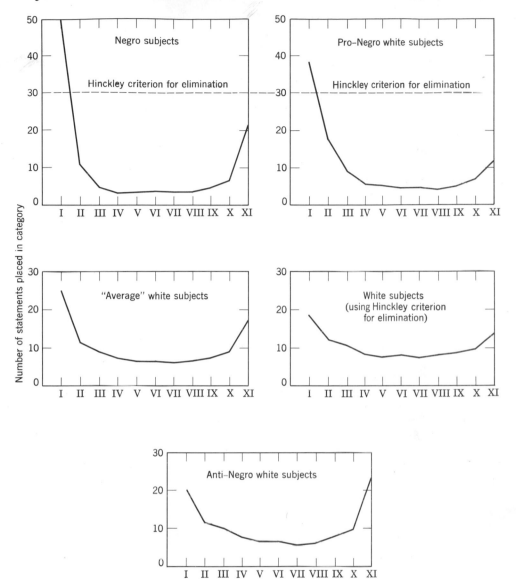

Figure 1. Number of statements placed in each of 11 categories by each group of judges.

commodates Negroes" or "My lack of contact with the Negro makes it impossible for me to pass judgment as to his social position" are not as relevant to Negro Ss as to whites. But it was possible to find 11 items which seemed equally appropriate for the Negro and white populations, and which were approximately equidistant in the original Hinckley scaling. Scale values were then found for each of these items for each of the present groups, using the conventional Thurstone procedure. The eleven items were all used in the final forms of the

Scale of Attitude toward the Negro.[5] They are numbered 5, 6, 10, and 16 in Scale A, and 1, 2, 3, 5, 8, 9, and 15 in Scale B.

The distributions of scale values for these eleven items derived from the responses of the various groups are presented graphically in Figure 2. For comparison, the scale values reported by Hinckley are given. It will be seen

[5] Hinckley, E. D. *Attitude toward the Negro*, Scale No. 3, Forms A and B. (L. L. Thurstone, Ed.) Chicago: Univer. of Chicago Press, 1930.

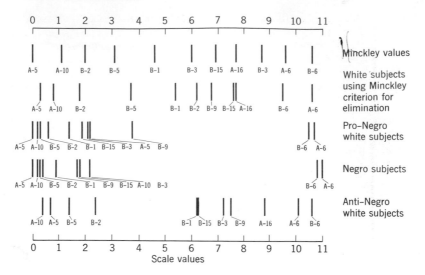

Figure 2. Scale values of 11 selected items for each of the four major groups.

that there is considerable similarity in the scale values for the average white Ss (with the Hinckley procedure of eliminating those with 30 or more statements in any category) and the scale values originally found by Hinckley. The correlation between the two sets of scale values is .96 (11 items). But the values for the strongly pro-Negro white judges and for the Negro judges do not correspond at all to those obtained by Hinckley. The distributions of the Negro groups show the majority of the items bunched up at the extreme anti-Negro end of the scale (in line with the results of Figure 1). The items which are neutral for Hinckley's group and for our "average" white Ss are displaced by the Negro judges to the extremes, principally to the anti-Negro end. The distribution of scale values for the pro-Negro white Ss is similar to that for the Negro Ss but again not quite as extreme. The results for the anti-Negro Ss also show a tendency for neutral items to be displaced toward the extremes, but in their case some displacement is also noticeable toward the pro-Negro end.

"Carelessness" as an Explanation for the Results

It will be recalled that Ss who placed 30 or more statements in any single pile were discarded by Hinckley on the grounds of carelessness. To obtain a check on this explanation for the large number of our Ss who placed this number of statements in the extreme position piles, after the sorting was completed and the cards placed in their envelope, a question was

asked concerning the Ss' impressions of the percentage of the statements which were "very unfavorable," "unfavorable," "neutral," "fairly favorable," and "very favorable" to the Negro. From these data we have evidence that the Ss who placed a large number of their cards in the extremely unfavorable categories may really have perceived the statements in that way and did not place them there through carelessness. The data are presented in Table 1

TABLE 1. Percentages of Statements Considered "Very Unfavorable" or "Unfavorable" to Negroes by Individuals Placing Varying Numbers of Statements in Category I (Anti-Negro)

Per Cent of Items Judged "Very Unfavorable" or "Unfavorable"	Percentages Making Various Estimates of Unfavorableness of Items among Individuals Who Placed		
	Less than 30 Items in Category I ($N = 119$)	30 to 59 Items in Category I ($N = 105$)	60 or More Items in Category I ($N = 34$)
60 or over	22.7	51.5	79.4
40–59	55.5	39.0	17.7
Less than 40	21.8	9.5	2.9
	$x^2 = 43.3$		
	$p = <.001$		

to show the difference in the evaluations of the number of unfavorable statements in the list among Ss who placed less than 30 statements at the anti-Negro end of the scale, among those who placed between 30 and 59, and among those who placed 60 or more in this category. The Ss who placed a greater number of statements in the anti-Negro category were definitely more inclined to believe that there were a high number of unfavorable statements in the list. The chi-square value for the distributions is 43.3, which gives a probability value of considerably less than .001. A very high degree of relationship is not to be expected in view of the fact that Ss had not been given any prior intimation that they would be required to make such a judgment. For the entire group of 258 Ss on whom the relevant information was available, a correlation of .32 was obtained between the percentage of statements considered "very unfavorable" and "unfavorable" and the number of cards placed in the extreme anti-Negro category. This correlation is significantly different from zero at considerably less than the .001 level. These data suggest that Ss who put a large number of statements into the extreme category do so not because of carelessness but because they actually perceive the statements differently.

DISCUSSION

The results just presented clearly support the three principal hypotheses investigated. Even though judges are not asked to state their own attitudes, the position of the judge on the issue does influence in a significant way his categorization of the items. The displacements are away from the individual's own position, supporting the notion that those with extreme positions are more selective in the statements they will accept at their own end of the scale (their "threshold of acceptance" is *raised*), and more inclined to reject items which are at variance with their position (their "threshold of rejection" is *lowered*). The degree of displacement is greater for the items in the middle of the scale, in line with the hypothesis that "neutral" items are more ambiguous[6] and less well structured, and hence are more readily subject to the personal interpretations of the judges.

6 Edwards (5) has called attention to "lower Q values at both extremes of the scale and higher Q values toward the center of the scale" (p. 163). On the basis of this tendency Edwards concluded "Clearly, then, we have evidence to indicate that the scale and Q values of items sorted by the method of equal-appearing-intervals are not independent, that *"neutral" items are relatively more ambiguous than items at either extreme of the continuum.*" (Italics ours.)

The present data do not indicate whether the distortions and displacements are caused by the fact that individuals with extreme positions lack the ability to discriminate between adjacent items at the opposite extreme, and hence place them in the same category, or whether they reflect variations in the judge's interpretation of the total scale and the magnitude of category intervals. On the surface, the second alternative is supported by the study of Ferguson (6) who found no differences in the distributions of paired comparisons for judges with differing attitudes toward war. But in the light of the present results a question is again raised as to the magnitude of differences in attitudes of his contrasted groups of judges and in the degree of their involvement in the issue) During the thirties, when the study was done, it is likely that variation in attitude toward war may not have been very pronounced, and Ferguson himself states that it was impossible "to secure any groups favorable toward war" (p. 116). The data of the present experiment suggest that it is quite likely that the effects are specific to methods of absolute scaling (the second alternative), since the rank orders of the items for the pro and con judges are very similar. An experiment is currently underway specifically on this problem, in which the Attitude toward the Negro issue is again used with Negro Ss in an attempt to see whether the items which are bunched together with the equal-appearing interval method are clearly differentiated with the method of paired comparison.

On the basis of the present study it appears quite likely that the startling difference between the present results and those of Hinckley is due to his elimination of the extreme cases. When his elimination procedure is followed and the sample restricted to white Ss, there is a close correspondence in results even though 20 years have elapsed since his original study.

Evidence against the explanation of the results as due to "carelessness" comes from several sources. The data already presented indicate that those who placed a large number of the statements in the extreme anti categories judged at a later time that more of the items had been unfavorable to Negroes. Further evidence comes from another study done in conjunction with the present one in which Ss were allowed to use as many or as few categories for sorting as they deemed necessary to distinguish among the items on the issue. The Ss who placed a large number of items in the extreme categories under the present instructions used fewer categories to express shades of opinion and again placed a large number in the extreme categories. A different type of evidence is the lawful nature of the phenomenon. It is the very subgroups with extreme positions (determined either by their own attitude statements or by their assignment to a criterion group) who place the large number at the extremes, and the items they displace are those in the middle of the scale (the more ambiguous items).

Our results do, as Thurstone (19) had clearly anticipated, raise serious questions as to the use of the method of equal-appearing intervals on issues where strong attitudes are involved. Further research is needed to determine whether under these conditions a single scale is involved for the different groups of judges or whether distinctive scales will be required. A Guttman or Lazarsfeld type of analysis will be required to answer this question (18). Even if a single scale is involved, great care will be required in the selection of judges, since their position may influence the scale values obtained. Obtaining an unbiased sampling of positions may constitute a difficult practical problem, since on many issues attitudes are related to educational and socioeconomic status. It may therefore be very difficult to secure representatives of all positions among those who are well enough educated and have sufficient sophistication to carry out the difficult task of categorizing the items.

From the present results there emerges an interesting possibility for developing a behavioral, "projective" method of attitude assessment through study of the way an individual sorts statements on an issue. If the tendencies found in the present experiment for individuals with extreme positions to bunch up the statements at the extremes are found for other issues, it may be possible to assess the attitude of an individual without ever asking him his opinion but by relying entirely on the way he distributes his judgments. Individuals with more or less neutral attitudes would be expected to space their judgments rather evenly over the entire range, those at the pro end would tend to reject neutral items and hence pile them up at the anti end, and those with anti attitudes would place them at the opposite end of the scale. As indicated previously, one may even carry this technique a step further by not using a fixed number of categories, but by deliberately letting the individual establish a scale of his own with whatever number of categories he sees fit. Then the extension or constriction of the scale he establishes, the number of categories he uses, the crowding or neglecting of certain categories, and the direction of concentration of items may all provide useful indices for analysis of the way the individual "perceives" the issue. In such a technique one would obviously want to insure the inclusion of a large number of ambiguous and unstructured items since these will be the ones which are more conducive to displacement. In another study done in conjunction with the present experiment, investigation has been carried out along these lines and the results will be reported in a forthcoming paper.

SUMMARY

1. Investigation was made of the apparent discrepancy between studies in the field of judgment, where the position of the individual on an issue affects the nature of his judgments, and those in the field of attitude scaling, where it has been reported that the scaling of statements is independent of the judge's stand on the issue.

One possible hypothesis for the discrepancy, based on an analysis of the original studies, was that prior experiments had not employed Ss with a sufficiently wide range of attitudes to represent adequately the strongly involved Ss who would be most likely to show the distortions and displacements typically obtained in the field of perception and judgment. Accordingly, every effort was made to secure samples of Ss who were deeply involved in the issue about which the items to be judged were written. Attitudes toward the social position of the Negro furnished an issue on which strong personal involvement could be secured, particularly on the part of Negro Ss. The materials to be judged were the 114 statements originally used by Hinckley (8), and his instructions and procedures were duplicated. In addition to Negro judges, groups of white Ss with known pro-Negro attitudes, "average" white Ss, and a small group of anti-Negro whites, were employed as judges.

2. It was found that Negro Ss and militantly pro-Negro white Ss tended to place a disproportionate number of statements in the extreme categories, in line with the predictions from

judgment theory that individuals with strong attitudes tend to see issues in "black and white" and displace neutral statements to the extremes. The numbers of statements assigned to the various categories by "average" white Ss are much more uniform.

3. Scale values for 11 statements spaced rather evenly over the entire scale in Hinckley's study were compared for each of the major groups. The distributions of scale values for the Negro and pro-Negro white Ss were compressed at the anti-Negro end of the scale, with a small number at the other extreme. Those for the "average" white Ss were spaced more evenly throughout the range in a manner closely approximating the distribution found by Hinckley. Anti-Negro Ss tended to displace neutral statements to the extremes, particularly toward the pro-Negro end.

4. The results support the notion that part of the discrepancy in results between the present study and those of previous experimenters may be attributable to the representation of a greater range of attitudes. In the experiment

of Pintner and Forlano (14) on attitude toward patriotism it is likely that there was considerable homogeneity in position and perhaps insufficient personal involvement. In Hinckley's study the procedure of eliminating Ss who placed 30 or more statements in any category may have eliminated the individuals with the strongest attitudes on the issue. His procedure would eliminate the majority of our Negro Ss and many of our pro-Negro white Ss.

5. The disproportionately large number of sortings in the extreme position does not appear to be due to carelessness, as thought by Hinckley. Evidence against this explanation is the fact that Ss who put a large number of statements in the extreme anti-Negro categories expressed the opinion on a questionnaire, after the cards were removed, that a high proportion of the statements were unfavorable to Negroes. Further evidence is the lawful regularity of the phenomenon obtained.

6. The implications of the present results for procedures used in the construction of attitude scales are discussed.

REFERENCES

1. Ansbacher, H. Number judgment of postage stamps: A contribution to the psychology of social norms. *J. Psychol.*, 1938, **5**, 347-350.
2. Asch, S. E., Block, H., and Hertzman, M. Studies in the principles of judgment and attitude I. Two basic principles of judgment. *J. Psychol.*, 1938, **5**, 219-251.
3. Cartwright, D. Relation of decision-time to the categories of response. *Amer. J. Psychol.*, 1941, **54**, 174-196.
4. Coffin, T. E. Some conditions of suggestion and suggestibility. *Psychol. Monogr.*, 1941, **53**, No. 4 (Whole No. 241).
5. Edwards, A. L. A critique of "neutral" items in attitude scales constructed by the method of equal appearing intervals. *Psychol. Rev.*, 1946, **53**, 159-169.
6. Ferguson, L. W. The influence of individual attitudes on construction of an attitude scale. *J. soc. Psychol.*, 1935, **6**, 115-117.
7. Fernberger, S. W. The effect of the attitude of the subject upon the measure of sensitivity. *Amer. J. Psychol.*, 1914, **25**, 538-543.
8. Hinckley, E. D. The influence of individual opinion on construction of an attitude scale. *J. soc. Psychol.*, 1932, **3**, 283-296.
9. Hinckley, E. D., and Rethlingshafer, D. Value judgments of heights of men by college students. *J. Psychol.*, 1951, **31**, 257-262.
10. Johnson, C. S. *Growing up in the Black Belt.* Washington: American Council on Education, 1941.
11. Luchins, A. S. On agreement with another's judgment. *J. abnorm. soc. Psychol.*, 1944, **39**, 97-111.
12. Marks, E. Skin color judgments of Negro college students. *J. abnorm. soc. Psychol.*, 1943, **38**, 370-376.
13. McGarvey, H. R. Anchoring effects in the absolute judgment of verbal materials. *Arch. Psychol.*, 1943, No. 281.
14. Pintner, R., and Forlano, G. The influence of attitude upon scaling of attitude items. *J. soc. Psychol.*, 1937, **8**, 39-45.
15. Proshansky, H., and Murphy, G. The effect of reward and punishment on perception. *J. Psychol.*, 1942, **13**, 295-305.
16. Rogers, S. The anchoring of absolute judgments. *Arch. Psychol.*, 1941, No. 261.

17. Sherif, M. A study of some social factors in perception. *Arch. Psychol.*, 1935, No. 187.

18. Stouffer, S. A., Guttman, L., et al. *Measurement and prediction*. Princeton: Princeton Univer. Press, 1950.

19. Thurstone, L. L., and Chave, E. J. *The measurement of attitude*. Chicago: Univer. of Chicago Press, 1929.

20. Volkmann, J. The anchoring of absolute scales. *Psychol. Bull.*, 1936, 33, 742-743.

21. Volkmann, J. Scales of judgment and their implications for social psychology. In J. Rohrer and M. Sherif (Eds.), *Social psychology at the crossroads*. New York: Harper, 1951. Pp. 273-294.

27. A Comparison of the Thurstone and Likert Techniques of Attitude Scale Construction

ALLEN L. EDWARDS and KATHRYN CLAIRE KENNEY

This is a study in the methodology of attitude measurement; a comparison and evaluation of two methods of attitude scale construction. Although various techniques for the measurement of social attitudes have been suggested,[1] the two most frequently used methods are probably the "method of equal appearing intervals" developed by Thurstone and Chave (18) and the "method of summated ratings"[2] developed by Likert (11). This study is concerned with the relative merits of the Thurstone and Likert techniques of scale construction.

METHOD OF EQUAL APPEARING INTERVALS

The method of equal appearing intervals begins with the collection of a variety of statements of opinion toward a particular issue which are then screened and edited in accordance with certain "informal criteria." Statements which appear to represent past rather than present attitudes are discarded or reworded, as are statements which appear to be double-barreled[3] or which contain confusing or ambiguous concepts. Inspection should also exclude statements which might be approved by individuals with opposed attitudes.[4]

After the statements have been edited, they are then presented to a group of judges who are instructed to sort them into various categories to represent a scale ranging from extremely favorable, through neutral, to extremely unfavorable expressions of opinion about the issue or institution in question. The judges are not asked to give their own opinions, but merely to estimate the degree of favorableness or unfavorableness expressed by each statement. When the sorting procedure is completed, tabulations are made indicating the number of judges who placed each item in each category. From these data accumulative proportions are computed for each item and ogives are constructed. Scale values of the individual items are then read from the ogives, the value of each item being that point along the base line, in terms of scale value units, above and below which 50 per cent of the judges placed the item.

A statistical criterion of the ambiguity of the items is provided in terms of the width of the range between the points on the scale marking off the 25th and 75th percentiles. This distance is called the Q value. A small Q value indicates that the middle 50 per cent of the judgments spread over a relatively small range or, in other words, that there is a good deal of agreement among the judges as to where the item belongs on the scale. A large Q value indicates lack of agreement among the judges and, indirectly, that something is probably wrong with the wording of the statement.

Items are selected for the final scale on the

• Reprinted from *Journal of Applied Psychology,* 1946, 30, 72-83, with permission of the senior author and the American Psychological Association.

[1] Excellent summaries can be found in Albig (1, pp. 181-213), Bird (3, pp. 149-167), LaPiere and Farnsworth (10, pp. 397-399), and Murphy, Murphy, and Newcomb (13, pp. 891-912).

[2] The term "method of summated ratings" was introduced by Bird (3, p. 159) to describe the procedure followed by Likert.

[3] But in this connection see the discussion by Edwards (4, p. 578) which points to the possible value of statements which contain a "rationalization" clause.

[4] A more detailed enumeration of the rules to be followed can be found in the monograph by Thurstone and Chave (18, pp. 56-58).

basis of the computed scale and Q values. An attempt is made to select about 20 or 22 items with low Q values and with scale values falling at relatively equally-spaced distances along the continuum. Two comparable forms of the scale, in terms of scale and Q values of the items included in each form, are constructed. The two forms are then given to a new group of subjects who are asked to check those statements with which they agree. The score for the individual subject is the mean or median scale value of the items which he has checked as being those with which he agrees. Reliability of the scales is found by correlating scores on the two forms of the scale.

METHOD OF SUMMATED RATINGS

The method of summated ratings also calls for a collection of various statements of opinion which are then edited in accordance with informal criteria similar to those used in the method of equal appearing intervals.[5] After the elimination and editing of items failing to meet the prescribed standards, the remaining statements are presented to a group of subjects who are asked to respond to each one in terms of their own agreement or disagreement with the statement. Usually a 1 to 5 scale of response is used; subjects check whether they strongly agree, agree, are undecided, disagree, or strongly disagree with each statement. A score is given for each item depending upon the response made. The five possible responses may be weighted 1-2-3-4-5 or 5-4-3-2-1.[6] Either 1 or 5 is consistently favorable or unfavorable, although the continuum is reversed in about half the statements. That is, about half the statements are worded so that a strongly agree response indicates a favorable reaction to the issue in question, while the other half of the statements are worded so that a strongly agree response indicates an unfavorable reaction. The score for the individual subject is the sum of all scores for the separate items.

In selecting items for the final scale, a criterion of internal consistency is used. Criterion groups consisting of the upper and lower 10 (or some other) per cent of the subjects in terms of total scores are compared to find whether the individual items will differentiate between the two groups. The means of the upper and lower groups for each item are found; items which show the largest difference between the means of the two groups are retained in the final scale.

Scales constructed by the method of summated ratings usually contain about 20 to 25 items, although Hall (8) has used scales with as few as 5, 7, and 10 items. Reliability of the scales is found by the split-half method of correlating scores for the odd versus even items.

CRITICISMS OF THURSTONE'S METHOD

The monograph by Thurstone and Chave, describing in detail the method of equal appearing intervals for measuring attitudes, appeared in 1929. By the time Likert's monograph describing his technique appeared in 1932, the Thurstone procedure was generally recognized as a major, if not the most important, development in the field of attitude scale construction. It is important, therefore, if we are to compare the two methods, to examine the motivation behind Likert's departure from the by then already well-established Thurstone technique. Some indication of this is given by the following quotation from Murphy and Likert:[7]

A number of statistical assumptions are made in the application of his (Thurstone's) attitude scales—e.g., that the scale values of the statements are independent of the attitude distribution of the readers who sort the statements—assumptions which, as Thurstone points out, cannot always be verified. The method is, moreover, exceedingly laborious. It seems legitimate to inquire whether it actually does its work better than the simpler scales which may be employed, and in the same breath to ask also whether it is not possible to construct equally reliable scales without making unnecessary statistical assumptions (12, p. 26).[8]

---

[5] See Murphy and Likert (12, pp. 281-283) and Rundquist and Sletto (16, pp. 6-8) for a discussion of these standards.

[6] This is a simplified method of scoring which was found to correlate .99 with the more complicated sigma method first used.

[7] We quote from Murphy and Likert rather than from Likert's original report because the Murphy and Likert publication is probably more readily available to the interested reader and since it contains, with but few corrections or omissions, the material originally reported by Likert and, in addition, a more detailed report of applications of scales constructed by the technique. The passage quoted, with but minor changes, is the same as that appearing in Likert (11, p. 6).

[8] The method of summated ratings also makes certain statistical assumptions as Murphy and Likert recognize (12, pp. 26 ff.). Cf. also the paper by Ferguson (6).

The main contentions of Murphy and Likert regarding the method of summated ratings seem essentially to be: (1) "it avoids the difficulties encountered when using a judging group to construct the scale" (12, p. 42); (2) "the construction of an attitude scale by the sigma method[9] is much easier than by using a judging group to place the statements in piles from which the scale values must be calculated" (12, p. 43); (3) "it yields reliabilities as high as those obtained by other techniques with fewer items" (12, pp. 42-43); (4) it gives results which are comparable to those obtained by the Thurstone technique.[10] More generally, the method of summated ratings "seems to avoid many of the shortcomings of existing methods of attitude measurement, but at the same time retains most of the advantages present in methods now used" (12, p. 42). These claims, it should be noted, have been vigorously contested, notably by Bird (3) and Ferguson (7). For our part, we shall, in the sections which follow, attempt to evaluate them in the light of available evidence.

INFLUENCE OF THE JUDGING GROUP

Several studies cast doubt upon Murphy and Likert's criticism that the attitudes of the judging group may influence the scale values of items when the method of equal appearing intervals is used. Using various approaches to the problem, these studies (5), (9), (15), seem to be in agreement that the attitude of the judging group is not a seriously disturbing factor. Hinckley's study (9), in particular, is clear cut. Groups of white students with differing attitudes toward the Negro were asked to sort items expressing opinions about the Negro. A high positive correlation was obtained between the scale values assigned to the items by the white students who were favorable and by those who were unfavorable in attitude toward the Negro. A high positive correlation was also obtained between scale values derived from judgments of an antagonistic white group and from the judgments of a group of Negroes.

SIMPLICITY OF THE LIKERT METHOD

Investigators who have used the Likert method seem to be in agreement that it is simpler than the method of equal appearing intervals. Hall reports that he used the method of summated ratings in his survey of the attitudes of employed and unemployed men "because of its relative simplicity and because it yields scales of high reliability" (8, p. 6), and Rundquist and Sletto, who used the Likert technique in constructing the Minnesota Survey of Opinions scales, agree that "it is less laborious than that developed by Thurstone" (16, p. 5). This evidence is, of course, in the nature of authoritative opinion, and Bird has raised some rather pertinent objections concerning it:

Will the experimenter spend more time, too, in scoring every item and summating them in these long scales than another might spend determining the mean or median value by the Thurstone technique? Then too, is it actually less time-consuming to validate items in terms of selected groups than to determine the Q values from a curve or a distribution of scores? The claim of greater or lesser laboriousness seems to have been put forward without due regard for all processes in scaling techniques; but, in the interest of constructing refined measuring instruments, time can be neglected. There is much to be said in favor of a psychologist's refining his instrument before actually applying it to experimental groups. The argument that the method of summated ratings is less laborious limps badly (3, p. 161).

Bird's points are well taken, particularly in the case of scales constructed by the method of summated ratings which contain more than, let us say, 25 items. But most investigators who have used the method of summated ratings have not found any need for the "long scales" to which Bird is objecting. After our own experience in constructing *both* Likert and Thurstone scales, we are inclined to agree with other investigators that scales can be constructed by the method of summated ratings more quickly and with less labor than by the equal appearing interval method. We found, for example, that construction of the Thurstone scales required about twice as much time, exclusive of the time spent by the judging group in sorting the items, as did the Likert scale. It is unfortunate that this is but an estimate and that our records do not permit a more precise statement of the time factor—a point that should be checked in future research and reported.

[9] Later replaced by the even simpler 1 to 5 method.
[10] We have failed to find a specific statement to this effect, yet the idea seems implied in the paragraph quoted above.

RELIABILITIES OF THE TWO METHODS

A note of confusion has centered around the subject of reliability largely as a result of Likert's study of the reliability of a Thurstone-type scale which was scored by both his and the Thurstone technique. The scale was given to a group of subjects with instructions to check the items in accordance with the usual Thurstone instructions. The same scale was then given to the subjects with instructions to check for each item one of the five alternatives (strongly agree, agree, undecided, disagree, strongly disagree) in accordance with the usual Likert instructions. Four of the items on the Thurstone scale were not adaptable to Likert-type responses and were omitted when the subjects were asked to check their reactions according to the method of summated ratings scoring system.

The reliability coefficient between the two forms of the scale (22 versus 22 items), when scored by the Thurstone method, was .88 (corrected). The reliability coefficient for the two forms (18 versus 18 items) as scored by the Likert method was .94 (corrected). What this demonstrates, of course, is that it is possible to take a scale constructed by the Thurstone technique and to apply to most of the items the Likert method of scoring. But one critic seems to think that because of this finding, Likert erroneously concluded that "his technique is the better one" (7, p. 52). The higher reliability coefficient obtained by the Likert method of scoring, he adds, may be due to the fact that "increasing the number of steps in a psychological scale increases reliability" (7, p. 52). As a matter of record, this is precisely the same explanation offered originally by Murphy and Likert (12, p. 55 and p. 47) for the higher reliability coefficient obtained by the 1 to 5 method of scoring. The entire discussion, pro and con, on this point, it seems to us, has little bearing upon the question of whether the *method* of summated ratings or the *method* of equal appearing intervals will yield scales of higher reliability. The real problem concerns the reliabilities of scales constructed by the two methods, not the reliability of a particular scoring scheme isolated from the technique of scale construction of which it is a part. And on this question there is ample evidence.

Ferguson has quoted Thurstone as reporting the reliabilities of scales constructed by the method of equal appearing intervals, under his editorship, as being "all over .8, most of them being over .9" (6, p. 670). We do not know whether these coefficients are for scales of 20 or 40 items, but Ferguson mentions that in his own studies he has found reliabilities for Thurstone scales ranging from ".52 to .80 for the 20-item forms and from .68 to .89 for the 40-item forms" (6, p. 670). If we take these coefficients as representative, how do they compare with those reported for scales constructed by the method of summated ratings?

Murphy and Likert found reliability coefficients for their Internationalism Scale of 24 items ranging from .81 to .90.[11] Their Imperialism Scale of 12 items gave coefficients ranging from .80 to .92; the Negro Scale of 14 items yielded coefficients ranging from .79 to .91 (12, p. 48). Rundquist and Sletto report coefficients ranging from .78 to .88 for various scales of 22 items each (16, p. 110).

That Likert-type scales with even fewer items will give high reliability coefficients is indicated by Hall. Reliability coefficients for his religious scale of 10 items ranged from .91 to .93; for the scale of 7 items measuring attitude toward employers the coefficients ranged from .77 to .87; and the morale scale of 5 items gave coefficients of .69 to .84 (8, p. 19). All of these coefficients compare favorably with those obtained from scales constructed by the method of equal appearing intervals. According to the evidence at hand, there is no longer any reason to doubt that scales constructed by the method of summated ratings and containing fewer items will yield reliability coefficients as high as or higher than those obtained with scales constructed by the Thurstone method.

THE NEED FOR A JUDGING GROUP

The confusion which followed Likert's rescoring of a Thurstone-type scale by the 1 to 5 method, unfortunately, has not been confined to the subject of reliability; it has spread to involve the question of whether or not there is need for a judging group in the construction of attitude scales. Ferguson seems to believe

[11] The reliability coefficients of the Likert scales are based upon split-half correlations, and all of those reported here have been "corrected" to indicate the reliability of the test taken as a whole. We feel that, at least for purposes of comparison, it is not valid to raise the coefficients for the Thurstone scales which are based upon equivalent forms of 20 to 22 items each. To do so would indicate the reliability to be expected from a Thurstone scale of 40 to 44 items, while in practice the scales generally used contain only half these numbers.

that Murphy and Likert implied, as a result of obtaining a higher reliability coefficient with the 1 to 5 method of scoring than with the customary Thurstone method of scoring, that they had demonstrated that the method of summated ratings does away entirely with the need for a judging group. He argues against this and bases his criticism on the following grounds: "Since the statements (used by Murphy and Likert in the above study) had been sifted through the sorting procedure (Thurstone's), it would seem unjustifiable to conclude that Likert's method did away with the need for a judging group. To test this point adequately one should compare scales constructed (independently of the Thurstone method) by the Likert technique with those constructed by the equal appearing interval method" (7, p. 52).

We are in complete agreement with this argument; therefore we find ourselves at a loss to understand the following statement of experimental design appearing in the same article:

A more adequate test can be provided by rescaling items using Thurstone's method in scales constructed by Likert's technique. If Likert's technique does away with the need for a judging group, the two methods of treating the statements should give the same result (7, p. 52).

But this particular experimental design will not give a test of the two *methods* of scale construction; it is an investigation of where Likert-selected items will fall along the continuum posited by Thurstone or, stated somewhat differently, what Thurstone scale values will be attached to the particular items included in a particular Likert-type scale.

What Ferguson found by following this line of investigation was that Likert-selected items, when scaled according to the method of equal appearing intervals, failed to spread evenly over the scale continuum of Thurstone; the statements failed to represent all degrees of attitude but fell largely at the favorable and unfavorable ends of the scale with the middle categories neglected. Only one of the Likert-type scales which Ferguson attempted to scale by the Thurstone technique, an economic conservatism scale, gave a fairly even spread of items, and the correlation between the Thurstone and Likert methods of scoring this scale was .70.[12]

Because of these findings, the failure of the Likert-selected items to spread evenly over the Thurstone continuum and the "low" correlation between the Thurstone and Likert methods of scoring the one scale that did, Ferguson believes that he has successfully demonstrated "that Likert's technique for the construction of attitude scales does not obviate the need for a judging group" (7, p. 57).

We cannot agree with this conclusion. What has been demonstrated, as we pointed out earlier, is that Likert-selected items do not necessarily fall at equally-spaced intervals along the theoretical continuum posited by Thurstone and Chave. That they do not may be of theoretical interest, but has little bearing upon the practical problem of whether or not there is need for a judging group. This question can only be answered in terms of whether or not scales constructed *independently* by each of the two methods will yield comparable scores, i.e., if an individual is a standard distance above the mean on one scale, he will be a comparable distance above the mean on the second.

It might seem that the correlation of .70 between the Thurstone and Likert method of scoring the economic conservatism scale would bear upon the problem. But this correlation is biased in that Ferguson failed to give the Thurstone method a fair trial, i.e., he limited the Thurstone scale to the items already selected by Likert's technique. Nor can we accept the correlations of .75 and .81 (corrected for attenuation) which Murphy and Likert report for their Internationalism Scale and scores on the Thurstone-Droba War Scale. These correlations also fail to do justice to the question of whether comparable results can be obtained with independently constructed Thurstone and Likert scales since it is possible that the attitudes under consideration are not the same.

COMPARATIVE STUDY OF THE TWO METHODS

A valid comparison of the Thurstone and Likert techniques, we believe, must start with an original set of items, not with items already sifted by the Thurstone procedure and then scored by Likert's method, and not with items sifted by the Likert procedure and then scaled by the Thurstone technique. We believe also

---

12 Assuming that the reliability coefficient of this scale when scored by the Thurstone method is approximately that obtained when the scale is

scored by the Likert method (reported by Rundquist and Sletto as .85), and correcting for attenuation, the correlation would be .82.

that the same group of subjects should be used in the construction of the two scales, but that the steps for each method should be carried through independently. To carry out this comparison, we used the original statements of opinion used by Thurstone and Chave in the construction of their scale designed to measure attitude toward the church.

Subjects used in the construction of the scale were 72 members of an introductory psychology class at the University of Maryland.[13] Half the class, selected at random, was asked to judge the degree of favorableness or unfavorableness expressed by the statements in accordance with the Thurstone method, while the other half of the class was requested to give Likert-type responses to the same statements. Two days later the procedure was reversed; the first half of the class gave Likert-type responses to the statements, while the other half gave Thurstone-type responses. The Seashore and Hevner (17) method of rating items was used instead of the Thurstone and Chave procedure of sorting items into piles.[14]

In constructing the Thurstone scale, tabulations were made indicating the number of judges who placed each item in each of the categories. From these data accumulative proportions were determined and ogives constructed for each item. Scale values of the items were found by dropping a perpendicular to the baseline of scale values at the point where the curve crossed the 50 per cent level.[15] Q values were determined in a similar fashion by dropping perpendiculars at the 25th and 75th per cent levels, the Q value being the scale distance between these two points.

Items were selected for two "equivalent" forms of the scale, each form containing 20 items. Selection was made on the basis of Thurstone's

13 Although Thurstone and Chave used a much larger group of subjects, subsequent research (14) indicates that groups as small as 25 or 50 can be used to obtain scale values of items and that these values are very similar to those obtained with larger groups.

14 Seashore and Hevner found that a technique of asking judges to rate statements on a scale instead of requesting that they sort the statements into piles yielded results which correlated very well with those obtained by Thurstone's original sorting procedure. See also the study by Ballin and Farnsworth (2).

15 The correlation coefficient between our scale values and those obtained by Thurstone and Chave 15 years earlier was .95. Our Q values, however, tended to differ considerably, the correlation coefficient being only .18.

informal standards, Q values, and scale values. Insofar as possible, the final scales contained items with low Q values and with scale values which were spread along the entire scale at relatively equally-spaced distances. Since only a few items, however, were found to have scale values near the center of the continuum and, at the same time, low Q values, this was not entirely possible.

In constructing the Likert scale, a total score for each subject was found by summing the weights of responses given for each of the items. The upper and lower 10 subjects in terms of total scores served as the groups for applying the criterion of internal consistency. Since many of the original items would not meet Likert's *a priori* screening standards, we thought it possible that total scores determined in part by these items would include in the criterion groups individuals who might otherwise not be represented, i.e., if these items had not been used in the scoring. Thurstone and Chave, we might emphasize, had included various ambiguous items in the original set in order to test Q as a means of statistically determining ambiguity. Total scores, therefore, were first determined by excluding those items which we felt did not meet Likert's criteria. Total scores were then found with these items included. Since we found that the criterion groups would contain essentially the same subjects using either score, the total scores based on all of the items were used.

Twenty-five items, all with a mean difference between the two criterion groups of 1.8 or higher, were selected for the final Likert scale. Approximately half of these items were weighted 5 for a strongly agree response and half were weighted 1 for a strongly agree response. Of the 25 items selected for the Likert scale, 3 were also used in Form A of the Thurstone scale and 2 were used in common with Form B.

RELIABILITY AND COMPARABILITY

To obtain data on the reliabilities of the scales and to find out the relationship existing between scores on the *independently* constructed Likert and Thurstone scales, members of another introductory psychology class and an applied psychology class at the University of Maryland were tested. One group of subjects was presented with the Thurstone scales followed by the Likert scale; for the second group of subjects the order of presentation was reversed. There were 80 subjects altogether, each group containing approximately half of this number.

The reliability coefficient for the Likert scale of 25 items was .94. This coefficient compares favorably with those usually reported for scales constructed by this method. The reliability coefficient for the equivalent forms of the Thurstone scales of 20 items each was .88. This is comparable to the reliability coefficients of .85 and .89 which Thurstone and Chave originally reported for scores on their Form A and B for two different groups of subjects (18, p. 66).

The correlation coefficient between scores on the Likert scale and Form A of the Thurstone was .72, which, when corrected for attenuation, becomes .79. On the other hand, the correlation between the Likert scale and Form B of the Thurstone was .92. When corrected for attenuation the coefficient indicates a perfect relationship. Unfortunately, we have no way of knowing which of these two coefficients is more representative of the "true" relationship existing between scores on independently constructed Likert and Thurstone scales in general. But the coefficient of .92 between the Likert and one of the Thurstone scales is surely sufficiently high to establish the fact that *it is possible* to construct scales by the two methods which will yield comparable scores. This is the question we set out to answer.

SUMMARY AND CONCLUSIONS

Now if we go back and examine the points on which we compared the Thurstone and Likert techniques of scale construction, we reach the following conclusions:

1. The evidence available indicates that the attitude of the judging group is not an important factor determining the scale values of items sorted by the Thurstone technique.[16]

16 We are not satisfied with the evidence on this

2. Scales constructed by the Likert method will yield higher reliability coefficients with fewer items than scales constructed by the Thurstone method.

3. What evidence we do have seems to indicate that the Likert technique is less time-consuming and less laborious than the Thurstone technique. But additional research is needed on this point and should be based on carefully kept time records.

4. It is true that Likert-selected items tend to be those which would fall at one or the other extreme on the Thurstone continuum, if scaled according to the Thurstone technique. But the implication of this finding is more theoretical than practical as far as the need for a judging group is concerned. The important problem is whether scores obtained from the two differently constructed scales are comparable and the evidence at hand indicates that they are. As far as we can determine there is nothing of a practical nature to indicate that a judging group, in the Thurstone sense, is a prerequisite for the construction of an adequate attitude scale.

point. Would similar results obtain from judgments derived from those with sympathetic attitudes toward fascism and those violently opposed to fascism in the construction of a scale measuring attitude toward fascism? And in the case of communist sympathizers and non-communists in the construction of a scale measuring attitude toward communism? When social approval or disapproval attaches to a favorable or unfavorable attitude toward an issue, different scale values might result from groups with differing attitudes. An individual with a highly generalized unfavorable attitude toward fascism, for example, might scale an item such as: "Superior races are justified in dominating inferior races by force" as very favorable toward fascism. But would "native fascists" tend to scale it toward the same end of the continuum? The research so far, it seems to us, also neglects the related problem of *ego-involved* attitudes and the bearing they might have upon scale values of items.

REFERENCES

1. Albig, W. *Public opinion.* New York: McGraw-Hill, 1939.
2. Ballin, M., and Farnsworth, P. R. A graphic rating method for determining the scale values of statements in measuring social attitudes. *J. soc. Psychol.,* 1941, **13**, 323-327.
3. Bird, C. *Social psychology.* New York: Appleton-Century, 1940.
4. Edwards, A. L. Unlabeled fascist attitudes. *J. abnorm. soc. Psychol.,* 1941, **36**, 575-582.
5. Ferguson, L. W. The influence of individual attitudes on construction of an attitude scale. *J. soc. Psychol.,* 1935, **6**, 115-117.
6. Ferguson, L. W. The requirements of an adequate attitude scale. *Psychol. Bull.,* 1939, **36**, 665-673.
7. Ferguson, L. W. A study of the Likert technique of attitude scale construction. *J. soc. Psychol.,* 1941, **13**, 51-57.

8. Hall, O. M. Attitudes and unemployment. *Arch. Psychol., N. Y.,* 1934, No. 165.
9. Hinckley, E. D. The influence of individual opinion on construction of an attitude scale. *J. soc. Psychol.,* 1932, **3,** 283-296.
10. LaPiere, R. T., and Farnsworth, P. R. *Social psychology.* New York: McGraw-Hill, 1942.
11. Likert, R. A technique for the measurement of attitudes. *Arch. Psychol., N. Y.,* 1932, No. 140.
12. Murphy, G., and Likert, R. *Public opinion and the individual.* New York: Harper, 1937.
13. Murphy, G., Murphy, L. B., and Newcomb, T. M. *Experimental social psychology.* New York: Harper, 1937.
14. Nystrom, G. H. The measurement of Filipino attitudes toward America by use of the Thurstone technique. *J. soc. Psychol.,* 1933, **4,** 249-252.
15. Pintner, R., and Forlano, G. The influence of attitude upon scaling of attitude items. *J. soc. Psychol.,* 1937, **8,** 39-45.
16. Rundquist, E. A., and Sletto, R. F. *Personality in the depression.* Minneapolis: Univ. Minnesota Press, 1936.
17. Seashore, R. H., and Hevner, K. A time-saving device for the construction of attitude scales. *J. soc. Psychol.,* 1933, **4,** 366-372.
18. Thurstone, L. L., and Chave, E. J. *The measurement of attitude.* Chicago: Univ. Chicago Press, 1929.

28. A Consideration of Beliefs, and Their Role in Attitude Measurement

MARTIN FISHBEIN

Two persons who are equally opposed to segregation may have quite different conceptions of its nature, causes, and consequences, and may hold different views concerning the actions which should be taken to eliminate segregation. In the language of this paper, these two persons are said to have the *same attitudes* toward segregation but to hold *different beliefs* about it. Attitudes are learned predispositions to respond to an object or class of objects in a favorable or unfavorable way. Beliefs, on the other hand, are hypotheses concerning the nature of these objects and the types of actions that should be taken with respect to them.

Many writers do not maintain this distinction between attitudes and beliefs. Both notions are commonly subsumed under the single term "attitude," which is said to have affective (evaluative), cognitive, and conative (action) components. According to this view, an "attitude" toward segregation would include not only a person's negative feelings toward segregation, but also his ideas about its causes and implications, and his conviction that it should be attacked through mass demonstrations and legislation. There is, of course, no overwhelming reason why the word "attitude" should not mean all of these things. Words are created by man for his own convenience, and they may be used in any manner that man finds appropriate. But certain considerations lead us to believe that "attitude" is a more useful scientific word when it is given restricted meaning.

• Revised and expanded for this book from "A Consideration of Beliefs, Attitudes, and Their Relationships," in I. D. Steiner and M. Fishbein (Eds.), *Current Studies in Social Psychology*, Holt, Rinehart, and Winston, New York, 1965, with permission of the publisher.

It is obvious that affect, cognition, and action are not always highly correlated. Different people like the same thing for different reasons, and a thin man who likes pastries may eat them because he believes they contain many calories while a fat man may spurn them for exactly the same reason. Consequently, a multi-component conception of attitude turns out to be a multidimensional conception, and the "attitude" of any one person toward an object or concept may fall at three very different positions on three different dimensions. But the operations by which attitudes are measured almost invariably yield a single score which is unlikely to reflect these three different components in any very precise fashion. As a matter of fact, people who construct "attitude scales" rarely maintain that their instruments are measuring three components; instead, they usually contend that their scales indicate people's evaluations (pro-con) of objects or concepts. Thus, although "attitudes" are often said to include all three components, it is usually only evaluation or "the affective component" which is measured and treated by researchers as the essence of attitude.

It is the contention of this paper that increased precision and understanding can be gained by bringing our definition of attitude into closer harmony with the techniques by which attitudes are measured. Multi-dimensional concepts are notoriously difficult to employ in rigorous theory, and they create almost unmanageable problems when theory is translated into research. A conceptual system in which only the affective component is treated as attitudinal, and the other two components are linked to beliefs, should permit a more productive approach to the study of attitudes.

I. ATTITUDE

Elsewhere in this book (pp. 108 to 116) C. E. Osgood has described techniques for measuring the meanings which objects or concepts have for people. Subjects rate the object or concept on a series of seven-step bipolar scales, the ends of which are identified by adjectives such as "good-bad," "clean-dirty," "strong-weak," or "fast-slow." Ratings obtained on a very large number of these scales have been subjected to a procedure called factor analysis which reveals the underlying dimensions of meaning along which people see various objects as falling. It is significant that Osgood has invariably found that one of the most critical aspects of meaning is an evaluative dimension. A very large share of the meaning of objects or concepts appears to be determined by the position which the object or concept is seen to occupy on a good-bad or pro-con continuum.

After reviewing many of the earlier definitions of attitude, Osgood and his associates (i.e., Osgood and Tannenbaum, 1955; Osgood, Suci, and Tannenbaum, 1957) concluded:

It seems reasonable to identify attitude, as it is ordinarily conceived in both lay and scientific language, with the evaluative dimension of the total semantic space. . . . The meaning of a concept is its location in a space defined by some number of factors or dimensions, and attitude toward a concept is its projection onto one of these dimensions defined as "evaluative."

Osgood's definition of attitude has many advantages. First, it has the virtue of treating attitude as a unidimensional concept. It equates attitude with the evaluative meaning of an object or concept, i.e., attitude refers only to the "evaluation" of a concept—its "favorableness" or "unfavorableness," its "goodness" or "badness." Other types of meaning which the object may have for a person (e.g., its size, shape, speed, etc.) are excluded from the notion of attitude except insofar as they may influence the placement which the person gives the object on the evaluative dimension. Second, as Osgood et al. (1957) point out, "every point in semantic space has an evaluative component (even though the component may be of zero magnitude when the evaluative judgments are neutral)." Thus, this definition makes it clear that with respect to any object or concept, an individual has a positive, negative, or neutral attitude. Third, it is consistent with the description of attitude as a learned predisposition to respond to a stimulus in a favorable or unfavorable way. According to Osgood, this definition characterizes attitude as a mediating evaluative response, i.e., a learned implicit response that varies in intensity and tends to "mediate" or guide the individual's more overt evaluative responses to an object or concept.

Considerable evidence supporting the reliability and validity of Osgood's instrument for measuring attitudes (called the Semantic Differential) has been presented by Osgood et al. (1957) and Fishbein and Raven (1962). Although the Semantic Differential is not the only technique by which unidimensional attitude scores may be obtained, it provides a clear operational definition of the term "attitude" as it will be used in this paper.

II. BELIEF

In another paper in this book, Fishbein and Raven (pp. 183 to 189) suggested a definition of belief that is analogous to the definition of attitude. According to these investigators, an individual may not only evaluate a concept (i.e., view it as "good" or "bad," "clean" or "dirty," etc.) but also he may believe or disbelieve in the existence of the concept (i.e., view it as "existent" or "non-existent," "probable" or "improbable," etc.). As we have seen above, the first type of judgment has been viewed as a measure of the evaluative dimension of a concept, or more specifically, as an attitude. The latter type of judgment may be viewed as a measure of the *probability* dimension of a concept, or more specifically, as a "belief." Just as Osgood and his associates demonstrated that valid and reliable measures of attitude could be obtained by having the subject judge the concept on a series of bipolar evaluative scales, Fishbein and Raven demonstrated that valid and reliable measures of belief could be obtained by having the subject judge the concept on a series of bipolar *probabilistic* scales (e.g., probable-improbable, likely-unlikely, possible-impossible, etc.). It is this definition of belief, i.e., the position of the object or concept on the probability dimension, that will be used throughout this paper.

At first glance, however, it may appear that this conception of belief is a highly specialized one. That is, this definition of belief appears to be concerned only with the probability of the existence of an object—it does not appear to deal with the type of belief that most psychologists have considered. Particularly in the area of attitude research, almost all psychologists have been concerned with beliefs about the object. As was pointed out above, both the "cognitive" and "action" components of attitude can be viewed as beliefs about the object. The cognitive component refers to beliefs about the nature of the object and its relations to other "objects," while the action component refers to beliefs about what should be done with respect to the object.

Fishbein and Raven recognized this problem and suggested a distinction between *belief in* an object and *belief about* an object. "Thus far, we have defined *belief in,* or more completely, *belief in the existence of,* an object. One could also consider *belief in the existence of a relationship* between that object and some other object or some quality." Thus, just as an individual may believe or disbelieve in the existence of "God," so too might he believe or disbelieve in the existence of relationships involving "God," e.g., "God is omnipotent," "God is omniscient," "God is vengeful," "God had a son," etc. Any of these statements could be placed above the probability scales, and the belief in the existence of that particular relationship could be measured. "The various *beliefs in the relationships* between an object and other objects or qualities would then be defined as *beliefs about* that object. While *belief in* refers to the existence of an object, *belief about* deals with the nature of that object, the manner in which it exists."

Thus, like *beliefs in, beliefs about* an object are also equated with the probability dimension of a concept. However, in the latter case, the "concept" is a relational statement, i.e., a statement associating the object of belief with some other object, concept, value, or goal. In general, then, a belief about an object may be defined as the probability or improbability that a particular relationship exists between the object of belief and some other object, concept, value, or goal.

This definition of beliefs about an object is consistent with the descriptions of beliefs that most investigators have suggested. That is, most investigators have reached implicit or explicit agreement that a belief about an object may be described as a relationship between the object (of belief) and some other object, value, goal, or "concept." Indeed, most investigators are agreed that any belief about an object may be diagrammed as (X) _____ (Y), where (X)

refers to the object of belief, (Y) refers to some other object or concept, and the line, i.e., _____, represents the relationship or assertion linking (X) and (Y). Thus, a belief about an object can, in part, be described as any statement that relates the object of belief to some other object, value, concept, or goal. This description, however, is really a definition of a belief statement; the belief *per se* is the position that an individual ascribes to the statement on the probability dimension, i.e., the probability or improbability that the particular relationship expressed in the statement does exist.

This conception of beliefs about objects appropriately represents the many different types of beliefs that an individual may hold. For example, consider the following different types of beliefs that have been referred to in the literature:

1. Beliefs about the component parts of the object.
2. Beliefs about the characteristics, qualities, or attributes of the object.
3. Beliefs about the object's relation with other objects or concepts.
4. Beliefs about whether the object will lead to or block the attainment of various goals or "valued states."
5. Beliefs about what should be done with respect to the object.
6. Beliefs about what the object should, or should not, be allowed to do.

With respect to the "object" Negro, these six types of belief may be illustrated as follows:

1. (Negroes) *have* (dark skin).
2. (Negroes) *are* (athletic).
3. (Negroes) *are equal to* (white men).
4. (Negroes) *inhibit* (free expression of ideas).
5. (Negroes) *should be* (respected).
6. (Negroes) *should not be allowed to hold* (government jobs).

It should be noted that these six types of beliefs are the kinds of beliefs that have typically been considered as comprising the "cognitive" and "action" components of attitude. That is, when most investigators are talking about an individual's "cognitive structure" or the "cognitive component," they are referring to beliefs to Type 1, 2, 3, or 4. Similarly, when they are talking about the "action component," they are usually referring to beliefs of Type 5 or 6.[1] In the present paper, however, rather than viewing "belief" as a part of "attitude," these concepts have been described and defined independently. "Attitude" has been characterized as a learned, implicit response that mediates evaluative behavior, and has been operationally defined as "a concept's position on the evaluative dimension." Similarly, "belief" was operationally defined as "a concept's position on the probability dimension," and a distinction between *beliefs in* and *beliefs about* an object has been made. Specifically, *belief in* refers to the probability that a particular object or concept exists, and *belief about* refers to the probability that a particular relationship involving the object or concept exists. Thus, like attitude, belief is defined as unidimensional concept, i.e., the term "belief" refers only to the "probability" or "improbability" that a particular object (belief in) or a particular relationship (belief about) exists. In addition, we have seen that beliefs about objects may be described as relationships between the object of belief and any other object, concept, value, or goal. In the following section, we shall consider some of the implications of this definition and description of beliefs about an object.

III. BELIEFS ABOUT OBJECTS

In the discussion of attitude, it was pointed out that every concept contains an evaluative component. That is, we have attitudes toward all concepts or objects. Thus, in considering a belief statement, an individual not only has an attitude toward the object of belief, but he also has an attitude toward the "related object." For example, with respect to the statement that "Negroes are athletic," an individual has an attitude toward "athletic" as well as toward "Negroes." Similarly, in the statement, "Negroes should not be allowed to hold gov-

ernment jobs," an individual has an attitude toward "government jobs." The attitude associated with the related concept shall henceforth be referred to as the *evaluative aspect of a belief about an object*. Thus, every belief about an object contains a positive, negative, or neutral evaluative aspect. In other words, every belief statement relates the object of belief to some other concept that is positively, negatively, or neutrally evaluated by an individual.

Further, the relation or assertion between the object of belief and the related object may be either positive or negative, "associative" or "dissociative." "Examples of associative (positive) relations are: is, has, includes, likes, produces, implies. Examples of dissociative (negative) relationships are: avoids, hates, hinders, defeats, destroys, is incompatible with." (Abelson, 1959, p. 345).

Thus, there are six basic types of belief statements:

1. The attitude object is positively associated with a positively evaluated concept.
2. The attitude object is positively associated with a neutrally evaluated concept.
3. The attitude object is positively associated with a negatively evaluated concept.
4. The attitude object is negatively associated with a positively evaluated concept.
5. The attitude object is negatively associated with a neutrally evaluated concept.
6. The attitude object is negatively associated with a negatively evaluated concept.

Each of these statements implies a favorable, neutral, or unfavorable attitude toward the attitude object. That is, as Thurstone (1928) and others have pointed out, beliefs (or "opinions") may be viewed as expressions of attitude; beliefs are often used "as the means for measuring attitude." Specifically, statements of Type 1 and Type 6 indicate favorableness toward the attitude object. Thus, if an individual holds beliefs of Type 1 or Type 6, this would suggest that he has a positive attitude toward the object. Similarly, statements of Type 2 and Type 5 imply neutral evaluations of the attitude object, while statements of Type 3 and Type 4 indicate negative evaluations. The more favorable or unfavorable the evaluative aspect of the belief statement, the more favorable or unfavorable is the attitude indicated. It is important to note, however, that if one is to judge whether a given statement suggests a favorable or unfavorable attitude, it is necessary to know

---

1 It should be noted, however, that in addition to beliefs about the attitude object, the "action component" has also been viewed in terms of beliefs about "the self." That is, subjects are often asked to indicate whether or not *they* would engage in certain activities with the attitude object (see Triandis' contribution to this book, pp. 208 to 219). For example, a subject might be asked to indicate whether he "would" or "would not" "respect Negroes." Diagrammatically, this type of belief may be represented as follows:

(I) *would* (respect Negroes).

(I) *would not* (allow Negroes to hold government jobs).

how the person making the statement (i.e., holding the belief) evaluates the related concept. For example, most people would agree that if an individual believed that "Negroes are equal to white men," this would suggest that he had a positive attitude toward Negroes. This judgment, however, is based on an implicit assumption that all individuals evaluate "white men" positively. Yet, it is possible to argue that for some individuals, holding this belief, i.e., agreeing with this statement, actually indicates a negative attitude toward Negroes. Consider the case of an Oriental respondent who has a strong negative attitude toward "white men." If this person believed that "Negroes are equal to white men," the belief would suggest that he had a negative attitude toward Negroes. That is, from his point of view, he is agreeing with a statement that associates Negroes with a negatively evaluated concept (i.e., a Type 3 statement). Thus, although two people may hold the same belief, this belief may mean quite different things to the people; and therefore, it may suggest that they hold quite different attitudes.

It is for this reason that careful attention is paid to item selection when one is attempting to construct an attitude scale. An attempt is made to select only those items that will have the same meaning for all respondents. For example, Thurstone Scales are usually constructed through the use of the methods of successive categories and equal-appearing intervals. That is, the experimenter selects a large number of statements involving the attitude object. These statements are then presented to judges who are asked to sort the statements into eleven categories ranging from "1," the statement indicates extreme unfavorableness toward the attitude object, to "6," the statement indicates neither favorableness nor unfavorableness toward the attitude object, to "11," the statement indicates extreme favorableness toward the attitude object. Essentially then, the judge is presented with a large number of belief statements; and he is asked to judge whether each of these statements indicates an unfavorable, favorable, or neutral attitude towards the attitude object. Since the major determinants of the degree of favorableness or unfavorableness indicated by a statement are (1) the nature of the association (positive or negative) and (2) its evaluative aspect (favorable, neutral, or unfavorable), and since the nature of the association is specified,

one of the major variables determining where a judge will place a statement is his evaluation of the related concept. Only those statements that result in a consistent sorting by the judges are retained. Wherever there is much disagreement among the judges' ratings, the item is eliminated. Each statement that is retained is given a value equal to the mean or median of the category placements it has received from the judges. The experimenter then selects a final set of items that range all along the favorable-unfavorable continuum, i.e., items that link the attitude object with other objects which represent varying positions on the evaluative dimension.

It is important to note, however, that the discarded items are *not* eliminated because they don't indicate favorableness or unfavorableness toward the attitude object. Indeed, it is because different judges see them as indicating different attitudes that they are eliminated. Thus, discarded items are not ordinarily irrelevant to the attitude which one wishes his instrument to measure. But items which have different attitudinal significance for different judges are likely to have uncertain attitudinal significance for other people as well. For example, a statement such as "Negroes are happy-go-lucky," is likely to be eliminated from the sample. This is because some judges will evaluate being "happy-go-lucky" as good, others will evaluate it negatively, and still others will consider it neutral. Because the statement has different evaluative aspects for different judges, it will be placed in quite different categories. On the other hand, a statement such as "Negroes are intelligent" is likely to be retained. That is, almost all judges will be in agreement that being "intelligent" is good; and thus, almost all judges will view the statement as indicating a favorable attitude. If one knew how a given individual evaluated being "happy-go-lucky," his agreement or disagreement with the statement "Negroes are happy-go-lucky" would be just as good an indication of *his* attitude as would his agreement or disagreement with the statement "Negroes are intelligent." It should be noted, however, that no one belief is likely to be a very reliable or valid "indicator" of attitude. As we shall see below, it is only when many beliefs are considered collectively that reliable estimates of attitude can be obtained.

Although the above discussion pointed out that the items eliminated on the basis of the judges' decisions are not irrelevant to an individual's attitude, Thurstone did establish a "criterion of irrelevance." Unlike the technique described above, this criterion, rather than being based on judgments of favorableness and unfavorableness, is based on subjects' agreement or disagreement with items that have already received scale values. That is, this criterion is only considered *after* a scale has been constructed through the method described above. Essentially, this criterion leads to the elimination of items that are responded to in the same manner (i.e., agreed with or disagreed with) by subjects with very different attitudes. More specifically, it should be recalled that each item selected for inclusion on a Thurstone Scale presumably represents a given point on an attitude continuum (ranging from favorableness to unfavorableness). In addition, each subject may also be viewed as falling on some point along that continuum. In order for an item to meet the criterion of relevance, the greatest amount of agreement with the item should come from subjects whose attitudes fall on the same point of the continuum as does the item. The bigger the discrepancy between the subject's attitude (i.e., his scale position) and the attitude expressed by the item (i.e., the item's scale position), the smaller should be the probability that the subject will agree with the item. Thus, for example, if subjects at every point on the continuum were equally likely to agree with a given item, the item would be eliminated as "irrelevant." Similarly, if subjects at two different points of the continuum (e.g., subjects with quite favorable and quite unfavorable attitudes) had higher probabilities of agreeing with an item than subjects at any other point, the item would be eliminated. Although little emphasis has been given to this criterion in Thurstone Scaling, it is essentially equivalent to the major criterion used in selecting items for a Likert Scale. Thus, let us briefly consider the construction of a Likert Scale.

As in Thurstone Scaling, the experimenter starts with a large set of items that relate the attitude object to other objects, concepts, etc. (i.e., belief statements). Rather than giving these items to judges, the experimenter simply decides which items indicate favorableness and which items indicate unfavorableness to the attitude object. If a statement indicates neither favorableness or unfavorableness to the experimenter, or if he has difficulty in determining whether the statement is favorable or unfavorable, it will usually be eliminated immediately. Having made these decisions, the experimenter then gives the set of remaining items to a group of subjects, who are asked to indicate their degree of agreement or disagreement with each statement (usually by responding to each item on a five-point scale ranging from "strongly agree" to "neither agree nor disagree" to "strongly disagree"). For statements judged as indicating favorableness toward the attitude object, "strong agreement" is given the value 5 and "strong disagreement" is given the value 1. The order of scoring is reversed for statements indicating unfavorableness toward the attitude object, i.e., "strong disagreement" is given the value 5. A total score is then obtained for each subject by summing his scores on each of the individual items. It is at this point that item selection actually begins. While many methods of item analysis have been used as a basis for rejecting statements, the most common (and probably the simplest) technique involves selecting the 25 per cent of the subjects with the highest total scores and also the 25 per cent of the subjects with the lowest total scores. It is assumed that these two groups provide criterion groups in terms of which the individual items can be analyzed. That is, it is assumed that the subjects in these two groups have maximally different attitudes toward the object; and thus, if the item is a good one, it should discriminate between the two groups. More specifically, the mean score on a given statement for the high group should be significantly different than the mean score on the same statement for the low group. If the mean scores are not significantly different, the item is eliminated. Thus, similar to Thurstone's *criterion of irrelevance,* if an item is responded to in the same way by subjects with different attitudes, the item is considered as a "bad" or "irrelevant" item, and is eliminated from the instrument.

After running significance tests on each item, the experimenter then constructs his final instrument by selecting the 20 (or 25) items that were the best discriminators (i.e., produced the largest significant differences between the groups). In addition, he attempts to include an equal number of statements that indicate favorableness and unfavorableness so that possible response sets of the subjects will be minimized.

Here again, however, it should be noted that

the items eliminated from Likert Scales on the basis of item analysis or from Thurstone Scales on the basis of the criterion of irrelevance are not necessarily "bad" or "irrelevant" attitude items. They are simply being eliminated because people with different attitudes tend to show the same amount of agreement with them. That is, the assumption is being made that if two people have different attitudes, but hold the same belief, then, "by definition," the belief is viewed as irrelevant and unrelated to their attitudes. As we saw above, however, this is a completely false assumption since the same belief may have totally different attitudinal significance for different individuals. In other words (similar to items eliminated by judges in Thurstone Scaling), the item is not being eliminated because it has no attitudinal significance (i.e., because it is unrelated to attitude), but rather it is eliminated because it does not indicate the same attitude for all individuals. For example, suppose an experimenter was constructing a Likert scale to measure attitudes toward a political candidate. One of the items that comes to his attention is the item "Candidate X is opposed to atmospheric nuclear testing." Being violently opposed to atmospheric nuclear testing himself, he (i.e., the experimenter) views the statement as one that is favorable toward "Candidate X," and thus leaves it in the set he will initially present to his subjects. Further, let us assume that Candidate X really is in favor of ending atmospheric nuclear testing, and has made his position clear to the public. Thus, all subjects will tend to agree strongly with this item. Since it does not discriminate between individuals with favorable and unfavorable attitudes toward Candidate X, the item will be eliminated. But this does not mean that the belief has no attitudinal significance. On the contrary, the belief may be strongly related to the individual's attitude; and it *can* serve as a good indicant of it. That is, many subjects, like the experimenter, will view "atmospheric nuclear testing" as a very bad thing; and thus their agreement with the statement "Candidate X is opposed to atmospheric nuclear testing" indicates that they have a favorable attitude toward Candidate X. (Indeed, holding this belief may actually be one of the reasons they are favorable to Candidate X.[2]) Many other

subjects, however, may see "atmospheric nuclear testing" as a very good thing. Thus, their agreement with the statement indicates an unfavorable attitude toward Candidate X. (Here, too, holding this belief may be a reason for being unfavorable.) Clearly then, if one knew the way a given individual evaluated "atmospheric nuclear testing," his belief that "Candidate X is opposed to atmospheric nuclear testing" would be as good an indicant of his attitude toward Candidate X as would any belief statement that met the criterion for inclusion on the Likert Scale. Although no one belief is likely to be a very reliable or valid indicator of attitude, all beliefs about an object may be viewed as indicants of attitude toward that object. It is unfortunate, however, that the necessity of obtaining items that have the same attitudinal meaning for all individuals often leads to the elimination of precisely those items that are probably most strongly related to attitude, and thus would serve as the best indicants of attitude. That is, as in the example given above, it will often be the case that many individuals will hold the same beliefs about any given object. For example, during the 1964 Presidential election, most of the population of the United States held at least the following six beliefs about Lyndon Johnson:

1. He is a Democrat.
2. He is in favor of the anti-poverty bill.
3. He is in favor of Medicare.
4. He is in favor of our present foreign policy in Viet Nam.
5. He is in favor of increased social security benefits.
6. He is in favor of the Nuclear Test Ban Treaty.

Although most people held these same beliefs, the evaluative aspects of these beliefs differed considerably among the people (i.e., some would evaluate "being a Democrat" positively and some negatively; some would evaluate one of the issues—Medicare, increased social security benefits, our present foreign policy in Viet Nam—positively, others would evaluate the same issue negatively). Thus, although most people held the same beliefs, these beliefs were quite likely to lead to different attitudes.[3] Yet, none of these statements would appear on either a Thurstone or a Likert Scale because they do have different attitudinal significance

---

2 For a discussion of beliefs as determinants of attitude, see Rosenberg (pp. 325 to 331 in this book) and Fishbein (pp. 389 to 400) in this book.

3 *Ibid.*

for different people. We shall return to this point below.

Consideration of the types of statements that are retained or eliminated from attitude scales also points out another important aspect of attitude research. Many investigators have attempted to distinguish between belief and attitude on the basis of "affect." Krech and Crutchfield (1948), for example, have stated that "beliefs, as such, are motivationally and emotionally neutral . . . attitude can be defined as either 'pro' or 'anti' while beliefs are conceived as neutral." Similarly, Katz and Stotland (1959) have asserted that a belief is not an attitude "unless there is an attribution of good or bad qualities accompanying the specific belief." As was pointed out above, however, all belief statements may be viewed as indicating some degree of favorableness or unfavorableness toward the attitude object. Further, a statement that may contain an implicit or explicit *neutral* evaluation of the attitude object for one person may contain an implicit or explicit *positive* or *negative* evaluation for another person.

In addition, the attempt to distinguish between belief and attitude on the basis of "affect" has resulted in much confusion when one attempts to distinguish between a belief and an attitude. For example, consider the following statements:

1. (Negroes) *are* (good).
2. (Negroes) *are* (dirty).
3. (Negroes) *are* (musical).
4. (Negroes) *are* (superstitious).
5. (Negroes) *are* (tall).
6. (Negroes) *are* (dark-skinned).

Many investigators would say that statement "1" and probably statement "2" express an "attitude." Similarly, there would be general agreement that statements "5" and "6" express "beliefs." With respect to statements "3" and "4," however, little agreement would be reached. Some investigators would say these statements reveal "beliefs" while others would associate them with "attitudes."

From the point of view presented in this paper, all of the statements are belief statements—all of the statements consist of an associative relationship between "Negro" and some other "concept." Further, there is an attitude, an evaluative response, associated with each of these related concepts; each of these statements contain an evaluative aspect. As Green (1954) has pointed out, the concept of "atti-

tude" is a hypothetical variable, abstracted from the *many* statements and actions that an individual makes with respect to a given object. Thus, none of the above statements may be viewed as an attitude. All, however, serve as indicators of attitude. If an individual positively evaluates a "concept," and if he believes that there is an associative relationship between "Negro" and that "concept," his holding of this belief suggests that he has a positive attitude toward Negroes. Similarly, if an individual negatively evaluates a "concept," his belief that there is an associative relationship between "Negro" and that "concept" suggests he has a negative attitude toward Negroes. Although each belief suggests an attitude, the attitude *per se* can only be reliably abstracted by considering the many beliefs an individual holds.

The problem is that most investigators have overlooked the fact that, for a given individual, all concepts have an evaluative component. Generally speaking, they have tended to label agreement with a statement or the statement *per se* as an "attitude" when the concept related to the attitude object appeared to be universally favored or unfavored. Where it could not be assumed that all individuals would evaluate the concept related to the attitude object in the same manner, most investigators have tended to label the statement as a "belief." The statements, however, are neither belief nor attitudes. They are all belief statements; the belief is the position an individual ascribes to the statement on the probability dimension. All belief statements do contain an evaluative aspect; all beliefs about an object carry some implicit or explicit evaluation of the attitude object. Thus, it would seem that the attempt to distinguish between "attitudinal" and "non-attitudinal" beliefs on the basis of "affect" is inappropriate.

One further point concerning beliefs about objects should be considered. In this section, we have seen that a Thurstone Scale consists of a series of carefully selected belief statements. Each of the statements has previously been assigned some evaluative weight between "1" and "11". Further, this evaluative weight is primarily determined by the judges' attitudes toward the concepts related to the attitude object. Thus, the respondent is confronted with a series of belief statements with *different evaluative aspects*. The respondent's task is simply to indicate by a check mark those statements "which come closest to his own feelings." His attitude is then considered to be indexed by the mean or median value of the statements with which he agrees. Thus, the *single score* that represents the respondent's degree of favorableness or unfavorableness toward the attitude object is obtained through a consideration of some of his beliefs about the object.

Likert Scales also consist of a series of carefully selected belief statements. However, rather than differentially weighting each of the statements, each statement is simply considered as indicating favorableness or unfavorableness toward the attitude object. Instead of checking only those statements with which he fully agrees, the respondent is asked to indicate how strongly he agrees with (i.e., believes) or disagrees with (i.e., disbelieves) each statement, usually by checking a five-step scale ranging from "strong agreement" to "strong disagreement." Each response is then given a score from 1 to 5, and the sum of the values is taken as the index of the respondent's attitude. The higher the sum, the more favorable the attitude. Thus, once again, it can be seen that the single score that represents the respondent's attitude is obtained through a consideration of some of his beliefs about the object.

Similar descriptions could be made for most other types of "attitude scales," e.g., Guttman Scales, Bogardus Scales, etc. Indeed, almost every attitude measurement instrument obtains its attitude index through a consideration of beliefs and their evaluative aspects. However, although there is this basic similarity among most attitude measuring instruments, there are also several important differences. For example, Thurstone and Likert Scales place different emphasis on the relative importance of belief strength and the evaluative aspects of belief in obtaining attitude scores. That is, in Thurstone's system, an individual either agrees with ("1") or does not agree with ("0") each statement, and the evaluation associated with the statements varies from "1" (extremely unfavorable) to "11" (extremely favorable). In Likert's system, the degree of agreement varies from "1" to "5," and each statement is simply considered as indicating favorableness ("+1") or unfavorableness ("−1"). Further, it should be recalled that in Thurstone Scaling, the attitude score is obtained by computing the mean or median scale value of the statements the respondent agreed with, while in Likert Scaling, the attitude score is obtained by summing the subject's responses to every item.

Thus, in a sense, when one uses a Thurstone or Likert Scale, he is implicitly accepting fundamentally different theoretical conceptions of attitude. More specifically, from the point of view of Thurstone Scaling, attitudes are primarily determined by the direction and intensity of the evaluation associated with an individual's beliefs about the attitude object. Neither the strength of these beliefs nor any "disbeliefs" are viewed as determinants of attitude. Further, the process of attitude organization is viewed as a process of cognitive averaging or cognitive balance.

In contrast to this, from the point of view of Likert Scaling, attitudes are primarily determined by the strength of an individual's beliefs *and* disbeliefs about the attitude object. Although the direction of the evaluation associated with each belief does serve as a determinant of attitude, the intensity of the evaluation does not. Finally, the process of attitude organization is viewed as a process of cognitive summation.

Although the above discussion has pointed out some major differences between Thurstone and Likert Scaling techniques, their essential similarity should not be overlooked. These scales, like most other attitude measurement instruments, obtain an attitude score through a consideration of a respondent's beliefs about the attitude object. Although the different measurement techniques may differ with respect to the type of items they contain (e.g., a Likert Scale will not include an item with a neutral evaluative aspect while a Thurstone Scale will), and the relative weights that are given to belief strength and the evaluative aspects of beliefs, the essential point is that they are in complete agreement about the basic elements that must be taken into account (i.e., the strength and evaluative aspects of beliefs) in order to measure attitude. However, as was noted above, many important belief statements will not appear on most standardized instruments because they do have different meanings for different people. Thus, most measures of attitude are based on a very restricted range of belief statements. It would seem then, that the best estimate (or measure) of attitude would be one which (*a*) did not restrict the range of belief statements, and which (*b*) put equal weight on belief strength and the evaluative aspect of belief. Although this will necessitate obtaining independent measures of the evaluative aspects of beliefs, the increase in work should be more than compensated for by increased precision in attitude measurement.

REFERENCES

Abelson, R. P. Modes of resolution of belief dilemmas. *Conflict Resolution,* 1959, **3**, 343-352 (see pp. 349 to 356 in this book).

Fishbein, M., and Raven, B. H. The AB scales: an operational definition of belief and attitude. *Hum. Relat.,* 1962, **15**, 35-44.

Green, B. F. Attitude measurement. In G. Lindzey (Ed.), *Handbook of social psychology.* Cambridge: Addison-Wesley, 1954.

Katz, D., and Stotland, E. A preliminary statement to a theory of attitude structure and change. In S. Koch (Ed.), *Psychology: a study of a science.* Vol. 3, *Formulations of the person and the social context.* New York: McGraw-Hill, 1959.

Krech, D., and Crutchfield, R. S. *Theory and problems of social psychology.* New York: McGraw-Hill, 1948.

Osgood, C. E., Suci, G. J., and Tannenbaum, P. H. *The measurement of meaning.* Urbana: University of Illinois Press, 1957.

Osgood, C. E., and Tannenbaum, P. H. The principle of congruity in the prediction of attitude change. *Psychol. Rev.,* 1955, **62**, 42-55.

Thurstone, L. L. Attitudes can be measured. *J. Sociol.,* 1928, **33**, 529-554.

29. *Intensity and a Zero Point for Attitude Analysis*

LOUIS GUTTMAN and EDWARD A. SUCHMAN

1. THE NEED FOR A ZERO POINT

In common parlance, people are said to be happy or unhappy, to be intelligent or stupid, to have a favorable or unfavorable attitude toward something, to be for or against a certain political candidate. Such dichotomizations are made with respect to characteristics that are recognized not to consist simply of two categories; in common parlance, *degrees* of happiness, intelligence, or favorableness are considered to exist. The problem that we wish to consider in this paper is: Is there any sense to dividing people into two kinds—positive and negative—when the variable under consideration comprises many differences in degrees?

This problem occurs in much of attitude analysis and especially in public opinion analysis. Public opinion polls attempt to state, for example, how many people are "pro-Russia" and how many are "anti-Russia," how many are "pro-labor" and how many are "anti-labor," how many are "in favor of" certain governmental policies and how many are "against" these governmental policies, etc., etc. The problem of how to determine such dichotomizations is not in general susceptible to solution by the use of an external criterion like going to the polls and voting, or contributing money, or some consideration. Such external criteria are important and of great interest, but seem to afford only an indirect approach to the problem of defining a cutting point which is intrinsic to the attitude or opinion. It is conceivable that a person is "against" a certain candidate but will vote for him because he is even more "against" the opposing candidate, or he is "against" a given proposition but will endorse it, if the only alternative is one he considers even worse; or he may be "for" a candidate but even more so "for" the opponent, or "for" a

proposition but even more so "for" an alternative one. Furthermore, different external criteria will produce different cutting points. For example, should a man be considered "pro-labor" or "anti-labor," if he contributes money to a labor welfare fund, but still crosses a picket line?

It seems, then, that an intrinsically meaningful cutting point should be defined in a manner that will not depend on an external criterion. If such an internal dichotomization can be made, then in addition to solving some current methodological problems, it will open up new avenues of research in attitude and public opinion analysis which should increase the understanding of the depth or intensity of feeling with which opinions are held, and should also facilitate predictions. For example, of all people who are favorable to a candidate, how many will turn out to vote for him? Of all people who are well-adjusted now in their marriage, how many will become divorced in the future?

The need for an internal definition of a zero point is especially vital for public opinion polls. Research workers in this field are acutely aware of the problem of "bias" in the wording of questions, and thus far there has been no satisfactory solution to this problem. It is well-known that the wording of questions, the order of presentation of questions, the wording of the check-list of answers, or the use of free responses in answers, and a whole host of related things, can change the apparent opinion of the respondent. Furthermore, any single question asked on an issue is but one example of all possible questions that could be asked on that same issue, and the proportion saying "agree" or "yes" to these questions can range from zero to 100 per cent.[1] For example, a

• Reprinted from *American Sociological Review*, 1947, **12**, 55-67, with permission of the senior author and the American Sociological Association.

[1] Compare the "tree" of public opinion in Hadley Cantril, ed., *Gauging Public Opinion*, Princeton University Press, 1944, pp. 26-27.

study of soldiers' attitudes toward the British asked, "Do you agree or disagree with the following statements about the British? . . .

. . . The British are doing as good a job as possible of fighting the war, everything considered.

. . . The British always try to get other countries to do their fighting for them."

We find 80 per cent of the soldiers *agreeing* to the first statement, but only 48 per cent *disagreeing* to the second statement (Table 1).

TABLE 1

Response	First Statement	Second Statement
Agree	80	47
Disagree	17	48
Undecided	3	5
Total	100	100

Which of these questions is an "unbiased" question with respect to the entire issue?

The problem of "bias," or differing results produced by differing questions, has been widely recognized by pollsters; indeed, the utility of most of their findings rests almost entirely on reaching a solution to this problem.

An approach to an internal definition of a zero point has been made by the Research Branch of the Information and Education Division of the War Department during the last year of the war. This approach begins with the idea of content scale analysis and, in fact, is a direct consequence or corollary of content scale analysis. It affords a determination of a zero point—if one exists for a given problem—that is completely objective. It does not depend upon the wording of any particular question and will divide the population into the same two parts on an issue regardless of the specific questions used. This means that the problem of "bias" of question wording or question selection is solved in an objective manner which does not depend on having "experts" judge the apparent "bias" of questions. One set of questions could be made up by a group of people with one particular axe to grind, and another set of questions with reference to the same issue could be made up by a group of people with the opposite axe to grind. No matter how these two sets of questions were worded, *provided only*

that the two sets pertain to the same single issue, they will both yield the same proportion of people positive and negative on the issue.

At first, it may seem like an impossibility to obtain such an invariant answer. That it is not impossible, but in fact highly plausible that such an answer can be obtained, will become clear from considerations of what is involved in content scale analysis and in its corollary, the intensity function.

2. CONTENT SCALE ANALYSIS

Before we can speak meaningfully about people being divided into positive and negative, it must be ascertained whether or not it is at all meaningful to arrange people in rank order *along a single continuum* with respect to the particular area being studied. This means that the area must be tested to see if it is *scalable* for the given population of people. The theory of scale analysis has been presented before to this Society.[2] Briefly, the procedure is to consider a universe of content that is to be studied, like attitude towards the Army, attitude towards one's job, attitude towards Russia, etc., etc. The universe is considered to be indefinitely large—it consists of all possible questions that could be asked about one's attitude towards the topic being studied. This universe is sampled by making up a series of questions on the issue. At least ten to twelve items are ordinarily to be used in practice for the pre-testing in a preliminary study. The population of people is also defined, and a random sample of the population is chosen. The responses of the sample of people are then observed with respect to the sample of questions. On the basis of these sample data, any of several equivalent techniques of scale analysis can be used to test the hypothesis that the universe of content is scalable for the population of individuals, e.g., has a single content variable for all respondents.

The Research Branch has been using scale analysis as a standard procedure for the past four years. Many areas of content have been found to be scalable, and very many have been

2 Louis Guttman, "A Basis for Scaling Qualitative Data," *American Sociological Review*, 1944, 9:139-150. A bibliography of published materials on scale and intensity analysis will be found in Louis Guttman, "Scale and Intensity Analysis for Attitude, Opinion, and Achievement," to appear in the *Proceedings of the Conference of Military Psychologists on Methodological Contributions to Psychology* to be published soon by the University of Maryland.

found not to be scalable for given populations of people.

3. THE SAMPLING OF ITEMS

For our present purposes, it is important to recognize the distinction between the sampling of items or questions and the sampling of people. The sampling of people can be analyzed according to ordinary statistical procedures since the sampling can be done at random (with or without stratification) in the strict sense of the term. On the other hand, for the sampling of items or questions a completely different problem exists. The process of item selection or construction is not at all a random sampling process; it is a psychological process undergone by the research worker which, thus far, has little analytical theory behind it. It seems certain at present that ordinary sampling theory is inappropriate for the problem of item selection. Scale analysis affords an approach to an answer in that its results *do not depend on the particular sample of questions used.* No matter what sample of questions is used (provided only that the marginal frequencies are sufficiently different) the hypothesis can be tested that they are from a scalable universe of questions. The reason for this relative independence of the sample of questions is that the hypothesis of scalability is an extremely simple and highly restrictive one. If the entire universe of questions is scalable, then any sample of questions must prove to be scalable no matter how it is chosen. Hence, if a sample of questions is not scalable, this proves the universe is not scalable. If a sample of questions is scalable and is large and diverse enough, then the inference is made that the universe is scalable.[3]

If a universe of content is scalable, it is meaningful to say that some people are higher than others on the universe and in fact to arrange the whole population in a rank order on the area from high to low. Furthermore, the ranking of the people on any sample of questions must be essentially that which would be obtained from the whole universe of questions. Any sample of items or questions from a scalable universe must rank the people in essentially the same order as any other sample of items. Thus, the rank order of individuals from high to low, or from more to less favorable, for

one set of attitude or opinion questions will be the same as the rank order from a completely different set of questions on the same topic. This is the first invariance property that makes obtaining an invariant zero point possible. By obtaining another invariant ranking, on intensity, and relating these two invariant rankings, we obtain an invariant zero point.

4. INTENSITY ANALYSIS

If a given universe of content is not scalable, then it is not meaningful to order people from high to low, and in particular it is not meaningful to speak of people being positive or negative on the area. The lack of scalability indicates that more than one content variable is involved and no single ranking or division into pro and con can be made.

If an area is scalable, what intrinsic properties must a zero point have? There is meaning in the statement that one person is higher than another on the area because of the scale pattern. What should it mean to say that one person is positive and another person is negative? If a zero point were to be defined, in what respect are two people the same if one is a certain distance *above* the zero point and the other is the *same* distance *below* the zero point? They are different in that the first is higher than the second in the content scale ordering, but they are the same in their distance from the zero point. What shall we name this second variable on which they are the same? The answer proposed here is to call this second variable the *intensity function.* If two people have the same intensity of feeling on an issue but differ in their position on the content scale, then they must be on opposite sides of the zero point.

If intensity of feeling goes up as one moves either to the right or to the left of the zero point, then intensity must be a U or J shaped function of the content scale order. The zero point can then be determined as that point on the content scale at which the intensity function reaches its minimum; that is, as that content point corresponding to the bottom of the U or J.

The problem is to measure the intensity function empirically. If this can be done, the zero point can be determined by plotting intensity of feeling against content score. This has been done by the Research Branch for many areas; in each scalable case, a U or J shaped curve emerged and a zero point was thereby approx-

---

[3] Like all inferences made about a population from a sample, this is, of course, not a completely certain inference.

imately determined. The technique used for measuring the intensity function is far from perfect and better suggestions will undoubtedly be forthcoming in the future. However, crude as it is, the technique does work and gives fairly satisfactory results. Several examples will be presented here of the use of this technique.

5. ILLUSTRATIONS OF THE INTENSITY FUNCTION

A survey was conducted in June, 1945, among a cross-section of 1,730 enlisted men in the United States to determine the soldier's attitude toward the Women's Army Corps (the WAC). A series of six questions was asked as a sample of all possible questions in the universe of "attitude toward the WAC." One of these questions was, for example:

(a) Suppose a girl friend of yours was considering joining the WAC, would you advise her to join?
—— Yes, I'm almost sure I would
—— Yes, I think I would, but I'm not sure
—— No, I probably would not
—— No, I'm sure I would not
—— Undecided

In order to measure intensity of feeling, each of the questions was followed by another question [part (b)] asking:

(b) How strongly do you feel about this?
—— Very strongly
—— Fairly strongly
—— Not so strongly
—— Not at all strongly[4]

The parts (a)—the content—and the parts (b)—the intensity—were analyzed separately for scalability. The six content questions proved to form a scale, and the intensity to form a quasi-scale. One essential difference between a scale and a quasi-scale is that from scale scores one can reproduce the response of each individual to each item (within the margin of error provided by the coefficient of reproducibility of the scale), while in a quasi-scale this internal repro-

[4] As will be reported in the forthcoming publication on the work of the Research Branch, intensity of feeling can be measured in many different ways. For example, the same results were obtained by asking after each attitude question, "How sure are you of your answer?" or "How hard was it for you to make this choice?"

ducibility is not possible. An important property that a scale and quasi-scale do have in common is that each provides an *invariant ordering* of people with respect to the sampling of questions, and this is all that we require for our present purpose. The rank order of respondents on a sample of items from a quasi-scale would be essentially the same rank order as that in the universe of all items that could have been used. Therefore, the ordering of the soldiers on content and on intensity is essentially invariant with respect to the particular sample of six questions used. Each of the six content and intensity questions were dichotomized to produce seven ranks. Each soldier received two scores: a content score ranging from 0 to 6 depending upon the number of questions upon which he held "positive" attitudes toward the WAC, and an intensity score ranging from 0 to 6 depending upon the number of answers about which he felt "strongly." Tabulating intensity score against content score for the 1,730 soldiers yielded the frequency distribution shown in Table 2.

If the pure intrinsic intensity function were being measured by the technique of using parts (b), then Table 2 should show intensity as a perfect U or J shaped function of content. Table 2 shows that this is not the case, that there is much error in the technique; but despite the considerable amount of error the essential shape of the intensity function is apparent. The italicized frequency in each column of Table 2 corresponds to the interval in which the median intensity lies for each content interval. A proper graphic presentation of the curve of medians is to express the data, not in the crude ranks observed, but in estimates of what the rank on the whole attitude universe would be if indefinitely many questions had been asked. The percentile metric is a way of doing this. The cumulative frequencies for the row (content) and column (intensity) marginals of Table 2 appear at the bottom and to the right of the table respectively. The last row of Table 2 indicates the estimated median percentile of each column. In Figure 1, the percentile metric is used for both content and intensity so that the people are considered to be arranged from zero to 100 per cent according to each of the two. Each plotted point corresponds to the midpoint of the interval on content and to the column median on intensity.

The curve in Figure 1 is essentially invariant. If a different sample of questions than these

TABLE 2. Attitude of Enlisted Men Toward the WAC

Intensity Rank	Content Rank (Negative)						(Positive)	Total Frequency	Cumulative Per Cent
	0	1	2	3	4	5	6		
6 (High)	92	78	47	21	21	13	20	292	100
5	37	50	34	21	21	6	9	178	83
4	17	50	46	22	28	11	10	184	73
3	26	27	65	39	36	13	15	221	62
2	4	22	65	60	60	27	18	256	49
1	4	20	48	45	123	34	10	284	35
0 (Low)	3	12	61	59	146	30	4	315	18
Total frequency	183	259	366	267	435	134	86	1730	
Cumulative per cent	11	25	47	62	87	95	100		
Midpoint of content percentiles	5	18	35.5	54	75	91	98		
Median of intensity percentiles	83	73	51	42	28	36	59		

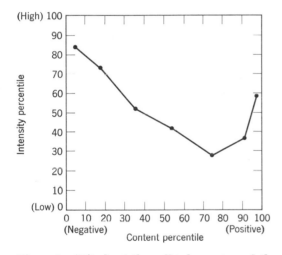

Figure 1. Attitude of the enlisted men toward the WAC.

particular six had been used, essentially the same curve would result if plotted by the percentile technique.[5]

In particular, *the region in which the zero point lies is invariant.* It is not possible to ascertain exactly where the zero point is, but clearly it should be between 54 and 91, the midpoints of the intervals surrounding the low-

[5] Several examples of similar curves and zero-points obtained from different samples of questions from the same attitude universe will be presented in the forthcoming publication on the work of the Research Branch. Despite the fact that these different samples of questions had widely different marginal distributions, the percentage of respondents to the right and left of the zero-point remained constant.

est point of the plotted curve. We can therefore say that, according to this sample of soldiers, 54 per cent of the Army had an unfavorable attitude toward the WAC; 9 per cent had a favorable attitude toward the WAC; and the remaining 37 per cent were in between. As more and more questions are added to the scale, the size of the zero-range will become more narrow and the exact location of the zero-point can be determined with greater accuracy. On the basis of the present sample of six questions, the zero-point is approximately at 75 per cent.

The fact that the curve in Figure 1 is suspended in mid-air and does not reach the bottom percentile of intensity is due to the presence of error in the technique for ascertaining intensity. The column medians are being plotted; since there is error, the medians are away from where they would be if there were no error. The essential shape of the intensity curve that would be obtained if there were no error seems rather apparent from Figure 1, and it seems safe to assume that the pure curve would actually touch bottom in a region within the zero interval obtained from the observed curve.

A technique for obtaining a *single point approximation* for the zero point is to use the *median content percentile of the people lowest on intensity.* In the perfect curve, the lowest person on intensity would be at the zero point on content. Since we have error present in practice, we can take an average of the content positions of the people lowest on intensity as an approximation to the ideal zero point. As small a percentage as possible should be used in order to avoid distortion, but the sample number of people included must be large enough to be reliable. If we consider only the bottom row in Table 2, the median content percentile of the 315 men therein is, by interpolation, 66 per cent, and we can use this as an estimate of the true zero point. This estimate does fall in the zero interval just previously obtained from the U curve.

The shape of the intensity function can vary considerably from problem to problem. An interesting example is afforded by a study of soldiers' opinions of the Army's demobilization score card plan. Two areas were to be studied. One was opinion of the *idea* of the score card, and the other was opinion of *how the plan was being carried out in practice*. Let us consider this second area first. Six questions were asked as a sample of the universe of content. As in the previous example, each question was actually in two parts; the first part concerned the content, and the second part elicited intensity of feeling. One of the questions was, for example:

(*a*) In general, do you think the Army is trying its best to carry out the Army score card plan as it should be carried out?
—— Yes, it is trying its best
—— It is trying some, but not hard enough
—— It is hardly trying at all
(*b*) How strongly do you feel about this?
—— Not at all strongly

—— Not so strongly
—— Fairly strongly
—— Very strongly

Each part (*a*) of the remaining five questions asked opinion about how the plan was being carried out; each part (*b*) was identical with the above for all the questions.

The joint distribution of content and intensity ranks for the attitude of soldiers on how the score card plan was being carried out is given in Table 3, and the approximate intensity function is plotted in Figure 2. The expected U curve of intensity on content results

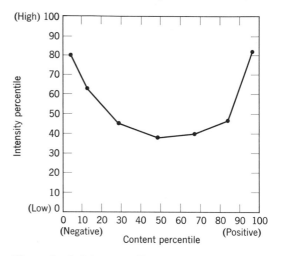

Figure 2. *Opinion of enlisted men on the administration of the Army score card system.*

TABLE 3. *Opinion of Enlisted Men on the Administration of the Army Score Card Plan*

Intensity Rank	Content Rank (Negative)						(Positive)	Total Frequency	Cumulative Per Cent
	0	1	2	3	4	5	6		
9 (High)	65	50	42	22	30	33	81	323	100
8	44	66	70	40	45	52	57	374	90
7	39	55	84	60	59	63	44	404	78
6	16	67	98	85	84	85	25	460	65
5	17	42	93	114	112	91	28	497	51
4	12	34	130	128	157	157	11	629	36
3	10	21	64	82	70	19	1	267	16
2	—	8	46	46	28	9	1	138	8
1	4	8	19	28	13	6	1	79	4
0 (Low)	4	18	23	15	7	4	—	71	2
Total frequency	211	369	669	620	605	519	249	3242	
Cumulative per cent	7	18	39	58	76	92	100		
Midpoint of content percentiles	3	12	28	48.5	67	84	96		
Median of intensity percentiles	79	63	45	38	40	47	81		

with the low point of the curve, the zero-point, falling between percentile 28 and 67 of the content scale. There is indicated a split among the soldiers in their attitude toward the *way in which the score card plan was being administered,* with half the soldiers having a favorable attitude and half having an unfavorable attitude. In general the curve has a rather flat bottom indicating a wide zero-range, or area of indifference. The shape of this curve is quite different from the curve on attitude toward the WAC.

The other aspect of the problem, the soldier's attitude toward the *idea* of the score card plan, produced an altogether differently shaped intensity curve. Seven questions, containing the content in part (*a*) and the intensity in part (*b*) were asked as a sample of all questions that could have been asked in this area.

The joint distribution of content and intensity ranks for soldiers' attitudes toward the *idea* of the score card plan is given in Table 4, and the approximate intensity function is plotted in Figure 3. The zero point seems to be indefinitely far to the left! This indicates that there was little or no unfavorable opinion about the idea of the score card—practically everybody was favorable. Such a conclusion could not be ascertained by looking at the marginal frequencies of the individual questions asked in this area. For example, one of the questions was, "In general, what do you think of the Army score card plan (the point system)?" The responses were as follows:

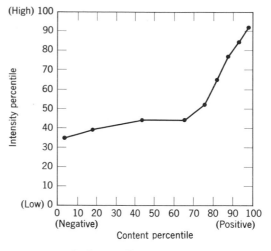

Figure 3. *Attitude of enlisted men toward the idea of the Army score card plan.*

23%	It is very good
49	It is fairly good
16	It is not so good
7	It is not good at all
5	Undecided
100%	

It is important to notice that the technique of single point estimation of the zero point by using the content median of the lowest intensity group breaks down in this instance. Using the lowest intensity technique is not safe if the intensity function is too asymmetric.

Illustrations of other shapes of curves are presented in Figure 4, but further discussion will

TABLE 4. *Attitude of Enlisted Men Toward the Idea of the Army Score Card Plan*

Intensity Rank	Content Rank (Negative)								(Positive)	Total Frequency	Cumulative Per Cent
	0	1	2	3	4	5	6	7	8		
8 (High)	26	58	75	26	17	30	46	54	104	436	100
7	15	62	60	27	16	28	34	45	12	299	87
6	18	46	73	32	19	30	34	19	8	279	77
5	13	54	102	32	36	31	10	10	4	292	69
4	19	55	113	67	38	28	18	5	—	343	60
3	20	91	144	84	42	23	11	3	2	420	49
2	15	80	157	66	29	22	7	3	3	382	36
1	32	119	177	70	27	8	6	2	—	441	24
0 (Low)	69	134	80	37	15	10	3	2	—	350	11
Total frequency	227	699	981	441	239	210	169	143	133	3242	
Cumulative per cent	7	29	59	72	79	85	90	96	100		
Midpoint of content percentiles	4	18	44	66	76	83	89	94	98		
Median of intensity percentiles	34	39	43	44	51	64	76	83	91		

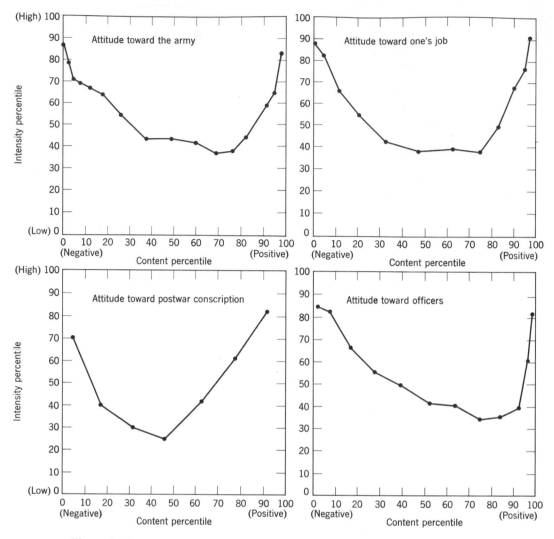

Figure 4. Four examples of approximate intensity curves of attitudes of enlisted men.

be reserved for the forthcoming publication of the Research Branch which will summarize the findings of its four years of work in surveying soldier attitudes and opinions. Briefly, we can say that flat-bottom U shaped curves indicate that there is not much difference between pros and cons; except for those relatively few people who are very extreme on either side, most of the people are relatively indifferent. Very sharp V curves indicate a clear distinction between being positive and being negative.

6. THE PROBLEM OF ERROR

The technique of asking "How strongly do you feel about this?" after each question is ad-

mittedly a crude one and accounts for much of the error in the observed relationship between intensity and content. If the intrinsic intensity could be ascertained, the relationship should be perfect. How error is introduced by the technique just described can be shown in several ways. Some men would say "undecided" to a question. When asked the part (*b*) about strength of feeling, they say they felt "very strongly." When they were asked why they said "very strongly" to part (*b*) when they were undecided on part (*a*), they would answer to the effect that by "very strongly" they meant that the problem was very important, or else that they were very sure that they were undecided, or some such thing. Thus, many of the responses were out of context and contributed to error in the frequency distribution.

Even if all the responses were in context, there is still a contribution to error from the fact that the degrees of meaning of the words vary from sub-group to sub-group of the population. Verbal habits of people are considerably different. Some people will say "strongly agree" to almost anything when they are in favor of it, where other people would say "agree" under the same circumstances. Especially with respect to the intensity questions, there are people who say "very strongly" to every question. This tendency to use or not to use strong adjectives, we shall call "generalized verbal intensity." That it exists as a quasi-scale for the Army population has been shown in several surveys, as will be reported in the forthcoming publication of the Research Branch. Generalized verbal intensity was measured by studying ten or so different universes of content (attitudes) in a single survey. One part (b) question on intensity was selected from each of the ten different areas at random, and it was found that the ten intensity questions formed a quasi-scale.

It was also found that responses to individual questions were related to this generalized intensity. This finding emphasizes all the more that responses to any single content question must be regarded with suspicion and re-emphasizes the need for an objective technique for obtaining a zero point such as that described in this paper.

An example of how "generalized" intensity can be related to responses to a particular content question is the following. The sample of soldiers was divided into three groups according to their generalized intensity: low, medium, and high. When asked the question, "All things considered, do you think the Army is run about as efficiently as possible, or do you think it could be run better?" the responses for the three groups turned out to be as shown in Table 5. The categories obviously mean different things to the different kinds of people; for this reason the interpretation of any frequency distribution of responses to a single question must take into account the verbal habits of the respondents.

This "generalized" intensity, of course, is a verbal variable and reflects verbal habits of people; it is worth much further exploration. A research study was undertaken to find out if this generalized verbal variable correlated with personality areas as investigated by conventional personality inventories. Four different personal-

TABLE 5

	General Intensity		
	Low	Medium	High
It is run as well as possible	38%	32%	28%
It could be run somewhat better	42	36	27
It could be run a lot better	20	32	45
Total per cent	100%	100%	100%
Total cases	441	800	525

ity areas were studied: inferiority, hypomania, psychopathic deviate, depression. All areas correlated to some degree with generalized intensity. These personality variables were also correlated with content of specific opinion questions. This suggests a rich field of exploration of the role that personality traits play in attitudes and opinions on political, social, and economic matters, and from a methodological point of view in determining respondents' verbal habits and modes of expression.

7. SUMMARY

1. One purpose of intensity analysis is to provide an objective method of determining an invariant cutting point for an attitude or opinion scale. This cutting point will enable the research worker to divide his population into favorable and unfavorable groups, a division which will be independent of the selection or "bias" of the specific questions asked.

2. The basis of intensity analysis is the theory of scaling which provides a test for the single meaning of a series of questions. Any single question or series of questions on an issue is considered as simply a sample of all other questions on the same issue which might have been asked instead. The problem of scaling is to test whether the particular sample of questions used can be considered as belonging to an attitude or opinion universe that contains only one dimension. Once a selected series of questions has been determined to be scalable, it is meaningful to rank the respondents from high to low on the attitude universe being studied.

3. In addition to the rank order of individuals on the content or attitude scale, it is also possible to determine the intensity with which an attitude is held. This intensity measurement is found to be a U or J shaped function of the

content scale. People on both ends of the content scale feel more strongly than people towards the middle of the scale. As one moves down the content scale, intensity of feeling decreases *until a point is reached* where intensity of feeling begins to increase again. This point is invariant for any single attitude area, and regardless of the sample of attitude questions used will always divide the population into the same *proportion* with positive and negative opinions. Thus, this cutting point is both invariant and objective.

4. The method used in this paper for measuring intensity of feeling was to ask, "How strongly do you feel about this?" after each attitude question. Correlating the content scale scores with the intensity scores produced the expected U or J shaped curve. This technique of measuring intensity is far from perfect and results in a large amount of variance around the curve. Further research will undoubtedly serve to reduce much of this variance. However, crude as it is, the present technique does work and has been used successfully in many instances.

30. Response Biases and Response Sets

J. P. GUILFORD

By "response bias" we mean that a response to a test item tends to be altered in such a way that it indicates something other than that which we intended it to measure. The biases in which we are particularly interested here are usually determined by mental sets on the part of the examinee that are other than optimal for ensuring valid measurement by means of the item. Cronbach (1, 2) has done us a great service by his systematic study of response sets and their effects. This subject will concern us in the next few paragraphs.

KINDS OF RESPONSE SETS

The following list of response sets is essentially Cronbach's, with some difference in terminology and one additional type of set.

1. The set to gamble. Whenever clear-cut response alternatives are presented, unless E is told to respond to every item, there will be individual differences in caution or lack thereof. Caution is negatively correlated with the right score to the extent that the gambler adds to his score by chance success.

Chance success contributes error variance, and this attenuates intercorrelations. . . . The parameter of item difficulty has much to do with the problem. As item difficulty increases, the amount of guessing increases, and the element of chance success increases in importance. Examinees who know all the answers make perfect scores, and chance success plays no role in them. Examinees who know all except 10 of the answers and who guess on the remaining 10 items will have scores of $n - 10 + e$, where e is a chance increment. . . . Thus the more difficult the test for the population, the larger is the element of chance and the lower will be the correlation between that test and anything else.[1]

There are other aspects to the problem when we consider tests of temperament and interest. In many such tests there is a neutral category, such as "indifferent," "uncertain," or "?." Caution, although it may be of a different kind than that in tests of ability, would be expected to favor the use of the neutral category. Cronbach reports (1) that a score based entirely on the number of neutral responses had a reliability coefficient of .73. The writer has found about the same reliability for number of "?" responses in different temperament inventories. Thus the tendency to use the neutral category is a consistent habit. There is considerable true variance in this kind of score. Does it mean caution and caution only? It could mean indecision, or lack of observation, or it could mean a genuinely moderate amount of the trait indicated by the keyed items. It could actually mean that the examinee is inclined in one direction or another on the trait continuum for which the keyed score was designed. The writer has found that when a "?" response is correlated with a criterion for the trait in item analysis it often correlates significantly and sometimes as high as one of the other responses. Thus the reliability such as Cronbach reports for a neutral-response-bias score may be loaded very much with variance in common factors we want to measure. It cannot all be attributed to caution or anything else without evidence.

2. Semantics. Where the categories of response are such as "agree," "strongly disagree," "dislike," and "sometimes," there is much room for individual interpretations. What one person calls "sometimes," another calls "often," and so on. Resulting constant errors may well

---

• Excerpted from *Psychometric Methods,* 2nd Ed., McGraw-Hill, New York, 1954, with permission of the author and the publisher.

[1] This paragraph has been added to the article by the editor. It is taken from page 437 of Guilford's original text.

cumulate to bias scores to degrees that should cause concern. Very little has been done to establish just how much difference in quantitative meaning such descriptive terms entail or how much they affect scores. The fact that we obtain high reliability coefficients of scores is no assurance of their lack of consequence, for these personal deviations in interpretation probably contribute to true variance. They would detract from validity.

We encounter the same kind of difficulty in the method of constant stimuli when doubtful judgments are used, and we find it in the use of rating scales where verbal cues are used to guide the rater. No doubt any method that will serve to stabilize individual interpretations of words will go a long way to improve psychological measurements of different kinds.

3. Impulsion. An "impulsion" set is seen operating when there is the alternative for E to respond or not to respond; to mark or not to mark. This situation occurs in multiple-choice tests in which, given a model object, E is to mark all those in a list that resemble it or are identical with it. Es differ in the number of marks that they make. The more marks they make, the greater their chance of hitting the right ones. Unless there is a penalty for errors of commission the score favors the liberal marker. The same kind of bias occurs in using check lists, where each item is to be marked or not marked. It occurs in essay examinations in which the amount written weighs heavily in the mark given.

4. Acquiescence. This is the error of the "yes man," at least for the "yes man" of a type. The set is to favor affirmative responses over negative responses. There may be a few negativistic persons who are inclined in the opposite direction. The point here is that each person has some general disposition on this continuum, positive or negative. It is found, however, that more individuals give an excess number of "true" responses in true-false tests, regardless of the actual composition of the test. This has several interesting consequences. For example, the poor student who guesses a great deal makes a good score on the true items but a very poor score on the false items. Sometimes the score based on only the false items correlates extremely high with that on the total test.

The same kind of set may be found in tests answered by "Yes" and "No." The number of "Yes" responses may be excessive on some papers. This may represent the actual situation

with respect to this person's status in the traits that are scored, but it may also represent distortions due to the acquiescence set.

5. Speed versus accuracy. This is a long recognized disturber that has received much attention. In the practice of group testing it is sometimes essential, or at least it is very convenient, for every examinee to be allotted the same limited working time on a test. This fact, particularly, has raised many questions concerning the effect of working time upon scores and upon measurement. . . . There are . . . fundamental questions concerning what psychological qualities are measured when time is liberal versus when time is short. . . . The number (of items) attempted means different things for different individuals. Some examinees make no responses until they feel confident of the answer, while others record an answer even when they know they are guessing. In a speed test, too, differences in motivation level may have an important bearing on the number of answers recorded. Thus, speed conditions where items are not very easy open the door to many uncontrolled determiners of individual differences in scores. It appears that speed of work is a relatively stable personal trait somewhat related to kind of task but not fully determined by kind of task or level of difficulty. The psychological nature of these speed factors is unknown, but it is a good hypothesis that they represent motivational and temperament variables as well as or instead of abilities.[2]

6. Falsification. Since the time when temperament and interest inventories became popular, we have had a new source of bias recognized and identified by various terms such as *faking-good* and *sophistication* as well as the term chosen here, *falsification.* The set is motivated by the desire to make a good score or to make a good appearance and to cover up defects and deficiencies. If the examinee has any idea about the kinds of traits being measured, as is more likely to be true of vocational-interest inventories, it has been shown that he can manage to increase certain scores by a judicious choice of responses, without regard to whether those responses describe him or not. In temperament inventories he is not so likely to guess successfully what traits are being scored, but as he comes to each item he may have his own ideas as to which response is

[2] This paragraph has been revised by the editor. To a large extent, it has been taken from the discussion on pages 365-370 of Guilford's original text.

more desirable to him or to his examiner. If his ideas of desirability are correlated with any trait key, he can thus increase that score. If his ideas are at random with respect to any trait key, he may not change his score, but he has added much chance variance to his total scores. If he is applying for or competing for a certain assignment, he will probably think what are the best responses to make to each item in the light of this assignment. He may be very mistaken about the way in which items are actually keyed and might make a poorer score rather than a better one; yet the score he makes does not describe him as it should and is therefore biased.

Many studies have shown that under obvious inducements much biasing of responses and of scores can occur, but no crucial study has been made showing how much actually does occur under normal testing conditions. It must not be supposed that all examinees attempt to make a good impression, for many are honest. There are some who actually "lean over backwards" when reporting upon themselves; there are the soul-searching ones and self-flagellating ones; and there are those who want to appear mentally incapacitated. The user of inventories must be ever alert to the occasions for any of these biases, positive or negative.

SOME PRINCIPLES OF RESPONSE SETS

Before we attempt to suggest corrective measures for response sets, it is desirable to extract some generalizations. The sources of response sets, like those for sets in general, are varied. Some of the sources in this connection will be implied in what follows.

1. Sets are consistent and persistent. While some sets of an examinee may shift from test to test and even from item to item, others represent apparently enduring qualities that can be called personality traits. Some are very persistent over time, and some are consistent from one test to another and from one administration to another of the same test. To the extent that consistency occurs, we find that the sets contribute to increased reliability of total scores. In other words, within the true variance of a test, perhaps even among its common-factor variances, we may find a contribution from one or more of these sets. It is this fact that makes possible the use of tests of ability, which are more objective, to provide, as by-products, scores for temperament traits. Unfortunately, such variance probably occupies a small part of the total-score variance and cannot therefore give an unadulterated index of status in a temperament trait. Perhaps with intentional cultivation this "bias" variance can in some tests be augmented and made to do duty as a measure of temperament.

2. Response sets make scores more ambiguous. To the extent that response sets contribute to the true variance of a test they are probably doing so at some expense of the common-factor variance that we intended to bring out in our measurements. Even if there is merely addition of more true variance, it alters the meaning of the score and of its interpretation in use. We should therefore strive to get rid of such biases even if to do so lowers reliability. The test will be a better diagnostic instrument even if the bias variance is replaced by error variance, because the latter is not focused systematically in any direction while the bias variance is.

3. Response sets operate most in ambiguous and unstructured situations. When the instructions leave too much to the imagination of the examinee, he invents his own goal and his own task. If each examinee has his own goal and task and if these differ among examinees, we have lost the experimental conditions necessary for meaningful scores. We hear much about the virtues of unstructured tests for diagnostic purposes. Since unstructured tests open very widely the way for personal response sets, and since personal sets lead to ambiguous scores and interpretations, the conclusion is inevitable that the "scores" from unstructured tests are largely uninterpretable. There is a sense in which the unstructured test can be of use, and that is in the direction of the measurement of the sources of response sets when these sources are personality traits. But there must be a structuring of some kind to make the outcome mean anything at all univocal concerning the particular trait we want to measure. In throwing away some of the controls in order to give response sets free play, the projective tester has thrown away controls that he very much needs for interpretable measurement.

4. Difficult tests open the way to response sets. In the multiple-choice test it is when the items are difficult for the examinee that he resorts most to response sets. This parallels very closely the situation in psychophysical judgment. When differences in stimuli become so small that it all seems like guesswork, the observer falls into habits that determine his sequences of judgments. Since the same test is easy for some and difficult for others, this poses a special problem, but it is not an insoluble problem.

THE CONTROL OF RESPONSE SETS

Some of the facts concerning response sets and the principles just stated almost suggest their own remedies. Some of the specific steps that may be taken to counteract them and their effects are suggested below.

1. Identify the set. We are much better prepared to do something about a disturbing response set if we can identify it and can know that it is present. There are various ways of finding indications that a certain suspected set is present. Bias scores can be developed and some have been in use. The Humm "no-count" score, which is the number of "No" responses given to the Humm-Wadsworth Temperament Scale, is used to indicate that the individual is attempting to give "good" answers rather than real answers. For the great majority of the items in that scale the answer "Yes" is in the pathological direction. With the *Minnesota Multiphasic Personality Inventory* there are a number of so-called validating scores used to indicate various types of departures from correct reporting on the part of the examinee. It would be important to factor analyze such scores to determine whether they are actually measuring what they are purported to measure, or to validate them in some other way.

2. Structure the test sufficiently. Administering a test is like conducting an experiment. If the outcome is to have meaning, experimental controls must be exerted. There is no escaping this scientific requirement. The administrator should set the goal and define the task for all examinees. This may be accomplished by writing better instructions. It might even be well to warn E against certain biases and their unfortunate effects. In administering check lists, one might instruct E to mark a stated number of items, or might set upper and lower limts for him.

3. Use good test forms. Some item forms are more subject to biases from sets than others. The multiple-choice form in which E selects one right answer only and in which the alternatives are objectively interpretable seems to be best. Yet, even in multiple-choice tests there

have been indications of bias, in the form of slight preference for some answer positions over others, especially for low-scoring individuals. Mosier and Price (6) have provided a system for randomizing the position of the right answer, also of the wrong answers. This should go far to prevent the test maker from hitting, by a position habit of his own, a response pattern that does or does not coincide with the examinee's habits.

Cronbach (2) recommends avoidance of certain item forms including the "yes-no" choice, the "same-different" choice, the "mark-or-not-to-mark" distinction, the categories "like," "indifferent," and "dislike," and of the neutral category in general. The writer can agree that this would remove much of the trouble with response biases, but it would also remove many useful tests because at present there are no good substitutes for some of these response categories. He has not found the indifference category so troublesome if it is given an empirical weight, as indicated earlier.

The forced-choice type of item is also sometimes recommended as a solution to some of the bias problems. Gordon (3, 4) has found slightly higher reliability and validity for inventory scores obtained from forced-choice items than from the usual type. The writer believes, however, that there are better ways of dealing with the same problems and that the forced-choice device introduces some measurement problems that may be worse than those they were intended to correct.

4. Make multiple-choice tests sufficiently easy. This advice has been emphasized a number of times. Where a population has considerable variability in the ability tested, it might even be wise to develop two or three tests at different levels of ability. Some preliminary rough testing would determine at which level each individual should be tested and the appropriate test would then be applied to him. By scaling procedures the scores from the three tests could be brought to a common scale. The use of limen scores also suggests itself in this connection.

5. Use a good scoring formula. After considering the nature of the test and the score distributions for rights, wrongs, and unattempted items, a favorable a priori formula may be chosen. The best solution would be to obtain factor-analysis information concerning each of these scores and to weight them accordingly.

Another good solution, if a known criterion is to be predicted, is to derive optimal weights using formula (15.27).

6. Use suppressors to remove effects of bias. Knowing what kind of bias is present, not having been able to prevent it, we may resort to a corrective procedure. This is to use a "suppressor" score to attempt to negate the bias variance in the score. In an inventory in which there may be successful falsification, each trait score might be summed with a "lie" score (the latter with appropriate negative weight) to lower the bias variance. Since this is a difference score, the suppression as well as the trait score should be of high reliability. Even then the difference score will be less reliable than the trait score, but since it is more univocal, it is more interpretable. The same suppression score should not be used in combination with all trait scores, since this would introduce correlation among the corrected trait scores due to a common element. Levine (5) has made the very pertinent suggestion that suppression items be planted in the inventory for use where suppression is needed. They should be

item analyzed and those correlating low with the criterion but high with the other trait items should be selected to provide the suppressors for that trait.

7. Refrain from using tests where biasing sets are invalidating. One may as well recognize the limitations to the application of tests whose scores can be effectively biased. Before accepting the scores from an inventory in a certain situation, some exploration might well first be instituted to determine whether the examinees can and do successfully bias scores. It may be that in spite of motivation to do so, little effective biasing occurs. Examinees may not be so sophisticated as some believe, and items can be written so as to make alternative responses seem equally attractive or equally unattractive. Schultz (7) administered an attitude-interest inventory to two successive freshmen classes, one before it was admitted to the college and the other after it had been admitted. He found that the students were apparently unable to detect the more valid items and that the inventory score remained valid in the interested (preadmission) group.

REFERENCES

1. Cronbach, L. J. Response sets and test validity. *Educ. psychol. Measmt.*, 1946, **6**, 475-494.
2. Cronbach, L. J. Further evidence on response sets and test design. *Educ. psychol. Measmt.*, 1950, **10**, 3-31.
3. Gordon, L. V. Validities of the forced-choice and questionnaire methods of personality measurement. *J. appl. Psychol.*, 1951, **35**, 407-412.
4. Gordon, L. V. The effect of position on the preference value of personality items. *Educ. psychol. Measmt.*, 1952, **12**, 669-676.
5. Levine, A. S. A technique for developing suppression tests. *Educ. psychol. Measmt.*, 1952, **12**, 313-315.
6. Mosier, C. I., and Price, H. G. The arrangement of choices in multiple choice questions and a scheme for randomizing choices. *Educ. psychol. Measmt.*, 1945, **5**, 379-382.
7. Schultz, D. G. Item validity and response change under two different testing conditions. *Research Bulletin.* Princeton, N. J.: Educational Testing Service, 1952.

31. Convergent and Discriminant Validation by the Multitrait-Multimethod Matrix

DONALD T. CAMPBELL and DONALD W. FISKE

In the cumulative experience with measures of individual differences over the past 50 years, tests have been accepted as valid or discarded as invalid by research experiences of many sorts. The criteria suggested in this paper are all to be found in such cumulative evaluations, as well as in the recent discussions of validity. These criteria are clarified and implemented when considered jointly in the context of a multitrait-multimethod matrix. Aspects of the validational process receiving particular emphasis are these:

1. Validation is typically *convergent,* a confirmation by independent measurement procedures. Independence of methods is a common denominator among the major types of validity (excepting content validity) insofar as they are to be distinguished from reliability.

2. For the justification of novel trait measures, for the validation of test interpretation, or for the establishment of construct validity, *discriminant* validation as well as convergent validation is required. Tests can be invalidated by too high correlations with other tests from which they were intended to differ.

3. Each test or task employed for measurement purposes is a *trait-method unit,* a union of a particular trait content with measurement procedures not specific to that content. The systematic variance among test scores can be due to responses to the measurement features as well as responses to the trait content.

4. In order to examine discriminant valid-

• Abridged from *Psychological Bulletin,* 1959, **56**, 81-105, with permission of the senior author and the American Psychological Association. The new data analyses reported in this paper were supported by funds from the Graduate School of Northwestern University and by the Department of Psychology of the University of Chicago.

ity, and in order to estimate the relative contributions of trait and method variance, *more than one trait* as well as *more than one method* must be employed in the validation process. In many instances it will be convenient to achieve this through a multitrait-multimethod matrix. Such a matrix presents all of the intercorrelations resulting when each of several traits is measured by each of several methods.

To illustrate the suggested validational process, a synthetic example is presented in Table 1. This illustration involves three different traits, each measured by three methods, generating nine separate variables. It will be convenient to have labels for various regions of the matrix, and such have been provided in Table 1. The reliabilities will be spoken of in terms of three *reliability diagonals,* one for each method. The reliabilities could also be designated as the monotrait-monomethod values. Adjacent to each reliability diagonal is the *heterotrait-monomethod* triangle. The reliability diagonal and the adjacent heterotrait-monomethod triangle make up a *monomethod block.* A *heteromethod block* is made up of a *validity* diagonal (which could also be designated as monotrait-heteromethod values) and the two *heterotrait-heteromethod* triangles lying on each side of it. Note that these two heterotrait-heteromethod triangles are not identical.

In terms of this diagram, four aspects bear upon the question of validity. In the first place, the entries in the validity diagonal should be significantly different from zero and sufficiently large to encourage further examination of validity. This requirement is evidence of convergent validity. Second, a validity diagonal value should be higher than the values lying

TABLE 1. *A Synthetic Multitrait-Multimethod Matrix*

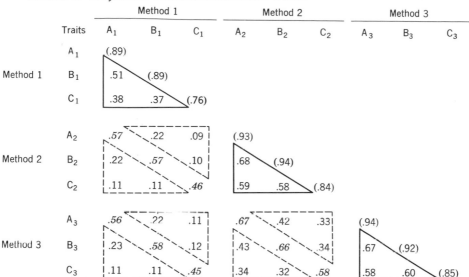

	Traits	Method 1			Method 2			Method 3		
		A_1	B_1	C_1	A_2	B_2	C_2	A_3	B_3	C_3
Method 1	A_1	(.89)								
	B_1	.51	(.89)							
	C_1	.38	.37	(.76)						
Method 2	A_2	*.57*	.22	.09	(.93)					
	B_2	.22	*.57*	.10	.68	(.94)				
	C_2	.11	.11	*.46*	.59	.58	(.84)			
Method 3	A_3	*.56*	.22	.11	*.67*	.42	.33	(.94)		
	B_3	.23	*.58*	.12	.43	*.66*	.34	.67	(.92)	
	C_3	.11	.11	*.45*	.34	.32	*.58*	.58	.60	(.85)

Note. *The validity diagonals are the three sets of italicized values. The reliability diagonals are the three sets of values in parentheses. Each heterotrait-monomethod triangle is enclosed by a solid line. Each heterotrait-heteromethod triangle is enclosed by a broken line.*

in its column and row in the heterotrait-heteromethod triangles. That is, a validity value for a variable should be higher than the correlations obtained between that variable and any other variable having neither trait nor method in common. This requirement may seem so minimal and so obvious as to not need stating, yet an inspection of the literature shows that it is frequently not met, and may not be met even when the validity coefficients are of substantial size. In Table 1, all of the validity values meet this requirement. A third common-sense desideratum is that a variable correlate higher with an independent effort to measure the same trait than with measures designed to get at different traits which happen to employ the same method. For a given variable, this involves comparing its values in the validity diagonals with its values in the heterotrait-monomethod triangles. For variables A_1, B_1, and C_1, this requirement is met to some degree. For the other variables, A_2, A_3 etc., it is not met and this is probably typical of the usual case in individual differences research, as will be discussed in what follows. A fourth desideratum is that the same pattern of trait interrelationship be shown in all of the heterotrait triangles of both the monomethod and heteromethod blocks. The hypothetical data in Table 1 meet this requirement to a very

marked degree, in spite of the different general levels of correlation involved in the several heterotrait triangles. The last three criteria provide evidence for discriminant validity.

Before examining the multitrait-multimethod matrices available in the literature, some explication and justification of this complex of requirements seems in order.

Convergence of Independent Methods: The Distinction Between Reliability and Validity

Both reliability and validity concepts require that agreement between measures be demonstrated. A common denominator which most validity concepts share in contradistinction to reliability is that this agreement represent the convergence of independent approaches. The concept of independence is indicated by such phrases as "external variable," "criterion performance," "behavioral criterion" (American Psychological Association, 1954, pp. 13-15) used in connection with concurrent and predictive validity. For construct validity it has been stated thus: "Numerous successful predictions dealing with phenotypically diverse 'criteria' give greater weight to the claim of construct validity than do . . . predictions involving very similar behavior" (Cronbach and Meehl, 1955, p. 295). The importance of independence recurs in most discussions of proof. For example, Ayer discussing a historian's belief about a past event, says "if these sources are numerous and independent, and if they agree with one another, he will be reasonably confident that their account of the matter is correct" (Ayer, 1954, p. 39). In discussing the manner in which abstract scientific concepts are tied to operations, Feigl speaks of their being "fixed" by "triangulation in logical space" (Feigl, 1958, p. 401).

Independence is, of course, a matter of degree, and in this sense, a reliability and validity can be seen as regions on a continuum. (Cf. Thurstone, 1937, pp. 102-103.) Reliability is the agreement between two efforts to measure the same trait through maximally similar methods. Validity is represented in the agreement between two attempts to measure the same trait through maximally different methods. A split-half reliability is a little more like a validity coefficient than is an immediate test-retest reliability, for the items are not quite identical. A correlation between dissimilar subtests is probably a reliability measure, but is still closer to the region called validity.

Some evaluation of validity can take place even if the two methods are not entirely independent. In Table 1, for example, it is possible that Methods 1 and 2 are not entirely independent. If underlying Traits A and B are entirely independent, then the .10 minimum correlation in the heterotrait-heteromethod triangles may reflect method covariance. What if the overlap of method variance were higher? All correlations in the heteromethod block would then be elevated, including the validity diagonal. The heteromethod block involving Methods 2 and 3 in Table 1 illustrates this. The degree of elevation of the validity diagonal above the heterotrait-heteromethod triangles remains comparable and relative validity can still be evaluated. The interpretation of the validity diagonal in an absolute fashion requires the fortunate coincidence of both an independence of traits and an independence of methods, represented by zero values in the heterotrait-heteromethod triangles. But zero values could also occur through a combination of negative correlation between traits and positive correlation between methods, or the reverse. In practice, perhaps all that can be hoped for is evidence for relative validity, that is, for common variance specific to a trait, above and beyond shared method variance.

Discriminant Validation

While the usual reason for the judgment of invalidity is low correlations in the validity diagonal [e.g., the Downey Will-Temperament Test (Symonds, 1931, p. 337ff)] tests have also been invalidated because of too high correlations with other tests purporting to measure different things. The classic case of the social intelligence tests is a case in point. [See below and also (Strang, 1930; R. Thorndike, 1936).] Such invalidation occurs when values in the heterotrait-heteromethod triangles are as high as those in the validity diagonal, or even where within a monomethod block, the heterotrait values are as high as the reliabilities. Loevinger, Gleser, and DuBois (1953) have emphasized this requirement in the development of maximally discriminating subtests.

When a dimension of personality is hypothesized, when a construct is proposed, the proponent invariably has in mind distinctions between the new dimension and other constructs already in use. One cannot define without implying distinctions, and the verification of these distinctions is an important part of the validational process. In discussions of construct validity, it has been expressed in such terms as "from this point of view, a low correlation with athletic ability may be just as important and encouraging as a high correlation with reading comprehension" (APA, 1954, p. 17).

The Test as a Trait-Method Unit

In any given psychological measuring device, there are certain features or stimuli introduced specifically to represent the trait that it is intended to measure. There are other features which are characteristic of the method being employed, features which could also be present in efforts to measure other quite different traits. The test, or rating scale, or other device, almost inevitably elicits systematic variance in response due to both groups of features. To the extent that irrelevant method variance contributes to the scores obtained, these scores are invalid.

This source of invalidity was first noted in the "halo effects" found in ratings (Thorndike, 1920). Studies of individual differences among laboratory animals resulted in the recognition of "apparatus factors," usually more dominant than psychological process factors (Tryon, 1942). For paper-and-pencil tests, methods variance has been noted under such terms as "test-form factors" (Vernon: 1957, 1958) and "response sets" (Cronbach: 1946, 1950; Lorge, 1937). Cronbach has stated the point particularly clearly: "The assumption is generally made . . . that what the test measures is determined by the content of the items. Yet the final score . . . is a composite of effects resulting from the content of the item and effects resulting from the form of the item used" (Cronbach, 1946, p. 475). "Response sets always lower the logical validity of a test. . . . Response sets interfere with inferences from test data" (p. 484).

While E. L. Thorndike (1920) was willing to allege the presence of halo effects by comparing the high obtained correlations with common sense notions of what they ought to be (e.g., it was unreasonable that a teacher's intelligence and voice quality should correlate .63) and while much of the evidence of response set variance is of the same order, the clear-cut demonstration of the presence of method variance requires both several traits and several methods. Otherwise, high correlations between tests might be explained as due either to basic trait similarity or to shared method variance. In the multitrait-multimethod matrix, the presence of method variance is indicated by the difference in level of correlation between the parallel values of the monomethod block and the heteromethod blocks, assuming comparable reliabilities among all tests. Thus the contribution of method variance in Test A_1 of Table 1 is indicated by the elevation of $r_{A_1B_1}$ above $r_{A_1B_2}$, i.e., the difference between .51 and .22, etc.

The distinction between trait and method is of course relative to the test constructor's intent. What is an unwanted response set for one tester may be a trait for another who wishes to measure acquiescence, willingness to take an extreme stand, or tendency to attribute socially desirable attributes to oneself (Cronbach: 1946, 1950; Edwards, 1957; Lorge, 1937).

DISCUSSION

Relation to Construct Validity

While the validational criteria presented are explicit or implicit in the discussions of construct validity (Cronbach and Meehl, 1955; APA, 1954), this paper is primarily concerned

with the adequacy of tests as measures of a construct rather than with the adequacy of a construct as determined by the confirmation of theoretically predicted associations with measures of other constructs. We believe that before one can test the relationships between a specific trait and other traits, one must have some confidence in one's measures of that trait. Such confidence can be supported by evidence of convergent and discriminant validation. Stated in different words, any conceptual formulation of trait will usually include implicitly the proposition that this trait is a response tendency which can be observed under more than one experimental condition and that this trait can be meaningfully differentiated from other traits. The testing of these two propositions must be prior to the testing of other propositions to prevent the acceptance of erroneous conclusions. For example, a conceptual framework might postulate a large correlation between Traits A and B and no correlation between Traits A and C. If the experimenter then measures A and B by one method (e.g., questionnaire) and C by another method (such as the measurement of overt behavior in a situation test), his findings may be consistent with his hypotheses solely as a function of method variance common to his measures of A and B but not to C.

The requirements of this paper are intended to be as appropriate to the relatively atheoretical efforts typical of the tests and measurements field as to more theoretical efforts. This emphasis on validational criteria appropriate to our present atheoretical level of test construction is not at all incompatible with a recognition of the desirability of increasing the extent to which all aspects of a test and the testing situation are determined by explicit theoretical considerations, as Jessor and Hammond have advocated (Jessor and Hammond, 1957).

Relation to Operationalism

Underwood (1957, p. 54) in his effective presentation of the operationalist point of view shows a realistic awareness of the amorphous type of theory with which most psychologists work. He contrasts a psychologist's "literary" conception with the latter's operational definition as represented by his test or other measuring instrument. He recognizes the importance of the literary definition in communicating and generating science. He cautions that the operational definition "may not at all measure the process he wishes to measure; it may measure something quite different" (1957, p. 55). He does not, however, indicate how one would know when one was thus mistaken.

The requirements of the present paper may be seen as an extension of the kind of operationalism Underwood has expressed. The test constructor is asked to generate from his literary conception or private construct not one operational embodiment, but two or more, each as different in research vehicle as possible. Furthermore, he is asked to make explicit the distinction between his new variable and other variables, distinctions which are almost certainly implied in his literary definition. In his very first validational efforts, before he ever rushes into print, he is asked to apply the several methods and several traits jointly. His literary definition, his conception, is now best represented in what his independent measures of the trait hold *distinctively* in common. The multitrait-multimethod matrix is, we believe, an important practical first step in avoiding "the danger . . . that the investigator will fall into the trap of thinking that because he went from an artistic or literary conception . . . to the construction of items for a scale to measure it, he has validated his artistic conception" (Underwood, 1957, p. 55). In contrast with the *single operationalism* now dominant in psychology, we are advocating a *multiple operationalism, a convergent operationalism* (Garner, 1954; Garner, Hake, and Eriksen, 1956), a *methodological triangulation* (Campbell, 1953, 1956), an *operational delineation* (Campbell, 1954), a *convergent validation.*

Underwood's presentation and that of this paper as a whole imply moving from concept to operation, a sequence that is frequent in science, and perhaps typical. The same point can be made, however, in inspecting a transition from operation to construct. For any body of data taken from a single operation, there is a subinfinity of interpretations possible; a subinfinity of concepts, or combinations of concepts, that it could represent. Any single operation, as representative of concepts, is equivocal. In an analogous fashion, when we view the Ames distorted room from a fixed point and through a single eye, the data of the retinal pattern are equivocal, in that a subinfinity of hexahedrons could generate the same pattern. The addition of a second viewpoint, as through binocular parallax, greatly reduces this equiv-

ocality, greatly limits the constructs that could jointly account for both sets of data. In Garner's (1954) study, the fractionation measures from a single method were equivocal—they could have been a function of the stimulus distance being fractionated, or they could have been a function of the comparison stimuli used in the judgment process. A multiple, convergent operationalism reduced this equivocality, showing the latter conceptualization to be the appropriate one, and revealing a preponderance of methods variance. Similarly for learning studies: in identifying constructs with the response data from animals in a specific operational setup there is equivocality which can operationally be reduced by introducing transposition tests, different operations so designed as to put to comparison the rival conceptualizations (Campbell, 1954).

Garner's convergent operationalism and our insistence on more than one method for measuring each concept depart from Bridgman's early position that "if we have more than one set of operations, we have more than one concept, and strictly there should be a separate name to correspond to each different set of operations" (Bridgman, 1927, p. 10). At the current stage of psychological progress, the crucial requirement is the demonstration of some convergence, not complete congruence, between two distinct sets of operations. With only one method, one has no way of distinguishing trait variance from unwanted method variance. When psychological measurement and conceptualization become better developed, it may well be appropriate to differentiate conceptually between Trait-Method Unit A_1 and Trait-Method Unit A_2, in which Trait A is measured by different methods. More likely, what we have called method variance will be specified theoretically in terms of a set of constructs. (This has in effect been illustrated in the discussion above in which it was noted that the response set variance might be viewed as trait variance.) It will then be recognized that measurement procedures usually involve several theoretical constructs in joint application. Using obtained measurements to estimate values for a single construct under this condition still requires comparison of complex measures varying in their trait composition, in something like a multitrait-multimethod matrix. Mill's joint method of similarities and differences still epitomizes much about the effective experimental clarification of concepts.

The Evaluation of a Multitrait-Multimethod Matrix

The evaluation of the correlation matrix formed by intercorrelating several trait-method units must take into consideration the many factors which are known to affect the magnitude of correlations. A value in the validity diagonal must be assessed in the light of the reliabilities of the two measures involved: e.g., a low reliability for Test A_2 might exaggerate the apparent method variance in Test A_1. Again, the whole approach assumes adequate sampling of individuals: the curtailment of the sample with respect to one or more traits will depress the reliability coefficients and intercorrelations involving these traits. While restrictions of range over all traits produces serious difficulties in the interpretation of a multitrait-multimethod matrix and should be avoided whenever possible, the presence of different degrees of restriction on different traits is the more serious hazard to meaningful interpretation.

Various statistical treatments for multitrait-multimethod matrices might be developed. We have considered rough tests for the elevation of a value in the validity diagonal above the comparison values in its row and column. Correlations between the columns for variables measuring the same trait, variance analyses, and factor analyses have been proposed to us. However, the development of such statistical methods is beyond the scope of this paper. We believe that such summary statistics are neither necessary nor appropriate at this time. Psychologists today should be concerned not with evaluating tests as if the tests were fixed and definitive, but rather with developing better tests. We believe that a careful examination of a multitrait-multimethod matrix will indicate to the experimenter what his next steps should be: it will indicate which methods should be discarded or replaced, which concepts need sharper delineation, and which concepts are poorly measured because of excessive or confounding method variance. Validity judgments based on such a matrix must take into account the stage of development of the constructs, the postulated relationships among them, the level of technical refinement of the methods, the relative independence of the methods, and any pertinent characteristics of the sample of Ss. We are proposing that the validational process be viewed as an aspect of an ongoing program for improving measuring procedures and that the "validity coefficients" obtained at any one stage in the process be interpreted in terms of gains over preceding stages and as indicators of where further effort is needed.

The Design of a Multitrait-Multimethod Matrix

The several methods and traits included in a validational matrix should be selected with care. The several methods used to measure each trait should be appropriate to the trait as conceptualized. Although this view will reduce the range of suitable methods, it will rarely restrict the measurement to one operational procedure.

Wherever possible, the several methods in one matrix should be completely independent of each other: there should be no prior reason for believing that they share method variance. This requirement is necessary to permit the values in the heteromethod-heterotrait triangles to approach zero. If the nature of the trait rules out such independence of methods, efforts should be made to obtain as much diversity as possible in terms of data-sources and classification processes. Thus, the classes of stimuli *or* the background situations, the experimental contexts, should be different. Again, the persons providing the observations should have different roles *or* the procedures for scoring should be varied.

Plans for a validational matrix should take into account the difference between the interpretations regarding convergence and discrimination. It is sufficient to demonstrate convergence between two clearly distinct methods which show little overlap in the heterotrait-heteromethod triangles. While agreement between several methods is desirable, convergence between two is a satisfactory minimal requirement. Discriminative validation is not so easily achieved. Just as it is impossible to prove the null hypothesis, or that some object does not exist, so one can never establish that a trait, as measured, is differentiated from all other traits. One can only show that this measure of Trait A has little overlap with those measures of B and C, and no dependable generalization beyond B and C can be made. For example, social poise could probably be readily discriminated from aesthetic interests, but it should also be differentiated from leadership.

Insofar as the traits are related and are expected to correlate with each other, the monomethod correlations will be substantial and heteromethod correlations between traits will also be positive. For ease of interpretation, it may be best to include in the matrix at least two traits, and preferably two sets of traits, which are postulated to be independent of each other.

In closing, a word of caution is needed. Many multitrait-multimethod matrices will show no convergent validation: no relationship may be found between two methods of measuring a trait. In this common situation, the experimenter should examine the evidence in favor of several alternative propositions: (a) Neither method is adequate for measuring the trait; (b) One of the two methods does not really measure the trait. (When the evidence indicates that a method does not measure the postulated trait, it may prove to measure some other trait. High correlations in the heterotrait-heteromethod triangles may provide hints to such possibilities.) (c) The trait is not a functional unity, the response tendencies involved being specific to the nontrait attributes of each test. The failure to demonstrate convergence may lead to conceptual developments rather than to the abandonment of a test.

SUMMARY

This paper advocates a validational process utilizing a matrix of intercorrelations among tests representing at least two traits, each measured by at least two methods. Measures of the same trait should correlate higher with each other than they do with measures of different traits involving separate methods. Ideally, these validity values should also be higher than the correlations among different traits measured by the same method.

Illustrations from the literature show that these desirable conditions, as a set, are rarely met. Method or apparatus factors make very large contributions to psychological measurements.

The notions of convergence between independent measures of the same trait and discrimination between measures of different traits are compared with previously published formulations, such as construct validity and convergent operationalism. Problems in the application of this validational process are considered.

REFERENCES

American Psychological Association. Technical recommendations for psychological tests and diagnostic techniques. *Psychol. Bull., Suppl.,* 1954, **51**, Part 2, 1-38.

Ayer, A. J. *The problem of knowledge.* New York: St. Martin's Press, 1954.

Bridgman, P. W. *The logic of modern physics.* New York: Macmillan, 1927.

Campbell, D. T. *A study of leadership among submarine officers.* Columbus: Ohio State Univ. Res. Found., 1953.

Campbell, D. T. Operational delineation of "what is learned" via the transposition experiment. *Psychol. Rev.,* 1954, **61**, 167-174.

Campbell, D. T. *Leadership and its effects upon the group.* Monogr. No. 83. Columbus: Ohio State Univ. Bur. Business Res., 1956.

Cronbach, L. J. Response sets and test validity. *Educ. psychol. Measmt.,* 1946, **6**, 475-494.

Cronbach, L. J. Further evidence on response sets and test design. *Educ. psychol. Measmt.,* 1950, **10**, 3-31.

Cronbach, L. J., and Meehl, P. E. Construct validity in psychological tests. *Psychol. Bull.,* 1955, **52**, 281-302.

Edwards, A. L. *The social desirability variable in personality assessment and research.* New York: Dryden, 1957.

Feigl, H. The mental and the physical. In H. Feigl, M. Scriven, and G. Maxwell (Eds.), *Minnesota studies in the philosophy of science.* Vol. II. *Concepts, theories and the mind-body problem.* Minneapolis: Univ. Minnesota Press, 1958.

Garner, W. R. Context effects and the validity of loudness scales. *J. exp. Psychol.,* 1954, **48**, 218-224.

Garner, W. R., Hake, H. W., and Eriksen, C. W. Operationism and the concept of perception. *Psychol. Rev.,* 1956, **63**, 149-159.

Jessor, R., and Hammond, K. R. Construct validity and the Taylor Anxiety Scale. *Psychol. Bull.,* 1957, **54**, 161-170.

Loevinger, J., Gleser, G. C., and DuBois, P. H. Maximizing the discriminating power of a multiple-score test. *Psychometrika,* 1953, **18**, 309-317.

Lorge, I. Gen-Like: Halo or reality? *Psychol. Bull.,* 1937, **34**, 545-546.

Strang, R. Relation of social intelligence to certain other factors. *Sch. and Soc.,* 1930, **32**, 268-272.

Symonds, P. M. *Diagnosing personality and conduct.* New York: Appleton-Century, 1931.

Thorndike, E. L. A constant error in psychological ratings. *J. appl. Psychol.*, 1920, 4, 25-29.

Thorndike, R. L. Factor analysis of social and abstract intelligence. *J. educ. Psychol.*, 1936, **27**, 231-233.

Thurstone, L. L. *The reliability and validity of tests.* Ann Arbor: Edwards, 1937.

Tryon, R. C. Individual differences. In F. A. Moss (Ed.), *Comparative Psychology.* (2nd ed. New York: Prentice-Hall, 1942. Pp. 330-365.

Underwood, B. J. *Psychological research.* New York: Appleton-Century-Crofts, 1957.

Vernon, P. E. Educational ability and psychological factors. Address given to the Joint Education-Psychology Colloquium, Univ. of Illinois, March 29, 1957.

Vernon, P. E. *Educational testing and test-form factors.* Princeton: Educational Testing Service, 1958. (Res. Bull. RB-58-3.)

PART III

Attitude Theory

A. Consistency Theories

32. An Approach to the Study of Communicative Acts

THEODORE M. NEWCOMB

This paper points toward the possibility that many of those phenomena of social behavior which have been somewhat loosely assembled under the label of "interaction" can be more adequately studied as communicative acts. It further points to the possibility that, just as the observable forms of certain solids are macroscopic outcomes of molecular structure, so certain observable group properties are predetermined by the conditions and consequences of communicative acts.

The initial assumption is that communication among humans performs the essential function of enabling two or more individuals to maintain simultaneous orientation toward one another as communicators *and* toward objects of communication. After presenting a rationale for this assumption, we shall attempt to show that a set of propositions derived from or consistent with it seems to be supported by empirical findings.

CO-ORIENTATION AND THE A-B-X SYSTEM

Every communicative act is viewed as a transmission of information, consisting of discriminative stimuli, from a source to a recipient.[1] For present purposes it is assumed that the discriminative stimuli have a discriminable object as referent. Thus in the simplest possible communicative act one person (A) transmits information to another person (B) about something

• Excerpted from *Psychological Review*, 1953, **60**, 393-404, with permission of the author and the American Psychological Association.

[1] This statement is adapted from G. A. Miller's definition: "'information' is used to refer to *the occurrence of one out of a set of alternative discriminative stimuli*. A discriminative stimulus is a stimulus that is arbitrarily, symbolically, associated with some thing (or state, or event, or property) and that enables the stimulated organism to discriminate this thing from others" (9, p. 41).

(X). Such an act is symbolized here as AtoBreX.

The term "orientation" is used as equivalent to "attitude" in its more inclusive sense of referring to both cathectic and cognitive tendencies. The phrase "simultaneous orientation" (hereinafter abbreviated to "co-orientation") itself represents an assumption; namely, that A's orientation toward B and toward X are interdependent. A-B-X is therefore regarded as constituting a system. That is, certain definable relationships between A and B, between A and X, and between B and X are all viewed as interdependent. For some purposes the system may be regarded as a phenomenal one within the life space of A or B, for other purposes as an "objective" system including all of the possible relationships as inferred from observations of A's and B's behavior. It is presumed that a given state of the system exists when a given instance of AtoBreX occurs, and that as a result of this occurrence the system undergoes some change (even though the change be regarded as only a reinforcement of the pre-existing state).

The minimal components of the A-B-X system, as schematically illustrated in Figure 1, are as follows:

1. A's orientation toward X, including both attitude toward X as an object to be approached or avoided (characterized by sign and intensity) and cognitive attributes (beliefs and cognitive structuring).

2. A's orientations toward B, in exactly the same sense. (For purposes of avoiding confusing terms, we shall speak of positive and negative *attraction* toward A or B as persons, and

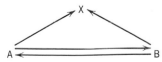

Figure 1. Schematic illustration of the minimal A-B-X system.

of favorable and unfavorable *attitudes* toward X.)

3. B's orientation toward X.
4. B's orientation toward A.

In order to examine the possible relationships of similarity and difference between A and B, we shall make use of simple dichotomies in regard to these four relationships. That is, with respect to a given X at a given time, A and B will be regarded as cathectically alike $(+ +$ or $- -)$ or different $(+ -$ or $- +)$ in attitude and in attraction; and as cognitively alike or different. We shall also make use of simple dichotomies of degree—i.e., more alike, less alike. We shall refer to lateral similarities of A's and B's orientations to X as *symmetrical* relationships.

This very simple system is designed to fit two-person communication. In the following discussion these additional limitations will be imposed, for simplicity's sake: (*a*) communicative acts will be treated as verbal ones, in face-to-face situations; (*b*) initiation of the communicative act is considered to be intentional (i.e., such acts are excluded as those which the actor assumes to be unobserved); (*c*) it is assumed that the "message" is received—i.e., that the communicative act is attended to by an intended recipient, though not necessarily with any particular degree of accuracy; and (*d*) A and B are assumed to be group members, characterized by continued association.

The assumption that co-orientation is essential to human life is based upon two considerations of complementary nature. First, the orientation of any A toward any B (assuming that they are capable of verbal communication) is rarely, if ever, made in an environmental vacuum. Even in what seems the maximally "pure" case of two lovers oblivious to all but each other, both singly and both jointly are dependent upon a common environment; and their continued attachment is notoriously contingent upon the discovery or development of common interests beyond themselves. It is not certain that even their most person-oriented communications (e.g., "I love you") are devoid of environmental reference. The more intense one person's concern for another the more sensitive he is likely to be to the other's orientations to objects in the environment.

Second, the orientation of any A capable of verbal communication about almost any conceivable X is rarely, if ever, made in a social

vacuum. There are few if any objects so private that one's orientations toward them are uninfluenced by others' orientations. This is particularly true with regard to what has been termed "social reality" (3); i.e., the less the possibility of testing one's assumptions by observing the physical consequences of those assumptions, the greater the reliance upon social confirmation as the test of what is true and valid. And even when assumptions can be put to the direct test (e.g., the child can find out for himself about the stove which he has been told is hot), social reality is often accepted as the quicker or the safer test. As various linguists have pointed out, moreover, a good deal of social reality is built into the very language with which we communicate about things. Under the conditions of continued association which we are assuming, A and B as they communicate about X are dependent upon each other, not only because the other's eyes and ears provide an additional source of information about X, but also because the other's judgment provides a testing ground for social reality. And to be dependent upon the other, in so far as such dependence influences behavior, is to be oriented toward him.

In short, it is an almost constant human necessity to orient oneself toward objects in the environment and also toward other persons oriented toward those same objects. To the degree that A's orientation either toward X or toward B is contingent upon B's orientation toward X, A is motivated to influence and/or to inform himself about B's orientation toward X. Communication is the most common and usually the most effective means by which he does so.

SYMMETRY OF ORIENTATION

Much of the remainder of this paper will deal with the relationships between A's and B's orientations toward X, within the postulated A-B-X system. The implications of this model are: (*a*) that while at any given moment the system may be conceived of as being "at rest," it is characterized not by the absence but by the balance of forces; and (*b*) that a change in any part of the system (any of the four relationships portrayed in Figure 1) may lead to changes in any of the others. We shall also make the assumption (not inherent in the model) that certain forces impinging upon the system are relatively strong and persistent, and that thus there are "strains" toward preferred states of equilibrium.

This assumption, related to the initial one concerning the co-orientation function of communication, is as follows. To the degree that A's orientation toward X is contingent upon B's orientation toward X, A's co-orientation will be facilitated by similarity of his own and B's orientation toward X. The first advantage of symmetry—particularly of cognitive symmetry—is that of ready calculability of the other's behavior; the more similar A's and B's cognitive orientations, the less the necessity for either of them to "translate" X in terms of the other's orientations, the less the likelihood of failure or error in such "translations," and thus the less difficult and/or the less erroneous the co-orientation of either. Second, there is the advantage of validation of one's own orientation toward X; the more similar A's and B's orientations, either cognitive or cathectic (particularly in the many areas where validation is heavily dependent upon "social reality"), the more confident each of them can be of his own cognitive and evaluative orientations. Co-orientation is of course possible with little or no symmetry, but the facilitative value of symmetry for co-orientation is considerable.

If these advantages are commonly experienced as such, communicative acts resulting in increased symmetry are likely to be rewarded, and symmetry is likely to acquire secondary reward value. This is the basis of our assumption of a persistent "strain toward symmetry," under the conditions noted.

These assumptions may now be brought together in terms of the following inclusive postulate: *The stronger the forces toward A's co-orientation in respect to B and X, (a) the greater A's strain toward symmetry with B in respect to X; and (b) the greater the likelihood of increased symmetry as a consequence of one or more communicative acts.* The latter part of the postulate assumes the possibility of modified orientations toward X on the part of both A and B, who over a period of time exchange roles as transmitters and receivers of information.

Several testable propositions are derivable from this postulate. First, if the likelihood of instigation to and achievement of symmetry varies as a function of forces toward co-orientation, the latter varies, presumably, with valence of the objects of co-orientation—i.e., of intensity of attitude toward X and of attrac-

tion toward B. That is, under conditions such that orientation toward either B or X also demands orientation toward the other, the greater the valence of B or of X the greater the induced force toward co-orientation, and thus the greater the likelihood of both instigation toward and achievement of symmetry.

Such research findings as are known to the writer are in support of these predictions. Experimental results reported by Festinger and Thibaut (5), by Schachter (12), and by Back (1) indicate that attempts to influence another toward one's own point of view vary as a function of attraction. In the second of these studies it is shown that communications within a cohesive group are directed most frequently toward those perceived as deviates, up to a point where the deviate is sociometrically rejected (i.e., attraction decreases or becomes negative), beyond which point communication to them becomes less frequent. It is also shown in this study that frequency of influence-attempting communication varies with degree of interest in the topic of group discussion.

Some of these same studies, and some others, present data concerning symmetry as a consequence of communication. Thus Festinger and Thibaut, varying "pressure toward uniformity" and "perception of homogeneous group composition," found actual change toward uniformity following a discussion to be a function of both these variables, but some change toward uniformity took place in every group, under all conditions. Back found that subjects who started with different interpretations of the same material and who were given an opportunity to discuss the matter were influenced by each other as a direct function of attraction.

Findings from two community studies may also be cited, as consistent with these laboratory studies. Newcomb (10), in a replicated study of friendship choices as related to political attitudes in a small college community, found on both occasions that students at each extreme of the attitude continuum tended to have as friends those like themselves in attitude. Festinger, Schachter, and Back (4), in their study of a housing project, found a correlation of +.72 between a measure of attraction and a measure of "conformity in attitude." No direct observations of communication are made in these two studies; the relevance of their findings for the present point depends upon the assumption that frequency of communication is a function of attraction. This assumption is clearly justified in these two particular investigations, since in both communities there was complete freedom of association. As noted below, this assumption is not justified in all situations.

Other testable propositions derivable from the general postulate have to do with A's judgments of existing symmetry between himself and B with respect to X. Such judgments (to which the writer has for some time applied the term "perceived consensus") are represented by the symbol B-X, within A's phenomenal A-B-X system. Such a judgment, under given conditions of demand for co-orientation with respect to a given B and a given X, is a major determinant of the likelihood of a given AtoBreX, since strain toward symmetry is influenced by perception of existing symmetry. Such a judgment, moreover, is either confirmed or modified by whatever response B makes to AtoBreX. The continuity of an A-B-X system thus depends upon perceived consensus, which may be viewed either as an independent or as a dependent variable.

According to the previous proposition, the likelihood of increased symmetry (objectively observed) as a consequence of communicative acts increases with attraction and with intensity of attitude. The likelihood of perceived symmetry presumably increases with the same variables. Judgments of symmetry, like other judgments, are influenced both by "reality" and by "autistic" factors, both of which tend, as a function of attraction and intensity of attitude, to increase the likelihood of perceived consensus. Frequency of communication with B about X is the most important of the "reality" factors, and this, as we have seen, tends to vary with valence toward B and toward X. As for the "autistic" factors, the greater the positive attraction toward B and the more intense the attitude toward X, the greater the likelihood of cognitive distortion toward symmetry. Hypothetically, then, perceived symmetry with regard to X varies as a function of intensity of attitude toward X and of attraction toward B.

A considerable number of research studies, published and unpublished, are known to the writer in which subjects' own attitudes are related to their estimates of majority or modal position of specified groups. Only a minority of the studies systematically relate these judgments to attraction, and still fewer to intensity of attitude. Among this minority, however, the

writer knows of no exceptions to the above proposition. The most striking of the known findings were obtained from students in several university classes in April of 1951, in a questionnaire dealing with the very recent dismissal of General MacArthur by President Truman (Table 1).

TABLE 1

	Pro-Truman Ss Who . . .	Anti-Truman Ss Who . . .
Attribute to "most of my closest friends"		
Pro-Truman attitudes	48	2
Anti-Truman attitudes	0	34
Neither	4	4
Attribute to "most uninformed people"		
Pro-Truman attitudes	6	13
Anti-Truman attitudes	32	14
Neither	14	13

If we assume that "closest friends" are more attractive to university students than "uninformed people," these data provide support for the attraction hypothesis. Comparisons of those whose own attitudes are more and less intense also provide support, though less strikingly, for the hypothesis concerning attitude intensity.

Perceived symmetry, viewed as an independent variable, is obviously a determinant of instigation to symmetry-directed communication. Festinger (3), with specific reference to groups characterized by "pressures toward uniformity," hypothesizes that "pressure on members to communicate to others in the group concerning item x increases monotonically with increase in the perceived discrepancy in opinion concerning item x among members of the group," as well as with "relevance of item x to the functioning of the group," and with "cohesiveness of the group." And, with reference to the choice of recipient for communications, "The force to communicate about item x to a particular member of the group will increase as the discrepancy in opinion between that member and the communicator increases [and] will decrease to the extent that he is perceived as not a member of the group or to the extent that he is not wanted as a member of the group" (3, p. 8). Support for all of these hypotheses is to be found in one or more of his and his associates' studies. They are consistent with the following proposition: the likelihood of a symmetry-directed AtoBreX varies as a multiple function of perceived discrepancy (i.e., inversely with perceived symmetry), with valence toward B and with valence toward X.

Common sense and selected observations from everyday behavior may also be adduced in support of these propositions. For example, A observes that an attractive B differs with him on an important issue and seeks symmetry by trying to persuade B to his own point of view; or A seeks to reassure himself that B does not disagree with him; or A gives information to B about X or asks B for information about X. From all these acts we may infer perception of asymmetry and direction of communication toward symmetry. Selected observations concerning symmetry as a consequence of communication are equally plentiful; there is, in fact, no social phenomenon which can be more commonly observed than the tendency for freely communicating persons to resemble one another in orientation toward objects of common concern. The very nature of the communicative act as a transmission of information would, on a priori grounds alone, lead to the prediction of increased symmetry, since following the communication both A and B possess the information which was only A's before. B will not necessarily accept or believe all information transmitted by A, of course, but the likelihood of his doing so presumably varies not only with attraction toward A but also with intensity of attitude toward X, since in the long run the more important X is to him the more likely it is that he will avoid communicating with B about X if he cannot believe him. Thus the propositions have a considerable degree of face validity.

But everyday observation also provides instances to the contrary. Not all communications are directed toward symmetry, nor is symmetry an inevitable consequence of communication, even when attraction is strong and attitudes are intense. A devoted husband may refrain from discussing important business matters with his wife, or two close friends may "agree to disagree" in silence about matters of importance to both. People who are attracted toward one another often continue to communicate about subjects on which they continue to disagree—and this is particularly apt to happen with regard to attitudes which are intense, contrary to our theoretical prediction.

In sum, the available research findings and a considerable body of everyday observation support our predictions that instigation toward, perception of, and actual achievement of symmetry vary with intensity of attitude toward X and attraction toward B. The readiness with which exceptions can be adduced, however, indicates that these are not the only variables involved. The propositions, at best, rest upon the assumption of *ceteris paribus;* they cannot account for the fact that the probabilities of A's instigation to communicate about a given X are not the same for all potential B's of equal attraction for him, nor the fact that his instigation to communicate to a given B are not the same for all X's of equal valence to him. We shall therefore attempt to derive certain further propositions from our basic assumption that both instigation to and achievement of symmetry vary with strength of forces toward co-orientation in the given situation.

DYNAMICS OF CO-ORIENTATION

The foregoing propositions represent only a slight extrapolation of Heider's general principle (6) of "balanced states" in the absence of which "unit relations will be changed through action or through cognitive reorganization." In a later paper devoted specifically to the implications of Heider's hypotheses for interrelationships among attitudes toward a person and toward his acts, Horowitz et al. (8) note the following possible resolutions to states of imbalance: (a) the sign-valence of the act is changed to agree with that of the actor; (b) the reverse of this; and (c) the act is cognitively divorced from the actor; in addition, of course, the disharmony may be tolerated.

Orientations as attributed by A to B are here considered as equivalent to acts so attributed, in Heider's sense, and symmetry is taken as a special case of balance. Assume, for example, the following asymmetry in A's phenomenal system: $+A:X$, $+A:B$, $-B:X$, $+B:A$ (i.e., A has positive attitude toward X, positive attraction toward B, perceives B's attitude toward X as negative, and B's attraction toward A as positive). Any of the following attempts at "resolution," analogous to those mentioned by Heider, are possible: (a) $-A:X$; (b) $-A:B$; or (c) cognitive dissociation. These can occur in the absence of any communication with B. Attempts at harmony (symmetry) may also be made via communications directed toward $+B:X$. And, if such attempts fail, the three alternatives mentioned as possible without communication are still available. Finally, there is the possibility of compromise, following communication (e.g., agreement on some midpoint), and the possibility of "agreeing to disagree."

Such acts of resolution are made necessary, according to the present theory, by the situational demands of co-orientation on the one hand and by the psychological strain toward symmetry on the other. But symmetry is only a facilitating condition for co-orientation, not a necessary one. While (as maintained in the preceding propositions) the probabilities of symmetry vary, *ceteris paribus*, with demand for co-orientation, the theory does not demand that a symmetry-directed AtoBreX occur in every instance of strong demand for co-orientation. On the contrary, the theory demands that it occur only if, as, and when co-orientation is facilitated thereby. We must therefore inquire more closely into the nature of the forces toward co-orientation as related to possible forces against symmetry.

One kind of situational variable has to do with the nature of the forces which result in association between A and B. Of particular importance are constrained (enforced) vs. voluntary association, and association based upon broad as contrasted with narrow common interests. The range of X's with regard to which there is demand for co-orientation is presumably influenced by such forces. The relevant generalization seems to be as follows: *The less the attraction between A and B, the more nearly strain toward symmetry is limited to those particular X's co-orientation toward which is required by the conditions of association.* This would mean, for example, that as attraction between two spouses decreases, strain toward symmetry would increasingly narrow to such X's as are required by personal comfort and conformity with external propriety; similarly, the range of X's with regard to which there is strain toward symmetry is greater for two friendly than for two hostile members of a chess club.

The problem of constraint has already been noted. In some of the studies cited above it was assumed that frequency of communication varies with attraction, but this is not necessarily true under conditions of forced association. Two recent theoretical treatises deal with this problem.

Homans, one of whose group variables is "frequency of interaction" (though not communication, specifically), includes the following among his other propositions: "If the frequency of interaction between two or more persons increases, the degree of their liking for one another will increase, and vice versa"; and "The more frequently persons interact with one another, the more alike in some respects both their activities and their sentiments tend to become" (7, p. 120). (The latter proposition, which closely resembles the one here under consideration, apparently takes a much less important place in Homans' system than the former.) Almost immediately, however, the latter proposition is qualified by the statement, "It is only when people interact as social equals and their jobs are not sharply differentiated that our hypothesis comes fully into its own." In nearly every chapter, moreover, Homans (whose propositions are drawn *post hoc* from various community, industrial, and ethnological studies) points to the limitations which are imposed by constraining forces—particularly those of rank and hierarchy—upon the relations among attraction, similarity of attitude, and communication.

Blake manages to incorporate these considerations in a more rigorous proposition. Noting that hostility cannot be considered as the simple psychological opposite of positive attraction, he proposes to substitute a curvilinear for Homans' linear hypothesis: ". . . when pressures operate to keep members of a group together, the stresses that drive toward interaction will be stronger in *both* positive and negative feeling states than in neutral ones" (2). This proposition seems consistent with the present argument to the effect that demands for co-orientation are likely to vary with the nature and degree of constraints upon association; hence communicative acts, together with their consequences, will also vary with such constraints.

Another situational variable deals with the fact that, under conditions of prescribed role differentiation, symmetry may take the form of "complementarity" (cf. 11) rather than sameness. For example, both a man and his small son may (following a certain amount of communication of a certain nature) subscribe to the *same norms* which prescribe *differentiated behavior* for man and boy with respect to a whiskey and soda. If the father drinks in the son's presence, there are demands upon both of them for co-orientation; but there is strain toward symmetry only with respect to "the code," and not with respect to personal orientation toward the whiskey and soda. The code becomes the X with regard to which there is strain toward symmetry. In more general terms, *under conditions of differentiation of A's and B's role prescriptions with regard to X, the greater the demand for co-orientation the greater the likelihood of strain toward symmetry with respect to the role system* (rather than with respect to X itself).

A third situational variable has to do with the possibility that symmetry may be threatening. Particularly under circumstances of shame, guilt, or fear of punishment there are apt to be strong forces against a symmetry-directed AtoBreX, even though—in fact, especially when—attitude toward X (the guilty act) and attraction toward B (a person from whom it is to be concealed) are strong. Under these conditions it is the demand for co-orientation which creates the problem; if A could utterly divorce X (his own act) from B, he would not feel guilty. Forces toward symmetry, however, are opposed by counterforces. Demand for co-orientation induces strain toward symmetry, but does not necessarily lead to a symmetry-directed AtoBreX.

A theoretically analogous situation may result from the omnipresent fact of multiple membership groups. That is, strains toward symmetry with B_1 in regard to X may be outweighed by strains toward symmetry with B_2, whose orientations toward X are viewed as contradictory with those of B_1. This is often the case when, for example, two good friends "agree to disagree" about something of importance to both. Thus in one study (13) it was found that those members least influenced by reported information concerning their own group norms were those most attracted to groups whose norms were perceived as highly divergent from those of the group in question.

Communicative acts, like others, are thus subject to inhibition. Such "resolutions" as "agreement to disagree," however, represent relatively stressful states of equilibrium. It is therefore to be expected, in ways analogous to those noted by Lewin in his discussion of the quasi-stationary equilibrium, that A-B-X systems characterized by such stress will be particularly susceptible to change. Such change need not necessarily occur in the particular region of the system characterized by maximal strain.

The dynamics of such a system are by no means limited to those of strains toward symmetry, but must include changes resulting from acceptance of existing asymmetry. The possible range of dynamic changes is illustrated in Figure 2. (In this figure, the A and B at either

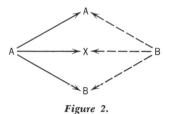

Figure 2.

side represent persons as communicators; the A and B in the center represent the same persons as objects of co-orientation. The broken lines represent A's judgments of B's orientations.) Given perceived asymmetry with regard to X, and demand for co-orientation toward B and X, the possibilities for A are such that he can do the following:

1. Achieve, or attempt to achieve, symmetry with regard to X:
   (a) By influencing B toward own orientation.
   (b) By changing own orientation toward B's.
   (c) By cognitively distorting B's orientation.

2. Introduce changes in other parts of the system:
   (a) Modify his attraction toward B.
   (b) Modify his judgment of own attraction for B.
   (c) Modify evaluation of (attraction toward) himself (A).
   (d) Modify his judgment of B's evaluation of himself (B).

3. Tolerate the asymmetry, without change.

As suggested by this listing of possible "solutions," the perception of asymmetry, under conditions of demand for co-orientation, confronts A with a problem which he can attempt to solve behaviorally (i.e., by communicative acts) and/or cognitively (i.e., by changing either his own orientations or his perception of B's orientations). Whatever his chosen "solution," it has some effect upon A's phenomenal A-B-X system —either to reinforce it or to modify it. As a result of repeatedly facing and "solving" problems of co-orientation with regard to a given B and a given X, a relatively stable equilibrium is established. If A is free either to continue or not to continue his association with B, one or the other of two eventual outcomes is likely: (a) he achieves an equilibrium characterized by relatively great attraction toward B and by relatively high perceived symmetry, and the association is continued; or (*b*) he achieves an equilibrium characterized by relatively little attraction toward B and by relatively low perceived symmetry, and the association is discontinued. This "either-or" assumption under conditions of low constraint presupposes a circular relationship between attraction and the perception of symmetry. The present theory demands this assumption of circularity, and empirical evidence (under conditions of relative freedom from constraint) seems to support it.

Under conditions of little or no freedom to discontinue association, no such circularity is assumed. The conditions which dictate continued association also dictate the requirements for co-orientation, which are independent of attraction. The empirical data suggest that the degree to which attraction is independent of symmetry varies with the degree of *perceived* (rather than the degree of objectively observed) constraint.

SUMMARY

Communicative acts, like other molar behaviors, may be viewed as outcomes of changes in organism-environment relationships, actual and/or anticipated. Communicative acts are distinctive in that they may be aroused by and may result in changes anywhere within the system of relations between two or more communicators and the objects of their communication. It seems likely that the dynamics of such a system are such that from an adequate understanding of its properties at a given moment there can be predicted both the likelihood of occurrence of a given act of communication and the nature of changes in those properties which will result from that act.

REFERENCES

1. Back, K. The exertion of influence through social communication. *J. abnorm. soc. Psychol.*, 1951, **46**, 9-23.
2. Blake, R. R. The interaction-feeling hypothesis applied to psychotherapy groups. *Sociometry*, 1953, **16**, 253-265.
3. Festinger, L. Informal social communication. In L. Festinger, K. Back, S. Schachter, H. H. Kelley, and J. Thibaut, *Theory and experiment in social communication*. Ann Arbor: Institute for Social Research, Univ. of Michigan, 1950.
4. Festinger, L., Schachter, S., and Back, K. *Social pressures in informal groups*. New York: Harper, 1950.
5. Festinger, L., and Thibaut, J. Interpersonal communications in small groups. *J. abnorm. soc. Psychol.*, 1951, **46**, 92-99.
6. Heider, F. Attitudes and cognitive organization. *J. Psychol.*, 1946, **21**, 107-112.
7. Homans, G. C. *The human group*. New York: Harcourt Brace, 1950.
8. Horowitz, M. W., Lyons, J., and Perlmutter, H. V. Induction of forces in discussion groups. *Hum. Relat.*, 1951, **4**, 57-76.
9. Miller, G. A. *Language and communication*. New York: McGraw-Hill, 1951.
10. Newcomb, T. M. *Personality and social change*. New York: Dryden, 1943.
11. Parsons, T., and Shils, E. A. (Eds.) *Toward a general theory of action*. Cambridge: Harvard Univ. Press, 1951.
12. Schachter, S. Deviation, rejection and communication. *J. abnorm. soc. Psychol.*, 1951, **46**, 190-207.
13. White, M. S. Attitude change as related to perceived group consensus. Unpublished doctoral dissertation, Univ. of Michigan, 1953.

33. The Principle of Congruity in the Prediction of Attitude Change

CHARLES E. OSGOOD and PERCY H. TANNENBAUM

The theoretical model presented in this paper, while not pretending to take account of all variables relating to attitude change, does attempt to cover those variables believed to be most significant with respect to the direction of change to be expected in any given situation. These variables are (a) existing attitude toward the source of a message, (b) existing attitude toward the concept evaluated by the source, and (c) the nature of the evaluating assertion which relates source and concept in the message. Predictions generated by the theory about the directions and relative amounts of attitude change apply to both sources and the concepts they evaluate.

UNDERLYING NOTIONS

Our work on attitude theory and measurement is an outgrowth of continuing research on experimental semantics, particularly the development of objective methods for measuring meaning (4, 5). From this viewpoint, the *meaning* of a concept is its location in a space defined by some number of factors or dimensions, and *attitude* toward a concept is its projection onto one of these dimensions defined as "evaluative." In the factor analytic work we have done so far, the first and most heavily loaded factor is always one clearly identifiable as evaluative by the labels of the scales it represents, e.g., good-bad, fair-unfair, valuable-worthless, pleasant-unpleasant, and the like. This conception of attitude as a dimension or factor in total meaning has a number of implications, including those explored in the present paper. It implies, for example, that

• Reprinted from *Psychological Review*, 1955, 62, 42-55, with permission of the senior author and the American Psychological Association.

people having the same attitude toward a concept, such as NEGRO, may be sharply differentiated in terms of other dimensions of the semantic space (e.g., some perceiving NEGRO as powerful and active, others as weak and passive).[1]

Attitudes toward the various objects of judgment associated in messages must be measured in the same units if comparative statements about attitude change are to be made. There have been attempts to devise *generalized attitude scales* in the history of this field (cf. 6, 7), but if one is to judge the criterion of acceptance and use, they have not been outstandingly successful. In applying the *semantic differential* (a label that has come to be applied to our measuring instrument), various objects of judgment, sources and concepts, are rated against a standard set of descriptive scales. To the extent that location on the evaluative dimension of the semantic differential is a reliable and valid index of attitude (as determined by correlation with other criteria), it is then necessarily a generalized attitude scale. We have some evidence for validity[2] and more is being obtained; reliability of the differential, particularly the evaluative dimension, is reasonably high, running in the .80's and .90's in available data.

Another underlying notion about human thinking we have been exploring is that *judgmental frames of reference tend toward max-*

[1] A study in progress exhibits precisely this phenomenon with respect to the concept NEGRO. Similar findings are evident with respect to THE CHURCH and CAPITAL PUNISHMENT.

[2] For example, the correlations between scores on the evaluative scales of the semantic differential and scores on the Thurstone scales on attitude toward THE CHURCH, NEGRO, and CAPITAL PUNISHMENT are .74, .82, and .81, respectively.

imal simplicity. Since extreme, "all-or-nothing" judgments are simpler than finely discriminated judgments of degree, this implies a continuing pressure toward polarization along the evaluative dimension (i.e., movement of concepts toward either entirely good or entirely bad allocations). We have evidence that extreme judgments have shorter latencies than more discriminative judgments (5), and that extreme judgments are characteristic of less intelligent, less mature, less well educated, or more emotionally oriented individuals (8). Furthermore, since assumption of identity is a simpler process than maintenance of distinction, this also implies a continuing pressure toward elimination of differences among concepts which are localized in the same direction of the evaluative framework. We have evidence that in the judging of emotionally polarized concepts all scales of judgment tend to rotate toward the evaluative, e.g., their correlations with good-bad tend to increase and therefore the relative loading on the evaluative factor tends to increase (5).

The most "simple-minded" evaluative frame of reference is therefore one in which a tight cluster of highly polarized and undifferentiated good concepts is diametrically opposed in meaning to an equally tight and polarized cluster of undifferentiated bad concepts. The same underlying pressure toward simplicity operates on any new or neutral concept to shift it one way or the other. For example, there is the tendency in American thinking, about which Pandit Nehru complains, requiring that India be either "for us or agin' us." This is, of course, the condition referred to by the general semanticists (e.g., Johnson, 2) as a "two-valued orientation," and it is unfortunately characteristic of lay thinking in any period of conflict and emotional stress. The more sophisticated thinker, according to this view, should show less tendency to polarize, more differentiation among concepts, and thus greater relative use of factors other than the evaluative.

THE PRINCIPLE OF CONGRUITY

The principle of congruity in human thinking can be stated quite succinctly: *changes in evaluation are always in the direction of increased congruity with the existing frame of reference.* To make any use of this principle in specific situations, however, it is necessary to elaborate along the following lines: When

does the issue of congruity arise? What directions of attitude change are congruent? How much stress is generated by incongruity and how is it distributed among the objects of judgment?

The Issue of Congruity

Each individual has potential attitudes toward a near infinity of objects. It is possible to have varying attitudes toward diverse concepts without any felt incongruity or any pressure toward attitude change, as long as no association among these objects of judgment is made. As anthropologists well know, members of a culture may entertain logically incompatible attitudes toward objects in their culture (e.g., ancestor worship and fear of the dead) without any stress, as long as the incompatibles are not brought into association. The issue of congruity arises whenever a message is received which relates two or more objects of judgment via an assertion.

The simplest assertion is merely a *descriptive statement:* "Chinese cooking is good," "Jefferson was right," 'This neurotic modern art." To the extent that the evaluative location of a particular qualifier differs from that of the thing qualified, there is generated some pressure toward congruity. Similar pressure is generated by ordinary *statements of classification:* "Senator McCarthy is a Catholic," "Tom is an ex-con," "Cigarettes contain nicotine." To the extent that the evaluative locations of instance and class are different, some pressure toward congruity exists. A more complex situation is that in which *a source makes an assertion about a concept:* "University President Bans Research on Krebiozen"; "Communists like strong labor unions." This is the most commonly studied situation, and one for which we have some empirical data against which to test our hypotheses. Assertions may be explicit linguistic statements of evaluation or implicit behavioral, situational statements. A newsphoto of Mrs. Roosevelt smiling and shaking hands with a little colored boy is just as effective in setting up pressures toward congruity as a verbal statement on her part.

Directions of Congruence and Incongruence

To predict the direction of attitude change from this general principle it is necessary to take into account simultaneuosly the existing attitudes toward each of the objects of judgment prior to reception of the message and the nature of the assertion which is embodied in the message. Attitudes can be specified as favorable (+), neutral (0), and unfavorable (−). Assertions can be specified as positive or associative (+) or negative or disassociative (−). They may also, of course, include evaluative loading (e.g., when X denounces Y, we have both a dissociative assertion and negative evaluation of Y). When attitudes toward both objects of judgment are polar, the nature of the assertion determines congruence or incongruence. For EISENHOWER (+) to come out in favor of FREEDOM OF THE PRESS (+) is, of course, congruent with the existing frame of reference of most people in this country, but for THE DAILY WORKER (−) to speak in favor of FREEDOM OF THE PRESS (+) is attitudinally incongruent. In this simplest of states in which human thinking operates, sources we like should always sponsor ideas we like and denounce ideas we are against, and vice versa.

When the existing attitude toward one of the objects of judgment is neutral and the other polar, we must speak of what directions *would be* congruent. If, for example, a favorable source like EISENHOWER were to make a favorable assertion about the MINISTER FROM SIAM (a neutral notion to most of us), it would be congruent *if* the latter were also favorable—hence pressure is generated toward attitude change in this direction. If PRAVDA (−) sponsors GRADUAL DISARMAMENT (0), the pressure is such as to make the relatively neutral notion of disarmament less favorable; similarly, if a PROFESSOR (0) as a source favors PREMARITAL SEXUAL RELATIONS (−) as making for better marriages, it is the PROFESSOR that becomes less favorable (this is not unlike the "guilt by association" technique). Conversely, for our neutral PROFESSOR (0) to speak out against MORAL DEPRAVITY (−) must have the effect of raising his esteem (this is the familiar "I am against sin" technique).

When both objects of judgment are neutral, there is no question of congruity between them, and movement is determined solely by the nature of the assertion, i.e., this becomes a case of simple qualification or classification. If MR. JONES denounces MR. SMITH, neither of whom is known, there is presumably some negative pressure on MR. SMITH by virtue of the sheer devaluation of "being denounced." Since the evaluation applies to the concept and not the source, the effect should be chiefly upon the concept. We shall find evidence for such an "assertion effect" in the available data.

We may now make a general statement governing the direction of congruence which will hold for any object of judgment, source or concept, and any type of assertion.

1. *Whenever one object of judgment is associated with another by an assertion, its congruent position along the evaluative dimension is always equal in degree of polarization (d) to the other object of judgment and in either the same (positive assertion) or opposite (negative assertion) evaluative direction.*

This is to say that we have attitude scores toward two objects of judgment, OJ_1 and OJ_2, and to each of these scores we assign a value, d, which represents the degree of polarization of that attitude. Thus we have d_{OJ_1} and d_{OJ_2}. Since the measuring instrument which has been used in our quantitative work so far (the semantic differential) treats the evaluative dimension as a 7-step scale with "4" defined as the neutral point, we have three degrees of polarization in each direction, i.e., $+3$, $+2$, $+1$, 0, $−1$, $−2$, $−3$. Given OJ_1 and OJ_2 associated with one another through either a positive $(OJ_1A + OJ_2)$ or negative $(OJ_1A − OJ_2)$ assertion, we define the congruent position (c) of either object of judgment as follows: If $OJ_1A + OJ_2$, then

$$dc_{OJ_1} = d_{OJ_2}, \tag{1}$$

$$dc_{OJ_2} = d_{OJ_1}. \tag{2}$$

If $OJ_1A − OJ_2$, then

$$dc_{OJ_1} = − d_{OJ_2}, \tag{3}$$

$$dc_{OJ_2} = − d_{OJ_1}. \tag{4}$$

Figure 1 provides some graphic illustrations. In example 1, we have a positive assertion (indicated by the + on the bar connecting source and concept) associating two equally favorable objects of judgment; in this situation maximum congruity already exists. In all the other illustrations given, the existing positions are not those of maximum congruence, and those positions which would be maximally congruent for each object of judgment are shown by dashed circles. In situation 3, for example, a congruent source would be at −2 and a congruent concept would be at +3, given the favorable assertion between two items of opposite sign.

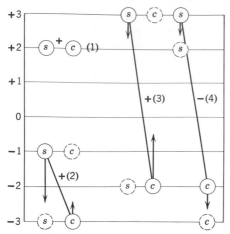

Figure 1. Graphic examples of four situations in which a source (s) makes an assertion (+ or −) about a concept (c). Positions of maximum congruity are indicated by dashed circles; predicted changes in attitude are indicated by arrows. See discussion in text.

Magnitude and Distribution of Pressure toward Congruity

Knowing the existing locations of maximum congruence under the given conditions (by applying Principle 1), it becomes possible to state the amount and direction of application of total available pressure toward congruity.

2. *The total available pressure toward congruity (P) for a given object of judgment associated with another by an assertion is equal to the difference, in attitude scale units, between its existing location and its location of maximum congruence along the evaluative dimension; the sign of this pressure is positive (+) when the location of congruence is more favorable than the existing location and negative (−) when the location of congruence is less favorable than the existing location.*

That is,

$$P_{OJ_1} = dc_{OJ_1} - d_{OJ_1}, \qquad (5)$$

$$P_{OJ_2} = dc_{OJ_2} - d_{OJ_2}. \qquad (6)$$

Therefore, substituting from equations 1 through 4, if $OJ_1 A + OJ_2$,

$$P_{OJ_1} = d_{OJ_2} - d_{OJ_1}, \qquad (7)$$

$$P_{OJ_2} = d_{OJ_1} - d_{OJ_2}. \qquad (8)$$

If $OJ_1 A - OJ_2$,

$$P_{OJ_1} = -d_{OJ_2} - d_{OJ_1}, \qquad (9)$$

$$P_{OJ_2} = -d_{OJ_1} - d_{OJ_2}. \qquad (10)$$

The resulting signs of equations 7 through 10 then represent the direction of P.

For example 2 in Figure 1, the total pressure toward congruity available for the source is −2 units and for the concept is +2 units. As can be seen by inspection of these examples, the total pressures toward congruity for both objects associated by an assertion are always equal in magnitude, although they may be the same or different in sign (i.e., $|P_{OJ_1}| = |P_{OJ_2}|$). The upper figures in each cell of Table 2 give the total pressures and directions of application for all possible relations among sources and concepts and both types of assertions. These computations are based upon the assumption of a 7-step scale with three degrees of polarization possible in each evaluative direction; they may be treated as general index numbers.

The third principle with which we shall operate incorporates the empirical generalization that intense attitudes are more resistant to change than weakly held ones (cf. 1, 3, 9), but does so in a way which generates more detailed predictions.

3. *In terms of producing attitude change, the total pressure toward congruity is distributed between the objects of judgment associated by an assertion in inverse proportion to their separate degrees of polarization.*

In other words, relatively less polarized objects of judgment, when associated with relatively more polarized objects of judgment, absorb proportionately greater amounts of the pressure toward congruity, and consequently change more.

Applying Principle 3 above, it is possible to predict relative attitude change according to the following formulas:

$$AC_{OJ_1} = \frac{|d_{OJ_2}|}{|d_{OJ_1}| + |d_{OJ_2}|} P_{OJ_1}, \qquad (11)$$

$$AC_{OJ_2} = \frac{|d_{OJ_1}|}{|d_{OJ_1}| + |d_{OJ_2}|} P_{OJ_2}, \qquad (12)$$

where AC refers to attitude change; where d_{OJ_1} and d_{OJ_2} are taken at their absolute values regardless of sign, and where P_{OJ_1} and P_{OJ_2} are determined from equations 7 through 10. Thus, the sign of the right-hand side of the equation is always that of the particular P_{OJ} under consideration, and thus represents the direction of change. In example 1 in Figure 1, there is no pressure and hence no change. In the other examples solid arrows indicate the direction and magnitude of predicted change. In example 2, the source must absorb twice as much pressure as the more polarized concept, and in a negative rather than a positive direction (e.g., BULGARIA −1 sponsors HATE CAMPAIGN −3). The unexpected prediction here, that the even more unfavorable concept, HATE CAMPAIGN, actually becomes a little less unfavorable under these conditions, derives directly from the theoretical model and will be discussed later.

If we associate OJ_1 with the source of an assertion, and OJ_2 with the concept, the numbers in Table 1 represent the results of applying formula 12 to the prediction of attitude change toward the concept for all combinations of original attitude toward source and concept when the assertion is positive.

Note that for all *incongruous relations* the predicted change is constant for a given original attitude toward source (upper right and lower left corners of matrix)—a highly favorable source favoring a negative concept produces just as much attitude change when that concept is −3 as when it is −1. This prediction assumes complete credulity of the message on the part of the receiver, a condition that exists only rarely, in all probability, for incongruous messages. Certainly, when presented with the incongruous message, EISENHOWER sponsors COMMUNISM, in an experimental situation, very few subjects are going to give it full credence. If we are going to make predictions, it is apparent that the variable of credulity must be taken into account.

4. *The amount of incredulity produced when one object of judgment is associated with another by an assertion is a positively accelerated function of the amount of incongruity which exists and operates to decrease attitude change, completely eliminating change when maximal.*

Since incongruity exists only when similarly evaluated concepts are associated by negative assertions or when oppositely evaluated concepts are associated by positive assertions, the correction for incredulity is limited to the upper right and lower left corners of the matrix in Table 1. Within these situations, the *amount* of this correction is assumed to increase with the degree of incongruity, e.g., with the total pressure toward congruity available. It is assumed that no incongruity, and hence no incredulity, can exist where one of the objects of judgment is neutral, e.g., EISENHOWER may come out either for or against a neutral concept like ST. LAWRENCE WATERWAY without the issue of incredulity arising. It is realized, of course, that other factors than those discussed here may affect incredulity.

Figure 2 provides graphic illustration of the corrections made for incredulity. The original curves, level for the neutral point and beyond, derive from the upper right corner of Table 1 and represent three degrees of favorable original attitude toward the source (OJ_1). The dashed lines represent postulated incredulity, positively accelerated functions of total pressure toward congruity. The shape of this function is, of course, based on pure hunch and will probably have to be modified; it simply

TABLE 1. *Predicted Attitude Change for Concept as a Function of Original Locations of Both Source and Concept—Positive Assertion* **(Uncorrected for incredulity)**

Original attitude toward source	Original Attitude Toward Concept						
	+3	+2	+1	0	−1	−2	−3
+3	0.0	+0.6	+1.5	+3.0	+3.0	+3.0	+3.0
+2	−0.4	0.0	+0.7	+2.0	+2.0	+2.0	+2.0
+1	−0.5	−0.3	0.0	+1.0	+1.0	+1.0	+1.0
0	0.0	0.0	0.0	0.0	0.0	0.0	0.0
−1	−1.0	−1.0	−1.0	−1.0	0.0	+0.3	+0.5
−2	−2.0	−2.0	−2.0	−2.0	−0.7	0.0	+0.4
−3	−3.0	−3.0	−3.0	−3.0	−1.5	−0.6	0.0

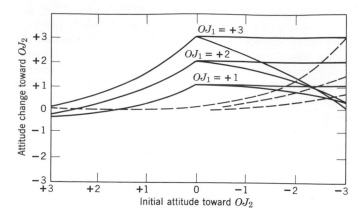

Figure 2. *Predicted change in attitude toward* OJ_2 *and correction for incredulity (postulated incredulity indicated by dashed lines).*

seems reasonable that a person's tendency to reject a message will be relatively much less for slightly incongruous relations (e.g., EISENHOWER +3 praises BULGARIANS −1) than for grossly incongruous ones (e.g., EISENHOWER +3 praises COMMUNISM −3). The light solid curves represent the result of subtracting incredulity functions from predicted attitude changes. The corrected values are given in Table 2. The same corrections, with appropriate regard to sign, apply to the lower left corner of Table 1 and are made in Table 2. For incongruous situa-

TABLE 2. *Total Pressure Toward Congruity (Upper Numbers) and Predicted Changes in Attitude (Lower Numbers) as Corrected for Incredulity**
(Positive assertion)**

Initial Location of OJ_2	Initial Location of OJ_1							
	+3	+2	+1	0	−1	−2	−3	M
+3	0	+1	+2	+3	+4	+5	+6	
	0.0	+0.6	+1.5	+3.0	+2.6	+1.5	0.0	+1.3
+2	−1	0	+1	+2	+3	+4	+5	
	−0.4	0.0	+0.7	+2.0	+1.8	+1.3	+0.5	+0.8
+1	−2	−1	0	+1	+2	+3	+4	
	−0.5	−0.3	0.0	+1.0	+0.9	+0.7	+0.4	+0.3
0	−3	−2	−1	0	+1	+2	+3	
	0.0	0.0	0.0	0.0	0.0	0.0	0.0	0.0
−1	−4	−3	−2	−1	0	+1	+2	
	−0.4	−0.7	−0.9	−1.0	0.0	+0.3	+0.5	−0.3
−2	−5	−4	−3	−2	−1	0	+1	
	−0.5	−1.3	−1.8	−2.0	−0.7	0.0	+0.4	−0.8
−3	−6	−5	−4	−3	−2	−1	0	
	0.0	−1.5	−2.6	−3.0	−1.5	−0.6	0.0	−1.3
/M/	0.3	0.6	1.1	1.7	1.1	0.6	0.3	

* The OJ whose change is being predicted, either source or concept, is always OJ_1 and the other is OJ_2.

** When dealing with negative assertions, reverse the sign of OJ_2 and look in that row.

tions, then, the formulas for predicting attitude change become:

$$AC_s = \frac{|d_c|}{|d_s| + |d_c|} P_s \mp i, \qquad (13)$$

$$AC_c = \frac{|d_s|}{|d_s| + |d_c|} P_c \mp i, \qquad (14)$$

where the sign of the second factor ($i =$ correction for incredulity) is always opposite to that of the first factor, i.e., of P, and thus serves to diminish the effect. The notations s and c refer, of course, to source and concept, respectively.

It is to be emphasized that formulas 13 and 14 apply only to situations of incredulity, or, to put it another way, $i = 0$ for all credulous situations. The precise nature of the i function remains to be empirically determined. The curve we have assumed for i approximates the function $i = a(d_s{}^2 + b)(d_c{}^2 + d_c)$, where the constants a and b are $1/40$ and 1 respectively. It is clear, however, that $i = f(d_s, d_c)$, and hence the attitude change is still a function of the two degrees of polarization and of direction of the assertion.

Incredulity, to the extent it is present, will not only operate to "damp" changes in attitude but should also appear in expressions of disbelief and rationalization. This makes it possible to ascertain the incredulity function independent of attitude change. A proposed experiment along these lines might be as follows: If subjects are presented with a number of messages and told that some are valid and others faked, we would expect the frequency of "fake" judgments to be some increasing function of the measured amount of incongruity (e.g., in terms of locations of original attitudes toward the associated objects of judgment). It is the shape of this function in which we would be particularly interested. If the same subjects were then assured that certain of the "fake" messages were actually valid, we would expect to record rationalizations and other attempts to interpret the message without modifying the evaluative frame of reference; e.g., told that RUSSIA is actually sponsoring a PEACE CONFERENCE, the subject is likely to rationalize this event as some subterfuge on the part of the Soviets in the Cold War. Use of the same messages on another group of subjects in a standard pre- and postmessage attitude change design should serve to test the prediction that attitude change for incongruous

assertions is damped in proportion to the degree of incredulity produced.

This independence of credulity as a variable also means that it should be possible to approximate the attitude change values in Table 1 (uncorrected) under special conditions where credulity is made more probable. For example, if EISENHOWER were actually to invite important COMMUNIST PARTY OFFICERS to a friendly dinner at the White House, the effects on devaluating EISENHOWER and vice versa should be extreme. The greater effectiveness of "event" as compared to "word" propaganda follows directly.

The lower numbers in each cell in Table 2 represent the predicted magnitudes and directions of attitude change for all combinations of original attitude—for SOURCES or CONCEPTS and for either positive assertions or negative assertions (see instructions in table footnotes) —as computed by applying formulas 11 and 12, or 13 and 14 in the case of incongruous assertions. Let us take illustration 2 in Figure 1 as an example: the original attitudes in this case are -1 (source) and -3 (concept), so we will be concerned with the cell defined by these values. Looking first for SOURCE CHANGE (e.g., SOURCE as OJ_1), we find a total pressure toward congruity of -2 (upper figure in cell) and a predicted attitude change of -1.5; looking then for CONCEPT CHANGE (e.g., CONCEPT as OJ_1), we find a total pressure of $+2$ and a predicted attitude change of $+0.5$. If this were the message BULGARIA praises COMMUNISM, we might expect a considerable increase in unfavorableness toward BULGARIA and a slight decrease in unfavorableness toward COMMUNISM. The reader may check the other illustrations against Table 2 if he wishes.

Predictions about attitude change are assumed to hold for any situation in which one object of judgment is associated with another by an assertion. In the special source-concept situation, we must take one additional factor into account—the fact that the *assertion itself*, whether positive or negative, typically applies to the concept rather than to the source. When X praises Y, the favorable effect of "praise" applies chiefly to Y; when X denounces Y, similarly, the unfavorable effect of "denounce" applies chiefly to Y. In other words, we must add to the equation predicting attitude change for concepts a constant ($\pm A$) whose sign is always the same as that of the assertion. In the data we have available, the existence of such an assertion constant applying to the concept but not the source is clearly evident.

A TEST OF THE CONGRUITY PRINCIPLE[3]

On the basis of a pretest of 36 potential objects of judgment, three source-concept pairs were selected which met the criteria of (a) approximately equal numbers of subjects holding favorable, neutral, and unfavorable original attitudes toward them, and (b) lack of correlation between attitude toward the source and the concept making up each pair. The three source-concept pairs finally selected were: LABOR LEADERS with LEGALIZED GAMBLING, CHICAGO TRIBUNE with ABSTRACT ART, and SENATOR ROBERT TAFT with ACCELERATED COLLEGE PROGRAMS. Another group of 405 college students was given a *before-test,* in which the 6 experimental concepts along with 4 "filler" concepts were judged against a form of the semantic differential including 6 scales highly loaded on the evaluative factor. The sum of ratings on these six 7-step scales constituted the attitude score for each concept, these scores ranging from 6 (most unfavorable) to 42 (most favorable). Five weeks later the same subjects were given highly realistic newspaper stories including positive or negative assertions involving the experimental source-concept pairs. Immediately afterward the subjects were given the *after-test,* again judging the same concepts against the semantic differential.

Original attitudes toward each source and concept were determined from the before-test scores, subjects being distributed into nine cells, s_+c_+, s_+c_0, s_+c_-, s_0c_+, etc. Attitude change amounts, for both source and concept, were obtained by subtracting the before-test score from the after-test score for each subject, a positive value thereby indicating increased favorableness.

Table 3 compares predicted attitude change scores (upper number in each cell) with obtained attitude change scores (lower number in each cell) for both sources and concepts and for both positive and negative assertions. The predicted values represent the algebraic mean of the attitude change scores in appropriate cells of Table 2 (e.g., the value for s_+c_+ with a positive assertion equals the average for the nine cells in the upper left corner); the ob-

[3] This experiment is described in detail in a separate report by one of the authors (9).

TABLE 3. *Predicted (Upper Values in Cells) and Obtained (Lower Values in Cells) Changes in Attitude*

Original Attitude Toward Source	Positive Assertions			Negative Assertions		
	Original Attitude toward Concept			Original Attitude toward Concept		
	+	0	−	+	0	−
	Source Changes					
+	+ 0.2 / + 25	0.0 / + 16	− 1.1 / − 42	− 1.1 / − 45	0.0 / + 1	+ 0.2 / + 34
0	+ 2.0 / + 150	0.0 / + 25	− 2.0 / − 94	− 2.0 / − 68	0.0 / + 17	+ 2.0 / + 96
−	+ 1.1 / + 49	0.0 / + 13	− 0.2 / − 7	− 0.2 / − 33	0.0 / − 3	+ 1.1 / + 34
	Concept Changes					
+	+ 0.2 / + 51	+ 2.0 / + 245	+ 1.1 / + 107	− 1.1 / − 88	− 2.0 / − 180	− 0.2 / − 39
0	0.0 / + 39	0.0 / + 80	0.0 / + 48	0.0 / − 72	0.0 / − 79	0.0 / − 34
−	− 1.1 / − 24	− 2.0 / − 52	− 0.2 / − 10	+ 0.2 / + 19	+ 2.0 / + 22	+ 1.1 / + 16

tained values represent the total attitude change scores, summed algebraically, for 45 subjects (15 subjects on each of 3 stories) on 6 evaluative scales. The reason for the gross difference in absolute magnitudes of predicted and obtained scores is therefore that the former are expressed in scale units and the latter in group totals. The general correspondence between predicted and obtained directions of attitude change is apparent from inspection of Table 3. In every case predicted positive changes (+) and predicted negative changes (−) show corresponding signs in the obtained data, and predicted lack of change (0) generally yields obtained changes of small magnitude.

The predictions obviously hold better for source changes than for concept changes, and it will be recalled that it was also predicted that *an assertion constant* ($\pm A$) would apply to the concept but not the source. This would mean that for comparable situations (e.g., s_+c_0 vs. s_0c_+, s_0c_- vs. s_-c_0, etc.) concept changes should be more in the favorable direction than source changes for positive assertions and more in the negative direction for negative assertions. Table 4 provides a test of this prediction. As can be seen, when comparable conditions for source and concept changes are arranged, the differences in magnitudes of attitude change are regularly positive for positive assertions (concept changes more toward favorable direction) and regularly negative for negative assertions (concept changes more toward unfavorable direction). With 17 of the 18 values

TABLE 4. Effects of Assertion Itself (A)

Source	Concept	Difference (A)
Positive Assertions (Predicted that A is +)		
s_+c_+ + 25	s_+c_+ + 51	+ 26
s_0c_+ +150	s_+c_0 +245	+ 95
s_-c_+ + 49	s_+c_- +107	+ 58
s_+c_0 + 16	s_0c_+ + 39	+ 23
s_0c_0 + 25	s_0c_0 + 80	+ 55
s_-c_0 + 13	s_0c_- + 48	+ 35
s_+c_- − 42	s_-c_+ − 24	+ 18
s_0c_- − 94	s_-c_0 − 52	+ 42
s_-c_- − 7	s_-c_- − 10	− 3
Negative Assertions (Predicted that A is −)		
s_+c_+ − 45	s_+c_+ − 88	− 43
s_0c_+ − 68	s_+c_0 −180	−112
s_-c_+ − 33	s_+c_- − 39	− 6
s_+c_0 + 1	s_0c_+ − 72	− 73
s_0c_0 + 17	s_0c_0 − 79	− 96
s_-c_0 − 3	s_0c_- − 34	− 31
s_+c_- + 34	s_-c_+ + 19	− 15
s_0c_- + 96	s_-c_0 + 22	− 74
s_-c_- + 34	s_-c_- + 16	− 18

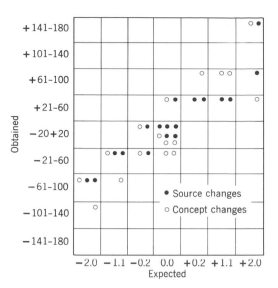

Figure 3. Correlation plot between predicted and obtained attitude changes after corrections for incredulity and for constant effect of assertion.

in the predicted direction, this is obviously significant.

A rough estimate of the size of this constant can be obtained from the average difference between source and concept changes for comparable situations: it turns out to be $A = \pm 46$ in total change score or $A = .17$ in units of the 7-step attitude scale employed. In other words, under the general conditions of this experiment, the assertion constant applied to concept changes equals about ⅙ of a scale unit.

That the magnitudes of attitude changes as well as their directions tend to follow predictions is also evident by inspection of Table 3. This can be seen more clearly in the correlation plot between predicted changes and obtained changes given as Figure 3. The predicted values are here treated as categorical and the obtained as continuous, and the latter have been corrected for the assertion constant by adding 46 to concept changes with negative assertions and subtracting 46 from concept changes with positive assertions. The correlation between predicted and obtained changes in attitude is high ($r = .91$).

A number of corollaries derive from the congruity principle, some of which can be tested

against Tannenbaum's data and others of which cannot. They are as follows:

1. *Shifts in evaluation always tend toward equalization of the degrees of polarization of the objects of judgment associated by an assertion.* If two unequally polarized concepts are associated, the less polarized one becomes more so and the more polarized less so; if a neutral concept is associated with a polarized one, it always becomes more polarized. In Tannenbaum's data this means that the less polarized object of judgment (neutral) should always change more than the more polarized object of judgment (plus or minus); this holds for all relevant conditions except one (s_0c_+, negative assertion), and even here when correction for the assertion constant is made. The comparisons shown in Table 5, where concept changes have been corrected for the assertion constant, clearly substantiate this prediction—in every case the neutral member shows a large shift and the polar member a small shift.

2. *When the total pressure toward congruity is constant, it is easier to make an object of judgment more polarized than less so.* That this prediction follows from the theory can be seen in Table 2 by comparing magnitudes of attitude change within the same row or column (for a given location of source or concept) when the total pressure is the same in amount but opposite in sign—amount of attitude change is always larger in the same direction

TABLE 5. Comparison of Attitude Changes for Neutral and Polar Objects of Judgment

Situation	Change for Neutral	Change for Polar
Positive Assertions		
$s_0 c_+$	+150 (s)	− 7 (c)
$s_+ c_0$	+199 (c)	+16 (s)
$s_- c_0$	− 98 (c)	+13 (s)
$s_0 c_-$	− 94 (s)	+ 2 (c)
Negative Assertions		
$s_0 c_+$	− 68 (s)	−26 (c)
$s_+ c_0$	−134 (c)	+ 1 (s)
$s_- c_0$	+ 48 (c)	− 3 (s)
$s_0 c_-$	+ 96 (s)	+12 (c)

as the sign of the row or column. This cannot be checked in Tannenbaum's data because he does not differentiate between degrees of original attitude in the same direction. It would be expected, however, from our general notion that evaluative frames of reference tend toward maximum simplicity.

3. *Attitude change toward an object of judgment is an inverse function of intensity of original attitude toward that object.* That weakly held attitudes are more susceptible to change is a widely held notion, but it is only valid, according to the present theory, for the *average* of all degrees of attitude toward the other object with which a given one is associated *regardless of sign* (the absolute means, $|M|$, given at the bottom of Table 2) or for maximally polarized attitudes toward the other object (+3 and −3 rows in Table 2). The "law" definitely does not hold for other degrees of attitude toward the second object of judgment, as can be seen by inspection of this table. The data in Table 6 compare predicted values (absolute means at bottom of Table 2) with those obtained by Tannenbaum, both being expressed in attitude scale units in this case. The close correspondence in trend is apparent, and the obtained trend is statistically significant. The difference in absolute magnitude presumably represents the limited effect of a single message upon attitude change. The theoretical model as developed so far takes account of neither learning via successive messages nor of intensity of assertions.

4. *Attitude change for a given object of judgment in the direction of the assertion is*

TABLE 6. Attitude Change Toward an Object of Judgment as a Function of Original Attitude Toward that Object Itself

	Original Attitude Toward Object of Judgment		
	+	0	−
Predicted	0.6	1.7	0.6
Obtained (source)	0.2	0.5	0.2
Obtained (concept)	0.3	0.7	0.2

an approximately linear function of the favorableness of the original attitude toward the other object of judgment with which it is associated. The more favorable the attitude toward a source, the greater the effect of a positive assertion on raising attitude toward the concept and the greater the effect of a negative assertion upon lowering attitude toward the concept. Strongly unfavorable sources have just the opposite effects. The same statements hold for changes in attitude toward sources when original attitudes toward concepts are varied. Table 7 compares predicted and obtained values. Again, the generally lower levels of obtained changes as compared with predicted changes are presumably due to the limited effects of a single message. Changes in

TABLE 7. Attitude Change Toward One Object of Judgment as a Function of Original Attitude Toward the Other Object of Judgment

Assertions	Original Attitude toward Other Object		
	+	0	−
Positive			
Predicted	+0.8	0.0	−0.8
Obtained (source)	+0.3	0.0	−0.2
Obtained (concept)	+0.3	0.0	−0.3
Negative			
Predicted	−0.8	0.0	+0.8
Obtained (source)	−0.2	0.0	+0.2
Obtained (concept)	−0.2	−0.1	+0.2

attitude have been corrected for the assertion constant, here as in Table 6. The obtained functions are in the direction predicted, and their trend is statistically significant.

5. *Whenever a congruent assertion associates two differently polarized objects of judgment, and neither of them is neutral, the more polarized object of judgment becomes less so.* This deduction includes the rather paradoxical situations noted earlier in this paper in which, for example, a highly favorable source comes out in favor of somewhat less favorable concept and becomes slightly less favorable itself in doing so, according to theory. The locations in Table 2 where this prediction arises are italicized. Here we are forced to predict, for example: when EISENHOWER +3 praises GOLFING +1, he loses a little prestige while giving a big boost to the concept; when EISENHOWER +3 denounces COMIC BOOKS −1, he may make the latter considerably more unfavorable, but he loses a little ground himself in the exchange. It is as if a highly favorable source should only favor equally good things or be against extremely bad things and a highly unsavory concept should be only sponsored by equally unsavory sources or condemned by highly noble sources.

If such an effect could be demonstrated, it would be convincing evidence for the whole theory. Tannenbaum's study provides only a partial test for this phenomenon in that the experi-

mental situation probably lacked the necessary sensitivity to get at the very minimal changes predicted. However, of 38 cases that met the necessary conditions, 21 (55.3 per cent) showed relatively small changes in the predicted direction, 15 (39.5 per cent) showed no change, and only 2 (5.3 per cent) changed in the opposite direction.

SUMMARY

This paper describes a general theory of attitude change which takes into account original attitude toward the source of a message, original attitude toward the concept evaluated by the source, and the nature of the evaluative assertion. Predicted changes in attitude toward both source and concept are based upon the combined operation of a principle of congruity, a principle of susceptibility as a function of polarization, and a principle of resistance due to incredulity for incongruous messages. Comparison of predictions with data obtained in a recent experiment provides a test of the theory. No attempt has been made to integrate this particular theoretical model with more general psychological theory, and we feel no urge at this time to attempt such detailed translations. We are, of course, aware that there are many variables other than those considered here which contribute to attitude change.

REFERENCES

1. Birch, H. G. The effect of socially disapproved labeling upon well-structured attitudes. *J. abnorm. soc. Psychol.*, 1945, **40**, 301-310.

2. Johnson, W. The communication process and general semantic principles. In W. Schramm (Ed.), *Mass communications.* Urbana: Univ. of Illinois Press, 1949. Pp. 261-274.

3. Klapper, J. T. The effects of mass media. Mimeographed manuscript, Bureau of Applied Social Research, Columbia Univ., 1949.

4. Osgood, C. E. The nature and measurement of meaning. *Psychol. Bull.*, 1952, **49**, 197-237.

5. Osgood, C. E. Report on development and application of the semantic differential. Unpublished manuscript, Institute of Communications Research, Univ. of Illinois, 1953. Privately distributed.

6. Remmers, H. H. (Ed.) Generalized attitude scales: studies in socio-psychological measurements. *Bull. Purdue Univ. Stud. higher Educ.*, 1934, **36**, No. 4.

7. Remmers, H. H., and Silance, E. B. Generalized attitude scales. *J. soc. Psychol.*, 1934, **5**, 298-312.

8. Stagner, R., and Osgood, C. E. An experimental analysis of a nationalistic frame of reference. *J. soc. Psychol.*, 1941, **14**, 389-401.

9. Tannenbaum, P. H. Attitudes toward source and concept as factors in attitude change through communications. Unpublished doctor's dissertation, Univ. of Illinois, 1953.

34. *Structural Balance: A Generalization of Heider's Theory*

DORWIN CARTWRIGHT and FRANK HARARY

A persistent problem of psychology has been how to deal conceptually with patterns of interdependent properties. This problem has been central, of course, in the theoretical treatment by Gestalt psychologists of phenomenal or neural *configurations* or *fields* (12, 13, 15). It has also been of concern to social psychologists and sociologists who attempt to employ concepts referring to social *systems* (18).

Heider (19), reflecting the general field-theoretical approach, has considered certain aspects of cognitive fields which contain perceived people and impersonal objects or events. His analysis focuses upon what he calls the *P-O-X* unit of a cognitive field, consisting of *P* (one person), *O* (another person), and *X* (an impersonal entity). Each relation among the parts of the unit is conceived as interdependent with each other relation. Thus, for example, if *P* has a relation of affection for *O* and if *O* is seen as responsible for *X*, then there will be a tendency for *P* to like or approve of *X*. If the nature of *X* is such that it would "normally" be evaluated as bad, the whole *P-O-X* unit is placed in a state of imbalance, and pressures will arise to change it toward a state of balance. These pressures may work to change the relation of affection between *P* and *O*, the relation of responsibility between *O* and *X*, or the relation of evaluation between *P* and *X*.

The purpose of this paper is to present and develop the consequences of a formal definition of balance which is consistent with Heider's conception and which may be employed in a more general treatment of empirical configu-

• Reprinted from *Psychological Review*, 1956, **63**, 277-293, with permission of the senior author and the American Psychological Association. This paper was prepared as part of a project sponsored in the Research Center for Group Dynamics by the Rockefeller Foundation.

rations. The definition is stated in terms of the mathematical theory of linear graphs (8, 14) and makes use of a distinction between a given relation and its opposite relation. Some of the ramifications of this definition are then examined by means of theorems derivable from the definition and from graph theory.

HEIDER'S CONCEPTION OF BALANCE

In developing his analysis of balanced cognitive units, Heider distinguishes between the two major *types* of relations. The first concerns attitudes, or the relation of liking or evaluating. It is represented symbolically as **L** when positive and as ~**L** when negative. Thus, *PLO* means *P* likes, loves, values, or approves *O*, and *P*~*LO* means *P* dislikes, negatively values, or disapproves *O*. The second type of relation refers to cognitive unit formation, that is, to such specific relations as similarity, possession, causality, proximity, or belonging. It is written as **U** or ~**U**. Thus, according to Heider, *PUX* means that *P* owns, made, is close to, or is associated with *X*, and *P*~*UX* means that *P* does not own, did not make, or is not associated with *X*.

A *balanced state* is then defined in terms of certain combinations of these relations. The definition is stated separately for two and for three entities.

In the case of two entities, a balanced state exists if the relation between them is positive (or negative) in all respects, i.e., in regard to all meanings of **L** and **U** . . . . In the case of three entities, a balanced state exists if all three relations are positive in all respects, or if two are negative and one positive (9, p. 110).

These are examples of balanced states: *P* likes something he made (*PUX, PLX*); *P* likes what his friend likes (*PLO, OLX, PLX*); *P* dislikes what his friend dislikes (*PLO, O~LX, P~LX*); *P* likes what his enemy dislikes (*P~LO, O~LX, PLX*); and *P*'s son likes what *P* likes (*PUO, PLX, OLX*).

Heider's basic hypothesis asserts that there is a tendency for cognitive units to achieve a balanced state. Pressures toward balance may produce various effects.

If no balanced state exists, then forces towards this state will arise. Either the dynamic characters will change, or the unit relations will be changed through action or through cognitive reorganization. If a change is not possible, the state of imbalance will produce tension (9, pp. 107-109).

The theory, stated here in sketchy outline, has been elaborated by Heider so as to treat a fuller richness of cognitive experience than would be suggested by our brief description. It has been used, too, by a number of others as a point of departure for further theoretical and empirical work. We shall summarize briefly some of the major results of this work.

Horowitz, Lyons, and Perlmutter (10) attempted to demonstrate tendencies toward balance in an experiment employing members of a discussion group as subjects. At the end of a discussion period each subject was asked to indicate his evaluation of an event (*PLX* or *P~LX*) which had occurred during the course of the discussion. The event selected for evaluation was one which would be clearly seen as having been produced by a single person (*OUX*). The liking relation between each *P* and *O* (*PLO* or *P~LO*) had been determined by a sociometric questionnaire administered before the meeting. Would *P*'s evaluation of the event be such as to produce a balanced *P-O-X* unit? If so, *P*'s evaluation of *O* and *X* should be of the same sign. The experimental data tend to support the hypothesis that a *P-O-X* unit tends toward a balanced state.[1]

The social situation of a discussion group

can be better analyzed, according to Horowitz, Lyons, and Perlmutter, by considering a somewhat more complex cognitive unit. The evaluation of *X* made by *P*, they argue, will be determined not only by *P*'s evaluation of *O* but also by his perception of the evaluation of *X* given by others (*Q*s) in the group. The basic unit of such a social situation, then, consists of the subject, a person who is responsible for the event, and another person who will be seen by the subject as supporting or rejecting the event. This is called a *P-O-Q-X* unit. The additional data needed to describe these relations were obtained from the sociometric questionnaire which indicated *P*'s evaluation of *Q* (*PLQ* or *P~LQ*), and from a question designed to reveal *P*'s perception of *Q*'s support or rejection of *X*, treated by the authors as a unit relation (*QUX* or *Q~UX*).[2]

Although these authors indicate the possibility of treating the *P-O-Q-X* unit in terms of balance, they do not develop a formal definition of a balanced configuration consisting of four elements. They seem to imply that the *P-O-Q-X* unit will be balanced if the *P-O-X* and the *P-Q-X* units are both balanced. They do not consider the relation between *Q* and *O*, nor the logically possible components of which it could be a part. Their analysis is concerned primarily with the two triangles (*P-O-X* and *P-Q-X*), which are interdependent, since both contain the relation of *P*'s liking of *X*. We noted above that the data tend to support the hypothesis that the *P-O-X* unit will tend toward balance. The data even more strongly support the hypothesis when applied to the *P-Q-X* unit; *P*'s evaluation of *X* and his perception of *Q*'s attitude toward *X* tend to agree when *P* likes *Q*, and to disagree when *P* dislikes *Q*. It should be noted, however, that there was also a clear tendency for *P* to see *Q*'s evaluation of *X* as agreeing with his own whether or not he likes *Q*.

In a rather different approach to the question of balanced *P-O-X* units, Jordan (11) presented subjects with 64 different hypothetical situations in which the **L** and **U** relations between each pair of elements was systematically varied. The subject was asked to place himself in each situation by taking the part of

---

[1] One of the attractive features of this study is that it was conducted in a natural "field" setting, thus avoiding the dangers of artificiality. At the same time the setting placed certain restrictions on the possibility of manipulation and control of the variables. The data show a clear tendency for *P* to place a higher evaluation on *X*s produced by more attractive *O*s. It is not clearly demonstrated that *P* likes *X*s produced by liked *O*s and dislikes *X*s produced by disliked *O*s.

[2] Whether this relation should be treated as **U** or **L** is subject to debate. For testing Heider's theory of balance, however, the issue is irrelevant, since he holds that the two relations are interchangeable in defining balance.

P, and to indicate on a scale the degree of pleasantness or unpleasantness he experienced. Unpleasantness was assumed to reflect the postulated tension produced by imbalanced units. Jordan's data tend to support Heider's hypothesis that imbalanced units produce a state of tension, but he too found that additional factors need to be considered. He discovered, for example, that negative relations were experienced as unpleasant even when contained in balanced units. This unpleasantness was particularly acute when *P* was a part of the negative relation. Jordan's study permits a detailed analysis of these additional influences, which we shall not consider here.

Newcomb (17), in his recent theory of interpersonal communication, has employed concepts rather similar to those of Heider. He conceives of the simplest communicative act as one in which one person *A* gives information to another person *B* about something *X*. The similarity of this *A-B-X* model to Heider's *P-O-X* unit, together with its applicability to objective interpersonal relations (rather than only to the cognitive structure of a single person), may be seen in the following quotations from Newcomb:

A-B-X is . . . regarded as constituting a system. That is, certain definable relationships between *A* and *B,* between *A* and *X,* and between *B* and *X* are all viewed as interdependent. . . . For some purposes the system may be regarded as a phenomenal one within the life space of *A* or *B,* for other purposes as an "objective" system including all the possible relationships as inferred from observations of *A*'s and *B*'s behavior (17, p. 393).

Newcomb then develops the concept of "strain toward symmetry," which appears to be a special instance of Heider's more general notion of "tendency toward balance." "Strain toward symmetry" is reflected in several manifestations of a tendency for *A* and *B* to have attitudes of the same sign toward a common *X*. Communication is the most common and usually the most effective manifestation of this tendency.

By use of this conception Newcomb reinterprets several studies (1, 4, 5, 16, 20) which have investigated the interrelations among interpersonal attraction, tendencies to communicate, pressures to uniformity of opinion among members of a group, and tendencies to reject devi-

ates. The essential hypothesis in this analysis is stated thus:

If *A* is free either to continue or not to continue his association with *B,* one or the other of two eventual outcomes is likely: (*a*) he achieves an equilibrium characterized by relatively great attraction toward *B* and by relatively high perceived symmetry, and the association is continued; or (*b*) he achieves an equilibrium characterized by relatively little attraction toward *B* and by relatively low perceived symmetry, and the association is discontinued (17, p. 402).

Newcomb's outcome *a* is clearly a balanced state as defined by Heider. Outcome *b* cannot be unambiguously translated into Heider's terms. If by "relatively little attraction toward *B*" is meant a negative **L** relation between *A* and *B,* then this outcome would also seem to be balanced. Newcomb's "continuation or discontinuation of the association between *A* and *B*" appear to correspond to Heider's **U** and ~**U** relations.

STATEMENT OF THE PROBLEM

This work indicates that the tendency toward balance is a significant determinant of cognitive organization, and that it may also be important in interpersonal relations. The concept of balance, however, has been defined so as to apply to a rather limited range of situations, and it has contained certain ambiguities. We note five specific problems.

1. *Unsymmetric relations.* Should all relations be conceived as symmetric? The answer is clearly that they should not; it is possible for *P* to like *O* while *O* dislikes *P*. In fact, Tagiuri, Blake, and Bruner (21) have intensively studied dyadic relations to discover conditions producing symmetric relations of actual and perceived liking. Theoretical discussions of balance have sometimes recognized this possibility—Heider, for example, states that unsymmetric liking is unbalanced—but there has been no general definition of balance which covers unsymmetric relations. The empirical studies of balance have assumed that the relations are symmetric.

2. *Units containing more than three entities.* Nearly all theorizing about balance has referred to units of three entities. While Horowitz, Lyons, and Perlmutter studied units with four

entities, they did not *define* balance for such cases. It would seem desirable to be able to speak of the balance of even larger units.

3. *Negative relations.* Is the negative relation the *complement* of the relation or its *opposite*? All of the discussions of balance seem to equate these, but they seem to us to be quite different, for the complement of a relation is expressed by adding the word "not" while the opposite is indicated by the prefix "dis" or its equivalent. Thus, the complement of "liking" is "not liking"; the opposite of "liking" is "disliking." In general, it appears that ~**L** has been taken to mean "dislike" (the opposite relation) while ~**U** has been used to indicate "not associated with" (the complementary relation). Thus, for example, Jordan says: "Specifically, '+**L**' symbolizes a positive attitude, '−**L**' symbolizes a negative attitude, '+**U**' symbolizes the existence of unit formation, and '−**U**' symbolizes the lack of unit formation" (11, p. 274).

4. *Relations of different types.* Heider has made a distinction between two types of relations—one based upon liking and one upon unit formation. The various papers following up Heider's work have continued to use this distinction. And it seems reasonable to assume that still other types of relations might be designated. How can a definition of balance take into account relations of different types? Heider has suggested some of the ways in which liking and unit relations may be combined, but a general formulation has yet to be developed.

5. *Cognitive fields and social systems.* Heider's intention is to describe balance of cognitive units in which the entities and relations enter as experienced by a single individual. Newcomb attempts to treat social systems which may be described objectively. In principle, it should be possible also to study the balance of sociometric structures, communication networks, patterns of power, and other aspects of social systems.

We shall attempt to define balance so as to overcome these limitations. Specifically, the definition should (a) encompass unsymmetric relations, (b) hold for units consisting of any finite number of entities, (c) preserve the distinction between the *complement* and the *opposite* of a relation, (d) apply to relations of different types, and (e) serve to characterize cognitive units, social systems, or any configuration where both a relation and its opposite must be specified.

THE CONCEPTS OF GRAPH, DIGRAPH, AND SIGNED GRAPH

Our approach to this problem has two primary antecedents: (a) Lewin's treatment (15) of the concepts of whole, differentiation, and unity, together with Bavelas' extension (2) of this work to group structure; and (b) the mathematical theory of linear graphs.

Many of the graph-theoretic definitions given in this section are contained in the classical reference on graph theory, König (14), as well as in Harary and Norman (8). We shall discuss, however, those concepts which lead up to the theory of balance.

A *linear graph*, or briefly a *graph*, consists of a finite collection of *points*[3] *A, B, C, . . .* together with a prescribed subset of the set of all unordered pairs of distinct points. Each of these unordered pairs, *AB*, is a *line* of the graph. (From the viewpoint of the theory of binary relations,[4] a graph corresponds to an irreflexive[5] symmetric relation on points *A, B, C, ...* Alternatively a graph may be represented as a matrix.[6])

Figure 1 depicts a graph of four points and four lines. The points might represent people,

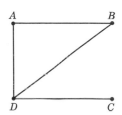

Figure 1. *A linear graph of four points and four lines. The presence of line **AB** indicates the existence of a specified symmetric relationship between the two entities **A** and **B**.*

and the lines some relationship such as mutual liking. With this interpretation, Figure 1 indicates that mutual liking exists between those pairs of people *A, B, C,* and *D* joined by lines. Thus *D* is in the relation with all other persons, while *C* is in the relation only with *D*. Figure 1 could be used, of course, to represent many

---

3 Points are often called "vertices" by mathematicians and "nodes" by electrical engineers.

4 This is the approach used by Heider.

5 A relation is irreflexive if it contains no ordered pairs of the form (a, a), i.e., if no element is in this relation to itself.

6 This treatment is discussed in Festinger (3). The logical equivalence of relations, graphs, and matrices is taken up in Harary and Norman (8).

other kinds of relationships between many other kinds of entities.

It is apparent from this definition of graph that relations are treated in an all-or-none manner, i.e., either a relation exists between a given pair of points or it does not. Obviously, however, many relationships of interest to psychologists (liking, for example) exist in varying degrees. This fact means that our present use of graph theory can treat only the structural, and not the numerical, aspects of relations. While our treatment is thereby an incomplete representation of the strength of relations, we believe that conceptualization of the structural properties of relations is a necessary first step toward a more adequate treatment of the more complex situations. Such an elaboration, however, goes beyond the scope of this paper.

A *directed graph,* or a *digraph,* consists of a finite collection of points together with a prescribed subset of the set of all ordered pairs of distinct points. Each of these ordered pairs $\overrightarrow{AB}$ is called a *line* of the digraph. Note that the only difference between the definitions of graph and digraph is that the lines of a graph are unordered pairs of points while the lines of a digraph are ordered pairs of points. An *ordered pair* of points is distinguished from an unordered pair by designating one of the points as the first point and the other as the second. Thus, for example, the fact that a message can go *from A to B* is represented by the ordered pair (A, B), or equivalently, by the line $\overrightarrow{AB}$, as in Figure 2. Similarly, the fact that A and D choose each other is represented by the two directed lines $\overrightarrow{AD}$ and $\overrightarrow{DA}$.

A *signed graph,* or briefly an *s-graph,* is obtained from a graph when one regards some of the lines as positive and the remaining lines as negative. Considered as a geometric representation of binary relations, an s-graph serves to

depict situations or structures in which both a relation and its opposite may occur, e.g., like and dislike. Figure 3 depicts an s-graph, employing the convention that solid lines are positive and dashed lines negative; thus A and B are represented as liking each other while A and C dislike each other.

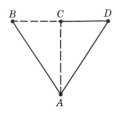

Figure 3. A signed graph of four points and five lines. Solid lines have a positive sign and dashed lines a negative sign. If the points stand for people and the lines indicate the existence of a liking relationship, this s-graph shows that **A** *and* **B** *have a relationship of liking,* **A** *and* **C** *have one of disliking, and* **B** *and* **D** *have a relationship of indifference (neither liking nor disliking).*

Combining the concepts of digraph and s-graph, we obtain that of an s-digraph. A *signed digraph,* or an *s-digraph,* is obtained from a digraph by taking some of its lines as positive and the rest as negative.

A *graph of type 2* (8), introduced to depict structures in which two different relations defined on the same set of elements occur, is obtained from a graph by regarding its lines as being of two different colors (say), and by permitting the same pair of points to be joined by two lines if these lines have different colors. A *graph of type* τ, $\tau = 1, 2, 3, \ldots$, is defined similarly. In an s-graph or s-digraph of type 2, there may occur lines of two different types in which a line of either color may be positive or negative. An example of an s-graph of type 2 might be one depicting for the same *P-O-X* unit both **U** and **L** relations among the entities, where the sign of these relations is indicated.

A *path* is a collection of lines of a graph of the form $AB, BC, \ldots, DE$, where the points $A, B, C, \ldots, D, E$, are distinct. A *cycle* consists of the above path together with the line EA. The *length* of a cycle (or path) is the number of lines in it; an *n-cycle* is a cycle of length n. Analogously to graphs, a *path of a digraph* consists of directed lines of the form $\overrightarrow{AB}, \overrightarrow{BC}, \ldots, \overrightarrow{DE}$, where the points are distinct. A *cycle* consists of this path together with the line $\overrightarrow{EA}$. In the later discussion of balance of an s-digraph we shall use the concept of a semicycle.

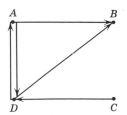

Figure 2. A directed graph of four points and five directed lines. An $\overrightarrow{AB}$ *line indicates the existence of a specified ordered relationship involving the two entities* **A** *and* **B**. *Thus, for example, if* **A** *and* **B** *are two people, the* $\overrightarrow{AB}$ *line might indicate that a message can go from* **A** *to* **B** *or that* **A** *chooses* **B**.

A *semicycle* is a collection of lines obtained by taking exactly one from each pair $\overrightarrow{AB}$ or $\overrightarrow{BA}$, $\overrightarrow{BC}$ or $\overrightarrow{CB}$, . . . , $\overrightarrow{DE}$ or $\overrightarrow{ED}$, and $\overrightarrow{EA}$ or $\overrightarrow{AE}$. We illustrate semicycles with the digraph of Figure 2. There are three semicycles in this digraph: $\overrightarrow{AD}$, $\overrightarrow{DA}$; $\overrightarrow{AD}$, $\overrightarrow{DB}$, $\overleftarrow{BA}$; and $\overrightarrow{AD}$, $\overrightarrow{DB}$, $\overleftarrow{BA}$. The last two of these semicycles are not cycles. Note that every cycle is a semicycle, and a semicycle of length 2 is necessarily a cycle.

BALANCE

With these concepts of digraphs, and signed graphs we may now develop a rigorous generalization of Heider's concept of balance.

It should be evident that Heider's terms, *entity, relation,* and *sign of a relation* may be coordinated to the graphic terms, *point, directed line,* and *sign of a directed line*. Thus, for example, the assertion that *P* likes *O* (*PLO*) may be depicted as a directed line of positive sign $\overrightarrow{PO}$. It should also be clear that Heider's two different kinds of relations (**L** and **U**) may be treated as lines of different type. It follows that a graphic representation of a *P-O-X* unit having positive or negative **L** and **U** relations will be an s-digraph of type 2.

For simplicity of discussion we first consider the situation containing only symmetric relations of a single type (i.e., an s-graph of type 1). Figure 4 shows four such s-graphs. It will be noted that each of these s-graphs contains one cycle: *AB, BC, CA.* We now need to define the sign of a cycle. The *sign of a cycle* is the product of the signs of its lines. For convenience

we denote the sign of a line by $+1$ or -1 when it is positive or negative. With this definition we see that the cycle, *AB, BC, CA* is positive in s-graph (*a*) $(+1 \cdot +1 \cdot +1)$, positive in s-graph (*b*) $(+1 \cdot -1 \cdot -1)$, negative in s-graph (*c*) $(+1 \cdot +1 \cdot -1)$, and negative in s-graph (*d*) $(-1 \cdot -1 \cdot -1)$. To generalize, a *cycle is positive* if it contains an even number of negative lines, and it is *negative* otherwise. Thus, in particular, a cycle containing only positive lines is positive, since the number of negative lines is zero, an even number.

In discussing the concept of balance, Heider states (see 9, p. 110) that when there are three entities a balanced state exists if all three relations are positive or if two are negative and one positive. According to this definition, s-graphs (*a*) and (*b*) are balanced while s-graphs (*c*) and (*d*) are not (Figure 4). We note that in the examples cited Heider's balanced state is depicted as an s-graph of three points whose cycle is positive.

In generalizing Heider's concept of balance, we propose to employ this characteristic of balanced states as a general criterion for balance of structures with any number of entities. Thus we define an *s-graph* (containing any number of points) as *balanced* if all of its cycles are positive.

Figure 5 illustrates this definition for four s-graphs containing four points. In each of these s-graphs there are seven cycles: *AB, BC, CA; AB, BD, DA; BC, CD, DB; AC, CD, DA; AB, BC, CD, DA; AB, BD, DC, CA;* and *BC, CA, AD, DB.* It will be seen that in s-graphs (*a*) and

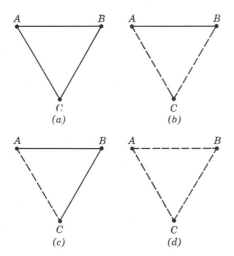

Figure 4. Four s-graphs of three points and three lines each. Structures (a) and (b) are balanced, but (c) and (d) are not balanced.

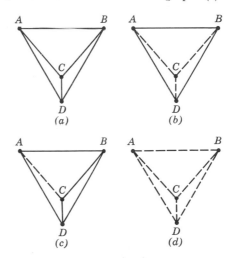

Figure 5. Four s-graphs containing four points and six lines each. Structures (a) and (b) are balanced, but (c) and (d) are not balanced.

(b) all seven cycles are positive, and these s-graphs are therefore balanced. In s-graphs (c) and (d) the cycle, *AB*, *BC*, *CA*, is negative (as are several others), and these s-graphs are therefore not balanced. It is obvious that this definition of balance is applicable to structures containing any number of entities.[7]

The extension of this definition of balance to s-digraphs containing any number of points is straightforward. Employing the same definition of *sign of a semicycle* for an s-digraph as for an ordinary s-graph, we similarly define an s-digraph as balanced if all of its semicycles are positive.

Consider now Heider's *P-O-X* unit, containing two persons *P* and *O* and an impersonal entity *X*, in which we are concerned only with liking relations. Figure 6 shows three of the

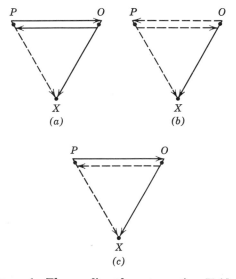

Figure 6. Three s-digraphs representing Heider's P-O-X units. Only structure (b) is balanced.

possible 3-point s-digraphs which may represent such *P-O-X* units. A positive $\overrightarrow{PO}$ line means that *P* likes *O*, a negative $\overrightarrow{PO}$ line means that *P* dislikes *O*. We assume that a person can like or dislike an impersonal entity but that an impersonal entity can neither like nor dislike a person.[8] We also rule out of consideration here

"ambivalence," where a person may simultaneously like and dislike another person or impersonal entity.

In each of these s-digraphs there are three semicycles: $\overrightarrow{PO}$, $\overrightarrow{OP}$; $\overrightarrow{PO}$, $\overrightarrow{OX}$, $\overleftarrow{XP}$; and $\overleftrightarrow{PO}$, $\overleftrightarrow{OX}$, $\overleftrightarrow{XP}$. If we confine our discussion to the kind of structures represented in Figure 6 (i.e., where there is no ambivalence and where all possible positive or negative lines are present), it will be apparent that: when *P* and *O* like each other, the s-digraph is balanced only if both persons either like or dislike *X* (s-digraph (a) is not balanced); when *P* and *O* dislike each other, the s-digraph is balanced only if one person likes *X* and the other person dislikes *X* (s-digraph (b) is balanced); and when one person likes the other but the other dislikes him, the s-digraph must be not balanced [s-digraph (c) is not balanced]. These conclusions are consistent with Heider's discussion of *P-O-X* units and with Newcomb's treatment of the *A-B-X* model.

The further extension of the notion of balance to s-graphs of type 2 remains to be made. The simplest procedure would be simply to ignore the types of lines involved. Then we would again define an *s-graph of type 2* to be balanced if all of its cycles are positive. This definition appears to be consistent with Heider's intention, at least as it applies to a situation containing only two entities. For in speaking of such situations having both **L** and **U** relations, he calls them balanced if both relations between the same pair of entities are of the same sign (see 9, p. 110). There remains some question as to whether this definition will fit empirical findings for cycles of greater length. Until further evidence is available, we advance the above formulation as a tentative definition. Obviously the definition of balance can be given for s-graphs of general type τ in the same way.

SOME THEOREMS ON BALANCE

By definition, an s-graph is balanced if and only if each of its cycles is positive. In a given situation represented by an s-graph, however, it may be impractical to single out each cycle, determine its sign, and then declare that it is balanced only after the positivity of every cycle has been checked. Thus the problem arises of deriving a criterion for determining whether or not a given graph is balanced without having to revert to the definition. This problem is the subject matter of a separate paper (6), in which

[7] If an s-graph contains no cycles, we say that it is "vacuously" balanced, since all (in this case, none) of its cycles are positive.

[8] In terms of digraph theory we define an *object* as a *point with zero output*. Thus a completely indifferent person is an object. If, psychologically, an impersonal entity is active and likes or dislikes a person or another impersonal entity, then in terms of digraph theory it is not an object.

two necessary and sufficient conditions for an s-graph to be balanced are developed. The first of these is no more useful than the definition in determining by inspection whether an s-graph is balanced, but it does give further insight into the notion of balance. Since the proofs of these theorems may be found in the other paper, we shall not repeat them here.

Theorem. An s-graph is balanced if and only if all paths joining the same pair of points have the same sign.

Thus, we can ascertain that the s-graph of Figure 7 is balanced either by listing each cycle

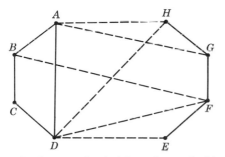

Figure 7. An s-graph of eight points and thirteen lines which, by aid of the structure theorem, can be readily seen as balanced.

separately and verifying that it is positive, or, using this theorem, by considering each pair of possible points and verifying that all possible paths joining them have the same sign. For example, all the paths between points A and E are negative, all paths joining A and C are positive, etc.

The following structure theorem has the advantage that it is useful in determining whether or not a given s-graph is balanced without an exhaustive check of the sign of every cycle, or of the signs of all paths joining every pair of points.

Structure theorem. An s-graph is balanced if and only if its points can be separated into two mutually exclusive subsets such that each positive line joins two points of the same subset and each negative line joins points from different subsets.

Using the structure theorem, one can see at a glance that the s-graph of Figure 7 is balanced, for A, B, C, D, and E, F, G, H are clearly two disjoint subsets of the set of all points which satisfy the conditions of the structure theorem.

It is not always quite so easy to determine balance of an s-graph by inspection, for it is

not always necessarily true that the points of each of the two subsets are connected to each other. Thus the two s-graphs of Figure 8 are balanced, even though neither of the two disjoint subsets is a connected subgraph. However,

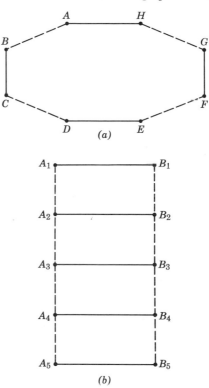

Figure 8. Two s-graphs whose balance cannot be determined easily by visual inspection.

the structure theorem still applies to both of the s-graphs of Figure 8. In the first graph the appropriate subsets of points are A, D, E, H and B, C, F, G; while in the second one we take A_1, B_1, A_3, B_3, A_5, B_5 and A_2, B_2, A_4, B_4.

In addition to providing two necessary and sufficient conditions for balance, these theorems give us further information about the nature of balance. Thus if we regard the s-graph as representing Heider's L-relation in a group, then the structure theorem tells us that the group is necessarily decomposed into two subgroups (cliques) within which the relationships that occur are positive and between which they are negative. The structure theorem, however, does not preclude the possibility that one of the two subsets may be empty—as, for example, when a connected graph contains only positive lines.

The first theorem also leads to some interesting consequences. Suppose it were true, for example, that when two people like each other they can influence each other positively (i.e., produce intended changes in the other), but when two people dislike each other they can only influence each other negatively (i.e., produce changes opposite to those intended). An s-graph depicting the liking relations among a group of people will, then, also depict the potential influence structure of the group. Suppose that Figure 7 represents such a group. If A attempts to get H to approve of something, H will react by disapproving. If H attempts, in turn, to get G to disapprove of the same thing, he will succeed. Thus A's (indirect) influence upon G is negative. The first theorem tells us that A's influence upon G must be negative, regardless of the path along which the influence passes, since the s-graph is balanced. In general, the sign of the influence exerted by any point upon any other will be the same, no matter what path is followed, since the graph is balanced.

By use of the structure theorem it can be shown that in a balanced group any influence from one point to another within the same clique must be positive, even if it passes through individuals outside of the clique, and the influence must be negative if it goes from a person in one clique to a person in the other. (It should be noted that in this discussion we give the term "clique" a special meaning, as above.) Thus, under the assumed conditions, any exerted influence regarding opinions will tend to produce homogeneity within cliques and opposing opinions between cliques.

Although we have illustrated these theorems by reference to social groups, it should be obvious that they hold for any empirical realizations of s-graphs.

FURTHER CONCEPTS IN THE THEORY OF BALANCE

The concepts of balance as developed up to this point are clearly oversimplifications of the full complexity of situations with which we want to deal. To handle such complex situations more adequately, we need some further concepts.

Thus far we have only considered whether a given s-graph is balanced or not balanced. But it is intuitively clear that some unbalanced s-graphs are "more balanced" than others! This suggests the introduction of some scale of balance, along which the "amount" of balance

possessed by an unbalanced s-graph may be measured. Accordingly we define the *degree of balance of an s-graph* as the ratio of the number of positive cycles to the total number of cycles. In symbols, let G be an s-graph,

$c(G) =$ the number of cycles of G,
$c_+(G) =$ the number of positive cycles of G, and
$b(G) =$ the degree of balance of G.

Then

$$b(G) = \frac{c_+(G)}{c(G)}.$$

Since the number $c_+(G)$ can range from zero to $c(G)$ inclusive, it is clear that $b(G)$ lies between 0 and 1. Obviously $b(G) = 1$ if and only if G is balanced. We can give the number $b(G)$ the following probabilistic interpretation: the degree of balance of an s-graph is the probability that a randomly chosen cycle is positive.

Does $b(G) = 50\%$ mean that G is exactly one-half balanced? The answer to this question depends on the possible values which $b(G)$ may assume. This in turn depends on the structure of the s-graph G. Thus, if G is the complete graph of 3 points and G is not balanced, then the only possible value is $b(G) = 0$, since there is only one cycle. Similarly, if the lines of G are as in Figure 9, some of which may be nega-

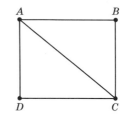

Figure 9. A graph of four points which can acquire degrees of balance of only .33 and 1.00 regardless of the assignment of positive and negative signs to its five lines.

tive, and if G is not balanced, then the only possible value is $b(G) = \frac{1}{3}$, and $b(G) = 50\%$ does not even occur for this structure. Thus any interpretation given to the numerical value of $b(G)$ must take into account the distribution curve for $b(G)$, which is determined by the structure of G.

We now consider the corresponding concept of the degree of balance for s-digraphs. Since an s-digraph is balanced if all of its semicycles are positive, the *degree of balance of an s-digraph* is taken as the ratio of the number of positive semicycles to the total number of semicycles.

In a given s-graph which represents the signed structure of some psychological situation, it may happen that only cycles of length 3 and 4 are important for the purpose of determining balance. Thus in an s-graph representing the relation **L** in a complex group, it will not matter at all to the group as a whole whether a cycle of length 100, say, is positive. To handle this situation rigorously, we define an s-graph to be *N-balanced* if all its cycles of length not exceeding N are positive. Of course the degree of N-balance is definable and computable for any s-graph. Examples can be given of unbalanced s-graphs which are, however, N-balanced for some N. Figure 10 illustrates this phenomenon

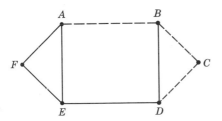

Figure 10. An s-graph which is 3-balanced but not 4-balanced.

for $N = 3$, since all of its 3-cycles are positive, but it has a negative 4-cycle.[9]

For certain problems, one may wish to concentrate only on one distinguished point and determine whether an s-graph is balanced there. This can be accomplished by the notion of local balance. We say an s-graph is *locally balanced at point P* if all cycles through P are positive. Thus the s-graph of Figure 11 is balanced at points A, B, C, and not balanced at D, E, F. If this figure represents a sociometric structure, then the concept of local balance at A is applicable provided A is completely unconcerned about the relations among D, E, F.

Some combinatorial problems suggested by the notions of local balance and N-balance have been investigated by Harary (7). The principal theorem on local balance, which follows, uses the term "articulation point" which we now define. An *articulation point*[10] of a connected

graph is one whose removal[11] results in a disconnected graph. Thus the point D is the only articulation point of Figure 11. We now state the main theorem on local balance, without proof.

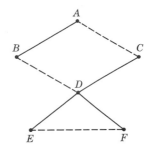

Figure 11. An s-graph which is locally balanced at points A, B, C, but not balanced at points D, E, F.

Theorem. If a connected s-graph G is balanced at P, and Q is a point on a cycle passing through P, where Q is not an articulation point, then G is also balanced at Q.

Figure 11 serves to illustrate this theorem, for the s-graph is balanced at A, and is also balanced at B but is not balanced at D, which is an articulation point.

In actual practice, both local balance and N-balance may be employed. This can be handled by introducing the combined concept of local N-balance. Formally we say that an s-graph is *locally N-balanced at P* if all cycles of length not exceeding N and passing through P are positive. Obviously the degree of local N-balance can be defined analogously to the degree of balance.

In summary, the concept of degree of balance removes the limitation of dealing with only balanced or unbalanced structures, and in addition is susceptible to probabilistic and statistical treatment. The definition of local balance enables one to focus at any particular point of the structure. The introduction of N-balance frees us from the necessity of treating all cycles as equally important in determining structural balance. Thus, the extensions of the notion of balance developed in this section permit a study of more complicated situations than does the original definition of Heider.

---

9 One way of viewing the definition of N-balance is to regard cycles of length N as having weight 1, and all longer cycles as of weight 0. Of course, it is possible to generalize this idea by assigning weights to each length, e.g., weight $1/2^n$ to length N.

10 A characterization of the articulation points of

a graph, or in other words the liaison persons in a group, is given by Ross and Harary (19), using the "structure matrix" of the graph. An exposition of this concept is given in Harary and Norman (8).

11 By the removal of a point of a graph is meant the deletion of the point and all lines to which it is incident.

ADEQUACY OF THE GENERAL THEORY OF BALANCE

In any empirical science the evaluation of a formal model must be concerned with both its formal properties and its applicability to empirical data. An adequate model should account for known findings in a rigorous fashion and lead to new research. Although it is not our purpose in this article to present new data concerning tendencies toward balance in empirical systems, we may attempt to evaluate the adequacy of the proposed general theory of balance in the light of presently available research.

Our review of Heider's theory of balance and of the research findings related to it has revealed certain ambiguities and limitations concerning (a) the treatment of unsymmetric relations; (b) the generalization to systems containing more than three entities; (c) the distinction between the complement and the opposite of a relation; (d) the simultaneous existence of relationships of different types; and (e) the applicability of the concept of balance to empirical systems other than cognitive ones. We now comment briefly upon the way in which our generalization deals with each of these problems.

Unsymmetric relations. It was noted above that, while theoretical discussions of balance have sometimes allowed for the possibility of unsymmetric relations, no rigorous definition of balance has been developed to encompass situations containing unsymmetric relationships. Furthermore, empirical studies have tended to assume that liking is reciprocated, that each liking relation is symmetric. By stating the definition of balance in terms of s-digraphs, we are able to include in one conceptual scheme both symmetric and unsymmetric relationships. And it is interesting to observe that, according to this definition, whenever the lines $\overrightarrow{PO}$ and $\overrightarrow{OP}$ are of different signs, the s-digraph containing them is not balanced. Thus, to the extent that tendencies toward balance have been effective in the settings empirically studied, the assumption of symmetry has, in fact, been justified.

Situations containing any finite number of entities. Heider's discussion of balance has been confined to structures containing no more than three entities. The definition of balance advanced here contains no such limitation; it is applicable to structures containing any finite number of entities. Whether or not empirical theories of balance will be confirmed by research dealing with larger structures can only

be determined by empirical work. It is clear, however, that our generalization is consistent with the more limited definition of Heider.

A relation, its complement, and its opposite. Using s-graphs and s-digraphs to depict relationships between entities allows us to distinguish among three situations: the presence of a relation (positive line), the presence of the opposite of a relation (negative line), and the absence of both (no line). The empirical utilization of this theory requires the ability to distinguish among these three situations. In our earlier discussion of the literature on balance, we noted, however, a tendency to distinguish only the presence or absence of a relationship. It is not always clear, therefore, in attempting to depict previous research in terms of s-graph theory whether a given empirical relationship should be coordinated to no line or to a negative line.

The experiment of Jordan (11) illustrates this problem quite clearly. He employed three entities and specified certain **U** and **L** relations between each pair of entities. The empirical realization of these relations was obtained in the following way: **U** was made into "has some sort of bond or relationship with"; $\sim$**U** into "has no sort of bond or relationship with"; **L** was made into "like"; and $\sim$**L** into "dislike." Viewed in the light of s-graph theory, it would appear that Jordan created s-graphs of type 2 (which may contain positive and negative lines of type **U** and type **L**). It would also appear, however, that the $\sim$**U** relation should be depicted as the absence of any **U**-line but that the $\sim$**L** relation should be depicted as a negative **L**-line. If this interpretation is correct, Jordan's classification of his situations as "balanced" and "imbalanced" will have to be revised. Instead of interpreting the $\sim$**U** relation as a negative line, we shall have to view it as no **U**-line, with the result that all of his situations containing $\sim$**U** relations are vacuously balanced by our definition since there are no cycles.

It is interesting to examine Jordan's data in the light of this reinterpretation. He presented subjects with 64 hypothetical situations, half of which were "balanced" and half "imbalanced" by his definition. He had subjects rate the degree of pleasantness or unpleasantness experienced in each situation (a high score indicating unpleasantness). For "balanced" situations the mean rating was 46 and for "imbalanced" ones, 57.

If, however, we interpret Jordan's $\sim$**U** relation as the absence of a line, his situations must be reclassified. Of his 32 "balanced" situations, 14 have no ~U relation and thus remain balanced. The mean unpleasantness score for these is 39. The remaining 18 of his "balanced" situations, having at least one ~U relation, become vacuously balanced since no cycle remains. The mean unpleasantness of these vacuously balanced situations is 51. Of Jordan's 32 "imbalanced" situations, 19 contain at least one ~U relation, thus also becoming vacuously balanced, and the mean unpleasantness score for these is 51. The remaining 13 situations, by having no ~U relations, remain imbalanced, and their mean score is 66. Thus it is clear that the difference in pleasantness between situations classed by Jordan as "balanced" and "imbalanced" is greatly increased if the vacuously balanced situations are removed from both classes (balanced, 39; vacuously balanced, 51; not balanced, 66). These findings lend support to our view that the statement "has no sort of bond or relationship with" should be represented as the absence of a line.[12]

Relations of different types. A basic feature of Heider's theory of balance is the designation of two types of relations (L and U). Our generalization of the definition of balance permits the inclusion of any number of types of relations. Heider discusses the combination of types of relations only for the situation involving two entities, and it is clear that our definition is consistent with his within this limitation. It is interesting to note that Jordan (11) finds positive liking relations to be experienced as more pleasant than negative ones. This finding may be interpreted as indicating a tendency toward "positivity" over and above the tendency toward balance. It is possible, however, that in the hypothetical situations employed by Jordan the subjects assumed positive unit relations between each pair of entities. If this were in fact true, then a positive liking relation would form a positive cycle of length 2 with the positive unit relation, and a negative liking relation would form a negative cycle

of length 2 with the positive unit relation. And, according to the theory of balance, the positive cycle should produce more pleasantness than the negative one. This interpretation can be tested only through further research in which the two relations are independently varied.

Empirical applicability of concept of balance. Heider's discussion of balance refers to a cognitive structure, or the life space of a single person. Newcomb suggests that a similar conception may be applicable to interpersonal systems objectively described. Clearly, our definition of balance may be employed whenever the terms "point" and "signed line" can be meaningfully coordinated to empirical data of any sort. Thus, one should be able to characterize a communication network or a power structure as balanced or not. Perhaps it would be feasible to use the same definition in describing neural networks. It must be noted, however, that it is a matter for empirical determination whether or not a tendency to achieve balance will actually be observed in any particular kind of situation, and what the empirical consequences of not balanced configurations are. Before extensive utilization of these notions can be accomplished, certain further conceptual problems regarding balance must be solved.

One of the principal unsolved problems is the development of a systematic treatment of relations of varying strength. We believe that it is possible to deal with the strength of relations by the concept of a graph of strength σ, suggested by Harary and Norman (8).

SUMMARY

In this article we have developed a generalization of Heider's theory of balance by use of concepts from the mathematical theory of linear graphs. By defining balance in graph-theoretic terms, we have been able to remove some of the ambiguities found in previous discussions of balance, and to make the concept applicable to a wider range of empirical situations than was previously possible. By introducing the concept *degree of balance,* we have made it possible to treat problems of balance in statistical and probabilistic terms. It should be easier, therefore, to make empirical tests of hypotheses concerning balance.

Although Heider's theory was originally intended to refer only to cognitive structures of

[12] A strict test of our interpretation of Jordan's data is not possible since he specified for any given pair of entities only either the L or U relation. We can but guess how the subjects filled in the missing relationship. In the light of our discussion of relations of different types, in the next section, it appears that subjects probably assumed a positive unit relation when none was specified, since there is a marked tendency to experience negative liking relations as unpleasant.

an individual person, we propose that the definition of balance may be used generally in describing configurations of many different sorts, such as communication networks, power systems, sociometric structures, systems of orientations, or perhaps neural networks. Only future research can determine whether theories of balance can be established for all of these configurations. The definitions developed here do, in any case, give a rigorous method for describing certain structural aspects of empirical configurations.

REFERENCES

1. Back, K. The exertion of influence through social communication. *J. abnorm. soc. Psychol.*, 1951, **46**, 9-23.

2. Bavelas, A. A mathematical model for group structures. *Appl. Anthrop.*, 1948, **7**, No. 3, 16-30.

3. Festinger, L. The analysis of sociograms using matrix algebra. *Hum. Relat.*, 1949, **2**, 153-158.

4. Festinger, L., Schachter, S., and Back, K. *Social pressures in informal groups.* New York: Harper, 1950.

5. Festinger, L., and Thibaut, J. Interpersonal communication in small groups. *J. abnorm. soc. Psychol.*, 1951, **46**, 92-99.

6. Harary, F. On the notion of balance of a signed graph. *Mich. math. J.*, 1953-1954, **2**, 143-146.

7. Harary, F. On local balance and N-balance in signed graphs. *Mich. math. J.*, 1955-1956, **3**, 37-41.

8. Harary, F., and Norman, R. Z. *Graph theory as a mathematical model in social science.* Ann Arbor, Mich.: Institute for Social Research, 1953.

9. Heider, F. Attitudes and cognitive organization. *J. Psychol.*, 1946, **21**, 107-112.

10. Horowitz, M. W., Lyons, J., and Perlmutter, H. V. Induction of forces in discussion groups. *Hum. Relat.*, 1951, **4**, 57-76.

11. Jordan, N. Behavioral forces that are a function of attitudes and of cognitive organization. *Hum. Relat.*, 1953, **6**, 273-287.

12. Koffka, K. *Principles of gestalt psychology.* New York: Harcourt, Brace, 1935.

13. Köhler, W. *Dynamics in psychology.* New York: Liveright, 1940.

14. König, D. *Theorie der endlichen und unendlichen Graphen.* New York: Chelsea, 1950 (originally published in Leipzig, 1936).

15. Lewin, K. *Field theory in social science.* New York: Harper, 1951.

16. Newcomb, T. M. *Personality and social change.* New York: Dryden, 1943.

17. Newcomb, T. M. An approach to the study of communicative acts. *Psychol. Rev.*, 1953, **60**, 393-404.

18. Parsons, T. *Essays in sociological theory.* (Rev. Ed.) Glencoe, Ill.: Free Press, 1954.

19. Ross, I. C., and Harary, F. Identification of the liaison persons of an organization using the structure matrix. *Mgmt. Sci.*, 1955, **1**, 251-258.

20. Schachter, S. Deviation, rejection and communication. *J. abnorm. soc. Psychol.*, 1951, **46**, 190-207.

21. Tagiuri, R., Blake, R. R., and Bruner, J. S. Some determinants of the perception of positive and negative feelings in others. *J. abnorm. soc. Psychol.*, 1953, **48**, 585-592.

35. *Cognitive Structure and Attitudinal Affect*

MILTON J. ROSENBERG

Understanding of the related processes of attitude learning and attitude change will probably be advanced by the investigation of structural relationships between attitudes and beliefs about the objects of attitudes. The present research is an attempt to verify a set of hypotheses about such relationships. These hypotheses have much in common with some that have already been presented by Cartwright (2), Hilliard (3), Smith (8), Tolman (9), and Woodruff (11, 12). However, they differ from these earlier formulations in attempting to delineate more explicitly certain variables that are assumed to covary with attitude (here defined as *relatively stable affective response to an object*). One of these variables is the intensity of a person's values. A second is the perceived importance of the attitude object in leading to or blocking the attainment of his values.

The general theoretical view underlying the present study includes the following points: (*a*) When a person has a relatively stable tendency to respond to a given object with either positive or negative affect, such a tendency is accompanied by a *cognitive structure* made up of beliefs about the potentialities of that object for attaining or blocking the realization of valued states; (*b*) the sign (positive or negative) and extremity of the affect felt toward the object are correlated with the content of its associated cognitive structure. Thus strong and stable positive affect toward a given object should be associated with beliefs to the effect that the attitude object tends to facilitate the attainment of a number of important values, while strong negative affect should be associated with beliefs to the effect that the attitude object tends to block the attainment of important values. Similarly, moderate positive or negative affects should be associated with beliefs that relate the attitude object to less important values or, if to important values, then with less confidence as to the existence of clear-cut instrumental relationships between the attitude object and the values in question.

From this view, three specific hypotheses were formulated for experimental test:

1. The degree and sign of affect aroused in an individual by an object (as reflected by the position he chooses on an attitude scale) vary as a function of the algebraic sum of the products obtained by multiplying the rated importance of each value associated with that object by the rated potency of the object for achieving or blocking the realization of that value.

2. The degree and sign of affect aroused in an individual by an object (as reflected by the position he chooses on an attitude scale) vary as a function of the algebraic sum of his ratings of the potency of that object for achieving or blocking the realization of his values (when the importance of these values is held constant).

3. The degree and sign of affect aroused in an individual by an object (as reflected by the position he chooses on an attitude scale) vary as a function of the algebraic sum of his ratings of the importance of the values whose attainment or blocking he perceives to be affected through the instrumental potency of that object (when the instrumental potency of that object for attaining or blocking each of these values is held constant).

METHOD

Subjects and Attitude Measure

One hundred and twenty *Ss*, recruited from undergraduate courses at the University of

• Reprinted from *Journal of Abnormal and Social Psychology*, 1956, **53**, 367-372, with permission of the author and the American Psychological Association. The study was supported by the U. S. Air Force, Human Resources Research Institute, under contract # AF33-(038)-26646.

Michigan and the Ypsilanti State Teachers College, took an attitude questionnaire that contained, among other items, one dealing with the issue of "whether members of the Communist Party should be allowed to address the public." Each S checked his first choice among five alternative statements. Seventeen Ss chose the alternative indicating extreme opposition to allowing members of the Communist Party to address the public, 31 Ss the alternative indicating moderate opposition, 44 Ss that indicating moderate approval, and 25 Ss that indicating extreme approval. Only three Ss chose the alternative indicating "neutrality" on the issue, and, because of their small number, were excluded from the research population. In a retest of 95 Ss on this measure after an interval of at least two months, a reliability coefficient of .72 was obtained ($p < .001$).

Value Measures

Three to five weeks after the administration of the attitude measure two card-sorting tasks were administered individually. These tasks required S to categorize each of a group of value items in terms of (a) *value importance*, i.e., its importance to him as a "source of satisfaction" and (b) *perceived instrumentality*, i.e., his estimate as to whether, and to what extent, the value in question would tend to be achieved or blocked through the "policy of allowing members of the Communist Party to address the public."

The pack of value-cards included 35 items constructed in the light of White's value-analysis technique (10) and Murray's analysis of major needs (6). (The value items used are given in Table 1.) In addition to these 35 items, the pack of cards presented to each S also contained value terms that had been coded out of his questionnaire answer to a verbal probe in conjunction with the item on "allowing members of the Communist Party to address the public." For most Ss the total number of such "salient" values came to two or three, the range among all Ss extending from zero to six.

For the "value importance" measure S was asked to rank each card so as to indicate how much satisfaction he gets, or would get, from the value state that it described. Each value was to be judged independently in terms of 21 categories ranging from "gives me maximum satisfaction" (Category +10) through "gives me neither satisfaction nor dissatisfaction" (Cate-

*TABLE 1. Value Items Used in Card-Sorting Tasks**

1. People sticking to their own groups.
2. People looking out for the welfare of others.
3. Being looked up to by others.
4. Change and variety; having new kinds of experience.
5. Sticking to a difficult task; solving difficult problems.
6. Making one's own decisions.
7. People being strongly patriotic.
8. Serving the interests of the group to which one belongs.
9. Giving expression to feelings of anger or hostility.
10. Keeping promises made to others.
11. Having one's family approve of one's views.
12. The uncompromising administration of punishment to anyone who deserves it.
13. Having interesting work to do.
14. Having power and authority over people.
15. Being well-informed about current affairs.
16. Having the value of property well protected.
17. People of different backgrounds getting to know each other better.
18. All human beings having equal rights.
19. Being good-looking; having attractive face, body, or clothes.
20. Having a steady income.
21. Believing in a relationship between the individual and some higher spiritual power.
22. America having high prestige in other countries.
23. Being liked or loved by the opposite sex or associating with the opposite sex.
24. Getting advice on important problems.
25. People having the right to participate in making decisions which will affect them.
26. Achieving superiority over others in such things as knowledge, work, or sports.
27. Complying with the wishes of persons in authority.
28. Being like others in general; having the same interests.
29. People being well educated.
30. People having strict moral standards.
31. The open expression of disagreement between people.
32. Everyone being assured of a good standard of living.
33. Being allowed to maintain the privacy of one's opinions and beliefs.
34. Being with other people; socializing.
35. Letting others make their own decisions.

* This list does not include the "salient" value items specially constructed for each S.

gory 0) to "gives me maximum dissatisfaction" (Category —10). For the measure of "perceived instrumentality" he was asked to judge and place each card in terms of 11 categories ranging from "the condition (value described on the card) is completely attained by allowing admitted Communists to address the public" (Category +5) through "whether or not admitted Communists are allowed to address the public is completely irrelevant to the attainment of the condition" (Category 0) to "the condition is completely blocked by allowing admitted Communists to address the public" (Category —5). In each of the two card-sorting tasks S was required, after the initial categorization was completed, to rank the cards *within* each category in terms of "value importance" and "perceived instrumentality" respectively.

The test-retest reliability of these two measures was studied with a subpopulation of 12 Ss, the second administration following the first by from four to five weeks. For each of these Ss Spearman's rho was computed as an estimate of the degree of correlation between the ranks assigned to the separate values on the first and second administrations respectively. For the measure of value importance, the median rho was .89 ($p < .01$); for that of perceived instrumentality, it was .74 ($p < .01$).

From the data obtained through the two card-sorting tasks ten indices were computed to permit testing the major hypotheses. Operational definitions of these indices are given in Tables 2 to 4.

RESULTS AND DISCUSSION[1]

Each hypothesis was tested by chi square,[2] computed from a 3×4 table. In each such table the four groups in terms of attitude position (extremely favorable, moderately favorable, moderately unfavorable, and extremely

[1] All of the results reported in this section have been successfully replicated with regard to the attitude area of "allowing Negroes to move into white neighborhoods." The replication was based on an analysis exactly parallel to the one described in the present report and upon identical measurement operations.

[2] This technique was used rather than correlational methods because it was felt that the assumptions required by correlational methods (particularly the assumptions of normality and equal-interval scales) were not fully met by the data. The method used for computing chi square was the "maximum likelihood test" of Mood (5) which is applicable to data plots with low cell counts.

unfavorable toward "allowing members of the Communist Party to address the public") were cross classified in terms of a threefold categorization of the Ss on one of the indices derived from the card-sorting value measures.

Hypothesis 1

All of the four indices used to test Hypothesis 1 provide, as the hypothesis requires, for representation of both the importance to the individual of some set of values and his perceptions as to how these values are affected (with regard to their attainment or blocking) through the instrumental agency of the attitude object (the policy of "allowing members of the Communist Party to address the public"). By algebraically summing the importance-instrumentality products for each of the values it is possible to represent appropriately the interaction between positive and negative values on the one hand and perceptions of positive and negative instrumentality on the other. Thus a positive value (rated say as +7 in its capacity to satisfy the S) may be perceived as being attained through the policy of "allowing members of the Communist Party to address the public" (to the extent say, of a rating of +3 on "instrumentality"). In this case the product would be +21. If on the other hand, the same value were rated as being *blocked* by the policy of "allowing members of the Communist Party to address the public" (for example a rating of —3 on "instrumentality") the resultant product would be —21. Similarly, a value rated as yielding dissatisfaction and thus bearing a minus sign on "value importance" would yield a negative product if multiplied by a rating of positive instrumentality and a positive product if multiplied by a rating of negative instrumentality. By summing all such products for a given set of values a single algebraic quantity is obtained representing the total import of the S's pattern of beliefs about the influence of the attitude object upon attaining or blocking various states that he values to differing degrees.

Since all four of the indices used to test Hypothesis 1 were found to be significantly related to attitude position (see Table 2), the hypothesis would appear to have been confirmed at an acceptable level. These findings, to generalize, lend support to the view that beliefs associated with an attitudinal affect tend to be congruent with it; i.e., that there exists within the individual an "organization" of the affective and cognitive properties of his total pattern of response to what is, for him, an "attitude object."

TABLE 2. Relationships between "Value Importance × Perceived Instrumentality" (Indices 1 to 4) and Attitude Position (N = 117)

Index	Description of Index	Chi Square	Proba-bility*
1	Algebraic sum of importance-instrumentality products for all value items	26.33	.001
2	Algebraic sum of importance-instrumentality products for the twenty values ranking highest on importance	30.82	.001
3	Algebraic sum of importance-instrumentality products for all "salient" values	45.09	.001
4	Algebraic sum of importance-instrumentality products for all "non-salient" values	15.10	.02

* Examination of the actual data plots reveals that all of these significant chi squares are due to positive, monotonic relationships.

One possible objection to such an interpretation might hold that the way in which S sorts the cards may reflect not his actual cognitive structure but rather an attempt to demonstrate to the experimenter and to himself that his beliefs are consistent with his attitudes. If striving for cognitive-affective consistency accounts in part for relationships obtained during the testing session, however, it seems appropriate to assume that similar motivation had been in operation before the testing session, i.e., that the motive to "rationalize" one's attitudes plays a role in the natural history of attitude development.

Still another line of evidence that limits the significance of this objection arises from the findings obtained with Index 3. This index is based solely upon the "value importance" and "perceived instrumentality" ratings of the S's "salient" values, which were coded out of his own verbal defense of his stated attitude position. Certainly the individual's estimates of the importance of these values and the ways in which their realization would be influenced by the attitude object must have had *pre-experimental* reality to have been given expression in response to the questionnaire probe.

It should be noted, however, that the historical relationship between affective and cognitive processes in the development of attitudes is not approachable through analysis of the present data. The province of the present study is to examine the relationships between cognitive and affective processes at a point in time after an attitude has been acquired and stabilized. Nevertheless, the present hypotheses may, if confirmed, suggest further hypotheses about the processes of attitude learning and attitude change.

Hypotheses 2 and 3

While the data just reviewed confirm the existence of a relationship between a measure of affect toward an object and a measure based upon both the "importance" and "perceived instrumentality" of values associated with it, the question may be raised as to whether each of these two latter variables may be demonstrated to covary with affect when the other is held constant. Hypotheses 2 and 3 assert the existence of such relationships. Indices 5-10 are based upon procedures for obtaining separate estimates of the "value importance" and "perceived instrumentality" variables. To isolate the one variable, it was possible to hold the other constant since the original card-sorting tasks had required S to rank the values *within* each of the categories used in sorting.

Thus, to test the relationship between "perceived instrumentality" of values and affect toward the attitude object, four indices (5-8) were developed, all of which have in common being based upon a summation of the "perceived instrumentality" ratings of a group of values defined and chosen in terms of their "value importance" ranks. Index 5 for example is obtained by choosing the value items ranked 1-20 by the S on the dimension of "value importance" and then obtaining the algebraic sum of the "perceived instrumentality" ratings of these same 20 values.

A similar procedure was employed with regard to the indices (9 and 10) used to test the relationship between "value importance" and affect toward the attitude object. These two indices are both based upon the "value importance" ratings of a group of values defined and chosen in terms of their "perceived instrumentality" ranks. Index 9 for example is obtained by choosing the five values ranked highest on "perceived positive instrumentality" and then obtaining the algebraic sum of the "importance" ratings of these same five values. Index 10 is identical except that it is computed from the five values ranked highest on "perceived negative instrumentality."

The results reported in Table 3 indicate that all four of the indices of "perceived instrumentality" are significantly related to attitude position. Furthermore it should be noted that the hypothesis has been verified at a number of different levels of "value importance" control, each of the four indices representing a different level. On the basis of these findings Hypothesis 2 appears to have been confirmed. To generalize, other things (particularly "value importance") being equal, extreme attitudinal affects are associated with perceptions of close positive or negative instrumental connection between the attitude object and related values, while moderate attitudinal affects are associated with perceptions of less clear-cut instrumental relationships. In terms of attitude theory this finding suggests the existence of a distinguishable and important dimension of attitude-related cognitive structures. Recent research (1) based upon the present study lends confirmation to the existence of this dimension as a separate and manipulable one and indicates that attitude-change effects (in the sense of affective change) may be achieved through its manipulation.

The results reported in Table 4 indicate that both of the indices of "value importance" are

TABLE 3. Relationships between "Perceived Instrumentality" (Indices 5 to 8) and Attitude Position (N = 117)

Index	Description of Index	Chi Square	Probability*
5	Algebraic sum of the instrumentality ratings of the values ranking 1st-20th on importance	35.51	.001
6	Algebraic sum of the instrumentality ratings of the values ranking 11th-30th on importance	21.27	.001
7	Algebraic sum of the instrumentality ratings of the values ranking 1st-10th on importance	20.82	.01
8	Algebraic sum of the instrumentality ratings of the values ranking 11th-20th on importance	38.47	.001

* Examination of the actual plots reveals that all of the significant chi squares are due to the presence of positive, monotonic relationships.

TABLE 4. Relationships between "Value Importance" (Indices 9 and 10) and Attitude Position (N = 117)

Index	Description of Index	Chi Square	Probability*
9	Algebraic sum of the importance ratings of the values ranking 1st-5th on positive instrumentality (attainment of values)	12.75	.05
10	Algebraic sum of the importance ratings of the values ranking 1st-5th on negative instrumentality (blocking of values)	16.46	.02

* Examination of the actual plots reveals that the significant chi square in the case of Index 9 is due to the presence of a positive monotonic relationship, while the significant chi square in the case of Index 10 is due to the presence of a negative monotonic relationship, both as predicted.

significantly related to attitude position. On the basis of these findings, Hypothesis 3 appears to have been confirmed.

Although the relationships reported in Table 4 reach an acceptable level of significance, however, their significance level is lower than most of the relationships reported in Tables 2 and 3. The present data leave it an open question as to whether this is an artifact of the measurements or computations employed or whether, on the other hand, "perceived instrumentality" actually controls more variance in attitudinal affect than does "value importance." The generalization is nevertheless supported that other things (particularly "perceived instrumentality") being equal, extreme attitudinal affects are associated with values of high importance while moderate attitudinal affects are associated with values of less importance. For attitude theory, these results suggest the existence of a second distinguishable and important dimension of attitude-related cognitive structures. Further research is needed to determine whether the individual's assessment of the importance of his values is manipulable and whether, if it is, such manipulation is sufficient to produce change in affect toward an object seen as having instrumental influence upon the attainment or blocking of these values.

Further Implications for Attitude Theory

It has been suggested that attitudinal effect toward an object may be altered by the prior modification of value importance and perceived instrumentality. A related implication is that one way in which attitudes may originally develop is through the prior acquisition of beliefs about the value-attaining or value-blocking powers of particular objects, be those objects individuals, groups, political proposals, or commercial products. Such a view, even if it has not been systematically elaborated, seems to underlie the attitude-creating and attitude-changing communication techniques of many propagandists in such fields as advertising, teaching, psychological warfare, and child-rearing.

A less obvious implication of the present findings suggests at least one other type of sequential process leading to the establishment of stabilized affective-cognitive patterns. It seems plausible that much original attitudinal learning (the acquisition of a stable affective response where none existed previously) may originate in experiences of being rewarded or punished for imitation or rehearsal of expressions of affect provided by others. A case in point may be found in the data on the acquisition of the anti-Negro attitude as reported by Horowitz (4). With an affect, or its beginnings, established through reinforcement procedures, something like a need for affective-cognitive consistency may set the person to acquire socially available beliefs that "rationalize" the acquired affect. When such beliefs are unavailable in the person's communicative surround, he may invent them. In real-life situations where attitudes are being instilled, there are generally available both cognitive supports for the advocated affect and direct reinforcements for its expression.

Recent research by the investigator seems to indicate that the production of *change* in an already established attitude may be obtained without any direct attempt to modify the associated cognitive structure, but rather through direct assault (with hypnotic techniques) upon the established affect. Such assault produces in some Ss a temporary affective reversal, and along with this reversal, a spontaneous, self-directed modification of the related cognitive structure.

SUMMARY

An attitude questionnaire on the issue of "allowing members of the Communist Party to address the public" was administered to 117 Ss. Three to five weeks later each S took a card-sorting test which required him to rate and rank each of a group of value items in terms of (a) the importance of the value as a source of satisfaction and (b) his perception as to the extent to which the value tends to be attained or blocked through the instrumental agency of the attitude object.

The data thus gathered were used in testing three hypotheses concerned with the relationships between stable affective response (attitude) toward an object and beliefs about that object. These hypotheses were derived from a general proposition to the effect that the sign and extremity of affect toward an object are functions both of whether it is perceived as facilitating or blocking the attainment of values and of whether or not the values involved are important ones. All three hypotheses were confirmed. Some of the data interpreted as suggesting that "value importance" and "perceived instrumentality" are separate and possibly, manipulable dimensions of attitude-related cognitive structures.

Some suggestions were presented as to the implications of the present study with regard to the phenomena of attitude learning and attitude change.

REFERENCES

1. Carlson, E. R. Attitude change and attitude structure. *J. abnorm. soc. Psychol.*, 1956, **52**, 256-261.
2. Cartwright, D. Some principles of mass persuasion. *Hum. Relat.*, 1949, **2**, 253-268.
3. Hilliard, A. E. *The forms of value.* New York: Columbia Univ. Press, 1950.
4. Horowitz, E. L. The development of attitude toward the Negro. *Arch. Psychol., N. Y.*, 1936, No. 194.
5. Mood, A. E. *Introduction to the theory of statistics.* New York: McGraw-Hill, 1950.
6. Murray, H. A. *Explorations in personality.* New York: Oxford Univ. Press, 1938.
7. Rosenberg, M. J. The experimental investigation of a value theory of attitude structure. Unpublished doctor's dissertation, Univ. of Michigan, 1953.
8. Smith, M. B. Personal values as determinants of a political attitude. *J. Psychol.*, 1949, **28**, 477-486.
9. Tolman, E. C. A psychological model, in T. Parsons and E. A. Shils (Eds.), *Toward a general theory of action.* Cambridge: Harvard Univ. Press, 1951.
10. White, R. K. *Value analysis: the nature and use of the method.* Society for the Psychological Study of Social Issues, 1951.
11. Woodruff, A. D. Personal values and the direction of behavior. *Sch. Rev.*, 1942, **50**, 32-42.
12. Woodruff, A. D., and DiVesta, F. J. The relationship between values, concepts, and attitudes. *Educ. psychol. Measmt.*, 1948, **8**, 645-660.

36. Attitudinal Consequences of Induced Discrepancies Between Cognitions and Behavior

ARTHUR R. COHEN

Many situations in daily life involve engaging in disagreeable behavior or considering information contrary to one's own attitudes and values. The reasons for becoming involved in situations of this discrepant character do not concern us here. Our major purpose is to deal with the psychological processes which occur in such situations and their consequences for attitude change.

THEORETICAL BACKGROUND

It has often been demonstrated that forcing a person to express an opinion position discrepant from what he privately believes results in a change of private opinion.[1] According to Festinger's analysis, expressing an opinion discrepant from one's privately held position creates "dissonance," or psychological tension having drive character. The tension may be

• Excerpted from *Public Opinion Quarterly*, 1960, **24**, 297-318, with permission of the publisher. This paper was prepared as part of the program of the Research Center for Human Relations, New York University. Most of the research cited was carried out by the author and J. W. Brehm while both were at Yale University.

1 H. Burdick, "The Compliant Behavior of Deviates under Conditions of Threat," Minneapolis, University of Minnesota, 1955, unpublished doctoral dissertation. I. L. Janis and B. T. King, "The Influence of Role Playing in Opinion Change," *Journal of Abnormal and Social Psychology*, Vol. 58, 1959, pp. 203-210. H. C. Kelman, "Attitude Change as a Function of Response Restriction," *Human Relations*, Vol. 6, 1953, pp. 185-214. D. McBride, "The Effects of Public and Private Changes of Opinion on Intra-group Communication," Minneapolis, University of Minnesota, 1955, unpublished doctoral dissertation. B. H. Raven, "Social Influence on Opinions and the Communication of Related Content," *Journal of Abnormal and Social Psychology*, Vol. 58, 1959, pp. 119-129.

reduced by changing one's private position to coincide more nearly with the position expressed.[2]

While the direction of attitude change may thus be understood, what, according to dissonance theory, controls just how much tension the person experiences? Or, more formally, we may ask: What are the factors controlling the magnitude of dissonance created and therefore the magnitude of consequent attitude change? One obvious controlling factor is the importance to the individual of the various cognitions, or bits of information, relevant to his behavior. Other things being equal, the more important to him his private opinion and whatever rewards or punishments that lead him to engage in a discrepant behavior, the greater will be the resulting amount of dissonance. In other words, inducing a person to express a discrepant position on an issue that is very important to him will create more dissonance than inducing him to express a discrepant position on a trivial issue.

Festinger's theory states that the cognitions that lead to the behavior are consonant with it. Those that deter the behavior are dissonant with it. A second, and more central, determinant of the amount of dissonance is, then, the ratio of dissonant to consonant cognitions. The greater this ratio, the greater will be the dissonance. In regard to a discrepant behavioral stand or opinion expression, the greater the importance and number of cognitions against having made it compared to the importance and number for it, the greater will be the dis-

2 L. Festinger, *A Theory of Cognitive Dissonance*, Evanston, Ill., Row, Peterson, 1957. The stimulation for the studies to be discussed comes from Festinger's theoretical statement. Most of the data were collected to test inferences made on the basis of these derivations.

sonance. It follows that if a person has a private opinion on an issue and is induced to behave in a way which is discrepant from it, then the greater the number and importance of cognitions leading to the discrepant behavior, the less will be the amount of dissonance produced. Or, to put it another way, the more compelling the reasons for taking the discrepant stand, the less will be the dissonance created by taking it.

Fortunately, there are many ways in which the individual can reduce dissonance. He can, in general, change any or all of the cognitions so that they will lead more strongly to the expression made. He can increase the felt importance of the intrinsic rewards or punishments that led to the discrepant behavior. And, more importantly for our interests, he can reduce or completely eliminate his dissonance by changing his private opinion so that it is more consistent with the expression made.

It is expected that the greater the amount of dissonance, the stronger will be the attempts to reduce it. Since dissonance can be reduced by attitude change, we should be able to predict the amount of attitude change as a function of the variables that control the amount of dissonance created. Thus, given the expression of opinion discrepant from the position held privately, the more equal the balance between cognitions leading toward and against the behavior, the greater will be the magnitude of dissonance and consequent attitude change in the direction of the behavior or expression. Finally, we may state the major idea: The greater the number and/or the importance of the cognitions leading to the behavior discrepant from one's private opinion, the less will be the dissonance created and the less will be the consequent amount of attitude change toward the expression or position represented by the behavior. In other words, the more compelling the reasons for taking a public stand that differs from what one really believes, the smaller will be the attitude change toward the expressed position.

We may now summarize our analysis. Whenever one's cognitions about extrinsic forces lead to a public expression different from one's private opinion, dissonance will inevitably result. The amount of dissonance will increase as the general importance of the guiding cognitions increases, and as the balance between the opposing cognitions increases. When a person experiences dissonance he will try to reduce or eliminate it in proportion to its strength. In general, he may do this by making his cognitions more consistent with the expression already made. Thus, one major consequence will be a change in one's private opinion to make it more consistent with the position expressed. And, finally, as the imbalance of cognitions leading to the alternate expressions becomes greater, the amount of dissonance and consequent attitude change will be smaller.

Let us now examine some evidence relevant to these theoretical considerations and see what additional issues important to communication and attitude change emerge.

RESEARCH EVIDENCE

Motivational Determinants of Cognitive Dissonance and Consequent Attitude Change

The foregoing analysis leaves some question as to what cognitions lead to an opinion expression or behavior discrepant from that privately held. One cognition is the promise of a reward or prize with monetary value. If the value of such a prize is meaningful, people can be induced to behave publicly in a way that is inconsistent with what they privately believe. In all the previously cited experiments, in which persons were induced to express positions discrepant from their private opinions, opinion change in the direction of the induced position was found. More specific evidence comes from the experiment by Kelman in which he induced children to write essays discrepant from their private opinions.[3] In one of his conditions everyone who wrote a discrepant essay was to get a prize, while in the other only the few best essays would earn a prize. Festinger has pointed out that certainty of getting a prize is a more compelling reason for compliance than is the uncertainty of a competitive situation and should consequently produce less dissonance and resultant opinion change.[4] Kelman does indeed report less opinion change where his subjects were certain of getting the prize, but he and others[5] have maintained that the opinion change he obtained, as well as that in the other previously cited experiments, may result simply from a person's persuading himself, much as a communicator might. In support of this explanation, the average essay strength, in terms of number of

3 Kelman, *op. cit.*
4 Festinger, *op. cit.*
5 Janis and King, *op. cit.*

arguments, in Kelman's experiment was greater in the condition that produced the most opinion change. What was needed, therefore, was an unequivocal test of each explanation.

An experiment by Brehm, generally patterned along the lines of Kelman's experiment, appears to give clear support to the dissonance theory analysis.[6] Junior high school students were asked to indicate on a questionnaire how they would like it if summer vacations were shortened to eight weeks, five weeks, or eliminated altogether. To each of these questions they were to check one answer of a seven-point scale ranging from, "I'm very much in favor of it," to "I'm very much against it." Though this questionnaire required their names, the essentially anonymous nature of it was stressed.

One week later the actual experiment was conducted. Four experimental conditions were created. The first was a control in which subjects were simply asked to fill out the questionnaires again, this time without putting their names on them. There was, of course, a method of identifying them. In the other three conditions the experimenter said he wanted to know what reasons the students might have for wanting shorter vacations. He said he was therefore willing to give a prize to anyone who would write a strong essay in favor of shorter vacations. In order to vary the imbalance of cognitions leading to and from compliance with the request, the magnitude of the prize value was varied. In the low-value condition, subjects could have any one of the following: a phonograph record, a movie ticket, or a ticket to a skating rink; in the medium-value condition they could have two of these; and in the high-value condition they could have four. Anyone who wanted could write in favor of keeping vacations long, but he would not get a prize. After the subjects completed their essays, they filled out the questionnaires again, without signing them.

In short, then, students were induced to write statements against their private opinions, in one case for an attractive prize, in a second, for a very attractive prize, and in a third, for an extremely attractive prize. Their private attitudes on the issue, their judgment about the fairness of giving prizes for compliance, and their perception of experimenter friendliness were measured before and after the induced behavior.

We might expect, according to dissonance theory, that, as the prize value increases, one's private opinion becomes relatively less important, thereby creating less and less dissonance. The results indicate this is indeed what happens. Persons complying for the high-value prize show less attitude change in the direction of compliance than do those in the medium- or low-value conditions.

It should be noticed that this effect is difficult to explain in terms of verbal self-persuasion. The analysis of essay strength in terms of number of words and arguments per essay indicates that as prize value increases there is a very slight, generally nonsignificant, trend for essay strength to increase. Thus this small trend for essay strength to increase is accompanied by less, rather than more, opinion change.[7]

Another experiment by Festinger and Carlsmith was designed to test similar derivations from the theory.[8] Subjects were given a very boring experience and then paid to tell someone that the experience had been interesting and enjoyable. After varying amounts of money were paid to the subjects, their private opinions concerning the experience were determined. The results show that if a person is induced to say something contrary to his private opinion, the larger the financial inducement, the weaker will be the tendency to change his opinion to correspond with what he has said.

Other research by Cohen, Brehm, and Fleming has shown that another type of inducing force has consequences for dissonance and attitude change.[9] College students were re-

---

[6] The theoretical account in the previous section and this brief description of Brehm's experiment on forced verbal compliance were adapted from a speech given by Brehm at the 1957 meeting of the American Association for Public Opinion Research, held in Washington, D.C. (J. W. Brehm, "Forced Verbal Compliance and Attitude Change," New Haven, Conn., Yale University, 1957, unpublished manuscript.)

[7] In general, however, where inducement varies, an attempt is made through experimental controls to keep essay strength constant. This makes it difficult to interpret the results in terms of self-persuasion or differing involvement.

[8] L. Festinger and J. M. Carlsmith, "Cognitive Consequences of Forced Compliance," *Journal of Abnormal and Social Psychology*, Vol. 58, 1959, pp. 203-210.

[9] A. R. Cohen, J. W. Brehm, and W. H. Fleming, "Attitude Change and Justification for Compliance," *Journal of Abnormal and Social Psychology*, Vol. 56, 1958, pp. 276-278.

quested to write essays supporting a position opposite to their own on a current-event issue. In one condition, they were given minimal reasons for writing the discrepant essay, while in another they were given numerous reasons, for example, that it would help the experimenter and social science, that everyone should cooperate, and that the college authorities were interested. The assumption was that each argument would add a compelling reason for performing the discrepant act so that the inducing force would be greater in the high-justification condition than in the low-justification condition. As expected, greater dissonance and consequent attitude change toward the discrepant position occurred in the low-justification condition. A further study by Rabbie, Brehm, and Cohen provides similar evidence concerning the inverse relationship between justification for taking a discrepant stand and attitude change toward that stand.[10]

A further derivation from the theory concerns the amount of discrepant behavior engaged in. It would seem that, other factors held constant, the amount of dissonance created will be a function of the amount of disliked behavior engaged in. Dissonance may be reduced by decreasing the magnitude of dislike (or increasing the magnitude of liking) for the behavior.

The experiments mentioned above were concerned with verbal processes. Another experiment, by Brehm, was designed to test some predictions concerning attitude change as a function of overt behavioral compliance.[11] Eighth-grade boys and girls were induced to eat a vegetable they had previously indicated they heartily disliked. For those who were told that the vegetable had low food value, the more they had to eat the more they liked it. Thus the dissonance engendered by choosing to eat a disliked vegetable can be reduced or eliminated by making one's attitude more consistent with one's behavior.

Taken together, these results clearly support the applicability of dissonance theory to this problem. When an individual is induced to make a public stand different from what he privately believes, dissonance or psychological tension will result. This tension will tend to be great where the balance between the opposing cognitions is about equal. The more compelling the forces leading to the discrepant expression, the less tension will result from making the discrepant expression. Thus increasing rewards or justifications for taking a discrepant stand will lead to decreasing dissonance; decreasing the motivation (beyond that necessary to elicit the behavior) will lead to greater dissonance. In any case, whenever the tension does exist, it can be relieved by making one's private opinion more consistent with the view expressed; the greater the dissonance the greater the attitude change.

The Importance of Choice

The assumptions presented above point to phenomena of post-decision behavior, to what happens to the person's attitude after he has chosen to comply with the request to engage in discrepant behavior. It should therefore be apparent that dissonance theory has explicit implications for situations of "free choice," where the person chooses between alternatives. According to this theory, all cognitive elements that favor the chosen alternative are consonant and all cognitive elements that favor the unchosen alternative are dissonant. Other things being equal, the greater the number of elements favoring the unchosen alternative (the greater its relative attractiveness), the greater the resulting dissonance. Dissonance can be reduced by making the chosen alternative more desirable and the unchosen alternative less desirable after choice than they were before.

Brehm and Brehm and Cohen have shown that an increase in the magnitude of dissonance and consequent pressure to reduce it by increasing the relative attractiveness of the chosen alternative depend at least upon (1) an increase in the degree to which the alternatives approach equal desirability, (2) a greater number of alternatives, and (3) greater qualitative dissimilarity or lack of cognitive overlap among alternatives.[12]

Given the centrality of the act of choice in

10 J. M. Rabbie, J. W. Brehm, and A. R. Cohen, "Verbalization and Reactions to Cognitive Dissonance," *Journal of Personality*, Vol. 27, 1959, pp. 407-417.

11 J. W. Brehm, "Attitudinal Consequences of Commitment to Unpleasant Behavior," *Journal of Abnormal and Social Psychology*, in press.

12 J. W. Brehm, "Post-decision Changes in the Desirability of Alternatives," *Journal of Abnormal and Social Psychology*, Vol. 52, 1956, pp. 384-389; J. W. Brehm and A. R. Cohen, "Re-evaluation of Choice Alternatives as a Function of Their Number and Qualitative Similarity," *Journal of Abnormal and Social Psychology*, Vol. 58, 1959, pp. 373-378.

either selecting an alternative or complying to an induced discrepant behavior, the question arises as to the importance of the act of volition for the creation of cognitive dissonance. The theory certainly implies that a person who is *forced* to behave in a manner he would avoid if he could experiences no dissonance. In this case maximum force would be motivationally equivalent to maximum financial inducement, and both should produce little consequent attitude change. On the other hand, a *fait accompli*, i.e. an event beyond the person's control, might conceivably produce dissonance if the same event would have led to the opposite behavior had it been predictable at the choice point.

Brehm reports an experiment in which a *fait accompli* does appear to have increased cognitive dissonance.[13] The previously mentioned study on behavioral compliance provided a framework for testing this hypothesis. The theoretical expectations were that if a person is induced by the promise of a small prize to eat a disliked food he should experience dissonance. A person who is experiencing dissonance should try, in proportion to its magnitude, to reduce it by convincing himself that he likes the food more than he originally thought. If, then, *after the initial decision to eat has occurred,* a *fait accompli* shows him that he must expect to eat more, and this is accompanied by increased liking, it may be concluded that a *fait accompli* can affect the magnitude of dissonance. Thus, after the eighth-grade children were induced to eat the disliked vegetable, some were additionally told, while eating, that their parents would learn what vegetable they had eaten, with the implication that they would have to eat more at home; others were told nothing further. A questionnaire measured liking before and after the experiment. It was found that the *fait accompli* of implied further eating produced a greater increase in attitude change toward liking the vegetable.

Thus, Brehm's experiment demonstrates that a chance event can affect the magnitude of dissonance. However, since choice was not varied it is not clear whether the effects of such an event depend upon there having been a prior relevant choice. Brehm and Cohen report an experiment designed to explore some of these

limiting conditions under which dissonance, and consequent attitude change, is produced.[14] In their experiment, perceived choice in submitting to an unpleasant event and a chance relative deprivation introduced after commitment were varied. Subjects were asked to and did commit themselves to a very disagreeable and time-consuming project. The results indicated that, under conditions of low perceived choice, the more relative deprivation they suffered, the more negative were their attitudes toward the project. The authors interpret this as a straightforward effect of motivation. However, under conditions of high perceived choice, the more relative deprivation the subjects suffered, the more *positive* were their attitudes toward the event. The latter effect is a clear expectation from dissonance theory: A person who chooses to behave in a way he would ordinarily avoid experiences dissonance; the more unpleasant the induced behavior, the greater the magnitude of dissonance and the greater the consequent attitude change in order to reduce it. Thus, a chance event or a *fait accompli* may be seen to affect the magnitude of dissonance in taking a discrepant position, but presumably only under conditions of high prior choice.

A further experiment by Cohen, Terry, and Jones also demonstrates the importance of choice.[15] It shows that at least some prior decision in which the person commits himself to a general negative situation is necessary for the creation of dissonance. In this experiment, choice in exposure to counterpropaganda was varied and the person's opinion on a salient attitude dimension was measured. Half the subjects who were extreme in their opinions and half who were moderate were exposed to information which they knew to be counter to their positions; the other halves of these groups were given a choice about exposing themselves to the contrary information. After exposure, their opinions were measured again. The results show that under conditions of low choice a direct resistance effect was obtained: the greater the discrepancy between the propa-

[13] J. W. Brehm, "Increasing Cognitive Dissonance by a *Fait Accompli*," *Journal of Abnormal and Social Psychology*, Vol. 58, 1959, pp. 379-382.

[14] J. W. Brehm and A. R. Cohen, "Choice and Chance Relative Deprivation as Determinants of Cognitive Dissonance," *Journal of Abnormal and Social Psychology*, Vol. 58, 1959, pp. 383-387.

[15] A. R. Cohen, H. I. Terry, and C. B. Jones, "Attitudinal Effects of Choice in Exposure to Counterpropaganda," *Journal of Abnormal and Social Psychology*, Vol. 58, 1959, pp. 388-391.

ganda and their initial opinion, the less the attitude change. However, under conditions of high choice, expectations from dissonance theory were fulfilled: Having chosen to behave in a discrepant fashion (chosen to expose themselves to contrary information), the greater the discrepancy between the information and their initial opinion the greater the dissonance and consequent attitude change.

An interesting experiment by Davis and Jones also illustrates the importance of prior choice in creating dissonance.[16] In this experiment, subjects changed their attitudes to become more negative toward a stimulus person, after publicly making a negative evaluation of him, only when they were given some choice in engaging in the behavior and assumed that their behavior was irrevocable (i.e. they did not anticipate explaining the behavioral deception to the stimulus person).

It should be clear that, in all these experiments, though choice is manipulated, subjects do not select themselves in complying or not complying. Although the subject perceives that he has a great deal of choice, he is not permitted to escape from the experimental situation. This eliminates the bias of self-selection. All subjects comply, even though, depending upon the experimental condition to which they are assigned, they may differ in their perceptions of choice in compliance. This issue will be discussed more fully later.

In any case, these experiments indicate that the perception of commitment to a choice may be a necessary precondition for the creation of cognitive dissonance. Where choice is varied, expectations from dissonance theory are fulfilled only under high-choice conditions; under low-choice conditions, straightforward motivational or resistance effects seem to account for the results. These findings imply that the mechanism through which variations in motivational inducements are operating in producing variations in attitude change may conceivably be the person's subjective perception of the choice he has in submitting or exposing himself to the undesirable event. Thus, it is possible that large rewards give the person the feeling that he cannot turn down the request. Small rewards, just over the threshold necessary to induce the discrepant behavior, may raise the subject's subjective perception of choice, i.e. raise the issue of his own control over the situation. Having chosen to take the discrepant stand, for whatever reason, there is dissonance between the event and his own actions in committing himself to it. The less the reward when he complies, perhaps the greater the subjective perception of choice, and the greater the consequent dissonance and attitude change.

These speculations are based only upon the most general inferences from the research discussed. To be more certain about these notions, it would be necessary to demonstrate two relationships: that variations in reward *do* lead to variations in subjective perception of choice; and that variations in choice *do* lead to variations in attitude change.

An experiment by Cohen and Brehm deals with this issue by studying the effects of coercive inductions.[17] It is clear from the data that variations in coercion (as means of inducing compliance in taking a discrepant stand) do lead to variations in perceived choice and attitude change. But the fact that coercion has complex effects depending upon the perceived reasonableness of the situation and the perceived legitimacy of the coercive agent made worthwhile a further but more simple demonstration using positive inducements.

On this point, Cohen performed two pilot experiments which are related in that they are both concerned with the variable of perceived choice in situations where persons comply to undesirable events.[18] In the first experiment, reward was manipulated, the subject took a discrepant stand by writing an essay against his own position on a salient issue, and his perceived choice as well as his attitude change on the issue were measured. In the second experiment, choice was manipulated directly, the subject took a discrepant stand by making a recorded speech against his position on another issue, and his attitude change was measured. The data tentatively confirm the above hypotheses. They indicate that the lower the financial inducements for taking the discrepant position, the greater may be the subjective perception

---

[16] K. E. Davis and E. E. Jones, "Changes in Interpersonal Perception as a Means of Reducing Cognitive Dissonance," *Journal of Abnormal and Social Psychology*, in press.

[17] A. R. Cohen and J. W. Brehm, "Coercion, Choice and Attitude Change," Yale University, 1958, unpublished manuscript.

[18] A. R. Cohen, "Forced Compliance through Positive Inducements, Perceived Choice and Attitude Change," New York University, 1959, unpublished manuscript.

of choice, and the greater the perception of choice in taking the discrepant stand, the greater may be the attitude change toward the discrepant position.

Thus it would seem that a good many of the experiments in which dissonance has been produced and studied can be integrated under the general rubric of situations in which there is subjective perception of choice. Examples of such experiments are: free-choice situations in which subjects choose between alternatives;[19] forced-compliance studies like those of Brehm, Festinger and Carlsmith, and Cohen, where rewards have been used;[20] experiments where deprivations and coercions have been manipulated to produce compliance;[21] studies where justification inducements have been used;[22] and studies in which choice in exposure to counter-propaganda has been manipulated.[23] The use of such a rubric might make possible more general theoretical statements. While the dissonance formulation as it stands deals with bundles of cognitions in opposition and is conceptualized at a very abstract level, a more adequate formulation might point to the conflict within the person as different aspects of his self become embroiled in opposition as a result of a choice or commitment on his part.

THEORETICAL STATUS OF DISSONANCE RESEARCH: PROBLEMS AND LIMITATIONS

The research mentioned above illustrates the power of the dissonance formulation to explain attitudinal effects of commitment to discrepant and other positions which produce dissonance. However, a number of problems should cause us to accept the general case with some caution. In the present section some of these problems and limitations will be briefly mentioned.

The Specificity of Decision

One limitation in the present research centers around the necessity in the dissonance formu-

lation to be pro or con and to take a clear stand on a contrary issue. While dissonance theory may work well where there are such clear-cut alternatives, it may not be so helpful where compromise positions may be taken. It seems reasonable that dissonance reduction via attitude change is dependent upon the individual's decision to commit himself to a discrepant position.

The Psychology of Choice

A related but more serious question concerns the theoretical status of choice. It is often not clear from the theory and experimental work just what creates the basic state of tension or dissonance. It is, for example, the discrepancy between a prior attitude and an undesirable behavior which creates dissonance or the discrepancy between a prior attitude and the individual's feelings of responsibility for having chosen to do something contrary to his cognitions? These issues raise the question of whether it is necessary to extend the conceptualization of dissonance into the sphere of conflicts within the individual as his self-feelings become engaged after having initiated behavior which is contrary to his cognitions. Another relevant question concerns the possible similarities and distinctions between the psychological processes involved in choice and those involved in commitment. Most generally, these issues concern more rigorous specification of just "what" the individual is choosing to do when he agrees, for example, to comply with or commit himself to a discrepant event.

Conflict versus Dissonance

Another difficult problem concerns the dual theoretical notions of conflict and dissonance. With regard to the free-choice situations, a conflict interpretation might claim that re-evaluation of alternatives occurs before choice, thereby changing the approach-avoidance gradients for the alternatives, and allowing finer discriminations so that a choice can be made. While both predecisional re-evaluation before choice owing to resolution of conflict and post-decisional re-evaluation after choice owing to resolution of dissonance undoubtedly occur, it is not clear to which process and therefore to which theoretical notion the major share of re-evaluation may be attributed. More realistically, it is at least important to specify the conditions under which one or the other process might be expected to occur.

---

[19] Brehm, "Post-decision Changes in the Desirability of Alternatives"; Brehm and Cohen, "Re-evaluation of Choice Alternatives."

[20] Brehm, "Forced Verbal Compliance and Attitude Change"; Festinger and Carlsmith, *op. cit.*; Cohen, "Forced Compliance through Positive Inducements, Perceived Choice and Attitude Change."

[21] Brehm and Cohen, "Choice and Chance Relative Deprivation"; Cohen and Brehm, "Coercion, Choice and Attitude Change."

[22] Cohen, Brehm, and Fleming, *op. cit.*; Rabbie, Brehm, and Cohen, *op. cit.*

[23] Cohen, Terry, and Jones, *op. cit.*

It is also possible to attempt an interpretation of the forced-compliance studies through the use of conflict theory assumptions. However, this would involve a coordination of the conceptual variables of conflict theory to those of dissonance theory. For example, as Brehm indicates, the dependent variables of attitude change would have to be directly related to the approach and avoidance gradients using reinforcement principles or they would have to be related to an assumed intermediate motive that might be called "conflict tension."[24] In any case, the task is a difficult one primarily because there exists no one conflict theory and because what exists has not laid the groundwork for the application of reinforcement principles to the effects of choice among alternatives. Nevertheless, this would appear to be an area for future crucial theory and experimentation.

Alternative Methods of Dissonance Reduction

While the theory predicts attitude change because of its assumption that behavior is relatively fixed and attitudes relatively flexible, it does not specify which of several methods of dissonance reduction other than attitude change might be expected in a given instance. In most of the studies cited, persons were experimentally prevented from dissociating themselves from their remarks, from repudiating their behavior, from leaving the field, from making negative attributions to others, from repudiating the experimenter, and so forth. (Zimbardo's paper illustrates the problems involved in closing off other avenues of dissonance reduction.[25]) However, since these are all devices for reducing the tension aroused by discrepant behaviors, specification of their comparative utilization depending upon the individual and upon situational limitations should be more explicitly built into the theory. Thus, for example, it might be possible to relate given ego-defensive behavior to a given method of dissonance reduction, as characteristic individual reactions to tension or conflict in discrepant situations. A recent experiment by Brock has made a beginning along these general lines: it deals with the restructuring of cognitive organization as an alternative to dissonance reduction through attitude change.[26]

Creating the Conditions for Choice

Still another problem concerns the experimental fostering of the individual's belief that he has relative freedom of choice about whether or not he complies with the discrepant request. If the person feels that he has been coerced, little dissonance and consequent attitude change will result. On the other hand, if subjects are actually allowed to agree or disagree freely with the request to comply, few may comply. After all, why should anyone agree to support a position with which he disagrees or engage in behavior which is unpleasant to him? To the degree that some people are allowed to refuse and some to comply, self-selection becomes a serious limitation of the experiment. Therefore, a great deal of experimental ingenuity must be exercised if the subject is to be made to feel that the choice is his, while at the same time the experimenter must be careful not to allow him to slip out of the experiment. Depending upon the experimental situation,[27] different procedures have been adopted to cope with this problem.

Definitions and Conceptualizations

For the most part, the above studies have made the most general assumptions about the conceptualization of cognition, attitude, opinion, choice, and so forth. Emphasis has usually been placed on the prior conditions of dissonance creation and their effects upon a verbal statement of opinion. The task of defining attitude as distinct from opinion, or the explicit separation of public from private opinion, has not been taken up here. Obviously, this imposes a limitation on the present research which, it is hoped, future work on communication and attitude change will correct.

Alternative Explanations

In a number of the studies mentioned, there are particular problems of interpretation. For example, in the "effort" and "choice in exposure" experiments, communication discrepancy was effected not through experimental manipulation but through premeasure of the subjects' attitudes. Because of this, it is possible to ascribe the effects in the high-choice and high-effort

24 Brehm, "Attitudinal Consequences of Commitment to Unpleasant Behavior."

25 Zimbardo, op. cit.

26 T. Brock, "The Role of Cognitive Restructuring in the Attitude Change Process," New Haven, Yale University, 1960, unpublished doctoral dissertation.

27 E.g. Festinger and Carlsmith, op. cit., and Cohen, "Forced Compliance through Positive Inducements, Perceived Choice and Attitude Change."

conditions not to dissonance but, for example, to an acquiescence effect. Thus, subjects in these conditions could have been disposed to take the counterpropaganda more seriously because they had chosen to expose themselves to it or felt that they had expended effort to understand it. They would then change more, the more change possibilities were inherent in their initial scale positions. A more satisfactory procedure, which would close off such an alternative explanation, would be to manipulate communication discrepancy through presentation of contrary communications of different strengths to subjects at all initial scale positions.

It is particularly tempting to concoct "personality explanations" for the results presented in the foregoing pages. Such reinterpretations could center around factors like "defensive rationalizations of conflicts occasioned by compliance" or "common personality sources of discrepant expression and various forms of attitude change." The difficulties with such alternative explanations are:

1. They are often *post hoc;* in such cases a reconstruction can be attempted only when a behavioral datum is given beforehand. It is usually difficult to point to any given behavior in advance as relevant or interesting or predictable.

2. Such explanations usually focus on restricted aspects of the experimental situation, often ignoring the situational factors which place demands and limits upon the individual.

3. They are nonspecific, in that they can usually be applied to most experimental situations, without necessarily distinguishing from other situations those typically dissonance-producing situations in which post-decision behavior is treated.

4. They usually involve different kinds of explanation for each particular experiment, so that an interpretation involving a given defense may be applied to one experiment, a different defense applied to another, a given conflict to a third, and hostility, for example, to a fourth.

5. The personality mechanisms isolated are not necessarily coordinate to the dissonance situation. Why, for example, should a "randomly chosen" psychosexual conflict or ego defense necessarily have implications for reactions to discrepant situations? The personality construct studied ought to be tailored to the dissonance-producing situation. Thus the selection of some notion like "need for cognitive consistency," for example, where the cue-arousing properties of the situation are especially relevant for the internal characteristic, might increase explanatory power.

In any case, it should be said that though there may be problems of interpretation in any experiment, the results of all experiments tend to be consistent with each other and with the theoretical model from which they were derived. The virtue of the dissonance formulation is that the different experiments are derived from and assimilated to a fairly general body of propositions.

Tolerance for Dissonance

The discussion above does not imply that "personality" explanations are valueless and irrelevant to the present discussion. One can isolate personality constructs which may be theoretically coordinate to the dissonance phenomena and particularly appropriate to study in interaction with them, rather than select an "arbitrary" construct from "general personality theory." Festinger, for example, has discussed the variable of what he calls "tolerance for dissonance," a personality variable which he feels has implications for behavior in dissonance-producing situations.[28] Individuals might be expected to differ in the magnitude of a given reaction like attitude change depending upon how much dissonance was created in them by a forced-compliance situation. The experiments discussed here have not studied individual differences in the degree to which dissonance is experienced in a given dissonance-producing situation. However, specification of these different personality styles might sharpen predictions about behavior in such situations.

28 Festinger, *op. cit.,* pp. 266-271.

37. Symbolic Psycho-Logic: A Model of Attitudinal Cognition

ROBERT P. ABELSON and MILTON J. ROSENBERG

Several lines of theoretical and research interest have gradually been converging upon the study of "cognitive structure," especially in the area of social attitudes. Attitudes, by the definitions of Smith, Bruner and White (15), Peak (12), Rosenberg (14), Green (6) and many others, involve both affective and cognitive components. These components interact intimately with one another, so that cognitions about attitudinal objects are not felt to be meaningfully analyzable without consideration of affective forces. Theorists are reluctant even to consider cognitive units of an attitude apart from other cognitive units, preferring to treat cognition as "structured" into meaningful wholes (10, 16). Krech and Crutchfield (9, p. 152) define attitude globally as "an enduring organization of motivational, emotional, perceptual and cognitive processes with respect to some aspect of the individual's world." They state (p. 108) "Each of our perceptions does not lead 'a life of its own' but is embedded in an organization of other perceptions—the whole making up a specific cognitive structure." Smith, Bruner, and White (15, p. 286), in discussing attitude measurement, caution, "Recent advances in the theory and technique of attitude measurement . . . have yet to take this complexity [of opinions] into account. Characteristically, they have conceived of attitudes as a matter of pro-ness and con-ness. . . . We would question whether it is reasonable to expect them to generate the dimensions required for an adequate description of opinion. [An adequate description] comes rather from intensive explorations. . . ." Asch (2) is another author who has employed a holistic concept of attitude structure. He seeks to explain certain attitude change phenomena in terms of the "restructuring" of the attitudinal object (3). Rokeach (13) treats structure as an individual difference variable of cognitive style, defining one extreme, dogmatism, as "a relatively closed cognitive organization of beliefs and disbeliefs about reality . . . which . . . provides a framework for patterns of intolerance and qualified tolerance toward others."

This Gestalt emphasis, motivated by the desire to construct an accurate model of the phenomenal organization of attitudes, has underscored the difficulties inherent in attempts to deal analytically with a set of cognitive units or elements. Nevertheless, if psychologists are to talk about "cognitive structure," they must do something about it; there must be a correspondence between theory and some sort of research operation. At least two important recent theoretical developments, Festinger's (5) "dissonance theory," and Heider's (7) "theory of cognitive balance," deal conceptually with the effects of organizing forces and affective forces upon cognitive elements. Both theories are concerned with changes in cognitive structure. Festinger's theory deals mainly with inconsistencies between belief and action, and attempts to specify certain circumstances under which there will be more or less change in belief as an outgrowth of cognitive "dissonance," due to such inconsistencies. The research operations which are used to test Festinger's theory are not addressed to the details of cognitive structure, but rather to single-response predictions derivative from the theory. Heider's theory is addressed to structural details of cognition, but there has been no research operation available to investigate these details with particular attitude contents. On the other hand, the recently proposed methodological devices of Rosenberg (14) and Abelson (1) are not completely anchored in a general theory of attitudes. A fresh approach to the measurement of cognitive structure is clearly called for.

This paper proposes one such approach. We have drawn some inspiration from Cartwright

• Excerpted from *Behavioral Science*, 1958, **3**, 1-8, with permission of the senior author and the publisher.

and Harary's (4) objective system for the examination of "structural balance," from Heider's (7) ideas on cognitive balance, and are also intellectually indebted to Zajonc (17), who has suggested clever procedural devices in eliciting cognitive material. Otherwise, the system to be proposed is our own, albeit with a strong historical tether. The paper is divided into two parts: the "Psychological Model" and the "Mathematical System."

THE PSYCHOLOGICAL MODEL

Cognitive Elements

Human thought, for all its complexity and nuance, must involve some cognitive representation of "things," concrete and abstract. These things or concepts are the *elements* of our system. Though it does not seem absolutely necessary, we shall for convenience assume that individuals can attach some sore of verbal labels to the elements of their thinking. We will refer, then, to cognitive elements by verbal labels.

We may distinguish three broad classes of elements: Actors, Means (Actions, Intrumentalities), and Ends (Outcomes, Values). These classes are not completely exhaustive nor mutually exclusive. We propose this classification merely to suggest the variety of possible cognitive elements. To exemplify each class, consider

the illustrative issue: "Having an honor system at Yale." The following elements were among those frequently elicited from Yale students in a pilot study.

Actors: myself, the Faculty, the Administration, the Student Body, a certain minority of students, the honest student. . . .

Means: the honor system, other honor systems, the present examination system, cheating, reporting those who cheat, social pressure from other students. . . .

Ends: the feeling of being trusted, mature moral standards, loyalty to friends, the University's reputation, having well-run examinations. . . .

Note that all elements are expressed here substantively to reflect their "thing-like" character.

Cognitive Relations

Of all the conceivable relations between cognitive elements, we choose to consider only four: *positive, negative, null,* and *ambivalent.* These will be denoted p, n, o, and a. (See also "Mathematical System.") We again conveniently assume that cognitive materials of a relational sort can be verbally labeled. Some typical examples of relations between elements are shown in Table 1. Ambivalent relations (a) are defined

TABLE 1.

		Positive (p)	Negative (n)	Null (o)
Actor vs.	Actor	likes; supports	dislikes; fights	is indifferent to
	Means	uses; advocates	opposes; undermines	is not responsible for
	End	possesses; aims for	inhibits; aims against	is indifferent to
Means vs.	Actor	helps; promotes	hinders; insults	does not affect
	Means	is equivalent to	is alternative to; counteracts	is unrelated to
	End	brings about	prevents	does not lead to
End vs.	Actor	serves; is vital to	is inimical to	does not interest
	Means	justifies	obviates	cannot ensue from
	End	is consistent with	is incompatible with	is unconnected to

as conjunctions of positive and negative relations; they are psychologically secondary or "derived," and have been omitted from the table.

Note that relations are expressed here as verbs.

Certain omissions from the above scheme may occur to the reader. Relations like "is next in line to," "is north of," etc. are certainly not included. Other phrases which imply relationship without specifying its sign, e.g., "depends upon," "is connected with," etc., are difficult to classify. Furthermore, notions of time sense, moral imperative, and conditionality or probability, e.g., "might have acted upon," "probably will help," "ought to seek," etc., are not dealt with explicitly. Time sense and conditionality are beyond the scope of the present treatment. We deal here only with cognitions of the psychological present, and temporarily set aside the past, conditional past, future, and conditional future. As for the other exceptions to the scheme, note that their phrasing tends to be affectless. Dispassionate descriptions of, say, the mating habits of flamingoes or the operation of a nuclear reactor or the economic situation in Viet Nam would probably contain many relations impossible to classify. But such descriptions are reportorial, not attitudinal. When cognition is invested with affect, when the Actors, Means, and Ends are responded to emotionally, then the relations become classifiable in terms of the present system. Our intent is to be able to code all relations occurring in attitudinal cognitions into these four broad categories.

Cognitive Units or Sentences

Cognitive units are built out of pairs of elements, connected by a relation. That is, the basic "sentences" of attitudinal cognition are of the form

$$A r B$$

where A and B are elements and r is a relation. Many sentences which at first seem more complicated than the simple ArB unit may be reduced to such a unit by broadening the definition of an element. For example, consider the sentence,

"Nasser (A) insists on (p) all Suez tolls (B) belonging to (p) Egypt (C)." (Here p denotes a positive relation.) This sentence, symbolically, is $Ap(BpC)$. But regard (BpC) as a new element D, the broader conception "all Suez tolls be-

longing to Egypt." Then we have simply ApD.

In this way, we reduce our catalogue of basic sentences to four:

$$A\ p\ B$$
$$A\ n\ B$$
$$A\ o\ B$$
$$A\ a\ B$$

The Conceptual Arena. The Structure Matrix

For the convenience of both theory and operation, we conceive of an attitude as being defined over a certain delimited though perhaps large *conceptual arena*. We restrict attention, in other words, to those elements which are (phenomenally) relevant to the given issue or attitude object.

Operationally, what one can do is this. Following Zajonc (17), we ask the subject to list all the words or short phrases that come to mind as he mulls over a given topic, such as "Having an Honor System at Yale" or "The State Department Ban on Reporters Going to Red China." Subjects will typically write several phrases in rapid-fire order, then pause, give one or two more, and finally stop. These words or phrases are not always "noun-like," but by simple instructions to the subject, they can be reworded satisfactorily and be treated subsequently as the cognitive elements. This procedure yields the conceptual arena idiosyncratic to each subject.[1]

After the arena is defined, the relations between pairs of elements may be mapped. We conceptualize a matrix setting forth the relations between each element and every other. This matrix we denote the *structure matrix*, R (see the "Mathematical System"). As an illustration of a structure matrix, consider that shown in Table 2.

The entries in this matrix were elicited by instructing a subject to fill in the *middles* of sentences linking his elements (the six listed). He wrote these "open-middled" sentences:

The honest student *feels very reluctant about* reporting cheaters.
The honest student *possesses* the feeling of being trusted.

---

1 For some experimental purposes, it is more convenient to define a common conceptual arena for a group of subjects. Some topics yield low overlap between subjects, but other topics possess sufficient overlap so that it is worthwhile to construct a group arena encompassing the most generally salient elements.

TABLE 2. Structure Matrix; Topic: Having an Honor System at Yale

	Ego	Honest Student	Report Cheater	Feel Trust	Cheating by Few	Honor System
Ego (the subject himself)	p	p	n	p	n	o
The honest student	p	p	n	p	o	p
Reporting cheaters	n	n	p	o	n	p
Feeling trusted	p	p	o	p	o	p
Cheating by a few	n	o	n	o	p	n
An honor system	o	p	p	p	n	p

The honor system *is fine for* the honest student.

The honor system *promotes* the feeling of being trusted.

Cheating by a few *is cut down by* reporting cheaters.

The honor system *is harmed by* cheating by a few.

The honor system *involves* reporting cheaters.

The verb forms in these sentences were coded[2] into the relations p and n shown in the matrix. In addition, the subject himself was asked whether he felt favorable, neutral, or unfavorable toward each element. His responses are shown in the first row (column) of the matrix in Table 2.

All relations between elements and themselves are taken to be positive. Also, relations are considered to be symmetric; i.e., if ArB, then BrA. Our preliminary work does not suggest a pressing need to revise these assumptions.

The structure matrix is our basic description of attitudinal cognition. One may wish to superimpose further refinements upon the structure such as the intensity of different relations, the confidence with which they are held, time perspective, and so on. In this paper, we can answer only the simplest question, "In what way can the structure matrix be used to characterize the fundamental structural varieties of attitudinal cognition, apart from specific content?"

[2] In order to circumvent the coding problem, one may require the subject to choose his verb forms from a precoded list. This version is presently being attempted. Full details of the entire procedure will be set forth elsewhere.

Thinking. Psycho-Logic

Individual cognitive units may originate in various ways—through exposure to written information, through social pressure, emotional need, thinking, etc. Once originated, these units may be manipulated in thought.

We propose a set of rules by which an individual imputes or discovers new symbolic sentences by combining two old sentences with an element in common. We hypothesize that *these rules apply only when the individual thinks about the topic*, or "rehearses the arguments" (8, p. 129).

Rule 1. ApB and BpC implies ApC.

Rule 2. ApB and BnC implies AnC.

Rule 3. AnB and BnC implies ApC.

Rule 4. AoB and BrC implies nothing about the relation between A and C, irrespective of r.

Rule 5. If ApC and AnC are both implied, or if one is held initially and the other implied, then AaC. This is the definition of the ambivalent relation.

Rule 6. AaC and CpD implies AaD.

Rule 7. AaC and CnD implies AaD.

Rule 8. AaC and CaD implies AaD.

Each rule above has several equivalent forms not listed, arising from the symmetry assumption $ArB = BrA$.

Though we have given formal status to these rules,[3] note that the verbal corollaries are not

[3] The entire set of rules may be organized into one with the aid of Tables 1 and 2 of The "Mathematical System." Letting R denote the structure matrix, derived or imputed sentences may be found from the matrix multiplication of R by itself. The

necessarily logical at all. Exemplify Rule 3 by the sentences:

India (A) opposes (n) U. S. Far Eastern policy (B)

U. S. Far Eastern policy (B) is directed against (n) Communism (C).

Therefore, India (A) is in favor of (p) Communism (C).

Such "reasoning" would mortify a logician, yet it can be found in much this form inside of millions of heads. Thus we speak of the formal system as *psycho-logic* rather than as *logic.*

We assume that thinking about a topic *must be motivated before it will occur.* Some possible motivating conditions[4] would be these:

1. Pressure to reach a decision on the topic.

2. Socially derived needs to appear informed on the topic, to converse well about it, to win over others, etc. Anticipation of the relevant social situations would motivate thinking.

3. Relevance of the topic to needs, conflicts, and persisting preoccupations. Activation of such processes would generate pressure to think.

4. A general "cognitive style" of the individual such that thinking per se is satisfying. For such individuals, mere mention of the topic might motivate thinking.

Suppose that a given individual is motivated to think about a given topic. He already possesses certain relevant cognitive units. Using psycho-logic, he imputes new units. These new units may or may not be compatible with his existing units. Referring back to the India-China example, if the individual had originally thought, "India (A) resists the influence of (n) Communism (C)," then he would be confronted with the coexistence of ApC and AnC. By Rule 5, this is expressed AaC, the ambivalent relation, which might translate back into words thus:

The relationship between India (A) and Red China (C) is very confusing (a).

---

powers R^2, R^3, etc., yield imputations which are successively more removed from the original sentences.

[4] The potency of these various motivating conditions could be subjected to empirical test, using before and after measures of cognitive structure and experimental manipulation of motivating conditions in-between. One such experiment has in fact been carried out by Zajonc (17), using a different theoretical context. See his discussion of "cognitive tuning."

On the other hand, had he originally held ApC, then the imputed sentence ApC would reinforce rather than contradict his original view.

Balance and Imbalance

Certain structure matrices are characterized by the interesting property that no amount of thinking (i.e., imputing of new relations according to the rules above) leads the individual into any inconsistency (i.e., ambivalent relation). The cognitive structures represented by such matrices are said to be *balanced.* When the structure matrix is such that one or more ambivalent relations will be discovered in thinking, the structure is said to be *imbalanced.* (Our statement of the mathematical condition for cognitive balance is given in the "Mathematical System.") In common-sense terms, a balanced cognitive structure represents a "black and white" attitude. The individual views some elements as good and the other elements as bad. All relations among "good elements" are positive (or null), all relations among "bad elements" are positive (or null), and all relations between good and bad elements are negative (or null).

Redressing Imbalance

Heider (7), Festinger (5), Osgood and Tannenbaum (11), and others have postulated that individuals strive to reduce or redress cognitive imbalance, or "dissonance." This is probably especially true for attitudinal cognitions. It is important to note, however, that potential imbalance will remain undiscovered by an individual unless he is motivated to think about the topic and in fact does so. Assuming these necessary preconditions, suppose that an individual does come upon a cognitive inconsistency in his attitude. What can he do about it? Three things:

1. Change one or more of the relations.

2. Redefine, "differentiate," or "isolate" one or more elements.

3. Stop thinking.

A simple example will illustrate the first two methods. The third method is self-explanatory. Take the three elements, E, C, G: Ego (a Yale student), Having Co-eds at Yale, and Getting Good Grades. The subject might tell us:

"I'm for having co-eds at Yale." (EpC)

"I want good grades." (EpG)

"Having co-eds at Yale would undoubtedly interfere with getting good grades." (CnG)

This attitudinal cognition

$$R = \begin{matrix} & \begin{matrix} E & C & G \end{matrix} \\ \begin{matrix} E \\ C \\ G \end{matrix} & \begin{matrix} p & p & p \\ p & p & n \\ p & n & p \end{matrix} \end{matrix}$$

is imbalanced. Never having been forced to take a consistent stand on the issue, however, our subject may readily tolerate (or even be unaware of) this imbalance. Now suppose that the issue is hotly debated and our subject thinks. The imbalance becomes apparent and he seeks a balance-producing resolution.

Method 1. He alters any one of the three relations, by abandoning the desire for good grades, by opposing the admission of co-eds, or by rationalizing to the effect that "Co-eds do not really interfere with getting good grades (in fact, they enhance the chances, etc.)"

Method 2. (The following is one of various possibilities.) He differentiates the concept "Getting good grades" into "Getting A's" and "Getting C's" and then reasons that while co-eds may interfere with getting A's, they don't interfere with getting C's, and what he really wants is not to get A's but to get C's.

It is assumed that under sufficient pressure to continue thinking, the individual will try Methods 1 and 2, presumably seeking a relatively effortless means to achieve balance. If these attempts fail, because certain relations are resistant to change and certain elements are difficult to redefine, the individual may resort to Method 3 which is to stop thinking. If, however, strong pressures, internal or external, do not permit him to stop thinking, he will re-examine the topic, seeking a more complex utilization of either or both of the first two methods. And so on. With extremely strong pressure to continue thinking, some cognitive units will in all probability ultimately yield to one attack or another.[5] With weak pressure and a structure that is highly resistant to change, the individual will most likely stop thinking, and his attitudinal structure will revert to its state before he started thinking.

In other words, we envision an extensive hierarchy of cognitive solutions to the problem of reducing imbalance. Experimental prediction of outcome is extremely difficult under these circumstances, and represents a considerable challenge. The next section presents a

crude preliminary step toward meeting the challenge.

Experimental Prediction of Cognitive Changes

Our present machinery is not refined enough to permit predictions with respect to Method 2 above, "redefining the elements." It would appear feasible, however, to restrict experimentally the availability of this alternative [the arguments of Asch (3) to the contrary] and focus upon Method 1.

The question we pose for ourselves is this: "Given an imbalanced structure[6] with highly stably defined elements, can we predict which particular set of relations in the whole conceptual arena will be changed in order to achieve balance?"

The mathematical system presented later in detail is helpful in providing what we hope will be an approximate answer. In that system, the *complexity of imbalance* of a structure is defined as the *minimum number of changes of relations necessary to achieve balance.*[7] The system also implies a way of identifying which particular changes constitute the minimum set, or, when there are alternative minimal sets, identifies all of them. In addition, the "next to minimal" sets of changes can be identified, and so on.

Working under the highly tentative heuristic assumption that all relations are equally resistant to change, the least effortful balancing operation on an imbalanced structure is the one that requires the fewest changed relations. A predicted set of changes can easily be generated under this assumption.

---

[5] So-called "conversion experiences" may be representative of the extreme case: very extensive cognitive changes are characteristic of this phenomenon.

[6] One may provoke imbalance experimentally by strong persuasive communication aimed at a given cognitive unit. We are presently launching an experiment of this type.

[7] Cartwright and Harary (4) have proposed a different index for degree of structural imbalance. The present index is simpler to compute, and has also the appealing feature that it refers to the dynamic property of change in structure. Harary, in a personal communication, has indicated that he has recently and independently hit upon an index equivalent to the present one. He calls it the "line index of balance." A "line" in his terminology is a relation in our terminology. His "line index of balance" is the minimal number of lines (relations) whose negation yields balance. He points out that negation in the sense of changed sign and negation in the sense of deletion or elimination are equivalent insofar as balancing is concerned. Where we say "change of relation," this may be taken to mean change from p to either n or o, and change from n to either p or o.

TABLE 3

		1	2	3	4	5	6
		Ego	Honest Student	Report Cheater	Feel Trust	Cheat by Few	Honor System
1.	Ego	p	p	n	p	n	o
2.	The honest student	p	p	n	p	o	p
3.	Reporting cheaters	n	n	p	o	n	p
4.	Feeling trusted	p	p	o	p	o	p
5.	Cheating by a few	n	o	n	o	p	n
6.	An honor system	o	p	p	p	n	p

The steps involved in the analysis are:

1. Write down the structure matrix.

2. Find the row (column) with the largest plurality of n's over p's, exclusive of the p in the main diagonal of the matrix. Change all n's to p's and p's to n's, in both the row and the corresponding column (leaving the diagonal entry p unchanged). Ignore the o entries.

3. Repeat the previous step on a new row (column).

4. Continue the change operations on selected rows and columns until the number of n's in the matrix cannot be further reduced.[8]

This irreducible minimum number defines the complexity of imbalance. Duplication due to symmetry is avoided by counting n's on one side of the diagonal only. The entries where the n's appear identify the minimal set. If the minimum number can be attained in more than one way, the sets so identified are alternative "solutions." If the minimum number is zero, then the structure is balanced. The entire procedure is based upon Theorem 13 of the "Mathematical System."

The method will now be illustrated with the Yale student's structure on "Having an honor system at Yale," presented in an earlier section. His structure matrix is shown in Table 3.

[8] A certain amount of trial-and-error may be required before reaching a final decision. This decision is not automatic; the change operation is sometimes useful on a row and column with a plurality of p's over n's—a temporary *increase* in the number of n's can lead to an ultimate further reduction in the minimum number of n's.

Row 5 contains three n's and one p. We then carry out the change operation on Row 5 and Column 5, carrying p into n (except in the diagonal) and n into p. The result is shown in Table 4.

TABLE 4

	1	2	3	4	5	6
1.	p	p	n	p	p	o
2.	p	p	n	p	o	p
3.	n	n	p	o	p	p
4.	p	p	o	p	o	p
5.	p	o	p	o	p	p
6.	o	p	p	p	p	p

Both remaining n's lie in Row 3. Three p's also lie in this row, but one of them is the unchanging diagonal element, so that essentially it is two n's versus two p's. The change operation on Row 3 and Column 3 would yield the matrix shown in Table 5.

TABLE 5

	1	2	3	4	5	6
1.	p	p	p	p	p	o
2.	p	p	p	p	o	p
3.	p	p	p	o	n	n
4.	p	p	o	p	o	p
5.	p	o	n	o	p	p
6.	o	p	n	p	p	p

The number of n's here is also two. It is evident that the number of n's cannot be further reduced by the change operation. It is also evident upon further inspection that no other set of change operations will yield as few as two *n*'s. Thus the structure matrix is of complexity *two* and there are two alternate minimal solutions to the balancing problem.

The first solution tells us that had the subject's initial relations between elements 3 and 1, and 3 and 2 not been as they were, there would not have been any imbalance. In other words, achieving balance requires changing the relations between elements 3 and 1, and elements 3 and 2. Looking back at his original structure matrix, this means that were he to *favor* reporting cheaters, or at least not be opposed, and also regard honest students as favoring or not opposing reporting cheaters, his structure would be balanced. The "good elements" would be *Ego, The honest student, Reporting cheaters, Feeling trusted,* and *The honor system,* while *Cheating by a few* would be a "bad element." In short, "We honest students would all feel trusted in an honor system. A few cheaters might violate the system, but they should be reported."

The second solution tells us that the subject must change the relations between elements 3 and 5, and elements 3 and 6 to achieve balance. In other words, were he to view *Reporting cheaters* as not identified with the honor system, and as in any case ineffective in cutting down *Cheating by a few* his structure would be balanced. *Ego, The honest student, Feeling trusted,* and *The honor system* would be "good elements," and *Reporting cheaters* and *Cheating by a few,* "bad elements." A hypothetical quote would read, "We honest students would all feel trusted in an honor system. A few cheaters might violate the system, but I wouldn't feel right about reporting them and it probably wouldn't work anyway. There are a few lousy guys who will always try to foul things up."

We make no claim that this subject would necessarily make one or the other of these changes in striving for a balanced structure. We only claim that if the strengths of all relations are equal, the above changes would be preferred for their simplicity.

We are now working on various means for empirical measurement of the strength of relations. Incorporation of the strength variable in the model will represent an important refinement.

REFERENCES

1. Abelson, R. P. A technique and a model for multi-dimensional attitude scaling. *Pub. opin. Quart.,* 1954, **18**, 405-418.
2. Asch, S. E. *Social psychology.* New York: Prentice-Hall, 1952.
3. Asch, S. E., Block, H., and Hertzman, M. Studies in the principles of judgments and attitudes: I. Two basic principles of judgment. *J. Psychol.,* 1938, **5**, 219-251.
4. Cartwright, D., and Harary, F. Structural balance: a generalization of Heider's theory. *Psychol. Rev.,* 1956, **63**, 277-293.
5. Festinger, L. *Theory of cognitive dissonance.* Evanston: Row Peterson, 1957.
6. Green, B. F. Attitude measurement. In G. Lindzey (Ed.) *Handbook of social psychology.* Cambridge: Addison-Wesley, 1954.
7. Heider, F. Attitudes and cognitive organization. *J. Psychol.,* 1946, **21**, 107-112.
8. Hovland, C. I., Janis, I. L., and Kelley, H. H. *Communication and persuasion.* New Haven: Yale Univ. Press, 1953.
9. Krech, D., and Crutchfield, R. *Theory and problems of social psychology.* New York: McGraw-Hill, 1948.
10. Lewin, K. *Field theory in social science.* New York: Harper, 1951.
11. Osgood, C. E., and Tannenbaum, P. H. The principal of congruity in the prediction of attitude change. *Psychol. Rev.,* 1955, **62**, 42-55.
12. Peak, H. Attitude and motivation. In M. Jones (Ed.) *Nebraska symposium on motivation, 1955.* Lincoln: Univ. of Nebraska Press, 1955.
13. Rokeach, M. The nature and meaning of dogmatism. *Psychol. Rev.,* 1954, **61**, 194-204.
14. Rosenberg, M. Cognitive structure and attitudinal affect. *J. abnorm. soc. Psychol.,* 1956, **53**, 367-372.
15. Smith, M. B., Bruner, J. S., and White, R. W. *Opinions and personality.* New York: Wiley, 1956.
16. Tolman, E. C. *Purposive behavior in animals and men.* New York: Century, 1932.
17. Zajonc, R. B. Structure of cognitive field. Unpublished doctoral dissertation, Univ. of Michigan, 1954.

38. Modes of Resolution of Belief Dilemmas

ROBERT P. ABELSON

INTRODUCTION

This is a paper about intrapersonal conflict resolution. We first identify the kind of conflict to be considered.

There are two levels of analysis of intrapersonal conflict: the action level and the belief level, the former dealing with external motor responses and the latter with internal affective and cognitive processes. Particular instances of conflict may, for theoretical convenience, be localized at one or another of these levels. For example, one may ask how a person acts when simultaneously motivated to approach and to avoid an external object (3, 9, 10). Or one may ask instead what happens to the cognitive representation of an external object when the object simultaneously incurs favorable and unfavorable cognitions (12). The present paper is addressed to the latter type of question. We shall not consider the problem of whether and how the action level is to be reduced to the belief level or vice versa. We only consider conflicts between one belief and another or, more generally, conflicts within a belief structure. The term "belief dilemma" is intended to enforce the distinction between the variety of conflict here considered and conflict in general.

BELIEF DILEMMAS

The model of cognitive structure to be described is similar at various points to other recent models (6, 8, 13).

First, we imagine a cognitive representation, a "cognitive element," corresponding to any attitude object. Associated with such a cognitive element is a numerical value, positive if the

• Reprinted from *Journal of Conflict Resolution*, 1959, 3, 343-352, with the permission of the author and the publisher.

object is liked, negative if the object is disliked. Next, we suppose that between each pair of cognitive elements there may exist some kind of perceived relation. Assigned to each relation is another numerical value, positive if the relation is "associative," negative if the relation is "dissociative" (11). Examples of associative relations are: is, has, includes, likes, helps, produces, implies. Examples of dissociative relations are: avoids, hates, hinders, defeats, destroys, is incompatible with. A zero value indicates a null, or irrelevant, relation.

Given an attitude issue or "conceptual arena" (1), a certain set of cognitive elements would be relevant for a given individual. The set of relevant elements and the particular relations among them define the *content* of the individual's belief system on the issue. The form, or *structure,* of belief may be expressed independently of the content according to the array of numerical affect values and relation values defined above.

A belief structure may or may not contain inconsistencies. By inconsistency is meant not logical inconsistency but psychological inconsistency, or, as it has been variously referred to, imbalance (7), incongruity (12, 13), or dissonance (5). We shall use the term "imbalance."

Heider (7), Festinger (5), and Osgood and Tannenbaum (12) have all postulated a motivation for the reduction of imbalance. There is said to be a tendency, a pressure, toward the attainment of cognitive balance. An essential qualification to this postulate has been pointed out by Abelson and Rosenberg (1). There are innumerable inconsistencies in anyone's belief system which may lie dormant and unthought about. Pressure toward cognitive balance, if always operative on all cognitive elements, would produce much more balance in belief systems than one finds empirically. It is much more plausible to assume that this pressure operates only when the issue is salient; that is, when the issue is being "thought about," or, if this is too rational a terminology, when "cognitive work" is applied on the issue. General methods for identifying the presence of imbalance in a structure of any size have been given elsewhere (1, 4). Here we confine our analysis to a simple case of imbalance: two elements and the relation between them.

There are six possible cases to be considered: two positively valued objects, related associatively or related dissociatively; one positively valued object and one negatively valued object, related dissociatively or related associatively; and two negatively valued objects, related associatively or related dissociatively. In each of these three pairs of cases, the first possibility is balanced, the second one is imbalanced. This may be clarified by reference to Figure 1.

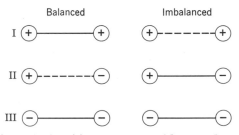

Figure 1. Cognitive structures with two elements and one relation. An unbroken line symbolizes an associative (positive) relation; a broken line a dissociative (negative) relation. The mechanism of denial aims toward the conversion of a structure on the right into one on the left, either through change of affect toward the element ("denial of the element") or change in the sign of the relation ("denial of the relation").

An imbalanced dyad will be said to constitute a belief dilemma when the intensity of affect toward the objects is strong and when the dyad is often salient (i.e., often present in thought).

MODES OF RESOLUTION

Four possible modes of resolution are specified below. Each can manifest itself in several ways. The modes are labeled: (a) denial, (b) bolstering, (c) differentiation, and (d) transcendence.

Denial refers to a direct attack upon one or both of the cognitive elements or the relation between them. The value felt toward the object, whether positive or negative, is denied, or the opposite is asserted; or the sign of the relation between the elements is explained away, or the opposite is asserted. Examples are: the man on a diet professing that he never liked rich foods anyway, the groom convincing himself of his avid belief in his bride's religion, John Calvin interpreting the scriptures to show that Christ never really condemned usury. If an attempt at denial is successful, it will convert an imbalanced structure into a balanced one. However, denial attempts may run into various difficulties, as, for example, when the denial is too great a distortion of reality or conflicts with other elements in the larger belief system. For example, the Boston colonists faced in 1773 with the odious taxation on tea went so far as to vote that "it is the sense of this Body that the use of tea is improper and pernicious." It is unlikely that this denial of the desirability of tea, albeit effective in encouraging group action, was effective in suppressing the taste for tea of the individuals concerned.

The mechanism called "bolstering" consists of relating one or the other of the two cognitive objects in a balanced way to other valued objects (Figure 2), thereby minimizing the relative imbalance in the structure. This mechanism plays an important part in Festinger's theory of cognitive dissonance (5). He points out many situations in which the introduction of new cognitive elements is useful in reducing dissonance. This is a mechanism not for eliminating

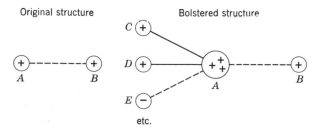

Figure 2. The mechanism of bolstering in reducing cognitive imbalance. In the bolstered structure (right) the units AC, AD, . . . are all balanced. The relative effect of the imbalanced unit AB is thus reduced.

balance entirely but only for drowning it out, so to speak. Examples are: the smoker who is worried about lung cancer telling himself that smoking is extremely enjoyable, good for his nerves, and socially necessary; and the proponent of a large standing army, unwelcome in peacetime, claiming that it is good character training for the nation's youth. The mechanism of bolstering may be used in conjunction with the mechanism of denial. For example, in the example of the large standing army the advocate might also say that the large standing army was not contrary to peaceful purposes; in fact, it aided the cause of peace to have a large standing army.

The two mechanisms listed thus far have the property that they preserve the identity of the cognitive elements. The meaning of the attitude objects remains the same even though attitude toward the objects may be weakened by denial or strengthened by bolstering. Another mode of resolution arises if we consider the possibility of differentiation of the cognitive elements. An element may be split into two parts with a strong dissociative relation between the parts.

To see how this mechanism might restore cognitive balance, consider the issue of hydrogen-bomb testing. For many people, continued hydrogen-bomb testing is positively valued, but poisoning of the atmosphere is negatively valued. These two cognitive objects are associatively related—there is a causal connection of some degree. This dyad is therefore imbalanced. But there is bomb testing and there is bomb testing: one might differentiate this attitude object into two—testing "dirty bombs" and testing "clean bombs." It is only the testing of dirty bombs that contributes to poisoning of the atmosphere; the testing of clean bombs presumably does not. Thus the imbalance is resolved. To take another example, the facts of evolution, positively valued, are contradictory to the Bible which is also positively valued. But there are two Bibles: the Bible as literally interpreted and the Bible as figuratively interpreted. The Bible as figuratively interpreted is not contradictory to the facts of evolution but may be seen as concordant with them. In a third example, from an experiment by Asch (2), subjects who feel unfavorable toward "politi-

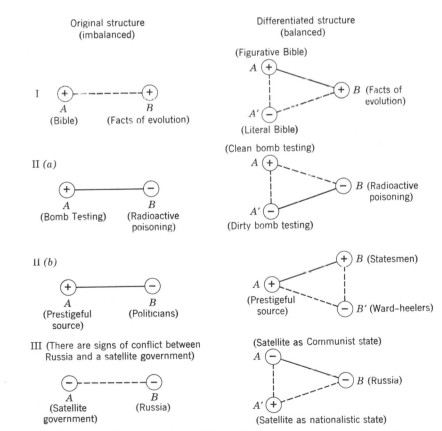

Figure 3. The mechanism of differentiation in restoring cognitive balance.

cians" are confronted with a highly prestigeful source who glorifies the political profession. Many subjects get off the hook by differentiating statesmen (good politicians) from wardheelers (bad politicians). In these examples one element is differentiated into two parts, a new part and an old part. The old part retains the relation with the other element in the structure, but the affect toward it is changed. The new part, on the other hand, retains the old affect toward the differentiated element, but the sign of the relation with the other element is changed. These changes are reviewed in Figure 3.

It is interesting to note the large number of dimensions along which objects can be differentiated. They may be differentiated according to the internal content of the object, the object as viewed in a social context versus a personal context, the object as it is versus as it should be, the object as it is versus the object as it will be, etc.

The mechanism of transcendence is in a sense obverse to the mechanism of differentiation. Elements, instead of being split down, are built up and combined into larger units organized on a superordinate level, as indicated in Figure 4. For example, the dilemma pitting science against religion is transcended by the consideration that both the rational man and the spiritual man must be jointly cultivated to reach a fuller life or a better society or a deeper understanding of the universe. Thus the dilemma is transcended by imbedding the conflicting parts in a new concept instrumental to

some higher purpose. The theosophical dilemma of God's presumed permissiveness toward evil is sometimes resolved by appeal to transcendent concepts. In the intriguing case study (6) of a group of individuals who prepared for a cataclysm that never occurred, it is reported that the group leader offered a transcendent resolution for the belief crisis: the cataclysm was said to have been stayed by God because of the group's devotion.

CHOICE AMONG THE MODES OF RESOLUTION

Presumably, the individual with an imbalanced cognition will strive to choose among the various modes of resolution. Imbalanced structure would then be under a variety of pressures to change. The theoretical specification of which particular changes are likely to take place is a complex problem. Several working propositions are sketched here. A more rigorous theory is in the process of development.

Proposition 1. There will be a hierarchy of resolution attempts in general proceeding in the following order: denial, bolstering, denial, differentiation, and transcendence.

The hierarchy of resolution attempts is based upon the relative ease of achieving success with each of the methods. The reason denial appears twice in the listing is that there are usually two points in the process at which denial may enter. If we consider the situation in which imbalance is introduced by forced or accidental exposure

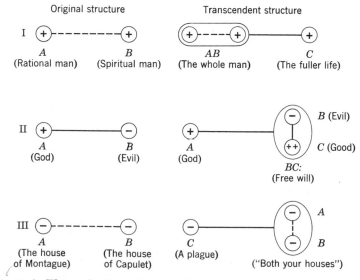

Figure 4. The mechanism of transcendence in restoring cognitive balance.

to propaganda or opinions seeking to establish new cognitive relations or to contradict previously held affect values, a first opportunity for denial may arise by a rejection of the relevance of the new material. If the initial denial fails, bolstering will be attempted and then another attempt at denial, this time buttressed by further thought about the issue. The presumption here is that denial and bolstering are simpler cognitive mechanisms than differentiation and transcendence, although they are not necessarily more effective in reducing cognitive imbalance. Differentiation is difficult because it requires intellectual ability, flexibility, and because, when there is strong affect toward a cognitive object, it is not easily split apart. Transcendence is presumably still more difficult, for it requires the existence of a compelling superordinate structure in which a given imbalance may be imbedded.

Proposition 2. When two cognitive elements stand in imbalanced relation to each other and the affect toward one is more intense than toward the other, the tendency will be to apply bolstering toward the more intensely affected element and/or denial toward (*a*) the less intensely affected element and/or (*b*) the relation between the elements.

Proposition 2a. The probability that an attempt will be made to bolster an element is high if other elements relevant to it are strong and stand in balanced relation to it (Figure 2) and is low if other relevant elements are weak or stand in imbalanced relation to it.

Corollary. Elements for which the individual's affect is intensely socially supported are readily subject to bolstering attempts when caught in a strong dilemma.

Proposition 2b. The probability that an attempt will be made to deny an element is high if other relevant elements are strong and stand in imbalanced relation to it and is low if other relevant elements are weak or stand in balanced relation to it.

Corollary. Elements with which considerable shame or guilt is associated (e.g., elements connoting the overindulgence of appetites) are readily subject to denial attempts when caught in a strong dilemma (i.e., when firmly related in imbalanced fashion to a strongly affected element). See Example 1.

Proposition 2c. Relations between cognitive elements are readily denied when the external evidence for the relation is remote, ambiguous, under suspicion of bias, or dependent upon specific circumstances which can readily be perceived as inapplicable in general.

Proposition 2d. A relation between cognitive elements *A* and *B* is readily subject to denial attempts when there is available an element *A'*, formally similar to *A* and standing in associative relation with it, such that *the relation between A' and B is of opposite sign as between A and B, and is stronger.*

Proposition 2e. A relation between cognitive elements *A* and *B* is readily subject to denial attempts when there is available an element *A'*, formally similar to *A*, yet standing psychologically in dissociative relation to *A*, such that *the relation between A' and B is of the same sign as between A and B, but stronger* (the "mote-beam" technique).

See Example 2 (from the point of view of a liberal but very proud southerner).

Proposition 3. If the affects toward two cognitive elements which stand in imbalanced relation to each other are nearly equal and the resolutions suggested in Proposition 2 fail, the converse resolutions will be attempted; that is, there will be attempts to bolster the less intense element and/or to deny the more intense element.

Original delemma   Attempted resolution

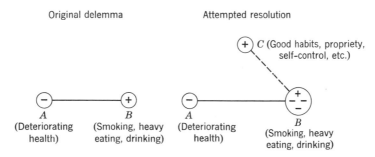

Example 1. *Note. **The element C must be compelling for the resolution to be stable. If original positive affect toward B is strong, the stability of the attempted resolution is jeopardized.***

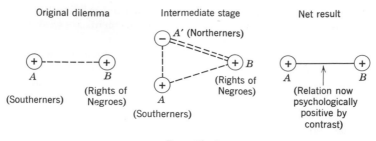

Example 2

Proposition 4. The classical relationship between the intensity and extremity of attitude may be explained in terms of a succession of dilemma resolutions in individual histories with the attitude object.

Explanation. The mechanism of bolstering used in the service of dilemma resolution increases the intensity of affect toward the object. An object which has been repeatedly bolstered is therefore the object of an intense attitude. But repeated bolstering also increases the extremity of attitude. In bolstering, the attitude object is connected with other objects. New reasons and supports are given for it; it is seen to be instrumental to other values; it is seen to be supported by various people and groups. In

short, it is imbedded in a cognitive system of ever widening circumference. If scope of cognitive support is equated with extremity of attitude, then the relationship between extremity and intensity follows.

Those individuals who do not invoke bolstering will in general be the ones with moderate attitudes of low intensity.

Proposition 5. If, in the search for new elements to bolster an original element in imbalance, further imbalance is created (usually because the new elements are imbalanced with each other), differentiation of the original element is encouraged.

See Example 3 (it is pointed out to an individual that universal public school education,

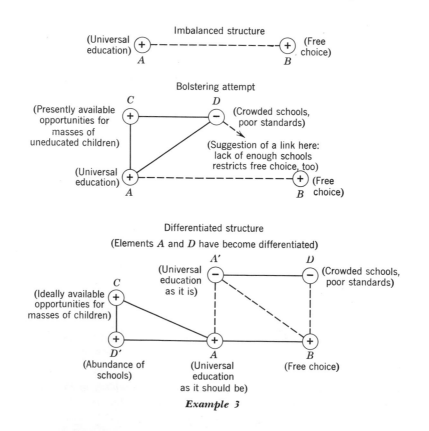

Example 3

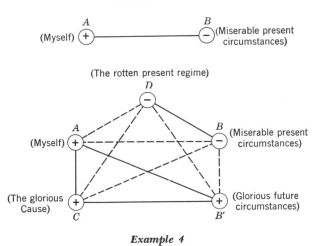

Example 4

by being compulsory, violates the democratic ideal of individual free choice—some parents might want to keep children out of school).

Proposition 6. When an element is differentiated it is crucial to the maintenance of the resolution that the old part and the new part of the element be strongly dissociated.

Proposition 7. Transcendent resolutions are likely to be invoked only in the case of chronically insoluble dilemmas. However, once a transcendent resolution is achieved, it may be found applicable to a variety of dilemmas.

Proposition 8. Mass propaganda efforts seek dilemma resolutions effective for a large number of people simultaneously.

See Example 4 (a nation in a period of hard times).

Revolutionary propaganda aims to bolster *A* and differentiate *B* along a time dimension.

The dissociated parts of *B* are each doubly bolstered, as follows:

(*English translation:* "You are now part of the glorious Cause. Reject with us your miserable present circumstances. Look forward to the glorious future when all will be different. The rotten present regime despises you and is responsible for your misery. The Cause will attack the regime and lead you to the glorious future. The regime will try to prevent this but we shall triumph.")

Explicit in this analysis is the reason revolutionists should be so concerned over public apathy. Those "Indifferents" who are not dissatisfied with their present circumstances have no dilemma to resolve, and consequently the propaganda does not "take" (unless the Indifferents can be convinced that their situation is indeed grim).

REFERENCES

1. Abelson, R. P., and Rosenberg, M. J. "Symbolic Psychologic: A Model of Attitudinal Cognition." *Behavioral Science,* III (1958), 1-13.
2. Asch, S. E. "Studies in the Principles of Judgments and Attitudes: II. Determination of Judgments by Group and Ego Standards." *Journal of Social Psychology,* XII (1940), 433-465.
3. Brown, J. S. "Principles of Intrapersonal Conflict." *Conflict Resolution,* I (1957), 135-154.
4. Cartwright, D., and Harary, F. "Structural Balance: A Generalization of Heider's Theory." *Psychological Review,* LXIII (1956), 277-293.
5. Festinger, L. *Theory of Cognitive Dissonance.* Evanston, Ill.: Row, Peterson and Co., 1957.
6. Festinger, L., Riecken, H., and Schachter, S. *When Prophecy Fails.* Minneapolis: University of Minnesota Press, 1956.
7. Heider, F. "Attitudes and Cognitive Organization." *Journal of Psychology,* XXI (1946), 107-112.
8. Heider, F. *The Psychology of Interpersonal Relations.* New York: John Wiley and Sons, 1958.
9. Lewin, K. "Environmental Forces in Child Behavior and Development." In C. Murchison (ed.), *A Handbook of Child Psychology.* Worcester, Mass.: Clark University Press, 1931.

10. Miller, N. "Experimental Studies of Conflict." In J. McV. Hunt (ed.), *Personality and the Behavior Disorders*. New York: Ronald Press Co., 1944.

11. Osgood, C. E., Saporta, S., and Nunnally, J. C. "Evaluative Assertion Analysis." *Litera*, III (1956), 47-102.

12. Osgood, C. E., and Tannenbaum, P. H. "The Principle of Congruity in the Prediction of Attitude Change." *Psychological Review*, LXII (1955) 42-55.

13. Osgood, C. E., Suci, G. T., and Tannenbaum, P. H. *The Measurement of Meaning*. Urbana: University of Illinois Press, 1957.

39. Cognitive Consistency and Attitude Change

WILLIAM J. McGUIRE

There has been a recent resurgence of interest among psychological researchers in the predictive value of a postulate that people tend to maintain logical consistency among their cognitions (and even between cognitions and more gross behavior). The most influential single source of this revived interest is probably Heider's (1946, 1958) "balance" theory, while Festinger's (1957) theory of cognitive dissonance is probably the most stimulating elaboration to date. Most of the approaches that employ this postulate recognize, implicitly or explicitly, that the tendency towards consistency is not absolute. Its expression is limited by other, potentially conflicting forces in the person and by the inadequacies of his cognitive apparatus, even in the absence of conflicting forces, to achieve full consistency. These coordinate hypotheses of cognitive consistency and its predictable limitations have been applied successfully to the prediction of behavior in many areas. The work reported here involves two applications in the area of persuasion.

The first of these applications involves what will be called the "Socratic method" of persuasion. The persuasion technique usually studied in the social sciences involves inducing a change in a person's opinion by presenting him with a persuasive message from an external source, either through a "mass" one-way communication channel or in a face-to-face reciprocal communication network. The postulate of cognitive consistency suggests that persuasion could be effected by the quite different technique of eliciting the persuasive material from the person's own cognitive repertory, rather than presenting it from outside. Specifically, this technique would involve asking the person his opinions on logically related issues, thus sensitizing him to

any inconsistencies that exist among his stands on these issues and producing a change towards greater mutual consistency. The technique has an obvious affinity to the "Socratic method" used in the Platonic dialogues (Jowett, 1937).

The derivation of the foregoing hypothesis requires, besides the postulate of a tendency to maintain cognitive consistency, the assumptions that various distorting factors (of which "wishful thinking" is given primary attention in this study) have introduced inconsistency among the initially elicited set of opinions, and that the temporally contiguous elicitation of these opinions brings the tendency towards consistency more strongly to bear upon them.

Part of the study described below was designed to test the hypothesis that a person tends to change his opinions on logically related issues in the direction of greater mutual consistency when he is merely asked to state these opinions in close temporal contiguity. Several additional hypotheses regarding the focus of the Socratic effect, that is, the type of opinion most likely to be adjusted in case of inconsistency, were also tested.

The second application of the cognitive consistency postulate to the area of persuasion in the present experiment dealt with the logical repercussions of persuasive communications. The effectiveness of a persuasive message is usually gauged by the amount of change in opinion that it induces on the issue with which it explicitly deals. From the postulated consistency tendency, however, it would follow that an induced change on the explicit issue tends also to produce changes on logically related (unmentioned) issues such as would tend to maintain internal consistency among beliefs.

From the additional, limiting assumption that there is a certain amount of inertia in the person's cognitive apparatus, two additional hypotheses were derived. It was hypothesized that the consistency-maintaining change ex-

• Reprinted from *Journal of Abnormal and Social Psychology*, 1960, **60**, 345-353, with permission of the author and the American Psychological Association.

pected on remote issues is less than the amount logically required for complete consistency with the induced changes on the explicit issues. Further, it was hypothesized that inertia would also result in temporal effects, such that the impact of the message on the remote issue occurs only gradually, the opinion on the remote issue continuing to change in the logically required direction for some time after receipt of the persuasive message.

Since most of these hypotheses involve predictions of fine graduations of change towards or away from a reference point of precise cognitive consistency, we need a quantitative definition of consistency. Such a definition is provided by a model combining formal logic and probability theory, the relevant aspects of which are summarized below.

Consider three issues so interrelated that a person taking Stands a and b on two of these issues would, if he were to be consistent, be logically required to take Stand c on the third. That is, the three stands are in a syllogistic relationship, with c following as a valid conclusion from the conjunction of a and b. If the person's opinions on these issues are obtained by having him indicate his adherence to each of the Stands, a, b, and c, on a probabilistic scale, we can specify that to be completely consistent, these probabilistically scaled opinions must be interrelated in the form

$$p(c) = p(a \,\&\, b) + p(k)(1 - p(a \,\&\, b)) \quad (1)$$

where $p(k)$ in his opinion of the probability of c on bases other than the conjunction of a and b. It can also be specified that if we induce a change of opinion on a and/or b (for example, by a persuasive communication) while $p(k)$ does not change appreciably, then the required change on c necessary for maintaining logical consistency among the opinions is

$$\Delta p(c) = \Delta p(a \,\&\, b) \quad (2)$$

which, assuming that a and b are independent events, i.e., that $p(a \,\&\, b) = p(a)\,p(b)$ becomes

$$\Delta p(c) = \Delta p(a)p(b) + \Delta p(b)p(a) + \Delta p(a)\Delta p(b) \quad (3)$$

where $p(a)$ and $p(b)$ refer to the initial opinions, before the communication induced changes. When, in the discussion below, we refer to the "logically required change on the conclusion," we are referring to the $\Delta p(c)$ value specified in Equation 3.

METHOD

Material. The Ss' opinions on sets of logically related issues were measured by means of a questionnaire that contained 48 statements. These statements comprised 16 sets of three syllogistically related propositions; that is, two of the propositions stated stands on a pair of issues, agreement with which would logically imply agreement with the stand taken in the proposition on the third issue.[1] The three propositions making up any one syllogism appeared in different parts of the questionnaire, being interspersed with the propositions of other syllogisms.

The Ss were asked to indicate in probabilistic terms the extent of their adherence to the stand taken in each proposition. For this purpose each proposition was followed by a graphic scale consisting of a five-inch horizontal line marked off at half-inch intervals and calibrated 0, 10, 20 . . . 90, 100. To the left of the scale was written "Very improbable end," and at the right, "Very probable end." The Ss were asked to decide how probable they felt the truth of each statement to be, and to indicate this subjective probability by drawing a line through the scale at the appropriate point.

In a later section of the questionnaire the propositions were repeated, this time with a scale consisting of five boxes labelled from left to right "very desirable," "somewhat desirable," . . . , "very undesirable." The S was instructed to indicate his feeling regarding the desirability of each proposition by putting an X in the appropriate box. (As explained below, these ratings of desirability were obtained to allow identification of initial inconsistencies, due to wishful thinking, among the probability ratings.)

The questionnaires were administered during each of the three experimental sessions. Be-

[1] A complete list of all syllogisms and persuasive messages used in the present study has been deposited with the American Documentation Institute. Order Document No. 6235, from ADI Auxiliary Publications Project, Photoduplication Service, Library of Congress, Washington 25, D. C., remitting in advance $1.25 for microfilm or $1.25 for photocopies. Make checks payable to Chief, Photoduplication Service, Library of Congress.

One of the 16 syllogisms used was as follows. Students who violate any regulation that has been made to safeguard the lives and property of other students will be expelled; the regulations against smoking in the classrooms and corridors were made to safeguard the lives and property of the student; students who violate the regulation against smoking in the classrooms and corridors will be expelled.

tween the first and second administrations of the opinion questionnaires, a series of persuasive messages were communicated to the Ss in mimeographed booklets.[2] There were 16 such messages, each directed at one premise of each of the 16 syllogisms. Each message argued that the proposition in question was true, i.e., was aimed at increasing the S's probabilistic estimate of the statement's truth. These messages were "one-sided," 200–300 words long, employed rational appeals, and based arguments on factual evidence. They were mild in tone and attributed to a purportedly competent and dependable source.

Procedure. There were three 50-min. experimental sessions. In the first, the questionnaires were administered to obtain "before communication" measures of opinions on the issues. The second session, which came one week after the first, was devoted to communicating the persuasive messages and then to a second administration of the opinion questionnaires in order to measure the immediate impact of the persuasive messages. One week later, the Ss participated in the third session during which the questionnaires were again administered (in order to ascertain the delayed effects of the persuasive messages). At this final session the Ss were also told the purpose of the experiment and the E pointed out the deceits that he had employed in the experiments and his reasons for so doing.

Until this final "catharsis," an attempt was made to conceal, or at least distract attention from, the persuasion aspect of the experiment and from the investigator's interest in cognitive consistency. The study was purported to be an investigation of people's ability to understand experts' discussions of controversial topics. The persuasive messages were alleged to be excerpts from such discussions, and after each message the Ss were required to answer a series of comprehension questions (to emphasize the contention that we were primarily interested in studying the Ss' understanding of the material). The opinion questionnaires were explained as required to ascertain whether the issues dealt with were actually controversial in the group being studied and whether they continued to be controversial throughout the period of the experiment.

Subjects and design. A total of 120 Ss par-

2 The text of all 16 persuasive messages can be obtained in the ADI Document No. 6235, cited in Footnote 1.

ticipated in the experiment. One-fourth of these were high school seniors and the remainder, college freshmen; the ratio of men to women was about 2:1 at both grade levels. To minimize the likelihood that the consistency hypotheses would receive specious confirmation by the employment of atypically rationalistic Ss, these Ss were selected from a group with a rather low level of intellectual attainment. Their modal high school grade average was below the 30th percentile for all high school students in their state. Each of these students reported that he had never had a course in formal logic or in probability theory.

In order that the Ss might have time to respond thoughtfully to the opinion items and to read the persuasive messages carefully, each S was required to provide data on only 8 of the 16 syllogistically related sets of propositions. On only four of these eight did he receive persuasive messages, the other four serving as no-communication "control" items. These no-communication syllogisms provided the data for testing the Socratic effect hypotheses. The syllogisms on which messages were communicated provided the data for testing the hypotheses concerning logical repercussions. Specific syllogisms were alternated between message and no-message conditions from S to S.

RESULTS AND DISCUSSION

Hypotheses Concerning the Socratic Effect

Initial inconsistencies among the opinions. In order to identify initial opinion inconsistencies we employed an auxiliary hypothesis that the subjective probabilities of the propositions would be distorted in the direction of wishful thinking. Internal evidence indicates that this assumption was a valid one. The 16 syllogisms were partitioned into two subsets: the eight in which the desirability of the conclusions was low relative to that of the premises; and the eight whose conclusions had relatively high desirabilities. Wishful thinking would tend to make the subjective probabilities of the conclusions low relative to those of their (more desirable) premises in the first subset of syllogisms, while the subjective probabilities of the conclusions in the second set should be high relative to their less desirable premises. This prediction is borne out by the subjective probability ratings obtained in the first session, as shown in Table 1. (To avoid confusing them with the significance levels, the obtained sub-

TABLE 1. *Subject Probability Scores (Multiplied by a Factor of 100) in the No-Communication Conditions*

	Session	Major Premises	Minor Premises	Joint of Premises	Conclusions	Excess of Conclusions over Premises
Syllogisms with conclusions less desirable than premises	1st	62.15	54.14	33.66	35.86	2.20
	Changes, 1st to 2nd	—3.04	1.45	—0.79	5.17	5.96
Syllogisms with conclusions more desirable than premises	1st	55.50	55.41	30.12	47.30	17.18
	Changes, 1st to 2nd	3.96	—1.98	2.06	0.35	—1.72

jective probability ratings given in this report are the obtained probability ratings, multiplied by 100.) The mean subjective probability of the conclusions exceeded the mean joint probability of the premises by only 2.20 points on the 100-point scale in the first eight syllogisms, while in the other eight syllogisms (the conclusions of which had relatively high desirability) the mean subjective probability of the conclusions exceeded the mean joint probability of the premises by 17.18 points. This difference between 2.20 and 17.18 points is significant beyond the .01 level. (All significance levels reported in this paper are based on analyses of variance and two-tailed tests.) Hence, the attempted manipulation of initial inconsistency by use of the tendency toward wishful thinking was successful.

The main effect. The changes in opinion obtained in the conditions in which no persuasive message was communicated on the given issues provide the test of the main Socratic hypothesis, that when the person's opinions on related issues are elicited in close temporal contiguity, his need for consistency is brought more fully to bear on them. Hence, when these opinions are again elicited on a later occasion, they will be found to have changed towards greater mutual consistency. In view of the initial distortions from consistency produced by wishful thinking, it would follow that in the no-communication conditions in the present experiment initial questioning should produce an increase in the subjective probabilities of the conclusions relative to those of the premises in the first eight syllogisms (those with the relatively undesirable conclusions); while for the second eight syllogisms, there would be a relative decline in the subjective probabilities of the conclusions.

The results bear out this prediction. As can be seen in Table 1, the gain in probability of the conclusions over that of the premises in the first eight syllogisms averaged 5.96 points. The probabilities of the conclusions of the second eight syllogisms, on the other hand, showed a loss of 1.72 points relative to the premises. This net difference of 7.68 points between means is significant at the .02 level. Hence, simply eliciting opinions on logically related issues does tend to move those opinions toward greater mutual consistency when subsequent elicitation occurs one week later.

The difference obtained between the two sets of syllogisms as regards internal changes is in the direction that would be expected on the basis of a simple regression from the initially obtained difference. In order to test whether there is a Socratic effect over and above simple regression, an additional covariance analysis was carried out. The obtained difference in change of probability scores between the two sets of syllogisms was adjusted for the difference in initial levels by means of the obtained within-set correlation between the initial probability scores and the changes therein. Even when the obtained changes are adjusted for initial levels by this analysis of covariance, the difference in changes remains significant at the .02 level, indicative that a significant Socratic effect remains, even when the effect of regression is partialed out.

The Socratic effect tends to be produced primarily by the first contiguous elicitation of the opinions, with only slight evidence of an accumulative effect from subsequent, additional elicitations. As discussed above, there was a net Socratic effect, from the first to second elicitation of the opinions, of 7.68 points. The corresponding net effect, from second to third elicitations was again in the predicted direction but amounted to only 2.62 points, which falls far short of the conventional levels of statistical significance.

Focus of the Socratic effect. An attempt was made to answer the further question of where this Socratic effect is focused; that is, which of the person's initially inconsistent opinions are most likely to be changed in bringing about the greater consistency? The present data were analyzed to ascertain whether the amount of change was related to any of three variables: the logical status of the propositions, their initial valence, or their ordinal position on the questionnaire in the first session.

As regards logical status of the proposition, we tested whether the major premise, minor, and conclusion contributed differentially to the change towards consistency. All of the syllogisms used in this study were of the "Barbara" type. Hence the major premise contained the M-P terms; the minor, the S-M terms; and the conclusion, the S-P terms (where S refers to the subject of the conclusion; P to its predicate; and M to the middle term).

Logical status of the proposition did have a significant overall impact on amount of opinion change. As can be seen in Table 1, the major premise contributed most of the change towards increased consistency, the mean change being 3.50 points on the 100-point scale. The conclusion showed the next greatest change towards consistency, a mean of 2.41 points; and the minor premise contributed least, in fact their mean change was slightly (1.71 points) away from consistency. These differences among the three means are significant at the .05 level by an overall analysis of variance.

The overall significance of the variance among the three means is due primarily to the greater change towards consistency (averaging 2.95 points) of the propositions with the P terms (namely, the major premises and the conclusions) than of those without these P terms (namely the minor premises), which averaged a 1.71 point change away from consistency. The difference between the two classes of propositions is significant at the .03 level. It appears to be explicable on the basis of initial distortion. In these "Barbara" syllogisms, the P terms tend to have the greatest emotional valence. Therefore, by the auxiliary hypothesis of wishful thinking, the propositions that include these emotionally-tinged terms would have been the most distorted originally. The minor premises, without the P terms, are typically statements of

class inclusion ("Socrates is a man") and therefore less likely to be distorted. Hence, the greater change towards consistency of the other propositions appear to be a consequence of the fact that the others had contributed more of the original inconsistency.

Two other propositional characteristics were investigated for possible relationship to the amount of change in opinion produced by the Socratic method: initial valence and initial order of presentation. It was found that somewhat more change towards consistency occurred on the highly valenced propositions—the 12 most and the 12 least desirable propositions—than on the 24 moderately valenced ones. The direction of this outcome tends to reverse the "polarity" prediction (Osgood and Tannenbaum, 1955; Tannenbaum, 1956), but it does not approach the conventional level of statistical significance. Regarding initial order, it was found that somewhat more change toward consistency occurred on those propositions which, in the first session, appeared earlier on the questionnaire than on those that appeared towards the end, but that this difference was not statistically significant. The difference has been predicted on the assumption that the later appearing propositions had already, on the first administration of the questionnaire, been brought into closer agreement with the opinions given on the propositions that had come earlier, so that less change remained to be made.

A number of other hypotheses, not tested in this study, regarding propositional characteristics that affect amount of change in cases of mutual inconsistency could be tested. Opinions on more familiar issues may be more stable than those on less familiar. Opinions on issues that show greater cognitive complexity and greater articulation with the rest of the person's cognitive system [as defined, for example, by Zajonc's (1954) procedures] might participate less in the change towards consistency than more isolated and undifferentiated opinions. Tannenbaum's (1956) finding (that when differently valenced sources and stands on issues are paired, the person's attitude on the issue shows less change than his attitude towards the source) is suggestive in this regard. Following Asch's (1952) thinking that persuasion involves a change of the issue being judged rather than change of judgment on the given issue, we might expect that in case of conflict, the greatest change would occur on the issues most easily redefined. Another hypothesis is that the relative proneness to readjustment of conflicting opinions is related to the bases for accepting the opinions. For example, following Kelman's (1956) terminology, we might conjecture that opinions based on internalization might be more prone to change, in case of internal conflict, than those based on identification or on compliance. These latter need not be consistent with one's other beliefs, because the adherence to them is based on extrinsic considerations.

Hypothesis Concerning Logical Repercussions

The results just reported regarding the Socratic effect hypotheses are all based on data in the no-communications conditions. The following results, which deal with the logical repercussions of persuasive messages are based on data from the conditions in which persuasive communications were received. The changes reported as due to the persuasive messages are computed from a baseline provided by the change from first to second session in the no-communication condition. Since the results concerning the Socratic effect indicate certain systematic changes in opinions occur from first to second session even in the absence of persuasive messages, the message-induced changes must be computed from a control baseline that will eliminate those other changes and also any regression trends.

Immediate postcommunication changes. The induced changes of opinion on the explicit target issues (the premises) were considerable. Each message argued that the stand taken in one of the premises of each syllogism was true and that, therefore, the receiver should increase his subjective probability regarding the truth of that proposition. As can be seen in Table 2, the mean induced increase on the 16 explicit propositions immediately after the communication was 17.56 points on the 100-point scale ($p < .001$).

In order to maintain cognitive consistency, the Ss should therefore have increased their subjective probabilities regarding the truth of the conclusions. Even though neither conclusions nor the additional premises needed for their derivation had been adverted to in the communications, a considerable immediate postcommunication increase was indeed produced on these conclusions. As can be seen in Table 2, there was an increase (as required for consistency) immediately after the messages on 14 of the 16 unmentioned conclusions, the mean in-

TABLE 2. Changes in Subjective Probabilities on Explicit Issue and on Derived, Unmentioned Issues Immediately After and One Week after Persuasive Messages

	Obtained Change on Premises	Logically Required Change on Conclusions	Obtained Change on Conclusions	Discrepancies of Obtained from Required Change on Conclusions
Changes from before to immediately after	17.56	11.57	5.96	—5.61
Changes from immediately to one week after	—8.43	—6.69	—1.48	5.20

crease being 5.96 points. A mean change of this magnitude is significant at the .01 level. Hence, the results do indicate a consistency tendency sufficiently strong to cause a persuasive message to have an impact on logically related issues not explicitly mentioned in the communication.

These obtained changes on the derivative issues are, however, less than the amount required for complete logical consistency as determined by substituting the amount of the obtained change on the explicit premise in Equation 3. The mean required increase on the conclusions so computed was 11.57 points, while the actually obtained increase was only 5.96 (see Table 2), a difference significant beyond the .05 level. Hence, persuasive messages, while they do produce changes on remote, unmentioned issues, produce less than the amount logically required, a finding that supports the hypothesis of a certain amount of cognitive inertia.

Delayed postcommunication changes. A considerable amount of the immediately induced persuasion on the explicit target issues had dissipated by the end of the week following the communication. As can be seen in Table 2, almost half of the immediately induced change on these explicit issues had dissipated one week later. The mean loss of 8.43 points was significant at the .02 level. On the other hand, the 9.13 points of change remaining after one week was also significant (at the .01 level), indicating that there is still a significant amount of change of opinion on the explicit issue one week after the persuasive communication.

When this loss on the premises is substituted in Equation 3 the amount of the originally induced change on the unmentioned derived issues that should logically have dissipated during the succeeding week was computed as 6.69 points (see Table 2). The obtained loss during the interim, however, was only a negligible 1.48 points, a gain of 5.20 points relative to the explicit premises for the week ($p = .10$). In fact, by the week after the persuasive communication, the net mean change on the conclusions from their precommunication level was an increase of 4.47 points, which was almost as much as the 4.89 points logically required in view of the net changes on the premises. The trivial extent to which the change on conclusions fell short of the required amount one week after, as compared with the significant extent to which it fell short immediately after the communication, gives some support to the hypothesis that the persuasive messages had a delayed-action effect on the derived issues. The net change on the derived issues did not actually increase with the passage of time, but it fell off less sharply than would have been expected on the basis of the usual rate of temporal decay of the immediately transmitted opinion change, suggesting that continued seepage of the impact on the explicit issue almost completely overcame the opposing decay effect on the derived, unmentioned issue.

Comparison with previous studies. One methodological artifact in the present study, the use of a before-after design, may have augmented the amount of the logical repercussions of the persuasive messages. In order to obtain each S's precommunication opinions he was required to fill out, one week prior to receipt of the persuasive messages, an opinion questionnaire containing all the issues, including the auxiliary premises and conclusions not mentioned in the message itself. It is possible that having stated his opinions on these related issues during the previous week may have somewhat increased their saliency so that they were more affected by the message than would have been the case had they not been raised the previous week.

On the other hand, the finding of logical repercussions in the present experiment is particularly convincing in view of the fact that the method included a number of conditions that have been shown in previous studies to militate against logical repercussions. In the first place, not only was the conclusion itself unmentioned in the messages but also one of the two premises necessary for its derivation was left unmentioned. Also, the Ss employed were of a type,

being below average in intelligence, that has been found (Cooper and Dinerman, 1951) to be relatively resistant to nonexplicit messages. Furthermore, no mention was made during the experiment of our interest in consistency, and the logically related propositions were widely interspersed with other propositions within the questionnaire. Finally the Ss gave their opinions on a scale with whose computational axioms they were unfamiliar, so that they could hardly have determined the extent of their inconsistencies even had they been interested in this matter.

Hence, the negative indications reported in some previous studies for the hypothesis that persuasive communications have logical repercussions require comment. While more persuasion has typically been found on a derived issue if that issue is explicitly mentioned rather than only implied, the data reported typically do show some change on the nonexplicit issue (Hovland, Lumsdaine, and Sheffield, 1949; Hovland and Mandell, 1952). Also, the relative lack of effect on the derived issue is most evident in the immediate postcommunication periods. Hovland, Lumsdaine, and Sheffield (1949, pp. 70–71) found that the "Why We Fight" films did have an impact on more general attitudes after the passage of a greater amount of time, and have postulated that there may be need for a "sinking in" period before these derivative effects are felt. Similarly, Katz, Stotland, Patchen, and Jochen (1957) report that giving Ss case history material regarding the roots of prejudice causes little immediate effect on their own prejudice, but after the passage of several weeks, the extrapolation of the intellectual knowledge to their opinions does occur. Furthermore, the magnitude of the logically required change on the derived issue is, as shown by Equation 3, less than that on the explicit issue. This logically consistent attenuation of the persuasive impact on derived issues due to a compounding of contingencies becomes more severe as the derived issue becomes more tenuously related to the explicit issue. For example, the more premises beside the explicit one needed for its derivation, the less the logically required change on the derived conclusion. Where the derived issues are as remote from those explicitly dealt with as was the case, for example, in the Hovland, Lumsdaine, and Sheffield "Why We Fight" studies (1949), very little change on the derived issues would be logically required even in a perfectly consistent S.

However, while only a small change in opinion is logically required on the derived issue, the amount actually occurring is even less. People's opinions seem to follow a "loose-link" model such that a considerable change can be induced on one cognition before any pull is exerted on related cognitions. This effect, however, is at least partially corrected by the continued seepage of change from the explicit issue to the derived one as time passes after the receipt of the communication.

The question of conscious awareness arises in connection with the psychodynamics of the present effect: to what extent is it necessary that the person be consciously aware of the inconsistencies among his beliefs in order that the effects occur? In the present study several procedures were employed in an attempt to minimize the degree of conscious awareness. (For example, no mention was made to the Ss that their consistency was being assessed; the related propositions were widely separated from one another in the questionnaire; a quantitative expression of opinion was required and the assessment of inconsistency involved a mathematical model unfamiliar to the Ss.) Hence, the present findings indicate that the effects occur even under conditions that attempt to avoid any suggestion of inconsistency.

The Ss' level of awareness of inconsistency was not systematically varied within the present experiment, but it is interesting to speculate on the results of such a manipulation. Increasing the person's awareness of his inconsistency by, say, explicitly pointing it out to him might produce greater changes towards consistency. On the other hand, such a procedure could well have the opposite effect by provoking the person's hostility or defensiveness, and so result, not in a greater change towards consistency, but in some other reaction such as the rejection of consistency, with Carlyle, as the hobgoblin of little minds; or in the repression of some of the conflicting issues.

SUMMARY

Two sets of hypotheses were derived from the postulate that people tend to maintain consistency among their opinions on logically related issues. First, it was hypothesized that opinion change would be effected by the Socratic method of simply asking the person to state contiguously his opinions on logically related issues, thus bringing the tendency towards

consistency to bear on any logical discrepancies among these opinions. Secondly, it was hypothesized that a persuasive communication directed at a person's opinion on some explicit issue tends to change also his opinions on logically related (even if unmentioned) derivative issues in a consistent direction. A procedure for quantitatively measuring the degree of logical consistency among opinions on related issues was described.

The Ss were 120 college students participating in three experimental sessions. In the first, before-communication opinions regarding the subjective probabilities and desirabilities of 16 sets of syllogistically related propositions were obtained. In the second session, 16 messages, each arguing for the truth of one premise of each syllogism, were communicated, and the immediate postcommunication opinion of the truth of each of the 48 propositions was obtained. Each S served in communication conditions with respect to some issues, and control, no-communication conditions with respect to others. In the third session, one week later, the delayed postcommunication opinions on the truth of the 48 propositions were obtained.

With respect to the Socratic effect hypothesis a significant amount of inconsistency attributable to wishful thinking was found, as postulated on the first elicitation of the opinions ($p < .01$). One week later, on a second elicitation of the opinions, there was a significant ($p = .02$) decline in the amount of this wishful thinking, indicating that the Socratic method did indeed produce the predicted change towards consistency. Several propositional variables were examined for possible relationship to the amount of change towards consistency. It was found that propositions with the predicate term (namely, major premises and conclusions) contributed significantly more ($p = .03$) of the change towards consistency than those without the predicate term.

With respect to the hypothesis concerning logical repercussions, it was found that immediately after the communication there was an induced opinion gain not only on the explicit target issues ($p < .001$) but also the derived issues ($p = .02$), even though neither the derived issues themselves nor even the auxiliary premises needed for their derivation were mentioned in the communication. This indirectly induced gain on the derived issues fell short, however, of the full amount needed for complete logical consistency ($p < .05$). One week later, there was some suggestion that the impact of the persuasive message had continued to seep down to the derived issues: immediately after the messages the opinions on the derived issues had shown only 52% of the logically required amount of change, while by one week after, this impact had risen to 91% of the required amount ($p = .10$).

REFERENCES

Asch, S. E. *Social psychology.* New York: Prentice-Hall, 1952.

Bagley, W. C. *The educative process.* N. Y.: Macmillan, 1906.

Cooper, Eunice, and Dinerman, Helen. Analysis of the film "Don't be a Sucker": A study in communication. *Publ. opin. Quart.,* 1951, **15**, 243-264.

Festinger, L. *A theory of cognitive dissonance.* Evanston: Row, Peterson, 1957.

Heider, F. Attitudes and cognitive organization. *J. Psychol.,* 1946, **21**, 107-112.

Heider, F. *The psychology of interpersonal relations.* New York: Wiley, 1958.

Hovland, C. I., Lumsdaine, A. A., and Sheffield, F. D. *Experiments on mass communication.* Princeton: Princeton Univer. Press, 1949.

Hovland, C. I., and Mandell, W. An experimental comparison of conclusion—drawing by the communicator and by the audience. *J. abnorm. soc. Psychol.,* 1952, **47**, 581-588.

Jowett, B. (Ed.) *The dialogues of Plato.* New York: Random House, 1937.

Katz, D., Stotland, E., Patchen, M., and Jochen, J. Research in methods for changing attitudes. I. Situational and personality determinants of the reduction of prejudice through self-insight. Univer. of Michigan, 1957. (Mimeo.)

Kelman, H. C. Three processes of acceptance of social influence: Compliance, identification and internalization. *Amer. Psychol.,* 1956, **11**, 261. (Abstract)

Osgood, C., and Tannenbaum, P. The principle of congruity and the production of attitude change. *Psychol. Rev.,* 1955, **62**, 42-55.

Tannenbaum, P. Initial attitude towards source and concept as factors in attitude change through communication. *Publ. opin. Quart.,* 1956, **20**, 413-425.

Zajonc, R. B. Cognitive structure and cognitive tuning. Unpublished doctoral dissertation, Univer. Michigan, 1954.

B. Behavior Theories

40. Attitude Formation: The Development of a Color-Preference Response through Mediated Generalization

BERNICE EISMAN LOTT

The present investigation of attitude development has had as its major stimulus Doob's 1947 discussion (7) and reinterpretation of the concept. His placement of attitude within the framework of behavior theory and his emphasis on attitude as a learned response to definable stimuli appears to be a more research oriented and potentially fruitful approach to the problem than has been taken in the past. An equally important source of stimulation for this study has come from the work on mediated and semantic generalization, particularly from the work of Birge (2), Cofer and Foley and associates (3, 4, 5, 8, 9), Keller (11), Razran (13, 14), and Reiss (15, 16).

An attitude is here defined, as suggested by Doob, as a learned implicit anticipatory response having both cue and drive properties. An anticipatory response is one which originally came after a rewarded response but as a result of being most closely associated with the reward moves forward in the behavior sequence. This results in its "anticipatory" occurrence directly to the external stimulus before its original time in the response series. As a response with stimulus properties, an attitude falls into

the class of "pure stimulus acts" defined by Hull (10) as responses whose major function is to serve as stimuli for other acts. It follows, therefore, that once such an implicit response-produced stimulus (r-s) has been established, it can be conditioned to evoke overt behavior. In this way an attitude acts as a mediator of responses. It is these responses, mediated by an attitude, which are measured by attitude questionnaires in attitude experiments, etc.

The property of drive value ascribed to an attitude is derived from the fact that an attitudinal response is assumed to produce strong stimulation. Any strong, persistent stimulus is considered by Miller and Dollard (6, p. 30) to constitute a drive. Reduction of the strong stimulus is drive reducing and therefore reinforcing. It is expected, therefore, that any overt response which leads to a significant reduction of the strong stimulus will be learned. Ascribing drive value to attitudes distinguishes them from other implicit, anticipatory response-produced stimuli and is in line with traditional views. Attitudes, wrote Allport (1), "both motivate and guide; they supply both drive and direction." Sherif and Cantril (17, p. 300) offer, as one criterion of an attitude, its affective property. Krech, too, speaks of attitudes as motivational, thus distinguishing them from beliefs (12, p. 152).

• Reprinted from *Journal of Abnormal and Social Psychology*, 1955, **50**, 321-326, with permission of the author and the American Psychological Association.

STATEMENT OF THE PROBLEM

The purpose of the present study has been to demonstrate experimentally that attitude formation is amenable to laboratory observation and control, and can be adequately conceptualized and explained by reinforcement learning theory. The general hypothesis of this study can be formally stated as follows: A positive preference or attitude toward an object with which an individual has had only neutral experience can be developed through mediated generalization. In more operational terms, it is predicted that if individuals are taught to attach the same label to two stimuli which differ from one another in all other relevant ways, and if these individuals subsequently have rewarding experience with one of these stimuli, then a positive preference for the other stimulus, as well as for stimuli resembling the latter, will be demonstrable. This type of learning experience follows the general paradigm for mediated generalization. In this study the subjects develop a positive response for a color after being subjected to such a series of learning experiences.

To test this general hypothesis four different test situations, in which a color preference could be demonstrated, were employed. These situations, differing in context, complexity, and social significance, will be described in detail below.

METHOD

Apparatus and Subjects

A wooden stage, 20.5 in. high, 30 in. wide, and 19 in. deep, with a raised, slanted platform, at an angle of about 35 degrees from the horizontal, was constructed and used for the presentation of various stimulus objects to the subjects. An unbleached muslin curtain could be pulled in front or away from the platform in order to hide or expose objects on it. Three small depressions about 8 in. apart were drilled into the platform to serve as receptacles for marbles which were used as rewards during certain portions of the training.

The following stimulus objects were used: (a) three wooden *geometrical blocks,* each painted white and .75 in. thick, triangular, circular, and square, respectively; (b) three *thin rectangular blocks,* each 2.5 in. by 6 in. and .75 in. thick, painted green, yellow, and black, respectively; (c) three metal *jar tops,* 2.5 in. in

diameter, also painted green, yellow, and black, respectively; (d) three *glasses,* 3.5 in. high, painted green, yellow, and black, respectively; (e) three *thick rectangular blocks,* 1.5 in. by 1.5 in. by 4.5 in., painted green, yellow, and black, respectively; (f) three white wooden *"nonsense" blocks,* .75 in. thick, and of three different nonsense shapes.

Eighty-one subjects (Ss) were used, 41 boys and 40 girls, ranging in age from 5 years, 10 months to 8 years, 10 months. All Ss were attending an elementary school operated by the Department of Education of U.C.L.A. All members of each of the classes used in this study were utilized by the experimenter (E), i.e., there was no arbitrary selection of Ss from within any class. The Ss were told that E had a new game she wanted to try out and that she would play with each of the children in a class, one at a time. Owing to the nature of the school, all children in it were accustomed to observation by strangers and many of them were also accustomed to leaving their classes for some time for testing or other "play"-research purposes.

Procedure

The 81 Ss were randomly divided into four groups with 9 Ss in Group I, 18 Ss in Group II, and 27 Ss each in Groups III and IV. One third of the Ss in each group was randomly selected to be trained positively for each of the three colors, yellow, green, and black. The E worked with one S at a time. Since the name of each S had been assigned to an experimental group prior to the start of the experiment, the order in which Ss came to E was not fixed, and either the teacher or the last S chose the next S.

Part 1. Name learning for the geometrical blocks. Each S sat facing E and the front of the stage. The Ss in all four groups were treated alike during this portion of the training. The three geometrical blocks were placed on the stage by E, and S was told that all three had names which S had to discover, the names being "egg" (for the triangle), "car" (for the circle), and "shoe" (for the square). Each S was shown one block at a time in a predetermined random order which was the same for all Ss. When a block was presented, S guessed at its name and E told S if he was right or wrong. The S was given as many trials as was necessary in order for him successfully to identify each of the three blocks five times in succession. Each S was told that learning the names of the blocks was necessary in order to proceed to the next part of the game during which he could win some marbles.

Part 2. Reward series. Here, too, Ss in all four groups were treated alike. The geometrical blocks were again placed on the platform and S was told that E would hide a marble under one of them when the curtains were closed and then ask S to guess where the marble was. The S was instructed to point to the block under which he thought the marble was hidden and to call the block by its *name,* the name learned in Part 1. When placing a marble under the proper block, E was careful to make extraneous noise so that sound would not serve as a reliable cue with respect to the hiding place of the marble.

A marble was always hidden under the same block for any given S. For those who were to be trained to prefer green, the marble was always placed under the triangle ("egg"); for those to be trained for yellow, the marble was placed under the circle ("car"); and for those to be trained for black, the marble was always placed under the square ("shoe"). The relative positions of the blocks were shifted per trial according to a random, predetermined order which was constant for all Ss.

Each time a marble was hidden S was permitted only one guess as to its location. If S guessed correctly, he kept the marble; if he guessed incorrectly, E closed the curtains and hid the marble again, under the same block but in a new position with respect to the other two. The reward series ended when S had made six consecutive correct guesses. If the criterion was not reached by the fourteenth trial, a correction procedure was instituted, i.e., when S guessed incorrectly, E lifted the correct block and showed S where the marble was.

The purpose of this part of the training was to provide differential reinforcement for one of the three names ("egg," "car," or "shoe") which S had learned in Part 1. This is the only portion of the training in which such differential reinforcement could be obtained.

Part 3. Name learning for the thin rectangular blocks. Immediately after the reward series, E presented the three colored rectangular blocks, instructing S that one was called "egg" (the green block), one was called "car" (the yellow block), and one was called "shoe" (the black block). The S was again asked to discover which block had what name. The procedure followed here was identical to that followed in

Part 1 and again Ss in all four groups were treated alike.

Part 4. Review series. Groups I and II. Immediately following Part 3, Ss in both of these groups were tested for recall of the names of the geometrical blocks and of the colored rectangles and for recall of the marble game (reward series).

Groups III and IV. For Ss in these groups a longer and more elaborate review was given in order to introduce more reward and color-naming experience. This was done because the results of a preliminary investigation had led to the conclusion that owing to the nature of the test situations (to be described below) given Ss in Groups III and IV, additional reward and naming experience would be necessary for mediated generalization to be demonstrable.

The E presented three new stimuli, the colored jar tops, and asked S to guess what their names were. The S received a marble each time he correctly named all three stimuli. When S reached the criterion of three correct identifications, the colored glasses were presented and the same procedure was followed. The E next presented the three thick rectangles and asked S to guess their names. Correct identifications were calling the green objects "egg," the yellow ones "car," and the black ones "shoe."

The Ss were then reviewed on the marble game (reward series). Then one jar top, one glass, and one rectangle, each of a different color, were presented. All three of the possible combinations were presented successively and S was asked to name the objects. No marble rewards were given.

Part 5. Test for mediated generalization and color preference. Here the major differential treatment for the four experimental groups was introduced. The tests were given immediately after the review.

Group I. The Ss in this group were presented with the three thin rectangular blocks used in Part 3 and told, "Now we'll play the marble game with these. You tell me where you think the marble is. Don't forget to tell me the name of the block you think the marble is under." With the curtains hiding the platform, E placed a marble under each block. Only one trial was given, and after S made his choice he was told that there would be no more games. A right choice was picking that colored rectangle which had the same name as the geometrical block under which S had consistently found marbles in Part 2.

Group II. The Ss in this group were also told that they were going to play the marble game again. The curtains were drawn, but instead of placing the three thin rectangles on the platform, as was done with Group I, E substituted three new stimuli, the colored jar tops, with which Ss in Group II had had no prior experimental experience. A marble was placed under each jar top. When the curtains were opened, S was told to choose that jar top under which he thought a marble was hidden and to give its name ("egg," "car," "shoe"). The E did not tell Ss that these were the names of the new objects, and Ss had had no experience in so naming them. Only one choice trial was given. A correct choice was picking that jar top which was the same color as the rectangle which S, in Part 3, had learned had the same name as the geometrical block under which marbles had consistently been found in Part 2.

Group III. The Ss in this group were presented with three new stimuli, the white "nonsense" blocks, and instructed that one was called "green," one "black," and one "yellow." The S was told that he had to discover which block had what name. The same name-learning procedure as was used in Parts 1 and 3 was utilized here, and again a criterion of five successive correct identifications of each block was employed. After S reached the criterion, he was asked, "If you could take one of these blocks home, which would you pick?"

The color name learned for each of the three "nonsense" blocks was varied from S to S in order to correct for possible preference for one of the blocks because of its shape. Thus, for example, of three subjects, all trained to prefer black ("shoe") by having been given differential reinforcement for the square block ("shoe") in Part 2, each learned to call a different "nonsense" block "black" in this test situation. Each of the three Ss was expected to choose that block which he had learned to call "black."

Group IV. The E told the Ss in this group a story about a pair of twins who had just moved into a new neighborhood. During the course of the story the twins meet three groups of children, a green, a yellow, and a black group. The play activities described for the three groups are almost identical. The climax of the story is reached when the twins decide to have a birthday party and their parents insist that they can invite only *one* of the groups of their new friends. The twins must choose only one of the groups for their party. Each S was asked by E to choose the group he would invite. A correct choice was picking that group having the same color as the rectangular block which S had learned, in Part 3, had the same name as the geometrical block under which he had consistently found marbles in Part 2.

RESULTS

Table 1 summarizes the generalization results obtained from S's responses in their respective

TABLE 1. Generalization Results: Responses of Subjects in All Groups in Their Respective Test Situations

Group	N	Number of Ss Making Correct Choice	Number of Ss Making Incorrect Choice	χ^2	p*
I	9	8 (3)	1 (6)	—	< .002**
II	18	14 (6)	4 (12)	16.00	< .001
III	27	16 (9)	11 (18)	8.17	< .01
IV	27	17 (9)	10 (18)	10.67	< .01

*Probability that the difference between obtained and expected frequencies could have occurred by chance alone.
**Since the theoretical frequencies and total N of Group I are too low for the reliable use of χ^2, the probability figure shown was obtained by evaluating the data by means of the binomial expansion (both tails of the distribution considered).

test situations. The numbers in parentheses represent expected frequencies. It was expected that since each S had to choose among three colors or three colored objects in the test situation, one third of the group could choose the correct (i.e., trained for) color and two thirds of the group could choose the incorrect color by chance alone. A significant deviation from these proportions in the direction of more than one third *Yeses* and less than two thirds *Noes* refutes the null hypothesis and lends support to the experimental hypothesis.

It can be seen from Table 1 that the performance of all groups verified the experimental hypothesis. The null hypothesis of no significant difference between obtained and theoretical frequencies can be safely rejected, and the training given each group is thus shown to be adequate for the generalization of a positive choice response from one stimulus to a previously neutral one.

A chi-square test of independence was also run on the data shown in Table 1 to see if there were any significant differences among the four groups in the success-failure ratio. No such differences were found ($\chi^2 = 3.0$; $p > .30$).

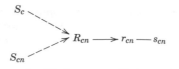

Conditioning assumed to have
occurred prior to the experiment

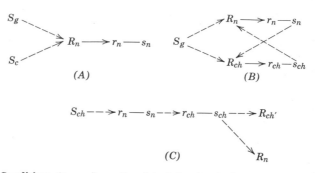

Figure 1. Conditions for and results of training for Ss in Group IV. S stands for stimulus of either geometric blocks (g) or colors (c); R stands for overt responses of either naming (n) or choosing (ch); r stands for implicit responses and s stands for stimuli produced by these implicit responses.

A test between Groups I and II combined and Groups III and IV combined also yielded insignificant results, although there is an indication that the more difficult task required of Ss in these latter two groups served to lower the number of correct responses ($\chi^2 = 3.37$; $p > .05$).[1]

GENERAL DISCUSSION AND CONCLUSIONS

The results of this experiment have shown that conditions which allow for mediated generalization, and which, in certain cases, offer Ss additional opportunities for reward and "labeling" experience, are sufficient to produce a positive response toward a previously neutral color with which Ss had had no differential reward experience. From this positive response, a favorable "attitude" towards this color is inferred. In addition, this favorable attitude has been demonstrated in more than one type of situation.

Space limitations do not permit a full presentation of the analysis of the results of this study in terms of learning theory concepts and

[1] The influence of age and sex on generalization in this experimental situation was tested by means of chi square. No significant differences were found to exist between Ss above and below the median age of their respective groups with respect to success and failure on the generalization tests. Similarly, no significant difference in the success-failure ratio was found to hold between the sexes.

principles. One illustration of the kind of analysis performed will have to suffice.

Figure 1 represents the conditions for and results of training for Ss in Group IV. Stage A represents Parts 1 and 3 of the experimental training, i.e., the name-learning sessions; Stage B represents Part 2, the reward session; and Stage C represents Part 5, the test situation. Stage A might have been better represented by three diagrams—one for each geometrical block and colored rectangle pair to which S learned to give the same name. For convenience, only one diagram, however, is used to represent all three. In stage B only one S_g is referred to, depending upon which geometrical block a particular S was consistently rewarded for choosing.

In stage C, the test situation, color names of three groups of children in a story were presented as oral stimuli to the Ss by E. S_{cn} represents these color-name stimuli. Each of the color-name stimuli can evoke a specific r_n-s_n because of the relationship shown in Figure 1 under the heading "conditioning assumed to have occurred prior to the experiment." It is assumed that the Ss, outside the experimental situation, have learned to make this same response to both S_c (a visual color stimulus) and S_{cn} (an auditory color stimulus, i.e., a color name). This same response is R_{cn} (naming the color, for example, "yellow"). If we now invoke the principle of mediated generalization we can say that any response subsequently conditioned to S_c will also be evocable by S_{cn}. In stage A such a new response was conditioned to S_c, namely the "egg," "car," or "shoe" response, R_n. As a result, when S_{cn} is presented in stage C, it can evoke the implicit and anticipatory component of R_n, namely r_n-s_n.

Once we have thus accounted for the evocation of r_n-s_n, we can see how this can evoke the anticipatory component of R_{ch}, namely r_{ch}-s_{ch}, the "attitude." This stems from the conditioning which took place in stage B and from the anticipatory nature of r_{ch}-s_{ch}. In this situation we see that r_{ch}-s_{ch} evokes, not the old R_{ch} of stage B, but a slightly different choice response ($R_{ch'}$). Both choice responses can be understood as being part of a habit family associated with the same stimulus, r_{ch}-s_{ch}, the "attitude." The evocation of the correct choice response, $R_{ch'}$, cannot be fully explained without assuming, as we have done, its evocation by its implicit component, the attitudinal response-produced stimulus r_{ch}-s_{ch}.

There is one part of our diagram which has thus far been ignored. We have said that in stage B r_n-s_n becomes conditioned to R_{ch} and that similarly r_{ch}-s_{ch} becomes conditioned to R_n. That this is indeed the case was demonstrated by the fact that many Ss, when choosing the colored group of their choice also used an "egg," "car," or "shoe" name to refer to it. Stage C, therefore, has been diagrammed to include the evocation of R_n by r_{ch}-s_{ch}.

Analyses of the conditions and results of training for Ss in Groups I, II, and III involve the application of similar principles.

It is hoped that the present study represents a step in the direction of experimentally validating certain principles of learning theory on a human level in more or less uniquely human situations. The author has shown that at least one of these principles (mediated generalization) can be used to predict a certain type of human behavior, preference for a class of stimuli with which individuals have had only neutral experience. This type of behavior is common and shows itself most dramatically in the exhibition of attitudes toward social or ethnic groups with which individuals have had little or no direct experience. That such attitudes may be directly taught by parents or other "teachers" and maintained by group reinforcement is one possibility. That they may also be formed in the indirect manner experimentally demonstrated by this study is another. It is not too big a step to assume that if children can learn to prefer the color yellow, for example, over the colors green and black as a result of the type of training given them in this investigation, they can also, as a result of similar training, learn to prefer people called Englishmen over those called Poles and Italians, even though they have had no differential reward or punishment experience with any of those three national groups. The essential requirement for this learning is that individuals should learn to attach the same labels to the word "Englishman" as to stimuli with which they have rewarding experience, and to attach the same labels to the words "Pole" or "Italian" as to stimuli with which they have had neutral or punishing experience.

SUMMARY

Eighty-one elementary school children of grades 1, 2, and 3 were trained to label a white triangular block and a green rectangular block "egg," to label a white square block and a black rectangular block "shoe," and to label a white circular block and a yellow rectangular block "car." In a subsequent situation all Ss were rewarded for choosing one particular geometrical white block. The Ss in Group I were then tested for mediated generalization by being asked to choose which of the colored rectangles they thought would bring a reward. The Ss in Group II were presented with three new, i.e., previously unexperienced, color stimuli and asked to guess which one would bring a reward. The Ss in Group III learned to label three different white "nonsense" blocks "yellow," "black," and "green," respectively, and then were asked to choose the block they would like to take home. The Ss in Group IV were told a story about three groups of children, a yellow, a black, and a green group, and then asked, which group they would invite to a hypothetical birthday party.

For each group it was predicted that Ss would choose that stimulus in the test having the same actual color or color name as the colored rectangle which they had learned had the same "egg," "car," or "shoe" name as the geometrical block for the choice of which they had previously been rewarded. These predictions were verified. Significantly more Ss in each group made the correct choices in the test than would have been expected by chance.

The investigation was designed to test the

general hypothesis that a color-preference response (positive attitude) could be developed through mediated generalization, and that this preference could be demonstrated in four situations differing in context, complexity, and social significance. An analysis, in terms of reinforcement learning theory principles and concepts, of the experimental conditions and results for Group IV was presented as illustrative of the type of analysis necessary for a full explanation of the behavior of Ss of all four groups in their respective test situations.

REFERENCES

1. Allport, G. W. Attitudes. In C. Murchison (Ed.), *A handbook of social psychology*. Worcester, Mass.: Clark Univer. Press, 1935. Pp. 798-844.
2. Birge, Jane S. The role of verbal responses in transfer. Unpublished doctor's dissertation, Yale Univer., 1941.
3. Cofer, C. N., and Foley, J. P., Jr. Mediated generalization and the interpretation of verbal behavior: I. Prolegomena. *Psychol. Rev.*, 1942, **49**, 513-540.
4. Cofer, C. N., and Foley, J. P., Jr. Mediated generalization and the interpretation of verbal behavior: II. Experimental study of certain homophone and synonym gradients. *J. exp. Psychol.*, 1943, **32**, 168-175.
5. Cofer, C. N., Janis, Marjorie G., and Rowell, Mary M. Mediated generalization and the interpretation of verbal behavior: III. Experimental study of antonym gradients. *J. exp. Psychol.*, 1943, **32**, 266-269.
6. Dollard, J., and Miller, N. E. *Personality and psychotherapy*. New York: McGraw-Hill, 1950.
7. Doob, L. W. The behavior of attitudes. *Psychol. Rev.*, 1947, **54**, 135-156.
8. Foley, J. P., Jr., and Mathews, M. A. Mediated generalization and the interpretation of verbal behavior: IV. Experimental study of the development of interlinguistic synonym gradients. *J. exp. Psychol.*, 1943, **33**, 188-200.
9. Foley, J. P., Jr., and MacMillan, Z. L. Mediated generalization and the interpretation of verbal behavior: V. Free association as related to differences in professional training. *J. exp. Psychol.*, 1943, **33**, 299-310.
10. Hull, C. L. Knowledge and purpose as habit mechanisms. *Psychol. Rev.*, 1930, **6**, 511-525.
11. Keller, Margaret. Mediated generalization: the generalization of a conditioned GSR established to a pictured object. *Amer. J. Psychol.*, 1943, **56**, 438-448.
12. Krech, D., and Crutchfield, R. S. *Theories and problems of social psychology*. New York: McGraw-Hill, 1948.
13. Razran, G. H. S. Salivating and thinking in different languages. *J. Psychol.*, 1935-36, **1**, 145-151.
14. Razran, G. H. S. A quantitative study of meaning by a conditioned salivary technique (semantic conditioning). *Science*, 1939, **90**, 89-90.
15. Reiss, B. F. Semantic conditioning involving the GSR. *J. exp. Psychol.*, 1940, **26**, 238-240.
16. Reiss, B. F. Genetic changes in semantic conditioning. *J. exp. Psychol.*, 1946, **36**, 143-152.
17. Sherif, M., and Cantril, H. The psychology of attitudes. *Psychol. Rev.*, 1945, **52**, 293-319.

41. An Outline of an Integrated Learning Theory of Attitude Formation and Function

ARTHUR W. STAATS

The history of psychology is a history of separatism, of clashes of men and theories. There have been many dimensions along which the field has split; for example, learning versus cognitive approaches. However, even within the general field of learning, there has been separatism. Even as it has been arrayed against other orientations, major efforts within learning have been expended in developing and maintaining separate experimental methods, separate general (philosophical) methodologies, and separate terminologies.

I see this as being very disadvantageous; it is a course that has prevented the development of a believable learning theory of human behavior. Simplistic learning approaches to human behavior, although frequently productive in their own research realms, have remained fragmented and vulnerable to criticism in more general considerations—it has been relatively easy to pick an example of behavior that the isolated approach could not handle. Consequently, I have attempted to integrate the basic principles of learning (classical and instrumental conditioning), the experimental findings from various areas of human learning experimentation, and the observations of the social and behavioral sciences, to constitute a comprehensive learning theory of human behavior (see Staats, 1961, 1964a, 1966, in press; Staats and Staats, 1963). This has involved an analysis of what we consider to be attitudes, some of the dimensions of which are presented here.

First, a theory of attitudes should include the study not only of attitude formation, but also of attitude *function*. The former, nevertheless, is usually the focus of the study of attitudes, while the latter is taken for granted. As this

• Prepared especially for this book.

outline will suggest, however, an analysis of both aspects of attitudes is more comprehensive, the analysis may be used to indicate how classical and instrumental conditioning principles are closely intertwined in the study of human behavior, and this in turn enables the study of attitudes to be interrelated with the considerations of human motivation relevant to the other social and behavioral sciences.

To begin, it may be suggested that what I mean by an attitude is an "emotional" response to a stimulus—usually a social stimulus or a stimulus that has social significance, although this is only an artificial demarcation. Emotional responses come to be elicited by many stimuli, social and otherwise, in a process of classical conditioning. Thus, if a new stimulus is paired with a stimulus that elicits an emotional response, the new stimulus will come to do so also. This can occur with negative emotional responses, elicited by aversive stimuli, as well as with positive emotional responses, elicited by pleasant (or rewarding) stimuli. Once a stimulus has come through classical conditioning to elicit an emotional response, it can "transfer" the response to a new stimulus with which it is paired. This process is called higher-order conditioning.

Thus classical conditioning may be said to account for the formation of attitudes, but it is still necessary to explicate the principles involved in attitude function—the reason why attitudes are so important to man's adjustment. It may be suggested, in making an integrated analysis, that the one process of classical conditioning actually endows the conditioned stimulus with two properties, or functions.

The rationale may be summarized as follows. Stimuli that elicit emotional responses in addition have another stimulus function. Although we consider the functions separately in laboratory study, the "emotional" stimuli that are used to elicit a response in the process of classical conditioning also have a function in an instrumental conditioning process. Thus, for example, food as a stimulus elicits the salivary response and other emotional responses, but in addition it will serve another function. When food is presented following an instrumental response, that response will occur more frequently—it will be instrumentally conditioned. Food, or sex stimulation, or some other positive emotional stimulus, will function as a reinforcer or reward, containing the power to effect instrumental behavior in the ways that rewards do. Electric shock, or any painful stimulus, may be seen as an example of a negative emotional stimulus that also has an instrumental function. Electric shock will elicit emotional responses, but in addition can be used as a negative reinforcer to suppress an instrumental behavior on which it is contingent (punishment), or to strengthen behaviors that escape from the shock.

Now, it has been suggested above that attitudinal stimuli are conditioned stimuli that through classical conditioning come to elicit emotional responses. It may also be suggested that in the process of classical conditioning *both* functions are "transferred" to the conditioned stimulus. That is, it would be expected that the conditioned attitudinal stimulus should also be capable of influencing the instrumental behaviors of the individual, as well as elicit an emotional response in the individual.

Let us take an extended example by which to illustrate these two aspects of attitude formation and function. Let us say that the word DANGEROUS has been paired with painful stimuli that elicit emotional responses. The word should come as a ^{C}S through this to elicit a conditioned emotional response. I and my associates (Staats et al., 1962) have shown that this emotional or attitudinal conditioning does indeed take place. That is, a word was paired with aversive stimuli, and the word came to elicit an emotional response (GSR). Furthermore, the subjects who were conditioned *rated* the word as unpleasant to an extent that was related to the extent of their emotional conditioning. These findings, which have been replicated by Maltzman et al. (1965), substantiate the analysis and also indicate that ratings can be used to index emotional, or attitudinal, conditioning.

To continue with the example, however, the word DANGEROUS should, after pairing with aversive stimuli, be capable of making other stimuli into attitudinal stimuli, according to the principle of higher-order classical conditioning. I and my associates have shown this in a number of studies (including the article that follows). That is, if the word DANGEROUS was paired with a new (social) stimulus, the new stimulus would be expected to come also to elicit the emotional response. To say that NEGROES ARE DANGEROUS would condition the negative emotional response elicited by DANGEROUS to the word NEGROES. This would be a process of higher-order conditioning.

Both this original conditioning and the higher-order conditioning have concerned only attitude *formation*. Following the preceding analysis, however, it would be expected that the word DANGEROUS, or the word NEGROES, would as a result of the conditioning also be capable of effecting the individual's instrumental behaviors. That is, the individual would be expected, for example, to learn escape behaviors that would take him away from the word DANGEROUS. He would avoid a bridge labeled DANGEROUS and so on. In the social area, following the example, he would also avoid people labeled as NEGROES. This learning would follow the principles of instrumental conditioning.

The experiment that is to be reprinted in the next article uses my experimental-theoretical method for the study of higher-order conditioning of attitudinal responses. Words that already elicit emotional responses are used to condition emotional responses to new words. The indication of the emotional (attitudinal) meaning of the words is obtained from ratings of the pleasantness or unpleasantness of the words. Although this study deals only with the *formation* of attitudes toward socially significant stimuli, it should be noted that the same attitudinal words would be expected to have also an instrumental conditioning *function*. This analysis (see Staats, 1964b) has already been tested in a study in which words that had been rated as pleasant or unpleasant, that is, positive and negative emotional words, were presented contingent on an instrumental response to assess their conditioning effect on the response. Three groups of subjects were used: for one group one of two alternative motor responses was followed on each occasion by a positive emotional word (like those used in the next study) such as HOLIDAY, SUPPER, BLOSSOM, VACATION, LAUGHTER; for another group negative emotional words were used such as BITTER, UGLY, FAT, HUNGER, LOST; for a third group words of neutral meaning were used such as BOX, WITH, TWELVE. Positive attitudinal words presented in a response-contingent manner strengthened the instrumental response, negative attitudinal words weakened the response, the neutral words had an in-between effect. The results showed that words that are ^CSs and elicit an emotional or attitudinal response, which can thus be used to condition emotional meaning to new stimuli, will also function as reinforcers in the learning of instrumental behaviors (Finley and Staats, in press).

The analysis and the various experimental results have important implications for understanding a powerful function of language in general, as well as for understanding the functions and the development of attitudes. Moreover, the analysis and findings are also relevant to attitude measurement—especially to rating procedures such as the semantic differential. Not only do such ratings indicate the attitude responses to stimuli, but in addition they indicate the reinforcement value of the stimuli—the extent to which such stimuli will condition and maintain behavior according to the principles of instrumental conditioning. It may be suggested that one of the important focuses of the study of attitudes must become the investigation of these principles by which attitude stimuli function.

In addition, showing the relationship of classical conditioning principles to the development of reinforcing, or attitudinal, stimuli has a great deal of significance in another way. That is, the consequent integration of the principles of reinforcement and the extension of the consideration of attitudes into the realm of instrumental behaviors brings a large area of significant human behavior into consideration by the analysis. This development revolves around the conception that what we consider to be attitude stimuli are a subclass of the larger class of reinforcing stimuli. Thus, in its broadest sense, the study of attitudes—and other reinforcing stimuli commonly described as *values* in social psychology and sociology, *needs* and *interests* in personality theory, evaluative meaning in experimental psychology, and *fetishes* and *urges* in abnormal psychology, to mention a few examples—is the study of human motivation. To appreciate fully the importance of an analysis of the development and function of such reinforcing stimuli, a word must be said of the importance of these stimuli in determining human behavior.

First, a great deal of information is given about the behavior of an individual (or, as we shall see, a group of individuals) when the nature of the reinforcers that are effective for the individual are described, as well as the *rules by which these reinforcers are applied*. For these two types of knowledge will tell us much about the types of behavior that the individual will develop.

For example, in our society some of the stimuli that have much reinforcing value (including many attitudinal stimuli) are: social and personal attention, acclaim, and respect; money, fine clothes, expensive cars, and houses; and various tokens such as awards and honors. In our society, also, there are "rules" (not formal or explicit) for the application of these stimuli. That is, they are delivered contingent on some kinds of behavior but not on others. Thus large amounts of these stimuli are delivered contingent on exceptionally skilled baseball, football, acting, dancing, or comic behaviors, among others. Relatively small amounts are delivered contingent on the behaviors of skilled manual work, teaching, unskilled manual work, nursing, and many others.

These characteristics of our reinforcing system and its rules of application, to continue with the example, have an effect on the manner in which behavior in our society is shaped. Consider, thus, a boy who has two classes of skilled behaviors—one a set of intellectual skills consisting of knowledge and well-developed study and scholarly work habits, and the other consisting of some form of fine athletic prowess. Let us say that either behavior could be developed to "championship" caliber. Now, in a situation in which the larger amount of reinforcing (attitudinal) stimuli is made contingent on the one behavior, this behavior will be strengthened, and as must be the case according to the principles of instrumental conditioning, it will be strengthened at the expense of the other behavior. In our society, of course, many of the strongest reinforcers are apt to be more liberally applied to athletic rather than scholarly behavior.

When groups are considered, it would also be expected that the reinforcer system and its rules of application will determine the types of behaviors that are dominant. A society that has a differing set of reinforcers and rules will evidence different behavior over the group of people exposed to that set of conditions. A society, for example, whose reinforcers are made contingent on scholarly research behaviors, will to a larger extent than another society create stronger behaviors of that type and in a greater number of people. In general, all of the different cultural, national, and class behaviors that have been observed in sociology, anthropology, and other behavioral sciences, can be considered to involve this aspect of human motivation—the reinforcer system and its rules of application.

The reinforcer system, including the many social attitudes, must also be considered to be of great importance in understanding abnormal behavior. An individual who has a markedly different reinforcer system than those in his group is likely to develop abnormal behavior. Thus the male for whom other males are strong sexual reinforcers is more likely to develop homosexual behaviors, for such behaviors will be strengthened by contact with those reinforcers. The problem of behavioral treatment may thus involve changing the nature of the individual's reinforcer (attitudinal) system.

These, of course, are simplified examples and take no account of other variables that will also contribute to the eventual outcome. [Moreover, not all of the learning principles that pertain to the study of attitudes, such as the discriminative control exerted by attitude stimuli (Staats, 1964a) can be discussed here.] However, in principle, it can be suggested that the nature of the individual's or group's reinforcer system and the rules of response-contingent application are crucial determinants of individual and group behavior.

This discussion has been conducted to indicate that the study of attitudes does not demarcate an area that is separate in principle from many other aspects of the human motivational system. The stimuli (and the responses they elicit) that we refer to under the term *attitudes* are in principle of the same type that we refer to in various social and behavioral sciences under the terms *values, emotions, needs, interests, group cohesiveness, goals, desires, utility* (in economics), *drive stimuli, reinforcers,* and so on. It may be suggested that the elaboration of an integration of learning principles, and the extension of the resulting model to the observations and concepts of the various social and behavioral sciences, is central to the development of a learning theory of human behavior, including a more comprehensive analysis of the acquisition and function of the motivational system.

REFERENCES

Finley, J. R., and Staats, A. W. Evaluative meaning words as reinforcing stimuli. *J. verb. Lg. and verb. Behav.*, in press.

Maltzman, I., Raskin, D. C., Gould, J., and Johnson, O. Individual differences in the orienting reflex and semantic conditioning and generalization under different UCS intensities. Paper presented at the Annual Meetings of the Western Psychological Association, Honolulu, June, 1965.

Staats, A. W. Verbal habit families, concepts, and the operant conditioning of word classes. *Psych. Rev.*, 1961, **68**, 190-204.

Staats, A. W. *Human Learning.* New York: Holt, Rinehart and Winston, 1964a.

Staats, A. W. Conditioned stimuli, conditioned reinforcers, and word meaning. In *Human Learning* (Staats, A. W. ed.). New York: Holt, Rinehart and Winston, 1964b.

Staats, A. W. An integrated-functional learning approach to complex human behavior. In *Problem Solving: Research, Method, and Theory* (Kleinmuntz, B., ed.). New York: Wiley, 1966.

Staats, A. W. Language Learning and Cognitive Development. New York: Holt, Rinehart and Winston, in press.

Staats, A. W., and Staats, C. K. *Complex Human Behavior.* New York: Holt, Rinehart and Winston, 1963.

Staats, A. W., Staats, C. K., and Crawford, H. L. First-order conditioning of meaning and the parallel conditioning of a GSR. *J. gen. Psychol.*, 1962, **67**, 159-167.

42. *Attitudes Established by Classical Conditioning*

ARTHUR W. STAATS and CAROLYN K. STAATS

Osgood and Tannenbaum have stated, ". . . The *meaning* of a concept is its location in a space defined by some number of factors or dimensions, and *attitude* toward a concept is its projection onto one of these dimensions defined as 'evaluative'" (9, p. 42). Thus, attitudes evoked by concepts are considered part of the total meaning of the concepts.

A number of psychologists, such as Cofer and Foley (1), Mowrer (5), and Osgood (6, 7), to mention a few, view meaning as a response—an implicit response with cue functions which may mediate other responses. A very similar analysis has been made of the concept of attitudes by Doob, who states, "'*An attitude is an implicit response . . . which is considered socially significant in the individual's society*'" (2, p. 144). Doob further emphasizes the learned character of attitudes and states, "The learning process, therefore, is crucial to an understanding of the behavior of attitudes" (2, p. 138). If attitudes are to be considered responses, then the learning process should be the same as for other responses. As an example, the principles of classical conditioning should apply to attitudes.

The present authors (12), in three experiments, recently conditioned the evaluative, potency, and activity components of word meaning found by Osgood and Suci (8) to contiguously presented nonsense syllables. The results supported the conception that meaning is a response and, further, indicated that word meaning is composed of components which can be separately conditioned.

The present study extends the original experiments by studying the formation of attitudes (evaluative meaning) to socially significant verbal stimuli through classical conditioning. The socially significant verbal stimuli were national names and familiar masculine names. Both of these types of stimuli, unlike nonsense syllables, would be expected to evoke attitudinal responses on the basis of the pre-experimental experience of the Ss. Thus, the purpose of the present study is to test the hypothesis that attitudes already elicited by socially significant verbal stimuli can be changed through classical conditioning, using other words as unconditioned stimuli.

METHOD

Subjects

Ninety-three students in elementary psychology participated in the experiments as Ss to fulfill a course requirement.

Procedure

The general procedure employed was the same as in the previous study of the authors (12).

Experiment I. The procedures were administered to the Ss in groups. There were two groups with one half of the Ss in each group. Two types of stimuli were used: national names which were presented by slide projection on a screen (CS words) and words which were presented orally by the E(US words), with Ss required to repeat the word aloud immediately after E had pronounced it. Ostensibly, Ss' task was to separately learn the verbal stimuli simultaneously presented in the two different ways.

Two tasks were first presented to train the Ss in the procedure and to orient them properly

• Reprinted from *Journal of Abnormal and Social Psychology*, 1958, **57**, 37-40, with permission of the senior author and the American Psychological Association. This article and the theoretical-experimental method were formulated by A. W. Staats as the principal investigator of a research project supported by the Office of Naval Research under Contract Nonr-2305(00). C. K. Staats aided in the conduct of the study and was responsible for the method of statistical analysis of the data.

for the phase of the experiment where the hypotheses were tested. The first task was to learn five visually presented national names, each shown four times, in random order. Ss' learning was tested by recall. The second task was to learn 33 auditorily presented words. Ss repeated each word aloud after E. Ss were tested by presenting 12 pairs of words. One of each pair was a word that had just been presented, and Ss were to recognize which one.

The Ss were then told that the primary purpose of the experiment was to study "how both of these types of learning take place together —the effect that one has upon the other, and so on." Six new national names were used for visual presentation: *German, Swedish, Italian, French, Dutch,* and *Greek* served as the CSs.

These names were presented in random order, with exposures of five sec. Approximately one sec. after the CS name appeared on the screen, E pronounced the US word with which it was paired. The intervals between exposures were less than one sec. Ss were told they could learn the visually presented names by just looking at them but that they should simultaneously concentrate on pronouncing the auditorily presented words aloud and to themselves, since there would be many of these words, each presented only once.

The names were each visually presented 18 times in random order, though never more than twice in succession, so that no systematic associations were formed between them. On each presentation, the CS name was paired with a different auditorily presented word, i.e., there were 18 conditioning trials. CS names were never paired with US words more than once so that stable associations were not formed between them. Thus, 108 different US words were used. The CS names, *Swedish* and *Dutch,* were always paired with US words with evaluative meaning. The other four CS names were paired with words which had no systematic meaning, e.g., chair, with, twelve. For Group 1, *Dutch* was paired with different words which had positive evaluative meaning, e.g., gift, sacred, happy; and *Swedish* was paired with words which had negative evaluative meaning, e.g., bitter, ugly, failure.[1] For Group 2, the order of *Dutch* and

Swedish was reversed so that *Dutch* was paired with words with negative evaluative meaning and *Swedish* with positive meaning words.

When the conditioning phase was completed, Ss were told that E first wished to find out how many of the visually presented words they remembered. At the same time, they were told, it would be necessary to find out how they *felt* about the words since that might have affected how the words were learned. Each S was given a small booklet in which there were six pages. On each page was printed one of the six names and a semantic differential scale. The scale was the seven-point scale of Osgood and Suci (8), with the continuum from pleasant to unpleasant. An example is as follows:

German
pleasant:—:—:—:—:—:—:—:unpleasant

The Ss were told how to mark the scale and to indicate at the bottom of the page whether or not the word was one that had been presented.

The Ss were then tested on the auditorily presented words. Finally, they were asked to write down anything they had thought about the experiment, especially the purpose of it, and so on, or anything they had thought of during the experiment. It was explained that this might have affected the way they had learned.

Experiment II. The procedure was exactly repeated with another group of Ss except for the CS names. The names used were *Harry, Tom, Jim, Ralph, Bill,* and *Bob.* Again, half of the Ss were in Group 1 and half in Group 2. For Group 1, *Tom* was paired with positive evaluative words and *Bill* with negative words. For Group 2 this was reversed. The semantic differential booklet was also the same except for the CS names.

Design

The data for the two experiments were treated in the same manner. Three variables were involved in the design: conditioned meaning (pleasant and unpleasant); CS names (*Dutch* and *Swedish,* or *Tom* and *Bill*); and groups (1 and 2). The scores on the semantic differential given to each of the two CS words were analyzed in a 2 x 2 latin square as described by Lindquist (4, p. 278) for his Type II design.

---

[1] The complete list of CS-US word pairs is not presented here, but it has been deposited with the American Documentation Institute. Order Document No. 5463 from ADI Auxiliary Publications Project, Photoduplication Service, Library of Congress, Washington 25, D. C., remitting in advance $1.25 for microfilm or $1.25 for photocopies. Make checks payable to Chief, Photoduplication Service, Library of Congress.

RESULTS

The 17 *S*s who indicated they were aware of either of the systematic name-word relationships were excluded from the analysis. This was done to prevent the interpretation that the conditioning of attitudes depended upon awareness. In order to maintain a counterbalanced design when these *S*s were excluded, four *S*s were randomly eliminated from the analysis. The resulting *N*s were as follows: 24 in Experiment I and 48 in Experiment II.

Table 1 presents the means and *SD*s of the meaning scores for Experiments I and II. The

TABLE 1. Means and SDs of Conditioned Attitude Scores

Experi-ment	Group	Names			
		Dutch		Swedish	
		Mean	SD	Mean	SD
I	1	2.67	.94	3.42	1.50
	2	2.67	1.31	1.83	.90

Experi-ment	Group	Tom		Bill	
		Mean	SD	Mean	SD
II	1	2.71	2.01	4.12	2.04
	2	3.42	2.55	1.79	1.07

Note. On the scales, pleasant is 1, unpleasant 7.

table itself is a representation of the 2×2 design for each experiment. The pleasant extreme of the evaluative scale was scored 1, the unpleasant 7.

The analysis of the data for both experiments is presented in Table 2. The results of the analysis indicate that the conditioning occurred in both cases. In Experiment I, the *F* for the conditioned attitudes was significant at better than the .05 level. In Experiment II, the *F* for the

TABLE 2. Summary of the Results of the Analysis of Variance for Each Experiment

Source	Experiment I			Experiment II		
	df	MS	F	df	MS	F
Between Ss						
Groups	1	7.52	4.36*	1	15.84	5.00*
Error	22	1.73		46	3.17	
Within						
Conditioned attitude	1	7.52	5.52*	1	55.51	10.47**
Names	1	.02	.01	1	.26	.05
Residual	22	1.36		46	5.30	
Total	47			95		

* $p < .05$.
** $p < .01$.

conditioned attitudes was significant at better than the .01 level. In both experiments the *F* for the groups variable was significant at the .05 level.

DISCUSSION

It was possible to condition the attitude component of the total meaning responses of *US* words to socially significant verbal stimuli, without *S*s' awareness. This conception is schematized in Figure 1, and in so doing, the way the

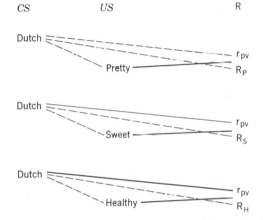

Figure 1. The conditioning of a positive attitude. The heaviness of line represents strength of association.

conditioning in this study was thought to have taken place is shown more specifically. The national name *Dutch,* in this example, is presented prior to the word *pretty*. *Pretty* elicits a meaning response. This is schematized in the figure as two component responses; an evaluative response r_{PV} (in this example, the words have a positive value), and the other distinctive responses that characterize the meaning of the word, R_P. The pairing of *Dutch* and *pretty* results in associations between *Dutch* and r_{PV}, and *Dutch* and R_P. In the following presentations of *Dutch* and the words *sweet* and *healthy,* the association between *Dutch* and r_{PV} is further strengthened. This is not the case with associations R_P, R_S, and R_H since they occur only once and are followed by other associations which are inhibitory. The direct associations indicated in the figure between the name and the individual words would also in this way be inhibited.

It was not thought that a rating response was conditioned in this procedure but rather an implicit attitudinal response which mediated the behavior of scoring the semantic differential scale. It is possible, with this conception, to interpret two studies by Razran (10, 11) which concern the conditioning of ratings. Razran found that ratings of ethnically labeled pictures of girls and sociopolitical slogans could be changed by showing these stimuli while Ss were consuming a free lunch and, in the case of the slogans, while the Ss were presented with unpleasant olfactory stimulation. The change in ratings could be thought to be due to the conditioning of an implicit evaluative response, an attitude, to the CSs by means of the lunch or the unpleasant odors. That is, part of the total response elicited by the food, for example, was conditioned to the pictures or slogans and became the mediation process which in turn elicited the positive rating.

It should be stated that the results of the present study do not show directly that Ss' behavior to the object (e.g., a person of Dutch nationality) has been changed. The results pertain to the Ss' attitudinal response to the signs, the national names themselves. However, Kapustnik (3) has demonstrated that a response generalized to an object when the response had previously been conditioned to the verbal sign of the object. Osgood states:

The aggressive reactions associated with *Nazi* and *Jap* on a verbal level certainly transferred to the social objects represented under appropriate conditions. Similarly, prejudicial behaviors established while reading about a member of a social class can transfer to the class as a whole . . . (7, p. 704).

The results of this study have special relevance for an understanding of attitude formation and change by means of verbal communication. Using a conception of meaning as a mediating response, Mowrer (5) has suggested that a sentence is a conditioning device and that communication takes place when the meaning response which has been elicited by the predicate is conditioned to the subject of the sentence. The results of the present study and the previous one of the present authors (12) substantiate Mowrer's approach by substantiating the basic theory that word meaning will

indeed condition to contiguously presented verbal stimuli. In the present study, the meaning component was evaluative, or attitudinal, and the CSs were socially significant verbal stimuli. The results suggest, therefore, that attitude formation or change through communication takes place according to these principles of conditioning. As an example, the sentence, "Dutch people are honest," would condition the positive attitude elicited by "honest" to "Dutch" —and presumably to any person called "Dutch." If, in an individual's history, many words eliciting a positive attitude were paired with "Dutch," then a very positive attitude toward this nationality would arise.

The reason for the group differences in each of the experiments is not clear. These differences could have arisen because there were actual differences in the Ss composing each group, or in some condition of the procedure occurring to one of the groups. Nothing the authors were aware of seem to indicate this as the explanation, and in the previous experiments of the authors (12) there were no group differences. Since in a 2×2 latin square the interactions are entirely confounded with the main effects, the group differences could also have arisen as a result of the interaction of the other two main effects (i.e., direction of conditioning and names).

SUMMARY

Two experiments were conducted to test the hypothesis that attitude responses elicited by a word can be conditioned to a contiguously presented socially significant verbal stimulus. A name (e.g., *Dutch*) was presented 18 times, each time paired with the auditory presentation of a different word. While these words were different, they all had an identical evaluative meaning component. In Experiment I, one national name was paired with positive evaluative meaning and another was paired with negative evaluative meaning. In Experiment II, familiar masculine names were used. In each experiment there was significant evidence that meaning responses had been conditioned to the names without Ss' awareness.

REFERENCES

1. Cofer, C. N., and Foley, J. P. Mediated generalization and the interpretation of verbal behavior: I. Prolegomena. *Psychol. Rev.,* 1942, **49**, 513-540.
2. Doob, L. W. The behavior of attitudes. *Psychol. Rev.,* 1947, **54**, 135-156.
3. Kapustnik, O. P. The interrelation between direct conditioned stimuli and their verbal symbols. (Trans. from Russian title) *Psychol. Abstr.,* 1934, **8**, No. 153.
4. Lindquist, E. F. *Design and analysis of experiments in psychology and education.* Boston: Houghton Mifflin, 1953.
5. Mowrer, O. H. The psychologist looks at language. *Amer. Psychologist,* 1954, **9**, 660-694.
6. Osgood, C. E. The nature and measurement of meaning. *Psychol. Bull.,* 1952, **49**, 197-237.
7. Osgood, C. E. *Method and theory in experimental psychology.* New York: Oxford Univer. Press, 1953.
8. Osgood, C. E., and Suci, G. J. Factor analysis of meaning. *J. exp. Psychol.,* 1955, **50**, 325-338.
9. Osgood, C. E., and Tannenbaum, P. H. The principle of congruity in the prediction of attitude change. *Psychol. Rev.,* 1955, **62**, 42-55.
10. Razran, G. H. S. Conditioning away social bias by the luncheon technique. *Psychol. Bull.,* 1938, **35**, 693.
11. Razran, G. H. S. Conditioned response changes in rating and appraising sociopolitical slogans. *Psychol. Bull.,* 1940, **37**, 481.
12. Staats, C. K., and Staats, A. W. Meaning established by classical conditioning. *J. exp. Psychol.,* 1957, **54**, 74-80.

43. A Concept-Formation Approach to Attitude Acquisition

RAMON J. RHINE

The purpose of this paper is to attempt a theoretical formulation of attitude development from a concept-formation point of view. Mediating responses have been employed by Osgood (21) to explain concept formation, and a mediating or implicit response has also been used as a main theoretical construct in Doob's (8) outline of attitude theory. To this extent, there is already an established theoretical link between concepts and attitudes.

Doob calls attitude "an implicit drive-producing response considered socially significant in the individual's society" (8, p. 136). This viewpoint has been criticized by Chein for a number of reasons, including the fact that it does not clearly indicate the evaluative nature of attitudes. Chein would rather call attitude a "disposition to evaluate certain objects, actions and situations in certain ways" (3, p. 177). Although many researchers in the field of attitudes might concur with Chein on this last point, a single meaning of attitude upon which there is close agreement is not available. Nelson's (20) review of the literature disclosed 23 more or less different definitions of attitude, and more recent statements could expand the list even further. No one definition seems clearly superior solely on logical grounds; if it were otherwise, there would not be so many alternatives.

The various definitions name constructs, and presumably some constructs have more scientific value than others. The psychologist, seeking a guide for his research among many alternatives, looks for a construct with heuristic and predictive value, particularly a construct which leads to informative research. Insofar as attitude change is concerned, Doob's type of approach has stimulated considerable research. But in the area of attitude development, very little carefully controlled experimentation has been done. Besides the research of Eisman (9), there is little experimentation available on attitude acquisition, although studies such as those by Horowitz (13) and by Clark and Clark (4) provide information about attitude growth. If it is possible to explain attitude learning in terms of concept formation, then attitude development is opened to controlled experimentation through concept-formation methods. A concept-formation approach to attitude learning also enables any systematic viewpoint which can account for concept formation to account at the same time for attitude formation.

THE GENERAL MEANING OF AN ATTITUDE

A concept is sometimes thought of as a psychological mechanism that represents a set of stimulus patterns; that is, a concept is considered a mental principle through which an individual can classify a number of objects in his stimulus world. Thus, redwood, elm, pine, fir, and oak fall into the class of "tall, nonanimal, living things," and *tree* is the name given to this principle. Similarly, the concept "a person who speaks with a drawl and has dark skin, thick lips, and kinky hair" classifies American Negroes for some people. Of course, the concepts learned in real life are not always verbalized into a precise principle. In fact, behavior in laboratory studies (19) indicates that a concept can be learned even though S is unaware of it and is unable to verbalize the principle on which the concept is based. The same phenomenon probably occurs with attitudes. People often betray by their behavior attitudes which they do not recognize as their own.

On a common-sense level, concepts are developed over a period of time through a series of experiences. The child learns the concept *cow*

• Reprinted from *Psychological Review*, 1958, **65**, 362-370, with permission of the author and the American Psychological Association.

because his parents and others point to objects in the field or in pictures and call them by that name. He learns that color alone is not the key to cow-ness, but that it is helpful. All black objects are not called cow, but green objects are never called by that name. The child soon learns to discriminate between cows and other objects as he learns that cow-ness is a feature of not one stimulus pattern but of a whole class of patterns.

The child learns about people in much the same manner. He discovers that one dimension of Negro-ness is dark skin, but that a deep suntan does not make one a Negro. He gradually learns that Negro-ness involves other dimensions such as facial characteristics and hair properties. This learning eventually enables him to make fairly accurate discriminations between Negroes and other persons. So far, the child has a concept of a Negro but not an attitude, because an attitude involves an evaluative dimension. Suppose, however, he has some unpleasant personal experiences with Negroes or receives adverse information about them from his parents. Then the child's concept might be based on the dimensions, "dark skin, kinky hair, thick lips, speaks with a drawl, and *bad*." Since an evaluative dimension now appears in the concept, he has acquired an attitude.

This approach to attitudes is not an arbitrary substitute for other meanings of attitude, but is representative of commonly used meanings, as may be seen from the following quotations:

"Most researchers in attitudes agree that one of the functions of attitudes is to integrate social perceptions and experiences. Thus our experiences with our mothers, sisters, girl friends and maiden aunts are integrated . . . into an attitude toward women" (16, p. 292). ". . . attitude [is] a more or less permanently enduring state of readiness of mental organization which predisposes an individual to react in a characteristic way to any object or situation with which it is related" (1, p. 13). "The attitude is a way of conceiving an object; it is the mental counterpart of an object" (10, p. 11). ". . . the *meaning* of a concept is its location in a space defined by some number of factors or dimensions, and *attitude* toward a concept is its projection onto one of these dimensions defined as 'evaluative'" (22, p. 42). "An attitude, roughly, is a residuum of experience, by which further activity is conditioned

and controlled . . . an inner mental organization takes place which predisposes the person to a certain type of activity towards objects, persons, and situations" (17, p. 238).

The thread which runs through these quotations—"experiences integrated into an attitude," "mental organization," "mental counterpart," "a way of conceiving"—is that an attitude is a kind of mental organization that is built through many experiences. In a sense, as a result of varied contacts with a class of objects, a concentrated representation of a set of stimuli is left within the person, which is the essence of what is generally meant by a concept.

AN EXPLANATION OF ATTITUDE

If an attitude is taken to be a concept with an evaluative dimension, its meaning may be derived from an explanation of concept formation. Consequently, any theory which can explain concept formation can also help to explain attitude development. One of several possible explanations of concept formation is provided by S–R Theory.

Borrowing from Osgood (21), a concept may be defined as the associations between a common response (often verbal) and a set of stimuli. These stimuli frequently comprise a class of phenomena which display certain common characteristics. The common characteristic of the set of phenomena may be the identical elements with which Hull (14) worked, such as a common shape embedded in each of several different Chinese characters. Or, as Smoke (30) has demonstrated, it may be common perceptual relations when, for instance, *S*s view a series of different figures and classify together all those having perpendicular lines in them. Although the stimuli mentioned in the definition of a concept often fall into a class, Osgood suggests that the only essential condition for concept formation is the associations between a common response and a variety of stimuli. There are no obvious stimulus characteristics common to hour-glass, ruler and mental test, all of which are *measuring instruments;* or to file cabinet, typewriter, and desk, all of which are *office equipment*. These items have in common the overt response of naming them, and, of greater theoretical importance, a common mediating process.

The mediating response, Hull's pure stimulus act, can be any fraction of a total response pattern. Partly as a result of the organism's capacity to discriminate, the mediating response will tend to become as fractionated as possible without destroying its cue function.

The greater the discriminatory capacity of an organism, the more reduced and implicit can become the "detachable" reactions finally included in the stable mediation process. The higher the organism in the evolutionary scale, the finer the discriminations it can usually make and the less gross its representing processes. Similarly, the more mature and intelligent the human individual, the less overt his symbolic processes. The hosts of fine discriminations that characterize language behavior are Nature's farthest step in this direction (21, p. 398).

Of all possible human mediators, probably the most significant are verbal mediators. Research by Cofer and Foley and associates (5, 6, 7, 12), Riess (28, 29), and others demonstrates the significance for language behavior of mediating responses. Other investigations by Reed (23, 24, 25), Kendler and Karasik (15), and by Goss and associates (2, 11) show the importance of verbal mediators in concept formation. Studies by Eisman (9), Rhine (26, 27), and Staats and Staats (31) show how verbal mediators enter into attitudes.

The general model for a simple, first-order concept based on either verbal or nonverbal mediators is illustrated in Part A of Figure 1. Many stimuli are conditioned to a common mediating response. By virtue of the common mediator, these stimuli become organized into one system. It is this system of associations between the stimuli and the common mediating process which is the concept. For the concept *gray*, the stimuli of Part A of Figure 1 would

be various acromatic shades all of which arouse the same mediating response. This response provides a stimulus generally conditioned in adults to the overt, verbal label *gray*.

A more complex or second-order concept is illustrated in Part B of Figure 1. Each set of stimuli with their associated mediators (r_1's) are first-order concepts. In the second-order concept, the stimuli produced by the first-order mediators are themselves associated with another common mediator. One set of first-order stimuli in Part B of Figure 1 might be different skin shades leading to the mediator representing *dark skin*; the second set of first-order stimuli might be various lip thicknesses which are associated with the mediator for *thick lips*; and each of the stimuli from these mediating responses may be associated with the mediator for *Negro* (r_2). This illustrates a second-order concept, but there is no attitude as yet because no evaluation is involved.

There is an attitude when the mediator of at least one of the first-order concepts is an evaluative reaction. Thus, attitudes are equivalent to that special class of concepts which is distinguished by the inclusion of an evaluative dimension. Part C of Figure 1 is a simplified illustration of an attitude. Suppose, as in the example of a second-order concept, that one r_1 of this figure is the mediator for *thick lips*, that the second r_1 represents *dark skin*, and that r_2 is the mediator for *Negro*. Suppose also that the stimuli (S_e) of the evaluative dimension are *dirty, stupid,* and *rude* and that r_{1_e}, the evaluative reaction, is *bad*. Now the stimuli associated with Negro are *dark skin, thick lips,* and *bad*. The inclusion of an evaluative dimension identifies Part C of Figure 1 as an attitude.

The mediating response produces a stimulus

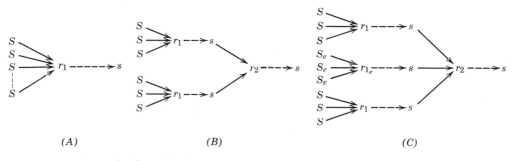

(A)   (B)   (C)

Figure 1. *A stimulus-response explanation of concepts and attitude.* (A) *First-order concept;* (B) *second-order concept;* (C) *attitude.* S = *evaluative stimuli;* r_1 = *a first-order mediator;* r_{1_e} = *a first-order evaluative mediator;* r_2 = *a second-order mediator;* s = *the stimulus produced by a mediator.*

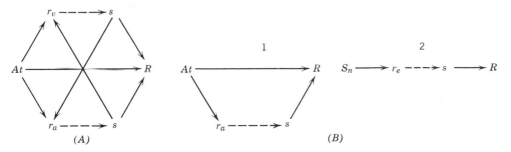

Figure 2. (A) *Major associations between the attitude* (At = *the attitude as shown in A of Figure 1), and verbal* (r_v) *and affective* (r_a) *mediators.* (B) *A stimulus-response explanation of prejudice through displaced aggression.*

which may then become conditioned to other mediating or instrumental reactions. Part A of Figure 2 shows some of the major associations possible between the attitude and these other mediating responses. It indicates how instrumental responses may depend upon a chain of associations involving two major types of mediators, namely, affective and verbal. Part A of Figure 2 is not meant to imply that in any given instance all the illustrated associations between the attitude and verbal or affective mediators will be formed. Instead, it indicates that one or more of the associations may be learned by a given individual. For instance, as is shown in Part B-1 of Figure 2, only some of the relations between the attitude, affect, and the instrumental response may be learned in an individual case.

One implication of Figure 2 is particularly interesting. A reaction conditioned to the attitude may be aroused by a stimulus which is associated with affect but not with the attitude. This situation suggests an explanation for prejudiced responses through displaced aggression. Suppose an individual has a negative attitude towards Negroes. Suppose further that the affect of Part B of Figure 2 is the mediator for *anger* and the instrumental response is aggression toward Negroes. Assume also, as Part B-1 of Figure 2 indicates, that the attitude leads to the simultaneous arousal of anger and of aggression against Negroes. Eventually, through conditioning, anger alone can lead to aggression. Now, as indicated by Part B-2 of Figure 2, any stimulus (S_n) which arouses anger will also have a tendency to evoke aggression towards Negroes, depending upon the degree to which this stimulus is supported by other stimuli. As a result, there is a tendency to displace aggression from S_n, the real source of anger, to Negroes.

Other specific predictions follow from the general relations shown in Part A of Figure 2. The relationship between verbal mediating responses and affect suggests one reason why attitudes are commonly accompanied by affective reactions. If a given verbal mediator, through past experience, has become associated with affect, then the arousal of this mediator by an attitude will also lead to an affective response: the attitude leads to the verbal mediator and the verbal mediator is associated with affect. Suppose, for instance, that an attitude supplies the conditioned stimulus which evokes the verbal mediator for *green vomit*. Then, insofar as this mediator evokes an emotional reaction, the attitude will be accompanied by affect. This particular verbal mediator was used as an example because in some cases it will make the illustration more vivid by actually arousing an emotional reaction in the reader.

There is probably a more important reason why attitudes are commonly linked to affect. It is quite often true that the experiences through which the attitude is developed occur in a charged atmosphere. In this case, the mediating response of the attitude is continuously aroused in conjunction with an emotional reaction, and the stimulus produced by the mediating response becomes a conditioned stimulus capable of evoking effect. As a result, the expression of this attitude is accompanied by an emotional response.

A METHOD FOR STUDYING ATTITUDE DEVELOPMENT

One of the main values of the concept-formation approach to attitude is that it suggests a simple laboratory method for studying attitude development. If an attitude is a kind of concept, then its acquisition may be investigated by the methods of concept formation. Such a method, depending on an evaluative dimension in the concept, has been employed by the writer. In order to construct an evaluative dimension, 100 Ss were asked to rate a large number of descriptive traits in terms of their desirability in a person. Some example traits are: ambitious, boring, calm, intelligent, obedient, and vain. All traits showing less than 90% agreement as to their desirability were discarded. The remaining traits can be employed to study the development of an attitude and to measure its strength and resistance to change. To do this, a group of Ss is told that anthropologists, missionaries and physicians have visited a group of people about which little is known, and that all the visitors agree on certain characteristics of this group of people. When these instructions are concluded, Ss are shown a number of traits, one by one, and are asked to predict whether each trait is or is not characteristic of the people. After each prediction they are told whether or not the word is indeed characteristic. For example, to develop a positive attitude, E would say "characteristic" after presenting each trait previously rated as desirable and "not characteristic" for words previously rated undesirable.

If S has learned the positive attitude, which might be labeled "pro-ness," he would be expected to respond accordingly. Hence, when he has completed the first list of traits, S is asked to continue responding in the previous manner to a second list of words without being told which traits are characteristic or not characteristic. Responses under this condition are taken as a measure of attitude strength. It is assumed that a strongly acquired, positive attitude will lead to a high proportion of positively rated traits being called "characteristic" and to most negatively rated traits being called not "characteristic."

Finally, resistance to attitude change is measured by using a third list of traits with E again saying "characteristic" or "not characteristic" after each prediction. But this time E's responses are reversed. For example, if S has previously acquired a positive attitude, change may be accomplished by calling "not characteristic" all positive traits in the third list and "characteristic" all negative traits.

This method is derived from the concept-formation approach to attitudes. The meaning of the many traits seen in a single session varies considerably, as can be observed from the ex-

amples given above. Although the traits are not synonyms, they do exhibit one common aspect, the evaluative element. The Ss are able to respond correctly when this evaluative element is consistently reinforced by E because the traits are stimuli which are capable of arousing a common, evaluative mediating response. The mediating process, in turn, determines S's further predictions of "characteristic" or "not characteristic."

The stimulus function of mediating responses in attitude development is demonstrated by two experiments which also illustrate the mediating response approach as applied through the concept-attitude method. A negative attitude was developed in both investigations. In one study (27), consistency of reinforcement was defined as the sum of the number of positive traits called "not characteristic" by E and the number of negative traits called "characteristic," divided by the total number of traits used during attitude development. Using five levels of consistency, it was shown that both attitude development and strength increase as a function of consistency of reinforcement, as would be predicted from the approach to attitude development based on mediating responses. The results for attitude change also suggest that attitudes exhibit properties of mediating responses. Research on acquired distinctiveness of cues (18) indicates that strong habits reverse more easily than weak ones when the cues arousing them have become distinct through learning. The distinctiveness of the stimulus dimension is believed to be related to the degree to which the stimuli are conditioned to a mediating process. The evaluative element of the stimulus traits should be most distinct when reinforcement is fully consistent; consequently, attitude change should be easiest under this condition. The Ss receiving the greatest consistency of reinforcement did in fact show least resistance to change.

A second experiment (26) illustrating the concept-attitude method investigated the effect on attitude development of peer responses. The traits were used with 100% and 84% consistency of reinforcement to develop a negative attitude. Some Ss made their predictions after first hearing the responses of three fellow students who were E's confederates, and other Ss made their predictions in private. The confederates' responses prior to S's predictions were always or almost always in contradiction with the statement E made after each prediction. Thus, when the confederates said a trait was characteristic, it was pretty certain that *E* would say the trait was not characteristic. The *Ss* who heard the confederates' responses learned the attitude with greater ease than those who responded in private. Apparently, peer responses provided cues which were an aid to *S* in attaining the attitude. This seemed to occur mainly with high consistency of reinforcement. With less than full consistency of reinforcement, peer responses were predictive of *E*'s behavior for a majority of the traits, but not all of them. When this ambiguity is introduced, cues from peer responses do not affect attitude development at a statistically significant level, although there is a slight trend in this direction.

These results may be explained by considering the effect of peer responses upon the arousal of the common, evaluative mediating response. With 100% consistency of reinforcement, a negative mediating reaction is aroused by a trait just prior to reinforcement and in conjunction with peer responses of "characteristic." Similarly, a positive mediating reaction is aroused in conjunction with peer responses of "not characteristic." In time, as a result of conditioning, the peer responses can be expected to help cue the appropriate positive or negative mediating response. With 84% consistency of reinforcement, the trend of conditioning is the same, but a minority of trials tend to establish competing, mediating responses: the same peer reactions are sometimes associated with positive mediating responses and sometimes with negative. Under these conditions, peer responses are a less stable and less predictive aspect of the stimulus environment. This would account for the statistically significant effect from peer responses with high consistency of reinforcement, which is diminished with lesser consistency.

Staats and Staats (31) have also studied attitudes using an approach similar to that employed in the preceding two studies. They associated given names, Tom or Bill, and nationalities, Dutch or Swedish, with positive or negative evaluative words. Subsequent ratings indicate that the given names and nationalities took on the same evaluative flavor as the words with which they were associated. The researchers explain their results by pointing to the common, evaluative mediating response made to the words which are paired with the nationalities and names. It is assumed that through conditioning the names (or nationalities) would also lead to the mediating response aroused by the words with which they were paired. This was reflected when the names (or nationalities) were rated on the evaluative scale.

The studies derived from the concept theory of attitudes illustrate the possibility of bringing attitude development under laboratory scrutiny. Despite the generally recognized significance of attitude development, as distinguished from attitude change, the literature reveals relatively little laboratory evidence bearing upon its nature. It is hoped that the concept theory of attitudes and the method it implies will help provide a means through which attitude development will be more accessible to experimental investigations.

SUMMARY

A theory of attitude development based upon concept formation was discussed, and similarities between this view and earlier meanings of attitude were pointed out. An attitude was defined as a concept with an evaluative dimension, and the mediating response was employed to explain attitude learning. A method for inducing an attitude in the laboratory was described along with illustrative studies employing this method.

REFERENCES

1. Cantril, H. Attitudes in the making. *Understanding the child,* 1934, **4**, 13-14, 18.
2. Carey, J. E., and Goss, A. E. The role of verbal labeling in the conceptual sorting behavior of children. *J. genet. Psychol.,* 1957, **90**, 69-74.
3. Chein, I. Behavior theory and the behavior of attitudes: Some critical comments. *Psychol. Rev.,* 1948, **55**, 175-188.
4. Clark, K. B., and Clark, Mamie P. Racial identification and preference in Negro children. In G. E. Swanson, T. M. Newcomb and E. L. Hartley (Eds.), *Readings in social psychology.* New York: Holt, 1952.
5. Cofer, C. N., and Foley, J. P. Mediated generalization and the interpretation of verbal behavior: I. Prolegomena. *Psychol. Rev.,* 1942, **49**, 513-540.

6. Cofer, C. N., and Foley, J. P. Mediated generalization and the interpretation of verbal behavior: II. Experimental study of certain homophone and synonym gradients. *J. exp. Psychol.*, 1943, **32**, 168-175.

7. Cofer, C. N., Janis, Marjorie E., and Rowell, Mary M. Mediated generalization and the interpretation of verbal behavior: III. Experimental study of antonym gradients. *J. exp. Psychol.*, 1943, **32**, 266-269.

8. Doob, L. W. The behavior of attitudes. *Psychol. Rev.*, 1947, **54**, 135-156.

9. Eisman, Bernice S. Attitude formation: The development of a color preference response through mediated generalization. *J. abnorm. soc. Psychol.*, 1955, **50**, 321-326.

10. Faris, E. The concept of social attitudes. In K. Young (Ed.), *Social attitudes.* New York: Holt, 1931.

11. Fenn, J. D., and Goss, A. E. The role of mediating verbal responses in the conceptual sorting behavior of normals and schizophrenics. *J. genet. Psychol.*, 1957, **90**, 59-67.

12. Foley, J. P., Jr., and Mathews, M. A. Mediated generalization and the interpretation of verbal behavior: IV. An experimental study of the development of interlinguistic synonym gradients. *J. exp. Psychol.*, 1943, **33**, 188-200.

13. Horowitz, E. L. The development of attitude toward the Negro. *Arch. Psychol.*, 1936, No. 194.

14. Hull, C. L. Quantitative aspects of the evolution of concepts. *Psychol. Monogr.*, 1920, **28**, No. 1 (Whole No. 123).

15. Kendler, H. H., and Karasik, A. D. Concept-formation as a function of competition between response produced cues. *J. exp. Psychol.*, 1958, **55**, 278-283.

16. Krech, D. Attitudes and learning: A methodological note. *Psychol. Rev.*, 1946, **53**, 290-293.

17. Krueger, E. T., and Reckless, W. C. *Social psychology.* New York: Longmans, Green, 1931.

18. Lawrence, D. H. Acquired distinctiveness of cues: II. Selective association in a constant stimulus situation. *J. exp. Psychol.*, 1950, **40**, 175-188.

19. Leeper, R. Cognitive processes. In S. S. Stevens (Ed.), *Handbook of experimental psychology.* New York: Wiley, 1951.

20. Nelson, E. Attitudes: I. Their nature and development. *J. genet. Psychol.*, 1939, **21**, 367-399.

21. Osgood, C. E. *Method and theory in experimental psychology.* New York: Oxford Univer. Press, 1953.

22. Osgood, C. E., and Tannenbaum, P. H. The principle of congruity in the prediction of attitude change. *Psychol. Rev.*, 1955, **62**, 42-55.

23. Reed, H. B. Factors influencing the learning and retention of concepts: I. The influence of set. *J. exp. Psychol.*, 1946, **36**, 71-87.

24. Reed, H. B. The learning and retention of concepts: II. The influence of length of series. III. The origin of concepts. *J. exp. Psychol.*, 1946, **36**, 166-179.

25. Reed, H. B. The learning and retention of concepts: IV. The influence of complexity of the stimuli. *J. exp. Psychol.*, 1946, **36**, 252-261.

26. Rhine, R. J. The effect of peer group influence upon concept-attitude development and change. *J. soc. Psychol.*, in press.

27. Rhine, R. J., and Silun, B. A. Acquisition and change of a concept attitude as a function of consistency of reinforcement. *J. exp. Psychol.*, 1958, **55**, 524-529.

28. Riess, B. F. Semantic conditioning involving the GSR. *J. exp. Psychol.*, 1940, **26**, 238-240.

29. Riess, B. F. Genetic changes in semantic conditioning. *J. exp. Psychol.*, 1946, **36**, 143-152.

30. Smoke, K. L. An objective study of concept formation. *Psychol. Monogr.*, 1932, **42**, No. 4 (Whole No. 191).

31. Staats, A. W., and Staats, Carolyn K. Attitudes established by classical conditioning. *J. abnorm. soc. Psychol.*, 1958, **57**, 37-40.

44. A Behavior Theory Approach to the Relations between Beliefs about an Object and the Attitude Toward the Object

MARTIN FISHBEIN

In another paper in this book, Fishbein (see pp. 257 to 266) presented a distinction between beliefs about an object and the attitude toward that object. Generally speaking, attitudes were conceptualized as learned predispositions to respond to an object or class of objects in a consistently favorable or unfavorable way, and beliefs about an object were viewed as hypotheses concerning the nature of the object and its relations to other objects. Consistent with the works of Doob (1947), Lott (1955), Osgood et al. (1957), Rhine (1958), and others, both of these phenomena (i.e., beliefs about an object and attitude) may readily be placed within the framework of behavior theory. As Lott has pointed out, the placement of attitude within the framework of behavior theory "appears to be a more research-oriented and potentially fruitful approach to the problem." (p. 321). Indeed, by following the principles of behavior theory, a model of attitude acquisition and a model of the relationships between beliefs about an object and the attitude toward the object can be generated. Before turning to these models, however, let us briefly consider the behavior theory view of attitudes and beliefs about an object.

ATTITUDE

Consistent with the work of Osgood and his associates (1957, 1965), an attitude may be characterized as a "mediating evaluative response," that is, as a learned implicit response that varies in intensity and tends to "mediate" or guide an individual's more overt evaluative

• Specially prepared for this book.

responses to an object or concept. Two points about this view should be noted. First, attitude is treated as a unidimensional concept; it refers only to the "evaluation" of a concept (i.e., its "goodness" or "badness"). In this respect, it is entirely consistent with Thurstone's (1931) definition of attitude as "the amount of affect for or against a psychological object." Second, as Osgood et al. have pointed out, "every point in semantic space has an evaluative component (even though the component may be of zero magnitude when the evaluative judgments are neutral)." Thus, with respect to any object, an individual has a positive, negative, or neutral attitude; that is, there is a mediating evaluative response associated with every stimulus.

BELIEF ABOUT AN OBJECT

As Fishbein (see pp. 257 to 266 in this book) has pointed out, any belief about an object can be defined in terms of the "probability" or "improbability" that a particular relationship exists between the object of belief (e.g., an attitude object) and any other object, concept, value, or goal. If the object of belief (i.e., the attitude object) is viewed as a "stimulus" and if the object or concept related to the object of belief is viewed as a "response," a belief statement may be viewed as a stimulus-response association. Thus a belief about an object may be seen as being highly related to the probability that the stimulus elicits the response, that is, to the probability that there is an association between the stimulus (the attitude object) and the response (any other concept). Furthermore, it should be noted that an individual has many beliefs about any aspect of

389

his world. That is, an individual associates many different concepts with any given attitude object. The totality of an individual's beliefs about an object can thus be viewed as a belief system. In addition, this system of responses associated with a given stimulus may also be viewed as a habit-family-hierarchy of responses (Hull, 1943). The higher the response in the hierarchy, the greater is the probability that the response is associated with the stimulus, that is, the stronger is the belief. Empirical evidence supporting this conception of a belief system has been presented by Fishbein (1963).

To summarize, both beliefs about an object and the attitude toward the object have been placed within a behavior theory framework. Attitudes have been viewed as learned, mediating evaluative responses, and beliefs about an object have been viewed in terms of the probability (or strength) of stimulus-response associations. Furthermore, a belief system has been conceptualized as a habit-family-hierarchy of responses. Given these descriptions, a model of attitude acquisition and a model of the relationships between beliefs and attitudes can be developed by following the principles of behavior theory and, in particular, the principle of mediated (i.e., secondary or conditioned) generalization (see Birge, 1941; Cofer and Foley, 1942; Murdock, 1952; Mednick, 1957).

1. A MODEL OF ATTITUDE ACQUISITION

In the foregoing article in this book (pp. 382 to 388), Rhine, working from Osgood's definition of attitude (i.e., "the evaluative dimension of a concept"), develops a model of attitude acquisition based on a consideration of the process of concept formation. Rhine's model may be seen in Figure 1. To review

briefly, Rhine argues that no attitude is present in either A (first-order concept) or B (second-order concept) of Figure 1. However, "there is an attitude when the mediator of at least one of the first-order concepts is an evaluative one." Thus, as Rhine views it, we first acquire the first-order mediators (or concepts) "thick lips" and "dark skin" from sets of first-order stimuli of lip thicknesses and skin shades. When the stimuli produced by these mediators come to elicit the second-order mediator "Negro," we have a second-order concept, but not an attitude (see Figure 1B). It is only when a series of first-order "evaluative stimuli" elicit a first-order evaluative mediator (e.g., "bad"), and the stimulus produced by this evaluative mediator also comes to elicit the second-order mediator "Negro," that an attitude is present (see Fig. 1C). Thus, according to this conceptualization, we may acquire the concept "Negro" and *not* have an attitude toward "Negro." The concept and the attitude can be learned independently or simultaneously. Similar views of the relationship between concept learning and attitudes have been presented by Clark and Clark (1958) and Allport (1954).

However, as was pointed out in the discussion of attitude, all concepts contain an evaluative component. That is, there is an attitude, an evaluative response associated with all concepts. Furthermore, it should be noted that as Osgood used the term "concept," it referred to any discriminable aspect of the individual's world; it might refer to any object, person, word, groups of words, and so on. Thus, as this term is used by Osgood, all "stimuli" and all "responses" (verbalizable or not) are viewed as concepts.

In A of Figure 1, then, all the "first-order stimuli" of various skin shades eliciting the

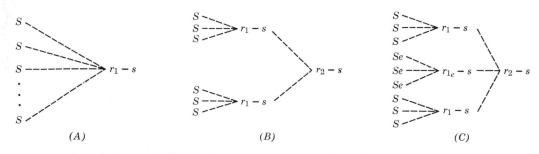

Figure 1. Ramon J. Rhine's theory of attitude acquisition (from Rhine, 1958). (A) *First-order concept;* (B) *second-order concept;* (C) *attitude.* S = *a first-order stimulus;* S$_e$ = *an evaluative stimulus;* r$_1$ = *a first-order mediator;* r$_{1_e}$ = *a first-order evaluative mediator;* r$_2$ = *a second-order mediator;* s = *the stimulus produced by a mediator.*

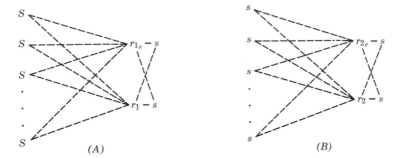

Figure 2. A general model of attitude acquisition. (A) First-order concept with attitude; (B) second-order concept with attitude. S = a stimulus; r_1 = a first-order mediator; r_{1_e} = a first-order evaluative mediator; r_2 = a second-order mediator; r_{2_e} = a second-order evaluative mediator; s = the stimulus produced by a mediator. The higher the stimulus in the stimulus hierarchy, the greater the probability that it will elicit the concept (either first-, second-, or n-order). The evaluative mediators represent a summation of the evaluative responses elicited by the stimuli. The strength of the evaluative mediator, i.e., the attitude, is a function of the evaluative dimension of each of the stimuli and the probability that the stimuli elicit the concept.

mediator or concept "dark skin" *also* elicit an evaluative response. These evaluative responses are seen as being summative; through the mediation process, the summated evaluative response is associated with the mediator or concept "dark skin." Thus, on future occasions, "dark skin" will elicit an evaluative response that is a function of the stimuli that elicit it (i.e., dark skin). This may be seen in *A* of Figure 2. Similarly, the stimuli produced by other first-order concepts or mediators (e.g., thick lips, curly hair) will elicit evaluative responses at the same time that they elicit the "second-order mediator" or concept "Negro." Therefore, on future occasions, the concept or stimulus "Negro" will elicit an evaluative response, an attitude, that is a function of the stimuli that elicit it (i.e., Negro). This may be seen in *B* of Figure 2.

The probability that the stimuli (e.g., dark skin, thick lips) elicit the mediator or concept "Negro," also influence the evaluation of (the attitude toward) "Negro." If a stimulus that elicits a strong evaluative response only elicits "Negro" 40 per cent of the time, while another stimulus that also elicits a strong evaluative response elicits "Negro" 80 per cent of the time, the latter will contribute more to the evaluation of "Negro" than will the former. Thus attitude toward any concept is a function of the evaluations of the stimuli that elicit the concept *and* the probability that these stimuli will elicit the concept.

This conception of attitude acquisition dif-

fers from Rhine's in that, following Osgood et al. (1957), all stimuli have evaluative responses associated with them. Furthermore, every time a new concept is learned, an attitude is automatically acquired with it. Attitude acquisition is an automatic, nonverbalized process that occurs in conjunction with concept learning.

2. A MODEL OF THE RELATIONSHIPS BETWEEN BELIEFS ABOUT AN OBJECT AND THE ATTITUDE TOWARD THE OBJECT

The theory of concept formation and attitude acquisition carries important implications for the study of beliefs about an object and the attitude toward it. If concepts are learned as the theory suggests, it follows that an individual's beliefs about the concept should be some function of the learning process. In the example above, we can assume that at least two of the individual's beliefs about "Negroes" are that (1) Negroes have dark skin, and (2) Negroes have thick lips. Furthermore, if "dark skin" has elicited "Negro" more frequently than "thick lips" has, his belief that Negroes have dark skin should be stronger than his belief that Negroes have thick lips. If, for the purpose of explication, we consider the process of concept formation as input, and beliefs about the object as output, then (even granting the asymmetry of backward and forward association) immediately after concept formation the output should be highly correlated with or equal to the input. This may be seen in Figure 3, which presents the theoretical model of the output side of the relationship, the model of the relations between beliefs about an object and the attitude toward that object.

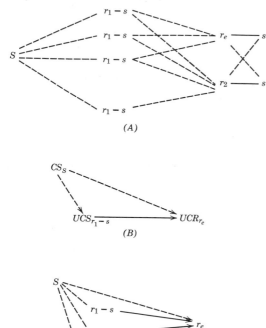

(A)

(B)

(C)

Figure 3. Some relations between beliefs about an object and the attitude toward the object. (A) A mediation model; (B) a classical conditioning model; (C) an extension of the classical conditioning model. S = *a stimulus (e.g., Negro);* r_1 = *a first-order mediator (e.g., dark skin);* r_2 = *a second-order mediator (e.g., Negro);* r_e = *an evaluative mediator;* s = *the stimulus produced by a mediator.*

In Figure 3*A*, it can be seen that immediately after concept formation, the concept (or stimulus) elicits the set of responses that have served to define it (e.g., "dark skin," "thick lips," etc.). Each of these mediating responses, however, also serve as stimuli. Viewing these responses in this way (i.e., as stimuli), it can be seen that the right-hand side of Figure 3*A* is identical to the model of attitude acquisition presented in Figure 2*B*. That is, "dark skin," "thick lips," etc., will each tend to elicit the concept "Negro" as well as a positive, negative,

or neutral evaluative response. As was discussed above, these evaluative responses summate; through the mediation process, the summated evaluative response becomes associated with the concept "Negro."

In addition, the summated evaluative response (i.e., the attitude) also becomes associated with the concept (or stimulus) through the process of classical conditioning. This can be seen in Figure 3*B*, where, for the purpose of presentation, only one belief is considered. Following the classical conditioning paradigm, it can be seen that, to a certain degree, the evaluative response (i.e., the UCR—unconditioned response) elicited by "dark skin" (i.e., the UCS—unconditioned stimulus) becomes associated with the concept "Negro" (i.e., the CS—conditioned stimulus). The stronger the association between "Negro" and "dark skin" (i.e., the stronger the belief that "Negroes have dark skin"), the more the evaluation of "dark skin" will become associated with "Negro." However, as already mentioned, an individual has many beliefs about any given concept, and the evaluation associated with each of these beliefs will also become associated, in part, with the attitude object or concept. This can be seen in Figure 3*C*. Again, it should be noted that the evaluative responses associated with each of the beliefs are viewed as summative; thus it is this summated evaluative response, i.e., this attitude, that becomes associated with the concept (e.g., Negro). Furthermore, the amount of the evaluative response associated with each belief that is available for summation is a function of the strength of the belief. That is, if "Negro" elicits "dark skin" 95 per cent of the time and "thick lips" 60 per cent of the time, the evaluation of "dark skin" will contribute more to the evaluation of "Negro" than will the evaluation of "thick lips."

An individual's attitude toward any object, then, is learned as a result of both mediation and conditioning. The complete model of the relations between beliefs about an object and the attitude toward that object can be seen in Figure 4. It should again be noted that the model of attitude acquisition is included within the model of the relations between beliefs and attitude. Thus it becomes apparent that beliefs about an object and the attitude toward that object are in a continuous, dynamic relationship. Changes in any one part of the system may produce changes in all the other parts. In addition, in Figure 4, it can be seen that

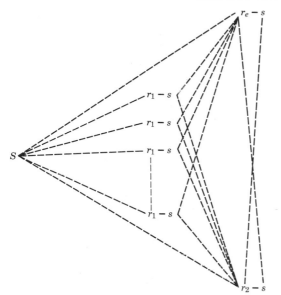

Figure 4. A model of the relation between belief about and attitude toward an object. S = the stimulus, i.e, attitude object; r_1 = first-order mediators elicited by S, indicating belief r, about S; r_e = an evaluative mediator; r_2 = a second-order mediator.

the summated evaluative response (i.e., the attitude) that is learned in concept formation is identical (for all practical purposes) to the summated evaluative response acquired through conditioning. However, it should be recalled that the discussion above was only concerned with the beliefs an individual held immediately following concept attainment. Once a concept has been learned (or once a given stimulus has been labeled), new beliefs are acquired and some of the original beliefs may be weakened or strengthened. That is, "new" concepts or "responses" become associated with the attitude object, and many of the original S-r asso-

ciations may be positively or negatively reinforced. Each of these changes in belief will affect the evaluation of the attitude object (i.e., the stimulus concept). This may be seen in Figure 5.

In A of Figure 5, it can be seen that, following concept formation, the presentation of a "stimulus" (e.g., Negro—S_N) will elicit a learned, mediating evaluative response (i.e., an attitude—r_e) and a response representing the stimulus (i.e., r_N). That is, the subject tends to read, or to repeat to himself, the stimulus toward which he is attending; he makes a "labeling" response (Hovland, Janis, and Kelly, 1953). Furthermore, it should be recalled that the learned mediating evaluative response is a function of the individual's initial beliefs about the attitude object. Figure 5 is identical to Figure 4, except that the mediating beliefs (e.g., "dark skin," "thick lips," etc.) have been omitted for purposes of presentation.

Once the individual has learned the concept, however, he may learn new associations to it. For example, he may now learn that "Negroes are athletic." This new response (i.e., athletic —r_a) becomes a part of the individual's habit-family-hierarchy of responses to the stimulus "Negro" (S_N). Similar to the other responses in the hierarchy, the response "athletic" may also be viewed as a stimulus that itself elicits a learned mediating evaluative response. This evaluative response elicited by "athletic" will summate with the evaluative response elicited by the attitude object (i.e., Negro), which, it will be recalled, is itself a summated response based on all the other beliefs in the individual's hierarchy. Through the processes of conditioning and mediated generalization, this "new" summated evaluative response becomes associated with the stimulus concept (i.e., Negro);

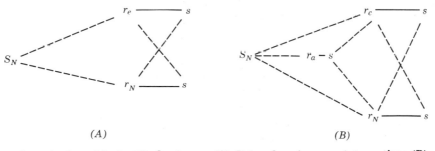

(A)   (B)

Figure 5. A model of attitude change. (A) Before learning new information; (B) after learning new information. S_N = the stimulus (e.g., Negro); r_e = an evaluative response; r_N = a mediating response representing the stimulus; r_a = a mediating response representing the newly learned information (e.g., Negroes are athletic); s = the stimulus produced by a mediator.

thus, on future occasions, the attitude object (i.e., Negro) will elicit this "new" summated mediating evaluative response (i.e., this attitude). This may be seen in B of Figure 5. It should again be recalled that the stronger the association between "Negro" and "athletic" (i.e., the stronger the S_N-r_a association or the stronger the belief that "Negroes are athletic"), the more the evaluation of "athletic" will contribute to the evaluation of "Negro." Similarly, any change in the strength of previously held beliefs (i.e., weakening or strengthening any of the S-r associations) will also change the evaluative influence of that belief on the final evaluation of the stimulus concept (S_N).

Because most learning probably occurs after the concept is learned (or the stimulus is "labeled"), attitudes can best be viewed as being functions of the individual's beliefs about the attitude object. Indeed, it is possible that many of the stimuli that originally influenced concept formation do not remain in the individual's belief system. That is, they may drop out of the response hierarchy completely either through replacement by new beliefs or through negative reinforcement.

To summarize, then, attitudes are most likely learned initially as part of the process of concept formation. Once the concept has been learned, however, the individual learns many new things about it, that is, he associates many different objects, concepts, values, or goals with the attitude object (the stimulus concept). This set of responses associated with the concept may be viewed as a belief system —a habit-family-hierarchy of responses. The higher the response in the hierarchy, the greater the probability that the response is associated with the stimulus concept, that is, the stronger the belief. Each of these associated responses may also be viewed as stimuli, which themselves elicit a learned mediating evaluative response. These mediating evaluative responses are viewed as summative; through the processes of mediated generalization and conditioning, this summated evaluative response becomes associated with the stimulus concept. Thus, when the concept is presented, it will elicit this summated evaluative response, that is, it will elicit this learned attitude. Finally, it should be noted that the higher the response in the hierarchy (i.e., the stronger the belief), the greater will be the amount of its evaluative response that is available for summation.

Thus, in its simplest form, the theoretical model (see Figure 4) leads to the prediction that an individual's attitude toward any object is a function of (1) the strength of his beliefs about the object (i.e., those beliefs in his response hierarchy) and (2) what Fishbein (1963) has called the evaluative aspect of those beliefs (i.e., the evaluation of the associated responses). Algebraically, this may be expressed as follows:

$$A_o = \sum_1^N B_i a_i$$

where A_o = the attitude toward object o
B_i = the strength of belief i about o, that is, the "probability" or "improbability" that o is associated with some other concept x_i
a_i = the evaluative aspect of B_i, that is, the evaluation of x_i
N = the number of beliefs about o, that is, the number of responses in the individual's habit-family-hierarchy

Before turning to a consideration of some of the evidence supporting this hypothesis, several points should be made:

1. It should be noted that this prediction is similar to predictions made by other investigators (e.g., Smith, 1949; Cartwright, 1949; Rosenberg, 1956, 1960; Zajonc, 1954; Peak, 1955). For example, Rosenberg, working from the point of view of a consistency principle, has predicted that the affect attached to an attitude object will be highly related to (a) "the perceived instrumentality of the attitude object," that is, the judged probability that the attitude object would lead to, or block, the attainment of "valued states," and (b) the "value importance," that is, the intensity of affect expected from these "valued states."[1] Similarly, Zajonc, working within the framework of a theory of "cognitive set," has predicted that the valence of (i.e., attitude toward)

---

[1] Algebraically, the central equation of Rosenberg's theory may be expressed as follows:

$$A_o = \sum_{i=1}^N I_i V_i$$

where A_o = the attitude toward the object, I_i = the belief or probability that the object will lead to or block the attainment of a given valued state "i," V_i = the "value importance" or the amount of affect expected from valued state "i," and N = the number of beliefs.

any object is a function of (a) the valence of its characteristics, and (b) the "prominence" of these characteristics, where "prominence" refers to "the ability of the characteristic to represent the object," that is, the belief that the characteristic is indeed a defining attribute of the object.[2] Although there are several theoretical and methodological differences between the various theories that have dealt with the belief-attitude relationship (e.g., see Fishbein, 1961), the important point is that all of them essentially lead to the hypothesis that an individual's attitude toward any object is a function of his beliefs about the object and the evaluative aspects of those beliefs.

2. It should also be noted that this hypothesis is entirely consistent with the way in which most standardized attitude measurement instruments obtain their estimates of attitude. That is, as Fishbein (see pp. 257 to 266 in this book) has pointed out, most of the standard attitude measurement instruments (e.g., Thurstone Scales, Likert Scales, Guttman Scales, etc.) obtain their estimates of attitude through a consideration of a set of the respondent's beliefs about the attitude object and the evaluative aspects of those beliefs. Thus, in a sense, the algebraic formula presented above may be viewed as a general formula for obtaining estimates of attitude. In Figure 3D, however, it can be seen that the only beliefs that serve as *determinants* of an individual's attitude are those that are present in his habit-family-hierarchy of responses. That is, although all of an individual's beliefs about an object serve as indicants of his attitude toward the object, it is only the individual's *salient* beliefs, i.e., those in his hierarchy, that serve as *determinants* of attitude. Although a complete discussion of the distinction between determinants and indicants of attitude is beyond the scope of the present paper, this distinction does suggest that the best estimates of attitude will be

2 Algebraically, the central equation of Zajonc's theory may be expressed as follows:

$$A_o = Va(o) = \frac{\sum_{i=1}^{N} Va(a) \ Prom(a)}{(N^2 + N)/2}$$

where A_o = attitude toward the object, $Va(o)$ = the valence of the object, $Va(a)$ = the valence of the characteristic "a," $Prom(a)$ = the prominence of characteristic "a," and N = the number of characteristics.

obtained when the estimate is based solely on a consideration of an individual's *salient* beliefs. Support for this hypothesis may be found in Rosenberg's contribution to this book (see pp. 325 to 331). He found that estimates of attitude based on a consideration of an individual's salient beliefs (i.e., those elicited by the subject) were considerably more accurate than estimates based on a consideration of 35 beliefs selected on an a priori basis.

It should be recalled that most attitude measurement instruments consist of a series of belief statements selected on some a priori grounds. Thus most of the beliefs that they contain are probably not salient for the respondents. Although these instruments will still provide valid estimates (or measures) of attitude, there is undoubtedly some loss in the precision of the estimate. Clearly, the greater the *proportion* and absolute number of salient beliefs contained in the instrument, the smaller will be the loss in validity.

This, however, raises a question about the number of beliefs that can be *salient* for an individual. That is, how many "objects, concepts, values, or goals" can an individual associate with an attitude object at any point in time? Studies on the span of attention or apprehension suggest that, in general, an individual can only perceive, and attend to, six to eleven objects at the same time (Woodworth and Schlossberg, 1954; Miller, 1956). Even though groupings do increase the number of objects that can be perceived, it seems likely that only six to eleven beliefs are salient, that is, are in the individual's hierarchy, at any one time. That is, although an individual may have many beliefs about any given attitude object, there are probably only six to eleven beliefs that actually appear in his hierarchy (i.e., that are above some response threshold) and function as determinants of attitude. Somewhat the same kind of notion has been suggested by March and Simon (1958) in their distinction between "satisficing" and "optimizing." According to these investigators:

Most human decision-making . . . is concerned with the discovery and selection of satisfactory alternatives; only in exceptional cases is it concerned with the discovery and selection of optimal alternatives. (p. 141)

From the point of view presented here, "satisficing" involves only the six to eleven immediately salient beliefs, whereas "optimizing" takes into account many more beliefs.

A recent study by Kaplan (1966) provides some support for the hypothesis that only six to eleven beliefs function as the primary determinants of an individual's attitude. Kaplan asked his subjects to list as many "characteristics, qualities, and attributes" of "Negroes" as they could. The number of beliefs presented by subjects varied from 3 to 25. Two estimates of attitude were computed for each subject— one based on a consideration of all his responses, and one based on a consideration of only "salient" beliefs, with *saliency* being operationally defined in terms of position in the response hierarchy. That is, Kaplan assumed that, at most, a subject might have nine salient beliefs. Thus, even though a subject might have listed more than nine beliefs, only the first nine that he listed were taken into account in this latter estimate of his attitude. Consistent with expectations, the estimates of attitude based only on the "salient" beliefs were more accurate predictors of attitude than estimates based on the total set of beliefs an individual listed.

Although the findings of Rosenberg and Kaplan support the hypothesis that an individual's attitude toward any object is primarily determined by his salient beliefs, and that there are probably only six to eleven beliefs that are salient, it must be made clear that these findings do *not* imply that valid estimates of attitude cannot be obtained from nonsalient beliefs. Indeed, both of these investigators did obtain valid estimates of attitude from considerations of nonsalient beliefs. However, the most precise estimates of attitude were those based solely on salient beliefs and their evaluative aspects. Furthermore, because only salient beliefs function as determinants of attitude, it will be only through a consideration of these beliefs that one will be able to gain an understanding of the genesis of attitude.

3. A final question concerns the types of beliefs that are related to and/or function as determinants of attitude. A review of the literature on attitude organization and change indicates considerable controversy about this question. For example, many investigators (e.g., Krech and Crutchfield, 1948, Katz and Stotland, 1959; Abelson and Rosenberg, 1958) have attempted to distinguish between beliefs that are attitudinal in nature (i.e., those that contain an implicit or explicit evaluation of the attitude

object) and beliefs that are unrelated to attitude (i.e., so-called "descriptive or reportorial" beliefs). Indeed, with very few exceptions (e.g., Campbell, 1950; Zajonc, 1954; Fishbein, 1963), investigators have tended to ignore these "descriptive or reportorial" beliefs in their investigations of attitude. Furthermore, due to the various techniques of item selection that are used, this type of belief is seldom, if ever, found as an item on one of the standard attitude measuring instruments. From the point of view of theory presented here, however, any type of belief (e.g., descriptive, reportorial, instrumental, etc.) may serve as a determinant or indicant of an individual's attitude. That is, any belief that is present in the individual's habit-family-hierarchy has an evaluative mediating response associated with it (i.e., all beliefs have evaluative aspects), and thus it will contribute to the individual's attitude. In addition, it seems reasonable to assume that the strongest beliefs about an object that an individual holds are those beliefs that serve to define and describe the object for him, that is, descriptive beliefs. Because these beliefs are likely to be high in the individual's hierarchy, they probably serve as some of the most important determinants of attitude. Thus, rather than ignore "descriptive or reportorial" beliefs, the present approach suggests that increased attention should be paid to them in future studies of attitude organization and change.

Because most investigators have tended to ignore "descriptive beliefs," it was felt that this type of belief would provide the most severe test of the hypothesis. Thus, in the initial test of the theory presented above, an attempt was made to predict subjects' attitudes toward Negroes from a consideration of their descriptive beliefs about Negroes (i.e., their beliefs about the characteristics and components of Negroes), and from the evaluative aspects of these beliefs. Specifically, following a procedure developed by Maltzman, Bogartz, and Breger (1958), 125 Ss listed what they believed to be the five characteristics that best described Negroes. The ten characteristics of Negroes that were most salient for the population, that is, the ten most frequent responses given by the subjects, were then selected for further consideration (e.g., dark skin, curly hair, athletic, musical, tall, etc.). Although it is clear that not all of the beliefs considered are "pure descriptive beliefs," many of them (e.g., Negroes have dark skin, Negroes have curly hair, etc.) would be considered as "non-evaluative" and/or unrelated to attitude by most investigators. Two weeks later, 50 of the subjects returned for a second session of the experiment. Using Fishbein and Raven's (1962) evaluative (A) and probability (B) Scales to measure attitude and belief respectively (see pp. 183 to 189 in this book), each subject rated each of the characteristics on the A Scale and each of the belief statements on the B Scale. In addition, all Ss rated the concept "Negro" on the A Scale. Using the algebraic formula presented above (i.e., $\Sigma B_i a_i$), estimated attitude scores were computed for each subject. That is, a subject's rating of each belief statement (i.e., B_i) was multiplied by his rating of the characteristic that was related to "Negroes" (i.e., a_i), and these ten products (one for each belief) were then summed. In support of the theory, the Spearman rank-order correlation between estimated and obtained attitudes (i.e., the direct evaluation of the concept "Negro" on the A Scale) equaled .801 ($N = 50$, $p < .001$).

In other studies, it has been found that a leader's attitudes toward the members of his group could be predicted from a knowledge of his beliefs about the members' behaviors (i.e., his rating of the "probability" or "improbability" that the member "listened attentively to others," "expressed his opinions tactfully," etc.) and the evaluations of those behaviors (Fishbein, 1965). Similarly, in an unpublished study, Fishbein and Feldman have obtained evidence that a voter's attitude toward a political candidate (on either the Presidential or the Congressional level) is a function of his (i.e., the voter's) beliefs about the characteristics of the candidate (e.g., "he has legislative experience," "he is a farmer") and the candidate's stands on various issues (e.g., "he is in favor of Medicare," "he is in favor of an immediate end to atmospheric nuclear testing"), and his (i.e., the voter's) evaluations of these characteristics and issues.

These findings, together with the previous findings of Rosenberg (1956, 1960), Zajonc (1954), and others, provide strong support for the hypothesis that an individual's attitude toward any object is a function of his beliefs about the object and the evaluative aspects of those beliefs. It should be noted, however, that these findings do not necessarily support the particular theoretical model of the relationships between beliefs and attitudes that has been proposed here. That is, as was mentioned earlier, other investigators have arrived at similar hypotheses from different theoretical viewpoints. Thus the findings reported above lend as much support to their theoretical models as they do to the one presented here. The model presented here, however, does provide an alternative way of viewing the belief-attitude relationship and thus suggests research hypotheses that would not necessarily follow from the other theories (e.g., the hypothesis that an individual's attitude is primarily determined by only six to eleven salient beliefs). Although a discussion of all the implications of the theory is beyond the scope of the present paper, a few implications are worth considering.

SOME IMPLICATIONS OF THE THEORY

The most obvious implications of the theory concern the question of attitude change. According to the theory, attitude change will occur when: (1) an individual's beliefs about an object change and/or (2) when the evaluative aspect of beliefs about an object change. It should be noted that beliefs about an object may change in two ways: (1) new beliefs may be learned, that is, new concepts may be related to the attitude object, new stimulus-response associations may be learned, and (2) the strength of already held beliefs may change, that is, the position of beliefs in the habit-family hierarchy may be altered through positive or negative reinforcement. Furthermore, referring back to Figure 5B, it can be seen that the amount and direction of attitude change will be a function of (1) the individual's initial attitude and, thus, the number, strength, and evaluative aspects of his salient beliefs, and (2) the number, strength, and evaluative aspects of the new beliefs he learns. Here, however, an important distinction must be made between learning the contents of an attitude change communication and learning something about the attitude object. That is, an individual's attitude toward some concept will only change if he learns something new about the concept, if he forms a new S-r association. Simply learning that "the communication says S is r" will not produce attitude change.[3] To use the terminology of Hovland,

[3] It should be noted that learning that "the communication says S is r" can produce delayed attitude change. That is, over time, the individual may forget the source of information and only recall that "S is r." This "new" belief about S may then lead to attitude change. This phenomenon of delayed change has been referred to as "the sleeper effect" by Hovland, Janis, and Kelley (1953).

Janis, and Kelley (1953), attitude change only occurs when the individual "accepts" the communication. Unfortunately, most so-called tests of "learning" that are conducted in attitude change studies are merely tests of retention or recall of the contents of the communication, that is, they are measures of the subjects' beliefs about what the communication said, rather than tests of whether the subjects have learned the *S-r* associations that the message was designed to teach them, that is, measures of the subjects' beliefs about the attitude object.

In addition, it should be noted that according to the theory, every time an individual learns a new belief that associates the attitude object with some positively evaluated concept, his attitude will change in a positive direction. Similarly, if the new belief associates the attitude object with a negatively evaluated concept, his attitude will change in a negative direction. That is, attitude change, as well as attitude per se, is viewed as a function of the *total* amount of affect associated with an individual's beliefs about the attitude object. In contrast to this, most theories based on a notion of "consistency" would predict that attitudes and attitude change are functions of the *mean* amount of affect associated with an individual's beliefs.[4] According to these theories, if an object is associated with other objects that are positively evaluated, it is "consistent" to have a positive attitude toward it. Similarly, if the object is associated with other objects that are negatively evaluated, it is "consistent" to have a negative attitude toward it. If the object is associated with some objects that are positively evaluated and some that are negatively evaluated, a relatively neutral attitude would be consistent. Furthermore, if the object is associated with "extremely good things," a high positive attitude is consistent; if it is associated with "slightly good things," a low positive attitude is consistent. From a strict consistency viewpoint, then, if an object is associated with some "extremely good things" and some "slightly good things," an individual's attitude toward it should be somewhere between high and low positive if it is to be consistent. Thus, if an individual originally believed that the object was associated with "extremely good things," and then learned some new beliefs associating the object with "slightly good things,"

according to most consistency theories these new beliefs (even though they associate the object with positively evaluated things) will actually serve to *lower* the individual's attitude. This prediction is explicitly made in Osgood's congruity theory, and implicitly follows from Heider's balance theory and Festinger's dissonance theory. Thus, although the theory proposed here views attitude organization and change as processes of "cognitive summation," most theories based on a notion of consistency view attitude organization and change as processes of "cognitive balance" or "cognitive averaging."[5]

Finally, it is worth noting that the theory also has implications for an understanding of the relationships between attitudes and behavior. In general, psychologists have had little success in attempting to predict overt behavior of the non-pencil-and-paper type from attitudes. At least one of the major reasons for this lack of success is the fact that the attitude that is measured is usually inappropriate. That is, the attitude that is measured is usually an attitude toward some concept "X," while the behavior that is predicted is Ss behavior with respect to some object "x" (a single instance of the general class of X). For example, an investigator might obtain measures of an individual's attitude toward "Negroes" or "Jews," and then attempt to predict the individual's behavior with respect to a particular Negro or a particular Jew. In the classic study by LaPiere (1934), restaurant, hotel, and motel owners, after giving service "with no trouble" to a Chinese couple, were later asked, "Will you accept members of the Chinese race as guests in your establishment?" Over 90 per cent of the responses to this question were negative. Thus, although these people responded negatively toward the general concept "Chinese," this was not reflected in their behavior toward specific individuals within the general class.

Generally speaking, the attitudes measured on attitude scales, at least when dealing with attitudes toward specific national and ethnic groups, are attitudes based on stereotypes. That is, the beliefs about the group that are salient for the individual are general characteristics (e.g., dark skin, curly hair, musical, athletic, lazy, etc.) that serve to define, describe, and differentiate the general class of stimuli (e.g.,

---

[4] A notable exception to this is Rosenberg (1956), who bases his theory on a notion of consistency, yet postulates cognitive summation.

[5] For a further discussion of the distinction between summation (adding) and balance (averaging), see pages 437 to 443 in this book.

Negroes) that the person is rating. When a person is confronted with a specific Negro, however, his beliefs are likely to be quite different than those that serve to describe "Negroes in general." Because an individual's attitude toward any object is a function of his salient beliefs about the object, it follows that his attitude toward "Negroes in general" (i.e., the attitude measured on the attitude scale) is likely to be quite different than his attitude toward any particular Negro. Clearly, if a relationship between attitude and behavior does exist (and there are some questions about this assump-

tion), it cannot be found until, at a minimum, attitudes toward the appropriate stimulus object are measured.

Although many of the implications described would also follow from other views of the belief-attitude relationship, the theory proposed in this paper does seem to provide a parsimonious explanation for a considerable number of phenomena in the area of attitude organization and change. The final test of the theory, however, will lie in its ability to generate testable hypotheses and to stimulate research in areas that might otherwise be overlooked.

REFERENCES

Abelson, R. P., and Rosenberg, M. J. Symbolic psychologic: a model of attitudinal cognition. *Behav. Sci.*, 1958, **3**, 1-13.

Allport, G. W. *The nature of prejudice.* New York: Doubleday and Co., 1954.

Birge, J. S. The role of verbal responses in transfer. Unpublished doctoral dissertation, Yale University, 1941.

Campbell, D. T. Indirect assessment of social attitudes. *Psychol. Bull.*, 1950, **47**, 15-38. (See pp. 163 to 179 in this book.)

Cartwright, D. P. Some principles of mass persuasion. *Hum. Relat.*, 1949, **2**, 253-267.

Clark, K. B., and Clark, M. P. Racial identification and preference in Negro children. In E. E. Maccoby, T. M. Newcomb, and E. L. Hartley (Eds.), *Readings in social psychology.* New York: Holt, Rinehart and Winston, 1958.

Cofer, C. N., and Foley, J. P. Mediated generalization and interpretation of verbal behavior: I. Prolegomena. *Psychol. Rev.*, 1942, **49**, 513-540.

Doob, L. W. The behavior of attitudes. *Psychol. Rev.*, 1947, **54**, 135-156. (See pp. 42 to 50 in this book.)

Fishbein, M. A theoretical and empirical investigation of the inter-relation between beliefs about an object and the attitude toward that object. Unpublished doctoral dissertation, U. C. L. A., 1961.

Fishbein, M. An investigation of the relationships between beliefs about an object and the attitude toward that object. *Hum. Relat.*, 1963, **16**, 233-240.

Fishbein, M. The prediction of interpersonal preferences and group member satisfaction from estimated attitudes. *J. pers. soc. Psychol.*, 1965, **1**, 663-667.

Fishbein, M. A consideration of beliefs and their role in attitude measurement. In M. Fishbein (Ed.), *Readings in attitude theory and measurement.* New York: John Wiley and Sons, 1967. (See pp. 257 to 266 in this book.)

Fishbein, M., and Raven, B. H. The AB scales: an operational definition of belief and attitude. *Hum. Relat.*, 1962, **15**, 35-44. (See pp. 183 to 189 in this book.)

Hovland, C. I., Janis, I. L., and Kelly, H. H. *Communication and persuasion.* New Haven: Yale University Press, 1953.

Hull, C. L. *Principles of behavior.* New York: Appleton Century, 1943.

Kaplan, K. J. A methodological comparison of two techniques of attitude measurement. Unpublished master's thesis, University of Illinois, 1966.

Katz, D., and Stotland, E. A preliminary statement to a theory of attitude structure and change. In S. Koch (Ed.), *Psychology: a study of a science.* Vol. 3, *Formulation of the person and the social context.* New York: McGraw-Hill, 1949.

Krech, D., and Crutchfield, R. S. *Theory and problems of social psychology.* New York: McGraw-Hill, 1948.

LaPiere, R. T. Attitudes vs. actions. *Social Forces,* 1934, **13**, 230-237. (See pp. 26 to 31 in this book.)

Lott, B. Eisman. Attitude formation: the development of a color preference response through mediated generalization. *J. abnorm. soc. Psychol.*, 1955, **50**, 321-326. (See pp. 366 to 372 in this book.)

Maltzman, I., Bogartz, W., and Breger, L. A procedure for increasing word association originality and its transfer effects. *J. exp. Psychol.*, 1958, **56**, 392-398.

March, J. G., and Simon, H. A. *Organizations.* New York: John Wiley and Sons, 1958.

Mednick, M. I. Mediated generalization and the incubation effect as a function of manifest anxiety. *J. abnorm. soc. Psychol.*, 1957, **55**, 315-321.

Miller, G. A. The magical number seven, plus or minus two: some limits on our capacity for processing information. *Psychol. Rev.*, 1956, **62**, 81-97.

Murdock, B. B., Jr. The effects of failure and retroactive inhibition on mediated generalization. *J. exp. Psychol.*, 1952, **44**, 156-164.

Osgood, C. E. Cross-cultural comparability in attitude measurement via multilingual semantic differentials. In I. D. Steiner and M. Fishbein (Eds.), *Current studies in social psychology.* New York: Holt, Rinehart and Winston, 1965. (See pp. 108 to 116 in this book.)

Osgood, C. E., Suci, G. J., and Tannenbaum, P. H. *The measurement of meaning.* Urbana: University of Illinois Press, 1957.

Peak, H. Attitude and motivation. In M. Jones (Ed.), *Nebraska symposium on motivation.* Lincoln: University of Nebraska Press, 1955.

Rhine, R. J. A concept-formation approach to attitude acquisition. *Psychol. Rev.*, 1958, **65**, 362-370. (See pp. 382 to 388 in this book.)

Rosenberg, M. J. Cognitive structure and attitudinal affect. *J. abnorm. soc. Psychol.*, 1956, **53**, 367-372. (See pp. 325 to 331 in this book.)

Rosenberg, M. J. A structural theory of attitude dynamics. *Pub. Opin. Quart.*, 1960, **24**, 319-340.

Smith, M. B. Personal values as determinants of a political attitude. *J. Psychol.*, 1949, **28**, 477-486.

Thurstone, L. L. Measurement of social attitudes. *J. abnorm. soc. Psychol.*, 1931, **26**, 249-269. (See pp. 14 to 25 in this book.)

Woodward, R. S., and Scholossberg, H. *Experimental Psychology.* New York: Holt and Co., 1954.

Zajonc, R. B. Structure of the cognitive field. Unpublished doctoral dissertation, University of Michigan, 1954.

C. Problems, Prospects, and Alternatives in Attitude Theory

45. The Current Status of Cognitive Consistency Theories

WILLIAM J. McGUIRE

It is a rather common occurrence in the history of science for a number of similar theories to be put forward contemporaneously by researchers who have little or no direct contact with one another. Merton has assembled several hundred cases of this sort (e.g., Merton, 1957). In the 1860's about six chemists suggested the essentials of the periodic law and Kuhn (1959) reports that the principle of energy conservation had a dozen different discoverers around the 1840's. It need not surprise us therefore that at least a half dozen of what we shall call "consistency theories" appeared in the psychological literature during the 1950's. These were proposed under various names (balance, congruity, symmetry, dissonance, etc.) but had in common the notion that the person tends to behave in ways that minimize the internal inconsistency among his interpersonal relations, among his intrapersonal cognitions, or among his beliefs, feelings, and actions. While resembling one another in their use of this fundamental predictive postulate, the various theories differed from one another in many respects, for example, in ways of defining consistency, in the additional assumptions made, and as regards the behavioral realms to which the derived predictions are applied. In this paper we shall touch upon both commonalities and diversities among the various theo-

ries, and both will be pursued in depth in later chapters.

After the appearance in print of these several consistency theories, research stemming from them grew rapidly, until currently they seem to us to furnish the point of theoretical departure for more personality and social psychological research than does any other one theoretical notion. This paper is restricted to five tasks that I shall turn to in the following order: (1) to cite the early sources of this flourishing of consistency theory; (2) to sketch out the diverse directions it has taken; (3) to review some of the unresolved problems and conflicts among consistency theories; (4) to suggest where consistency theory fits within the larger framework of psychological theory and research; and (5) to deliver a final word of prognostication about the future of consistency theory.

EARLY WORK ON CONSISTENCY THEORY

As Ebbinghaus (1909) said of psychology as a whole at the turn of the century, the currently lively theoretical notion of cognitive consistency has a long past but a short history. It must be admitted that there is some suspicion of descent from the medieval notion of logical man or the notion of rational man in economics which was so popular as a guiding postulate for explaining human behavior in the early days of that science. Yet these notions were ambiguously used in those contexts. "Rationality" was used to

• Excerpted from S. Feldman (Ed.), *Cognitive Consistency: Motivational Antecedents and Behavioral Consequences*, Academic Press, New York, 1966, with permission of the author and the publisher.

refer sometimes to reality orientation and sometimes to internal logical consistency. The latter is closer to the current meaning of cognitive consistency, but currently we use "consistency" more in the sense of operating in accord with the rules of psycho-logic (Abelson and Rosenberg, 1958) than with those of logic.

Beginnings of Formal Consistency Theory

History began with Heider's (1946) paper on attitude and cognitive organization in three-element structures which posit, for example, that if person p likes other person o, and o likes object x, then p will tend to like x also. In brief, it was argued, there will be a tendency towards balance such that in a triad there are likely to be either two minus (e.g., "dislike") links or none. Put more generally, such cycles will tend to have an even number of minuses, so that the product of the link signs will yield a positive value. Newcomb (1953, 1956) applied this theory to communicative acts, examined its motivational basis, and elaborated it in terms of role theory, in his A-B-X model. Cartwright and Harary (1956) generalized these three-element systems to structures of any number of elements, solving for consistency level by the use of graph theory and postulating a number of principles that yield predictions about empirical situations involving interpersonal relations.

Abelson and Rosenberg (1958) developed a system using matrix algebra to define the consistency level in a multielement structure, and a series of postulates for applying their notions to intrapersonal cognitive systems. While most of the earlier researchers dealt with interpersonal situations, the work of Abelson and Rosenberg concerned consistency within one skull.

Still another intrapersonal consistency approach, quite simple in its postulates but with wide-range and provocative applications, is the theory of cognitive dissonance proposed by Festinger (1957) and since then greatly elaborated (J. W. Brehm and Cohen, 1962; Festinger, 1964; Festinger and Aronson, 1960). While remaining frustratingly sparse and informal regarding its specific statement, dissonance theory has been exceedingly productive in terms of the amount of experimentation it has inspired.

Two other consistency theories of more diverse content and origin had in common an attempt at quantifying the links between cognitions. Osgood and Tannenbaum (1955) developed their congruity model to account for changes in evaluations that result from outside information linking cognitions that have different valences. They introduced quantification of the individual links, the polarity principle, the assertion constant, and the correction for incredulity into the theory. McGuire (1960a, 1960c) attempted to define consistency among propositions included in the individual's belief system and to handle quantitatively the gradations in assent to each proposition; he also attempted to identify sources of cognitive inconsistency and the probable foci of changes to reduce it. In brief, he has posited that the individual acts as honest broker among contending beliefs, seeking a least-squares solution for discrepancies among them. He concentrates particularly on reconciling "logical thinking" (minimizing discrepancies between the beliefs on a given issue and on logically related issues) with "wishful thinking" (minimizing discrepancies between belief and desire on each individual issue). One's least-squares solution, he argues, may favor the logical or the wishful realm of consistency, depending on situational manipulations of the salience of the two (McGuire, 1960b).

Another source of cognitive consistency theorizing is the trichotomy as regards the existential stances man can take—feeling, knowing, and acting form a trichotomy that goes back at least to Plato. In psychology, Allport's old (1935), but still respectable, review of the attitude area attributed to the ancients the perennial analysis of attitudes into three corresponding components: affective, cognitive, and conative. Many students of attitudes have developed this notion in detail (e.g., D. T. Campbell, 1947; Chein, 1948; Doob, 1947; Harding, Kutner, Proshansky, & Chein, 1954; Krech, Crutchfield & Ballachey, 1962). The terminology has changed and the level of sophistication in the research has varied, but interest in the analysis has been a persisting one. Recently, Fishbein (e.g., 1963) has brought much precision to the area. The work of Rosenberg (1960a, 1960b) on this problem is also noteworthy for its imaginativeness.

DIRECTIONS TAKEN BY CONSISTENCY THEORY

Those of us who have found the consistency formulation useful in our work have used it to raise and to suggest answers for a wide variety of questions. In this section we propose to exhibit the heuristic power of this formulation by reviewing a wide range of the types of problems towards which attention has been attracted by consistency theory. First, we shall discuss notions of how, if we have the tendency towards consistency, there is so much inconsistency in our experimental subjects to start with. Next, we shall review experimental procedures used to bring these consistency needs to bear more fully on a domain of cognitions. Third, we shall survey the various modes of consistency reduction that have been subjected to experimental study. Fourth, we shall discuss findings regarding the relative likelihood that consistency will be restored by changing one kind of cognition rather than another. A fifth topic for review will be the types of consistency that seem to be preferred. Finally, we shall consider predictions derived from consistency theory regarding communication, persuasion, and action effects.

Origins of Inconsistency

It may seem paradoxical or even embarrassing for the theory that we posit a strong tendency towards consistency and yet always manage to find sufficient inconsistency within the system to allow predictions to be made and tested regarding modes of resolving inconsistencies. It may be worthwhile, then, to list a half-dozen of the ways in which inconsistencies enter into the cognitive system in the first place and in which they are maintained there.

First, there may be inconsistencies among the person's cognitions because of methodological artifacts, such as acquiescence response sets, that cause him to agree with both a statement and its contradictory in "balanced" inventories (Couch and Keniston, 1960; O'Donovan, 1965; Rorer, 1965); likewise, context effects, such as those dealt with in assimilation-contrast theory (M. Sherif and Hovland, 1961; C. W. Sherif, M. Sherif, and Nebergall, 1965), can lead him into mutually inconsistent positions. Second, there are the logical shortcomings of the human cognitive apparatus that lead to material fallacies (the ambiguous "some," amphibology, etc.) or to formal fallacies (such as illicit process of the major, atmosphere effect, experimental wariness, a fortiori effect, etc.) that have been reviewed by McGuire (1960c).

Third, the fault may lie in the stars and not in ourselves. The notion of a society free of inherent contradictions is going out of fashion. Cognitions that reflect an inconsistent social world (e.g., see Myrdal, 1944, on the American Dilemma) must be internally contradictory.

People are cast in conflicting roles. They are called upon to serve God and man when the two may be at odds. The public safety officer at a time of disaster is torn between his duty to the broader public and to his own family. And even if the universe is inherently consistent in the eyes of God, man sees only a sample of information and so, unaware of the higher synthesis (cf. Abelson, 1959, p. 346), he may be left with a contradiction in his partial and even biased sample.

Fourth, the world may change, leaving the person encumbered with conceptual baggage that no longer accords with reality. He may labor to put his political leader into office only to see the sought-after patronage plum lifted past his waiting hands into those of the vanquished opponent as a gesture of reconciliation or to witness his victorious champion adopt the despised policy of the opposition to gain a consensus. Or, fifth, he may have been forced by external pressure to behave in ways inconsistent with his principles and be left with the problem of reconciling his behavior with his ideals. Or, sixth, he may be presented with new information, via persuasive communications, interpersonal interactions, or direct experience with the object that does not coincide with his previous beliefs.

Ways of Bringing the Consistency Need to Bear on a Given Cognitive Realm

Given that a certain degree of inconsistency has entered the cognitive system and maintained itself by some mechanism such as has been discussed in the preceding section, how can the person be made to feel the pressure of the consistency need so as to shift to a new quasi-stationary equilibrium of higher internal consistency? A number of procedures towards this end have been used experimentally and all probably have their real-life analogues. For example, in some studies, the need for consistency has been brought to bear by the forced recall of conflicting cognitions (Abelson and Rosenberg, 1958; Festinger, 1957; McGuire, 1960a). Another procedure (one which some of us find methodologically unattractive) is to have the person "role-play" certain cognitive constellations (Jordan, 1953; Morrissette, 1958; Rosenberg and Abelson, 1960). Still another method is to force the individual to make some kind of behavioral commitment (J. W. Brehm and Cohen, 1962) or to confront him with appropriate communications (Newcomb, 1953). Or, as

Abelson and Rosenberg (1958, p. 5) have conjectured, there may be a personality dimension with people at one pole which enables them to adopt as an intellectual style the reexamination of their own positions. For them, and for all of us to a degree, the unexamined life may not be worth living. No doubt we can stimulate this need for self-examination by suitable external manipulations (Glass, in press).

Modes of Resolving Cognitive Inconsistencies

The individual who is confronted with a cognitive inconsistency has many possible alternative responses to the situation. Here, we can take the time to briefly review a few of these modes of responding (others are described in D. T. Campbell, 1961). It should be understood that the use of one of these modes is more likely to be complementary to, rather than mutually exclusive of, use of the others.

First, one can always stop thinking, repress the matter, put the inconsistency out of mind, as Freud and St. Augustine (not necessarily in that order) have suggested—as have Dollard and Miller (1950, pp. 203–204), Newcomb (1953, pp. 400–401), Abelson and Rosenberg (1958, p. 5), and Harary (1959).

Another mode is "bolstering" (Abelson, 1959, p. 345; Festinger, 1957, pp. 21–22) which does not remove the inconsistency, but submerges it among a larger body of consistencies so that it looms relatively less large. The person using this mode, when confronted by a contradiction between one of his beliefs and another, amasses a great body of other beliefs that are consistent with the conflicting one. Or there is the somewhat related "mote" method where the believer, faced with his own inconsistency, draws solace in pointing out that other people are more inconsistent still, as did the Moscovite who was showing the American visitor the beauty of the mosaics in his home-town subway. When the American said, "Very nice indeed, but the trains? There seem to be no trains on these tracks," the Moscovite replied, "Yes, and what about the plight of the Negro in the South?"

Two other modes are the somewhat antithetical processes that Abelson (1959, pp. 345–346) calls "differentiation" and "transcendence." For example, the man who loves the Bible and also loves the theory of evolution, on becoming aware that his two loves are not in complete agreement, might try differentiating. For example, he might distinguish between the figurative Bible and the literal Bible and then decide he loves the former, while it is only the latter that conflicts with evolutionary theory. Or he might try transcendence: he would decide the Bible and evolution are the two faces of a higher reality, subsumed under a dynamic equilibrium of opposites. Those who find this process of Hegelian synthesis hard to follow are urged to use another mode of conflict resolution, or to see Abelson (1959) or Weil (1951), for further instructions.

Still other modes touch on Asch's (1940) notions about attitude change involving changing the object about which the opinion is held rather than the opinion about the given object. For example, the college student who moves up the status of "politican" after being told his peers ranked the profession much higher than he, may merely be redefining "politician" as meaning "statesman" after hearing their high ranking, whereas he had at first taken it to mean "ward-heeler." Alternatively, he may indeed resolve the dilemma of peer disagreement by devaluating the peer or by actually changing his opinion about the object, as well as by changing the object he is giving his opinion about. A final mode that we shall mention is devaluating the task when the inconsistency is noted. Both Newcomb (1953) and Festinger (e.g., 1957, p. 22) have suggested that, when confronted with an inconsistency, the person will tend to make it more tolerable by downrating the importance of the conceptual area in which it occurs.

In addition to all these modes of responding that reduce the inconsistencies, there is always, of course, the alternative stance of simply bearing it. Indeed, one may make a virtue out of it. We can say with Carlyle that consistency is the hobgoblin of little minds; or adopt the *credo quia absurdum* and find solace in contradictions such as Tertullian's irascible notion that the Christian creed is impossible and therefore it is evident, or Pascal's admission that the existence of God is incredible and therefore one believes. (But let us not claim for the West any exclusive possession of this profundity. It is written somewhere in Sikh scripture that if there be found any two passages in that work that are mutually contradictory, they are both true.)

But the fact that the layman or even the scientist seems able to tolerate a certain amount of ignorance and even inconsistency in his cognitive arena does not invalidate the general proposition of the consistency theorists that inconsistency reduction is reinforcing in much the same sense as pain reduction is reinforcing. The latter drive also is far from absolute. We all learn to tolerate pain and carry on our work even when bothered by a moderate degree of pain, when this must be endured because we lack the response possibility to elude it or choose to allow it as the lesser of evils. Indeed, we even seek out pain under certain circumstances, as evinced by our proceeding frequently if unenthusiastically to the dentist [save exceptions like Silvan Tomkins (1963), who is not bothered by dental pain]. Here pain is sought, at least in part, because of the need to avoid greater pain, and thus is supportive evidence for, rather than against, the existence of a pain-reduction drive. Hence, we can admit that toleration and continuance is indeed one mode of responding to inconsistency, without deserting our proposition that there is a drive to reduce inconsistency to low or even zero levels.

The eight or so responses to inconsistency that we have reviewed here—most of which serve to provide the protagonist an at least apparent reduction in his inconsistency—indicate a serious problem for consistency theorists. The availability of these many alternative modes is quite convenient for the person confronted with an inconsistency among his cognitions, but it is an embarrassment for the theorist trying to predict what the person will do. It is unclear even whether we should expect the use of the alternative modes to be positively or negatively correlated. If the persons are in a "zero-sum" situation where everyone has a given amount of inconsistency, then a negative correlation would be expected, the use of one mode serving to reduce the inconsistency so that use of other modes would be less necessary. But we usually cannot assume such a uniform level of internal inconsistency. On the contrary, we usually must work backwards, and if the individual makes more use of a mode than do others, it is usually a sign that he has experienced more internal inconsistency and will thus find it necessary to make greater use of alternative modes as well (Steiner and Johnson, 1964). The consistency theorist, in this difficult situation, typically tries to measure one or a few modes of reduction while blocking off the use of other modes, either a priori or a posteriori. In either case he leaves himself open to criticism. If he uses a priori tactics—such as elaborate inductions that attempt to restrain the subject within certain

conceptual limits (e.g., Festinger and Carlsmith, 1959)—for closing off some modes, he lays himself open to alternative explanations and the charge that his experimental conditions were so complex as to be unreplicable (cf. Rosenberg, 1965). If he attempts a posteriori closing off, such as by eliminating subjects who seem to use other modes than the one under study (cf. Festinger, 1957, pp. 211 ff.), then he becomes liable to charges of selecting his evidence and obscuring the generalizability of his results (cf. Chapanis and Chapanis, 1964, pp. 12–17). Some theorists are proceeding to handle this problem by examining individual difference factors (Glass, in press; Steiner and Rogers, 1963) or situational factors (Brock and Buss, 1962) that allow predictions that one mode or another will be the preferred route to inconsistency reduction.

Relative Likelihood of Various Aspects of the Cognitive System Changing in Case of Inconsistency

Given that an inconsistency exists between elements and that the person responds by changing his cognitions, there are several degrees of freedom regarding what might be changed to restore balance. For example, if one's expectation and his wish regarding a future contingency are in conflict, the person can bring them into line by adjusting his expectation or his wish or both. Or, if there is an imbalanced triad, such that A likes B and X, but B dislikes X, balance can be restored by A changing his attitude toward B or toward X, or by B changing his toward X. Consistency theorists have offered a wide range of suggestions regarding which elements in the system are most likely to be changed in order to restore consistency. The range of these suggestions and findings will be indicated here by mentioning a dozen or so of the relevant variables.

One of the best known predictions regarding which cognition is most likely to change in an inconsistent system is the Osgood and Tannenbaum (1955) polarity principle. In accordance with their postulate, if two related concepts are incongruously valenced, they will shift toward each other, with the less polarized cognition (i.e., the less extremely valenced one) shifting the more. The empirical validity of this postulate is as questionable (Rokeach and Rothman, 1965) as its fame is widespread. A second suggestion by Osgood and Tannenbaum is the assertion principle which states that if a source makes an incongruous assertion about a concept they are adjusted toward one another with the concept shifting more than the source. (If you do not believe these two theorists, then they will even give you a constant— ±.17 in the usual seven-step semantic differential scale—for this differential.) Perhaps this can be generalized to say that in a discrepant subject-object pairing, more adjustment will be made on the latter than the former.

Two principles that are not logically contradictory to one another if read closely, but will in practice tend to make opposite predictions, have been suggested by Abelson and Rosenberg (1958) and McGuire (1960a). According to the former, the cognition least cathected with affect is the one most likely to change. According to McGuire, the more distorted (e.g., by wishful thinking) cognition will change the most. These two positions will tend to conflict, since the most affectively charged cognition will usually be the most distorted. The Abelson and Rosenberg prediction will usually agree with that made from the Osgood and Tannenbaum polarity principle; McGuire (1960a) offers some post factum support for his prediction. Both positions could be put to a test rather easily by an appropriately designed experiment.

Cartwright and Harary (1956), Festinger (1957, p. 27), Abelson and Rosenberg (1958), Rosenberg (1960a, pp. 59–64), and Zajonc (1960, pp. 293–295) have all argued that the least "bolstered" cognition (i.e., the one most isolated from relational ties to other cognitions and needs) is the one most likely to change. We have here a least-effort notion. The person tries to avoid a change to reduce one cognitive incongruity that might introduce more imbalance than it removes. In addition, Festinger suggests that in working out this "bolstering" principle we should multiply the number of cognitive ties by their importance. J. W. Brehm and Cohen (1962, pp. 201–220) emphasize that we must also consider the degree of volition the person exercised in the establishment of the tie. Many of the dissonance people (e.g., J. W. Brehm and Cohen, 1962) have pointed out further that we must also consider how irrevocably committed the person is to each of the cognitions.

The Michigan group have demonstrated that when balance can be restored by changing either instrumentality or goal (i.e., either the person's perception of the utility of a given cognition for achieving some goal or his perception of the attractiveness of the goal itself), the perceived instrumentality is the more likely to change

(Carlson, 1956; Rosenberg, 1956). A somewhat related position given in terms more appropriate to the Osgood and Tannenbaum and the Abelson and Rosenberg formulations is that the sign of the relationship between concepts is more likely to change than the sign of the concepts themselves. We believe these various formulations could be summarized by postulating that the valence of the links between concepts is more likely to change when one of the concepts is not "ego" than when ego is involved as one of the concepts.

Jordan (1953) and Harary (1959) offer the suggestion that, in a system of three or more cognitions or individuals, when balance can be restored either by making a positive sign negative or a negative sign positive, the latter will be preferred.

McGuire (1960a) has argued that when we elicit the person's opinion on a series of issues on which he holds inconsistent positions, our questioning produces a "Socratic method" effect such that the opinions shift toward greater mutual consistency on a later occasion for having been elicited in close temporal contiguity earlier. He has argued (McGuire, 1960a) that the shift is greater on the opinions listed earlier in the series than on the ones elicited later. In another study (McGuire, 1960b) he has presented some evidence that when a persuasive communication argues in an inconsistency-increasing direction, the impact is absorbed on unmentioned but logically related issues as well as on the explicit issue. Immediately after the message the impact is mainly on the explicit issue, but as time passes, relatively more of the effect filters down to the remote issues.

This list by no means exhausts the proposed answers to the question of "which cognitions change more" when internal consistency is being restored. Some of the hypotheses have received substantial empirical confirmation; none can as yet be ruled out on the basis of available evidence. The range of these hypotheses and their somewhat untidy hodgepodge appearance give testimony to the wide-ranging investigation stemming from the diversity of the various consistency theories.

Relative Preference for Different Types of Consistency

A system of cognitions can be in perfect balance in a variety of ways. The system can, for example, always be put in vacuous balance by deleting all the relationships among the cognitions. A completely fractionated man who keeps each of his cognitions in a separate logic-tight compartment will never be bothered with cognitive inconsistency. At the other extreme, we might have a man who has perfect cognitive consistency by being a combination of William Wordsworth, seeing everything as connected to everything else, and Dr. Pangloss, seeing every relationship between things as positive. Such a person's cognitive system would be in a completely connected, and a perfect positive balance. Alternatively, the person could be in a partly connected, perfect positive balance; or he could be in perfect balance with the right mixture of positive and negative relations, either completely or partially connected.

It seems generally agreed on theoretical and psychological grounds that connected balance is preferred psychologically to unconnected balance, and unconnected structures tend towards connected balance (A. Campbell, Converse, Miller, and Stokes, 1960; Cartwright and Harary, 1956; Horowitz, Lyons, and Perlmutter, 1951; Jordan, 1953; Newcomb, 1961). It has also been suggested (Jordan, 1953) that positive balance is preferred to negative or to mixed positive and negative balance.

We have discussed these tendencies to positivity and to completeness as possible paths toward balance. However, in so far as there are such tendencies to a pronounced degree, they contain a possibility of conflict with the tendency toward consistency. We feel this area is a rather interesting one, and that it offers a fertile field for future research.

Resolving Inconsistencies by Communication, Opinion Changes, and Actions

What are the uses of consistency theory? What realms of behavior of traditional psychological interest does it help us predict? Even more important, are there new realms of behavior, previously neglected by psychology, that consistency theories open to scientific predictability? The answers to these questions are so rich that one is tempted to say simply, "Yes," and go on to the next topic. Rather than be embarrassed by such riches, we choose to review briefly some of the implications of consistency theories chosen from just three of the many areas to which it has been applied.

The first area of application is to communication behavior, the question of who sends messages to whom. The early work of the Lewin group, though undertaken with different theo-

retical inspiration, fits nicely into the consistency theory paradigm (Festinger and Thibaut, 1951; Festinger, Schachter, and Back, 1950). The classic "deviation" experiment of Schachter (1951), which perhaps represents the highpoint of Lewinian research, suggests still further directions that consistency theory could take. Newcomb (1953), particularly, has concerned himself with the communication implications of consistency theory. The traditional areas of selective avoidance and selective exposure have likewise been investigated in much detail under the inspiration of consistency theory, particularly by dissonance people (Adams, 1961; Brock, 1965; Mills and Ross, 1964; Mills et al., 1959; Rosen, 1961; Sears and Freedman, 1965). This is one area, however, where refutations of the theories have come at a rapid rate (J. W. Brehm and Cohen, 1962, pp. 48–49, 51–52, 92–97; Steiner, 1962).

The notion of proselytizing after the disconfirmation of a belief is a particularly intriguing notion of consistency theory. This is the prediction that if a person has irrevocably committed himself by action on the basis of a belief (e.g., he takes public and costly action because he believes the world is going to end on a certain day) and then the belief is disconfirmed (the day comes, but not The End), then he rather paradoxically proselytizes for his belief more avidly after the disconfirmation than before, in order to convert others and thus bolster his sagging confidence in his wisdom in having committed himself to this belief. This notion would explain some historical occurrences of more than a little importance that have puzzled many. It is an appealing proposition and deserves to be true. So far, however, the empirical evidence for it has not been overwhelming (Brodbeck, 1956; Festinger, Riecken, and Schachter, 1956; Hardyck and Braden, 1962).

A second area to which consistency theory has been applied with considerable success is that of attitude change. We may here review only a very skimpy selection of the large body of research in this area. McGuire (1960a) has shown that opinions can be changed by the Socratic method of simply asking questions on related issues, sensitizing the individual to the fact that on the basis of his own premises, his conclusions do not follow. This sensitization has proved sufficient to produce a significant trend toward greater internal consistency when the same beliefs are later tapped a second time.

McGuire (1960b) has also shown that the persuasive impact is felt, not only on the explicit issues, but also on unmentioned logically related issues. He has shown (1960c), further, that the persuasive impact is greater when the message argues in an inconsistency-decreasing direction than when it increases consistency, and that there tends to be a delayed-action persuasive effect on beliefs logically related to the ones with which the persuasive message explicitly deals. He has also studied the implications of consistency theory regarding ways of inducing resistance to persuasion (McGuire, 1964).

Another persuasion area to which consistency theories have been applied with a stimulating degree of theoretical controversy and an attractive amount of empirical ambiguity has been that of the discrepancy-involvement question. How does the amount of obtained opinion change vary as a function of the amount of change urged, and how does this relationship vary as the believer's "involvement" increases? There seem to be opposite predictions on the basis of dissonance theory (Zimbardo, 1960) and of assimilation-contrast theory (M. Sherif and Hovland, 1961; C. W. Sherif et al., 1965). Zimbardo (1960) has proposed a plausible reconciliation, but the issue is still in doubt (Bergin, 1962; Freedman, 1964; Greenwald, 1964).

A final area of application of consistency theory that we shall review briefly is to the relations of belief and action. It was long believed that, at least to some extent, belief was a determinant of action. Consistency theories (particularly the dissonance formulation of Festinger and his followers) have called attention to the frequent occasions on which this direction of causality is reversed and the person's action produces a belief to justify it. Instead of the classical *actio sequitur esse,* we have "as the person acts, so he becomes."

At the moment there is a lively controversy between a conflict theory (Janis, 1959), which suggests that the cognitive resolution occurs before the decision, and dissonance theory (Festinger, 1964), which suggests that the cognitive adjustments are postdecisional. So far, the dissonance theorists seem a little ahead, but the game is in the early innings and the country is yet to be heard from. Another quite lively scene in this same area involves internalization of forced compliance as a result of role-playing belief in a position that one does

not at the time really accept. From Kelman (1953), through Janis and King (1954) and the dissonance theorists (J. W. Brehm and Cohen, 1962, pp. 117–121, 248–258), this has been a fertile field of inquiry, and quite suggestive regarding cognitive functioning. Equal activity is found in the area of postdecisional reorganization following choice among alternatives; this area was opened by J. W. Brehm (1956; Brehm & Cohen, 1962). As one other of the less investigated but ingenious notions about beliefs and action investigated by consistency theorists, we might mention the Aronson and Mills (1959) study on attachment to a group as a consequent of traumatic initiation into it. The current state of the question in a number of the areas just reviewed has been summarized recently by McGuire (1966).

Clearly, the consistency theorists have been moving ahead on many fronts. It will come as no shock, though, when I say not all questions have been answered to everyone's satisfaction. What are some of these unanswered questions that confront consistency theories today? A review of some of these outstanding issues will constitute our next section.

ISSUES CURRENTLY CONFRONTING CONSISTENCY THEORY

A number of issues and points of disagreement have arisen among consistency theorists which have stimulated work in the past and will undoubtedly provoke research for some time to come. Some of these issues constitute unresolved puzzles for all the theories; on other issues, conflicting solutions have been proposed by the various theories. We shall in this section review a wide range of such issues. Some of these arise in connection with all or most of the approaches; others are relevant to only a few of our approaches. Also the several issues differ widely as to relative importance. We have attempted to cast a wide net in this review of unresolved problems. For convenience, we have listed them under three headings: definitional, empirical, and methodological problems.[1]

1 In November, 1963, four of us who participated in this symposium (Abelson, Aronson, Rosenberg, and myself) plus two others (Percy Tannenbaum and Theodore Newcomb) met at Newcomb's house in Ann Arbor, Michigan, to review problems in consistency theory—especially those issues on which we felt our respective theories might yield different predictions. The following month, I wrote a review

Issues Involving Definitions

We include here some outstanding questions regarding the elements, cognitive or otherwise, to which consistency theory should be applied. Besides those regarding definitions of the units, questions arise regarding the relationships among those units that are to be considered. And, as always in the empirical sciences, we are groping toward exactitude; therefore problems of definition lead to problems of quantification.

Interpersonal versus intrapersonal units. Some of the consistency theories (e.g., that of Cartwright and Harary, 1956) have been advanced to apply to interpersonal relations in social systems, so that the units they deal with are persons and the relations whose consistency is being considered are, e.g., the likes and dislikes among these people. Other consistency theories (e.g., those of Abelson and Rosenberg, 1958; Festinger and Aronson, 1960; Fishbein, 1963; Fishbein, 1965; McGuire, 1960*a*); McGuire, 1960*c*; Osgood and Tannenbaum, 1955) apply to cognitions within persons, so that the units are concepts or propositions and the relations are, e.g., implications or other logical relations among these intrapersonal cognitions. Some of these intrapersonal systems deal with the consistency among cognitions on related issues (McGuire, 1960*c*); others deal with consistency of different aspects of the cognitions on a single issue (Fishbein, 1963; McGuire, 1960*a*; Rosenberg, 1960*b*). Other consistency theorists (Newcomb, 1959; Heider, 1958) deal with mixed interpersonal and intrapersonal systems.

It seems likely that the different-appearing mathematics advanced for these two domains [e.g., Harary's graph-theoretical approach (cf. Cartwright and Harary, 1956; Harary, 1959) and Abelson's matrix algebraic approach (cf. Abelson and Rosenberg, 1958)] are isomorphic, but the point could bear further scrutiny. Even if the various mathematical formulations are equivalent, it is highly probable that the two domains differ substantially as regards the psychological and sociological propositions needed to predict tolerance for inconsistency, effects of inconsistency, and the preferred modes of

---

of the problems in the area (McGuire et al., 1963), based partly upon that Ann Arbor conference. That review has been circulated in preprint form, but to make it more generally available, I shall repeat here most of what I said in that informal report.

consistency restoration. Analogies might be useful in cross-fertilizing both applications of the model; e.g., restoration of consistency in the contentious social system by schism into noncommunicating factions seems analogous to the individual's restoring consistency to his cognitive system by segregating sets of beliefs into logic-tight compartments. An examination of the means, efficacy, and problems involved in each analogue should be suggestive regarding the other analogue.

Definition of negative relations. The basic problem of defining a negative relationship between two units remains unsettled in a number of regards. It seems clear that "psychological" implication is much broader than logical implication (Rosenberg and Abelson, 1960). Festinger's unfortunate choice of "obverse" (1957, p. 13) is illustrative of the confusion in the field. Whether a cognition should be opposed with its contradictory or contrary for best empirical applicability has been raised by a number of theorists (Cartwright and Harary, 1956, pp. 280–281, 290–291; Heider, 1946, p. 107), but remains unanswered. The question has also been raised (cf. Harary, 1959, p. 317) whether or not any relations can be defined per se as negative: e.g., Deutsch (Deutsch and Solomon, 1959; Deutsch, Krauss, and Rosenau, 1962) has suggested that for a person with a negative self-concept, another person's dislike for him would be a positive relationship (cf., also, Heider, 1946, p. 111; Heider, 1958, p. 210). Studies need to be designed to clarify and answer these questions.

Types of relationship. It has been argued, particularly by those who apply consistency theory to mixed inter- and intrapersonal structures, that in many cases the relationships involved in the structure should be partitioned into two or more subsets with the consistency measure having to be applied separately to each subset. Heider's (1946; 1958) type U and L relationship is an example. The question mentioned above, of whether the negation of relation should, psychologically, be its contrary or its contradictory, may have to be resolved differentially for different types of relations. Cartwright and Harary (1956) have suggested type-τ graphs as a method of handling systems involving different classes of relations. Both psychological and mathematical questions need consideration before we can make a beginning here.

Another problem involves bi-directional relationships, which arise particularly (though not exclusively) in connection with interpersonal links: The bond from A to B may be "likes" and that from B to A may be "dislikes." Such asymmetrical links provide much drama in human relations, actual and fictional, and much technical difficulty for consistency theorists. The mathematics of digraphs has been suggested (Cartwright and Harary, 1956) and Abelson's matrix method (cf. Abelson and Rosenberg, 1958) seems capable of handling the problem by allowing noncorresponding signs above and below the diagonal.

Quantification issues. As in almost every other behavioral science, problems of measurement abound in consistency theory and the state of the art as regards scaling is pitiful. We shall restrict mention here to quantification issues that are critical for our contending conceptions of basic models of how humans operate. For example, in Festinger's "dissonance" version of consistency theory, the tension or pressure to change as a result of inconsistency is defined in terms of the *ratio* of dissonant to total (or sometimes to consonant) elements (1957, p. 17). Obvious alternative definitions are suggested in early works of Kurt Lewin (e.g., 1951) and Neal Miller (e.g., 1944) on conflict resolution where the resulting tension is an intervening variable defined in terms of simply the magnitude of the weaker force or of the absolute difference (rather than ratio) between the two forces. Consistency theory experiments could be designed, we hope, to distinguish between these formulations as regards empirical relevance, thus providing findings whose implications would extend outside consistency theory. A possible resolution would be to develop an index that reflected both the relative and absolute level of the inconsistent cognitions (cf. J. S. Brown and Farber, 1951, pp. 483–486; Worell, 1962).

Another quantification problem that needs study has to do with the strength of the individual links in the structure. Most current theories (Abelson and Rosenberg; Heider, Cartwright and Harary; Newcomb; etc.) restrict the system to three-valued links (+1, 0, −1). Festinger has, in principle, the beginnings of more precise quantification in the "weighting by importance" notion. Osgood and Tannenbaum allow, in effect, a seven-point scale in their evaluation of the individual concepts on a plus-three to minus-three scale. McGuire in principle allows a continuous scale in his

probabilistic gradations of assent (1960c, p. 75), and has recently also developed an IPL-V program evaluating consistency in structures in which the links can have any value between plus one and minus one—in effect, a continuous scale. The issue is not just a question of precision, but a fundamental question of whether organisms behave as if they operate on continuous or discrete scales, in infinite gradations or quantum jumps, as an analogue computer or as a digital computer. It is conceivable that experiments be designed to test between such alternative depictions, which have implications far beyond consistency theory.

Still another quantification problem is that all the present consistency models posit a multiplicative basis for determining the signs of cycles; i.e., they assume that two minuses make a plus, or, psychologically speaking, that humans operate on the principle that "my enemy's enemy is my friend." However, an alternative additive model is conceivable, in which two minuses would make a still more minus result; i.e., that humans say in effect, "if even this creature A, whom I hate, hates B, then I would find B doubly odious." Further examination might yield a solution such that, in some domains of behavior, the multiplicative model is more appropriate, and in others, the additive one.

A similar-sounding, but quite different question is the additive versus averaging controversy, regarding resolution of cognitive conflict. For example, given that a stimulus person is described by several exceedingly good traits, what is the effect of ascribing to him several additional traits that are mildly good? Is an additive model correct, such that the additional (mildly) positive traits result in his being even more favorably evaluated (Abelson, 1961; Fishbein and Hunter, 1964; Gulliksen, 1956; Hammond, 1955; Triandis and Fishbein, 1963)? Or is the averaging model more appropriate, so that adding the only mildly positive traits results in an averaging out to a lower net evaluation than would the extremely positive trait alone (Anderson, 1962; D. T. Campbell, 1961; Feldman, 1962; Osgood and Tannenbaum, 1955; Rimoldi, 1956; Weiss, 1963)? The question is an attractive one in that it is accessible to precise empirical study which promises an answer that will improve the question. As might be expected, there is evidence of both trends and a sophisticated reconciliation seems in the offing (Anderson, 1965).

A final quantitative problem that we shall advert to here is that of weighting certain substructures in determining the inconsistency level. For example, it has been suggested by several theorists that cognitive cycles should be somehow weighted inversely as their length, on the plausible conjecture that an inconsistency in a long chain of cognitive associations (or of social relations) is psychologically more tolerable than one in a short chain, and thus yields less pressure to change. Alternative weighting procedures have been suggested by Cartwright and Harary (1956, p. 289). If we adopt McGuire's (1960c) procedure, mentioned above, of scoring the individual link on a continuous plus-one to minus-one scale, this problem of weighting for chain length would tend to be handled automatically.

Empirical Issues

A second large class of issues we group here as empirical issues. The distinction from the "theoretical" issues listed above is somewhat arbitrary. However, above we grouped as theoretical those issues having to do with the higher-order postulate and the fundamental inspiration of the theory; whereas here, as empirical issues, we include problems of further specification that must get tacked on to the core theory by empirical exploration or theoretical inspiration deriving from other viewpoints, rather than from the intrinsic character of consistency theory per se. For example, we shall discuss: (1) variations in tolerance for inconsistency as a function of personality, situational, and other factors; (2) alternate modes of dissonance reduction and factors affecting the preferential ordering among these; (3) factors purportedly necessary for arousal of the need for consistency, such as awareness, choice, commitment, etc.; (4) conjectures regarding the acquisition of the need for consistency, having to do, e.g., with child-rearing practice or later role assignment; and (5) time factors involved in the operation of consistency need.

Tolerance of inconsistency. One would expect to find reliable individual differences in tolerance for inconsistency. Aronson and Festinger (1958) did early work in this field. Steiner (1954; Steiner and Johnson, 1963) has had some success in teasing out personality and demographic correlates of tolerance for inconsistency. Bieri (1961) has worked on personality

correlates, as has Rosen (1961). Sex, intelligence, maturity, age, and many personality variables have been found (or theorized) to be related to tolerance for inconsistency. Others have found it more appropriate to look for interactions than main effects. Steiner and Johnson (1963), e.g., find that the individual difference variables tend to be related to preferred modes of dissonance reduction as well as to general tolerance. Rosenberg and Hovland (1960) point to interactions beween personality and situational (e.g., type of issue) variables in determining inconsistency tolerance. This important individual-differences aspect of consistency theory is still underinvestigated and underanalyzed. David Glass (in press) has recently supplied an extensive review of work in this area.

Also needing further investigation are situational determinants of tolerance for inconsistency. There is a complex pattern of confirmations and disconfirmations of consistency-theory predictions running through the literature (cf., e.g., Chapanis and Chapanis, 1964; Silverman, 1964; McGuire, 1966). There seem to be some regularities to the partition into positive and negative results, but so far these are seen through a glass, darkly. Rather than a continuing debate about the general validity of consistency theory, we hope for a situational analysis of the two well-filled classes of studies, to tease out variables that will better delimit the proper sphere of applicability of consistency theory and help place the fundamental postulates of this theory into their proper place among the principles of behavior.

Alternative modes of inconsistency reduction. As we discussed earlier in this chapter, inconsistency assumes multiple components, and hence it can be reduced in multiple ways. Identifying the likely target of change is a most interesting aspect of consistency theory that has preoccupied most of us from the start. Abelson (1959) has written at length on different cognitive strategies for restoring balance. Festinger and Aronson (1960) have also discussed this problem. McGuire (1960c) has studied the logical character of propositions that make them most likely to change in restoring consistency. Newcomb has studied the relative likelihood of perceptual changes and objective relational changes in the strain toward symmetry (cf. 1961, pp. 254–257). Rosenberg has long studied this problem in such terms as the relative likelihood of means and ends changes (1956) and of affective versus informational changes (1960*b*). Tannenbaum (1956) has investigated the probability of change as a function of initial polarization and in quantifying the "assertion constant." Yet despite (or because of) all this work, the issue remains conceptually confused and cries for further, less haphazard study with these diverse approaches made relevant to one another.

Purportedly necessary conditions for inconsistency arousal. A number of characteristics, mostly having to do with the subjective state of the subject (sometimes operationally defined), have been posited as necessary for the occurrences of the predicted inconsistency effects. "Awareness" has not been made especially troublesome. McGuire (1960*a*) has argued that his data imply that awareness of the inconsistency is unnecessary. The "felt discomfort" of dissonance theory (Festinger, 1957) apparently should not be taken to imply a necessary phenomenological experience on the part of the subject, though Brehm and Cohen, in their contrasting of psychoanalytic and dissonance theory, are ambivalent on this point (1962, pp. 167–168). Yet the revival of interest in "awareness" in connection with studies on verbal conditioning (Eriksen, 1962) and experimenter bias (Rosenthal, 1964) invites a reanalysis in the present case: e.g., it is necessary to be aware at least of the elements themselves, even if not of the inconsistency between them, in order for the consistency theory predictions to be borne out.

The most investigated of the proposed "necessary condition" variables is probably that of choice or volition. Left rather vague in Festinger's original formulation of dissonance theory (1957), the *fait accompli* experiments of his interpreters, Brehm and Cohen (cf., e.g., 1962, pp. 188–220), purport to show that the subject must feel he, to some degree, voluntarily entered the subsequently dissonant situation, though he did not necessarily foresee the dissonant element in it. The subsequent empirical study and theoretical extension of this notion has yielded a seemingly contradictory set of results. The theoretical and empirical status of the choice variable badly needs further analysis.

Still another such variable whose empirical status is ambiguous and whose theoretical interpretation is debated is that called "commitment." It remains uncertain to what extent various manipulations under this concept can be considered equivalent; viz., active participa-tion (King and Janis, 1956), overt compliance (Festinger, 1957, pp. 84-122), response restriction (Kelman, 1953), public versus private commitment (Bennett-Pelz–v. Bennett, 1955), external commitment (Rosenbaum and Franc, 1960), and somewhat more distantly related, reactance (J. W. Brehm, 1963). Further examination of the theories, the experimental operations, and the apparently conflicting results should help clarify the processes involved in the effects of these overlapping manipulations.

Origins of the need for consistency. It has purportedly been shown (Lawrence and Festinger, 1962) that animals other than men operate according to consistency theory. On the other hand, it has been amply demonstrated in the work on alternation and exploratory behavior, effects of infantile stimulation, etc. (Berlyne, 1960; Fiske and Maddi, 1961; Fowler, 1965), that various *albinus Rattus norvegicus* also have the somewhat opposite "need for complexity." All of this suggests we might look for the acquisition of need consistency in our phylogenetic origins, rather than the life history of the individual. However, two ontogenetic sources of need-consistency have been suggested and might repay a closer look: child-rearing practices and role assignment. Harvey, Hunt, and Schroeder (1961) have analyzed extensively how parents' rearing practices and the child's own maturational level may interact to affect the level of complexity which the individual subsequently finds optimal. Newcomb's role-theory approach suggests that subsequent life experiences and late status changes can influence the person's need for consistency.

Even cross-cultural data are available on the point at issue. Child, Barry, and their coworkers have presented a number of studies (e.g., Barry, 1957) based on data from the Human Relations Area Files showing societal and cultural variables related to modal preference for openness and complexity as symmetry and balance in art (and to a lesser extent, theological systems). Hovland, Lumsdaine, and Sheffield (1949, pp. 310–311) have commented on the "consistency reaction" one purportedly gets with American subjects when using the before-after design as contrasted with the "inconsistency reaction" such a procedure elicits from Syrian subjects.

Temporal factors. It is always captivating to deal with predictions involving the time variable because, as few others encountered in the behavioral sciences, this dimension is easily measurable and has well-understood scaling properties. Consistency theory has encountered this variable in at least two contexts. Leaving aside the question of awareness, McGuire (1960a) has considered to what extent the elicitation of two de facto inconsistent cognitions must be temporally contiguous for the need for consistency to produce a change in them. Put more elegantly, the question is asked: To what extent does the pressure toward consistency decay as a function of time beween elicitation of the inconsistent elements?

A second temporal issue is raised by the work of Elaine Walster (1964; Festinger and Walster, 1964); it shows that under some conditions the postdecision reevaluation towards consistency shows a nonmonotonic relationship to time. There is an immediate postdecision "regret" period with reevaluations away from greater consistency with the choice, but a long-term trend toward greater consistency.

These openings of the temporal issue have obviously raised more questions than they have answered, as has McGuire's (1960b) study on rate of return to the initial "inconsistent" state as time passed from the occasion on which it had been made salient. Freedman (1965) also has presented interesting data on this relationship.

Methodological Issues

This third rubric under which we group issues for discussion is, again, only imperfectly distinguishable from the other two types of issues (definitional and empirical) considered above. We group here, for convenience, those problems of manipulating variables or analyzing data that seem to arise again and again in connection with consistency-theory experiments and in regard to which work in the area has been subjected to severe criticism—both the self-criticism of the practitioners and the rather harsher criticisms of outside observers (see McGuire, 1966, for a review). None of the problems to be mentioned is found only in the consistency-theory area, nor are these the only methodological problems in the area, but these four arise frequently enough to bear mention. They include: (1) analytic and procedural problems arising from the availability of multiple modes of inconsistency reduction; (2) problems of interpretation and replication, arising from the tendency toward using rather complex social settings and complicated and subtle manipulations in many consistency-

theory experiments; (3) generalization problems arising from the frequent use, in consistency-theory experiments, of techniques which are not themselves well understood, such as role-playing, hypnosis, and computer simulation; and (4) the problem of obtaining a direct measure of inconsistency. We shall mention briefly problems in each of these areas.

Problem of multiple modes of resolution. It has already been pointed out that in any inconsistency situation there are inevitably alternative ways in which the system can return to consistency. Indeed, as was mentioned above, the consistency theorists have been quite active in positing new ways of reducing inconsistency. Problems of method arise when the investigator manipulates inconsistency to study the effect on one particular mode of inconsistency reduction. Strategies for dealing with the likelihood that other modes will also be utilized for inconsistency reduction have exposed these researchers to much criticism. The tactic of "blocking off" the alternative modes has usually resulted in the devising of very complicated and artificial situations, which gives rise to questions of interpretation and generalization (see next section). The alternative tactic of closing off these other avenues post factum by eliminating subjects who make extensive use of other modes has also been severely criticized. We need to consider alternative tactics and superior methods of computation (e.g., covariance and multivariate analysis) for handling this problem which is intrinsic to research on consistency theory and, indeed, to many other areas of research.

The complex manipulation problem. Consistency-theory researchers are frequently criticized also because of a tendency to use extremely complicated experimental situations and to carry out rather difficult manipulations of variables in testing their hypotheses. As a result, there arise questions of how the subject perceived the situation (Rosenberg, 1965), and of extraneous variables operating, unappreciated by the experimenter, but perhaps more important in producing the obtained effect than were the variables to which he attributed these effects. Numerous studies have been criticized as hard to interpret and generalize on these grounds. For example, the studies manipulating choice avoided subject self-selection by giving the subjects a pseudochoice utilizing a complicated sleight-of-hand induction. In this way all the subjects, even those in the "high" choice condition, will make the same choice as the subjects in the low choice conditions, but some will feel they had more volition in so choosing. The complexity and subtlety of the experimental situations not only make interpretation equivocal but also render replication in other laboratories difficult, a very serious shortcoming for a supposedly scientific theory. Hopefully, further discussion and analysis of this problem will yield methods of circumventing these complex subtle inductions or at least will indicate to what extent consistency theory predictions depend on such elaborate techniques or are confirmed even without their employment.

Questionable techniques. For practical reasons, consistency theory researchers have made more use of methodological techniques that are themselves not well understood than have workers in most other fields of psychology. For example, several investigators have tested predictions in a role-playing situation, which always leaves it open to question whether the subject's responses can be generalized to his ordinary behavior, or whether they instead represent his conception of what the experimenter wants him to do or what a rational man would do. Also open to question is the use of hypnosis in some consistency studies. The hypnotic processes are themselves more poorly understood than those consistency processes that they are being used to elucidate (Hilgard, 1965). Still others of us have used computer simulation, even though we are well aware that this strategy leaves the theorist with an embarrassing number of degrees of freedom. Each of these techniques, of course, has its defenders as well as its attackers; cf., e.g., R. Brown (1962, p. 74) on the value of role playing. We can hardly hope in this volume to solve the problems of role playing, hypnosis, and computer simulation. But we can hope to get an inkling of whether a substantial enough body of consistency-theory results is confirmed by both these and more prosaic techniques so that we can feel freer in the future to use these more venturesome procedures to study new processes that might otherwise remain uninvestigated.

The criterion problem. The motivational state of imbalance, asymmetry, discomfort, dissonance, etc., postulated by consistency theory is an intervening variable. The predictions by which the theory is tested typically use as their dependent variables quite derivative behavior only distantly related to inconsistency and affected also by many antecedents other than in-

consistency. As a result, the experiments are often insensitive as tests of consistency theory, and each individual experiment usually can be plausibly explained on bases other than consistency theory. It would be useful if we had more direct measures of this postulated internal state. The two obvious roads to making it a hypothetical construct would be to give it surplus meaning in phenomenological or in physiological terms. In this way we could hope to measure inconsistency level more directly by means of the subject's verbal reports of his felt inconsistency (a course which is unattractive for several reasons), or by means of physiological indexes. A start has been made toward developing the latter, e.g., by M. L. Brehm, Back, and Bogdonoff (1964) who have used blood cholesterol, and by Gerard (1964) who has employed electrophysiological indexes. The latter has also used simple physical response indexes like reaction time. It would be useful to examine the possibilities of further developing indexes along these lines.

THE PLACE OF CONSISTENCY THEORY IN THE LARGER PSYCHOLOGICAL SCENE

Our remarks so far may have revealed our belief that consistency theory is a Big Thing in current psychological thinking and that it has in the recent past constituted a very fertile approach for those experimenting in social and personality psychology. In closing, we should like to suggest where consistency theory fits within the larger psychological picture—how it relates to some other general formulations, especially motivation theory and the functional approaches. Also, we should like to point out that while, at the moment, consistency theory may be a big thing, it has not always been so and it will again not be so, in the foreseeable future. We shall glance ahead and suggest that the inevitable corrective to consistency theory is already visible on the horizon.

Relation to Other Approaches

Consistency among the motives. What is "consistency" as used in this discussion? It is a state of interrelation among cognitions and interpersonal bonds. We speak of the individual tending toward this state. Hence we view consistency as a tendency, a drive, a motive. Should we then consider consistency as one more motive, and seek to answer the questions about consistency that are being framed with more and more sophistication (J. S. Brown, 1961; Cofer and Appley, 1964) regarding motives in general? Should a book called "The Consistency Motive" take its place on the shelf along with "The Achievement Motive" (McClelland, Atkinson, Clark, and Lowell, 1953), "The Affiliation Motive" (Schachter, 1959), "The Approval Motive" (Crowne and Marlowe, 1964), etc.? My personal feeling is that if this process of finding new motives continues, the psychologist with his set of motives will offer the intelligent onlooker as absurd a prospect as the current spectacle of the physicist and his ludicrous set of particles. I would feel like King Alfonso who, after hearing a description of the later epicyclic theory of the solar system, said, "It may be so. But let me tell you, had I been the creator, I could have done the thing more simply."

Yet while we would be grieved to see consistency tending raised to the status of a motive, like a battle-weary British politician elevated to Lords, we agree that the concept can perhaps be fitted into current psychological thinking more appropriately as a motive than as anything else [not withstanding that long ago Summer argued that consistency was only a strain found in the realm of social systems and not in the heads of individual irrational man (cf. 1906, pp. 4–5, 473)]. We feel that clarification of the concept and heuristic suggestions for further research will come more from the motivational analysis of need for consistency than from any other single endeavor. I am quite hopeful that this advances us toward a clearer notion of consistency as a motive and better formulated research questions on the motivational issues than we had at the outset. The question has not been neglected before. Dissonance theorists have often presented derivations that seem in conflict with those derived from SR reinforcement theory (Aronson, 1961; Aronson, 1963; Lawrence and Festinger, 1962; Lott, 1963; Mowrer, 1963) or from more traditional hedonic theories (Aronson and Carlsmith, 1962; Festinger and Carlsmith, 1959; Janis and Gilmore, 1965; Rosenberg, 1965).

Other past discussions of consistency as a motive have included Newcomb's (1953) analysis of possible advantages of consistency in our usual environment. He suggests that whether or not it is intrinsically rewarding, consistency does pay off and thus would tend in any case to have secondary reward value. Several of the consistency theorists have questioned whether the motivational state involves consistency per se. J. W. Brehm and Cohen (1962, pp. 223–231) suggest that the evidence indicates that inconsistency is not ipso facto motivating but becomes so only when it frustrates another motive. Osgood (1957) suggests that consistency is important psychologically only insofar as it subserves the need for meaning.

Consistency among the functions. Several theorists have approached the attitude area from a "functional" point of view, which attempts to explain and predict the person's attitudes, their interrelations and susceptibility to change, and their relation to action, in terms of the functions they may serve in his total psychological economy. This approach obviously also entails an analysis of human motivation. Various workers have employed this approach, with the "authoritarian personality" study (Adorno, Frenkel-Brunswik, Levinson, and Sanford, 1950) being the best known of the early work. Smith has also been long working in this area (Smith, 1949; Smith, Bruner, and White, 1956) as has DiVesta (DiVesta and Merwin, 1960; Woodruff and DiVesta, 1948). Perhaps the most active group has been that at Michigan around Katz, Sarnoff, Stotland, et al. (cf. Katz, 1960; Katz and Stotland, 1959, for reviews).

Attitudes have been analyzed as serving many functions: utility, expression, meaning, ego, defensiveness, etc. It seems likely that maintenance of consistency plays an important role in all of these functions; certainly, in the last two. We feel that an integration into the functional approach is another avenue by which consistency theories, to the mutual benefit of both kinds of approach, could be brought into heuristically provocative interaction with other approaches.

The Rise and Fall of Consistency Theory: End of the Classic Phase

We have mentioned that the consistency approach was not always so dominant a theme in psychological thinking as currently. In fact, until the late 1940's it was decidedly out of fashion. Perhaps in the early nineteenth century the notion of consistency and the rational man reached its height of popularity for the Modern Era. The idealism and grand syntheses of the German philosophers such as Kant and Hegel were exceedingly popular in Nineteenth century America from the Mississippi to the

Charles and even in the few cultural enclaves beyond the old frontier.

But there was an extreme swing away from this rationalism in American psychology in the first half of this century. Whether inspired by the biologism of Darwin or the preoccupation with psychopathology stemming from Freud, it was *ganz Amerikanisch* to view behavior as nonrational, fragmented, unintegrated. Perhaps one could imagine a Pavlov or a Thorndike smiling tolerantly at the consistency theorists; but J. B. Watson would have exploded violently and Clark Hull would have refused to believe they existed, except perhaps as another bad joke from the West Coast extremists.

Still, there is a Yin and Yang in the course of scientific progress as in other human processes, and once again the consistency approach is highly popular in some circles and at least tolerated or recognized as worthy of attack (Chapanis and Chapanis, 1964; Lott, 1963; Mowrer, 1963) by psychologists in general. It seems that on the broad dimension of theorizing, like rationality-irrationality, there is a continuing slow oscillation between the two poles. At one time most of the theorists are gathered towards one pole using that notion as a point of departure for their thinking about behavior. In time, the heuristic potential of that pole becomes exhausted and novel predictions and nonobvious hypotheses get harder to come by As this happens, the natural corrective sets in, and the precursors of the new establishment swing to the opposite pole to continue the upward and onward sweep of psychological knowledge from that new vantage point.

It is of some parenthetical interest to me that this swing back and forth does not seem to be correlated across disciplines. Take psychology and philosophy. The 1925–1950 period was one in which the dominant psychological interest and approach involved the nonrational nonintegrated themes of isolated habits, nonphenomenal, noncognitivistic constructs, automatic and compartmentalized behaviors, etc. At the same time in philosophy, we witnessed unusual interest in systematics, symbolic logic, logical empiricism, the study of systematic theory, etc. Since 1950 psychology has been shifting toward an interest in integration and rationalism; we see the opposite shift in philosophy, with the dominant theme there of irrational man (Barrett, 1958). The voices we hear from the philosophical circles are no longer Hegel or Kant, or even the Wienerkreis but rather those of Kierkegaard, Husserl, Heidegger, Marcel, Merleau-Ponty (my own favorite), Jaspers, Sartre, etc. It appears that while philosophy yins, psychology yangs. One field's classic period tends to be another's romantic period.

Where are we today in this oscillation between the romantic and classic? I personally would venture the guess that we are at or near the quantitative peak of interest for this swing of the pendulum, but I suspect research activity will be sustained at the present level for at least five more years. I do see, however, the inevitable correction already setting in. This antithetical trend I shall call "complexity theory."

It is an interesting phenomenon that while many bright young men have been drawing heuristic inspiration from the consistency approach another group of men, a little younger, not so numerous, but perhaps just as bright, have been drawing their inspiration from the rather opposite complexity approach which, if not logically contradictory to the consistency theory, is at least the reverse of it in psychological flavor.

Under the unsatisfactory rubric of "complexity theories" I include the diverse approaches reviewed in such recent books as Berlyne (1960), Fiske and Maddi (1961), and Fowler (1965). Here we come upon a romantic notion of the organism, very different from the classic notion of consistency theories. The latter classic organism has a penchant for stability, redundancy, familiarity, confirmation of expectance, avoidance of the new, the unpredictable. Complexity theory's romantic organism works on a quite different economy. It has a stimulus hunger, and exploratory drive, a need curiosity. It takes pleasure in the unexpected, at least in intermediate levels of unpredictability. It wants to experience everything; it shows alternation behavior; it finds novelty rewarding.

It is an interesting incident for the sociologists of science that these two rather opposed themes of consistency need and complexity need have coexisted in the same field with very little hard feelings and, unfortunately, very little confrontation. Like that earlier-mentioned contributor to the Sikh scripture, I feel that even when the two approaches are contradictory, both are true. The resolution is encapsulated in a hypothetical non-monotonic relationship between our dependent and independent variables with the inflection point for the behavior lying at an intermediate level of our consistency manipulation.

I am tempted to go further into the work of the complexity theories, presenting their research in as much detail as I have given to the consistency theorists. However, the chapter is already long, and the claims of justice must yield to the weakness of the flesh and so we must here bring these extended remarks to a close.

REFERENCES

Abelson, R. P. Modes of resolution of belief dilemmas. *J. conflict Resolut.*, 1959, **3**, 343-352.

Abelson, R. P. Do predispositional factors summate? *Amer. Psychologist*, 1961, **16**, 377.

Abelson, R. P., and Rosenberg, M. J. Symbolic psychologic: a model of attitudinal cognition. *Behav. Sci.*, 1958, **3**, 1-13.

Adams, J. S. Reduction of cognitive dissonance by seeking consonant information. *J. abnorm. soc. Psychol.*, 1961, **62**, 74-78.

Adorno, T. W., Frenkel-Brunswik, Else, Levinson, D. J., and Sanford, R. N. *The authoritarian personality*. New York: Harper & Row, 1950.

Allport, G. W. Attitudes. In C. A. Murchison (Ed.), *A handbook of social psychology*. Worcester, Mass.: Clark Univer. Press, 1935. Pp. 798-844.

Anderson, N. H. Application of an additive model to impression formation. *Science*, 1962, **138**, 817-818.

Anderson, N. H. Averaging versus adding as a stimulus-combination rule in impression formation. *J. exp. Psychol.*, 1965, **70**, 394-400.

Aronson, E. The effect of effort on the attractiveness of rewarded and unrewarded stimuli. *J. abnorm. soc. Psychol.*, 1961, **63**, 375-380.

Aronson, E. Effort, attractiveness, and the anticipation of reward: a reply to Lott's critique. *J. abnorm. soc. Psychol.*, 1963, **67**, 522-525.

Aronson, E., and Carlsmith, J. M. Performance expectancy as a determinant of actual performance. *J. abnorm. soc. Psychol.*, 1962, **65**, 178-182.

Aronson, E., and Festinger, L. Some attempts to measure tolerance for dissonance. USAF, WADC, Tech. Rep. No. 58-492, 1958.

Aronson, E., and Mills, J. The effect of severity of initiation on liking for a group. *J. abnorm. soc. Psychol.*, 1959, **59**, 177-181.

Asch, S. E. Studies in the principles of judgments and attitudes: II. determination of judgments by group and by ego standards. *J. soc. Psychol.*, 1940, **12**, 433-465.

Barrett, W. *Irrational man*. Garden City, N. Y.: Doubleday, 1958.

Barry, H., III. Relationships between child training and the pictorial arts. *J. abnorm. soc. Psychol.*, 1957, **54**, 380-383.

Bennett, Edith B. Discussion, decision, commitment, and consensus in "group decision." *Hum. Relat.*, 1955, **8**, 251-273.

Bergin, A. E. The effect of dissonant persuasive communications upon changes in a self-referring attitude. *J. Pers.*, 1962, **30**, 423-438.

Berlyne, D. E. *Conflict, arousal, and curiosity*. New York: McGraw-Hill, 1960.

Bieri, J. Complexity-simplicity as a personality variable in cognitive and preferential behavior. In D. W. Fiske and S. R. Maddi (Eds.), *Functions of varied experience*. Homewood, Ill.: Dorsey, 1961. Pp. 355-379.

Brehm, J. W. Postdecision changes in the desirability of alternatives. *J. abnorm. soc. Psychol.*, 1956, **52**, 384-389.

Brehm, J. W. Reduction of freedom and its consequences: a theory of psychological reactance. Unpublished manuscript, Duke Univer., 1963.

Brehm, J. W., and Cohen, A. R. *Explorations in cognitive dissonance*. New York: Wiley, 1962.

Brehm, Mary L., Back, K. W., and Bogdonoff, M. D. A physiological effect of cognitive dissonance under stress and deprivation. *J. abnorm. soc. Psychol.*, 1964, **69**, 303-310.

Brock, T. C. Commitment to exposure as a determinant of information receptivity. *J. pers. soc. Psychol.*, 1965, **2**, 10-19.

Brock, T. C., and Buss, A. H. Dissonance, aggression, and evaluation of pain. *J. abnorm. soc. Psychol.*, 1962, **65**, 197-202.

Brodbeck, May. The role of small groups in mediating the effects of propaganda. *J. abnorm. soc. Psychol.*, 1956, **52**, 166-170.

Brown, J. S. *The motivation of behavior*. New York: McGraw-Hill, 1961.

Brown, J. S., and Farber, I. E. Emotions conceptualized as intervening variables—with suggestions toward a theory of frustration. *Psychol. Bull.*, 1951, **48**, 465-495.

Brown, R. Models of attitude change. In R. Brown, E. Galanter, E. H. Hess, and G. Mandler (Eds.), *New directions in psychology*. I. New York: Holt, Rinehart, and Winston, 1962. Pp. 1-85.

Campbell, A., Converse, P. E., Miller, W. E., and Stokes, D. E. *The American voter*. New York: Wiley, 1960.

Campbell, D. T. The generality of social attitudes. Unpublished doctoral dissertation. Univer. of California, 1947.

Campbell, D. T. Conformity in psychology's theories of acquired behavioral dispositions. In I. A. Berg and B. M. Bass (Eds.), *Conformity and deviation*, New York: Harper & Rowe, 1961. Pp. 101-158.

Carlson, E. R. Attitude change through modification of attitude structure. *J. abnorm. soc. Psychol.*, 1956, **52**, 256-261.

Cartwright, D., and Harary, F. Structural balance: a generalization of Heiders theory. *Psychol. Rev.*, 1956, **63**, 277-293.

Chapanis, Natalia P., and Chapanis, A. Cognitive dissonance: five years later. *Psychol. Bull.*, 1964, **61**, 1-22.

Chein, I. Behavior theory and the behavior of attitudes: some critical comments. *Psychol. Rev.*, 1948, **55**, 175-188.

Cofer, C. N., and Appley, M. H. *Motivation: theory and research.* New York: Wiley, 1964.

Couch, A., and Keniston, K. Yeasayers and naysayers: agreeing response set as a personality variable. *J. abnorm. soc. Psychol.*, 1960, **60**, 151-174.

Crowne, D. P., and Marlowe, D. *The approval motive: studies in evaluative dependence.* New York: Wiley, 1964.

Deutsch, M., and Solomon, L. Reactions to evaluations by others as influenced by self-evaluations. *Sociometry*, 1959, **22**, 93-112.

Deutsch, M., Krauss, R. M., and Rosenau, Norah. Dissonance or defensiveness? *J. Pers.*, 1962, **30**, 16-28.

DiVesta, F. J., and Merwin, J. C. The effects of need-oriented communications on attitude change. *J. abnorm. soc. Psychol.*, 1960, **60**, 80-85.

Dollard, J., and Miller, N. E. *Personality and psychotherapy*, New York: McGraw-Hill, 1950.

Doob, L. W. The behavior of attitudes. *Psychol. Rev.*, 1947, **54**, 135-156.

Ebbinghaus, H. *Abriss der psychologie.* Leipzig: Veit, 1909.

Eriksen, C. W. (Ed.) *Behavior and awareness: a symposium of research and interpretation.* Durham, N. C.: Duke Univer. Press, 1962. Suppl. to *J. Pers.*, 1962, **30**.

Feldman, S. Evaluative ratings of adjective-adjective combinations, predicted from ratings of their components. Unpublished doctoral dissertation, Yale Univer., 1962.

Festinger, L. *A theory of cognitive dissonance.* Stanford, Calif.: Stanford Univer. Press., 1957.

Festinger, L. (Ed.) *Conflict, decision, and dissonance.* Stanford, Calif.: Stanford Univer. Press, 1964.

Festinger, L., and Aronson, E. The arousal and reduction of dissonance in social contexts. In D. Cartwright and A. Zander (Eds.), *Group dynamics: research and theory*. (2nd ed.) Evanston, Ill.: Row, Peterson, 1960. Pp. 214-231.

Festinger, L., and Carlsmith, J. M. Cognitive consequences of forced compliance. *J. abnorm. soc. Psychol.*, 1959, **58**, 203-210.

Festinger, L., and Thibaut, J. Interpersonal communication in small groups. *J. abnorm. soc. Psychol.*, 1951, **46**, 92-99.

Festinger, L., and Walster, Elaine. Post-decision regret and decision reversal. In L. Festinger (Ed.), *Conflict, decision, and dissonance.* Stanford, Calif.: Stanford Univer. Press, 1964. Pp. 100-110.

Festinger, L., Schachter, S., and Back, K. *Social pressures in informal groups.* New York: Harper & Row, 1950.

Festinger, L., Riecken, H. W., and Schachter, S. *When prophecy fails.* Minneapolis, Minn.: Univer. of Minnesota Press, 1956.

Fishbein, M. An investigation of the relationships between beliefs about an object and the attitude toward that object. *Hum. Relat.*, 1963, **16**, 233-239.

Fishbein, M. A consideration of beliefs, attitudes, and their relationships. In I. D. Steiner & M. Fishbein (Eds.), *Current studies in social psychology.* New York: Holt, Rinehart and Winston, 1965. Pp. 107-120.

Fishbein, M., and Hunter, Ronda. Summation versus balance in attitude organization and change. *J. abnorm. soc. Psychol.,* 1964, **69**, 505-510.

Fiske, D. W., and Maddi, S. R. *Functions of varied experience.* Homewood, Ill.: Dorsey, 1961.

Fowler, H. *Curiosity and exploratory behavior.* New York: Macmillan, 1965.

Freedman, J. L. Involvement, discrepancy, and change. *J. abnorm. soc. Psychol.,* 1964, **69**, 290-295.

Freedman, J. L. Long-term behavioral effects of cognitive dissonance. *J. exp. soc. Psychol.,* 1965, **1**, 145-155.

Gerard, H. B. Physiological measurement in social psychological research. In P. H. Liederman and D. Shapiro (Eds.), *Psychobiological approaches to social behavior.* Stanford, Calif.: Stanford Univer. Press, 1964. Pp. 43-58.

Glass, D. Theories of consistency and the study of personality. In E. F. Borgatta and W. W. Lambert (Eds.), *Handbook of personality theory and research.* Chicago: Rand-McNally, in press.

Greenwald, H. The involvement-discrepancy controversy in persuasion research. Unpublished doctoral dissertation, Columbia Univer., 1964.

Gulliksen, H. Measurement of subjective values. *Psychometrika,* 1956, **21**, 229-244.

Hammond, K. R. Probabilistic functioning and the clinical method. *Psychol. Rev.,* 1955, **62**, 255-262.

Harary, F. On the measurement of structural balance. *Behav. Sci.,* 1959, **4**, 316-323.

Harding, J., Kutner, B., Proshansky, H., and Chein, I. Prejudice and ethnic relations. In G. Lindzey (Ed.), *Handbook of social psychology.* Reading, Mass.: Addison-Wesley, 1954. Pp. 1021-1061.

Hardyck, Jane A., and Braden, Marcia. Prophecy fails again: a report of a failure to replicate. *J. abnorm. soc. Psychol.,* 1962, **65**, 136-141.

Harvey, O. J., Hunt, D. E., and Schroder, H. M. *Conceptual systems and personality organization.* New York: Wiley, 1961.

Heider, F. Attitudes and cognitive organization. *J. Psychol.,* 1946, **21**, 107-112.

Heider, F. *The psychology of interpersonal relations.* New York: Wiley, 1958.

Hilgard, E. R. *Hypnotic susceptibility.* New York: Harcourt, Brace, 1965.

Horowitz, M. W., Lyons, J., and Perlmutter, H. V. Induction of forces in discussion groups. *Hum. Relat.,* 1951, **4**, 57-76.

Hovland, C. I., Lumsdaine, A. A., and Sheffield, F. D. *Experiments on mass communication.* Princeton, N. J.: Princeton Univer. Press, 1949.

Janis, I. L. Motivational factors in the resolution of decisional conflicts. In M. R. Jones (Ed.), *Nebraska symposium on motivation, 1959.* Lincoln, Nebr.: Univer. of Nebraska Press, 1959. Pp. 198-231.

Janis, I. L., and Gilmore, J. B. The influence of incentive conditions on the success of role playing in modifying attitudes. *J. pers. soc. Psychol.,* 1965, **1**, 17-27.

Janis, I. L., and King, B. T. The influence of role playing on opinion change. *J. abnorm. soc. Psychol.,* 1954, **49**, 211-218.

Jordan, N. Behavioral forces that are a function of attitudes and of cognitive organization. *Hum. Relat.,* 1953, **6**, 273-287.

Katz, D. The functional approach to the study of attitudes. *Publ. Opin. Quart.,* 1960, **24**, 163-204.

Katz, D., and Stotland, E. A preliminary statement to a theory of attitude structure and change. In S. Koch (Ed.), *Psychology: a study of a science.* Vol. 3. New York: McGraw-Hill, 1959. Pp. 423-475.

Kelman, H. C. Attitude change as a function of response restriction. *Hum. Relat.,* 1953, **6**, 185-214.

King, B. T., and Janis, I. L. Comparison of the effectiveness of improvised versus non-improvised role-playing in producing opinion changes. *Hum. Relat.,* 1956, **9**, 177-186.

Krech, D., Crutchfield, R. S., and Ballachey, E. L. *Individual in society.* New York: McGraw-Hill, 1962.

Kuhn, T. S. Energy conservation as an example of simultaneous discovery. In M. Clagett (Ed.), *Critical problems in the history of science.* Madison, Wis.: Univer. of Wisconsin Press, 1959. Pp. 321-356.

Lawrence, D. H., and Festinger, L. *Deterrents and reinforcement.* Stanford, Calif.: Stanford Univer. Press, 1962.

Lewin, K. (Ed.) Behavior as a function of the total situation. *Field theory in social science.* New York: Harper & Brothers, 1951.

Lott, Bernice E. Secondary reinforcement and effort: comment on Aronson's "The effect of effort on the attractiveness of rewarded and unrewarded stimuli." *J. abnorm. soc. Psychol.*, 1963, **67**, 520-522.

McClelland, D. C., Atkinson, J. W., Clark, R. A., and Lowell, E. L. *The achievement motive.* New York: Appleton-Century-Crofts, 1953.

McGuire, W. J. Cognitive consistency and attitude change. *J. abnorm. soc. Psychol.*, 1960, **60**, 345-353. (*a*)

McGuire, W. J. Direct and indirect persuasive effects of dissonance-producing messages. *J. abnorm. soc. Psychol.*, 1960, **60**, 354-358. (*b*)

McGuire, W. J. A syllogistic analysis of cognitive relationships. In M. J. Rosenberg and C. I. Hovland (Eds.), *Attitude organization and change.* New Haven, Conn.: Yale Univer. Press, 1960. Pp. 65-111. (*c*)

McGuire, W. J. Inducing resistance to persuasion: some contemporary approaches. *Advanc. exp. soc. Psychol.*, 1964, **1**, 191-229.

McGuire, W. J. Attitudes and opinions. *Annu. Rev. Psychol.*, 1966, **17**, 475-514.

McGuire, W. J., Abelson, R. P., Aronson, E., Newcomb, T. M., Rosenberg, M. J., and Tannenbaum, P. H. Proposal for a work group on consistency theory. Unpublished manuscript, Columbia Univer., 1963.

Merton, R. K. Priorities in scientific discovery: a chapter in the sociology of science. *Amer. soc. Rev.*, 1957, **22**, 635-659.

Miller, N. E. Experimental studies of conflict. In J. McV. Hunt (Ed.), *Personality and the behavior disorders.* Vol. 1. New York: Ronald, 1944. Pp. 431-465.

Mills, J., Aronson, E., and Robinson, H. Selectivity in exposure to information. *J. abnorm. soc. Psychol.*, 1959, **59**, 250-253.

Mills, J., and Ross, A. Effects of commitment and certainty upon interest in supporting information. *J. abnorm. soc. Psychol.*, 1964, **68**, 552-555.

Morrissette, J. O. An experimental study of the theory of structural balance. *Hum. Relat.*, 1958, **11**, 239-254.

Mowrer, O. H. Cognitive dissonance or counter-conditioning?—a reappraisal of certain behavioral "paradoxes." *Psychol. Rec.*, 1963, **13**, 197-211.

Myrdal, G. *An American dilemma.* New York: Harper & Row, 1944.

Newcomb, T. M. An approach to the study of communicative acts. *Psychol. Rev.*, 1953, **60**, 393-404.

Newcomb, T. M. The prediction of interpersonal attraction. *Amer. Psychologist*, 1956, **11**, 575-586.

Newcomb, T. M. Individual systems of orientation. In S. Koch (Ed.), *Psychology: a study of a science.* Vol. 3. New York: McGraw-Hill, 1959. Pp. 384-422.

Newcomb, T. M. *The acquaintance process.* New York: Holt, Rinehart, and Winston, 1961.

O'Donovan, D. Rating extremity: pathology or meaningfulness? *Psychol. Rev.*, 1965, **72**, 358-372.

Osgood, C. E. Motivational dynamics of language behavior. In M. R. Jones (Ed.), *Nebraska symposium on motivation, 1957.* Lincoln, Nebr.: Univer. of Nebraska Press, 1957. Pp. 348-424.

Osgood, C. E., and Tannenbaum, P. H. The principle of congruity in the prediction of attitude change. *Psychol. Rev.*, 1955, **62**, 42-55.

Rimoldi, H. J. A. Prediction of scale values for combined stimuli. *Brit. J. statist. Psychol.*, 1956, **9**, 29-40.

Rokeach, M., and Rothman, G. The principle of belief congruence and the congruity principle as models of cognitive interaction. *Psychol. Rev.*, 1965, **72**, 128-142.

Rorer, L. G. The great response-style myth. *Psychol. Bull.*, 1965, **63**, 129-156.

Rosen, S. Postdecision affinity for incompatible information. *J. abnorm. soc. Psychol.*, 1961, **63**, 188-190.

Rosenbaum, M. E., and Franc, D. E. Opinion change as a function of external commitment and amount of discrepancy from the opinion of another. *J. abnorm. soc. Psychol.*, 1960, **61**, 15-20.

Rosenberg, M. J. Cognitive structure and attitudinal affect. *J. abnorm. soc. Psychol.*, 1956, **53**, 367-372.

Rosenberg, M. J. An analysis of affective-cognitive consistency. In M. J. Rosenberg and C. I. Hovland (Eds.), *Attitude organization and change.* New Haven, Conn.: Yale Univer. Press, 1960. Pp. 15-64. (*a*)

Rosenberg, M. J. Cognitive reorganization in response to the hypnotic reversal of attitudinal affect. *J. Pers.*, 1960, **28**, 39-63. (*b*)

Rosenberg, M. J. When dissonance fails: on eliminating evaluation apprehension from attitude measurement. *J. pers. soc. Psychol.*, 1965, **1**, 28-42.

Rosenberg, M. J., and Abelson, R. P. An analysis of cognitive balancing. In M. J. Rosenberg and C. I. Hovland (Eds.), *Attitude organization and change.* New Haven, Conn.: Yale Univer. Press, 1960. Pp. 112-163.

Rosenberg, M. J., and Hovland, C. I. Cognitive, affective, and behavioral components of attitudes. In M. J. Rosenberg and C. I. Hovland (Eds.), *Attitude organization and change.* New Haven, Conn.: Yale Univer. Press, 1960. Pp. 1-14.

Rosenthal, R. The effect of the experimenter on the results of psychological research. *Progr. exp. pers. Res.*, 1964, **1**, 79-114.

Schachter, S. Deviation, rejection, and communication. *J. abnorm. soc. Psychol.*, 1951, **46**, 190-207.

Sears, D. O., and Freedman, J. L. Effects of expected familiarity with arguments upon opinion change and selective exposure. *J. pers. soc. Psychol.*, 1965, **2**, 420-426.

Sherif, Carolyn W., Sherif, M., and Nebergall, R. E. *Attitude and attitude change: the social judgment-involvement approach.* Philadelphia: Saunders, 1965.

Sherif, M., and Hovland, C. I. *Social judgment.* New Haven, Conn.: Yale Univer. Press, 1961.

Silverman, I. In defense of dissonance theory: reply to Chapanis and Chapanis, *Psychol. Bull.*, 1964, **62**, 205-209.

Singer, J. E. Brains, beauty, birth order and Machiavellism. *J. Pers.*, in press.

Smith, M. B. Personal values as determinants of a political attitude. *J. Psychol.*, 1949, **28**, 477-486.

Smith, M. B., Bruner, J. S., and White, R. W. *Opinions and personality.* New York: Wiley, 1956.

Steiner, I. D. Ethnocentrism and tolerance of trait "inconsistency," *J. abnorm. soc. Psychol.*, 1954, **49**, 349-354.

Steiner, I. D. Receptivity to supportive versus nonsupportive communications. *J. abnorm. soc. Psychol.*, 1962, **65**, 266-267.

Steiner, I. D., and Johnson, H. H. Authoritarianism and "tolerance of trait inconsistency." *J. abnorm. soc. Psychol.*, 1963, **67**, 388-391.

Steiner, I. D., and Johnson, H. H. Relationships among dissonance reducing responses. *J. abnorm. soc. Psychol.*, 1964, **68**, 38-44.

Steiner, I. D., and Rogers, E. D. Alternative responses to dissonance. *J. abnorm. soc. Psychol.*, 1963, **66**, 128-136.

Sumner, W. G. *Folkways.* Boston: Ginn, 1906.

Tannenbaum, P. H. Initial attitude toward source and concept as factors in attitude change through communication. *Publ. Opin. Quart.*, 1956, **20**, 413-425.

Tomkins, S. S. *Affect, imagery, consciousness,* Vol. 2. *The negative affects.* Berlin: Springer, 1963.

Triandis, H. C., and Fishbein, M. Cognitive interaction in person perception. *J. abnorm. soc. Psychol.*, 1963, **67**, 446-453.

Walster, Elaine. The temporal sequence of post-decision processes. In L. Festinger (Ed.), *Conflict, decision, and dissonance.* Stanford, Calif.: Stanford Univer. Press, 1964, Pp. 112-127.

Weil, Simone. *Les intuitions pré-chrétiennes.* Paris: La Colombe, 1951. Transl. and ed. by Elisabeth C. Geissbuhler, in *Intimations of Christianity among the ancient Greeks.* London: Routledge & Kegan Paul, 1957.

Weiss, W. Scale judgments of triplets of opinion statements. *J. abnorm. soc. Psychol.*, 1963, **66**, 471-479.

Woodruff, A. D., and DiVesta, F. J. The relation between values, concepts, and attitudes. *Educ. psychol. Measmt.*, 1948, **8**, 645-659.

Worell, L. Response to conflict as determined by prior exposure to conflict. *J. abnorm. soc. Psychol.*, 1962, **64**, 438-445.

Zajonc, R. B. The concepts of balance, congruity, and dissonance. *Publ. Opin. Quart.*, 1960, **24**, 280-286.

Zimbardo, P. G. Involvement and communication discrepancy as determinants of opinion conformity. *J. abnorm. soc. Psychol.*, 1960, **60**, 86-94.

46. *Cognitive Dynamics in the Conduct of Human Affairs*

CHARLES E. OSGOOD

Over the past two decades a great deal of social-psychological research has been converging on a conclusion about human thinking that common sense had already isolated as the consistency which is the "hobgoblin of little minds." It appears, however, that "consistency" can plague big minds as well as little, in high places as well as low. Indeed, the difficulties we face today on both national and international levels can be traced, in part at least, to these dynamics of human thinking. Research that is relevant to our problem cuts a wide swathe through the social sciences—attitude formation and change; the effects of context upon the interpretation of both perceptual and linguistic signs; interpersonal perception and group dynamics; the interactions among beliefs, decisions, and social behavior; and even public affairs. The researchers have come from a diversity of theoretical molds. Accordingly, the purposes of this paper are to provide a brief purview of this research on cognitive dynamics, to indicate the essential similarities in the theoretical notions that have been proposed, and to point up the significance of such cognitive dynamics for contemporary human affairs. But first we need a few specimens of the phenomena we wish to study.

Specimen 1: International affairs. Before the delegates to the United Nations Khrushchev makes sweeping proposals for world disarmament. A large segment of the American press editorializes about the deceptive nature of these proposals, that, rather than sincere overtures toward peaceful solutions of problems, his proposals are carefully planned moves in the Cold War. It is cognitively inconsistent for us to think of people we dislike and distrust making honest, conciliatory moves, behaving as human beings ought to behave, and assuming noble postures.

Specimen 2: Internal affairs. A noted counterspy is invited to speak in the high school auditorium of a university town. In the course of his talk, he emphasizes the fact that the university hasn't invited any *anti*-Communists (including himself) to make public appearances in its halls. Although no allegations are directly made, many people in his audience are led to conclude (*a*) that the university has invited *pro*-Communists (which it hasn't), or at least (*b*) that the university must include some powerful Communist supporters.

Specimen 3: Individual behavior and belief. Some time after stories in the mass media about the relation between smoking and lung cancer had saturated the public, a survey in Minneapolis inquired about both the smoking habits of respondents and whether they thought the relationship between smoking and lung cancer had been proven or not proven. The results showed that 29 per cent of nonsmokers, 20 per cent of light smokers, but only 7 per cent of heavy smokers believed it had been proven. It is cognitively inconsistent to believe one way and behave another; people who smoke heavily find it easier to *dis*believe information that it is damaging to their health.[1]

Specimen 4: Interpersonal affairs. Fraternity men were asked to (*a*) name the men in their group they liked best and liked least, (*b*) rate themselves on a series of traits, and (*c*) rate the other men on the same series of traits. The results showed that these men *assumed* greater similarity in personality traits between people they liked and themselves than actually existed.[2]

[1] Leon Festinger, *A Theory of Cognitive Dissonance*, New York, Row, Peterson, 1957, p. 155.

[2] F. E. Fiedler, W. G. Warrington, and F. J. Blaisdell, "Unconscious Attitudes as Correlates of Sociometric Choice in a Social Group," *Journal of*

• Reprinted from *Public Opinion Quarterly*, 1960, 24, 341-365, with permission of the author and the publisher.

It has also been shown that husbands and wives attribute more similarity between them than actually exists, and this is more true for happily married than for unhappily married couples.[3] It is "natural" to assume that people we like must think and feel as we do—at least, to the extent that we like ourselves.

Specimen 5: Making inferences about people. If we observe, or are told, that so-and-so is *intelligent* and *considerate,* and this is all the information we have, we are nevertheless able to generate many inferences about him—he is also likely to be *sensitive, socially adept, alert,* and so forth, we assume. The traits we infer are not haphazard: they are generated from the region of intersection of the meanings of the traits we know about, according to laws of cognitive interaction.[4] Many of the predictions we make about people and the expectations we have of them are based on inferences of this type.

Specimen 6: Perceptual affairs. In his *Film Technique and Film Acting*[5] Pudovkin describes a little experiment in film editing. A simple, passive close-up of the well-known Russian actor, Mosjukhin, was joined to three different strips of film. In one this close-up was followed by a shot of a bowl of soup on the table; in another it was followed by shots showing a dead woman in a coffin; in the third it was followed by shots of a little girl playing with a funny toy bear. The effects on an unsuspecting audience were terrific, according to Pudovkin. "The public raved about the acting of the artist. They pointed out the heavy pensiveness of his mood over the forgotten soup, were touched and moved by the deep sorrow with which he looked at the dead woman, and admired the light, happy smile with which he surveyed the girl at play. But we knew that in all three cases the face was exactly the same."

Specimen 7: A matter of naming. "A rose by any name would smell as sweet," we have been told—but would it? I do not know of any experiments on the influence of labels upon per-

ception of odors, but this should be easily demonstrated, smells being the elusive, subjective business they are. But from the myth of suburbia we can gather many examples of the same sort—the cramped, standardized, insignificant little house with its postage-stamp yard in "Briarwood Valley," in "Larchmont Hills," or in "Sunnyvale Downs" somehow assumes a splendor and grace it could never have in "Southside Brighton Avenue, subdivision No. 7." The cheap panel-and-paste bedroom set, produced by the hundreds of thousands but garnished with the name "Beverley Charm by Rudet," acquires a distinction far beyond its cost and worth.

Specimen 8: Attitudinal affairs. Suppose that we are favorably disposed toward Eisenhower, both as a person and as the President of our country. In Uruguay, let us say, he is greeted with flowers and smiles, but in Paraguay an unruly mob of students boos him and has to be dispersed with tear gas. Having little information, and generally neutral attitudes, toward both Uruguay and Paraguay, we find ourselves considerably more favorable toward the former than toward the latter. Subsequent news that Uruguay lives under a harsh dictatorship will be discounted—it must really be "benevolent" —and the fact that Paraguay has a democratic form of government, much like our own, is somehow difficult to assimilate. As this hypothetical example shows, we strive to maintain internal consistency among our attitudes and beliefs, often at the price of doctoring reality.

So much for specimens of cognitive interaction in human affairs. Such examples could be elaborated *ad infinitum.* The important thing is that they are all cut from the same cloth; they are all instances of a basic dynamism according to which human judgment, belief, perception, and thought are transformed in midflight, so to speak.

SOME THEORY OF COGNITIVE INTERACTION

Insight into the dynamics of human thinking has been available in the writings of brilliant men of all periods. Certainly Aristotle was aware of these dynamics when he dealt with the principles of rhetoric; Shakespeare imposes the rules of psycho-logic[6] on the thought and be-

Abnormal and Social Psychology, Vol. 47, 1952, pp. 790-796.

[3] M. G. Preston, W. L. Peltz, E. H. Mudd, and H. B. Froscher, "Impressions of Personality as a Function of Marital Conflict," *Journal of Abnormal and Social Psychology,* Vol. 47, 1952, pp. 326-336.

[4] J. S. Bruner and R. Tagiuri, "The Perception of People," in G. Lindzey, editor, *Handbook of Social Psychology,* Vol. 2, Cambridge, Mass., Addison-Wesley, 1954.

[5] V. I. Pudovkin, *Film Technique and Film Acting,* London, Vision, 1954.

[6] This term has been used by R. P. Abelson and M. J. Rosenberg in their article, "Symbolic Psycho-

havior of his characters; and Machiavelli could not have had the understanding he did of politics without an intuitive grasp of the same rules. But intuitive grasp and common sense—essential though they may be to discovery in science —are not the same thing as explicit and testable principles of human behavior.

Among psychologists who have dealt with cognitive interaction in recent times, Fritz Heider undoubtedly has given the earliest and richest analysis, in his two papers in the middle forties[7] and particularly as elaborated in his new book, *The Psychology of Interpersonal Relations,*[8] which is a much broader study of human perception and thinking than the title implies. Working in the area of human communication, particularly in small groups, Theodore Newcomb has utilized very similar theoretical notions to Heider's.[9] In his *A Theory of Cognitive Dissonance,* Leon Festinger has probably given the clearest statement of this type of theory and, through his own ingenious experiments, has extended it into the whole area of relations between cognitions and overt behavior.[10] Osgood and Tannenbaum, working in the area of attitude change, have presented what they call "the congruity hypothesis"—which again has similar features to the Heider-Newcomb-Festinger approaches.[11] The most explicit statement of this hypothesis appears in *The Measurement of Meaning* in the context of Osgood's mediation theory of meaning and the measurement procedures of the semantic differential.[12] Rather than try to describe each of these theories in isolation, it will be more useful to describe them comparatively in terms of certain common and differential features.

---

logic: A Model of Attitudinal Cognition," *Behavioral Science,* Vol. 3, 1958, pp. 1-13.

[7] F. Heider, "Social Perception and Phenomenal Causality," *Psychological Review,* Vol. 51, 1944, pp. 358-374. F. Heider, "Attitudes and Cognitive Organization," *Journal of Psychology,* Vol. 21, 1946, pp. 107-112.

[8] F. Heider, *The Psychology of Interpersonal Relations,* New York, Wiley, 1958.

[9] T. M. Newcomb, "An Approach to the Study of Communicative Acts," *Psychological Review,* Vol. 60, 1953, pp. 393-404.

[10] Festinger, *op. cit.*

[11] C. E. Osgood and P. H. Tannenbaum, "The Principle of Congruity in the Prediction of Attitude Change," *Psychological Review,* Vol. 62, 1955, pp. 42-55.

[12] C. E. Osgood, G. J. Suci, and P. H. Tannenbaum, *The Measurement of Meaning,* Urbana, Ill., University of Illinois Press, 1957.

I. Cognitive Modification Results from the Psychological Stress Produced by Cognitive Inconsistencies

We have here a kind of motivation, analogous to other drive states like hunger, sex, and anxiety, but purely cognitive in origin. It is necessary, of course, to define the states of cognitive "consistency" and "inconsistency" and in terms as close as possible to observables. Heider himself speaks in terms of *balance and imbalance* (from within a gestalt framework), but he does not provide us with a very clear statement, beyond the fact that "a balanced state is . . . a situation in which the relations among the entities fit together harmoniously; there is no stress toward change."[13] In order to give meaning and order to the flux of distal stimuli (things, persons, events), the individual strives to maintain balance among the proximal signs (cognitions) of these external affairs.[14]

Newcomb sees human communication as a means of achieving or maintaining *symmetry* in the orientations of individuals with respect to objects or events.[15] Festinger's theory is expressed in terms of *consonance and dissonance.* These terms refer to the relations which may exist between pairs of cognitive elements (bits of knowledge about the world, other people, the self, one's own behavior).[16]

---

[13] Heider, *The Psychology of Interpersonal Relations,* p. 201.

[14] Thus, if person P likes another person O, and desires a certain object X, it is fitting (balanced) that he strive to be with the other person and acquire the object, that he assume that the other person also likes him and that the object is of value intrinsically, that he assume the other person also likes the object he finds desirable, and so forth. States of imbalance, e.g., when P discovers that an admired O does *not* like X the way he does, produce stress and tension; it is these stresses that generate cognitive dynamics.

[15] In Newcomb's system the minimal communicative act is that where A communicates to B about some event, X. The important variables are A's orientation (attitude and meaning) toward X, A's orientation toward B, B's orientation toward X, and B's orientation toward A, each such orientation conceived as being potentially positive or negative in sign. To the extent that A's behavior with respect to X depends upon B's orientations, and to the extent nonsymmetrical relations exist, there will be stress toward communicating about X, on the one hand, and toward increasing or decreasing the cohesiveness of the group relation between A and B, on the other.

[16] Cognitive elements are consonant when one implies the other logically (e.g. knowledge that it is raining out and knowledge that you are putting on

Where Heider has not attempted a formal definition of balance in his system, Cartwright and Harary have done so in terms of the mathematical theory of linear graphs.[17] To handle Heider's types of situation in graph theory requires, according to these authors, *signed, directed graphs of type 2*. We start with the cognitive elements (people, objects, etc.) defined as points. If these elements are involved in interactions (and they need not be, cf. section 2 below), then we connect them with a line; the line must be *directed* by means of an arrow in order to take into account Heider's distinction between agent and recipient (e.g., in Figure 1A, it is P who likes O, the reverse relation not being given). Since Heider talks about both sentiments (liking vs. disliking) and cognitive units (belonging vs. not belonging) as being two-valued, we also require a *signed* line— which Cartwright and Harary accomplish by means of solid vs. dashed lines. Finally, since Heider distinguishes the two types of relations, "liking" vs. "belonging," it is suggested that a type 2 graph, using two colors, for example, should be employed. However, Cartwright and Harary make little use of this last distinction and, in fact, criticize the ambiguity in Heider's "cognitive unit" conception (see section 2 below).[18] In a more recent paper Harary has further elaborated this type of analysis, with special reference to the measurement of structural balance in small groups.[19]

your raincoat), dissonant when the obverse of one would follow from the other (e.g., knowledge that it is raining and planning to go on a picnic), and irrelevant when one implies nothing about the other (e.g., knowledge that it is raining and knowledge that you were married in 1939). Although analyzed in pairs, cognitive elements are assumed to exist in clusters, presumably on the basis of either external patterning of signs in the environment or internal patterning of meaningful associations. Dissonant elements in such clusters create the stress toward cognitive modification.

[17] D. Cartwright and F. Harary, "Structural Balance: A Generalization of Heider's Theory," *Psychological Review*, Vol. 63, 1956, pp. 277-293.

[18] A number of deductions about balanced states are derived from this model: (1) An S-graph is balanced if and only if all paths joining the same pair of points have the same sign. In Figure 1A the relation between M and N is balanced; it would not be if M liked N, but not vice versa. (2) Any cycle within an S-graph is balanced if it contains an even number of negatively signed lines (0, 2, 4, etc.); otherwise it is unbalanced. A cycle is any recursive path through any set of points connected by lines. The M-N-X cycle in Figure 1A is balanced; the P-O-X cycle is not. (3) A structure

This brings up a source of confusion in this field that has hardly been recognized, as far as I am aware, but must be cleared up before we proceed. Cognitive interactions, obviously, transpire within the nervous systems of single individuals. The "maps" we draw to represent such interactions necessarily reflect person-person and person-object relations *as some individual perceives them*. Festinger is clearly aware of this; Heider also seems to be working on this basis— to the extent that his book might better have been titled "The Psychology of Interpersonal *Perceptions*." But both Newcomb and Cartwright and Harary seem to shift too easily from the subjective (cognitive interactions in individuals) to the objective (group structure and dynamics) frame of reference. Now it may be that the laws which apply to the interactions, stresses, and resolutions among the cognitive processes of individuals can be directly transferred to interactions within groups of people —where persons are the elements rather than cognitions—but this remains to be proven. The bridge between the two levels presumably lies in the fact that the structuring of a group depends upon the cognitive "maps" individual members have of it.

Osgood et al.[20] equate "cognitive elements" with the *meanings* of signs, and these are indexed in terms of n bipolar dimensions or factors. However, since interactions are assumed to occur on each dimension independently of the others, we may restrict our attention to the dominant evaluative factor of the meaning space— which is the one which has interested all other investigators. In the measurement system provided by the semantic differential, the evaluative factor runs from +3 (extremely good) through 0 (neutral) to −3 (extremely bad). The *evaluative meaning* of a concept (cognitive element) is its location along such a scale; the *polarization* of a concept is its distance from 0, regardless of sign. Now, it is assumed that evaluative meanings are mediated by a representational reaction system (perhaps here the autonomic nervous system and its connections with the central nervous system) which can only

theorem states that an S-graph is balanced if and only if its points can be separated into two mutually exclusive subsets such that each positive line joins two points of the same subset and each negative line joins points from different subsets.

[19] F. Harary, "On the Measurement of Structural Balance," *Behavioral Science*, Vol. 4, 1959, pp. 316-323.

[20] Osgood, Suci, and Tannenbaum, *op. cit.*

do one thing, assume one "posture," at one time. It must follow, therefore, that if two (or more) signs associated with different evaluative meanings occur near-simultaneously, only one cognitive reaction can occur in the system, and this must be a compromise. According to Osgood et al., *congruity* exists when the evaluative meanings of interacting signs are equally polarized or intense—either in the same or opposite evaluative directions (see section 2 on types of *assertions*). To the extent that there are differences in polarization, some degree of *incongruity* must exist to be resolved in the process of cognizing these signs.

Although this theory will be shown to lead to similar conclusions about human thinking, it developed from a very different conceptual background than the others we have been considering, and certain critical differences should be noted at this point. First, *it attributes degrees of incongruity to single pairs of elements* rather than the all-or-nothing relations found in Heider and Festinger. Coupled with a measuring device like the semantic differential, this can lead to more refined predictions. Second, *it assigns affective or attitudinal values to the cognitive elements themselves,* and not to their relations, whereas Heider, at least, assigns both affective and connecting properties to the relations between cognitive elements. This double function of the relational variable is, to my mind, the major weakness in Heider's theory.

This distinction becomes clear in connection with the signed digraphs of Cartwright and Harary. The positive sign of the line P *likes* O in Figure 1*A* says nothing about the evaluations of either P or O per se—a bowery bum may be perceived as liking a slut by the particular Ego for whom our map is constructed! Now, giving the elements values may be unnecessary when dealing with group structures (where the points

represent people), but when we are dealing with cognitive interactions (and the points represent concepts) we know that the elements have varying values. When I see P *dancing with* O, and O is my girl or wife, the impact of this cognition obviously depends upon my attitude toward P (to say nothing of my attitude toward O), quite apart from the cognitive implications of *dancing with*.

Figure 1*B* suggests an alteration of the Cartwright-Harary graphic technique that may take account of this added property of cognitive maps. Let us enlarge each point to a circle and in it place a sign corresponding to the evaluative meaning of the cognitive element represented, +, 0 or −. Then, since we will later wish to use dashed lines to represent *inferred* relations (not given in the verbal or behavioral data), let us use only solid lines for the relations between elements and sign them by means of + or −. The basic test for balance (or congruity) of a cognitive structure must now be changed: *A cognitive structure is congruent if, and only if, all its included assertions have either zero or two negative signs*—where an "assertion" is any pair of cognitive elements connected by a line. Applying this test to the graph in Figure 1*B*, we can see that in this cognitive map the only assertion that fails to be congruent is that where +O is in favor of −X. There may be other, more complex, laws of balance or congruence derivable from this model, but I have not yet explored this possibility.

Is this elaboration of the Cartwright-Harary model psychologically necessary? The following seems to be a crucial test: Imagine a three-element triangular system in which all three pathways are signed +. Such a cycle would have to be cognitively balanced in the Cartwright-Harary system (as well as for Heider). It would also have to be congruent in my system, *pro-*

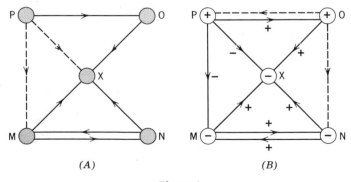

(A)   (B)

Figure 1

vided that the three elements were either all positive or all negative (e.g., "I love Mommy, Mommy loves Daddy, Daddy loves Me"). But what if one of the elements is negative? Here we would have two "good" people, both liking each other, but also liking an evil person, object or act (e.g., I love Mommy, Mommy loves a murderer, I love a murderer, etc.). If we agree that it is psychologically incongruent for a "good" thing to be positively associated with a "bad" thing, then the Cartwright-Harary model is untenable without elaboration.

2. If Cognitive Elements Are to Interact, They Must Be Brought into Some Relation with One Another

Contiguity is a necessary, but not a sufficient, condition for interaction among cognitive elements. In "Tom is a thief; Paul will catch him," "Paul" is spatially and temporally closer to "thief" than is "Tom," but the *structure* of the sentence brings "Tom" and "thief" into interaction. We have varying attitudes toward myriad people, things, and events, many of them *potentially* incongruent, imbalanced, or dissonant as one's theory would have it, but these cognitions are not continuously interacting—only when they are brought together in some way.

Festinger's theory fails to give explicit recognition to this variable. Implicit recognition of the need for linkage in some unit appears in the design of his experiments, however—dissonance only occurs when a person has been forced to make a choice between two gifts, when he has been exposed to information consistent or inconsistent with his beliefs, and so on. Analysis into "relevant" and "irrelevant" pairs of cognitive elements is not sufficient; cognitions of the attractiveness of an electric toaster and an electric clock are always potentially relevant, but only become effectively relevant when, by forced choice, the implied negative assertion that one is better than the other is made.

Heider, on the other hand, does give explicit recognition to this variable,[21] treating it in terms of gestalt perceptual factors. "Separate entities comprise a unit when they are perceived as belonging together. For example, members of a family are seen as a unit; a person and his deed belong together." Such factors as similarity, proximity, common fate, good continuation, set and past experience are cited as contributing to the formation of cognitive units, but it is evident in his examples that much more than perceptual organization in the traditional sense is involved. The difficulty with Heider's analysis, as Cartwright and Harary have implied, is that belonging in a unit (U or not U) is given the same status as liking (L vs. DL), both as relations between cognitive elements. Thus the triad, P *worships* O (P L O), O *told a lie* (O U X), and P *disapproves of lying* (P DL X), is said to be unbalanced because it has only one negative relation. One could also say that since O is + in evaluation and X is − in evaluation for P, the single assertion that O *told a lie* (i.e., +O + −X) is itself cognitively unbalanced or dissonant for P.

Osgood et al. make an absolute distinction between structure and content in the representation and analysis of cognitive interactions. In order for two cognitive elements to interact, they must be related in some kind of *assertion*. Assertions may be linguistic ("Eisenhower *favors* Big Business," as read in an editorial) or behavioral (a picture of Eleanor Roosevelt *patting the head of* a little colored boy), and they may be either associative (X *favors, likes, owns, is a member of*, etc., Y) or dissociative (X *attacks, dislikes, throws away, is excluded from*, etc., Y). But whether a particular cognitive pattern is congruent or not depends on both the structure *and* the content. Thus, in contradistinction to Heider, the assertion P *likes* O merely indicates an associative or positive structure; if both P and O have the same sign evaluatively, the assertion is congruent (e.g., "God is on our side" and "The Devil aids the enemy" are both congruent assertions), but if P is + and O −, or vice versa, then P *likes* O becomes incongruent (e.g., "God is with the enemy").

Although it is significant that Heider came to his theory via a very penetrating study of the ordinary *language* of human relations—which he calls a "naïve psychology"—it does not seem to me that he has fully explored the possibilities in rigorous linguistic (structural) analysis. Osgood, Saporta, and Nunnally[22] have developed a technique for abstracting the affective content of messages, called *evaluative assertion analysis*: (1) Objects of attitude are isolated from common-meaning terms and then masked by substituting nonsense letter pairs like AZ, BY, and CW for them. (2) Complex utterances in the

21 Heider, *The Psychology of Interpersonal Relations*, pp. 176ff.

22 C. E. Osgood, S. Saporta, and J. C. Nunnally, "Evaluative Assertion Analysis," *Litera*, Vol. 3, 1956, pp. 47-102.

masked message are broken down into component assertions of the actor-action-complement form. (3) Evaluative weights are given to the symbols for attitude objects in terms of their structural relations to evaluative common-meaning terms and other attitude objects. (4) The attitudinal consistency of the original utterances is checked by applying the congruity test (an even number of negative signs in each assertion).

Take, for example, the masked sentence, "AZ attacks *the expansionist ambitions* of both BY and CX." This breaks into three component assertions: /AZ/attacks/*expansionist ambitions*/, /BY/has/*expansionist ambitions*/, and /CX/ has/*expansionist ambitions*/. The circles and solid lines in Figure 2 provides a signed digraph

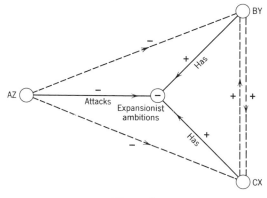

Figure 2

of the structural relations actually given. However, if one is also given the valence of the common-meaning cognitive element, "expansionist ambitions," he can fill in by the rules of inference of psycho-logic what the valences of all of the attitude-object circles must be: AZ must be +, BY must be —, and CX must be —, otherwise we would have an assertion line with an odd number of negatives.[23] But note that we still cannot decide whether or not this is a congruent or incongruent pattern until we know that, in fact and for some particular language user, AZ *is* + in evaluation, BY *is* —, and so forth. If AZ (e.g., Franco Spain) is in fact somewhat negative for a person, then it is incongruous psycho-logically for it to be "attacking" something (e.g., the "expansionist ambitions") belonging to two bad things (e.g., Russia and the Arab League), and he is under some pressure to modify his cognitive map.

The process of inference through psycho-logic—hence the possibility of predicting the

effects of implicit assertions in linguistic and behavioral situations—is also illustrated in Figure 2 by the dashed lines. Given that AZ is +, BY is —, and CX is — (i.e., a balanced situation), even though nothing is *said* about other relations, we can predict (1) that AZ should be against BY and vice versa, (2) that AZ should be against CX and vice versa, and (3) that BY should be in favor of CX and vice versa. Much of what is communicated attitudinally by messages and by behavior is based on such inferences; that is, of course, the chief tool of the propagandist, the technique of "innuendo." The syntax of language and of behavior provides a structural framework within which meaningful contents are put; the structure indicates what is related to what, and how, but only when the meaningful values are added does the combination of structure and content determine psycho-logical congruence or incongruence.

It was Abelson and Rosenberg[24] who introduced the term "psycho-logic" and contrasted it with "logic." They give a number of the rules of psycho-logic rule 1—A *likes* B and B *likes* C implies that A likes C also; rule 2—A *likes* B and B *dislikes* C implies that A dislikes C; rule 3—A *dislikes* B and B *dislikes* C implies that A likes C, and so forth. It is important to point out that the inferences from psycho-logic are not necessarily invalid; they are simply illogical. For example, if Khrushchev were to indicate that he favors a particular American presidential hopeful—the so-called "kiss of death"— many people would, psycho-logically, become suspicious of this candidate. Now, Khrushchev's support might be valid grounds for suspicion, but the inference is not logically necessary.

Abelson and Rosenberg also make an assertional analysis of linguistic statements, very much as Osgood, Saporta, and Nunnally have done, and they extend this type of analysis to interlocking sets of statements on the same topic. If the connectives (positive, *p*, and negative, *n*) in the following assertions—"*I'm for having coeds at Yale*," "*I want good grades*," and "*Having coeds would undoubtedly interfere with getting good grades*"—are arranged in a matrix in this fashion,

	Ego	Coeds	Good Grades
Ego	*p*	*p*	*p*
Coeds	*p*	*p*	*n*
Good grades	*p*	*n*	*p*

23 It should be pointed out that not all syntactical structures allow such inference of concept valences.

24 Abelson and Rosenberg, *op. cit.*

the degree and locus of incongruity can be clearly indicated. Since we cannot change the signs of any corresponding row and column in the matrix (always leaving the diagonal entries signed p) and thereby reduce the number of n's in one half of the matrix, the minimum complexity or imbalance is 1. If the first statement were changed to "I am against having coeds at Yale," similar analysis shows that all entries could be changed to the same sign, and hence the matrix of statements would then be congruent. This approach is similar to that of Cartwright and Harary, but is based on matrix algebra rather than the mathematical theory of graphs.

3. Magnitude of Stress Toward Modification Increases with the Degree of Cognitive Inconsistency

Most of the theories we have been considering express this relation, but it only becomes useful when a theory permits quantification. Heider's own statements remain essentially qualitative. Newcomb, on the other hand, states his principles in quantitative form, e.g., "the stronger the forces toward A's co-orientation in respect to B and X, . . . the greater A's strain toward symmetry with B in respect to X . . . ,"[25] but the units in which "forces toward co-orientation" and "strain toward symmetry" are to be measured remain obscure. Festinger specifies that the magnitude of dissonance increases (1) with the importance of the dissonant elements and (2) with the weighted proportion of all elements in a cognitive cluster that are dissonant. But again it is not clear how "importance" or "weighted proportion of elements that are dissonant" are to be quantified.

Association of the Osgood and Tannenbaum congruity hypothesis with the semantic differential provides quantification of cognitive inconsistency, but it also limits the types of situation that can be studied. Total *pressure toward congruity, P,* is stated to be equal to the difference between the initial scale position of a cognitive element (prior to interaction) and its location of perfect congruence (under the conditions of interaction). Perfect congruence between two elements was defined earlier as equal polarization (intensity), either in the same evaluative direction (for associative assertions) or in opposite evaluative directions (for dissociative assertions). Thus, for a hypothetical

individual for whom Eisenhower is $+3$ and Uruguay is $+1$, the assertion "Eisenhower was greeted with flowers in Uruguay" *would* be congruent *if* Eisenhower were only $+1$ or Uruguay were $+3$. We therefore have 2 units of pressure toward congruity, P, in this situation—and it may be noted in passing that the P's associated with the various interacting elements are always equal according to this hypothesis.

Cartwright and Harary arrive at the *degree of balance* of an S-digraph by taking the ratio of the number of positive semicycles to the total number of semicycles (cf., above). They state that such an index makes it possible to deal with cognitive inconsistencies in probabilistic and statistical fashions; they do *not* state any relation between degree of balance and the total stress toward consistency, however. Abelson and Rosenberg define the *complexity of imbalance* as the minimum number of changes of relations necessary to achieve balance. In the example given earlier about having coeds at Yale, the sign of one of the three assertions would have to be changed to achieve psychological consistency. Again, however, there is no statement to the effect that amount of stress toward consistency varies with the "complexity of imbalance." It is possible, of course, that total pressure toward cognitive modification does *not* vary in any simple way with degree of inconsistency. This may be the case particularly when only the structural relations and not the affective values of the contents are considered. Both Festinger and Osgood, who express the magnitude principle explicitly, deal with the properties of the cognitive elements themselves, not just their structural relation to each other.

4. The Dynamics of Cognitive Interaction Are Such That Modifications Under Stress Always Reduce Total Cognitive Inconsistency

We have here a kind of "mental homeostasis"[26]—cognitive inconsistencies set up pressures toward their own elimination. But we must say at the outset that modifications do not necessarily occur at all. People simply may not think about the matter or, as Festinger has shown, they may avoid exposing themselves to dissonance-arousing information. Furthermore, as Heider points out, some people seem to be able to "live with it" or even actively seek cogni-

25 Newcomb, *op. cit.*

26 R. Stagner, "Homeostasis as a Unifying Concept in Personality Theory," *Psychological Review,* Vol. 58, 1951, pp. 5-18.

tively disturbing situations; they are more "tolerant of ambiguity," to borrow an older phrase. Such tolerance probably increases with intelligence and education, and it certainly decreases under states of heightened emotion. But even here there may be a larger consistency operating: it may be intrinsically disturbing for some people to follow the simple-minded dictates of psycho-logic, at least to the extent they are aware of them.

But let us assume that our subjects are exposed to inconsistency, that they are thinking about it, and that they are susceptible to psychologic—what are the alternative resolutions available and how can we decide which will occur? We will find that theories in this field have been better at stating alternatives than at deciding among them.

(a) *The sign, or even existence, of a relationship may be changed.* For theories like Heider's that deal only with relations and not with the values of the included elements, this is the only type of resolution. However, since he deals with several types of relations, e.g., *L* vs. *DL* and *U* vs. *not U,* the situation is complicated. In the simplest diadic case, if P *L* O but also P *not U* O, either P may decide he doesn't like O or he may try to join O in some unit—what happens presumably depends upon the relative strengths of *L* vs. *not U*. In the triadic case of imbalance, where P *L* O, P *L* X, but O *DL* X, for example, as well as in the more complex cases treated by Cartwright and Harary, any one of the relations may be changed to produce an even number of negatives, or none—but again, which one? Whether P will change toward disliking O or disliking X, or O change toward liking X, seems to require more information than the model itself provides. When new relations are brought into existence (Heider uses the term "induced"), they will be in balance with the existing structure, e.g. if P *L* O, the relation O *L* P tends to be inferred. Conversely, relations may be wiped out of existence in the interest of balance.

(b) *The sign, or even existence, of a cognitive element may be changed.* Although Festinger does not attribute evaluations per se to cognitive elements, he does deal with changes of these elements in the direction of consonance. When dissonance between behavior and cognition exists, a person may (1) change his behavior so as to be consonant with his cognition, (2) change his cognition so as to be consonant with his behavior, (3) add new support-

ing elements to reduce the total dissonance, or (4) eliminate old dissonant elements to reduce the total dissonance. In the case of our heavy smoker confronted with information about lung cancer, for example, he may (1) take up filter cigarettes, (2) question the validity of the information, (3) seek information showing how much more likely one is to die in automobile accidents, or (4) avoid reading or thinking about it any more—or, of course, just live with it as many of us do! By making certain assumptions about the importance of different elements and other factors in particular experimental situations, Festinger is able to select among alternative resolutions.

Osgood and Tannenbaum have formulated a general law governing interactions among cognitive events: *Interacting elements are modified in inverse proportion to their intensity or polarization,* i.e., the congruity formula,

$$mc_1 = \frac{|p_2|}{|p_1| + |p_2|} P$$

$$mc_2 = \frac{|p_1|}{|p_1| + |p_2|} P$$

in which *mc* refers to *meaning change* on some dimension (e.g., attitude), *p* refers to *polarization* (deviation from neutrality regardless of sign), *P* refers to total *pressure toward congruity* (cf. section 3 above), and the subscripts 1 and 2 refer to the interacting cognitive elements. Given the assertion, "Eisenhower was greeted with flowers in Uruguay," and known values of +3 for Eisenhower and +1 for Uruguay, we can predict that three-fourths of the attitude change should be exerted on Uruguay and only one-fourth on Eisenhower. Similarly, in Heider's triadic P *L* O, P *L* X, O *DL* X, imbalance situation, if the attitude toward O were more intensely favorable than that toward X the formula would have to predict that most of the pressure in this dissociative assertion would be on making X much less favorable. The Eisenhower/Uruguay example illustrates another characteristic of the congruity hypothesis—it predicts changes on a quantitative basis even where relations are qualitatively balanced (here a + associated with a +).

However, some insufficiencies of the congruity hypothesis of Osgood and Tannenbaum appear when it is applied experimentally. First, although the associative or dissociative nature of assertions (relations) determines the direction of congruence (and hence the sign of P) in this model, the formula deals entirely with the changes in the meanings of the cognitive elements. Yet change in sign or even denial of the assertion itself is obviously one type of resolution. The assertion that Eisenhower is a card-carrying Communist produces incredulity and is denied. In order to generate accurate predictions in his attitude-change experiment, Tannenbaum had to apply a "correction for incredulity" that increased with the magnitude of P between values of 3 and 6, i.e., highly incongruous assertions. Second, the formula gives no weight to the direction of an assertion (cf. Heider's distinction between agent and recipient)—P *praises* O has the same effects upon the elements as O *praises* P, as far as the formula is concerned. Yet Tannenbaum's evidence, where Sources come out for or against Concepts, suggests that a greater share of the impact is exerted upon the recipient than the agent. The inverse proportionality formula underlying the congruity hypothesis may be valid in the "other things equal" sense, but there are certainly other factors to be considered.

In a recent paper titled "Modes of Resolution of Belief Dilemmas," Abelson presents a considerable variety of resolution types.[27] He limits his consideration to the simplest diadic situations, in which A is either associated with or dissociated from B by assertions, but follows Osgood et al. in attributing positive or negative values to the cognitive elements A and B, themselves. His first type—which he unfortunately calls *denial*—includes both the major forms of resolution discussed above, (1) where the sign of the relation is changed and (2) where the sign of one or both of the cognitive elements is changed. The term "denial" implies an all-or-nothing quality and a consciousness of decision which certainly do not apply to many of the interactions we would like to handle, e.g., in perceptual modification or in semantic adjustments to word mixtures. But let us now look at some of these other resolution types.

(c) *Other cognitive elements that are in balanced relation with one or the other of the dissonant elements may be adduced (bolstering).* As Abelson points out, this does not eliminate the imbalance but tends to "drown it out." This is a type of resolution stressed by Festinger, e.g., the heavy smoker who says that one is more

27 R. P. Abelson, "Modes of Resolution of Belief Dilemmas," unpublished paper, 1959.

likely to die in an automobile accident, that he has a large chest expansion, that he wouldn't be among the unlucky 15 per cent anyway, and so forth. Abelson also points out that it is usually the more strongly entrenched (attitudinally polarized?) element that receives bolstering: if one is a devout Catholic, yet intellectually agrees with the use of contraceptives, he is likely to react to the Church's condemnation of this practice by thinking of the Church's long history of being right, of God relying on him to exercise will power, and so on.

(d) *Other cognitive elements that are in a relation of imbalance with one or the other of the dissonant elements may be adduced (undermining).* Abelson does not distinguish this type of resolution from "bolstering," perhaps because it is the converse. Here new cognitive elements that have a dissociative (imbalance) relation to the less firmly entrenched element are adduced—the familiar process of rationalization. Our devout Catholic above is likely to decide that contraceptives are physically injurious, that their use weakens a person's will power, and so forth. Of course it must be recognized that adducing new relations, whether bolstering or undermining, must also produce shifts in the meanings of the elements involved *à la* congruity—which is presumably why Abelson says that, when failure of denial is followed by bolstering techniques, this in turn is usually followed by a new phase of denial.

In most real-life situations we are dealing with complex clusters of cognitive elements, each with its valence and each connected with others by an interlocking set of assertions, explicit or implicit. Patterns of bolstering and undermining relations already exist, without need for adducing them. We may, following Abelson's analysis, suggest a general rule for resolution in complex cases: *those cognitive modifications* (changes in assertions or in element valences) *will occur which require the minimum restructuring of the entire cognitive map.*

By way of illustration, let us look back at Figure 1B and verbalize a cognitive situation it might map: "I (P) am going around with an attractive young lady named O. She wants me to grow one of those filthy beards (X) that lowbrow beatniks like M (whom I know and despise) and his friend N wear." The source of dissonance for this poor Ego can be shown by congruity analysis to lie in the assertion $+O$ favors $-X$ (beards). Now, if Ego were to grow a beard ($+P$ *has* $-X$), he would not only have to change his attitude toward beards (so that $+P$ *has* $+$ X), but he would also have to change his attitude toward beatniks M and N—or perhaps induce them to shave off their beards! The simplest solution, of course, involving changing the sign of only one assertion, is to get his lady friend to give up the beard-growing project (thus produce $+O$ *against* $-X$), and we could confidently expect P to communicate vigorously (cf. Newcomb) with O along these lines. A second-best solution would be for this very proper Ego to change his evaluation of the girl, which in turn would require him to stop seeing her ($+P$ *not* U $-O$) if he has any sense of consistency at all. This analysis is obviously insufficient because we have not taken into account the relative evaluation weights of the elements; selection among these alternatives will also depend upon how much he likes O vs. how much he is against X—including all their supports in his total cognitive map.

(e) One or the other of the dissonant cognitive elements may be split into two parts, these parts being of opposed valence and dissociatively related (differentiation). This would be another possible resolution for our disturbed Ego above—he might decide there are "distinguished beards" and "pretentious beards" and then proceed to grow himself a "distinguished" one. Everything would then be in good cognitive order, with P, O, and X as one positive set opposed to M, N, and X' as a negative set. It may be interesting to note that what is involved in differentiation is a denotative reclassification of cognitive units forced by a connotative (affective) stress. Behaving the same way, having the same attitude, toward all members of a class (racial group, religious group, teachers, students, fried foods, sport-car owners, cats, etc.) often runs us into cognitive conflicts of an affective, psycho-logical sort, and intellectual redifferentiation provides one way out.

(f) Dissonant cognitive elements may be combined into a larger unit which, as a whole, is in balance with other cognitive elements (transcendence). Abelson gives as an example of this the typical resolution of the dissonance between "rational man" (A) and "spiritual man" (B): joined together in a larger unit, "the whole man," they become congruent with positive concepts (C) like "the full life," "a balanced education," and so forth. Or another example: Cain and Abel are always squabbling with each other; their father manages to avoid

choosing between them by saying, "You are both my sons, and I love my sons." In itself, transcendence does not resolve incongruities—it merely hides them. However, as Heider has pointed out, simply being included within a common unit implies a consonant relation among the dissonant elements, and this must weaken the total dissonance—the father is impelled toward believing that Cain and Abel really love one another, and our educator is impelled toward believing that religion can be rationalized.

SOME EVIDENCE ON COGNITIVE INTERACTION

Here some indication will be given of the diversity of phenomena which appear to follow the rules of cognitive interaction. These rules may be summarized as follows: When, in the course of human thinking, inconsistent cognitive elements are forced together by linguistic or behavioral assertions, stress is produced in proportion to the magnitude of the inconsistency, this stress producing cognitive modifications which—by changing the nature of the assertion, changing the connotative meanings of the elements, differentiating or integrating the denotations of the elements—serve to re-establish cognitive consistency. No attempt will be made to cover the experimental literature exhaustively; it has become quite extensive.

1. Attitude Change

Whenever a person reads a book or newspaper, listens to the belief statements of others, or even ruminates within his own storehouse of concepts, he is exposing himself to assertions which are likely to be incongruent to some degree with his existing frame of reference.[28] In experiments we try to measure some part of his existing attitude structure, produce messages which are congruent or incongruent to some definable degree, predict what the effects on him should be, and then measure his attitude structure again to determine the correctness of these predictions.

Tannenbaum[29] devised three supposed news-

[28] For a discussion of the relation between the affective and cognitive components of attitudes, see M. J. Rosenberg, *Public Opinion Quarterly*, Vol. 24, 1960, pp. 319-340.

[29] P. H. Tannenbaum, "Attitudes toward Source and Concept as Factors in Attitude Change through Communications," University of Illinois, 1953, unpublished doctoral dissertation.

paper messages in which a source (the *Chicago Tribune,* Senator Taft, labor leaders) comes out either in favor of or against a concept (abstract art, accelerated college programs, legalized gambling); the source/concept combinations (in the order given) were known by pre-test to divide college students about equally into 3-by-3 patterns, +S+C, +S—C, —S—C, etc., in terms of initial attitudes. On the basis of these original attitude measures, predictions of the direction and relative magnitude of attitude change were made, for both sources and concepts, by applying the congruity formula. The direction of attitude change was as predicted in every case, and the correlation between predicted and obtained magnitude of change was highly significant (.91). However, to obtain these results the data had to be corrected in a uniform way for incredulity (denial of the asserted relation when highly incongruent) and for directional effect (shifts in concept attitudes being regularly greater than shifts in source attitudes).

Kerrick has tested the congruity hypothesis under more realistic conditions.[30] The effects of an editorial (message) in a weekly newspaper (source) urging election of certain people to the school board (concept) were predicted from pre-exposure attitude scores in a sample of the readers of this weekly. The average effect of the editorial was nil, but when the sample was broken into two groups—those relatively favorable toward this weekly and those relatively unfavorable—it was found that attitudes toward the concept went up for the group favorably disposed toward the source and went down for the other group.

2. Cognition and Behavior

Pressures toward consistency in what one believes and how one behaves have been studied most intensively by Festinger and his associates in a variety of ingeniously contrived, realistic experiments.[31] Two examples will have to suffice.

(a) *Consequences of decisions.* The need for making a decision implies that there are dissonant elements in either course; therefore, to a degree dependent on the importance of the decision, the relative attractiveness of the unchosen course, and the degree of overlap of

elements in the two courses, decisions will leave some dissonance to be reduced.

(b) *Exposure to information.* Dissonance theory also leads to the prediction that people will avoid exposure to dissonance-increasing information and seek exposure to dissonance-decreasing information; if exposure to dissonant information is forced, they will defend against fully cognizing it.[32]

3. Interpersonal Perception

Although Heider himself has not contributed heavily on the experimental side, many other people have done research either inspired by or at least relevant to his theoretical notions. Jordan directly tested Heider's prediction that people prefer balanced to imbalanced situations.[33] Sixty-four hypothetical (and, unfortunately, very abstract) triadic situations were given to subjects to rate for degree of pleasantness, half of them being cognitively balanced and half unbalanced. An example would be: "I dislike O; I have a sort of bond or relationship with X; O likes X." The ratings for balanced triads were significantly more "pleasant" than ratings for unbalanced triads, and Cartwright and Harary have shown that if the ambiguous *not U* situations are eliminated, the difference becomes even greater. Heider cites a great deal of experimental evidence by others,[34] which cannot be reported in detail here, in support of various deductions about interpersonal relations that follow from cognitive balance theory: Egos tend to like Alters who are similar to themselves and dislike Alters who are dissimilar; Egos assume that Alters they like are more similar, and that Alters they dislike are less similar, to themselves than is the case; Egos tend to join in groups with Alters they like and to come to like Alters in groups they join; Egos tend to like what they own and to own what they like.

4. Communication and Group Cohesiveness

Newcomb cites experiments by Festinger and Thibaut,[35] by Schachter,[36] and by Back[37] which

[30] J. S. Kerrick, "The Weekly Newspaper as a Source: Prediction of an Editorial's Effectiveness," unpublished paper, 1959.

[31] Festinger, *op. cit.*

[32] For results of the experiments related to this proposition, see A. R. Cohen, "Attitudinal Consequences of Induced Discrepancies between Cognitions and Behavior," *Public Opinion Quarterly,* Vol. 24, 1960, pp. 297-318.

[33] N. Jordan, "Behavioral Forces That Are a Function of Attitudes and of Cognitive Organization," *Human Relations,* Vol. 6, 1953, pp. 273-287.

[34] Heider, *The Psychology of Interpersonal Relations,* Chap. 7.

[35] L. Festinger and J. Thibaut, "Interpersonal

demonstrate (*a*) that attempts to influence others increase with the attractiveness of the others to Ego, (*b*) that communications in cohesive groups tend to be directed toward those perceived as most deviant (up to the point where the sign of the relation shifts and a deviate is ejected from the group), and (*c*) that communications within groups typically result in both increased uniformity (co-orientations toward relevant X's) and increased cohesiveness (co-attractions among members). There are many other experiments in which the role of interpersonal communication can legitimately be inferred even though it was not directly observed, e.g., in a study by Festinger, Schachter, and Back[38] where a correlation of +.72 was found between a measure of interpersonal attractiveness and a measure of attitudinal conformity among people in a housing project.

5. Semantic Interactions

Finally, we will look briefly at a series of experiments which—precisely because of their remoteness from familiar everyday matters like attitudes, beliefs, and interpersonal relations—may serve to indicate the generality of our principles. All these studies are alike in that *meaning* as measured with a form of semantic differential is the dependent variable. They are also alike in general design: subjects first judge the meanings of a set of component stimuli and then judge the meanings of various combinations of these stimuli; predicted meanings of the combinations, derived from applying the congruity formula to the component meanings, are checked against the actual meanings of the combinations derived from subject ratings.

(*a*) *Word mixture.*[39] All subjects first rated the meanings of eight adjectives ("sincere," "breezy," "listless," etc.) and eight nouns ("nurse," "husband," "prostitute," etc.). Then

they rated eight of the sixty-four possible combinations ("sincere husband," "breezy prostitute," "listless nurse," etc.), eight groups being required to complete the design. Problem: Can the meanings of the combinations be predicted from the measured meanings of the components? Correlations between predicted and obtained meanings were high, .86, .86, and .90 for the evaluative, potency, and activity factors respectively. A constant error appeared for the evaluative factor, however—obtained evaluations of the mixtures were consistently less favorable than predicted evaluations. No obvious explanation for this error is at hand.

(*b*) *Fusion of facial expressions.*[40] The affective meanings of five facial expressions posed by the same person (intended to convey glee, rage, optimistic determination, complacency, and passive adoration) were obtained from thirty subjects in terms of two dominant factors, *pleasantness* and *activation*. Then the same subjects viewed all possible combinations of these expressions when fused in a stereoscope under conditions designed to minimize eye dominance. The apparent meanings of these fused expressions proved to be predictable via the congruity formula to a high degree. The median intra-subject correlation (across the ten combinations) between predicted and obtained scores was .84 for pleasantness and .82 for activation. Furthermore, as must be predicted from the congruity hypothesis, the semantic profiles for combinations regularly correlated more highly with the more polarized component; that is, the more intensely meaningful expression dominated in the process of interaction.

(*c*) *News photos and captions.* Kerrick[41] devised two unrelated captions ("A Quiet Minute Alone" and "Exiled Communist") to go with each of five pictures (e.g., a full profile shot of a well-dressed man on a park bench). Subjects judged the captions and pictures alone and then in combination (the design was such that subjects judging one set of captions alone would get the other set linked with the pictures). The results were strikingly different from those of (*a*) and (*b*) above: if picture and caption in isolation had opposed meaning, the meaning of their combination was predictable via congruity; but if picture and caption in isolation had

---

Communications in Small Groups," *Journal of Abnormal and Social Psychology*, Vol. 46, 1951, pp. 92-99.

36 S. Schachter, "Deviation, Rejection, and Communication," *Journal of Abnormal and Social Psychology*, Vol. 46, 1951, pp. 190-207.

37 K. Back, "The Exertion of Influence through Social Communication," *Journal of Abnormal and Social Psychology*, Vol. 46, 1951, pp. 9-23.

38 L. Festinger, S. Schachter, and K. Back, *Social Pressures in Informal Groups*, New York, Harper, 1950.

39 Osgood, Suci, and Tannenbaum, *op. cit.*, pp. 275-284.

40 A. Hastorf and C. E. Osgood, unpublished research.

41 J. S. Kerrick, "News Pictures, Captions and the Point of Resolution," *Journalism Quarterly*, Vol. 36, 1959, pp. 183-188.

similar meanings, their effects *summated* in combination, contrary to the congruity principle. In other words combining a slightly "happy" picture with a slightly "happy" caption produced a very "happy" whole.

(*d*) *Sound movies.* A similar summation effect was found by Gregory in an unpublished study on the combinations of words with sight in sound movies.[42] Five short "takes" of an actor saying five phonetically similar things with different meanings, with appropriate facial expressions and gestures, were recorded on sound film (e.g., "I can't get over the death of my wife," or, "This is the happiest day of my life"). Subjects judged the heard words alone, the viewed movies alone, the original combinations, and crossed combinations produced by splicing the words of one "take" with the sight of another. The results of the crossed combinations were generally predictable from the components via congruity, but the meanings of the "natural" combinations were more polarized than either component alone. We can only guess at why meaningful summation occurs in experiments (*c*) and (*d*) but not in experiments (*a*) and (*b*); both situations (*c*) and (*d*) involve interactions *across modalities,* and it may be that in such situations something other than simple congruity is operating.

COGNITIVE DYNAMICS IN PUBLIC AFFAIRS

In the absence of a science of public affairs, national and international, we can at least hypothesize that laws governing the thinking and behaving of individuals also govern the "thinking" and "behaving" of groups. The leap from individual cognitive maps to the structuring of relations within small groups has already been made—in some cases apparently without any self-consciousness of the shift in reference. However, application of the laws of cognitive dynamics to public affairs can be justified on several grounds: first, with nothing but communication to bind us together, it is clear that "decisions" and "behaviors" of nations must come down to myriad decisions in individual nervous systems and myriad behaviors of individual human organisms. Second, to the extent that government is popular, we can work on the basis of averaging over individuals, and to the extent that government is not, we are back to individuals anyhow. Finally, evidence abounds

that we do "personalize" groups and issues—not so much by an error of oversimplification as by an intuitive grasp of the underlying laws.

The analogue of a cognitive element for an individual is what we may call a *cultural meaning* (stereotype, public image, etc.) for a group. Although individuals within groups may be expected to vary in their private meanings, it is characteristic of cohesive groups, as Newcomb has shown, for interpersonal communication to produce increased uniformity of opinion and attitude. Mass communications have this function for the larger groupings of individuals in modern society, such as nations. Many of the applications of the semantic differential—in the study of information about mental health and illness, of images of political personalities and issues, of commercial institutions and products, and so forth—have dealt with cultural meanings based on reasonably representative groups of people. The degree of conformity on issues is often striking, 90 to 100 per cent of subjects frequently choosing the same side, if not the same intensity. This happens both for common meanings (tornadoes are *active*) and for attitude objects (the Bible is *good*).

Now, to the extent that the cultural meanings of two socially significant referents have different evaluative locations, increasing proportions of individuals will necessarily experience pressures toward congruity when these items are forced into interaction by assertions in the mass media. If, under accusation by his rival or perhaps a mantle of honesty, a candidate for public office admits that he, John Jones, *does not believe in* God, we have for large numbers of people a somewhat unfamiliar and neutral source making a negative assertion about a deeply entrenched and favorably polarized concept. The result is inevitable—all the pressure toward consistency is on John Jones to move in a negative direction. Whenever political candidates, particularly unfamiliar ones, run into conflict with the mores—become associated with bad things, like gambling, call girls, and divorce, or become dissociated from good things, like Mother, God, and Country—they lose out. Conversely, political candidates themselves try to establish associative assertions with good things and dissociative assertions with bad, by their statements and by their behavior. Even if the private attitudes and beliefs of the elites in popular governments may be at variance with such a simple-minded organization of the universe, they rarely run counter to the tide. These

42 J. Gregory, unpublished research.

are all very familiar facts about public affairs, but I think they illustrate the underlying laws.

Among our store of cultural meanings are a large number of "personalized" national stereotypes. Whether it is valid or not, populations in various countries do react to nations *as if* they were a collection of people, having certain "personality" traits and being organized into unstable group structures. The findings of Buchanan and Cantril in their book, *How Nations See Each Other*,[43] are quite consistent with this idea. Following Heider, if P *likes* O (e.g., O *is an ally* of P) and P *dislikes* X (e.g., X *is an enemy* of P), then P should attribute favorable characteristics to O and unfavorable ones to X. We find that Americans most often attribute to the British the traits of being *intelligent, hardworking, brave,* and *peace-loving,* whereas they most often attribute to the Russians the traits of being *cruel, backward, hard-working,* and *domineering* (being "hard-working" is obviously independent of general evaluation). We would also expect people to view their own countrymen favorably, in the interest of cognitive balance; the four most frequent self-attributions (across the eight countries sampled) were *peace-loving, brave, intelligent,* and *hard-working.* Although Buchanan and Cantril did not get into this matter, Heider's notions of cognitive balance would lead us to expect that if P *likes* O and P *likes* Q, but P *dislikes* X, then P would infer that O *likes* Q and that O and Q *dislike* X, and vice versa. Americans expect the British to favor the French, and vice versa, but they expect both to be as antagonistic to the Russians as we are. If P *likes* O, he also must infer that O *likes* P reciprocally; but as studies like *The Ugly American*[44] show only too clearly, this doesn't necessarily follow.

The operation of psycho-logic in national

and international affairs shows up quite generally once you start to look for it. All nations in time of conflict, for example, create "bogey men" on this basis. If we are *good, kind,* and *fair* and they are our enemy, then psycho-logic dictates that they must be *bad, cruel,* and *unfair.* However, when we are exposed to live Russians, as tourists in their country or as hosts to them in our homes and farms, and we find them in many ways *just like us,* cognitive disturbance is produced; it may be eliminated by the technique of differentiation—it is the Russian *leaders* who are bad, not the Russian *people.* And we confidently wait for the good *Russian people* to overthrow the bad *Russian leaders*—just as the Russians, no doubt, confidently wait for the good *American workers* to begin the revolution against their bad *capitalist leaders.* Abelson illustrates how differentiation works with a different example, the conflict over hydrogen bomb testing (+) being associated with poisonous fallout (−): if one can accept a distinction between using "clean bombs" and "dirty bombs," then a cognitively consistent resolution is achieved.[45]

Such examples could be adduced *ad infinitum,* but they would not further prove the thesis. The essential argument of this paper has been as follows: (1) there has been a considerable *confluence* (if not unanimity) *in theories* of cognitive interaction, sufficient at least to make it possible here to formulate several general principles; (2) there is a great deal of evidence for the operation of such principles *in the thinking and behaving of human individuals,* in areas as diverse as interpersonal relations and the semantics of word combination; and (3) we can at least hypothesize the operation of the same laws *at the level of groups, national and international,* and find illustrations which seem to support the hypothesis. How useful such a model would be for predicting in the area of public affairs remains to be seen.

43 W. Buchanan and H. Cantril, *How Nations See Each Other*, Urbana, Ill., University of Illinois Press, 1953.

44 W. J. Lederer and E. Burdick, *The Ugly American*, New York, Norton, 1958.

45 Abelson, *op. cit.*

47. Prediction of Attitude from the Number, Strength, and Evaluative Aspect of Beliefs about the Attitude Object: A Comparison of Summation and Congruity Theories

LYNN R. ANDERSON and MARTIN FISHBEIN

In a recent series of articles, Fishbein (1961, 1963, 1965) has presented a theory of attitude organization and change based on the relationships between beliefs about an object and the attitude toward that object. Consistent with Osgood, Suci, and Tannenbaum (1957), attitude is defined as the evaluative dimension of a concept, where the term "concept" refers to any discriminable aspect of an individual's world, verbalizable or not. In Osgood's behavior theory terminology, an attitude can be described as a mediating evaluative response associated with any stimulus (Osgood et al., 1957). Operationally, an individual's attitude toward any concept can be assessed by having the individual rate the concept on a series of bipolar evaluative scales (e.g., good-bad, clean-dirty) of the semantic differential form.

Similar to the definition of attitude, belief is defined as the probability dimension of a concept. Belief *in* a concept is seen as the probability that the concept per se (e.g., ESP) does exist, while belief *about* a concept is defined as the probability that a specific relation exists between the concept and some other object, concept, value, or goal (e.g., ESP is mystical, ESP is useful). Beliefs can be measured by having the subject rate the assertion (belief about) or the concept per se (belief in) on a series of bipolar probabilistic scales (e.g., probable-improbable, likely-unlikely) of the semantic

• Reprinted from *Journal of Personality and Social Psychology*, 1965, 3, 437-443, with permission of the authors and the American Psychological Association. This study was supported in part by a grant from the University of Illinois Research Board. The authors would like to express their special appreciation to C. E. Osgood for suggesting the test of his new extension of congruity theory.

differential form. This latter instrument has been called the B scale by Fishbein and Raven (1962), and considerable support for its reliability and validity has been presented.

Essentially, Fishbein's theory leads to the prediction that an individual's attitude toward any object is a function of his beliefs about the object and the evaluative aspects of those beliefs. The prediction can be expressed by the following formula:

$$A_o = \sum_{i=1}^{N} B_i a_i$$

where

$A_o =$ the attitude toward object "o"

$B_i =$ the strength of belief i about o (i.e., the probability that o is related to some other object "x_i")

$a_i =$ the evaluative aspect of B_i (i.e., the evaluation of x_i)

$N =$ the number of beliefs

As can be seen from the formula, the attitude toward the object is predicted to be a part function of the *total* amount of affect associated with each of the beliefs about the object. Fishbein (1961) and his associates (Fishbein and Hunter, 1964; Triandis and Fishbein, 1963) have previously pointed out that this prediction is opposed to the predictions which would follow from most of the theories of attitude change based on a notion of "consistency." In general, the consistency theories state that an individual's attitude toward an object is essentially based on *a mean*, or weighted mean, of the affect associated with each of the beliefs about the object. For example, both the principle of congruity (Osgood et al., 1957; Osgood and Tannenbaum, 1955) and Heider's (1958) balance theory would predict that if an individual held two beliefs about one object, one belief containing a high positive evaluative aspect and the other a low positive evaluative aspect, the individual's attitude toward the object would essentially represent a convergence or mean of these two evaluative aspects.[1] In contrast, Fishbein's theory would predict that the attitude is a function of the algebraic sum of the evaluative aspects of the beliefs. To summarize, a basic difference between Fishbein's theory and the various consistency theories is that Fishbein views attitude organization and change as a process of *cognitive summation,* while consistency theories view attitude organization and change as a process of *cognitive balance.*

Two recent studies provide support for the summation approach. Triandis and Fishbein (1963) compared predicted and obtained values of subjects' attitudes toward complex stimuli. One set of predictions was based on an extension of congruity theory, while another set of predictions was based on summation theory. The results clearly indicated the superiority of the summation theory predictions. Fishbein and Hunter (1964) provided four groups of 40 subjects with different amounts of positively evaluated information about a fictitious person. The information was presented in such a way that the *total* amount of affect associated with the information *increased* as a function of the amount of information, while the *mean* amount of affect associated with the information *decreased* as a function of the amount of information presented. Consistent with summation theory, the amount of attitude change was a function of the *total* amount of affect associated with the information presented. In addition, indirect evidence suggesting cognitive summation has also been obtained by Feldman (1962), Kerrick (1959), Podell and Podell (1963), and Tanaka (1964).

The present investigation is a further attempt to test Fishbein's theory. While all of the above studies provide support for a summation theory, none are strict tests of Fishbein's position. That is, in none of the above studies was the strength of belief (B_i) utilized in the prediction of attitudes. In addition, with the exception

of the Triandis and Fishbein study, none of the above studies has attempted to compare the explicit quantitative predictions of two different theories. With respect to this latter study, however, Osgood (1963) has recently presented an extension of congruity theory that differs from the earlier extension utilized by Triandis and Fishbein. This extension was in part presented in response to studies "which suggest an additive rather than a polarity-weighted function." As Osgood points out, however, "Whether differences would be obtained in predictions under these two conditions . . . [the new as opposed to the "old" extension] . . . remains to be seen."

Thus, the purpose of the present paper is threefold: to provide a further test of the hypothesis that attitude change is a function of the total affect associated with each of a person's beliefs about the attitude object; to provide an explicit comparison between Fishbein's summation theory and Osgood's congruity theory; and to compare Osgood's new extension of congruity theory with the extension previously utilized by Triandis and Fishbein.

METHOD

Subjects

One hundred undergraduate subjects (50 males and 50 females) were randomly assigned to five groups. The only restriction placed on the random assignments was that there would be an equal number of males and females in each group.

Procedure

The experiment was administered under the guise of a Literary Preference test in which the subjects were to evaluate each of four mimeographed paragraphs[2] taken from a short story. The attitude object was an incidental character, Mrs. Williams, who was mentioned in each of the four paragraphs. In order to provide a pretest measure of evaluation, the subjects, before reading the paragraphs, rated the name Mrs. Williams and other characters in the story

---

[1] For a more complete discussion of the distinction between summation and balance theory see Fishbein (1961), Triandis and Fishbein (1963), and Fishbein and Hunter (1964).

[2] A copy of the paragraphs used has been deposited with the American Documentation Institute. Order Document No. 8463 from ADI Auxiliary Publications Project, Photoduplication Service, Library of Congress, Washington, D. C. 20540. Remit in advance $1.25 for microfilm or $1.25 for photocopies and make checks payable to: Chief, Photoduplication Service, Library of Congress.

on the *A* Scale of Fishbein and Raven (1962). The *A* Scale consists of five empirically determined, evaluative scales of the semantic differential form. Since each polar pair of adjectives had a 7-point scale, a rated concept could obtain a score ranging from −15 (negative evaluation) to +15 (positive evaluation). The five scales used were: harmful-beneficial, foolish-wise, dirty-clean, bad-good, and sick-healthy.

After the pretest all subjects were then instructed to read and to evaluate each of the four paragraphs by circling a letter grade beneath each paragraph. The paragraphs were identical in each of the five experimental groups except for the inclusion of the evaluative adjectives used to describe Mrs. Williams.

Group I. This group represents a control in that no adjectives or evaluative characteristics were used to describe Mrs. Williams in any of the four paragraphs.

Group II. For the subjects in this group, the adjective "honest" was inserted before the noun "Mrs. Williams" in the first paragraph. The three remaining paragraphs were identical to those of Group I.

Group III. The adjective "honest" again described Mrs. Williams in the first paragraph, and the adjective "friendly" was attributed to her in the second paragraph. The remaining two paragraphs were identical to the control paragraphs.

Group IV. The adjective "honest" was inserted in the first paragraph, "friendly" was inserted in the second paragraph, and "helpful" was used to describe Mrs. Williams in the third paragraph. The fourth paragraph was again identical to the control group.

Group V. This group was similar to Group IV in having Mrs. Williams described as "honest," "friendly," and "helpful" in the first three paragraphs, respectively. In the fourth paragraph, however, the adjective "helpful" was repeated. Thus, for the subjects in this group, Mrs. Williams was described as being helpful in both the third and fourth paragraphs of the short story. Group V was included in the experiment in order to assess the effects of a single repetition of a belief statement on attitude change.

After the subjects had read and evaluated each of the four paragraphs, they were told that the experimenter was also interested in determining the type of impression which the paragraphs had created regarding each of the characters in the story. The subjects were asked

again to describe the fictional characters, including Mrs. Williams, on the *A* Scale. This measure provided the posttest attitude score.

In order to determine if the subjects had actually learned the experimental characteristics attributed to Mrs. Williams, three assertive statements ("Mrs. Williams is honest," "Mrs. Williams is friendly," and "Mrs. Williams is helpful") were each rated by all subjects on Fishbein and Raven's (1962) *B* Scale. This scale is also of the semantic differential form and contains five, empirically determined, probabilistic scales (impossible-possible, false-true, nonexistent-existent, improbable-probable, unlikely-likely). The scale provides a measure of each subject's beliefs about Mrs. Williams, and thus provides the belief score (B_i) utilized in Fishbein's prediction formula. The subjects were finally asked to evaluate each of the descriptive adjectives (honest, friendly, and helpful) on the *A* Scale. These ratings provide a measure of the evaluative aspect of each belief (a_i) used in Fishbein's prediction formula *and* a measure of the evaluation and polarity of each of the adjectives used in the congruity prediction formulas.

RESULTS

Obtained Evaluations of the Attitude Object

The pretest measure indicated that the five experimental groups were comparable in initial evaluation of the attitude object ($F = .414$, $df = 4/90$). Thus, analyses were conducted only on the data obtained on the posttest *A* Scale. The main hypothesis predicted that the subject's evaluation of the attitude object, Mrs. Williams, would be a function of the total amount of affect associated with each of the characteristics attributed to the object. Since only positively evaluated adjectives were presented to the experimental groups, the mean evaluative score should increase with the number of adjectives presented if the hypothesis is to be supported. The mean posttest score for each of the five experimental groups is presented in Table 1. When tested by an analysis of variance, these means proved to be significantly different ($F = 6.31$, $df = 4/90$, $p < .01$).[3]

[3] The significance test was made on the data obtained from all five experimental groups. Although four adjectives were presented in Group V, only three different adjectives were utilized. Hence, the data from this group may not represent a direct test of the hypothesis. However, when a similar

TABLE 1. Obtained Mean Evaluation Scores for the Experimental Groups

Experimental Group	Number of Adjectives Presented	Obtained M
I	0	.95
II	1	3.15
III	2	2.85
IV	3	5.90
V	4*	7.10

* Although four adjectives were used in describing Mrs. Williams in Group V, only three different adjectives were presented with one adjective being presented twice.

In addition, the slope of the regression of attitude scores on number of adjectives presented was tested and found to be significantly different from zero ($F = 11.98$, $df = 1/90$, $p < .001$). Thus, in support of a summation theory, attitude scores do increase significantly with the number of adjectives presented, and therefore, with the total amount of affect associated with each belief.

Differential Predictions of Attitude towards the Attitude Object

Three predicted attitude scores were computed for each subject: based on Fishbein's summation theory, based on Triandis and Fishbein's extension of congruity theory, and based on Osgood's more recent extension of congruity theory.

Summation theory predictions. According to the prediction formula presented by Fishbein, an individual's attitude toward any object should be a function of the sum of the products of beliefs about the object (B_i) and the evaluative aspect of these beliefs (a_i). Each subject had indicated the strength of his beliefs that "Mrs. Williams is 'honest,' 'friendly,' and 'helpful,'" and had evaluated each of the three descriptive adjectives. Thus, by direct application of the formula (i.e., the predicted attitude $= \Sigma_{i=1}^{N} B_i a_i$) a predicted attitude score was computed for each subject.

Congruity theory predictions: Triandis and Fishbein's extension. In a recent paper, Triandis and Fishbein (1963) presented a simple mathematical extension of congruity theory

that permitted the consideration of more than a single adjective-noun combination. The formula is identical to the one presented by Osgood et al. (1957), but it allows for the case where more than one adjective is associated with the noun. The formula is given as follows:

$$\text{Predicted attitude} = \frac{\left[\sum_{i=1}^{N} |a_i|(a_i) \right] + |a_n|(a_n)}{\left[\sum_{i=1}^{N} |a_i| \right] + |a_n|}$$

where

$|a_i| = $ the absolute evaluation of polarity of adjective "i"

$(a_i) = $ the algebraic evaluation of adjective i

$|a_n| = $ the absolute evaluation or polarity of the noun

$(a_n) = $ the algebraic evaluation of the noun

$N = $ number of adjectives associated with the noun

By direct application of the formula, predictions were made for each subject based on his pretest evaluation of the noun "Mrs. Williams" and his posttest evaluations of each of the descriptive adjectives. It should be noted, however, that only those adjectives which were presented to the subject in the communication were utilized in computing his predicted attitude score.[4] Although only three different adjectives were presented in Group V, the second presentation of the adjective "helpful" was treated in the formula as a separate adjective.

Congruity theory predictions: Osgood's new extension. Osgood (1963) has recently stated that the formula proposed by Triandis and Fishbein may be inadequate in representing the actual cognitive "balancing" that takes place as the individual is given more information about an attitude object. The objection is based mainly on the notion that a phrase such as "he is a wise, unscrupulous man" should be viewed as two separate assertions: the man is wise, and the man is unscrupulous.

"According to this view, the meaning of man resulting from *the man is wise* should first be determined and then 'plugged' into the second assertion, *the man* (as qualified) *is unscrupulous* [Osgood, 1963, p. 103]." Thus, the major

analysis of variance test was made using only the data from the first four groups, the F ratio was significant beyond the .05 level.

[4] In the case where only one adjective was presented the formula is identical to the one presented by Osgood et al. (1957).

objection to the formula proposed by Trandis and Fishbein is that it does not take into account this step-by-step convergence of evaluation, but rather, assumes that convergence occurs in one cognitive operation. Although Osgood's extension was formulated specifically to handle the prediction of complex stimuli (e.g., the wise, unscrupulous man; honest, friendly Mrs. Williams), it can be seen that his objection is particularly apropos in the present experiment since the subjects actually received separate assertions about Mrs. Williams in the communication. The general formula for the new extension is given as follows:

$$\text{Predicted attitude} = \frac{|a_i|\,(a_i) + |a_{n_{i-1}}|\,(a_{n_{i-1}})}{|a_i| + |a_{n_{i-1}}|}$$

where

$|a_i|$ and (a_i) = the absolute and algebraic evaluation of the "i^{th}" adjective

$|a_{n_{i-1}}|$ and $(a_{n_{i-1}})$ = the absolute and algebraic evaluation of the noun modified by $i-1$ adjectives

For example, the predicted attitude for a group receiving two adjectives and a noun would be a function of the evaluation of the second adjective and the evaluation of the noun after it had been modified by the first adjective. Once again, the subjects' evaluations of the adjectives and their pretest evaluation of Mrs. Williams were used to compute the predicted scores. Here too, only those adjectives actually presented to the subjects were included in the computations. It should also be recalled that in Group V, which received the adjective helpful twice, the adjective was considered as two separate adjectives (i.e., Mrs. Williams, modified by honest, friendly, and helpful, is again modified by helpful for the final predicted score).

The intercorrelations of the three predicted scores and the obtained scores may be seen in Table 2. All three of the predictors are significantly correlated with the obtained scores ($p <$ .001). However, consistent with previous findings, the predictions based on Fishbein's summation theory are significantly more accurate than the predictions based on either form of the congruity theory ($Z = 2.74$, $p < .01$ for both comparisons). These findings provide further support for Fishbein's theory and once again suggest that attitude organization and change

TABLE 2. *Intercorrelations of the Various Predicted Scores and the Actual Posttest Evaluation of the Attitude Object ($N = 100$)*

	Congruity Prediction (1)	Congruity Prediction (Extended) (2)	Fishbein Prediction (3)	Obtained Posttest Evaluation (4)
1	—	.86	.46	.38
2		—	.47	.39
3			—	.66
4				—

Note. All correlations are significant beyond the .001 level.

is a function of cognitive summation rather than cognitive balance. Table 2 also indicates that Osgood's new extension of congruity is highly correlated with the extension previously utilized by Triandis and Fishbein ($r = .86$) and perhaps more importantly, indicates that the new extension adds no predictive power over the original formulation.

Two basic objections could be raised concerning the intercorrelations presented in Table 2. First, with respect to the comparison between summation and congruity theory, it should be noted that in computing the summation theory predictions all of an individual's beliefs are taken into account in the computation, regardless of whether or not they were actually included in the communication. The congruity formulas, on the other hand, use only the evaluation of those adjectives actually included in the message presented to the subject. Thus, the obtained differences between summation and congruity may be artifacts produced by the utilization of different amounts of information in the prediction formulas. Second, with respect to the comparison of the two extensions of congruity theory, it is possible that much of the correlation is spurious. Both extensions lead to identical predictions when only one adjective is associated with the noun (Group II) or when no adjective is associated with the noun (Group I). Thus, 40 of the 100 scores predicted by both formulas are identical.

In order to check against both of those objections, the correlations reported in Table 2 were computed again for only those subjects in Group IV (i.e., the group receiving all three adjectives in the communication). Thus, for these 20 subjects, all three predicted scores are obtained from the same amount of data, and hence maximal differences between the two extensions of congruity theory should be obtained. While subjects in Group V also received all three adjectives, it should be recalled that in the computation of the congruity predictions the repeated adjective was treated as a fourth adjective and thus the same problem of utilizing different amounts of information would be encountered if Group V had been used in the present analysis.

The intercorrelations of the three predicted scores and the obtained scores for the 20 subjects in Group IV may be seen in Table 3. The

TABLE 3. *Correlation of the Various Predicted Scores and the Actual Posttest Evaluation of the Attitude Object for Group IV (N = 20)*

	Congruity Prediction (1)	Congruity Prediction (Extended) (2)	Fishbein Prediction (3)	Obtained Posttest Evaluation (4)
1	—	.69**	.30	.38
2		—	.46*	.34
3			—	.66**
4				—

* $p < .05$.
** $p < .01$.

results of the analyses based on the smaller sample are virtually identical to the results presented in Table 2. Thus, the higher accuracy of prediction obtained from the summation theory formulation is obviously not a statistical artifact of the number of adjectives included in the formula. Similarly, although the correlation between the two extensions of congruity theory is slightly lower ($r = .69$), it is still highly significant ($p < .01$). Finally, it can once again be noted that Osgood's extension of congruity theory does not lead to an increase in predictability. To summarize briefly then, these results strongly support a summation theory, and in particular, Fishbein's theory of the relationships between beliefs and attitudes. In addition they seriously question the utility of Osgood's new extension of congruity theory, as well as the older extension suggested by Triandis and Fishbein.

Effect of repetition on attitude change. Subjects in Group V were presented with the three different adjectives as well as a repetition of one of the adjectives (helpful). A comparison of this group's attitude toward Mrs. Williams with the mean attitude of Group IV, which received only the three adjectives, constitutes a test for the effect of repetition on attitude change. Subjects in **Group V** were significantly more favorable toward Mrs. Williams than were subjects in **Group IV** (7.10 versus 5.90,

$t = 7.31$, $df = 38$, $p < .001$).[5] Thus it appears that attitudes can be changed by even one repetition of the "message." According to Fishbein's theory, this change should result primarily from an increase in the strength of belief that "Mrs. Williams is helpful." If presenting the adjective twice in Group V did serve to strengthen the subjects' beliefs, then the statement "Mrs. Williams is helpful" should have been rated higher (i.e., more probable) in Group V than in Group IV. Consistent with this prediction, the obtained difference between the means (7.45 versus 3.75) was significant ($t = 1.79$, $df = 38$, $p < .05$ using a directional test of significance).

Indeed, one would expect that the main locus of effect of a communication would be to change and/or increase subjects' beliefs about the attitude object. That is, subjects whose communications mentioned "honest Mrs. Williams," should believe that "Mrs. Williams is honest" more strongly than subjects who did not receive this information. Similarly, subjects receiving information about "friendly Mrs. Williams" should believe that "Mrs. Williams is friendly" more strongly than subjects not receiving this information. While the overall effects suggest that this is true (the mean belief scores on those statements contained in the communications $= 6.26$, while the mean belief scores on those statements not contained in the communications $= 5.19$; t, corrected for correlated scores, $= 2.09$, $df = 298$, $p < .05$), analyses of the individual belief statements suggest a more complex relationship between information contained in the communication and belief change. For example, although subjects in Group II only had the adjective honest paired with Mrs. Williams, this information produced a significant increase in their belief that "Mrs. Williams is friendly," as well as the expected increase in the belief that "Mrs. Williams is honest." Although these findings suggest some generalization, the results are not indicative of any simple or systematic effect. A fuller discussion and interpretation of these data must await additional research.

SUMMARY AND CONCLUSIONS

This paper presented a comparison between two competing theories of attitude organization and change. On the basis of Fishbein's (1961)

[5] Unless otherwise noted, all t tests are two-tailed.

summation theory, it was predicted that an individual's attitude toward any object would be a part function of the *total* amount of affect associated with each of the individual's beliefs about the object. In contrast to this, Osgood's congruity theory, and indeed, most theories based on a principle of consistency or balance, predicts that attitude is a part function of the *mean* amount of affect associated with an individual's beliefs. The results strongly supported the summation theory hypothesis.

In addition, an explicit comparison of summation and congruity theory was made. Predictions based on Fishbein's summation theory correlated significantly higher with obtained attitude scores than predictions based on congruity theory. This result held true for Osgood's more recent extension of congruity theory, as well as an earlier extension proposed by Triandis and Fishbein. Indeed, predictions derived from Osgood's extension were no more highly correlated with the obtained attitudes than were the predictions based on the earlier extension. Further, the two sets of congruity predictions were highly correlated with each other. Thus, these results add further support to the hypothesis that attitude organization and change is a process of cognitive summation and not a process of cognitive balance, and point once again to the necessity of reexamining the validity of the consistency principle in attitude research.

REFERENCES

Feldman, S. Evaluative ratings of adjective-adjective combinations, predicted from ratings of their components. Unpublished doctoral dissertation, Yale University, 1962.

Fishbein, M. A theoretical and empirical investigation of the relationships between beliefs about an object and the attitude toward that object. Unpublished doctoral dissertation, University of California, Los Angeles, 1961.

Fishbein, M. An investigation of the relationships between beliefs about an object and the attitude toward that object. *Human Relations,* 1963, **16**, 233-239.

Fishbein, M. Prediction of interpersonal preferences and group member satisfaction from estimated attitudes. *Journal of Personality and Social Psychology,* 1965, **1**, 663-667.

Fishbein, M., and Hunter, Ronda. Summation versus balance in attitude organization and change. *Journal of Abnormal and Social Psychology,* 1964, **69**, 505-510.

Fishbein, M., and Raven, B. H. The *AB* scales: An operational definition of belief and attitude. *Human Relations,* 1962, **15**, 35-44.

Heider, F. *The psychology of interpersonal relations.* New York: Wiley, 1958.

Kerrick, Jean S. The effect of relevant and nonrelevant sources on attitude change. *Journal of Social Psychology,* 1958, **47**, 15-20.

Osgood, C. E. On understanding and creating sentences. Paper read at American Psychological Association, Philadelphia, September 1, 1963.

Osgood, C. E., Suci, G. J., and Tannenbaum, P. H. *The measurement of meaning.* Urbana: Univer. Illinois Press, 1957.

Osgood, C. E., and Tannenbaum, P. H. The principle of congruity in the prediction of attitude change. *Psychological Review,* 1955, **62**, 42-55.

Podell, J. E., and Podell, Harriett A. Effect of number of trait referent adjectives on impressions of persons. Paper read at Western Psychological Association, April 1963.

Tanaka, Y. *A test of congruity hypothesis across three language/culture communities.* (Doctoral dissertation, University of Illinois) Ann Arbor, Mich.: University Microfilms, 1964, No. 64–5589.

Triandis, H. C., and Fishbein, M. Cognitive interaction in person perception. *Journal of Abnormal and Social Psychology,* 1963, **67**, 446-453.

48. An Experimental Analysis of Self-Persuasion

DARYL J. BEM

Self-awareness, one's ability to respond differentially to his own behavior and its controlling variables, is a product of social interaction (Mead, 1934; Ryle, 1949; Skinner, 1953; Skinner, 1957). Among the responses that comprise self-awareness, verbal statements that are self-descriptive are perhaps the most common, and the general procedures by which the socializing community teaches an individual to describe his own overt behavior would not seem to differ fundamentally from the methods used to teach him to describe other events in his environment. The community, however, faces a unique problem in training the individual to make statements describing internal stimuli to which only he has direct access, for the conditioning of the appropriate verbal responses must necessarily be based on the public stimuli and responses that often accompany or resemble these private events. Skinner (1953, 1957) has provided a detailed analysis of the limited resources available to the community for training its members thus to "know themselves," and he has described the inescapable inadequacies of the resulting knowledge.

One implication of Skinner's analysis is that many of the self-descriptive statements that appear to be exclusively under the discriminative control of private stimulation may, in fact, remain under the control of the same public events which members of the community themselves must use in "inferring" the individual's inner states. In our well-fed society, for example, it is not uncommon to find a man consulting his wrist watch to answer the question, "Are you hungry?" There is also direct experimental evidence that an individual relies on external cues for describing his emotional states (Schachter and Singer, 1962). Attitude

• Reprinted from *Journal of Experimental Social Psychology*, 1965, **1**, 199-218, with permission of the author and the publisher.

statements may be similarly controlled. For example, when the answer to the question, "Do you like brown bread?" is, "I guess I do, I'm always eating it," it seems unnecessary to invoke a font of privileged self-knowledge to account for the reply. In this example, it is clear that the discriminative stimuli controlling the attitude statement reside in the individual's overt behavior; indeed, the man's reply is functionally equivalent to the reply his wife might give for him: "I guess he does, he is always eating it."

It is the major thesis of this report, then, that an individual's belief and attitude statements and the beliefs and attitudes that an outside observer would attribute to him are often functionally equivalent in that both sets of statements are "inferences" from the same evidence: the public events that the socializing community originally employed in training the individual to make such self-descriptive statements. The three experiments reported below provide support for this hypothesis by demonstrating that an individual's belief and attitude statements may be predicted and controlled by manipulating his overt behavior and the stimulus conditions under which it occurs in ways that would lead an *outside* observer to infer that the individual held the "belief" or "attitude" we wish to obtain. The individual, in short, is regarded as an observer of his own behavior and its controlling variables; accordingly, his belief and attitude statements are viewed as "inferences" from his observations.

TACTS, MANDS, AND COMMUNICATOR CREDIBILITY

A descriptive statement, a verbal response that is under the discriminative control of some portion of the environment, is classified as a "tact" (Skinner, 1957). A speaker is trained to describe or "tact" his environment for the benefit of his listeners who provide generalized social reinforcement in return. An individual's belief and attitude statements are often tacts of stimuli arising from himself (e.g., "I am hungry"), his behavior (e.g., "I am generous"), or the effects of stimuli on him (e.g., "It gives me goosepimples"). Attitude statements in particular have the properties of tacts of the reinforcing effects of a stimulus situation on the individual (e.g., "I detest rainy weather," "I'd walk a mile for a Camel").

Verbal responses that are under the control of specific reinforcing contingencies are called "mands." A speaker who emits a mand is asking for, requesting, or "manding" a particular reinforcer (cf. demands, commands). Only a characteristic consequence will serve to reinforce the response, and often this reinforcer is specified explicitly by the response (e.g., "Please pass the milk"). Mands need not be verbal in the usual sense; for example, pointing to the milk pitcher may be functionally equivalent to the vocal request. Mands are often disguised as tacts as in "I believe you have the sports page" or as in the case of the television announcer who praises a product he is selling; his verbal behavior is a mand for the salary he receives and may not at all be under the actual discriminative control of the features of the product he appears to be tacting. A lie is often a mand for escape from aversive consequences; it, too, is a mand disguised as a tact. Any particular verbal response, then, may have both mand and tact characteristics in differing degrees. Thus, until the controlling circumstances are specified, it is not possible to determine the functional classification of a remark like "Darling, you look beautiful tonight"; the probabilities are high that it is a subtle blend of mand and tact.

It is clear, then, that in attempting to infer a speaker's "true" beliefs and attitudes, the listener must often discriminate the mand-tact characteristics of the communication. This is, in fact, an important dimension of "communicator credibility." A communicator is credible to the extent that his communication is discriminated as a set of tacts, and his credibility is vitiated to the extent that he appears to be manding in the form of disguised tacts. Thus, a communication attributed to J. Robert Oppenheimer is more persuasive than the same communication attributed to *Pravda* (Hovland and Weiss, 1951); the white coat and stethoscope on the television announcer are intended to indicate to the viewer that the announcer is one whose verbal behavior is under discriminative control of the product, not one who is manding money. Not only is a credible communicator more likely to persuade his listeners, but to the extent that his verbal responses appear to be "pure" tacts, they will be judged, by definition, to be his own "true" beliefs and attitudes. We turn now to evidence that the beliefs and attitudes of the communicator himself may be viewed as self-judgments based partially upon his credibility as a communicator; and, to the extent that this is so, they will coincide with judgments of his beliefs and attitudes that outside observers would make.

In an experiment by Festinger and Carlsmith (1959), two experimental groups of 20 undergraduates were employed as subjects. In the $1 condition, the subject was first required to perform long repetitive laboratory tasks. He was then hired by the experimenter as an "assistant" and paid one dollar to tell a waiting fellow student that the tasks were enjoyable and interesting. In the $20 condition, the subjects were hired for $20 to do the same thing. A panel of judges, in a blind rating procedure, rated the $20 persuasive communications as slightly but insignificantly more persuasive than $1 communications. Attitude measurement showed that subjects paid $1 evaluated the tasks and the experiment *more* favorably than did $20 subjects. We may interpret these findings within the present framework by considering the viewpoint of an outside observer who hears the individual making favorable statements about the tasks, and who further knows that the individual was paid $1 or $20 to engage in this behavior. When asked to judge the "true" attitude of the communicator, an outside observer would almost certainly judge a $20 communication to be a mand, behavior not at all under the control of the actual features of the laboratory task the individual appears to be tacting. Although a $1 communication also has mand properties, an outside observer would be more likely to judge it than the $20 communication to be a set of tacts, and hence, by definition, to be the "true" attitudes of the individual. If one places our hypothetical outside observer and the communicator in the same skin, the findings obtained by Festinger and Carlsmith are the result.

Blind evaluations of the persuasive communications were an elegant control feature of the Festinger-Carlsmith design, and, as mentioned, showed $1 communications to be no more persuasive than $20 communications *when the mand-tact conditions under which the verbal behavior was emitted were not available to the observer.* But this is precisely the information which makes one communicator more credible than another.

Cohen (Brehm and Cohen, 1962, p. 73) performed an experiment similar to the Festinger-Carlsmith study in order to rule out the interpretation that the $20 payment in the latter study was so large that it engendered suspicion and resistance, leading subjects to think, "It must be bad if they're paying me so much for it." (See also, Rosenberg, 1965). Since this alternative interpretation is not unlike the mandtact conceptualization offered here, it is relevant to examine Cohen's subsequent experiment in some detail.

Cohen's subjects were offered $.50, $1, $5, or $10 to write an essay against their initial opinions on a current issue. The post-essay belief statements essentially duplicated the Festinger-Carlson results: the higher the inducement, the less the belief statement coincided with the view advocated in the essays. (The $5 and $10 conditions did not differ significantly from the control group who were simply asked their opinions on the issue.) The crux of Cohen's arguments resides in the fact that significant differences in post-essay belief statements emerged between the $.50 and the $1 conditions, and between them and the control condition. Since these payments were small and close to one another, Cohen's argument implies, the mand-tact discrimination could not account for the results.

This is, of course, an empirical question. The following study was designed to answer it by demonstrating that the belief statements made by Cohen's subjects when they were asked for their "true" opinions may be viewed as judgments based on the mand-tact characteristics of their own behavior, that is, on their own credibility as communicators.

EXPERIMENT I. AN INTERPERSONAL REPLICATION OF THE ESSAY STUDY

If the suggested interpretation of Cohen's results is correct, then an external observer should be able to replicate the true belief statement of one of Cohen's subjects with an interpersonal judgment if this observer is told the behavior of the subject and the apparent controlling circumstances of that behavior.

The subjects in the present study thus served as external observers; each subject judged one —and only one—volunteer in one of Cohen's experimental conditions.

Method

Sixty undergraduates were randomly assigned to "$.50," "$1," and "control" conditions. The first two groups were given the following instructions on a single sheet of paper; it consists of a description of the experimental situation employed by Cohen:

In the Spring of 1959, there was a student "riot" at Yale University in which the New Haven Police intervened with resulting accusations of police brutality toward the students. The issue was a very bitter and emotional one, and a survey of student opinion showed most of the student body to be extremely negative toward the police and their actions and sympathetic toward the students.

As part of a research project, a student member of a research team from the Institute of Human Relations at Yale selected a student at random and asked him to write a strong, forceful essay entitled, "Why the New Haven Police Actions Were Justified," an essay which was to be unequivocally in favor of the police side of the riots. The decision to write such an essay or not was entirely up to the student, and he was told that he would be paid the sum of $.50 [$1.00] if he would be willing to do so. The student who was asked agreed to do so, and wrote such an essay.

The scale shown below was used in the original poll of student opinion on the issue. From this description, estimate as well as you can the actual opinion of the student who was willing to write the essay. Indicate your estimate by drawing a line through the appropriate point on the scale.

"Considering the circumstances, how justified do you think the New Haven police actions were in the recent riot?"

| . . . |. . . .| . . . | . . . | . . . | . . .| . . . .|
NOT   VERY LITTLE   LITTLE   SOMEWHAT   QUITE   VERY   COMPLETELY
JUSTIFIED JUSTIFIED JUSTIFIED JUSTIFIED JUSTIFIED JUSTIFIED JUSTIFIED
AT ALL

The control Ss in the present study received the same instructions except that the entire second paragraph was deleted and the third paragraph was altered to read: "From this description, estimate as well as you can the actual opinion of a student selected at random on the Yale campus. . . ."

In Cohen's experiment the subjects first wrote the essay and were then asked to indicate their own opinions on the scale. The scale employed in the present study is identical to Cohen's. The "control" condition in the present study also provides a check on the adequacy with which the situation on the Yale campus has been described.

Results and Discussion

Figure 1 shows the interpersonal judgments of Ss in the present experiment compared to the belief statements collected by Cohen. Two-tailed probability levels based on t tests are also shown. It is seen that Cohen's results are closely replicated.

These results show the mand-tact interpretation of the general inverse relation between amount of payment and subsequent belief statements is still viable: (the lower the payment, the less the mand properties of the observed behavior predominate in the eyes of both intra- and inter-personal observers.) To the extent

that the behavior has non-mand properties, it will be discriminated by an observer (including the individual himself) as indicating the "true" beliefs of that individual.

It should be noted that Ss in the experiment just presented did not actually read any of the essays written by Cohen's Ss. The successful interpersonal replication of his results, then, suggests that it may not have been necessary for his Ss to write the essays; that is, the behavior of *volunteering* may be the source of discriminative control over the beliefs. The "communication" may be contained in the commitment to write the essay, and it is the *commitment* that has the crucial mand or non-mand properties depending upon the payment offered. Brehm and Cohen (1962, pp. 115–116) cite a number of studies which, indeed, do demonstrate that commitment alone is sufficient; the essays themselves do not have to be written. In order to provide direct support for our interpretation that the individual's subsequent belief statement in such experiments may be viewed as self-judgments based on his behavior of *volunteering* and its mand characteristics, it seemed desirable to attempt an interpersonal replication of a study in which persuasive communication *per se* did not play a part. The study chosen is of additional interest because the dependent variable is a judg-

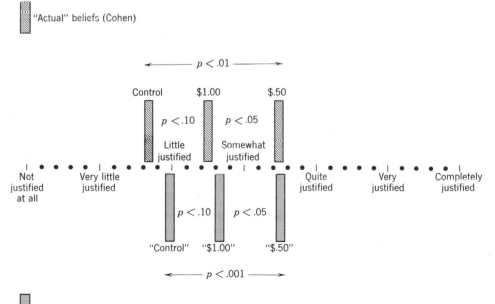

Figure 1. A comparison of "actual" beliefs and interpersonal judgments of belief.

ment of hunger, a tact that is not only self-descriptive, but is typically considered to be under the exclusive control of private internal stimuli.

EXPERIMENT II. AN INTERPERSONAL REPLICATION OF THE HUNGER STUDY

Volunteer male Ss in an experiment by Brehm (Brehm and Cohen, 1962, pp. 133–136) were required to go without food for a number of hours before an individual experimental session disguised as an investigation on hunger and intellectual performance. At the beginning of the session, the S indicated on a questionnaire scale how hungry he felt. After engaging in a number of tasks, the S was asked to volunteer for further testing, which would entail continued food deprivation. Half of the Ss were offered $5 for volunteering; others were offered nothing. A second self-evaluation of hunger, administered after the S had volunteered, showed that those offered the money rated themselves significantly more hungry than those who had volunteered for nothing.

As before, we interpret these results by assuming the standpoint of an outside observer who sees the S volunteering, and is then asked to judge the volunteer's hunger. If the observer

The design of the present experiment is the same as the interpersonal replication of the essay study; each S in the present experiment judges only one "other."

Method   *some people*

Fifty male college students were randomly assigned to a "$5" or a "no-pay" condition. Those in the "$5" condition were given the following instructions on a single sheet of paper.

Volunteer male subjects in a psychology experiment on the effect of hunger on motor and intellectual functioning were required to go without food from the time they got up in the morning until the afternoon testing session. The volunteers received experimental credit points in their introductory psychology course for this experiment.

When the subject arrived, he was shown the sandwiches, cookies, and milk on the testing table and told he would be able to eat as much of these as he wanted after the testing session. The subject then indicated how hungry he was on the rating scale shown below; the arrow shows the *average* degree of hunger for all the subjects who participated in this research at the beginning of this session.

"How hungry are you?"

```
                              ↓
|............|............|.........|.............|.............|...........|
NOT AT      VERY      SLIGHTLY   MODER-      QUITE      VERY    EXTREMELY
 ALL      SLIGHTLY              ATELY
```

were to see an S volunteering for the sum of $5, he would discriminate the mand properties of that behavior, which is to say that he would be able to conclude very little about the S's hunger; the internal discriminative stimuli arising from "hunger," the observer would assume, would not be a controlling variable of the decision to volunteer. If the observer had been told the volunteer's initial hunger rating, he would probably conclude that the S had simply increased his hunger somewhat over the intervening time. The behavior of the unpaid volunteer, however, has no obvious mand properties; *specific monetary* reinforcement is not a controlling variable. Hence, by volunteering, the S tells the outside observer (and himself) that he is not very hungry; his volunteering, relative of course to Ss paid $5, is not a mand.

If this interpretation of the Brehm results is correct, then external observers should be able to replicate with interpersonal judgments the self-ratings of hunger obtained by Brehm.

After giving this rating, the subject engaged in a number of motor and intellectual tasks. One of the subjects was then asked if he would be willing to return for further testing in the evening; this, it was explained, would require him to continue going without food until about eight or nine that evening. He was told, "Unfortunately, we cannot give you any more experimental credit points for the evening testing session. However, we can pay anyone willing to come back since we do need your help. The amount is $5.00."

This individual agreed to continue his participation. From this description, try to estimate how hungry this particular person must have been at the end of the first session just described. Indicate your estimate by drawing a line through the appropriate point on the scale above.

Subjects in a "no-pay" condition received identical instructions except that the reported offer of $5 was replaced by the following: "You get your point for having taken part this afternoon so don't think you have to come again this evening. But we would appreciate your help. If, however, you don't feel like doing it, that's okay because we can get someone else to do it."

The scale and reported instructions to the volunteers are identical to those employed by Brehm. The arrow given on the present instruction sheet represents the initial hunger rating of Brehm's $5 subjects.

Results and Discussion

Figure 2 shows the interpersonal judgments of Ss in the present experiment compared to the self-rating data collected by Brehm. (Brehm's result for the no-pay condition has been expressed as a displacement from the arrow rather than from the actual initial hunger rating of his no-pay Ss.) The separation between the results of the treatments in Brehm's study was statistically significant at the .01 level; the separation in the interpersonal data is significant at the .025 level (two-tailed t test). It is clear that Brehm's results for intrapersonal judgments are closely replicated by the results for interpersonal judgments in the present study.

We conclude that the self-ratings of hunger obtained by Brehm were partially under the control of the mand characteristics of the behavior of volunteering, and that the judgments made by Brehm's subjects *vis-a-vis* their own behavior does not differ significantly from judgments based on their behavior made by an external observer.

Alternative Manipulations of the Self-Credibility Parameter

The crux of the present interpretation is that the control over beliefs exercised by an individual's own behavior will vary as the contingencies of specific reinforcement for engaging in the behavior are made more or less prominent as a controlling variable. As the contingencies of reinforcement are made more subtle, less discriminable, the mand properties of the S's own behavior will be lessened and the behavior will, thereby, have maximum control over his subsequent beliefs. In the studies discussed in detail so far, this self-credibility discrimination has been manipulated by varying the magnitude of reinforcement offered for engaging in the overt behavior: the larger the reinforcement, the more likely it was that the S would discriminate his own behavior as a mand. We turn now to studies which employed a number of different stimulus operations, all with the effect of manipulating the mand properties of the induced behavior.

In an experiment by Aronson and Carlsmith

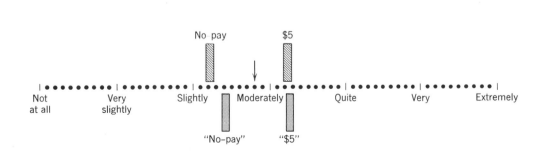

Figure 2. A comparison of self-judgments and interpersonal judgments of hunger.

(1963), school children approximately four years of age gave preference rank-orderings on a set of five toys. The experimenter then told the subject that he could play with any of the toys but one while the experimenter ran an errand. The forbidden toy was the one which ranked second in the child's preference ordering. Children assigned to a mild-threat condition were further told that the experimenter would be annoyed if the child played with the forbidden toy; children assigned to a strong-threat condition were told that if they disobeyed, the experimenter would be very angry, take all of the toys away, never come back, and think that the child was "just a baby." The experimenter then left the room and observed the child through a one-way mirror for ten minutes. None of the subjects played with the forbidden toy. After this interval, preference orderings on the five toys were again obtained from the subject. The final preference ranking of the forbidden toy was the dependent variable under investigation. It was found that subjects in the mild-threat condition assigned significantly lower final preference rankings to the toy than did children in the strong-threat condition. Rankings obtained 45 days later still showed some evidence of the differential effects of the treatments.

In interpreting these results, it is again instructive to assume the standpoint of an outside observer who sees the child playing with all the toys but one; in addition, we assume that the observer has been told that the child was given a mild [strong] threat of aversive consequences if he played with the toy. The outside observer is now asked to estimate the child's ranking of the forbidden toy. We may infer that the behavior of avoiding the toy on the part of subjects in the mild-threat condition has less the property of a mand (for withholding aversive consequences) than the behavior of subjects in the strong-threat condition. Thus, a hypothetical observer of a subject in the mild-threat condition would be more likely to assume that the actual reinforcing properties of the toy were partially controlling the observed behavior than would an observer judging the behavior of a subject in the strong-threat condition. The former observer would, then, assign a lower preference rating to the toy than the latter observer. These are the obtained findings, which are, then, consistent with the interpretation that the final ranking of the toy given by the child himself is primarily a self-judgment based on his own behavior and its controlling variables, rather than a tact of the reinforcing properties of the toy being ranked.

The studies which have been discussed so far are among several "forced compliance" experiments conducted within the framework of Festinger's theory of cognitive dissonance (1957). Each of these studies yields data consistent with the present analysis: when the operations employed are submitted to a careful analysis in terms of the discriminative stimuli presented to the subject, then those conditions in which specific reinforcing contingencies are enhanced or made more prominent (the mand conditions) are always found to yield weaker control over the subsequent belief statements than those conditions in which the subject is given "no good reason" for engaging in the behavior. For example, other experiments have manipulated the degree of choice permitted the subject, degree of commitment evoked, amount of justification given, and the reinforcing properties of the experimenter—all with the same results (Brehm and Cohen, 1962, pp. 303–306): when the contingencies of reinforcement are made less significant or more subtle, the non-mand properties of the behavior predominate and subsequent belief statements may be predicted by assuming them to be the inferences of an observer of the behavior.

Other studies from the literature are also amenable to the self-credibility interpretation. King and Janis (1956) compared improvised versus non-improvised role playing in producing belief change and found that subjects who read a communication and then played the role of a sincere advocate of the communication's point of view changed their beliefs more than those who read the fully prepared script aloud. It seems likely that the subjects who simply read the script clearly discriminated that their behavior was under the control of the text (cf. Skinner, 1957), whereas in the case of the subject who actually played out the role, every measure possible was taken to insure that he was surrounded by stimuli that would characteristically control the behaviors of an individual who "believed" the point of view. It should also be noted that subjects who were permitted to "improvise" would be expected to select precisely those arguments that had initial tact properties for themselves. It seems consonant with our analysis, then, to find that these subjects were more "persuasive" to themselves than the script readers.

In an experiment by Scott (1957), pairs of students were asked to debate different issues in front of a class; each student argued the position contrary to his initial beliefs. The experimenter manipulated the conditions so that a predetermined member of each pair "won" the debate. Later measurement of belief showed that the "winners" changed in the direction of the position that they had defended in the debate, but "losers" did not; in fact, "losers" shifted slightly toward the "winning" side. In a replication of the experiment in which a panel of judges rather than a class vote "decided" the winner of the debates, some of the debaters defended positions they actually held (Scott, 1959). Among these subjects, "winners" shifted still further in the direction of their arguments, and "losers" again shifted slightly in the direction of the "winning" side, a shift that was against the arguments they themselves presented *and* their initial beliefs.

Since the winners had been reinforced by winning and the losers had not, Scott interprets these results as showing that the reinforcement of overt verbal responses leads to a change in the beliefs. Such an interpretation, however, runs into difficulty in accounting for the results of the dissonance experiments previously described, which show an inverse relation between reinforcement and belief change. The present analysis suggests that the (falsified) class vote or judge's decision gave an additional tact property, or measure of credibility, to the beliefs stated in the "winning" argument; hence, the "winner" himself discriminated these beliefs as tacts, which is to say as his "true" beliefs. The fact that "losers" also shifted slightly toward the winning side is consistent with this interpretation. Further support for this interpretation comes from a study by Kelley and Woodruff (1956). College students who heard a recording of "prestigeful" members of their college group applaud a speech that opposed their initial beliefs changed their beliefs more than did a control group that was told that the applauding audience was a group of townspeople. These subjects thus based their credibility discriminations of the communicator on the judgment of other listeners, just as the debaters in the debate studies, it is suggested, based the credibility of their own communications on the decisions of the judges. The self-perception interpretation is thus consistent with the data from both the debate experiments and the dissonance theory experiments.

EXPERIMENT III. SELF-CREDIBILITY AND THE CONTROL OF ATTITUDE STATEMENTS

The stimulus operations that we have interpreted as controlling self-credibility discriminations in all the experiments discussed and replicated so far have always had other functional properties. Thus, money payoffs and the winning of debates also have reinforcing properties; manipulations of justification, choice, commitment, etc. involve a veritable tangle of complex and ambiguous stimulus operations. The present experiment was designed to provide more direct support for the present formulation by "raising stimuli from birth" in the laboratory that would have no functional properties other than those we have imputed to the stimulus operations in the other experiments discussed.

The dependent variable in this study is an attitude statement concerning the "funniness" of magazine cartoons. The cartoons employed are those that the S has previously marked as "neutral"; that is, neither funny nor unfunny. During the experimental session, which is disguised as a tape recording session for the preparation of experimental stimulus materials, the S is required to state that each cartoon is either "very funny" or "very unfunny." Each overt statement is made in the presence of a visual stimulus (a colored light) that has been previously paired with the S's verbal behavior: one of the colored lights, which we shall call the truth light, had always been illuminated previously when the S was giving true answers to a set of questions concerning personal information. The other light was always illuminated when the S was giving false answers to the questions; we shall call this light the lie light. After the S has made an overt statement about the cartoon, he rates his "true" attitude on a rating scale.

The prediction is that the S's "true" attitude will be controlled by his overt statements to a greater degree when the statement is emitted in the presence of the truth light than when it is emitted in the presence of the lie light. A post-experimental questionnaire tests for the S's "awareness" of any of the obtained effects. It will be noted that each S is his own control, and that each S provides a complete replication of the experiment.

Method

Eight college students were hired for two forty-minute sessions on consecutive days to "help prepare materials for use in experimental research on voice-judgment." In the first session, the S ranked each of 200 cartoons for "funniness" on the 100 millimeter scale shown below by drawing a short vertical line across the scale line at any appropriate point.

	VERY	UNFUNNY	SLIGHTLY	SLIGHTLY	FUNNY	VERY
Cartoon W-2	UNFUNNY		UNFUNNY	FUNNY		FUNNY

The cartoons, arranged two to a page in a loose-leaf notebook, were taken from *The New Yorker, The Saturday Evening Post, Look,* and *McCalls* magazines. This session, then, provided a baseline measure for the dependent variable, ratings of funniness of cartoons.

In the experimental session the following day, the S was seated at a desk in a small acoustically-tiled recording room for the alleged purpose of making a tape recording of his voice for the voice-judgment experiments. The S's first task was to fill out a form with 49 questions concerning personal information. The instructions and sample items from this form are reproduced below:

This information form will provide some of the materials you will be recording on tape for the voice-judgment experiment. It should be filled out completely and accurately. THIS INFORMATION WILL REMAIN CONFIDENTIAL AND ANONYMOUS. YOUR NAME WILL NOT APPEAR ON THE TAPE OR ELSEWHERE IN THE EXPERIMENT.

(1) First Name ———

(10) Are you generally favorable or unfavorable to fraternities and sororities? ——

(22) Do you feel that full socialism would be preferable to the free enterprise system in America? ———

(29) Do you believe in a Supreme Being? ———

After obtaining the completed information form, E left the recording room, and all further communication with the S was conducted with an intercom. The following training procedure was then employed to establish two lights as discriminative stimuli which would indicate that verbal behavior in the presence of the one was tacting ("truth-telling") and in the presence of the other, lying, a form of behavior which is characteristically a mand. The following instructions were given to the S:[1]

As I mentioned, you are going to be making a tape of your own voice to be used in some research we will be doing on an individual's ability to judge another person's voice. In particular, we are going to be examining an individual's ability to judge whether the speaker on the tape is telling the truth or not. To do this, some of the things you will say on the tape will be true statements; others will be untrue. The procedure will be as follows: I will ask you questions, one at a time, from the list of information you just filled out. After I ask you a question, I will start the tape recorder, and you should answer the question into the microphone in front of you. Whenever I turn on the tape recorder, one of two colored light bulbs in the ceiling fixture will also go on automatically. If the amber light goes on [amber light turned on], you are to answer the question truthfully; if, however, the green light turns on [green light turned on; amber light turned off], you should make up an untrue answer and speak it into the microphone as convincingly and as naturally as possible. My questions will not be recorded on the tape, so your answers must be complete statements, not just single word answers. For example, I will ask: "What is your first name?" When the ceiling light goes on, you should answer, "My first name is such-and-such." If the light is amber, then you would, of course, give your real first name. If the light is green, you would make up some other name. As you can see, we wanted this to be spontaneous, which is why you will not know until the tape actually starts whether you are going to give a true or an untrue answer; you have to be on your toes. The lighting circuitry is set to select the two colored lights automatically and in random sequence. I will be checking your responses on your information form; when you respond in the appropriate way, I will stop the tape, the colored light will go out, and we will proceed to the next question. If you happen to make a mistake, or do not answer with a com-

---

[1] Instructions were designed to sound matter-of-fact so that it would not be apparent to S that they were being read verbatim. Hence, in written form they seem wordy and ungrammatical.

plete sentence we will repeat that item. Are there any questions? [pause] Okay, remember the amber light means you are to give a true answer; the green light, an untrue one.

The training procedure then proceeded as described. Half of the questions required untrue responses, and half required true responses. The two lights were reversed for some Ss: green light for true responses, amber light for false responses. At the end of the training session, E continued as follows:

We have now completed all the questions on the information form. In the second part of our voice-judgment experiments, the subjects will be asked to look at some of the cartoons you judged earlier. The cartoons we have decided to use have been placed in the notebook in front of you. The subjects will be asked to give their opinions of each cartoon on a rating scale like the one on the notebook cover by drawing a line through the scale line at the appropriate point. You will note that this scale is less detailed than the ones you used earlier. [See scale below.] Before judging each cartoon, the subject will listen to a comment made by you on the tape stating that you found the cartoon very funny or very unfunny. We are interested in seeing whether your comment can influence the subject's opinion of the cartoon in the direction of your own opinion. Our procedure now, then, will be as follows: You will glance at each cartoon and decide whether it is funny or unfunny, that is, whether in your opinion it falls to the right or to the left of the neutral point on the scale. When you decide, tell me your decision and I will start the tape recorder. If you think the cartoon is a funny one, you should then record the comment, "I think cartoon such-and-such is a *very funny* cartoon." If the cartoon lies on the left side of the scale in your opinion, you should record the comment, "I think cartoon such-and-such is a *very unfunny* cartoon." In every case you should identify the cartoon by its code letter and say that

it is either very funny or very unfunny, whichever is closer to your own opinion. Aside from that, however, you should use whatever words seem most natural and convincing to you, such as "I find cartoon such-and-such to be etc." or "I think cartoon such-and-such is . . . etc." Are there any questions? [pause] Just so you will know when I turn the tape recorder on and off, I will leave the ceiling recording lights hooked up to the tape recorder; so, the two colored lights will continue to flash on and off with the recorder in random sequence. Okay, glance at the first cartoon and let me know which half of the scale it falls in, and I will start the recorder for your comment.

The following scale was used in this session:

```
|————————————————|————————————————|
```

VERY   VERY
UNFUNNY   FUNNY

At this point, S glanced at the first cartoon, and indicated his binary decision. E then turned on the lie light; S made his comment, the colored light went out, and the white desk light went on simultaneously. E continued as follows:

It is also necessary that we have a record of your *exact* opinion of the cartoon at the time the comment was recorded. For this reason, you should now turn the page and mark your exact opinion of the cartoon on the scale provided by placing a mark through the scale line at the appropriate point. [E waited for this to be done.] Okay, turn to the second cartoon and tell me which half of the scale it falls in.

For each S, the twenty cartoons employed in this session had been ranked within ten millimeters of the neutral point (that is, between SLIGHTLY FUNNY and SLIGHTLY UNFUNNY), on the scale presented in the preexperimental session. The cartoons were further matched and alternated in the sequence of presentation to control for the smaller variations around the neutral point. (This precaution was probably unnecessary because of the high variability of such rankings over time.)

The following sequence of lights was used for the 20 cartoons:

1. Lie	5. Truth	9. Lie	13. Truth	17. Lie
2. Truth	6. Lie	10. Truth	14. Lie	18. Truth
3. Truth	7. Lie	11. Truth	15. Lie	19. Truth
4. Lie	8. Truth	12. Lie	16. Truth	20. Lie

After the S followed the procedure for the first cartoon, E did not communicate further with him except to announce the code number of the next cartoon after the S had completed his ranking of the previous one.

This procedure, then, assessed the control of attitudes exercised by overt verbal behavior emitted in the presence of two discriminative stimuli, one of which had a history of pairing with true responses, the other with false responses. In order to assess awareness of the effects, in the event that they occurred, each S was instructed to respond in writing to the following four questions at the end of the session.

Each of the attached sheets contains a question which will be helpful to us in revising our procedures for the voice-judgment experiment. Please do not look ahead to the next question until you finish the preceding one.

As far as you can tell, did your ratings of the 20 cartoons you looked at today change from your previous ratings of them? If so, in what way?

As far as you can tell, were your cartoon ratings today affected in any way by the other procedures involved? If so, in what way?

Did you pay attention to the color of the recording lights during the cartoon portion of the session? As far as you can tell, did the recording lights affect your cartoon judgments in any way? If so, in what ways?

Each S was then paid $2.50 and told the true purpose of the experiment.

Results and Discussion

The prediction is that the 10 cartoons commented upon by the S in the presence of the truth light would be ranked further from the neutral point in the direction of the self-persuasion ("very funny" or "very unfunny") than the 10 cartoons commented upon by the S in the presence of the lie light. This one-tailed hypothesis is tested on each S with the Mann-Whitney U test.

Because separate analyses of attitudes toward the cartoons called "very funny" and "very unfunny" yielded comparable results, these data have been combined; the scores given in Table 1 represent mean absolute deviation in millimeters from the neutral point (0) in the direction of the self-persuasion on the 100 millimeter scale. Accordingly, the scores can range from 0 to 50, where a score of 50 represents a rating of either "very funny" or "very unfunny," depending upon the S's overt statement. The S's responses to the final awareness question are also displayed.

It is seen in Table 1 that seven of the eight Ss were persuaded to a greater extent by comments made in the presence of the truth light than by comments made in the presence of the lie light. The null hypothesis (no difference between attitude ratings affected by the truth versus lie treatments) is rejected by a sign test applied to the relative position of these ratings on the scale of each S ($p = .035$; one-tailed). In addition, the results from five of the Ss considered individually attain a significance level smaller than 5% by a one-tailed Mann-Whitney U test.

The reverse trend displayed by S 7 is due primarily to the final cartoon—a lie-light cartoon—which was marked at 48 (VERY FUNNY). On the awareness questionnaire she responded: "I didn't think any of them were too funny so toward the end maybe I tried to think that they were funny so I wouldn't seem so unhappy."

In pretesting the experimental procedures, a foreign student (Chinese undergraduate) served as an S. A slightly different procedure was employed with him in that only twelve cartoons, which he had previously marked as neutral, were employed, and E dictated the comment which was to be made for each cartoon rather than first obtaining the S's preference. For this reason, the attitude rating can be displaced from the neutral point in the negative direction, that is, in the direction away from the overt comment "very funny" or "very unfunny." The mean deviation from the neutral point for the lie-light cartoons was -9; the mean deviation for the truth-light cartoons was $+28$, a difference significant at the .004 level. In addition to indicating no awareness of the effect of the lights, he commented that "Some of the cartoons are not too obvious in their meanings. So it is quite hard to give them the correct ratings." The powerful control exercised by the lights over the attitude statements of this S is thus interpreted as reflecting the effect of the weak stimulus control exercised by the cartoons themselves ("stimulus ambiguity"). The control is even more striking because E dictated the comment which was to be made for each cartoon, rather than first obtaining the S's preference; this adds a strong mand property to the subse-

TABLE 1. A Comparison of the Effectiveness of Self-Persuasion in the Presence of the Truth Light and in the Presence of the Lie Light

Subject	Mean Deviation (in Millimeters) from the Neutral Point in the Direction of the Self-Persuasion		One-Tailed Mann-Whitney U Test	Response to the Awareness Question: "Were Your Ratings Affected by the Color of the Lights?"
	Truth Light ($N = 10$ Cartoons)	Lie Light ($N = 10$ Cartoons)		
1 (Male, 21 yrs.)	23	14	$U = 16$ $p < .01$	"The lights, as far as I know, did not affect me."
2 (Male, 22 yrs.)	4	3	$U = 20$ $p < .05$	"I do not believe so."
3 (Male, 20 yrs.)	24	14	$U = 24$ $p < .05$	"I made my judgment before the recording light came on—I don't think the light affected my judgment in any way."
4 (Male, 27 yrs.)	35	17	$U = 29$ $p < .06$	"No."
5 (Male, 24 yrs.)	27	13	$U = 38$ n.s.	"No."
6 (Female, 20 yrs.)	20	9	$U = 24$ $p < .05$	"Yes. They didn't affect the judgments (I don't think)."
7 (Female, 18 yrs.)	10	17	$U = 73$ Non-predicted direction	"I didn't even notice the colored lights."
8 (Male, 18 yrs.)	32*	20*	$U = 19$ $p < .05$	"I did not pay any particular attention to the lights and as far as I know they did not influence my answers."

* Subject made two incorrect overt statements at the beginning of the series. The analysis is based on the remaining nine truth-light and nine lie-light cartoons.

455

quent behavior. (It will be recalled that a manipulation of "amount of choice" was cited earlier as a demonstrated manipulation of the self-credibility parameter.) In fact, when this same procedure was attempted with ten American S's, no effect of stimulus control by the lights was obtained. These interpretations are not, of course, unequivocal since the cultural differences between this S and the American Ss would imply variation of many more parameters than just the ambiguity of the cartoons.

None of the Ss in the present experiment was able to identify the effect of his comments or the lights on his subsequent attitude statements. Again, it is evident that "self-awareness" is a set of behaviors which must be learned from a socializing community that sets up the necessary contingencies of reinforcement for establishing the discriminations (Skinner, 1953). In the present experiment, there is no theoretical reason to suppose that an S's tact of the conditions controlling his behavior should be causally relevant to the outcome of the experiment.

In sum, it is concluded that the data from the experiments reported provide support for the hypotheses advanced at the outset: self-

descriptive statements known as beliefs and attitudes are often under the partial control of the individual's overt behavior and its apparent controlling variables. Since these public stimuli and responses are those which the socializing community itself must use initially in training the individual to "know himself," the individual's belief and attitude statements are functionally equivalent to those that an outside observer would attribute to him. They are "inferences" from the same evidence. The two interpersonal replications of experiments by Brehm and Cohen (1962) illustrated the similarity between an individual's "true" beliefs and attitudes and the inferences drawn by an outside observer of his behavior. The final experiment demonstrated the direct control over an individual's attitude statements exerted by his own overt behavior and the stimulus conditions in which it occurs. Finally, it is suggested that the present functional analysis also provides an alternative formulation of several other experiments in the literature, especially the "forced compliance" studies conducted within the framework of Festinger's theory of cognitive dissonance (1957).

REFERENCES

Aronson, E., and Carlsmith, J. M. Effect of the severity of threat on the devaluation of forbidden behavior. *J. abnorm. soc. Psychol.,* 1963, **66**, 584-588.

Brehm, J. W., and Cohen, A. R. *Explorations in cognitive dissonance.* New York: Wiley and Sons, 1962.

Festinger, L. *A theory of cognitive dissonance.* Evanston: Row, Peterson, 1957.

Festinger, L., and Carlsmith, J. M. Cognitive consequences of forced compliance. *J. abnorm. soc. Psychol.,* 1959, **58**, 203-210.

Hovland, C. I., and Weiss, W. The influence of source credibility on communication effectiveness. *Publ. Opin. Quart.,* 1951, **15**, 635-650.

Kelley, H. H., and Woodruff, Christine L. Members' reactions to apparent group approval of a counternorm communication. *J. abnorm. soc. Psychol.,* 1956, **52**, 67-74.

King, B. T., and Janis, I. L. Comparison of the effectiveness of improvised vs. non-improvised role-playing in producing opinion change. *Hum. Relations,* 1956, **9**, 177-186.

Mead, G. H. *Mind, self, and society.* Chicago: University of Chicago Press, 1934.

Rosenberg, M. J. When dissonance fails: on eliminating evaluation apprehension from attitude measurement. *J. pers. soc. Psychol.,* 1965, **1**, 28-42.

Ryle, G. *The concept of mind.* London: Hutchinson, 1949.

Schachter, S., and Singer, J. Cognitive, social, and physiological determinants of emotional state. *Psychol. Rev.,* 1962, **69**, 379-399.

Scott, W. A. Attitude change through reward of verbal behavior. *J. abnorm. soc. psychol.,* 1957, **55**, 72-75.

Scott, W. A. Attitude change by response reinforcement: replication and extension. *Sociometry,* 1959, **22**, 328-335.

Skinner, B. F. *Science and human behavior.* New York: Macmillan, 1953.

Skinner, B. F. *Verbal behavior.* New York: Appleton-Century-Crofts, 1957.

49. *The Functional Approach to the Study of Attitudes*

DANIEL KATZ

EARLY APPROACHES TO THE STUDY OF ATTITUDE AND OPINION

There have been two main streams of thinking with respect to the determination of man's attitudes. The one tradition assumes an irrational model of man: specifically it holds that men have very limited powers of reason and reflection, weak capacity to discriminate, only the most primitive self-insight, and very short memories. Whatever mental capacities people do possess are easily overwhelmed by emotional forces and appeals to self-interest and vanity. The early books on the psychology of advertising, with their emphasis on the doctrine of suggestion, exemplify this approach. One expression of this philosophy is in the propagandist's concern with tricks and traps to manipulate the public. A modern form of it appears in *The Hidden Persuaders,* or the use of subliminal and marginal suggestion, or the devices supposedly employed by "the Madison Avenue boys." Experiments to support this line of thinking started with laboratory demonstrations of the power of hypnotic suggestion and were soon extended to show that people would change their attitudes in an uncritical manner under the influence of the prestige of authority and numbers. For example, individuals would accept or reject the same idea depending upon whether it came from a positive or a negative prestige source.[1]

The second approach is that of the ideologist who invokes a rational model of man. It assumes that the human being has a cerebral cortex, that he seeks understanding, that he consistently attempts to make sense of the world about him,

that he possesses discriminating and reasoning powers which will assert themselves over time, and that he is capable of self-criticism and self-insight. It relies heavily upon getting adequate information to people. Our educational system is based upon this rational model. The present emphasis upon the improvement of communication, upon developing more adequate channels of two-way communication, of conferences and institutes, upon bringing people together to interchange ideas, are all indications of the belief in the importance of intelligence and comprehension in the formation and change of men's opinions.

Now either school of thought can point to evidence which supports its assumptions, and can make fairly damaging criticisms of its opponent. Solomon Asch and his colleagues, in attacking the irrational model, have called attention to the biased character of the old experiments on prestige suggestion which gave the subject little opportunity to demonstrate critical thinking.[2] And further exploration of subjects in these stupid situations does indicate that they try to make sense of a nonsensical matter as far as possible. Though the same statement is presented by the experimenter to two groups, the first time as coming from a positive source and the second time as coming from a negative source, it is given a different meaning dependent upon the context in which it appears.[3] Thus the experimental subject does

• Excerpted from *Public Opinion Quarterly,* 1960, **24,** 163-204, with permission of the author and the publisher.

1 Muzafer Sherif, *The Psychology of Social Norms,* New York, Harper, 1936.

2 Solomon E. Asch, *Social Psychology,* New York, Prentice-Hall, 1952.

3 *Ibid.,* pp. 426-427. The following statement was attributed to its rightful author, John Adams, for some subjects and to Karl Marx for others: "those who hold and those who are without property have ever formed distinct interests in society." When the statement was attributed to Marx, this type of comment appeared: "Marx is stressing the need for a redistribution of wealth." When it was attributed to Adams, this comment appeared: "This social division is innate in mankind."

his best to give some rational meaning to the problem. On the other hand, a large body of experimental work indicates that there are many limitations in the rational approach in that people see their world in terms of their own needs, remember what they want to remember, and interpret information on the basis of wishful thinking. H. H. Hyman and P. Sheatsley have demonstrated that these experimental results have direct relevance to information campaigns directed at influencing public opinion.[4] These authors assembled facts about such campaigns and showed conclusively that increasing the flow of information to people does not necessarily increase the knowledge absorbed or produce the attitude changes desired.

The major difficulty with these conflicting approaches is their lack of specification of the conditions under which men do act as the theory would predict. For the facts are that people do act at times as if they had been decorticated and at times with intelligence and comprehension. And people themselves do recognize that on occasion they have behaved blindly, impulsively, and thoughtlessly. A second major difficulty is that the rationality-irrationality dimension is not clearly defined. At the extremes it is easy to point to examples, as in the case of the acceptance of stupid suggestions under emotional stress on the one hand, or brilliant problem solving on the other; but this does not provide adequate guidance for the many cases in the middle of the scale where one attempts to discriminate between rationalization and reason.

RECONCILIATION OF THE CONFLICT IN A FUNCTIONAL APPROACH

The conflict between the rationality and irrationality models was saved from becoming a worthless debate because of the experimentation and research suggested by these models. The findings of this research pointed toward the elements of truth in each approach and gave some indication of the conditions under which each model could make fairly accurate predictions. In general the irrational approach was at its best where the situation imposed heavy restrictions upon search behavior and response alternatives. Where individuals must

give quick responses without adequate opportunities to explore the nature of the problem, where there are very few response alternatives available to them, where their own deep emotional needs are aroused, they will in general react much as does the unthinking subject under hypnosis. On the other hand, where the individual can have more adequate commerce with the relevant environmental setting, where he has time to obtain more feedback from his reality testing, and where he has a number of realistic choices, his behavior will reflect the use of his rational faculties.[5] The child will often respond to the directive of the parent not by implicit obedience but by testing out whether or not the parent really meant what he said.

Many of the papers in this issue, which describe research and theory concerning consistency and consonance, represent one outcome of the rationality model. The theory of psychological consonance, or cognitive balance, assumes that man attempts to reduce discrepancies in his beliefs, attitudes, and behavior by appropriate changes in these processes. While the emphasis here is upon consistency or logicality, the theory deals with all dissonances, no matter how produced. Thus they could result from irrational factors of distorted perception and wishful thinking as well as from rational factors of realistic appraisal of a problem and an accurate estimate of its consequences. Moreover, the theory would predict only that the individual will move to reduce dissonance, whether such movement is a good adjustment to the world or leads to the delusional systems of the paranoiac. In a sense, then, this theory would avoid the conflict between the old approaches of the rational and the irrational man by not dealing with the specific antecedent causes of behavior or with the particular ways in which the individual solves his problems.

In addition to the present preoccupation with the development of formal models concerned with cognitive balance and consonance, there is a growing interest in a more comprehensive framework for dealing with the complex vari-

[4] Herbert H. Hyman and Paul B. Sheatsley, "Some Reasons Why Information Campaigns Fail," *Public Opinion Quarterly*, Vol. 11, 1947, pp. 413-423.

[5] William A. Scott points out that in the area of international relations the incompleteness and remoteness of the information and the lack of pressures on the individual to defend his views results in inconsistencies. Inconsistent elements with respect to a system of international beliefs may, however, be consistent with the larger system of the personality. "Rationality and Non-rationality of International Attitudes," *Journal of Conflict Resolution*, Vol. 2, 1958, pp. 9-16.

ables and for bringing order within the field. The thoughtful system of Ulf Himmelstrand, presented in the following pages, is one such attempt. Another point of departure is represented by two groups of workers who have organized their theories around the functions which attitudes perform for the personality. Sarnoff, Katz, and McClintock, in taking this functional approach, have given primary attention to the motivational bases of attitudes and the processes of attitude change.[6] The basic assumption of this group is that both attitude formation and attitude change must be understood in terms of the needs they serve and that, as these motivational processes differ, so too will the conditions and techniques for attitude change. Smith, Bruner, and White have also analyzed the different functions which attitudes perform for the personality.[7] Both groups present essentially the same functions, but Smith, Bruner, and White give more attention to perceptual and cognitive processes and Sarnoff, Katz, and McClintock to the specific conditions of attitude change.

The importance of the functional approach is threefold:

1. Many previous studies of attitude change have dealt with factors which are not genuine psychological variables, for example, the effect on group prejudice of contact between two groups, or the exposure of a group of subjects to a communication in the mass media. Now contact serves different psychological functions for the individual and merely knowing that people have seen a movie or watched a television program tells us nothing about the personal values engaged or not engaged by such a presentation. If, however, we can gear our research to the functions attitudes perform, we can develop some generalizations about human behavior. Dealing with nonfunctional variables makes such generalization difficult, if not impossible.

2. By concerning ourselves with the different functions attitudes can perform we can avoid the great error of oversimplification—the error of attributing a single cause to given types of attitude. It was once popular to ascribe radical-

ism in economic and political matters to the psychopathology of the insecure and to attribute conservatism to the rigidity of the mentally aged. At the present time it is common practice to see in attitudes of group prejudice the repressed hostilities stemming from childhood frustrations, though Hyman and Sheatsley have pointed out that prejudiced attitudes can serve as normative function of gaining acceptance in one's own group as readily as releasing unconscious hatred.[8] In short, not only are there a number of motivational forces to take into account in considering attitudes and behavior, but the same attitude can have a different motivational basis in different people.

3. Finally, recognition of the complex motivational sources of behavior can help to remedy the neglect in general theories which lack specification of conditions under which given types of attitude will change. Gestalt theory tells us, for example, that attitudes will change to give better cognitive organization to the psychological field. This theoretical generalization is suggestive, but to carry out significant research we need some middle-level concepts to bridge the gap between a high level of abstraction and particularistic or phenotypical events. We need concepts that will point toward the types of motive and methods of motive satisfaction which are operative in bringing about cognitive reorganization.

Before we attempt a detailed analysis of the four major functions which attitudes can serve, it is appropriate to consider the nature of attitudes, their dimensions, and their relations to other psychological structures and processes.

NATURE OF ATTITUDES: THEIR DIMENSIONS

Attitude is the predisposition of the individual to evaluate some symbol or object or aspect of his world in a favorable or unfavorable manner. Opinion is the verbal expression of an attitude, but attitudes can also be expressed in nonverbal behavior. Attitudes include both the affective, or feeling core of liking or disliking, and the cognitive, or belief, elements which describe the object of the attitude, its characteris-

[6] Irving Sarnoff and Daniel Katz, "The Motivational Bases of Attitude Change," *Journal of Abnormal and Social Psychology*, Vol. 49, 1954, pp. 115-124.

[7] M. Brewster Smith, Jerome S. Bruner, and Robert W. White, *Opinions and Personality*, New York, Wiley, 1956.

[8] Herbert H. Hyman and Paul B. Sheatsley, "The Authoritarian Personality: A Methodological Critique," in Richard Christie and Marie Jahoda, editors, *Studies in the Scope and Method of the Authoritarian Personality*, Glencoe, Ill., Free Press, 1954, pp. 50-122.

tics, and its relations to other objects. All attitudes thus include beliefs, but not all beliefs are attitudes. When specific attitudes are organized into a hierarchical structure, they comprise *value systems*. Thus a person may not only hold specific attitudes against deficit spending and unbalanced budgets but may also have a systematic organization of such beliefs and attitudes in the form of a value system of economic conservatism.

The dimensions of attitudes can be stated more precisely if the above distinctions between beliefs and feelings and attitudes and value systems are kept in mind. The *intensity* of an attitude refers to the strength of the *affective component*. In fact, rating scales and even Thurstone scales deal primarily with the intensity of feeling of the individual for or against some social object. The cognitive, or belief, component suggests two additional dimensions, the *specificity* or *generality* of the attitude and the *degree of differentiation* of the beliefs. Differentiation refers to the number of beliefs or cognitive items contained in the attitude, and the general assumption is that the simpler the attitude in cognitive structure the easier it is to change.[9] For simple structures there is no defense in depth, and once a single item of belief has been changed the attitude will change. A rather different dimension of attitude is the *number and strength of its linkages to a related value system*. If an attitude favoring budget balancing by the Federal government is tied in strongly with a value system of economic conservatism, it will be more difficult to change than if it were a fairly isolated attitude of the person. Finally, the relation of the value system to the personality is a consideration of first importance. If an attitude is tied to a value system which is closely related to, or which consists of, the individual's conception of himself, then the appropriate change procedures become more complex. The *centrality* of an attitude refers to its role as part of a value system which is closely related to the individual's self-concept.

An additional aspect of attitudes is not clearly described in most theories, namely, their relation to action or overt behavior. Though behavior related to the attitude has other determinants than the attitude itself, it is also true that some attitudes in themselves have more of what Cartwright calls an action struc-

ture than do others.[10] Brewster Smith refers to this dimension as policy orientation[11] and Katz and Stotland speak of it as the action component.[12] For example, while many people have attitudes of approval toward one or the other of the two political parties, these attitudes will differ in their structure with respect to relevant action. One man may be prepared to vote on election day and will know where and when he should vote and will go to the polls no matter what the weather or how great the inconvenience. Another man will only vote if a party worker calls for him in a car. Himmelstrand's work is concerned with all aspects of the relationship between attitude and behavior, but he deals with the action structure of the attitude itself by distinguishing between attitudes where the affect is tied to verbal expression and attitudes where the affect is tied to behavior concerned with more objective referents of the attitude.[13] In the first case an individual derives satisfaction from talking about a problem; in the second case he derives satisfaction from taking some form of concrete action.

Attempts to change attitudes can be directed primarily at the belief component or at the feeling, or affective, component. Rosenberg theorizes that an effective change in one component will result in changes in the other component and presents experimental evidence to confirm this hypothesis.[14] For example, a political candidate will often attempt to win people by making them like him and dislike his opponent, and thus communicate affect rather than ideas. If he is successful, people will not only like him but entertain favorable beliefs about him. Another candidate may deal primarily with ideas and hope that, if he can change people's beliefs about an issue, their feelings will also change.

10 Dorwin Cartwright, "Some Principles of Mass Persuasion," *Human Relations*, Vol. 2, 1949, pp. 253-267.

11 M. Brewster Smith, "The Personal Setting of Public Opinions: A Study of Attitudes toward Russia," *Public Opinion Quarterly*, Vol. 11, 1947, pp. 507-523.

12 Daniel Katz and Ezra Stotland, "A Preliminary Statement to a Theory of Attitude Structure and Change," in Sigmund Koch, editor, *Psychology: A Study of a Science*, Vol. 3, New York, McGraw-Hill, 1959, pp. 423-475.

13 Ulf Himmelstrand, "Verbal Attitudes and Behavior," *Public Opinion Quarterly*, Vol. 24, 1960, pp. 224-250.

14 Milton J. Rosenberg, "A Structural Theory of Attitude Dynamics," *Ibid.*, pp. 319-340.

9 David Krech and Richard S. Crutchfield, *Theory and Problems of Social Psychology*, New York, McGraw-Hill, 1948, pp. 160-163.

FOUR FUNCTIONS WHICH ATTITUDES PERFORM FOR THE INDIVIDUAL

The major functions which attitudes perform for the personality can be grouped according to their motivational basis as follows:

1. *The instrumental, adjustive, or utilitarian function* upon which Jeremy Bentham and the utilitarians constructed their model of man. A modern expression of this approach can be found in behavioristic learning theory.

2. *The ego-defensive function* in which the person protects himself from acknowledging the basic truths about himself or the harsh realities in his external world. Freudian psychology and neo-Freudian thinking have been preoccupied with this type of motivation and its outcomes.

3. *The value-expressive function* in which the individual derives satisfactions from expressing attitudes appropriate to his personal values and to his concept of himself. This function is central to doctrines of ego psychology which stress the importance of self-expression, self-development, and self-realization.

4. *The knowledge function* based upon the individual's need to give adequate structure to his universe. The search for meaning, the need to understand, the trend toward better organization of perceptions and beliefs to provide clarity and consistency for the individual, are other descriptions of this function. The development of principles about perceptual and cognitive structure have been the contribution of Gestalt psychology.

Stated simply, the functional approach is the attempt to understand the reasons people hold the attitudes they do. The reasons, however, are at the level of psychological motivations and not of the accidents of external events and circumstances. Unless we know the psychological need which is met by the holding of an attitude we are in a poor position to predict when and how it will change. Moreover, the same attitude expressed toward a political candidate may not perform the same function for all the people who express it. And while many attitudes are predominantly in the service of a single type of motivational process, as described above, other attitudes may serve more than one purpose for the individual. A fuller discussion of how attitudes serve the above four functions is in order.

1. The Adjustment Function

Essentially this function is a recognition of the fact that people strive to maximize the rewards in their external environment and to minimize the penalties. The child develops favorable attitudes toward the objects in his world which are associated with the satisfactions of his needs and unfavorable attitudes toward objects which thwart him or punish him. Attitudes acquired in the service of the adjustment function are either the means for reaching the desired goal or avoiding the undesirable one, or are affective associations based upon experiences in attaining motive satisfactions.[15] The attitudes of the worker favoring a political party which will advance his economic lot are an example of the first type of utilitarian attitude. The pleasant image one has of one's favorite food is an example of the second type of utilitarian attitude.

In general, then, the dynamics of attitude formation with respect to the adjustment function are dependent upon present or past perceptions of the utility of the attitudinal object for the individual. The clarity, consistency, and nearness of rewards and punishments, as they relate to the individual's activities and goals, are important factors in the acquisition of such attitudes. Both attitudes and habits are formed toward specific objects, people, and symbols as they satisfy specific needs. The closer these objects are to actual need satisfaction and the more they are clearly perceived as relevant to need satisfaction, the greater are the probabilities of positive attitude formation. These principles of attitude formation are often observed in the breach rather than the compliance. In industry, management frequently expects to create favorable attitudes toward job performance through programs for making the company more attractive to the worker, such as providing recreational facilities and fringe benefits. Such programs, however, are much more likely to produce favorable attitudes toward the company as a desirable place to work than toward performance on the job. The company benefits and advantages are applied across the board to all employees and are not specifically relevant to increased effort in task performance by the individual worker.

Consistency of reward and punishment also contributes to the clarity of the instrumental object for goal attainment. If a political party bestows recognition and favors on party workers in an unpredictable and inconsistent fashion, it will destroy the favorable evaluation of the im-

[15] Katz and Stotland, *op. cit.*, pp. 434-443.

portance of working hard for the party among those whose motivation is of the utilitarian sort. But, curiously, while consistency of reward needs to be observed, 100 per cent consistency is not as effective as a pattern which is usually consistent but in which there are some lapses. When animal or human subjects are invariably rewarded for a correct performance, they do not retain their learned responses as well as when the reward is sometimes skipped.[16]

2. The Ego-Defensive Function

People not only seek to make the most of their external world and what it offers, but they also expend a great deal of their energy on living with themselves. The mechanisms by which the individual protects his ego from his own unacceptable impulses and from the knowledge of threatening forces from without, and the methods by which he reduces his anxieties created by such problems, are known as mechanisms of ego defense. A more complete account of their origin and nature will be found in Sarnoff.[17] They include the devices by which the individual avoids facing either the inner reality of the kind of person he is, or the outer reality of the dangers the world holds for him. They stem basically from internal conflict with its resulting insecurities. In one sense the mechanisms of defense are adaptive in temporarily removing the sharp edges of conflict and in saving the individual from complete disaster. In another sense they are not adaptive in that they handicap the individual in his social adjustments and in obtaining the maximum satisfactions available to him from the world in which he lives. The worker who persistently quarrels with his boss and with his fellow workers, because he is acting out some of his own internal conflicts, may in this manner relieve himself of some of the emotional tensions which beset him. He is not, however, solving his problem of adjusting to his work situation and thus may deprive himself of advancement or even of steady employment.

Defense mechanisms, Miller and Swanson point out, may be classified into two families on the basis of the more or less primitive nature of the devices employed.[18] The first family,

more primitive in nature, are more socially handicapping and consist of denial and complete avoidance. The individual in such cases obliterates through withdrawal and denial the realities which confront him. The exaggerated case of such primitive mechanisms is the fantasy world of the paranoiac. The second type of defense is less handicapping and makes for distortion rather than denial. It includes rationalization, projection, and displacement.

Many of our attitudes have the function of defending our self-image. When we cannot admit to ourselves that we have deep feelings of inferiority we may project those feelings onto some convenient minority group and bolster our egos by attitudes of superiority toward this underprivileged group. The formation of such defensive attitudes differs in essential ways from the formation of attitudes which serve the adjustment function. They proceed from within the person, and the objects and situation to which they are attached are merely convenient outlets for their expression. Not all targets are equally satisfactory for a given defense mechanism, but the point is that the attitude is not created by the target but by the individual's emotional conflicts. And when no convenient target exists the individual will create one. Utilitarian attitudes, on the other hand, are formed with specific reference to the nature of the attitudinal object. They are thus appropriate to the nature of the social world to which they are geared. The high school student who values high grades because he wants to be admitted to a good college has a utilitarian attitude appropriate to the situation to which it is related.

All people employ defense mechanisms, but they differ with respect to the extent that they use them and some of their attitudes may be more defensive in function than others. It follows that the techniques and conditions for attitude change will not be the same for ego-defensive as for utilitarian attitudes.

Moreover, though people are ordinarily unaware of their defense mechanisms, especially at the time of employing them, they differ with respect to the amount of insight they may show at some later time about their use of defenses. In some cases they recognize that they have been protecting their egos without knowing the reason why. In other cases they may

[16] William O. Jenkins and Julian C. Stanley, "Partial Reinforcement: A Review and Critique," *Psychological Bulletin*, Vol. 47, 1950, pp. 193-234.
[17] Irving Sarnoff, "Psychoanalytic Theory and Social Attitudes," *Public Opinion Quarterly*, Vol. 24, 1960, pp. 251-279.
[18] Daniel R. Miller and Guy E. Swanson, *Inner*

Conflict and Defense, New York, Holt, 1960, pp. 194-288.

not even be aware of the devices they have been using to delude themselves.

3. The Value-Expressive Function

While many attitudes have the function of preventing the individual from revealing to himself and others his true nature, other attitudes have the function of giving positive expression to his central values and to the type of person he conceives himself to be. A man may consider himself to be an enlightened conservative or an internationalist or a liberal, and will hold attitudes which are the appropriate indication of his central values. Thus we need to take account of the fact that not all behavior has the negative function of reducing the tensions of biological drives or of internal conflicts. Satisfactions also accrue to the person from the expression of attitudes which reflect his cherished beliefs and his self-image. The reward to the person in these instances is not so much a matter of gaining social recognition or monetary rewards as of establishing his self-identity and confirming his notion of the sort of person he sees himself to be. The gratifications obtained from value expression may go beyond the confirmation of self-identity. Just as we find satisfaction in the exercise of our talents and abilities, so we find reward in the expression of any attributes associated with our egos.

Value-expressive attitudes not only give clarity to the self-image but also mold that self-image closer to the heart's desire. The teenager who by dress and speech establishes his identity as similar to his own peer group may appear to the outsider a weakling and a craven conformer. To himself he is asserting his independence of the adult world to which he has rendered childlike subservience and conformity all his life. Very early in the development of the personality the need for clarity of self-image is important—the need to know "who I am." Later it may be even more important to know that in some measure I am the type of person I want to be. Even as adults, however, the clarity and stability of the self-image is of primary significance. Just as the kind, considerate person will cover over his acts of selfishness, so too will the ruthless individualist become confused and embarrassed by his acts of sympathetic compassion. One reason it is difficult to change the character of the adult is that he is not comfortable with the new "me." Group support for such personality change is almost a necessity, as in Alcoholics Anonymous, so that the individual is aware of approval of his new self by people who are like him.

The socialization process during the formative years sets the basic outlines for the individual's self-concept. Parents constantly hold up before the child the model of the good character they want him to be. A good boy eats his spinach, does not hit girls, etc. The candy and the stick are less in evidence in training the child than the constant appeal to his notion of his own character. It is small wonder, then, that children reflect the acceptance of this model by inquiring about the characters of the actors in every drama, whether it be a television play, a political contest, or a war, wanting to know who are the "good guys" and who are the "bad guys." Even as adults we persist in labeling others in the terms of such character images. Joe McCarthy and his cause collapsed in fantastic fashion when the telecast of the Army hearings showed him in the role of the villain attacking the gentle, good man represented by Joseph Welch.

A related but somewhat different process from childhood socialization takes place when individuals enter a new group or organization. The individual will often take over and internalize the values of the group. What accounts, however, for the fact that sometimes this occurs and sometimes it does not? Four factors are probably operative, and some combination of them may be necessary for internalization. (1) The values of the new group may be highly consistent with existing values central to the personality. The girl who enters the nursing profession finds it congenial to consider herself a good nurse because of previous values of the importance of contributing to the welfare of others. (2) The new group may in its ideology have a clear model of what the good group member should be like and may persistently indoctrinate group members in these terms. One of the reasons for the code of conduct for members of the armed forces, devised after the revelations about the conduct of American prisoners in the Korean War, was to attempt to establish a model for what a good soldier does and does not do. (3) The activities of the group in moving toward its goal permit the individual genuine opportunity for participation. To become ego-involved so that he can internalize group values, the new member must find one of two conditions. The group activity open to him must tap his talents and abilities so that his chance to show what he is worth can be tied into the group effort. Or else the activities of the group must give him an active voice in group decisions. His particular talents and abilities may not be tapped but he does have the opportunity to enter into group decisions, and thus his need for self-determination is satisfied. He then identifies with the group in which such opportunities for ego-involvement are available. It is not necessary that opportunities for self-expression and self-determination be of great magnitude in an objective sense, so long as they are important for the psychological economy of the individuals themselves. (4) Finally, the individual may come to see himself as a group member if he can share in the rewards of group activity which includes his own efforts. The worker may not play much of a part in building a ship or make any decisions in the process of building it. Nevertheless, if he and his fellow workers are given a share in every boat they build and a return on the proceeds from the earnings of the ship, they may soon come to identify with the ship-building company and see themselves as builders of ships.

4. The Knowledge Function

Individuals not only acquire beliefs in the interest of satisfying various specific needs, they also seek knowledge to give meaning to what would otherwise be an unorganized chaotic universe. People need standards or frames of reference for understanding their world, and attitudes help to supply such standards. The problem of understanding, as John Dewey made clear years ago, is one "of introducing (1) *definiteness* and *distinction* and (2) *consistency* and *stability* of meaning into what is otherwise vague and wavering."[19] The definiteness and stability are provided in good measure by the norms of our culture, which give the otherwise perplexed individual ready-made attitudes for comprehending his universe. Walter Lippmann's classical contribution to the study of opinions and attitudes was his description of stereotypes and the way they provided order and clarity for a bewildering set of complexities.[20] The most interesting finding in Herzog's familiar study of the gratifications obtained by

housewives in listening to daytime serials was the unsuspected role of information and advice.[21] The stories were liked "because they explained things to the inarticulate listener."

The need to know does not of course imply that people are driven by a thirst for universal knowledge. The American public's appalling lack of political information has been documented many times. In 1956, for example, only 13 per cent of the people in Detroit could correctly name the two United States Senators from the state of Michigan and only 18 per cent knew the name of their own Congressman.[22] People are not avid seekers after knowledge as judged by what the educator or social reformer would desire. But they do want to understand the events which impinge directly on their own life. Moreover, many of the attitudes they have already acquired give them sufficient basis for interpreting much of what they perceive to be important for them. Our already existing stereotypes, in Lippmann's language, "are an ordered, more or less consistent picture of the world, to which our habits, our tastes, our capacities, our comforts and our hopes have adjusted themselves. They may not be a complete picture of the world, but they are a picture of a possible world to which we are adapted."[23] It follows that new information will not modify old attitudes unless there is some inadequacy or incompleteness or inconsistency in the existing attitudinal structure as it relates to the perceptions of new situations.

The articles by Cohen, Rosenberg, Osgood, and Zajonc[24] discuss the process of attitude change with respect to inconsistencies and discrepancies in cognitive structure.

DETERMINANTS OF ATTITUDE AROUSAL AND ATTITUDE CHANGE

The problems of attitude arousal and of attitude change are separate problems. The first has to do with the fact that the individual has many predispositions to act and many influences playing upon him. Hence we need a

---

[19] John Dewey, *How We Think,* New York: Macmillan, 1910.

[20] Walter Lippmann, *Public Opinion,* New York, Macmillan, 1922.

[21] Herta Herzog, "What Do We Really Know about Daytime Serial Listeners?" in Paul F. Lazarsfeld and Frank N. Stanton, editors, *Radio Research 1942-1943,* New York, Duell, Sloan & Pearce, 1944, pp. 3-33.

[22] From a study of the impact of party organization on political behavior in the Detroit area, by Daniel Katz and Samuel Eldersveld, in manuscript.

[23] Lippmann, *op. cit.,* p. 95.

[24] *Public Opinion Quarterly,* Vol. 24, 1960.

more precise description of the appropriate conditions which will evoke a given attitude. The second problem is that of specifying the factors which will help to predict the modification of different types of attitude.

The most general statement that can be made concerning attitude arousal is that it is dependent upon the excitation of some need in the individual, or some relevant cue in the environment. When a man grows hungry, he talks of food. Even when not hungry he may express favorable attitudes toward a preferred food if an external stimulus cues him. The ego-defensive person who hates foreigners will express such attitudes under conditions of increased anxiety or threat or when a foreigner is perceived to be getting out of place.

The most general statement that can be made about the conditions conducive to attitude change is that the expression of the old attitude or its anticipated expression no longer gives satisfaction to its related need state. In other words, it no longer serves its function and the individual feels blocked or frustrated. Modifying an old attitude or replacing it with a new one is a process of learning, and learning always starts with a problem, or being thwarted in coping with a situation. Being blocked is a necessary, but not a sufficient, condition for attitude change. Other factors must be operative and will vary in effectiveness depending upon the function involved.

GENERALIZATION OF ATTITUDE CHANGE

Perhaps the most fascinating problem in attitude change has to do with consequences to a person's belief systems and general behavior of changing a single attitude. Is the change confined to the single target of the attitude? Does it affect related beliefs and feelings? If so, what types of related belief and feeling are affected, i.e., on what does the change rub off? Teachers and parents, for example, are concerned when a child acquires an immoral attitude or indulges in a single dishonest act, for fear of the pernicious spread of undesirable behavior tendencies. Responsible citizens are concerned about the lawless actions of extremists in the South in combating integration, not only because of the immediate and specific implications of the behavior but because of the general threat to legal institutions.

Research evidence on the generalization of attitude change is meager. In experimental work, the manipulations to produce change are weak and last for brief periods, sometimes minutes and at the most several hours. It is not surprising, therefore, that these studies report few cases of change which has generalized to attitudes other than the one under attack. Even in the studies on self-insight by Katz et al., where the change in prejudice toward Negroes was still in evidence some two months after the experiment, there were no consistent changes in prejudice toward other minority groups.[25] In real-life situations outside the laboratory, more powerful forces are often brought to bear to modify behavior, but again the resulting changes seem more limited than one would expect on an a priori logical basis. Integration of whites and Negroes in the factory may produce acceptance of Negroes as fellow workers but not as residents in one's neighborhood, or as friends in one's social group. Significant numbers of Democrats were influenced by the candidacy of Dwight Eisenhower to help elect him President in 1952 and 1956, but, as Campbell *et al.* have established, this change in voting behavior did not rub off on the rest of the Republican ticket.[26] Most of the Democratic defectors at the presidential level voted for a Democratic Congress. Nor did they change their attitudes on political issues. And the chances are that this change will not generalize to other Republican presidential candidates who lack Eisenhower's status as a national figure.

It is puzzling that attitude change seems to have slight generalization effects, when the evidence indicates considerable generalization in the organization of a person's beliefs and values. Studies of authoritarian and equalitarian trends in personality do find consistent constellations of attitudes. It is true that the correlations are not always high, and Prothro reports that, among his Southern subjects, there was only a slight relationship between anti-Semitism and Negro prejudice.[27] But studies of the generalization hypothesis in attitude structure give positive findings. Grace confirmed his prediction that the attitudes people displayed in interpersonal relations toward their friends and colleagues carried over

25 Stotland and Katz, *op. cit.*
26 Campbell, Converse, Miller, and Stokes, *op. cit.*
27 E. Terry Prothro, "Ethnocentrism and Anti-Negro Attitudes in the Deep South," *Journal of Abnormal and Social Psychology*, Vol. 47, 1952, pp. 105-108.

to their attitudes toward international matters.[28] He studied four types of reaction: verbal hostility, direct hostility, intropunitiveness, and apathy. People characteristically giving one type of response in everyday situations would tend to respond similarly in professional and international situations. Stagner concluded on the basis of his empirical investigation of attitudes toward colleagues and outgroups that the evidence supported a generalization theory rather than a displacement or sublimation theory.[29] Confirmation of the generalization hypothesis comes from a Norwegian study by Christiansen in which reactions were classified on two dimensions: (1) threat-oriented versus problem-oriented and (2) outward-directed versus inward-directed. Thus, blaming oneself would be a threat-oriented, inwardly directed reaction. Christiansen found that (a) people tend to react consistently toward everyday conflict situations, (b) they react consistently to international conflicts, (c) there is a correlation between reactions to everyday conflicts and to international conflicts, and (d) this correlation is lower than the correlations among reactions to everyday conflicts and among reactions to international conflicts, respectively.[30]

Three reasons can be suggested for the failure to find greater generalization effects in attitude change:

1. The over-all organization of attitudes and values in the personality is highly differentiated. The many dimensions allow the individual to absorb change without major modification of his attitudes. A Democrat of long standing could vote for Eisenhower and still remain Democratic in his identification because to him politics was not involved in this decision. Eisenhower stood above the political arena in the minds of many people. He was not blamed for what his party did, as the Gallup polls indicate, nor did his popularity rub off on his party. In 1958, in spite of Eisenhower's urgings, the people returned a sizable Democratic majority to Congress. There are many standards of judgment, then, which pertain to content areas of belief and attitude. An individual uses one set of standards or dimensions for a political decision but will shift to another set when it is more appropriate.

2. The generalization of attitudes proceeds along lines of the individual's own psychological groupings more than along lines of conventional sociological categories. We may miss significant generalized change because we do not look at the individual's own pattern of beliefs and values. One man may dislike foreigners, but to him foreigners are those people whose English he cannot understand; to another person foreigners are people of certain physical characteristics; to a third they are people with different customs, etc.

People will utilize many principles in organizing their own groupings of attitudes: (a) the objective similarities of the referents of the attitudes, (b) their own limited experiences with these referents, (c) their own needs, and (d) their own ideas of causation and of the nature of proper relationships. Peak has used the concept of psychological distance and difference between events in psychological space to describe attitude structure and generalization.[31]

The liberal-conservative dimension, for example, may be useful for characterizing large groups of people, but individuals may differ considerably in their own scaling of attitudes comprising liberalism-conservatism. Some conservatives can stand to the left of center on issues of the legal rights of the individual or on internationalism. Social classes show differences in liberal and conservative ideology, the lower socio-economic groups being more liberal on economic and political issues and the upper income groups more liberal on tolerance for deviants and on democratic values in interpersonal relationships. Stouffer found that during the McCarthy period the low-status groups were more intolerant, and other studies have shown more authoritarian values among these groups.[32]

3. Generalization of attitude change is limited by the lack of systematic forces in the social environment to implement that change.

28 H. A. Grace, *A Study of the Expression of Hostility in Everyday Professional and International Verbal Situations*, New York, Columbia University Press, 1949.

29 Ross Stagner, "Studies of Aggressive Social Attitudes," *Journal of Social Psychology*, Vol. 20, 1944, pp. 109-120.

30 Bjorn Christiansen, *Attitudes towards Foreign Affairs as a Function of Personality*, Oslo, Norway, Oslo University Press, 1959.

31 Helen Peak, "Psychological Structure and Person Perception," in Renato Tagiuri and Luigi Petrullo, editors, *Person Perception and Interpersonal Behavior*, Stanford, Calif., Stanford University Press, 1958, pp. 337-352.

32 Samuel A. Stouffer, *Communism, Conformity and Civil Liberties*, New York, Doubleday, 1955.

Even when people are prepared to modify their behavior to a considerable extent they find themselves in situations which exert pressures to maintain old attitudes and habits. The discharged convict who is ready to change his ways may find it difficult to find a decent job and his only friends may be his former criminal associates. It does not necessarily help an industrial firm to train its foremen in human relations if the foremen must perform in an authoritarian structure.

ASSESSMENT OF MOTIVATIONAL BASES OF ATTITUDES

If an understanding of the nature of attitudes and the conditions for their change depends upon a knowledge of their functional bases, then it becomes of first importance to identify the underlying motivational patterns. The traditional advertising approach is to give less attention to the research assessment of needs and motives and more attention to multiple appeals, to gaining public attention, and to plugging what seems to work. Multiple appeals will, it is hoped, reach some members of the public with an effective message. In political campaigns, there is more concern with gearing the approach to the appropriate audience. If the political party makes serious mistakes in its assessment of the needs of particular groups, it is not a matter of losing a few potential customers but of losing votes to the opposing party, and so losing the election. Political leaders are, therefore, making more and more use of public opinion polls and a number of the major candidates for high office enlist their own research specialists. So true is this that we may no longer have political conventions naming a dark-horse candidate for the presidency. If the leaders are not convinced by poll results that a candidate has a good chance to win, they are not likely to support him.

There are no reliable short-cuts to the assessments of the needs which various attitudes satisfy. Systematic sampling of the population in question by means of interviews or of behavioral observation is a necessity. A growing number of devices are becoming available to supplement the depth interview. Objective scales for determining personality trends, such as the F-scale or the Minnesota Multiphasic Inventory, have been widely used. Projective methods which call for the completion of sentences and stories or furnishing stories about ambiguous pictures are just beginning to be exploited. In a nationwide survey of attitudes toward public health, Veroff et al. successfully used a picture test to obtain scores for people with respect to their needs for achievement, for affiliation, and for power.[33] Methods for measuring motivation are difficult, but the basic logic in their application is essentially that of any research tool. If early abuses of these instruments do not prejudice the research field, they will in the future have almost as wide a use as the polls themselves. Moreover, polling methods can be adapted to measuring people's needs with indirect questions which have been validated against more projective tests.

In many situations inferences can be made about people's needs without elaborate measures. If farm income has fallen drastically in a given section of the country, or if unemployment has risen sharply in a certain city, obvious inferences can be drawn. The extent and depth of the dissatisfaction will be better known through adequate measurement.

Measures of the four types of motivational patterns discussed indicate wide individual differences in the extent to which the patterns characterize the person. Though all people employ defense mechanisms, there are wide differences in the depth and extent of defensiveness. And Cohen has shown that the need for knowledge varies even in a college population.[34]

In spite of characteristic differences in the strength of needs and motives, we cannot predict attitude change with precision solely on the basis of measures of need. We must also have measures of the related attitudes. Knowledge of the need state indicates the type of goal toward which the individual is striving. But the means for reaching this goal may vary considerably, and for this reason we need to know the attitudes which reflect the evaluation of the various means. Farmers with depressed incomes may still vote for the Republican Party if they have confidence in Nixon's farm program. Some need patterns furnish more di-

33 Joseph Veroff, John W. Atkinson, Sheila C. Feld, and Gerald Gurin, "The Use of Thematic Apperception to Assess Motivation in a Nationwide Interview Study," *Psychological Monographs*, in press.
34 Arthur R. Cohen, "Need for Cognition and Order of Communication as Determinants of Opinion Change," in Carl Hovland et al., editors, *The Order of Presentation in Persuasion*, New Haven, Conn., Yale University Press, 1957, pp. 79-97.

rect predictions than others. The defensive person who is extrapunitive will be high in prejudice toward outgroups. Even in this case, however, his prejudices toward specific outgroups may vary considerably.

SUMMARY

The purpose of this paper was to provide a psychological framework for the systematic consideration of the dynamics of public and private attitudes. Four functions which attitudes perform for the personality were identified: the *adjustive function* of satisfying utilitarian needs, the *ego-defensive function* of handling internal conflicts, the *value-expressive function* of maintaining self-identity and of enhancing the self-image, and the *knowledge function* of giving understanding and meaning to the ambiguities of the world about us. The role of these functions in attitude formation was described.

50. *Compliance, Identification, and Internalization: Three Processes of Attitude Change*

HERBERT C. KELMAN

A crucial issue in communication research relates to the *nature* of changes (if any) that are brought about by a particular communication or type of communication. It is not enough to know that there has been some measurable change in attitude; usually we would also want to know what kind of change it is. Is it a superficial change, on a verbal level, which disappears after a short lapse of time? Or is it a more lasting change in attitude and belief, which manifests itself in a wide range of situations and which is integrated into the person's value system? Or, to put it in other terms, did the communication produce public conformity *without* private acceptance, or did it produce public conformity coupled with private acceptance? (Cf. 1, 4.) Only if we know something about the nature and depth of changes can we make meaningful predictions about the way in which attitude changes will be reflected in subsequent actions and reactions to events.

These questions about the nature of attitude changes are highly significant in the study of international attitudes. For example, we may have observed changes in opinion toward certain international issues—e.g., aspects of foreign policy, international organization, or disarmament—among the population of a given country. The implications that we draw from these changes will depend on their depth and

• Reprinted from *Journal of Conflict Resolution*, 1958, **2**, 51-60, with permission of the author and the publisher. The experiment reported here was conducted while the author was at Johns Hopkins University as a Public Health Service Research Fellow of the National Institute of Mental Health. Additional financial support was received from the Yale Communication Research Program, which is under the direction of Carl I. Hovland and which is operating under a grant from the Rockefeller Foundation.

on the psychological meanings that can be assigned to them. Let us assume that we find an increase in favorable attitudes toward the United Nations among the population of the United States at a particular juncture. This change in attitude may be due primarily to recent pronouncements by high-placed figures and may thus represent an aspect of "social conformity." On the other hand, the change may result from a series of international events which have led large segments of the population to re-evaluate American foreign policy and to ascribe a more central role to the UN. Depending on which of these *motivational processes* underlies the change in attitude, we would make different predictions about the manifestations and consequences of the new attitudes: about their durability, about the number of different attitudinal areas that will be affected by them, and about the ways in which they will be translated into action and will determine reactions to international events. Similarly, our predictions about the subsequent history of the new attitudes will depend on their *cognitive links,* i.e., the particular attitude structure within which the new attitude toward the UN is imbedded. For example, Americans may have become more favorable toward the UN because an important resolution sponsored by the United States delegate has been accepted. The new attitude toward the UN is thus an aspect of attitudes toward one's own nation and its prestige and international success. On the other hand, favorableness toward the UN may have increased because UN action has successfully averted war in a very tense conflict situation. In this case, the new attitude toward the UN is imbedded in an attitude structure revolving around the whole question of war and effective means of preventing its outbreak. Again, we would draw different implications from the changed attitudes, depending on which of these attitude areas was primarily involved in the occurrence of change.

The same considerations apply when we interpret the effects of international communications. For example, if we find changes in the way in which nationals of different countries perceive one another, it would be important to know at what level these changes have occurred and to what motivational and cognitive systems they are linked. These questions are important not only for the analysis of changes in attitude toward various international issues, objects, or events which may have occurred as a result of various kinds of communication or experience but also for the development of propositions about the conditions for change. In international relations, as in other areas of social behavior, one of our ultimate concerns is the exploration of the conditions under which lasting changes occur, changes which are generalized to many situations and which represent some degree of value reorganization.

In the present paper I should like to describe briefly an experimental study which is concerned with some of the conditions that determine the nature of attitude changes produced by communications on social issues. The specific content of the attitudes that were investigated in this study was in the area of race relations rather than international relations. The hypotheses refer, however, to general processes of attitude change, irrespective of the specific attitudinal area. Relationships found should be equally applicable, therefore, to the analysis of international attitudes.

THEORETICAL FRAMEWORK

The experiment reported here grows out of a broader theoretical framework concerned with the analysis of different processes of attitude change resulting from social influence. It is impossible to present this framework in detail in the present paper, but I should like to outline its main features.[1]

The starting point of the theoretical analysis is the observation discussed in the preceding paragraphs, i.e., that changes in attitudes and actions produced by social influence may occur at different "levels." It is proposed that these differences in the nature or level of changes that take place correspond to differences in the *process* whereby the individual accepts influence (or "conforms"). In other words, the underlying processes in which an individual engages when he adopts induced behavior may be different, even though the resulting overt behavior may appear the same.

Three different processes of influence can be distinguished: compliance, identification, and internalization.[2]

Compliance can be said to occur when an individual accepts influence because he hopes to achieve a favorable reaction from another person or group. He adopts the induced behavior not because he believes in its content but because he expects to gain specific rewards or approval and avoid specific punishments or disapproval by conforming. Thus the satisfaction derived from compliance is due to the *social effect* of accepting influence.

Identification can be said to occur when an individual accepts influence because he wants to establish or maintain a satisfying self-defining relationship to another person or a group. This relationship may take the form of classical identification, in which the individual takes over the role of the other, or it may take the form of a reciprocal role relationship. The individual actually believes in the responses which he adopts through identification, but their specific content is more or less irrelevant. He adopts the induced behavior because it is associated with the desired relationship. Thus the satisfaction derived from identification is due to the *act* of conforming as such.

Internalization can be said to occur when an individual accepts influence because the content of the induced behavior—the ideas and actions of which it is composed—is intrinsically rewarding. He adopts the induced behavior because it is congruent with his value system. He may consider it useful for the solution of a problem or find it congenial to his needs. Behavior adopted in this fashion tends to be integrated with the individual's existing values. Thus the satisfaction derived from internalization is due to the *content* of the new behavior.

The three processes represent three qualitatively different ways of accepting influence. A systematic treatment of the processes might,

[1] A detailed description of the theoretical framework and of the experiment reported here will be published elsewhere (5).

[2] A similar distinction, between four processes of conformity, was recently presented by Marie Jahoda (3).

therefore, begin with an analysis of the determinants of influence in general. These determinants can be summarized by the following proposition: The probability of accepting influence is a combined function of (*a*) the relative importance of the anticipated effect, (*b*) the relative power of the influencing agent, and (*c*) the prepotency of the induced response. A variety of experimental findings can be cited in support of this proposition.

Compliance, identification, and internalization can each be represented as a function of these three determinants. For each process, however, these determinants take a qualitatively different form. Thus the determinants of the three processes can be distinguished from one another in terms of the *nature* of the anticipated effect, the *source* of the influencing agent's power, and the *manner* in which the induced response has become prepotent.

In other words, each process is characterized by a distinctive set of *antecedent* conditions, involving a particular qualitative variation of a more general set of determinants. Given the proper set of antecedents, then, influence will take the form of compliance, identification, or internalization, respectively. Each of these corresponds to a characteristic pattern of internal responses (thoughts and feelings) in which the individual engages while adopting the induced behavior.

Similarly, each process is characterized by a distinctive set of *consequent* conditions, involving a particular qualitative variation in the subsequent history of the induced response. Responses adopted through different processes will be performed under different conditions, will be changed and extinguished under different conditions, and will have different properties.

Since each of the three processes mediates between a distinct set of antecedents and a distinct set of consequents, the proposed distinctions between the three processes can be tested by experiments which attempt to relate the antecedents postulated for a given process to the consequents postulated for that process. The present experiment was designed to vary one of the antecedents—the source of the influencing agent's power—and to observe the effects of this variation on one of the consequents—the conditions of performance of the induced response.

Power is defined as the extent to which the influencing agent is perceived as instrumental to the achievement of the subject's goals. The sources of the agent's power may vary (cf. 2). The following hypotheses are offered regarding the variations in source of power:

1. To the extent to which the power of the influencing agent is based on means-control, conformity will tend to take the form of compliance.
2. To the extent to which the power of the influencing agent is based on attractiveness, conformity will tend to take the form of identification.
3. To the extent to which the power of the influencing agent is based on credibility, conformity will tend to take the form of internalization.

Now let us look at the consequent side. One of the ways in which behaviors adopted through different processes can be distinguished is in terms of the conditions under which the behavior is performed. The following hypotheses are offered regarding the conditions of performance:

1. When an individual adopts an induced response through compliance, he tends to perform it only under conditions of surveillance by the influencing agent.
2. When an individual adopts an induced response through identification, he tends to perform it only under conditions of salience of his relationship to the agent.
3. When an individual adopts an induced response through internalization, he tends to perform it under conditions of relevance of the issue, regardless of surveillance or salience.

PROCEDURE

The subjects in this experiment were Negro college Freshmen in a border state. The experiment was conducted in the spring of 1954, just prior to the announcement of the Supreme Court decision on desegregation in the public schools. The social influence situation to which the students were exposed consisted of a fixed communication designed to change their attitudes on an issue related to the impending Court decision. Specifically, each of the communications employed in the study presented essentially the following message: If the Supreme Court rules that segregation is unconstitutional, it would still be desirable to maintain some of the *private* Negro colleges as all-Negro institutions, in order to preserve Negro culture, history, and tradition. Preliminary testing indicated that a large majority of the subjects would initially oppose the message presented in the communication.

The communications were tape-recorded interviews between a moderator and a guest (the communicator). They were presented to the subjects as recordings of radio programs which we were interested in evaluating. By varying the nature of these communications, it was possible to manipulate experimentally the source and degree of the communicator's power, while keeping the message of the communication constant. Four different communications were used, as can be seen from Table 1, which outlines the basic design of the experiment (see left-hand column).

In one communication the attempt was made to present the communicator in such a way that he would be perceived as possessing high means-control. He was introduced as the president of the National Foundation for Negro Colleges. In the course of the interview it became evident that his foundation had been supporting the college in which the study was being conducted; that he had almost complete control over the funds expended by the foundation; and that he was the kind of person who would not hesitate to use his control in order to achieve conformity. He made it clear that he would withdraw foundation grants from any college in which the students took a position on the issue in question which was at variance with his own position.

In the second communication the communicator was presented in such a way that he would be perceived as possessing high attractiveness. He was introduced as a Senior and president of the student council in a leading Negro university. He was also chairman of his university's chapter of an organization called Student Poll, which recently did a study on the attitudes of Negro college Seniors on issues relating to the Supreme Court decision. He presented the same message as the first communicator, but he made it clear that he was presenting not simply his own opinions but the overwhelming consensus of opinion of the college students represented in the polls. He was portrayed as a representative of one of the subjects' reference groups and as a person who was in a position to supply valid information on the group norms.

In the third communication the communicator was presented in such a way that he would be perceived as possessing high credibility. He was introduced as a professor of history in one of the country's leading universities. In the course of the interview, it became evident that he was one of the top experts on the history and problems of minority groups; that he was highly respected both by his colleagues and by members of minority groups; and that he had a profound concern for the welfare of the American Negro community. He presented the same position as the other speakers, but he made it clear that this position was based on his research and on the evidence of history.

For purposes of comparison, a fourth communication was used in which the communi-

TABLE 1. *Design of the Experiment and Predictions**

Experimental groups: Variations in Communicator Power	Questionnaires: Variations in Conditions of Performance		
	Questionnaire I Surveillance Salience Issue-Relevance	Questionnaire II Non-surveillance Salience Issue-Relevance	Questionnaire III Non-surveillance Non-salience Issue-Relevance
High power, based on means-control	H	L	L
High power, based on attractiveness	H	H	L
High power, based on credibility	H	H	H
Low-power	L	L	L

* H = high probability that attitude will be expressed; L = low probability that attitude will be expressed.

cator was presented in such a way that he would be perceived as possessing low power, that is, as being low in means-control, attractiveness, *and* credibility. He was introduced as an "ordinary citizen," who had no control over the subjects and no special knowledge about the topic. His attractiveness and credibility were further undermined by the fact that he was portrayed as a white man with a southern accent, who had recently come from Mississippi and who did not clearly dissociate himself from a pro-segregation point of view.

Each of the four communications was presented to a different experimental group. There was also a control group, which was not exposed to any communication at all. This group provided a base line for postcommunication attitudes, since we did not obtain before-scores from the experimental subjects.

After exposure to the communication, the subjects in each experimental group filled out attitude questionnaires, designed to measure the extent of their agreement with the communicator. The questionnaire consisted of eighteen statements which were directly or indirectly related to the central message of the communication. Subjects were asked to respond to each item on a six-point scale. Scores for each item ranged from 1 for extreme disagreement with the communicator's position to 7 for extreme agreement (the score of 4 was not used, since the scale did not contain a neutral position). A total score for each subject was computed by adding up the individual scores on the 18 items. Thus the range of possible total scores was from 18 (complete disagreement) to 126 (complete agreement).

To vary the conditions of performance, we presented these eighteen statements to each subject on three separate questionnaires. As can be seen from Table 1, it is assumed that issue-relevance was present on all three questionnaires, since the attitude items dealt with the issues involved in the communication. The questionnaires differed, however, with respect to surveillance and salience.

Questionnaire I was completed under conditions of salience and surveillance. In order to maximize the salience of the communicator and the communication, the questionnaire was administered immediately after the communication. In order to maximize surveillance by the communicator, it was made clear—both by the appearance of the questionnaire and by the instructions—that this questionnaire was being administered at the communicator's request and that he would see each subject's answers. Moreover, the subjects were asked to sign their names and to give other identifying information.

Questionnaire II was completed under conditions of salience and non-surveillance. In order to maximize salience, the questionnaire was administered immediately after Questionnaire I, so that the relationship between the questionnaire and the communication was still clearly apparent. In order to minimize surveillance, Questionnaire II was anonymous, and it was made clear to the subjects that their responses would not be seen by the communicator or by anyone other than the research staff.

Questionnaire III was completed under conditions of non-salience and non-surveillance. In order to minimize the salience of the communicator and the communication, the questionnaire was administered from one to two weeks after the communication session, in a different place, under different auspices, and by a different experimenter. The questions were imbedded in a large number of other attitudinal items; and no mention of the communication was made. In order to minimize surveillance, Questionnaire III was anonymous and was in no way tied in to the communication.

HYPOTHESES

The specific hypotheses that were tested were as follows:

1. Attitudes adopted from a communicator whose power is based on means-control will tend to be expressed only under conditions of surveillance by the communicator. The mediating process postulated here is compliance.

The specific prediction can be noted in Table 1. In the means-control group there will be a greater amount of acceptance of the communicator's position on Questionnaire I than on Questionnaires II and III, since Questionnaire I is the only one completed under conditions of surveillance. There should be no significant difference between Questionnaires II and III.

2. Attitudes adopted from a communicator whose power is based on attractiveness will tend to be expressed only under conditions of salience of the subject's relationship to the

communicator. The mediating process postulated here is identification.

Specifically, it is predicted that in the attractiveness group there will be a smaller amount of acceptance of the communicator's position on Questionnaire III than on Questionnaires I and II, since Questionnaire III is the only one completed under conditions of non-salience. There should be no significant difference between Questionnaires I and II.

3. Attitudes adopted from a communicator whose power is based on credibility will tend to be expressed under conditions of relevance of the issue, regardless of surveillance or salience. The mediating process postulated here is internalization.

The specific prediction for the credibility group is that there will be no significant differences between the three questionnaires, since they were all completed under conditions of issue-relevance.

RESULTS

Before proceeding to examine the data which bear directly on the hypotheses, it was necessary to check on the success of the experimental variations. Did the subjects really perceive each of the variations in communicator power in the way in which we intended it? To provide an answer to this question, Questionnaire II included a series of statements about the speaker and the communication to which the subjects were asked to react. An analysis of these data indicated that, by and large, the experimental manipulations succeeded in producing the conditions they were intended to produce, thus making possible an adequate test of the hypotheses.

The findings which are directly relevant to the hypotheses are summarized in Tables 2 and 3. Table 2 presents the mean attitude scores for the four experimental groups on each of the three questionnaires. All subjects who had completed the three questionnaires were used in this analysis.

It can be seen from the summary of the significance tests that all the experimental predictions were confirmed. In the means-control group, the mean score on Questionnaire I is significantly higher than the mean scores on Questionnaires II and III; and there is no significant difference between the scores on Questionnaires II and III. In the attractiveness

TABLE 2. *Effects of Variations in Communicator Power on Acceptance of Induced Attitudes under Three Conditions of Measurement*

Groups	N	Mean Attitude Scores		
		Questionnaire I	Questionnaire II	Questionnaire III
Means-control (compliance)	55	63.98	60.65	58.04
Attractiveness (identification)	48	56.81	55.94	49.67
Credibility (internalization)	51	59.51	56.39	56.10
Low power	43	49.33	50.58	53.35

Summary of Significance Tests

	Sources of Variation	F	p
Means-control	(1) Between questionnaires	3.6	<0.05
	(2) I versus II and III	5.8	<0.05
	(3) II versus III	1.4	n.s.
Attractiveness	(1) Between questionnaires	7.2	<0.01
	(2) I and II versus III	14.2	<0.01
	(3) I versus II	0.2	n.s.
Credibility	Between questionnaires	2.3	n.s.
Low power	Between questionnaires	2.0	n.s.

group, the mean score on Questionnaire III is significantly lower than the mean scores on Questionnaires I and II; and there is no significant difference between the scores on Questionnaires I and II. In the credibility group, there are no significant differences beween the three questionnaires.

While these results are all in line with the hypotheses, examination of the means in Table 2 reveals that the findings are not so clear-cut as they might be. Specifically, we should expect a relatively large drop in mean score for the means-control group from Questionnaire I to Questionnaire II. In actual fact, however, the drop is only slightly higher than that for the credibility group. This might be due to the fact that the analysis is based on *all* subjects, including those who were not influenced by the communication at all. The hypotheses, however, refer only to changes from questionnaire to questionnaire for those people who *were* initially influenced.

It was not possible to identify the subjects who were initially influenced, since there were no before-scores available for the experimental groups. It was possible, however, to approximate these conditions by using only those subjects who had a score of 60 or above on Questionnaire I. If we make certain limited assumptions (which I cannot spell out in this brief report), it can be shown that the use of a cutoff point of 60 "purifies" the experimental groups to some degree. That is, the subsamples selected by this criterion should have a higher ratio of influenced to uninfluenced subjects than the total groups from which they were selected. It was anticipated that an analysis based on these subsamples would provide a better test of the hypotheses and would yield more clear-cut results. This did, in fact, happen, as can be seen from Table 3.

Table 3 presents the mean attitude scores for the three high-power groups, using only those subjects who had scores of 60 or above on Questionnaire I. Examination of the means reveals a pattern completely consistent with the hypotheses. In the means-control group, agreement with the communicator is relatively high on Questionnaire I and declines on Questionnaires II and III. In the attractiveness group, agreement is high on Questionnaires I and II and declines on Questionnaire III. In the credibility group, changes from questionnaire to questionnaire are minimal.

TABLE 3. Effects of Variations in Communicator Power on Acceptance of Induced Attitudes under Three Conditions of Measurement*

		Mean Attitude Scores		
Groups	N	Questionnaires I	Questionnaires II	Questionnaires III
Means-control (compliance)	30	78.20	70.76	67.56
Attractiveness (identification)	23	71.30	69.57	59.70
Credibility (internalization)	26	73.35	71.04	69.27

Summary of Significance Tests

	Sources of Variation	F	p
Means-control	(1) Between questionnaires	5.2	<0.01
	(2) I versus II and III	9.4	<0.01
	(3) II versus III	0.9	n.s.
Attractiveness	(1) Between questionnaires	14.5	<0.01
	(2) I and II versus III	28.4	<0.01
	(3) I versus II	0.6	n.s.
Credibility	Between questionnaires	1.1	n.s.

* Data based on a selected sample, containing a higher proportion of influenced subjects. Criterion for selection was a score of 60 or above on Questionnaire I.

Analyses of variance clearly confirmed all the experimental predictions.

CONCLUSIONS

It would be premature to accept the hypotheses tested in this experiment as general principles that have been proved. The experiment does, however, lend considerable support to them. To the extent to which the hypotheses were substantiated, the experiment also gives support to the theoretical framework from which these hypotheses were derived. The mediating concepts of compliance, identification, and internalization seem to provide a unified and meaningful way of organizing the present experimental findings and of relating them to a more general conceptual framework.

The framework presented here can be applied directly to the analysis of the effects of various communications and other forms of social influence on attitudes and actions in the international sphere. In the study of public opinion, for example, it should help us identify some of the conditions which are likely to produce one or another of these processes and predict the subsequent histories and action implications of attitudes adopted under these sets of conditions. This framework may also be helpful in the study of the social influences which affect decision-making processes and negotiations on the part of various elites.

Some of the concepts presented here might be useful not only for the study of change but also for the analysis of existing attitudes and their motivational bases. Let us take, for example, people's attitudes toward their own country's system of government. Even if we look only at those individuals who have favorable attitudes, various distinctions suggest themselves. For some individuals, acceptance of their system of government may be based largely on compliance: they may go along with the accepted norms in order to avoid social ostracism or perhaps even persecution. For others, attitudes toward their government may be largely identification-based: their relationship to their own nation and its major institutions may represent an essential aspect of their identity, and acceptance of certain political attitudes and beliefs may serve to maintain this relationship and their self-definition which is anchored in it. For a third group of individuals, belief in the country's system of government may be internalized: they may see this political form as fully congruent and integrated with their value systems and likely to lead to a maximization of their own values. Our evaluation of the meaning of "favorable attitudes" on the part of a particular individual or group or subpopulation and our prediction of the consequences of these attitudes would certainly vary with the motivational processes that underlie them. The conditions under which these attitudes are likely to be changed, the kinds of actions to which they are likely to lead, and the ways in which they are likely to affect reactions to particular events will be different, depending on whether these attitudes are based on compliance, identification, or internalization.

REFERENCES

1. Festinger, L. "An Analysis of Compliant Behavior." In M. Sherif and M. O. Wilson (eds.), *Group Relations at the Crossroads*. New York: Harper & Bros., 1953.
2. French, J. R. P., Jr. "A Formal Theory of Social Power," *Psychological Review*, LXIII (1956), 181-194.
3. Jahoda, Marie. "Psychological Issues in Civil Liberties," *American Psychologist*, XI (1956), 234-240.
4. Kelman, H. C. "Attitude Change as a Function of Response Restriction," *Human Relations*, VI (1953), 185-214.
5. Kelman, H. C. *Social Influence and Personal Belief: A Theoretical and Experimental Approach to the Study of Behavior Change* (to be published).

51. Attitude and the Prediction of Behavior

MARTIN FISHBEIN

Throughout this book, relatively little has been said about the relations between attitude and behavior. To a large extent, this omission reflects the present state of the field. After more than seventy-five years of attitude research, there is still little, if any, consistent evidence supporting the hypothesis that knowledge of an individual's attitude toward some object will allow one to predict the way he will behave with respect to the object. Indeed, what little evidence there is to support any relationship between attitude and behavior comes from studies showing that a person tends to bring his attitude into line with his behavior rather than from studies demonstrating that behavior is a function of attitude (e.g., Cohen, 1960; Gerard, 1965; Landy, 1966).

It is my contention that we psychologists have been rather naïve in our attempts to understand and to investigate the relationships between attitude and behavior. More often than not, we have attempted to predict some behavior from some measure of attitude and found little or no relationship between these variables. Yet, rather than questioning our basic assumption that there is a strong relationship between attitude and behavior, we have tended to blame our failures on our measuring instruments, on our definition of attitude, or on both. Thus, from its relatively simple beginning as a unidimensional concept that referred to the amount of affect for or against some psychological object, the concept of attitude has grown into a complex, multidimensional concept consisting of affective, cognitive, and conative components.

While this view has done a great deal to stimulate new types of research and, more spe-

• Revised and expanded for this book from "The Relationships between Beliefs, Attitudes, and Behavior," in S. Feldman (Ed.), *Cognitive Consistency: Motivational Antecedents and Behavioral Consequents*, Academic Press, New York, 1966, with permission of the publisher.

cifically, to improve our understanding of the relationship between belief and attitude (i.e., between cognition and affect), and while it has recently led to investigations of the relationships between attitude and behavioral intentions (i.e., between affect and conation), it has not, to the best of my knowledge, contributed very much to our understanding of the specific relationships between attitude and behavior.

THE CONCEPT OF ATTITUDE

Before turning to a consideration of these relationships, however, let us first briefly review the concept of attitude. Perhaps the best way to begin is to provide a brief (and admittedly selective) historical sketch. In 1935, Gordon Allport reviewed the general area of attitude theory and research. After considering more than one hundred different definitions of attitude, Allport concluded that most investigators basically agreed that an attitude is a learned predisposition to respond to an object or class of objects in a consistently favorable or unfavorable way. Furthermore, he pointed out that this bipolarity in the direction of an attitude (i.e., the favorable versus the unfavorable) is often regarded as the most distinctive feature of the concept. Thus attitude was conceptualized as a simple unidimensional concept.

However, as Allport noted, research based on this conception of attitude had not resulted in behavioral prediction, and it appeared to him that this unidimensional view was oversimplified. Indeed, from Allport's point of view, two people could be equally favorable toward an object, yet feel differently about components or characteristics of the object. For example, two people could feel equally favorable toward the church but feel quite differently about characteristics or practices of the church. Similarly, two people could be equally in favor of change but disagree on the modus operandi of a reform movement. Thus, according to Allport, although two people may have the same degree of affect toward an object, they may differ *qualitatively* in their attitude toward it. Obviously, one reason why we cannot predict behavior from attitude, he continued, is that our measures of attitude are unidimensional and do not take this qualitative nature of attitude into account.

Allport argued, therefore, for the consideration of the qualitative nature of attitude. Allport's plea was not accompanied by a technique for measuring these qualitative differences, however, and this, in part, may explain why the plea fell on deaf ears. Indeed, following Allport's review, investigators still continued to measure attitude by obtaining single scores that essentially placed the respondent somewhere along a single dimension of favorableness or unfavorableness toward the attitude object. In fact, it is worth noting that two of the major attitude measuring instruments that have been introduced since Allport's review have been designed specifically to obtain unidimensional scores (i.e., the Guttman Scale and the Semantic Differential). Nevertheless, the prediction of behavior remained a major concern, *and* an unsolved problem.

I think the second major step came when Leonard Doob (1947) suggested that there may not be any one-to-one relationship between attitude and behavior. Doob's argument was quite straightforward, and it seems surprising that so little attention has been paid to it.

Basically, Doob's argument was as follows: Attitude is a learned predisposition to respond; that is, it is a learned mediating response (r_g). Thus one has to learn the attitude—the appropriate predisposition toward any given object. But once one has learned the attitude, he also must learn what response to make to it—that is, there is no innate relationship between the attitude and behavior; one still has to learn a behavioral response. Two people may learn to hold the same attitude toward a given stimulus; clearly, however, they may also learn to make different responses given the same learned attitude.

For example, two students may learn to feel equally favorable toward a given instructor. Furthermore, this feeling may initially elicit the same overt response in both students (e.g., calling the instructor by his first name). From Doob's point of view, the probability that this behavior will persist is a function of the reinforcement the students get for making this response. For example, with respect to one student, the instructor might say, "Well, I'm glad you finally decided to drop that 'professor' nonsense," while he might tell the other student, "I'd prefer it if you wouldn't call me by my first name." If this were the case, Doob's theory would predict that the behavior would continue for the first student, but not for the second.

Obviously, there may be some problems with this approach. More specifically, it is possible that the students' attitudes toward the instructor may also change differentially over time as a function of this reinforcement. However, even if this is the case, the main point is that Doob provided a reasonable partial answer, or at least an approach to an answer, to the problem of the relation between attitude and behavior. Doob was essentially arguing that attitude and behavior could be unrelated; that it was perfectly reasonable for two people with the same attitude to behave differently. Unfortunately, Doob's major point was not only not accepted, but it actually produced something akin to a "boomerang effect." That is, in Chein's (1948) critique of Doob's article, he essentially thanked Doob for pointing out what was wrong with our measures and definitions of attitude. Indeed, said Chein, Doob has pointed out that two people may feel the same amount of affect toward an object but may behave differently with respect to that object, or they may hold different beliefs about what should be done with respect to that object, or both. Clearly then, because the "action" component of attitude is different, these people must have different attitudes. Similarly, Chein continued, two people may be equally favorable toward the object, but they may also have different cognitions about the object; they may believe different things about it. Here again, these people must have different attitudes. An attitude, then, has several components. Now, this was not the first time that a multicomponent definition was advanced, nor was it the last. Indeed, if you pick up almost any social psychology textbook, you will find that attitude is currently defined as a concept containing an affective, a cognitive, and a conative component.

In contrast to this, I prefer, following Thurstone (1931), to view attitude as a relatively simple unidimensional concept, referring to *"the amount of affect for or against a psychological object"* (p. 261). Rather than viewing beliefs and behavioral intentions as a part of attitude, I prefer to define them independently and to view them as phenomena that are related to attitudes. More specifically, I see beliefs and behavioral intentions as determinants or consequents of an individual's attitude. As Green (1954) has pointed out, the concept of attitude is a hypothetical variable, abstracted from the many statements and actions that an individual makes with respect to a given object. Thus, rather than viewing statements about the object (i.e., beliefs) and statements about actions that one would take with respect to the object (i.e., behavioral intentions) as part of attitude or as the attitude per se, I feel that these statements can best be viewed as indicants of an individual's attitude.

One argument for the unidimensional viewpoint is a pragmatic one. If one accepts a multidimensional view of attitude, this implies that the "attitude" of any one person toward an object may fall at three very different positions on three different dimensions. Nevertheless, the operations by which attitudes are measured almost invariably yield a single score that is unlikely to reflect these three different components in any very precise fashion. As a matter of fact, people who construct "attitude scales" rarely maintain that their instruments are measuring three components; instead, they usually contend that their scales indicate people's evaluations of, or affect toward, an object or concept. Thus, although attitudes are often said to include all three components, it is usually only evaluation or "the affective component" that is measured and treated by researchers as the essence of attitude.

Furthermore, there is considerable evidence showing that this single "affective" score is highly related to an individual's beliefs about the object. The research of Rosenberg (1956, 1960), Zajonc (1954), Fishbein (1963, 1965a, 1965b), and others has demonstrated that an individual's attitude (or affect) toward any object is a function of his beliefs about the object (i.e., the probability or improbability that the object is related to some other object, value, concept, or goal) and the evaluative aspects of those beliefs (i.e., the evaluation of—or attitude toward—the "related concept").

In addition, as Fishbein (see pp. 257 to 266 in this book) has pointed out, a consideration of most standardized instruments for measuring attitudes will also demonstrate that the single "affective" score they obtain is in fact derived from a consideration of a subject's beliefs and the evaluative aspects of those beliefs. For example, in Thurstone Scaling and Likert Scaling the subject is confronted with a series of belief statements. In both cases, the attitude score is indexed from a consideration of the respondent's beliefs (i.e., his agreement or disagreement with each of the statements) or, as Green suggests, it is abstracted from several of his statements about the attitude object.

Similarly, the single "affective" score obtained from Bogardus' Social Distance Scales is based on a consideration of an individual's behavioral intentions and their evaluative aspects.

Thus, from my point of view, this hypothetical variable that we call an "attitude" can be measured by considering either beliefs or behavioral intentions, or by attempting to get at evaluation per se (e.g., through the use of such instruments as the Semantic Differential). It seems that these different types of instruments, or approaches, are attempting to measure the same thing; each is attempting to arrive at a single score that will represent how favorable or unfavorable the individual is toward the attitude object in question.

THE RELATIONSHIPS BETWEEN ATTITUDE AND OTHER PHENOMENA

Taking a unidimensional view of attitude does not imply that one should ignore cognition and conation. Rather, it implies that beliefs and behavioral intentions must be studied in their own right, as independent phenomena that may be related to attitude and behavior. Thus the problem is not simply to investigate relationships between attitude and behavior; rather, one must be concerned with at least four things: attitudes, beliefs, behavioral intentions, and behavior. The problem, then, is to investigate the interrelations among all four of these concepts.

Although considerable progress has been made in understanding the relationships between beliefs and attitudes, little has been done in investigating the relationships between beliefs and behavioral intentions, attitudes and behavioral intentions, or any of these three and behavior per se. In the remainder of this paper, I should like to consider some of these interrelationships.

The Relations between Beliefs and Attitudes (That Is, Cognition and Affect)

As already mentioned, it appears that we now have fairly conclusive evidence that a person's attitude toward any object can be seen as a function of his beliefs about the object (i.e., the probability or improbability that the object has a specific relationship with some other object, value, concept, or goal) and the evaluative aspects of those beliefs (i.e., the subject's attitude toward, or evaluation of, the "related object").[1]

It should be noted, however, that although this evidence provides strong support for the general hypothesis that an individual's attitude toward any object is a function of his beliefs about the object and their evaluative aspects, it does *not* imply that any given belief will be correlated with the attitude. Indeed, this relationship between beliefs and attitudes indicates that it is quite probable that an individual will have some beliefs that appear "inconsistent" with his attitude. As Fishbein (pp. 257 to 266 in this book) has pointed out, "Although each belief suggests an attitude, the attitude per se can only be reliably abstracted by considering the many beliefs an individual holds" (p. 264). Thus, while an individual's attitude will be highly correlated with an estimate based on a consideration of many of his beliefs, it may be uncorrelated or even negatively correlated with any single belief considered in isolation. Although the implications of this for the various "consistency theories" are beyond the scope of the present paper, it should be noted that this view suggests that it is not necessarily "inconsistent" for an individual (a) to have a favorable attitude toward some "object" and (b) to believe that the "object" has some negative characteristics, qualities, or attributes.

In addition to its implications for "consistency theories," the strong relationship between beliefs and attitudes also suggests one major reason why many investigators have failed to find relationships between attitudes and behavior: often the attitude being measured may be inappropriate. For example, in many cases an individual's attitude toward a class of people or objects has been measured, and this attitude has been used in an attempt to predict the individual's behavior with respect to a particular member of that class.

Thus one frequently measures a subject's attitude toward "Negroes," and then attempts to predict his behavior with respect to a particular Negro individual. However, it is very unlikely that the subject's beliefs about this particular

Negro individual are even similar to his beliefs about "Negroes in general." Clearly, if a subject were asked to describe a "Negro," he would give a very different set of responses than if he were asked to describe Martin Luther King or Cassius Clay. Because his beliefs about these stimuli would differ, his attitudes toward them would also differ. Indeed, probably the only reason why even minimal correlations between attitude and behavior have been obtained in some cases is the fact that one belief about the particular stimulus person is that "he is a Negro"; this belief, being quite strong, will contribute heavily to the attitude. However, even this may not occur with respect to other stimulus persons who cannot be readily identified as members of a given group (e.g., Jews, Catholics, etc.). It seems fairly obvious that the chances of predicting behavior from attitude are practically nil until we at least start measuring attitudes toward the appropriate stimulus.

The problem often becomes even more complex, however. For example, we are often concerned with predicting different types of sociometric choices. Thus we may try to predict which group members a particular member will choose as friends or as co-workers. Bales' (1958) research has provided strong evidence that the person we may like the best and the person we would most like to work with are usually two different people. This implies that our attitude toward a person as a co-worker may be quite different from our attitude toward the same person as a friend. This should not be surprising; if an individual were asked to describe a particular person as a card player, he would give a different set of beliefs about that person than if he were asked to describe the same person as a co-worker. Thus, as a minimal initial step in trying to understand the relationships between attitudes and behavior, we must first start measuring attitudes toward the appropriate stimuli, vis-à-vis the behaviors we are attempting to predict.

The Relations between Attitude and Behavioral Intentions (That Is, Affect and Conation)

In a recent series of papers, Triandis (see pp. 208 to 219 in this book) and his associates (e.g., Triandis and Davis, 1964; Fishbein, 1964; Triandis, Fishbein, Hall, Tanaka, and Shanmugan, 1967) have been exploring the "behavioral" or "conative" component of attitude. In the first paper in this series, Triandis developed an instrument called the Behavioral Differential.

[1] For two studies providing evidence for this hypothesis, see pages 325 to 331 and 389 to 400 in this book. The algebraic expression of the hypothesis appears on page 489.

This instrument consists of a series of behavioral statements (e.g., "accept as an intimate friend," "go fishing with," "admire the ideas of," etc.) similar to those found on Bogardus' (1925) Social Distance Scales. The respondent is asked to indicate (usually on a nine-place scale) the extent to which he "would" or "would not" engage in these behaviors with respect to a given stimulus person. Starting with a large set of behaviors obtained from a content analysis of novels, Triandis initially selected behavioral items on the basis of a facet analysis, and further reduced the number of items through factor analyses. Generally speaking, factor analyses of a large number of item-by-item intercorrelation matrices (obtained in several different studies, utilizing different behavioral items and different stimuli) have indicated five basic clusters of items. That is, items always seem to cluster together into the five types shown in Table 1.

It should be noted that these five types of intentions have not been referred to as different dimensions of behavioral intentions, but only as clusters or types. Depending largely on the types of stimulus persons that are rated, these different clusters tend to go together in different ways (i.e., they may load on the same or different dimensions in any given factor analysis). For example, in one study, admiration and friendship items may load on one factor, while social distance and subordination intentions

may load on a second factor. In another study, admiration and subordination intentions may load on one factor, while friendship and social distance intentions may load on a second factor. Thus, although Triandis has essentially identified five different general types of behavioral intentions, it should be made clear that these five types are usually not independent and, furthermore, that their relations to one another depend largely on the type of stimulus person being rated.

Turning to the question of the relations between these five types of behavioral intentions and attitude (i.e., affect), it should first be noted that because these behavioral intentions intercorrelate differentially with one another, they also are differentially related to attitude. That is, in one study attitude may be more highly correlated with friendship intentions than with social distance intentions, while in another study the findings may be reversed. Generally speaking, however, the results of several studies seem to indicate that attitudes are most highly correlated with admiration and friendship intentions $(\bar{r} = .55)$, are moderately correlated with subordination and social distance intentions $(\bar{r} = .35)$, and are least correlated with marital intentions $(\bar{r} = .15)$.

While the correlations between attitude and the different types of behavioral intentions vary considerably, the correlation between attitude and the sum of the behavioral intentions tends

TABLE 1. Item Clusters in Behavioral Differential

Cluster	Typical Items
1. Marital	I would: go on a date with fall in love with marry
2. Admiration	I would: admire character of believe admire idea of praise suggestions
3. Social distance	I would: invite to my club exclude from my neighborhood accept as a close kin by marriage
4. Friendship	I would: accept as an intimate friend treat as equal eat with
5. Subordination- superordination	I would: be commanded by elect to political office treat as a subordinate work for

to be quite stable and high ($\bar{r} = .70$). Thus, just as any given belief may be uncorrelated with an individual's attitude, any given behavioral intention (e.g., "I would elect this person to political office") or any one type of behavioral intention (e.g., subordination-superordination intentions) may also be uncorrelated with an individual's attitude. However, when one considers the totality (or at least a large set) of an individual's behavioral intentions, good estimates of attitude can be obtained. We shall return to this point shortly; first, however, it is worth noting that it is with respect to behavioral intentions (and behavior per se) that Doob's argument seems most appropriate.

More specifically, if we consider what has been happening in the South, we can get a clear picture of what Doob was referring to. That is, the Civil Rights Act of 1964 and various judicial decisions have had a profound effect on some behavioral intentions and behaviors of many Southerners. Many individuals in the South, if asked today, would say that they would admit Negroes to their hotels, motels, or restaurants. (And, indeed, Negroes have been admitted to various places that previously had refused to serve them.) I doubt very much, however, if any of us would really want to say that these individuals have thereby changed their attitudes toward Negroes.

As Doob pointed out, however, behavioral intentions (as well as overt behaviors) can be either positively or negatively reinforced. If our initial behavioral intentions or behaviors were always positively reinforced, it is likely that there would always be a clear relationship between attitude and behavioral intentions. Behavioral intentions are not always positively reinforced; indeed, they are often negatively reinforced. Furthermore, we are often positively reinforced for having behavioral intentions that are inconsistent with our attitudes. Once again, I think we can all see many examples of this in the South today.

Before going any further, one point should be made clear. Namely, although everything that has been said about the relationship between attitude and behavioral intentions is also true of the relationship between attitude and behavior per se, this *does not* imply that there is any given relationship between behavioral intentions and behavior. As we shall see below, the size of the correlation between a behavioral intention and behavior is determined largely by the specificity of the behavioral intention that is being considered. Indeed, everything that has been said about the relationships between attitudes and behavioral intentions may also apply to the relationships between Triandis' five types of behavioral intentions and overt behaviors.

This is important, for I do not think a change in a behavioral intention leads necessarily to a change in attitude unless the change in behavioral intention is accompanied by a change in behavior per se. That is, a change in behavior implies a new set of relationships between the individual and the attitude object. This may then lead to the learning of new beliefs about the attitude object, and thus to attitude change. These beliefs will not be learned overnight, however, and the change in attitude may lag well behind the change in behavior.

Thus, although an individual's attitude might initially influence and be related to specific behavioral intentions (or to specific behaviors), this relationship may or may not persist, depending on the nature and schedule of reinforcement associated with the behavioral intentions. Furthermore, unlike a change in belief that immediately produces an attitude change, changes in a behavioral intention may not produce a change in attitude unless the change in behavioral intention eventually leads to changes in behavior and thus changes in belief about the attitude object.

Therefore, rather than being viewed as parts of attitude, behavioral intentions should be viewed as independent phenomena. Just as a consideration of beliefs (or the cognitive component) yields a single score that indicates how favorable or unfavorable an individual is with respect to the attitude object, so, too, does a consideration of behavioral intentions (or the conative component). That is, as was mentioned earlier, an individual's attitude toward any object may be assessed by measuring affect or evaluation per se, by considering his beliefs or his behavioral intentions, or some combination of all of these.

It appears, then, that the multicomponent view of attitude is misleading and inappropriate. Indeed, in contrast to the major criticism leveled at the unidimensional view of attitude, this single "affective" score does, in a sense, take into account and reflect an individual's beliefs and his behavioral intentions. Although two people may have the same attitudes, however, these attitudes may be based on different beliefs or may be related to different behavioral intentions. As the multicomponent theorists have pointed out, this may well be one of the major reasons why attitudes are uncorrelated with behavior. But here I would argue that it is not because the attitude measure is inappropriate or incomplete. Rather, it is because attitude is a hypothetical variable abstracted from the *totality* of an individual's beliefs, behavioral intentions, and actions toward a given object. Any given belief, behavioral intention, or behavior, therefore, may be uncorrelated or even negatively correlated with his attitude. Thus, rather than viewing specific beliefs or classes of beliefs and specific behavioral intentions or types of behavioral intentions as part of attitude, these phenomena must be studied as variables in their own right, which, like attitudes, may or may not function as determinants of a specific behavior.

The Relationships between Attitude and Behavior (That Is, Affect and Behavior)

On this note we may finally turn our full attention to the presumed topic of this paper. First, however, I want to make it clear that when I use the term "attitude," I am simply referring to a learned predisposition to respond to any object in a consistently favorable or unfavorable way. Operationally, I do not care whether we have obtained our estimate of attitude through a consideration of affect per se, through a consideration of beliefs and their evaluative aspects, or through a consideration of behavioral intentions and their evaluative aspects. That is, I am talking about a single score that places an individual along a continuum ranging from favorableness toward the attitude object to unfavorableness. Let us further assume that this measure is reliable and valid (at least insofar as tapping a true underlying dimension of favorableness or unfavorableness toward the attitude object is concerned).

Thus far, I have indicated two possible reasons for our failure to predict behavior from attitude:

1. We have often measured attitude toward an inappropriate stimulus object—for example, we have often measured attitude toward a class of people or objects when we should have been measuring attitude toward a particular member of the class.

2. The particular behavior being studied

may be completely or partially unrelated to attitude. This point must be emphasized because most investigators of attitude have been unwilling to accept it. To a large extent, however, their unwillingness to accept this statement is surprising since most investigators firmly believe that any behavior is determined by a large number of variables. Yet time and again, a behavior is investigated because the experimenter assumes that it should be a function of attitude and then he is surprised and disappointed to find that his measure of attitude failed to predict the behavior.

Unfortunately, one of the most common responses to this failure has been to question the attitude measure; it is criticized for measuring only affect and not taking into account the so-called cognitive or conative dimensions of attitude. What one should be questioning however, is the initial assumption that the behavior being considered is a function of the attitude being measured. Furthermore, even if measures of specific sets of beliefs or types of behavioral intentions were available, the chances would still be high that the behavior could not be predicted. That is, it must be realized that the appeal to beliefs and behavioral intentions may be based on the same false assumption that led to the expectation of an attitude-behavior relationship —namely, the assumption that the behavior being investigated is a function of some type of belief or behavioral intention.

Granted, this assumption may be true in some cases, in most cases however, it is quite likely that the particular beliefs or behavioral intentions we would choose to measure would themselves be highly correlated with attitude. Thus they would add little, if anything, to our predictive ability. The only times when it may be useful to consider beliefs and behavioral intentions (in addition to attitude) are those situations in which the particular beliefs or behavioral intentions that we wish to consider are not themselves highly correlated with the individual's attitude. However, even in those cases we must be willing to recognize that the beliefs or behavioral intentions that we do select may also be unrelated to the behavior itself. That is, just as we must be willing to accept the fact that two people with the same attitudes may behave differently, so, too, must we be willing to accept the fact that two people with the same beliefs or two people with the same behavioral intentions may also behave quite differently.

BEHAVIORAL PREDICTION AND MEASURES OF BEHAVIOR

If you will notice, however, I have stopped discussing the relations between attitudes and behavior and started discussing the general problem of behavioral prediction. Essentially what I have been pointing out is how we might predict behavior in those situations where attitude is not a relevant variable. More specifically, I have indicated that when most attitude researchers fail to find a relation between attitude and behavior, they usually suggest that if we were to take one or two other variables into account, we might be able to predict the behavior. Although this is reasonable if our primary concern is to predict *behavior*—and this is what I believe our primary concern really is —it is unfortunate that two of the variables most commonly suggested (i.e., belief and behavioral intention) are arrived at through a consideration of the predictor, rather than through a consideration of the behavior per se. Here, I think, is where our major problem lies: we psychologists have never really studied behavior per se. By this I mean that we have usually taken behavior as a *given*; to the best of my knowledge, we—at least in the attitude area— have seldom, if ever, subjected our behavioral criteria to the same rigorous analyses to which we subject our paper-and-pencil tests. Yet this is what we must do if we are to thoroughly understand the relations between attitudes and behavior (i.e., if we are ever going to predict the conditions under which, and the extent to which, behavior is determined by, or related to, attitudes—or to any other variable, for that matter). In the remainder of this section, I shall try to clarify this by discussing a hypothetical example.

First, let me describe a very simple behavioral situation. A naïve subject shows up for an experiment and is asked to wait in an adjoining room while the experimenter sets up the experiment. The adjoining room is fairly small, containing only four chairs, arranged so that they form the four corners of a square. Seated in one of the chairs is a confederate of the experimenter. When the naïve subject enters the room, the confederate looks up and says, "Hello, my name is Robert Springer." The two people then remain in the room for a five-minute period.

Now let us suppose that, as the experimenter, I want to make an hypothesis about the sub-

ject's communicative behavior. Furthermore, let us assume that I have a highly valid and reliable instrument for measuring the number, duration, or type of communicative acts that the subject makes. Finally, let us also assume that I have a well-trained confederate who behaves in a highly standardized manner.

Now, to return to my hypothesis, let us suppose I have a strong hunch that the more the subject likes the confederate, the more he will talk to him. Thus I have essentially made the assumption that the amount of the subject's communicative behavior is a function of his attitude. To put it another way, I have implicitly made the assumption that this behavior is a good indicator of the subject's attitude toward the confederate. That is, rather than viewing the behavior as a criterion, I can also view it as a measure of the variable I assume it reflects. In this case, then, I would essentially be estimating the subject's attitude toward the confederate through a consideration of his communicative behavior.

Once we start considering the behavioral measure as an estimate of attitude (or any other variable), we can start subjecting the behavior to the same types of critical analyses to which we subject our paper-and-pencil measures. For example, one of the most obvious questions that should be asked concerns the reliability of the behavior. That is, even in the simple situation I have described, we could bring the subject back at the same time on another day and obtain a measure of test-retest reliability. Even this simple test provides us with a considerable amount of new information; if the behavior is unreliable, that finding almost immediately suggests that this behavior is not a direct function of any variable that *is* reliable or has not changed from Time 1 to Time 2. "Unreliability" provides a clear indication that the behavior is not determined directly by any of the controlled variables that are part of our experimental situation, whether they can be specified or not. More specifically, "unreliability" allows us to conclude that this behavior is neither situationally determined, nor solely a function of any factor that is consistently related to or based upon a consideration of the stimulus person, that is, the confederate.[2]

If the behavior is shown to be reliable, this

---

[2] Obviously, a change in behavior could be a function of a change in attitude. This example, however, is only concerned with the case where attitude does not change.

knowledge permits us to go on to the more important question of validity. Obviously, I am not talking about the validity of the behavior per se (for, by definition, behavior is "real"), but rather about the validity of the behavior as an indicant or measure of some other variable.

Here, rather than starting with the usual question of convergent validity (i.e, the extent to which two different estimates or measures of a given variable are correlated), I should like first to discuss briefly what Campbell and Fiske (1959) have called discriminant validity. According to these authors, a valid test should not only measure what it is supposed to measure, but also it should not measure anything else. To quote them, "tests can be invalidated by too high correlations with other tests from which they were intended to differ" (p. 81).

Furthermore, they point out that every test or task employed for measurement purposes should be viewed as a trait-method unit, that is, as "a union of a particular trait [or variable] content with measurement procedures not specific to that content." Thus, they continue, "The systematic variance among test scores can be due to responses to the measurement features as well as responses to the trait content" (p. 81).

To return to our simple situation, it can be seen that what I have described is a general, content-independent measurement procedure. Essentially, I have described a behavioral method for measuring a subject's attitude toward any given stimulus person. Variations in the characteristics or behavior of the stimulus person (or the situation per se) are analogous, then, to what Campbell and Fiske have called variations in trait content.

Continuing, Campbell and Fiske point out that "In order to examine discriminant validity, and in order to estimate the relative contributions of trait and method variance, *more than one trait* as well as *more than one method* must be employed in the validation process" (p. 81). Thus, in contrast to our usual validation technique of correlating some pencil-and-paper measure of attitude with one or more behavioral criteria (that we assume or hypothesize to be correlated with attitude), we should, *at a minimum,* be obtaining measures of attitude toward at least two stimulus objects and measuring the subject's behavior with respect to each of them. It is only in this way that we can start to obtain some indication of a more general pattern of relationships between attitude and behavior. That is, we must start to

pay more attention to the question of discriminant validity if we ever hope to distinguish between those behaviors that are functions of the situation and those that are related to characteristics associated with the attitude object.

Although a complete discussion of Campbell and Fiske's multitrait, multimethod matrix technique is beyond the scope of the present paper, it appears that this technique (with some modifications) provides a simple and straightforward procedure for beginning to analyze the relationship between attitude and behavior. Because Campbell and Fiske's original concerns were with the measurement of personality traits (which are usually assumed to be independent), at least one modification in interpretation should be mentioned. Specifically, the Campbell and Fiske analysis suggests that when the same method is used to measure two or more traits and the monomethod, multitrait correlations are high, a large (and irrelevant) "methods" factor may be influencing the responses. This is not necessarily the case in attitude research, because subjects' attitudes toward two or more stimuli may often be highly intercorrelated.

While this relationship does not require change in any of the criteria that Campbell and Fiske propose for analyzing discriminant validity, it does suggest that one alternative criterion may be useful in considering discriminant validity in attitude research. Specifically, variations in the attitude object should produce reliable variation in the attitude scores. For example, although individuals' attitudes toward two stimuli may be highly correlated (e.g., authoritarian subjects' attitudes toward Negroes and Jews), the method used to measure these attitudes would have discriminant validity with respect to the two stimulus persons if, in addition to Campbell and Fiske's criteria, one found a reliable mean difference between the two attitude scores, that is, if the subjects' attitudes toward Negroes were significantly different from their attitudes toward Jews. A similar argument applies to the behavioral measures. This may be seen more clearly below.

THE RELATIONSHIP OF ATTITUDE AND BEHAVIOR AS SEEN IN A MULTIATTITUDE OBJECT, MULTIMETHOD MATRIX

To return to the main point, it appears that in those cases where the attitudinal and behavioral measures are uncorrelated (i.e., where there is no convergent validity), the multitrait (or multiattitude object), multimethod approach provides a considerable amount of information that would not be obtained in other ways. This is not to say that one will not obtain convergent validity between some attitudes and some behaviors, nor that these findings are unimportant or uninformative. However, the Campbell and Fiske approach is probably most useful in respect to the further leads it provides in those cases where convergent validity is not obtained. This may perhaps be seen most clearly if we discuss some of the major cases that are possible.

Case A: Discriminant Validity in the Attitudinal, but not in the Behavioral Measures

Suppose that in our hypothetical situation we find that, irrespective of variations in the characteristics or behaviors of our confederate, the behavior in this situation does not vary. That is, suppose the results indicate that the number of communicative acts do not vary whether the confederate is Negro or White, male or female, Catholic or Protestant, dressed neatly or sloppily; or whether the confederate is instructed to agree or disagree with the subject, to respond with long sentences or short phrases, etc. In other words, suppose we find that, at least with respect to the variables we are manipulating, our behavioral measure has no discriminant validity. Let us further suppose that, in contrast, our paper-and-pencil measure does reflect these differences, that is, that as we manipulate certain characteristics of the confederate, the subject's attitudes toward the confederate change. Thus our attitude measure does have discriminant validity. Finally, let us assume that this particular paper-and-pencil measure has a high degree of convergent validity with respect to other measures of attitude, that is, that it has construct validity.

Clearly, then, our failure to obtain convergent validity with the behavioral measures in this situation does not imply that our measure of attitude is invalid; rather, it strongly indicates that this behavior is not sensitive to or not related to the attitude we have measured—nor to any variable that is likely to correlate with either the attitude or any of the characteristics or actions that were manipulated. Indeed, rather than concern ourselves with attitudes, we can be fairly certain that this behavior is either a function of some stable individual difference variable or some nonstimulus (i.e., nonconfederate) associated variable or variables in this situation.

Case B: Discriminant Validity in the Behavioral, but not in the Attitudinal Measures

Alternatively, of course, the lack of convergent validity could derive from the finding that variations in the stimulus object produce variations in the behavior but not in the paper-and-pencil measure. In this case our behavioral measure would have discriminant validity, but, at least with respect to the particular variables we have manipulated, our paper and pencil measure would not. Furthermore, let us again assume that the particular paper-and-pencil test does have a high degree of construct validity. This is an interesting case, for here we have a change in behavior that is related to the manipulation of a specified variable but is not correlated with the attitude measured. Here again, I would argue that our failure to obtain convergent validity does not imply that our measure of attitude is invalid; it would only indicate that this behavior is not related to the attitude measured, nor to any variable that is likely to correlate with the attitude measured. Indeed, what we have found is that certain variables that function as determinants of behavior with respect to a given stimulus person are unrelated to attitude toward that person. Thus, if our main interest is in predicting the behavior, we should concentrate on measuring those particular variables rather than on measuring attitudes toward the person.

Before continuing, I should mention one other possible reason for not obtaining convergent validity in this case, namely, it could be that we have measured attitude toward an inappropriate stimulus object. For example, E measured attitudes toward "Catholics" and "Protestants" rather than toward the specific Catholic individual and the specific Protestant individual who served as confederates. The failure to find discriminant validity in our attitude measure argues against this, however. That is, inappropriate stimuli are likely to be fairly general or stereotypic, and because our instrument has construct validity, this type of error would increase, rather than decrease, the degree of discriminant validity. Although this type of error is not indicated in the present case, it is indicated in the final set of alternatives I shall discuss.

Case C: Discriminant Validity in Both the Attitudinal and the Behavioral Measures

Consider the case where both our behavioral and our pencil-and-paper measures have discriminant validity but are not correlated with each other. Again, this lack of convergent validity does not imply that our measure of attitude is invalid. Here, however, the alternatives are two-fold: (1) as mentioned above, this may well be a situation in which we have measured attitudes toward an inappropriate attitude object; (2) this is also the kind of situation where we may want to look for some other variable that is some-what related both to our attitude measure and to our manipulations. That is, this is the type of situation in which variables such as beliefs or behavioral intentions are truly likely to in-crease our ability to predict behavior.

Obviously, there are many other alternatives that may be differentiated when one uses a multiattitude object, multimethod approach (e.g., both attitude and behavioral measures may have low discriminant validity; convergent validity may be obtained with only one set of the attitude and behavioral measures). Although a complete discussion of these alternatives is beyond the scope of the present paper, it is worth noting that each alternative carries dif-ferent implications for an understanding of the attitude-behavior relationship. In contrast to this, the usual procedure of obtaining a single-attitude measure and attempting to predict one or more behaviors provides us with little or no information in those cases where convergent validity is not obtained. That is, the failure to find convergent validity in such cases can be interpreted in many ways. As was pointed out above, the most common interpretation has been that there was something wrong with the measure of attitude (e.g., it was inappropriate; it was only a measure of affect and did not take the cognitive and the action component into account). However, as was also pointed out above, this lack of convergent validity can also be interpreted as indicating that the be-havior under consideration is unrelated to the attitude that was measured. More specifically, the multiattitude object, multimethod approach clearly indicates that many of an individual's behaviors with respect to a given object are likely to be primarily under the control of vari-ables other than the individual's attitude toward that object. In particular, it emphasizes the importance of the situation as a factor deter-mining behavior.

Although many investigators have often rec-ognized the importance of situational and "other" variables as determinants of behavior, most treatments of attitude have not dealt with these factors explicitly. Rather, they have usu-ally been viewed as sources of "error" variance. The conception of attitude as a "predisposition to respond" has generally led to the assumption that an individual's behavior with respect to some object is a direct function of his attitude toward the object, and "other" factors are viewed as "noise" in the system. In the final section of this paper, a theory will be presented that attempts to deal with this larger constella-tion of behavioral determinants within a single formulation of the attitude problem. Rather than starting with the assumption that there is a strong underlying relationship between atti-tude and behavior, the theory to be presented emphasizes the importance of situational, mo-tivational, and normative variables as factors influencing overt behavior.

THE ATTITUDE-BEHAVIOR RELATIONSHIP: A REANALYSIS

The theory to be presented below can best be seen as an adaptation of Dulany's (1961, 1964) theory of propositional control. Although Dulany's theory has largely been developed within the context of studies of verbal condi-tioning and concept attainment, it is essentially a theory that leads to the prediction of overt behavior. It is hoped that the present approach will provide a more complete understanding of the relationships between attitudes and be-havior, by identifying some of the ways in which other variables interact with attitudes as determinants of overt behavior. More spe-cifically, the present approach may be viewed as an attempt to bridge the gap between tradi-tional measures of attitude toward a stimulus object and behavior with respect to that object in a given situation.

As mentioned above, Dulany's theory has largely been developed within the context of studies of verbal conditioning and concept attainment. More specifically, Dulany has been concerned with predicting the probability with which an individual will make a particular verbal response or class of verbal responses. The central equation of the theory can be ex-pressed as follows:

$$BI = [(RHd)(A)]w_0 + [(BH)(Mc)]w_1$$

where

$BI =$ the subject's intention to make a par-ticular response or class of responses

$RHd =$ a "hypothesis of the distribution of reinforcement," that is, the subject's hypothesis that the occurrence of the particular response will lead to a certain event or class of events

A = the affective value of the reinforcement, that is, the subject's evaluations of (or attitudes toward) those events

BH = the subject's "behavioral hypothesis," that is, his belief as to what he is *expected* to do, or what he *should* do in the situation

Mc = the subject's "motivation to comply," that is, how much the subject *wants* to do what he believes is expected of him

w_0 and w_1 = beta weights, which may take any value

Two additional points about the theory should be mentioned:

1. According to the theory, behavioral intention is the immediate antecedent of overt behavior. Unlike the general types of behavioral intentions that most attitude researchers (e.g., Triandis, 1964; Triandis, Fishbein, and Hall, 1964) have been concerned with (e.g., intentions to marry, to show social distance, to subordinate, to accept as a friend), Dulany has been concerned with a more precise and specific type of behavioral intention—namely, an individual's intention to perform a given action in a given situation.

That is, it will be recalled that in order to obtain a measure of an individual's behavioral intention (to show social distance, for example), Triandis would ask the subject to indicate whether he (i.e., the subject) "would" or "would not" engage in a specific set of behaviors (e.g., "invite to my club," "exclude from my neighborhood," "accept as a close kin by marriage," etc.) with a given stimulus person. Triandis would then sum the responses to these items, and this sum would be taken as the measure of the respondent's behavioral intention (to show social distance). In contrast to this, Dulany has been concerned with measuring the subject's intention to perform the specific behavior he is interested in predicting. Furthermore, unlike Triandis, Dulany would not ask the subject to indicate his intention to engage in the act "in general," (e.g., measure his intention to "obey" the stimulus person), but rather he would measure the subject's intentions to engage in the act in a particular situation. Because of this close correspondence between the measure of the behavioral inten-

tion and the actual behavior that Dulany wants to predict, the correlation between the measure of behavioral intention and the actual overt behavior is almost perfect (i.e., the correlations are always in the mid .90's). Thus if one can predict the specific behavioral intention, one may, with only slightly attenuated accuracy, predict the overt behavior. It must be emphasized, however, that these near-perfect correlations between behavioral intentions and behavior are only obtained, and are only expected, when one considers an individual's intention to perform a specific act in a specific situation. The more abstract or generalized the intention becomes, the lower will be its correlation with a specific behavior.

2. As can be seen above, the algebraic expression of the theory takes the form of a linear multiple regression equation. That is, $[(RHd)(A)]$ is viewed as one component influencing behavioral intentions and $[(BH)(Mc)]$ is seen as a second component. The precise weights to be given these two components as determinants of behavioral intentions within a given situation may be determined by standard multiple-regression procedures.

A liberal interpretation of this theory as applied to social behavior may be given as follows. An individual's intention to perform a specific act, with respect to a given stimulus object, in a given situation, is a function of the following:

1*a*. His beliefs about the consequences of performing a particular behavior (in a given situation), that is, the probability or improbability that the performance of behavior X will lead to some consequence y_i (B_i).

1*b*. The evaluative aspect of B_i, that is, the S's evaluation of y_i (a_i).

2*a*. A normative belief, that is, the S's belief about what he *should* do in this situation (NB).

2*b*. His motivation to comply with the norm, that is, his desire, or lack of desire, to do what he thinks he should do (Mc).

Thus in the present adaptation of Dulany's theory, RHd (the hypothesis of the distribution of a reinforcer) is conceptualized as being analogous to an individual's beliefs about the consequences of performing a specific behavior, and A (the affective value of the reinforcer) is conceptualized as being equivalent to the evaluative aspects of those beliefs. It is interesting to note that this conceptualization redefines the first component of Dulany's theory $[(RHd)(A)]$ as a measure of attitude. That is, as was mentioned above, the work of Rosenberg (1956, 1965), Zajonc (1954), Fishbein (1963, 1965b, 1967a, 1967b), and others has provided strong evidence that an individual's attitude toward any object can be predicted from a knowledge of the individual's beliefs about the object and the evaluative aspects of those beliefs. Algebraically, this may be expressed as follows:

$$A_o = \sum_{i-1}^{n} B_i a_i$$

where

A_o = the attitude toward some object "o"
B_i = belief i about o, that is, the probability that o is related to some other object x_i
a_i = the evaluative aspect of B_i, that is, the respondent's attitude toward x_i
n = the number of beliefs

It must be emphasized, however, that the attitude under consideration is an attitude toward performing a given behavioral act, and is *not* an attitude toward a given object, person, or situation. That is, the algebraic formula presented above leads to the hypothesis that an individual's attitude toward any object is a function of the individual's beliefs about *that object*. In the present analysis, we are concerned with an individual's beliefs about the performance of a given behavioral act, and thus the attitude being assessed is the individual's attitude toward the performance of that act. More specifically, from the point of view of Dulany's theory, we should be assessing the individual's beliefs about what will happen if he performs behavior X with respect to stimulus Y in situation Z, and the evaluative aspects of those beliefs, that is, we should be assessing the individual's attitude toward the performance of a given act, with respect to a given stimulus object, in a given situation. Although these beliefs *may* vary considerably as a function of the stimulus object (e.g., the person) toward which the act is directed and the situation in which the act is to occur (e.g., in public or in private), these beliefs are still beliefs about the performance of the act, and not beliefs about the stimulus object or the situation. We shall return to this point below.

Turning to the second component of Dulany's theory $[(BH)(Mc)]$, it can be seen that BH (the behavioral hypothesis) has been conceptualized as a normative belief, that is, a belief about what *should* be done in the situation. More specifically, this is a belief about whether the particular act *should* or *should not* be performed. Here, however, it may be necessary to distinguish between two types of normative beliefs: (1) the individual's belief about what he *personally* feels he should do (i.e., a personal norm or rule of behavior); and (2) the individual's belief about what "society" (i.e., most other people, his "significant others," etc.) "says" he should do (i.e., a social or group norm). Although an individual's personal norms will often coincide with, or reflect, the social norms, this is not necessarily the case. For example, while social norms concerning interracial relations are markedly different in some Northern and Southern communities, a given individual in a Southern community may hold the same personal normative belief as an individual in a Northern community. Thus it may be necessary to take both of those types of normative beliefs into account. This can easily be done, for as was mentioned above, the central equation of Dulany's theory takes the form of a multiple regression equation. Thus, as Dulany has pointed out, this theory is an open theory, and additional components can be taken into account. We shall discuss this more fully below.

The final element in the equation (Mc—an individual's motivation to comply) is self-explanatory. Here we are concerned with the degree to which the individual "wants" to comply with the norm. Clearly, if two types of norms are considered, it will be necessary to measure the individual's motivation to comply with each of them.

Returning to the central hypothesis, it can be seen that in its adapted form Dulany's theory essentially leads to the prediction that an individual's intention to perform any behavior (and his actual performance of the behavior) is a function of (1) his attitude toward performing the behavior in a given situation, and (2) the norms governing that behavior in that situation and his motivation to comply with those norms. Algebraically, this can be expressed as follows:

$$B \approx BI = [A_{\text{act}}]w_0 + [(NB)(Mc)]w_1$$

However, as was discussed above, it is not clear

whether the second component $[(NB)(Mc)]$ can best be viewed as referring to a personal norm, a social norm, or both. The simplest way to handle this problem within the framework of the theory is to expand the algebraic formulation as follows:

$$B \approx BI = [A_{\text{act}}]w_0 + [(NB_p)(Mc_p)]w_1 \\ + [(NB_s)(Mc_s)]w_2$$

where the subscripts p and s refer to personal and social norms respectively.[3]

Thus, as mentioned previously, the present approach suggests a radical change in investigating and understanding the attitude-behavior relationship. Instead of assuming some underlying relationship between an individual's attitude toward a given object and his behavior with respect to that object, the proposed theory recognizes the importance of situational variables, norms, and motivation as factors influencing behavior. Rather than viewing attitude toward a stimulus object as a major determinant of behavior with respect to that object, the theory identifies three kinds of variables that function as the basic determinants of behavior: (1) attitudes toward the behavior; (2) normative beliefs (both personal and social); and (3) motivation to comply with the norms. Furthermore, although the theory suggests that other variables can also influence behavior, it indicates that these other variables operate *indirectly*, that is, by influencing one or more of the three basic determinants.

Thus under certain conditions an individual's attitude toward a stimulus object may be related to his behavior with respect to that object. For example, it is quite possible that an individual's beliefs about the consequences of performing some behavior (X) will be quite different if the behavior is to be performed with respect to someone he likes (p_1) than with respect to someone he dislikes (p_2). If this were the case, we would expect the individual to have a different attitude toward performing X with respect to p_1, than toward performing X with

respect to p_2. In other cases, however, the consequences of performing a given act may not vary with variation in p, and here attitude toward performing X may not change. In the former case, it is possible that we would obtain a correlation beween attitude toward p and behavior with respect to p, while in the latter case this is unlikely.

Similarly, we might also expect an individual's attitude toward a given stimulus person to influence his motivation to comply with a norm. That is, if we assume that an individual believes that he *should* perform behavior X with respect to individual p in situation X and, further, if we assume that the individual views behavior X as a behavior that indicates friendship (e.g., "invite to my club"), then it seems likely that the more positive the individual's attitude is to p, the more he will want to comply with the norm. Similarly, the more negative his attitude is to p, the less he may want to behave in "a friendly manner" even though he believes he should. Here again, however, it must be recognized that there will be cases where the individual's motivation to comply may be completely unrelated to his attitude toward p.

Along these same lines, it can be seen that variations in the situation may also influence one or more of the primary determinants of behavior. Clearly, an individual is likely to have quite different beliefs about the consequences of performing a given behavior in a public situation than in a private situation. Similarly, we would also expect that the individual has different normative beliefs (both personal and social) for different situations. Here too, however, it must be noted that if the situational variables that are being considered do *not* influence the individual's attitude toward the act, or his personal or social normative beliefs, or his motivation to comply with these beliefs, then, according to the theory, they will not influence his behavior. Indeed, one of the advantages of the theory is that it provides an explanation for a large number of results that may initially appear inconsistent. That is, from the point of view presented here, one would expect a considerable amount of variation in the relationship between any given variable and behavior.

In addition, it should be recalled that the specific weights given to the three basic components [i.e., (A_{act}), $(NB_p \times Mc_p)$, and $(NB_s \times$

---

[3] An alternative formulation can be seen as follows:

$$BI = [A_{\text{act}}]w_0 + \left[\sum_{i=1}^{n} NB_i Mc_i \right] w_1$$

This formulation suggests that it may be necessary to consider many different types of normative beliefs; for example, beliefs about what one's (a) parents, (b) friends, (c) co-workers, (d) religious group, etc., "says" the individual *should* do.

Mc_s)] of the theory must be determined; indeed, these weights are expected to vary from behavior to behavior. That is, with respect to some behaviors, the attitude toward the behavior may be a more important determinant of behavior than either type of normative belief and the motivation to comply with these norms, while for other types of behaviors the weightings may be reversed. Similarly, while some behaviors may be primarily determined by personal normative beliefs, other behaviors may be more under the control of social normative beliefs.

Furthermore, just as the weightings of the three components may vary with the type of behavior that is being considered, they may also vary for different individuals. That is, for some individuals, behavior may be primarily determined by norms and motivation to comply with the norms, while for other individuals behavior may be primarily determined by their attitudes toward the behavior. For example, it is possible that the behavior of high authoritarian individuals may be largely under the control of normative beliefs and motivation to comply with the norms.

Thus, even though an "outside" variable (e.g., attitude toward a stimulus object) may be related to one of the basic determinants of behavior (e.g., attitude toward the behavior), the outside variable may still be unrelated to the actual performance of that behavior.

SUMMARY

The present approach clearly indicates that traditional measures of attitude (i.e., toward a given object, person, or class of people) are *not* likely to be related to behavior in any consistent fashion. Indeed, the main purpose of the present paper has been to reconsider, and seriously question, the basic assumption that an individual's attitude toward an object is a major determinant of his behavior with respect to the object. While other investigators have also argued that traditional attitude measures will not predict behavior, they have usually questioned the measure of attitude rather than the assumption of an attitude-behavior relationship. More specifically, they have argued that most traditional measures of attitude are oversimplified; that most measures only consider an individual's "affective feelings," and fail to take his cognitions and conations into account. Thus most investigators

have attempted to resolve the attitude-behavior problem by expanding the definition of attitude to include affective, cognitive, and conative components.

In contrast to this, the present paper has attempted to show that beliefs (cognitions) and behavioral intentions (conations) can best be viewed as determinants or consequents of attitude; that rather than being viewed as parts of attitude, these variables should be viewed as independent phenomena that are related to, and serve as indicants of, an individual's attitude. Furthermore, it was argued that even if an individual's beliefs about an object and/or his behavioral intentions toward the object are considered, it is not likely that behavioral prediction will be improved. First, these variables may be highly correlated with traditional measures of attitude, and thus they will not explain additional variance in behavior. Second, even if this is not the case (i.e., even if beliefs and behavioral intentions that are unrelated to attitude are selected for consideration), they may still be unrelated to the behavior.[4] That is, viewing the attitude-behavior relationship within the framework of a multiattitude object–multimethod approach, it becomes clear that the most important determinants of behavior may be other variables than an individual's beliefs about, attitude toward, or general behavioral intentions toward, a given object. Indeed, this approach clearly indicates that behavior toward an object may be completely determined by situational or individual difference variables, rather than any variable associated with the stimulus object per se. In other words, this approach points out that behavior toward a given object is a function of many variables, of which attitude toward the object is only one.

Consistent with this position, a theory of behavioral prediction was suggested. In contrast to previous attempts to resolve the attitude-behavior problem by expanding the definition of attitude, the proposed theory attempts to understand the attitude-behavior relationship by (1) considering a limited set of variables that function as primary determinants of behavior, and (2) analyzing the relations between these variables and traditional methods of attitude.

[4] It should be recalled that the size of the relationship between a behavioral intention and a behavior is primarily a function of the specificity of the behavioral intention.

REFERENCES

Allport, G. W. Attitudes. In C. Murchison (Ed.), *A handbook of social psychology*. Worcester, Mass.: Clark University Press, 1935, pp. 798-844.

Bales, R. F. Task roles and social roles in problem-solving groups. In E. Maccoby, T. Newcomb, and E. Hartley (Eds.), *Readings in social psychology*. New York: Holt, Rinehart and Winston, 1958, pp. 437-447.

Bogardus, E. S. Measuring social distance. *J. Appl. Sociol.*, 1925, **9**, 299-308.

Campbell, D. T., and Fiske, D. W. Convergent and discriminant validation by the multitrait-multimethod matrix. *Psychol. Bull.*, 1959, **56**, 81-105.

Chein, I. Behavior theory and the behavior of attitudes: some critical comments. *Psychol. Rev.*, 1948, **55**, 175-188.

Cohen, A. R. Attitudinal consequences of induced discrepancies between cognitions and behavior. *Publ. Opin. Quart.*, 1960, **24**, 297-318.

Doob, L. W. The behavior of attitudes. *Psychol. Rev.*, 1947, **54**, 135-156.

Dulany, D. E. Hypotheses and habits in verbal "operant conditioning." *J. abnorm. soc. Psychol.*, 1961, **63**, 251-263.

Dulany, D. E. *The separable effects of the information and affect conveyed by a reinforcer.* Paper presented at the annual meeting of the Psychonomic Society, October 1964.

Fishbein, M. An investigation of the relationships between beliefs about an object and the attitude toward that object. *Hum. Relat.*, 1963, **16**, 233-240.

Fishbein, M. *The relationship of the behavioral differential to other attitude instruments.* Paper presented at APA Symposium, September 1964.

Fishbein, M. A consideration of beliefs, attitudes, and their relationships. In I. D. Steiner and M. Fishbein (Eds.), *Current studies in social psychology*. New York: Holt, Rinehart and Winston, 1965a, pp. 107-120.

Fishbein, M. The prediction of interpersonal preferences and group member satisfaction from estimated attitudes. *J. pers. soc. Psychol.*, 1965b, **1**, 663-667.

Fishbein, M. A consideration of beliefs, and their role in attitude measurement. In M. Fishbein (Ed.), *Readings in attitude theory and measurement*. New York: John Wiley and Sons, 1967a.

Fishbein, M. A behavior theory approach to the relations between beliefs about an object and the attitude toward the object. In M. Fishbein (Ed.), *Readings in attitude theory and measurement*. New York: John Wiley and Sons, 1967b.

Gerard, H. B. Deviation, conformity, and commitment. In I. D. Steiner and M. Fishbein (Eds.), *Current studies in social psychology*. New York: Holt, Rinehart and Winston, 1965, pp. 263-277.

Green, B. F. Attitude measurement. In G. Lindzey (Ed.), *Handbook of social psychology*. New York: Addison-Wesley, 1954, pp. 335-369.

Landy, E. An investigation of the relationships between attitude and two classes of overt behavior. Unpublished master's thesis, University of Illinois, 1966.

Rosenberg, M. J. Cognitive structure and attitudinal affect. *J. abnorm. soc. Psychol.*, 1956, **53**, 367-372.

Rosenberg, M. J. A structural theory of attitude dynamics. *Publ. Opin. Quart.*, 1960, **24**, 319-340.

Rosenberg, M. J. Inconsistency arousal and reduction in attitude change. In I. D. Steiner and M. Fishbein (Eds.), *Current studies in social psychology*. New York: Holt, Rinehart and Winston, 1965, pp. 121-134.

Thurstone, L. L. The measurement of social attitudes. *J. abnorm. soc. Psychol.*, 1931, **26**, 249-269.

Triandis, H. C., and Davis, E. E. *Negotiation of White and Negro students on civil rights issues.* Paper presented at APA Symposium, September 1964.

Triandis, H. C., Fishbein, M., Hall, E. R., Tanaka, Y. C., and Shanmugam, A. V. Affect and behavioral intentions (in preparation).

Zajonc, R. B. Structure of the cognitive field. Unpublished doctoral dissertation, University of Michigan, Ann Arbor, 1954.

Name Index

Abelson, R. P., 141, 145, 146, 147-153, 260, 266, 341-348, 349-356, 396, 399, 402, 403, 404, 406, 409, 410, 411, 417, 420, 421, 423, 428, 429, 431, 432, 436
Ach, N., 12
Adams, J. S., 407, 417, 457
Adorno, T. W., 224, 233, 415, 417
Albig, W., 249, 255
Allport, F. H., 7, 9, 10, 11, 12, 83
Allport, G. W., 3-12, 45, 50, 175, 177, 183, 189, 220, 230, 233, 234, 366, 372, 390, 399, 402, 417, 477, 478, 492
Ames, A., 286
Anderson, L. R., 437-443
Anderson, N. H., 410, 411, 417
Ansbacher, H., 247
Appley, M. H., 415, 418
Archer, W. K., 108
Aristotle, 423
Aronson, E., 402, 408, 409, 411, 415, 417, 418, 420, 449, 456
Arsenian, S., 58
Asch, S. E., 236, 247, 341, 346, 348, 351, 355, 361, 365, 404, 417, 457
Atkinson, J. W., 415, 420, 467
Attneave, F. A., 148, 149
Ayer, J. J., 284, 288

Back, K. W., 226, 235, 295, 300, 324, 407, 414, 417, 418, 433, 434
Bagby, J. W., 230, 233
Bagehot, W., 5
Bagley, W. C., 365
Bain, A., 4, 12
Bain, R., 3, 9, 12, 175, 177
Baldwin, J. M., 4, 5, 7, 12
Bales, R. F., 480, 492
Ballachey, E. L., 402, 419
Ballin, M., 254, 255
Barclay, J., 202, 206
Barker, R. G., 209, 219
Barnett, E. O., 230, 234
Barrett, W., 416, 417
Barron, F. X., 206
Barry, H., 412, 417
Bartlett, F. C., 169, 177
Bass, B. M., 221, 233, 418

Bavelas, A. A., 315, 324
Bem, D. J., 444-456
Bennett, E. B., 412, 417
Bentham, J., 461
Berelson, B., 135
Berg, I. A., 418
Bergin, A. E., 408, 417
Berlyne, D. E., 412, 416, 417
Bernard, L. L., 6, 12, 50
Bernberg, R. E., 222, 235
Bieri, J., 411, 417
Birch, H. G., 311
Bird, C., 249, 251, 255
Birge, J. S., 366, 372, 390, 399
Black, J. D., 9, 11, 12
Blaisdell, F. J., 422
Blake, R. R., 298, 300, 314, 324
Block, H., 236, 247, 348
Bogardus, E. S., 3, 7, 8, 10, 12, 32, 33, 71-76, 148, 199, 200, 206, 208, 210, 219, 265, 479, 481, 492
Bogartz, W., 396, 400
Bogdonoff, M. D., 414, 417
Borgatta, E. F., 419
Boring, E. G., 14
Braden, M., 407, 419
Braly, K., 32-38, 49, 50
Bray, D., 230, 234
Breger, L., 396, 400
Brehm, J. W., 332, 334-338, 339, 402, 403, 406-408, 412, 414, 415, 417, 446-450, 456
Brehm, M. L., 414, 417
Brengelmann, J. C., 206
Brentano, F., 8
Bridgman, P. W., 286, 288
Brock, T. C., 339, 405, 407, 417
Brodbeck, M., 407, 417
Brown, J. F., 177, 229, 234, 235
Brown, J. S., 355, 410, 415, 417, 418
Brown, R., 414, 418
Brown, S. W., 165
Brown, W., 168, 171, 174, 175
Bruner, J. S., 58, 314, 324, 341, 348, 415, 421, 423, 459
Bryan, G. L., 157
Buchanan, W., 436
Budner, S., 206